XENOPHON

VII

LCL 183

XENOPHON

SCRIPTA MINORA

TRANSLATED BY

E. C. MARCHANT

PSEUDO-XENOPHON

CONSTITUTION OF THE ATHENIANS

TRANSLATED BY

G. W. BOWERSOCK

HARVARD UNIVERSITY PRESS
CAMBRIDGE, MASSACHUSETTS
LONDON, ENGLAND

ISBN 0-674-99202-4

Printed in Great Britain by St Edmundsbury Press Ltd,
Bury St Edmunds, Suffolk, on acid-free paper.
Bound by Hunter & Foulis Ltd, Edinburgh, Scotland.

CONTENTS

INTRODUCTION   vii

HIERO   1

AGESILAUS   59

CONSTITUTION OF THE LACEDAEMONIANS   135

WAYS AND MEANS   191

THE CAVALRY COMMANDER   233

ON THE ART OF HORSEMANSHIP   295

ON HUNTING   365

CONSTITUTION OF THE ATHENIANS   459

INDEX   509

INTRODUCTION

" WELL, Xenophon, I had been told that you are
an Athenian ; and that was all I knew about you :
but now I praise you for your words and deeds, and
I should wish as many as possible to be like you.
That would be good for everybody."—Cheirisophus
the Lacedaemonian, in *Anabasis*, III. i. 45.

Various modern writers have challenged the
ascription to Xenophon of every one of the works
included in this volume. The *Agesilaus* and the
Ways and Means have suffered much from the on-
slaughts of the critics, the *Agesilaus* on account of
its style, the *Ways and Means* for its subject matter
It must suffice here to say that no case has been
made out against any one of them, with the exception of (a) the *Hunting* ; (and, even in this case, it is
impossible to state with confidence that the main
portion of the treatise was not written by Xenophon)[1];
and (b) *The Constitution of the Athenians*. This work
is manifestly spurious, very interesting though it is.

Undoubtedly there is something unusual about
the miscellany, when regarded as the product of
one author. Most authors write only in one
manner ; and when we have read some of their
works, we easily recognise their hand in the rest.
With Xenophon it is not so ; for there is an obvious
difference of manner in different parts of the

[1] See below, VII (p. xxxvi).

INTRODUCTION

Hellenica. Xenophon tried his hand at several kinds of prose literature—history, dialogue, the encomium, the technical treatise, the essay—and he had his ideas, gleaned from his reading, of the style appropriate to each kind. In the early part of the *Hellenica* we find him trying to write in the manner of Thucydides; in the rhetorical parts of the *Agesilaus* he clearly has the model of Gorgias before him. But of course for us it is not always possible to understand just *why* he regarded this or that manner as appropriate. Thus in the historical portion of the *Agesilaus,* he repeats passages of the *Hellenica* almost but not quite exactly; here he changes, there adds a word or two; but no modern reader can appreciate his reason for these minute alterations. But even in a translation, however inadequate, a reader must detect a difference in style between his rhetoric and his history.

More interesting for us is the variety of subjects that Xenophon knows and can expound. Of course he is better at some things than at others; but even about matters of which he is not a master he can tell us a good deal that is worth knowing. He flounders in the high finance; but even at that he is far from being such a duffer as some moderns have declared him to be. His speculations on forms of government and the secrets of national greatness are not profound, but they come from a singularly lucid, well-ordered mind. Of the theory of war he is a master. About horses, riding, the organisation and command of cavalry he knew everything that could be known in his day. His treatise on *Horsemanship*, especially, is in its way a masterpiece.

Like Socrates himself, he is continually trying to

make himself useful. Perhaps for us there is rather too much of the don about him : his books are too full of instruction, admonition and reproof; nor is it surprising that some think that he intended them to form a series of educational manuals for the use of his sons. What is abundantly clear to anyone who reads all his works is that his real purpose was to do good to everybody; and, generous man that he was, everybody meant to him the people of Athens—those by whom he had been driven into banishment. Exiles do not, as a rule, spend their time in heaping coals of fire on their fellow-countrymen. Happily his fellow-countrymen showed themselves not ungrateful ; they annulled the decree of banishment, though too late to entice him back to Athens. He died at Corinth. In these lesser productions of a virtuous and versatile Athenian gentleman there is, even in our age, not a little that is worth reading, apart from the information about ancient Greek life and manners that we owe to them. Their brevity too is a merit; for owing to his pedantry, Xenophon in his longer works is apt to be tedious.

In style Xenophon is simple and natural; he avails himself, indeed, of the resources of rhetoric, but he uses them moderately, and, except occasionally in the *Agesilaus*, he uses them soberly and sensibly. By the Atticists and the later Sophists he was taken as a model of simplicity.

Few traces of these *opuscula*, with the exception of the *Constitution of the Lacedaemonians*, occur in literature anterior to the Christian era; but the Atticist Demetrius of Magnesia, friend of Cicero's friend Atticus, included all of them in his list of

Xenophon's works.[1] They are not cited by name by
any extant Greek or Latin author earlier than Cicero,
who refers in laudatory terms to the *Agesilaus,* and
has made use of its design in his *Pro Lege Manilia.*
But echoes may be heard here and there by an
attentive listener. The *Constitution* quickly attained
an importance disproportionate to its merit. Isocrates
in his *Panathenaicus* makes some combative remarks
that certainly apply, though not perhaps exclusively,
to Xenophon's *Constitution.* All those who wrote on
the Spartan institutions, including Aristotle, and
especially the early Stoics, Zeno and his followers,
used it as an authority. Nor was its influence
exerted solely on the compilers of such works.
Thinkers who speculated on the balanced or mixed
form of Constitution also found it serviceable. Plato,
indeed, as we should expect, ignores it in his *Laws ;*
but Aristotle in his *Politics* does not ; and Polybius,
in his sixth book, is clearly indebted to it. From the
Hiero Isocrates has borrowed the matter and even
some of the language in his address *On the Peace*
(§ III f.), and this is interesting, because Xenophon in
the same year returned the compliment by borrowing
from this address of Isocrates in his *Ways and Means.*
We may safely hazard a guess that the *Hiero* was a
favourite work with the Cynics, amongst whom the
unhappiness of the despot was a common theme.[2]
In the age of Polybius, the traveller Polemon of
Ilium wrote a book with the curious title, *About the*

---

[1] It is inconceivable that Demetrius, as the text of Diogenes
Laertius says, challenged the *Constitution of the Lacedaemonians.* Most of what follows, and much more, may be
found in R. Münscher's *Xenophon in der griechisch-römischen
Literatur* (*Philologus, Sup.* xiii. 1920).

[2] The writer of [Diogenes] ep. 29, which is an onslaught on
Dionysius II., drew from a Cynic source.

INTRODUCTION

Car in Xenophon (Agesilaus, c. viii. 7), in which he
gave an account of Spartan customs that is not to be
found in Xenophon's *Constitution.*[1] Nepos used the
Agesilaus in his life of the king.[2] The *Ways and
Means* does not turn up once; but this is not
surprising, since the brochure was written for a
special occasion, and contains very little of general
application. We may anticipate here by mentioning
the adaptation of the passage (c. i. 2–8) on the nature
of Attica by Aristides, the Sophist of the second century A.D., in his *Panathenaicus.*[3] About the earlier history of the *Cavalry Commander* and the *Horsemanship*
there is a strange circumstance worthy of mention.
Cato the Censor, as we know from Cicero, read, and
highly esteemed Xenophon. The method of the
opening of Cato's *de Re Rustica* has given rise to a
suspicion that he had included these two treatises
in his studies.[4] Considering the age at which Cato
began Greek, he must have found the *Horsemanship*
" a tough proposition," if he really tackled it. The
Horsemanship did not oust Simon's work on the same
subject from its position as an authority ; but it is often
impossible to be sure on which of the two treatises
later writers draw.[5] Pollux came across a commentary on the *Horsemanship ;* we cannot tell whether it
was written before the Christian era. Probably
Theophrastus already culled something from the

[1] Athenaeus iv. p. 138 E.
[2] It is now said that he did not use it directly ; but I
cannot believe this.
[3] A. Brinkmann, *Rhenisches Museum,* lxvii, 1912, p. 135.
Among the Xenophontine works cited by Aristides are the
Agesilaus and the *Hunting* (Persson, p. 74).
[4] Leo started this.
[5] Oder in his *Anecdota Cantabrigiensia,* credits to Simon
all the repetitions of matter that is common to Simon and
Xenophon.

Hunting.[1] It is not clear that Grattius, who wrote his poem between 30 B.C. and 8 A.D., owes anything to the *Hunting ;* nor is it likely, since he did not go to Simon or to Xenophon for his treatment of the horse.

Into the complicated history of Xenophon's shorter works in the Christian era we cannot enter.

To speak generally, the *Hiero* and *Agesilaus* seem to have been most read by the Atticists and Sophists ; while the Romans, for the most part, neglected all of them.[2] But mention of one Greek author cannot be omitted, owing to the unique position that he occupies in the history of Xenophontine literature. Dio of Prusa (fl. 90 A.D.) not only, like Arrian, took Xenophon as his model of style, but his mind is saturated with Xenophon's thoughts and words. There is much of the *Hiero* and *Agesilaus* in Dio's discourses on kingship and despotism (I, II, III, VI, LXII). There is also, I think, a clear echo of the *Hunting* in Dio III. 135-6. The *Agesilaus* is cited by Dionysius of Halicarnassus as the type of the encomium. To Roman encomiasts it furnished a model. Its influence is felt in the design of Nepos' *Atticus,* in the *Agricola* of Tacitus, in the *Panegyric* of the younger Pliny, and, according to Leo, in the balanced estimate of the Emperor Valentinian in Ammianus Marcellinus (fl. 370 A.D.), book xxx.[3]

---

[1] περὶ φυτῶν αἰτιῶν vi. 19-20 compared with *Hunting* v. and viii.

[2] Only the *Cyropaedia* and *Memorabilia* of Xenophon's works gained a strong footing among the Romans.

[3] I am not myself conscious of this. Resemblances are rather readily detected by keen investigators. Thus Rademacher says that Oppian used the *Hunting* in his *Cynegetica,* but I have waded through Oppian without detecting any reminiscence of it.

INTRODUCTION

Finally, we may refer to an amusing passage in the *Apollonius* of the Athenian Philostratus (age of Caracalla), which appears to be a "dig" at the *Hunting,* as the scholiast says it is. "They (Apollonius and his companion in India) came in," writes Philostratus, "for a dragon hunt which I must tell about, for it is highly absurd that the devotees of hunting should have found so much to say about the hare, and how she is, or shall be, caught, and we should pass over the record of this noble and marvellous sport." [1]

I. *Hiero*

"Government of unwilling subjects and not controlled by laws, but imposed by the will of the ruler, is despotism."—*Memorabilia,* IV. vi. 12.

"Despotic rule over unwilling subjects the gods give, I fancy, to those whom they judge worthy to live the life of Tantalus, of whom it is said that in hell he spends eternity, dreading a second death."—*Oeconomicus, the end.*

The *Hiero* is an imaginary conversation between King Hiero, who ruled Syracuse from 478 to 467 B.C., and the poet Simonides of Ceos, one of the many famous strangers whom the hospitable despot entertained at his court. Its purpose is twofold—first to show that a despot, ruling without regard to the interests of his subjects, is less happy than the private citizen ; and secondly, to show by what means a despot may succeed in winning the affection of his subjects, and, by so doing, may gain happiness for himself. This subject was a common topic of

---

[1] *Apollonius* III. 6, Phillimore's translation.

speculation among the Socratics[1]: it had been discussed by Socrates himself; and we are told that Plato during his first visit to the court of Syracuse had spoken his mind upon it to Dionysius the Elder. Had it been possible for Xenophon to bring Socrates and a great despot together, we might have found just such a conversation in the *Memorabilia*.[2] Isocrates, in his oration addressed to Nicocles (374 B.C.), says that many doubt whether the life of men who live virtuously or the life of a despot is preferable, and in the letter which he wrote to the children of Jason, the "tagus" of Thessaly (359 or 358 B.C.), he declares that the private citizen is the happier.[3]

Modern writers, anxious to discover the date at which the *Hiero* was written, have ransacked the records of the despots contemporary with Xenophon to find some special event or events that may have prompted him to compose it. Grote, for example, refers to an incident that occured at the Olympic Festival of 388 or 384 B.C. In one of those years the orator Lysias delivered his *Olympic* oration, in which he stirred up hatred of despots,[4] and incited the Greeks to unite in ridding Syracuse of Dionysius. The despot on that occasion was represented at the festival by a magnificent mission. The date of composition has therefore been placed at about 383 B.C. Another view is that Xenophon wrote his

---

[1] Dio of Prusa, in his third discourse, puts into the mouth of Socrates a discussion on the question of the happiness of the despot.

[2] Just as Dio (VI) brings Diogenes and the Persian king together.

[3] Cf. Aristotle, *Politics*, p. 1325 A, and Stobaeus XLIX.

[4] The tone of Antisthenes' *Archelaus* was similar (Dümmler, *Akademika*, p. 13).

dialogue as a warning to Dionysius the Younger soon after his accession to the throne of Syracuse in 367 B.C. A third opinion is that the career of Jason of Pherae, who was assassinated in 370 B.C., was specially in Xenophon's mind ; and a modification of this view is that our author had lately read the letter of Isocrates already referred to, and that his dialogue, like Isocrates' epistle, is a warning to Jason's children who now shared the power in Thessaly. This last opinion is supported by reference to the passage in which Hiero remarks that many despots have been destroyed by their own wives (iii. 8); for Jason's nephew, Alexander, joint "tagus" of Thessaly, was murdered by his brothers-in-law at the instigation of his wife Thebé in 359 B.C.

But it is surely unnecessary to suppose that Xenophon had any special purpose or event in mind when he wrote the *Hiero*. The thing is merely a "Socratic" dialogue on a theme that interested him. He thought of despots in general, as the Socratics supposed them to be; and of course, like Plato in the ninth book of his *Republic,* when he writes of despotism he has an eye on the career of Dionysius I.[1] All that can be said about the date of composition is that, to judge from the language and the rhetoric of the *Hiero*, it appears to have been written in the author's later years.

There is no attempt at characterisation in the

[1] There is a close resemblance between *Republic*, ix. p. 579 B and *Hiero*, c. i. 11. Were the *Hiero* the later work it would be impossible to resist the impression that Xenophon had lately read the *Republic*. This may be so, since the *Republic* was written between 380 and 370 B.C.

persons of the dialogue. Hiero is not in the least the historical Hiero whom we know from the Odes of Pindar and Bacchylides. He is not the great warrior nor the enlightened ruler; and of course there is no indication of the true basis of his power and of his constitutional position. He is just a despot of the better type. As for Simonides, Xenophon, in drawing his favourite analogy from the Choruses, once faintly alludes to his craft (c. ix. 4); but he makes no attempt anywhere to represent the courtier poet; had he done so he must have made Simonides bring in the subject of verse pane-gyrics on princes at c. i. 14. The remark of the poet at c. i. 22 is singularly inappropriate to a man who had a liking for good living. At c. viii. Xenophon discards the thin disguise, and Simonides stands clearly revealed as Xenophon himself. To some of the recommendations offered to rulers that he makes in these concluding chapters we have parallels in the *Cavalry Commander* and the *Ways and Means.*

The *Hiero* is a naïve little work, not unattractive : in this case, as in that of the *Banquet,* it is unfortunate for our amiable author that Plato has written on the same subject with incomparably greater brilliancy.

The gist of Xenophon's counsel to despots is that a despot should endeavour to rule like a good king. The same counsel is given by Isocrates in his *Helen,* which was written about 370 B.C.[1] No man, in Xenophon's opinion, is fit to rule who is not better than his subjects.[2]

---

[1] Aristotle in the *Politics* (p. 1313 A) agrees.
[2] *Cyropaedia,* VIII. i. 37.

INTRODUCTION

II. *Agesilaus*

" What is government, and what is a governor ? "—
Memorabilia, I. i. 16.

" Government of men with their consent and in
accordance with the laws of the State is kingship."—
Memorabilia, IV. vi. 12.

Agesilaus became one of the two joint kings of
Sparta in 398 B.C. Though over forty at the time
of his accession,[1] he reigned for nearly forty years,
and died on active service, probably in the winter
of 361–60 B.C. His long career as a commander in
the field began with his expedition to Asia Minor
in 396 B.C. We do not know for certain when
Xenophon joined Agesilaus in Asia, and it is impossible to say with confidence whether or not he
was an eye-witness of the campaign of Agesilaus
against Tissaphernes, the satrap of Lydia, in 395 B.C.[2]
But he was certainly with Agesilaus in the following
year, and returned with him from Asia to Greece.
He fought under the king at the battle of Coronea
in the summer of 394 B.C. against his fellow-citizens,
and was banished in consequence. He spent some

---

[1] Xenophon calls him "still young" at the time of his
accession, no doubt having in mind the great age to which
he lived in full activity, and using the pardonable exaggera-
tion of an "encomiast." Similarly Isocrates implies that
Evagoras (who was really assassinated) died a happy death.

[2] Xenophon's account of the campaign is utterly different
from that which may now be read in a fragment of another
history. But even if Xenophon was in Greece in 395 B.C.,
he of course heard the facts from Agesilaus himself. Busolt
has successfully defended the accuracy of his account. In one
instance (c. i. 33) X. tacitly corrects the account he had
given in the *Hellenica* (III. iv. 24). At c. ii. 7 he defends what
he had said in *Hell.* IV. iii. 15.

time at Sparta, and thence removed to Scillus, near Olympia, to an estate that had been presented to him by the Lacedaemonians, doubtless at the suggestion of Agesilaus.

Xenophon, always a hero-worshipper, and an admirer of the ideal Spartan character and the institutions of Lycurgus, saw in Agesilaus the embodiment of his conception of a good king. Doubtless, he, like Isocrates,[1] regarded the Spartan kingship as the best form of monarchy. Shortly after the death of his hero he produced this tribute to his memory. In spite of its rhetorical embellishments, there are signs of hasty composition in the *Agesilaus*. Haste probably accounts for the extensive borrowing from the *Hellenica*. Now why should Xenophon be in a hurry? From some pretty strong hints that all did not consider the king to be above adverse criticism, we may conclude that there was adverse criticism[2]; quite possibly something had been writen about Agesilaus that was not entirely complimentary. The *Agesilaus*, in the main an encomium, is incidentally a defence.

A few years before, Isocrates had produced his encomium on Evagoras, king of Salamis in Cyprus, who was assassinated in 374 B.C. Isocrates says that he is the first to "praise a man's virtues in prose." If he means to say that nobody had written a prose encomium of an historical personage before him, it is very doubtful whether his claim can be sustained.[3] But perhaps he means only that he was the first to combine an account of a man's actions with praise of his character, pointing out the significance of

---

[1] Isocrates, *de Pace*, §§ 142–143.
[2] c. ii. 21 ; iv. 3 ; v. 6 ; viii. 7.
[3] Wilamowitz in *Hermes*, xxxv. p. 533.

the actions as indicating the virtues of his hero.[1]
That is just what he does in the *Evagoras*. Now
in the first portion of the *Agesilaus* (c. i.–ii.),
Xenophon has clearly taken the *Evagoras* for his
model. The king's exploits, judiciously selected,
are narrated in chronological order, passages from
certain portions of the *Hellenica* being repeated
with trifling alterations of the language; and into
the narrative are woven comments on the king's
character, as it is illustrated by his deeds.

Having finished with the king's actions, Xenophon
gives an account of his virtues (c. iii.–ix.). This
portion of his work has no counterpart in the
Evagoras. But even here Xenophon's idea is not
original. The great virtues—piety, justice, self-
control, courage, wisdom—are treated elsewhere in
the same order. In Plato's *Banquet* the poet Agathon
praises the justice, self-control, courage and wisdom
of Love, and Socrates remarks that the encomium
reminds him of Gorgias. Xenophon himself at the
end of the *Memorabilia* writes of the piety, justice,
self-control and wisdom of Socrates.[2] The order of
the categories no doubt goes back to Gorgias. To
these great virtues Xenophon adds patriotism, and
several minor excellences. He rounds off his encomium with a formal epilogue (c. x.).

To the epilogue is appended a summary (c. xi.)
of the king's virtues, and here again the categories
are arranged in the same order.[3] The summary

[1] So Usener.
[2] In *Cyropaedia*, VIII. i. 23–33, Xenophon enumerates the
piety, justice and self-control of Cyrus.
[3] The indications of the order are fainter, but they can be
discerned. But the disposition does not agree closely with
that of the second part of the work.

was a device introduced by the sophist Corax, and
the use of it is alluded to as an established practice
at the end of the *Palamedes,* an oration ascribed to
Gorgias. The extant fragment of Gorgias' *Funeral
Oration* appears to belong to a summary. There
are examples of the summary also in Isocrates.[1]
To the material of the eleventh chapter a passage
of the *Evagoras* has contributed something.[2]

What is peculiar in the structure of the *Agesilaus*
is the separate treatment of the actions and the
virtues of the hero. Xenophon has followed Isocrates
in one section of his encomium and Gorgias in the
other.[3] The result is, of course, a want of unity
in the design. The work, however, was much
admired by Cicero and by Nepos;[4] and the latter's
sketch of Cicero's friend Atticus is evidently modelled
on it.

III. *Constitution of the Lacedaemonians.*

" Lycurgus the Lacedaemonian now—have you
realised that he would not have made Sparta to
differ from other cities in any respect, had he not
established obedience to the laws most securely in
her ? "—*Memorabilia,* IV. iv. 15.

"When will Athenians show the Lacedaemonian
reverence for age . . . when will they adopt the
Lacedaemonian system of training . . . when will
they reach that standard of obedience to their rulers

[1] *e.g. Antidosis,* §§ 127, 128, the character of Timotheus.
[2] *Evagoras,* §§ 43–46. The notion that the eleventh chapter
of the *Agesilaus* is spurious is wrong. Compare the character
sketches of Proxenus and Menon in *Anabasis* II.
[3] All the little tricks of rhetoric that have been adversely
criticised by modern writers come in this second part.
[4] Nepos, *Agesilaus,* c. i.

INTRODUCTION

. . . or when will they attain that harmony?"—
Memorabilia, III. v. 16.

Xenophon's purpose in this work was to show
that the greatness and fame of the Lacedaemonians
were due to "the laws of Lycurgus." He had no
intention of writing a treatise on the Lacedaemonian
constitution; and though here and there he refers
to details of that constitution as things familiar to
his readers, it is only in the last chapter, about the
position and privileges of the kings, that he even
mentions the word "constitution." Even the remarks
on the constitutional powers of the Ephors in c. viii.
are merely illustrative. After the tenth chapter he
gradually loses sight of his subject. For if the
eleventh and the twelfth, on the excellence of the
Spartan army, have a loose connexion with it, the
thirteenth, on the powers of the kings, has none.
The fourteenth is clearly an afterthought, an
appendix; and the same is true of the fifteenth.

The title, then, is inaccurate; nevertheless there can
be no doubt that it was chosen by the author himself.
The first ten chapters are homogeneous, and they
have the appearance of a complete essay. For
evidently when he started Xenophon did not intend
to trace the "power" of Sparta to the organisation
of its army: he says clearly at the beginning that
he attributes her power to her institutions or
"principles"; and one of these principles turns out
to be (c. ix.) that a glorious death is preferable to
a base life—which is a good enough reason, in an
essay, to account for the power of the state on the
military side. Possibly, after writing the first ten
chapters, Xenophon kept them by him, and added
later on the appendices on the army and the functions

of the kings in war, on the violation of the "laws of Lycurgus,"[1] and on the constitutional position of the kings. The thesis of the appendix on the army is not the thesis of the essay proper; for the thesis of this appendix is not that the Lacedaemonians owe their power and fame to their army, but that the Lacedaemonians are artists in warfare, and the rest of the Greeks, in comparison with them, are mere amateurs (c. xiii. 6). In the last chapter he supports no thesis; he is merely stating certain facts about the kings, is, indeed, writing a fragment of a "Constitution."

The fourteenth chapter is strange and bewildering, and many have maintained that it is spurious. It is written in a spirit of disillusion, and it contradicts some of the statements made in earlier chapters. Internal evidence shows that it was written certainly before the battle of Leuctra (371 B.C.), and probably after 378 B.C. Observe, however, that Xenophon is not indicting the people: his wrath falls only on a small section of powerful Spartans, on the governors, "harmosts," whose conduct was a violation of the "laws of Lycurgus" and of the principles so strictly adhered to by his hero Agesilaus.

But the change of tone is manifest. It is tempting to seek the cause of the change in the impression made on Xenophon's mind by the scandalous seizure of the Theban citadel by the Spartan Phoebidas in 381 B.C. In the *Hellenica* Xenophon denounces that

---

[1] Some hold that the first thirteen chapters describe what *had been* the state of affairs at Sparta in better times. Though such great authorities as E. Meyer and Köhler agree that all the fifteen chapters were written at the same time, I cannot believe that they are right.

crime as an outrage against heaven. Again, in
378 B.C., Sphodrias, a Spartan governor, was persuaded
or bribed by the Thebans to make an attempt on
the Peiraeus. The plan miscarried and Sphodrias
was put on his trial for his gross act of treachery;
but he was acquitted. There is probably a covert
reference to Sphodrias in the second section of this
fourteenth chapter. The part taken by King
Agesilaus in the inquiries that followed both these
crimes was highly discreditable, and naturally
Xenophon makes no allusion to it in his *Agesilaus*.

As for the essay (c. i.-x.), one reads it with a
feeling of regret that the author, who during his
sojourn at Sparta had such excellent opportunities
for observation, did not undertake the task of writing
an account of the Lacedaemonian constitution. Even
what he tells us of the primitive institutions of the
Spartans in support of his thesis comes to very little;
but the facts that he selects are sufficient for his
purpose. He touches on the surprising marriage
customs of the Lacedaemonians, but not with entire
accuracy; and of course he disguises the extraordinary
laxity of the relations between the sexes at Sparta.
He gives no connected or detailed account of the
class organisation of boys and youths. Thus in
c. ix. 5 he refers incidentally to the "sides in a
game of ball"; but does not trouble to explain that
the term "ball-players" had a special meaning
among the Spartans;[1] the proper place for mentioning them, if he had been writing a treatise, would
have been at c. iv. 6. In speaking of the common
meals he uses, almost consistently, the Spartan

---

[1] Those who were no longer Ephebi and were not quite
men (Pausanias III. xiv. 6).

technical term Syskania and its cognate words, without giving their explanation.[1] The reference in c. ii. 9 to the ceremonial rite of flagellation at the altar of Artemis Orthia[2] is so confused that it is quite impossible that Xenophon, who must have witnessed it, can have written what stands in the text.

Whatever we may think of the method of the essay it is characteristic of Xenophon that he borrowed it from a predecessor in the same field.[3] Critias the politician, once a disciple of Socrates, had already produced a prose and a verse *Constitution of the Lacedaemonians*.[4] In the prose work he compared the usages of different states with those of Sparta ; and though, like Hellanicus and Thucydides, he ignored Lycurgus, the existing fragments of his work show that Xenophon is indebted to Critias, certainly for the method, and perhaps for some of the details of his essay.[5] No doubt it is the *Constitution* of Critias that is used by Plato, to the exclusion of Xenophon's, in the *Laws*.

The excellence of the Spartan institutions was of course a stock theme among the Socratics. Overemphasis led to the inevitable protest. Isocrates in his *Panathenaicus* makes some caustic remarks about those who are for ever harping on the subject.

---

[1] Also in c. xv.

[2] The rite is a substitute for human sacrifice.

[3] Köhler in *Sitzungsberichte der Berliner Akademie* 1896, p. 361.

[4] The quotation from the verse *Constitution* in Athenaeus x. 432 D, about drinking, corresponds closely with what Xenophon says on the same subject (c. v. 6).

[5] *e.g.* for the view he takes of the "Syssitia," or common meals, as neither a military nor a political institution. At c. ii. 1 Xenophon echoes Plato, *Protag.* p. 325 D.

INTRODUCTION

Amongst other things he says that some talk of
the Spartans as if the demi-gods had been Spartan
statesmen, and that Lycurgus borrowed his best
ideas from Athens! The date of the *Panathenaicus*
is 342 B.C. or thereabouts.

IV. *Ways and Means*

" Now tell me, from what sources are the city's
revenues at present derived and what is their total?
No doubt you have gone into this matter, in order
to raise the amount of any that are deficient and
supply any that are lacking."—*Memorabilia*, III. vi. 5.

The *Ways and Means* appears from internal
evidence to have been written in 355 B.C. There
are no convincing reasons for refusing to believe
that Xenophon is the author. The diction and
style are his, and there is nothing in the opinions
expressed that renders his authorship impossible,
or even unlikely. In the opening sentence he
repeats a remark that he has made at the end of
the *Cyropaedia* (VIII. viii. 4); [1] there are passages
that have a parallel in the *Hiero* and the *Cavalry
Commander*; and the epilogue both in language and
sentiment is thoroughly Xenophontine. We might,
no doubt, have expected more moralising than we
find, and we miss evidence of his interest in agriculture. But if the brochure was intended to support the financial policy of the statesman Eubulus,
the reason why these features are lacking becomes
apparent. This, then, is Xenophon's last work.
He probably died a few months after writing it.

Since 370 B.C., or thereabouts, Xenophon had

---

[1] A similar remark occurs in Isocrates *On the Peace*.

lived at Corinth. Some years later his banishment
from Athens was annulled on the proposal of
Eubulus. He did not, however, return to his
native city ; but he sent his two sons home to serve
in the Athenian cavalry.

In 355 B.C. Athens emerged in a state of serious
financial exhaustion from a disastrous war with her
most powerful allies. It was through Eubulus that
the peace was concluded. In the following year
Eubulus practically assumed control of the state
finances,[1] and he at once set to work to increase
the revenue and to relieve the poverty of the
citizens. The citizen body at this time, as we can
see from the *Ways and Means,* was in a deplorable
condition. Lazy and poverty-stricken, the people
looked to the state for maintenance. Trade was
in the hands of the resident aliens, among whom
were many Asiatics (c. ii. 3). How precisely Eubulus
dealt with the problems that faced him we do not
know. But as Controller of the "theoric" fund
he raised enough money from this tax upon the
well-to-do to enable him to make distributions to
the people on an unprecedented scale. From a
passage in the orator Deinarchus we infer that
Eubulus also introduced measures for the improvement of the cavalry. And when his administration
came to an end, probably in 339 B.C., the mines at
Laurium, which had been neglected, were once
again being vigorously worked by men in partnership
and by private companies.

The resemblance between these operations of
Eubulus and some of the proposals contained in

[1] See especially Beloch, *Attische Politik seit Perikles,*
p. 177 f.

INTRODUCTION

Xenophon's brochure is obvious. The brochure is addressed, apparently, to the Council of Five Hundred. The author confines himself rigidly to proposals of a practical nature. It is not his business here to probe the causes of the prevalent distress. The author of the *Memorabilia* knew well enough what was wrong with the Athenians; but when the problem of the moment is how to raise cash, it is useless to demand a change of national habits: you must take the conditions as they are, and make the best of them. The recognition of the demoralising dole system was, of course, unavoidable. Then, according to Xenophon's plan, capital is to be raised by the imposition of an income tax—whether for one year or more is not stated—and expended on the erection of hotels, the provision of accommodation for merchants and visitors both in the Peiraeus and in the city, and on a fleet of state-owned merchant vessels. Much space is given to measures to be adopted for the improved working of the mines: amongst them are a measure of state socialism (c. iv. 30) and a proposal for the formation of a great Joint-Stock Company (c. iv. 32). To encourage internal trade, it is essential to encourage the resident aliens; their status must be improved. It is a shock to find Xenophon proposing to make these aliens—including Lydians, Phrygians and Syrians—eligible for the aristocratic cavalry.

The insistence on the necessity of maintaining peace as an essential condition of financial recovery is in accordance with the policy of Eubulus.

Earlier in this same year, 355 B.C., Isocrates, now an octogenarian, issued his pamphlet *On the Peace*, in which he exhorted the Athenians to endeavour to conciliate the Greek world. His pamphlet is ostensibly a harangue addressed to the Assembly, and its subject is political morality. There are clear indications that Xenophon had read it before writing the *Ways and Means*.[1]

V. *The Cavalry Commander* [2]

"Perhaps you think you can do something for the good of the State as a cavalry leader, in case there is any occasion to employ that arm."— *Memorabilia*, iii. iii. 2.

The discourse on the duties of the cavalry commander was written at a time when there was some reason to anticipate the outbreak of war between Athens and Thebes (c. vii. 3), probably in 365 B.C. It is ostensibly addressed to an individual about to enter on that exalted office; but the convention is not consistently maintained, especially towards the end of the treatise. It is almost certain that Xenophon in his younger days had himself been a member of the Athenian cavalry corps, in 409 B.C. and the years following; and he had lately sent his two sons home to Athens to serve in the force. His profound interest in cavalry and his knowledge of its use are, of course, apparent in the *Cyropaedia*, the *Anabasis* and the *Memorabilia*. Our treatise may, indeed, be viewed as a commentary on the statement of a cavalry commander's duties that is put into the mouth of Socrates in the last mentioned work (iii. iii. 1).

[1] He has levied toll on §§ 21, 30, 42, 53 and 138.
[2] Literally the Greek title means "A discourse on the command of cavalry."

INTRODUCTION

When Xenophon wrote the discourse Athens was at peace. But even in peace time the duties of the cavalry, though ornamental, were important, since the cavalry procession was a prominent feature of all the great state festivals. And of course training for war was always being carried on with more or less vigour. Things were at the moment in a pretty bad way with the corps. Owing to the prevailing poverty, and the slackness of the Council and their immediate agents, the two annually elected commanders of cavalry ("hipparchs"), the number of troopers had apparently fallen from the thousand required by law to about six hundred and fifty; and the quality of the horses and the efficiency of the riders left much to be desired. It is probable that in this case, as in others, Xenophon's exhortations were not without practical result, for at the time of the battle of Mantinea (361 B.C.) the Athenian cavalry was able to play a creditable part in the field.

Xenophon recommends the use of infantry among the cavalry (c. v. 13); and his words imply that at the time infantry were not regularly provided for this service. In the *Constitution of Athens*, written some forty years later, Aristotle mentions such a body of infantry as a normal appendage to the cavalry. In the *Memorabilia*, as in our treatise, the cavalry commander is urged to require that the horses incapable of going the pace should be rejected. Aristotle, repeating the very expression used by Xenophon, says that the Council marked and rejected such horses. Both reforms may be due to Xenophon, at least in part. For it is hardly likely that the advice of such an authority can have gone entirely unheeded.

INTRODUCTION

Each of the ten tribes was supposed to furnish a hundred cavalrymen. The roll was drawn up annually by ten officials elected for the purpose,[1] who acted apparently under the direction of the two commanders. At the head of each of these ten regiments was a colonel ("phylarch"), who was responsible for the details of control, for the instruction, condition and equipment of his regiment. Each of the two commanders had five of these regiments under him, because in the field the chief duty of the cavalry was to protect the flanks of the infantry. On ceremonial occasions each colonel rode at the head of his regiment in the procession, and each commander at the head of his five regiments.

Preparation for service in the cavalry began while a youth was still under the control of his guardian (c. i. 11), that is to say, before the age of eighteen. The service, at any rate at this time, was continuous. The object of the annual enrolment, therefore, was to fill the places of those who retired through old age or other causes. It also appears that not all the recruits were young men: no doubt the difficulty of obtaining a sufficient number of young men of means led to the inclusion of persons of maturer years, men who could not be trained to vault on to a horse, but had to be assisted to mount by means of a leg-up, "in the Persian fashion."

Every recruit had to appear with his horse before a committee of the Council and to pass a test. On being approved the recruit had a legal right to receive a sum of money to defray the cost of his horse and equipment; but the colonels had sometimes to intervene to get the money paid over to

---

[1] At any rate this was so when Aristotle wrote.

the men. The cavalryman received, in addition, a daily allowance of a *drachma* for the keep of his horse in peace as well as in war; and the annual cost to the state of this wage amounted, says Xenophon, to nearly forty talents. The cost of the initial sum paid to the recruits did not fall on the state, as each man who left the service had to pay the amount over to his successor.

Each man was attended by a mounted groom (c. v. 6), but the grooms did not ride in the ranks, and were not armed. There were also mounted aides-de-camp (c. iv. 4).[1] The commanders had about them a corps of couriers (c. i. 25), of whom we know only that they had to pass a test before the Council (Aristotle, *Ath. Pol.* c. 49).

The author's purpose is, of course, to make recommendations for the improvement of the cavalry. Incidentally the *Cavalry Commander* is our chief authority on the organisation and employment of the Athenian cavalry, and it contains many details about the ceremonial processions.

None of Xenophon's shorter writings is more entirely characteristic of the writer. Note especially the frequent exhortation to "work with God"; it is the first and the last duty that he insists on. "If," he says, "you are surprised that I say this so often, I assure you that you will cease to wonder if you find yourself often in danger." He speaks from experience.

---

[1] Xenophon in the *Cyropaedia* assigns many functions to the aides in the army of Cyrus, including attention to the wounded.

INTRODUCTION

VI. *On the Art of Horsemanship*

"Seeing you are forced to meddle with horses, don't you think that common sense requires you to see that you are not ignorant of the business?"—*Oeconomicus*, iii. 9.

The treatise on *Horsemanship*, the oldest complete treatise on the subject in existence, was written soon after the *Cavalry Commander* (c. xii. 14). It is a masterly production. The text has suffered considerably from corruption, and even with the aid of restoration it is not easy reading; nevertheless, it presents no serious problems that still await solution. Bearing in mind the cardinal differences between the Greek cavalry horse of which Xenophon writes, and the modern riding horse, we shall have no serious difficulty in following the author. The Greek cavalry horse, familiar to everybody from the Parthenon sculptures, was small and cob-like. He was a troublesome creature to ride, and given the conditions, although the cavalry was not always an efficient arm in the field, it is a mistake to suppose that the individual Greek rider was a poor horseman ; nor is the supposition borne out by the Parthenon figures. The horses were ungelded and unshod; they were given to biting, and the rider had neither stirrups, nor saddle, nor curb to assist him. The well-to-do young Athenian rode, but did not often ride merely for pleasure: he rode commonly as a member or a prospective member of the cavalry —it is significant that the same word is used for a "horseman " and a " cavalryman "; occasionally he rode in order to compete in the horse-races at the Games; or if he were rich he hunted on horseback.[1] Naturally, therefore, the only gaits in use were the walk, the trot and the gallop.

The practical horseman will no doubt notice certain details in which modern practice differs from the Greek usage. But he will assuredly be surprised to find that so much of Xenophon's doctrine survives unchanged in the modern lore of the horse and his rider; and he will acknowledge that Xenophon was both an excellent judge of a horse and a highly accomplished horseman.

Xenophon recommends a "flexible" in preference to a "stiff" bit (c. x). Two "flexible" bits now in the Berlin Museum are figured and described by E. Pernice in his monograph entitled *Griechisches Pferdegeschirr* (Berlin, 1896). The bits, which are of bronze, and belong to the fourth century, B.C., were found along with a beautiful bronze muzzle and bronze ornaments of the headstall in a grave in Boeotia. They are complete in every detail, including the curved branches at the ends to which the straps of the headstall were fastened and the branches to which the reins were attached. Xenophon is concerned only with the bit itself. This, in the two examples referred to, consists of two axles joined in the middle by two links, one link within the other. Next to the links are discs; then on either side a cylinder covered with four rows of sharp teeth. Next to the cylinders come the branches to be attached to the headstall, and outside these the branches for the reins. Discs,

[1] Thus Ischomachus (*Oeconomicus*, xi. 17 f.), an excellent horseman (20), says that he has his horse led to and from his farm: he mounts at the farm, and goes through military exercises. Xenophon is, of course, describing his own practice.

cylinders and branches move on the axles. From each of the central links hangs a little chain, of three or four rings (see c. x. 9).

When the horse was led out to be groomed or to give him a roll, a muzzle was used. The muzzle is depicted on several vases. For example, a black-figured amphora in the Ashmolean Museum (No. 212) shows a led horse wearing the muzzle, and, in this case, bridled as well. The muzzles for ordinary use were made either of straps or of wicker. The Ashmolean horse's muzzle is attached by a strap passing under the ears. In another example figured in E. Walpole's *Memoirs of European and Asiatic Turkey*, we have two horses muzzled and tied together by the leading reins that hang from the muzzle. A groom is cleaning the back of the horse on the right with a strigil (cf. c. v. 5). Another groom is examining the uplifted forefoot of the horse on the left, crouching beneath the horse in a manner not approved by Xenophon. A halter was also attached to the bridle and used in mounting or in leading the horse when not muzzled (c. vii. 1). The halter is clearly seen on one of the horses depicted on an Attic *cylix* in the Berlin Museum, of which the subject is the examination of the cavalry recruits; and there are other extant examples.

In the twelfth chapter Xenophon recommends that the horse should be protected in war with a frontlet, breastplate and thigh-pieces.[1] It is not unlikely that these came into use in Greece as the result of his recommendation. Their origin is

---

[1] From this chapter it is clear that the rider's thighs were not protected by thigh-pieces.

INTRODUCTION

Asiatic, and of course Xenophon had seen them used during the expedition of the Ten Thousand.

The methodical construction of this treatise contrasts strongly with the want of arrangement that we find in the *Discourse on Hunting*. The author starts with a modest reference to his skill in horsemanship; and here let the translator, whose own acquaintance with horses has been brief and disastrous, offer an apology to any practical horseman into whose hands this version, or perversion, may fall, for any absurdities that he may—it is but too likely—detect in the English equivalents used in the translation to represent the technical terms of the original. After this brief and characteristic exordium the author falls at once to business. Here is a list of the contents: (1) Buying a colt—points and size of the young horse (c. i.). (2) Breaking a young horse (c. ii.). (3) Buying a horse already ridden (c. iii.). (4) Stable and yard (c. iv.). (5) The groom's duties (c. v.–vi.). (6) Instructions to the rider—mounting, starting, exercises (c. vii.–viii.). (7) Management of a fiery horse (c. ix.). (8) How to make the best of a war-horse (c. x. 1–5). (9) Bits, their form and use (c. x. 6). (10) The horse for ceremonial occasions (c. xi.). (11) Armour of rider and horse (c. xii. 1–10). (12) Offensive weapons and their use (c. xii. 11). (13) Brief reference to the *Cavalry Commander* for further information. The exposition is as clear as the arrangement.

In his opening words, and elsewhere, Xenophon refers to the treatise of Simon, of which an important fragment survives in the library of Emmanuel College, Cambridge.[1] There is much matter common to both

---

[1] There are several modern editions.

treatises, but it is unfair to represent Xenophon as merely repeating Simon.[1] Both authors begin their description of the parts of the horse at the hoofs and work upwards to the head. All later writers on the horse, Greek and Roman, start at the head. Very likely Xenophon consciously followed Simon's method: it would be like him to do that.

VII. *Hunting*

When an Englishman tells you that he is "going to hunt," you understand him to mean that he intends to hunt the fox on horseback. Had you heard a young Greek of the fourth century B.C. make the same remark, the odds would have been that he was going to hunt the hare on foot. Two other branches of the sport in which the average young Greek then indulged were the hunting of the red deer and the boar. But if either of these creatures was to be the object of his pursuit, he would have said so; and in either case he would have been intending to go unmounted,[2] unless he had said definitely that he was going on horseback. These simple facts explain the absence of a statement early in this treatise (c. ii.), that its author intends to deal first with hare hunting, and also explain why there is nothing in the treatise about hunting on horseback, apart from an incidental reference in the appendix on hunting abroad (c. xi. 3). Sons of aristocratic houses often rode to hounds;

[1] Oder in his *Anecdota Cantabrigiensia*, a mine of information on the ancient horse-literature, is hardly just to Xenophon.

[2] The term κυνηγετεῖν, consistently used for hunting in the treatise, is normally confined in classical authors to hunting *on foot*.

and no doubt Xenophon's boys were mounted when they hunted boars, gazelles and red deer at Scillus.[1] But this treatise is addressed to the average young hunter, and is confined to those forms of the sport that were open to him.

The art of hunting, like other arts and crafts, was a gift of the gods to the centaur Chiron, who imparted it to many heroes, all of whom enjoyed the special favour of the gods. To this topic is devoted a lengthy rhetorical exordium, which differs entirely by its elaborate style from the rest of the treatise, in which the rules of formal composition are almost entirely disregarded. There is no parallel to this exordium in Greek literature anterior to the Christian era.[2] To Xenophon, indeed, a long exordium of any kind is alien.

The writer's object is instruction of the novice. He undertakes to enumerate and to explain all the paraphernalia required in hunting (c. ii. 2). But his promise is but indifferently fulfilled in the sequel. He is excellent in description; but, like so many modern teachers, he unconsciously reckons on too much knowledge in his pupils. Especially confusing is his use of the same term for the track and the scent of the hare; and the directions for unravelling the tracks and for setting up the nets, the parts of which he does not explain, are anything but clear.

---

[1] *Anabasis*, v. iii. 10. We see that this treatise was not written, as is sometimes supposed, for the use of Xenophon's sons.

[2] As for the date of the exordium see below. J. Mewaldt (*Hermes*, xlvi. p. 76), has pointed out a remarkable parallel in the exordium to the *Physician* falsely attributed to Galen, but contemporary with him.

INTRODUCTION

Nor is his arrangement of his matter in the section on the hare wholly satisfactory. For most of the seventh chapter and the whole of the eighth consist of remarks, in the nature of an appendix, on the subject of the third chapter.

It is surprising to find that nets were not used in Greece for hunting the red deer on foot, though the "net-keeper" accompanied the hunt (c. ix. 6). Their place was taken by the abominable traps or caltrops, which are carefully and clearly described. We wonder how an unmounted hunter was to get among the deer and to isolate a member of the herd (c. ix. 10).

To the survey of the three branches of hunting the author appends a few irrelevant remarks on the hunting of big game abroad, apparently just because the subject interested him and might be expected to interest his young readers. These remarks, it may be observed, do not include varieties of hunting that Xenophon had witnessed in Asia, and would be expected to describe if he had written the *Hunting at Scillus.*

Having finished with the technical side of the subject, our author launches out into an enumeration of the benefits to be derived from hunting on foot (c. xii. 1–9). It is good for the health, fits men for their military duties, and affords a fine moral training. Some, he says, meaning, probably, Aristippus and his followers, object to hunting on the ground that it leads men to waste the time that ought to be given to their business and to the service of the state. These objectors are utterly wrong, and many of them are even vicious. But hunters are a virtuous folk, because they love toil (c. xii. 10, end). The argument here, and in the last chapter, is sloppy, but the writer disarms criticism by his zeal.

The task that the writer set himself at the beginning is now completed, and we should have expected him to end here. But he is in a fighting mood, and is determined to warn his young readers against all the enemies of his theories. Chief among these are the "sophists," that is, the professors of other systems of education than that in which he believes. They have never made a man virtuous, and their writings, for all the care lavished on their style, do nobody any good. Very likely one of them will attack this treatise for its slipshod style and want of "beauty." What does the author care? He seeks to do good, not to train the young in sophistry. Beware of the professors and cleave to the lovers of wisdom! Then there are the unscrupulous self-seekers and reckless politicians. Don't emulate them! The best of them incur envy,[1] and the bad ones are rogues. But hunters are genial and kindly, and they seek only to do good.

The technical portion of this treatise (c. ii.–xi.) and the curious epilogue (c. xii.–xiii.) are certainly contemporary with Xenophon; and—as all competent critics now agree—both were written by one man. The attack on the "sophists" in the last chapter must have been written in the fourth century B.C., when "philosophers" and "sophists" wrangled over the theory and practice of education, and flooded the world with books on the subject. The descriptive portions of the technical part are worthy of Xenophon; and the sentiments expressed in the

[1] This, I think, must have been the meaning of c. xiii. 10 before the text was corrupted.

epilogue strongly remind us of his sentiments. The difficulty in accepting the treatise as his lies mainly in the jerkiness of the style and the looseness of the grammar. We miss the combination of short simple sentences with long periods that is characteristic of his manner; and the constant indulgence in "ellipse," "asyndeton," "chiasmus," "infinitive of command," and so on, is not at all like what we find in his acknowledged works. On the whole, when the pros and cons are weighed and re-weighed, it does not appear utterly impossible that he wrote it as a first experiment in authorship before leaving Athens for Asia. The work is full of his zest for hunting, his pietism, his insistence that before you try to do a thing, you must understand how to do it, and, above all, his belief in the efficacy of diligence and toil. The author of the treatise is clearly an Athenian; and though his opinions bear a strong resemblance to those of the older Cynics, and especially of Antisthenes, the founder of the Cynic school, I see no decisive reason for thinking it impossible— though it is certainly difficult to believe—that Xenophon wrote it in the last years of Socrates' life. He was then aged thirty,[1] and might employ a didactic tone towards the youth of eighteen. If he did, he must have adopted a manner of writing that he judged appropriate to a didactic treatise addressed to the young.[2] We must suppose that he deliberately

---

[1] Xenophon was born 430 B.C.; Apollodorus (fl. 150 B.C.) in his *Chronica* wrongly suggested 440 B.C. From Apollodorus the error passed into Diogenes Laertius and Suidas.

[2] There is a similar manner in one or two didactic sentences quoted from Antisthenes by Diogenes Laertius (vi. 12). Mewaldt detects a similarity in the style of Simon's treatise on *Horsemanship*. The manner is common enough in technical

avoided formal rhetoric, of which there are only
very few examples in the treatise. Xenophon in
the *Hellenica* and the *Agesilaus* does experiment in
different styles of writing, though within limits that
he passes far beyond in the *Hunting*, if this work
be really his. But a great difficulty confronts us.
In the thirteenth chapter (3–7) the writer, in his
most rhetorical passage, says in effect that he despises
rhetoric as practised in his day, and has no belief
in its value. Now the rhetoric of the fourth-century
sophists is based on the teaching of Gorgias and
Prodicus. Xenophon elsewhere always writes respect-
fully of these two great stylists, and he shows both
by his statements and by his practice that he has a
keen appreciation of rhetoric as an aid to persuasion.[1]
Already at the beginning of the *Hellenica* (i. i. 30–31)
he attributes the reputation of Hermocrates the
Syracusan "as speaker and adviser" to the attention
that he paid to oratory; and Sicilian oratory without
rhetoric is unthinkable. Can it be that between,
say, 401 B.C. and 393 B.C. he so entirely changed his
opinion? It is possible that he did so, in consequence
of his experience in Asia, where the influence of
oratory on the soldiers was continually made manifest.[2]

In at least two parts of the epilogue it is highly
probable that Aristippus is attacked, first as object-

---

[1] The results of his study of Gorgias can be traced in the
Constitution of the Lacedaemonians and the *Ways and Means*
as well as in the *Agesilaus*.

[2] Note especially what he says about Proxenus (*Anabasis*,
II. vi. 16), that in his youth he had an ambition to become
a man of affairs, and therefore put himself under Gorgias.

---

writings. A pretty specimen of it is to be found in Plato's
description of the two horses (*Phaedrus*, p. 253 D).

ing to toil, and further on as a self-seeker (xii. 10; xiii. 10); Aristippus was, in fact, the first of the Socratics to take fees from his pupils.[1] Now we know that Xenophon had an aversion to Aristippus, whose opinions and conduct naturally jarred on him. What is more likely than that Xenophon should warn his young readers against such an alluring but dangerous teacher?

Here we may leave the problem. The style does not in the least suggest Xenophon: much of the matter, both in the technical part and in the epilogue, does suggest him. Absurdities have been pointed out[2] in the reasoning of the epilogue; but some of these absurdities are probably due to the corrupt state in which the text of it has come down to us. For whereas in the technical part we have the powerful aid of Pollux in correcting the text, he cites nothing from the epilogue.

The laborious exordium is not contemporary with the rest of the work. Certain rhythms are persistently used in it that were not in vogue earlier than the first half of the third century B.C.[3] But the "sophistic" list of Chiron's pupils and, still more, the highly artificial order of the words show that the date is much later than the third century. Norden, the highest authority in these matters, states confidently that the exordium belongs to the period of the "second sophistic."[4] We may con-

---

[1] Diogenes Laertius, ii. 65.

[2] Especially by Hartman in his *Analecta Xenophontea*.

[3] Especially the *dichoreus* ($-\smile-\smile$) at the end of the sentence, which is characteristic of the *Asianic* style. (Radermacher in *Rheinisches Museum*, lii.).

[4] In *Die Antike Prosakunst* (p. 433) he cites some striking parallels from the Lemnian Philostratus' *Imagines* and from *Aelian*.

xlii

clude without hesitation that it was composed in the reign of Hadrian (A.D. 117–138), when also the reference to it in c. xiii. 18 was added.[1] Somewhere about A.D. 150 Arrian must have come across a copy of the *Hunting* in Athens, with the exordium already prefixed. He took the exordium at its face value, and assumed that it too was written by Xenophon.[2] In the *Heroicus* (p. 308), written between A.D. 213 and 219, the Lemnian Philostratus includes Telamon, Theseus and Palamedes among the disciples of Chiron. These heroes are mentioned nowhere else as pupils of the Centaur except in our epilogue.[3]

The earliest author who alludes to the *Hunting* as Xenophon's work is Plutarch; but Demetrius of Magnesia, a contemporary of Cicero, already recognised it as his.[4]

The principal manuscripts are the following :—

1. For the *Hiero, Agesilaus, Constitution of the Lacedaemonians* and *Ways and Means :*

A. (*Vaticanus*, 1335), tenth or eleventh century. Of the *Ways and Means* only a part (c. i. 5 to c. iii. 5) has survived.

[1] This passage furnished, as it were, a text to the writer of the exordium.

[2] Arrian, *Cynegeticus* i. It is odd that Arrian, no mean judge of style, accepted the whole work, including the exordium, as certainly genuine.

[3] The coincidence at least shows that these names were introduced into the list by the late sophists. K. Münscher (*Philologus, Supplementband*, x., p. 503) doubts whether Philostratus consciously repeats the author of the exordium ; nor do I think it certain that he does so.

[4] Diogenes Laertius, ii. 57.

B. (*Vaticanus*, 1950), fifteenth century. Probably
    copied from A.

C. (*Mutinensis*, 145), fifteenth century. This MS.
    does not include the *Agesilaus*. It contains
    many peculiar readings, of which many are
    conjectures.

M. (*Marcianus*, 511), probably thirteenth century.

A papyrus fragment of the *Ways and Means*, c. i.
5–6, belonging to the second century A.D., is edited
by Wilcken in the *Archiv für Papyrusforschung*,
vol. i.

The copious extracts contained in the *Florilegium*
of Stobaeus are specially important for checking the
text of the *Constitution of the Lacedaemonians*.

2. For the *Cavalry Commander, Horsemanship* and
    Hunting.

A. (*Vindobonensis*, IV. 37), sixteenth century.
    This MS. does not include the *Cavalry
    Commander*. It is derived from an arche-
    type of the twelfth century, and is the best
    MS. of the *Horsemanship* and *Hunting*. Its
    version of c. i. of *Hunting* is peculiar,
    evidently because the MS. from which it
    was copied was blurred and partly illegible.

B. (*Vaticanus*, 989), thirteenth century. The best
    MS. of the *Hipparchicus*, and the next best
    to A. of the other two. The first chapter
    of *Hunting*, and the opening words of the
    second are missing.

M. (*Marcianus*, 511).

The lexicon of Pollux is of the utmost value in
checking and restoring the corrupted text of the

xliv

treatise on *Horsemanship* and the technical parts of that on *Hunting*.

An excellent critical edition of the text of the first four treatises by A. Thalheim and of the last three by E. Ruehl is included in the Teubner Series.

There is also a recent text of the whole in Vol. V. of *Xenophontis Opera Omnia* (Scriptorum Classicorum Bibliotheca Oxoniensis).

A translation of the *Horsemanship* with notes by R. Berenger is included in his *History of the Art of Horsemanship* (1671). Paul Louis Courier's translation of the *Cavalry Commander* and *Horsemanship* (1st ed. 1807) contains many valuable notes, and his contribution to the purification and elucidation of the text is of the first importance. The MS. that he followed was *Vaticanus* 989.

The Art of Horsemanship translated, with chapters on the Greek Riding-Horse, and with notes, by Morris H. Morgan (1894) is excellent.

The German translation of the last-mentioned work by E. Pollack (1912) includes a commentary and a full bibliography and is indispensable to students.

O. Manns, *Uber die Jagd bei den Griechen* (1888–1890), has given a complete exposition of the technical portions of the treatise on *Hunting*.

R. M. Radermacher's articles in the *Rheinisches Museum*, li., lii., mark an epoch in the criticism of the *Hunting*.

All recent textual criticism of the *Constitution of the Lacedaemonians* and of the last three treatises included in this volume is based on the exhaustive work of three Italian scholars. The results arrived

INTRODUCTION

at by them are contained in the following Berlin
editions:—

G. Pierleoni: Xenophontis *Respublica Lacedae-*
moniorum, 1905.
„ „ „ *Cynegeticus,* 1902.
P. Cerocchi: „ *Hipparchicus,* 1901.
V. Tommasini: „ *de Re Equestri,* 1902.

The Greek text of this volume follows that of
Sauppe (= S. in the footnotes) except where stated.

The earliest printed edition of the collected works
is that of Filippo Giunta (Florence, 1516); but it
does not include the *Agesilaus* and *Ways and Means.*
The *Agesilaus* was first printed by J. Reuchlin in
1520 (with the *Apology* and *Hiero*), and the *Ways
and Means* in the Aldine ed. (1525).
The Constitution of the Athenians, a work not included in this volume in 1925 or in subsequent
reprints, has now been added (1968).

Recent modern work includes:—

Hiero. Text and Spanish Translation and Notes·
M. F. Galiano. Madrid, 1954.
Constitution of the Lacedaemonians. Text and French
Translation and Commentary. F. Ollier. Lyon,
1934.
Edition by M. R. Gomez and M. F. Galiano. 1957.
A study by K. M. T. Chrimes (Mrs. D. Atkinson).
'*The Respublica Lacedaemoniorum.*' Manchester,
1948.

INTRODUCTION

On the Art of Horsemanship.   Edition by K. Widdra.
   Leipzig.   Teubner, 1964.

   Edition and German translation by K. Widdra.
   Berlin, 1965.

   Edition and French Translation.   E. Delebecque.
   Paris, 1950.

Constitution of the Athenians.   See the Bibliography
   in G. W. Bowersock's Introduction to this work
   in this Volume, pp. 470 ff.

HIERO

ΞΕΝΟΦΩΝΤΟΣ ΙΕΡΩΝ

I. Σιμωνίδης ὁ ποιητὴς ἀφίκετό ποτε πρὸς Ἱέρωνα τὸν τύραννον. σχολῆς δὲ γενομένης ἀμφοῖν εἶπεν ὁ Σιμωνίδης· Ἆρ᾽ ἄν μοι ἐθελήσαις, ὦ Ἱέρων, διηγήσασθαι ἃ εἰκὸς εἰδέναι σε βέλτιον ἐμοῦ;

Καὶ ποῖα ταῦτ᾽ ἐστίν, ἔφη ὁ Ἱέρων, ὁποῖα δὴ ἐγὼ βέλτιον ἂν εἰδείην σοῦ οὕτως ὄντος σοφοῦ ἀνδρός;

2 Οἶδά σε, ἔφη, ἐγὼ καὶ ἰδιώτην γεγενημένον καὶ νῦν τύραννον ὄντα· εἰκὸς οὖν ἀμφοτέρων πεπειραμένον καὶ εἰδέναι σε μᾶλλον ἐμοῦ, πῇ διαφέρει ὁ τυραννικός τε καὶ ὁ[1] ἰδιωτικὸς βίος εἰς εὐφροσύνας τε καὶ λύπας ἀνθρώποις.

3 Τί οὖν, ἔφη ὁ Ἱέρων, οὐχὶ καὶ σύ, ἐπεὶ νῦν γε ἔτι ἰδιώτης εἶ, ὑπέμνησάς με τὰ ἐν τῷ ἰδιωτικῷ βίῳ; οὕτως γὰρ ἄν σοι οἶμαι μάλιστα ἐγὼ δύνασθαι δηλοῦν τὰ διαφέροντα ἐν ἑκατέρῳ.

4 Οὕτω δὴ ὁ Σιμωνίδης εἶπε· Τοὺς μὲν δὴ ἰδιώτας ἔγωγε, ὦ Ἱέρων, δοκῶ μοι καταμεμαθηκέναι διὰ μὲν τῶν ὀφθαλμῶν ὁράμασιν ἡδομένους τε καὶ ἀχθομένους, διὰ δὲ τῶν ὤτων ἀκούσμασι, διὰ δὲ τῶν ῥινῶν ὀσμαῖς, διὰ δὲ τοῦ στόματος σίτοις τε καὶ ποτοῖς, τὰ δ᾽ ἀφροδίσια δι᾽ ὧν δὴ πάντες 5 ἐπιστάμεθα· τὰ δὲ ψύχη καὶ θάλπη καὶ σκληρὰ καὶ μαλακὰ καὶ κοῦφα καὶ βαρέα ὅλῳ τῷ σώματί μοι δοκοῦμεν, ἔφη, κρίνοντες ἥδεσθαί τε

2

XENOPHON'S HIERO

I. SIMONIDES, the poet, once paid a visit to Hiero, the despot. When both found time to spare, Simonides said: "Hiero, will you please explain something to me that you probably know better than I?"

"And pray what is it," said Hiero, "that I can know better than one so wise as yourself?"

"I know you were born a private citizen," he [2] answered, "and are now a despot. Therefore, as you have experienced both fortunes, you probably know better than I how the lives of the despot and the citizen differ as regards the joys and sorrows that fall to man's lot."

"Surely," said Hiero, "seeing that you are still [3] a private citizen, it is for you to remind me of what happens in a citizen's life; and then, I think, I could best show you the differences between the two."

"Well," said Simonides, taking the suggestion, [4] "I think I have observed that sights affect private citizens with pleasure and pain through the eyes, sounds through the ears, smells through the nostrils, meat and drink through the mouth, carnal appetites —of course we all know how. In the case of cold [5] and heat, things hard and soft, light and heavy, our sensations of pleasure and pain depend on the

---

[1] δ A. Sauppe omits with the other MSS.

καὶ λυπεῖσθαι ἐπ' αὐτοῖς· ἀγαθοῖς δὲ καὶ κακοῖς
ἔστι μὲν ὅτε δι' αὐτῆς τῆς ψυχῆς μοι δοκοῦμεν
ἥδεσθαί τε καὶ λυπεῖσθαι, ἔστι δ' ὅτε κοινῇ διά
6 τε τῆς ψυχῆς καὶ διὰ τοῦ σώματος. τῷ δ'
ὕπνῳ ὅτι μὲν ἡδόμεθα, δοκῶ μοι αἰσθάνεσθαι,
ὅπως δὲ καὶ ᾧτινι καὶ ὁπότε, ταῦτα μᾶλλόν πως,
ἔφη, δοκῶ μοι ἀγνοεῖν. καὶ οὐδὲν ἴσως τοῦτο
θαυμαστόν, εἰ τὰ ἐν τῷ ἐγρηγορέναι σαφεστέρας
ἡμῖν τὰς αἰσθήσεις παρέχεται ἢ τὰ ἐν τῷ ὕπνῳ.
7 Πρὸς ταῦτα δὴ ὁ Ἱέρων ἀπεκρίνατο, Ἐγὼ μὲν
τοίνυν, ἔφη, ὦ Σιμωνίδη, ἔξω τούτων ὧν εἴρηκας
σύγε οὐδ' ὅπως ἂν αἴσθοιτό τινος ἄλλου ὁ
τύραννος ἔχοιμ' ἂν εἰπεῖν, ὥστε μέχρι γε τούτου
οὐκ οἶδ' εἴ τινι διαφέρει ὁ τυραννικὸς βίος τοῦ
ἰδιωτικοῦ βίου.
8 Καὶ ὁ Σιμωνίδης εἶπεν, Ἀλλ' ἐν τοῖσδε, ἔφη,
διαφέρει· πολλαπλάσια μὲν δι' ἑκάστου τούτων
εὐφραίνεται, πολὺ δὲ μείω τὰ λυπηρὰ ἔχει.

Καὶ ὁ Ἱέρων εἶπεν· Οὐχ οὕτως ἔχει, ὦ Σιμωνίδη, ταῦτα, ἀλλ' εὖ ἴσθ', ὅτι μείω πολὺ
εὐφραίνονται οἱ τύραννοι τῶν μετρίως διαγόντων
ἰδιωτῶν, πολὺ δὲ πλείω καὶ μείζω λυποῦνται.
9 Ἄπιστα λέγεις, ἔφη ὁ Σιμωνίδης. εἰ γὰρ
οὕτω ταῦτ' εἶχε, πῶς ἂν πολλοὶ μὲν ἐπεθύμουν
τυραννεῖν, καὶ ταῦτα τῶν δοκούντων ἱκανωτάτων
ἀνδρῶν εἶναι ; πῶς δὲ πάντες ἐζήλουν ἂν τοὺς
τυράννους ;
10 Ὅτι ναὶ μὰ τὸν Δί', ἔφη ὁ Ἱέρων, ἄπειροι ὄντες
ἀμφοτέρων τῶν ἔργων σκοποῦνται περὶ αὐτοῦ.
ἐγὼ δὲ πειράσομαί σε διδάσκειν, ὅτι ἀληθῆ λέγω,
ἀρξάμενος ἀπὸ τῆς ὄψεως· ἐντεῦθεν γὰρ καὶ σὲ
δοκῶ μεμνῆσθαι ἀρξάμενον λέγειν.

4

whole body, I think. In good and evil we seem to feel pleasure or pain, as the case may be—sometimes through the instrumentality of the moral being only, at other times through that of the moral and the physical being together. Sleep, it seems clear 6 to me, affects us with pleasure; but how and by what means and when are puzzles that I feel less able to solve. And perhaps it is no matter for surprise if our sensations are clearer when we are awake than when we are asleep."

"For my part, Simonides," said Hiero in answer 7 to this, "I cannot say how a despot could have any sensations apart from those you have mentioned. So far, therefore, I fail to see that the despot's life differs in any respect from the citizen's."

"In this respect it does differ," said Simonides: 8 "the pleasures it experiences by means of these various organs are infinitely greater in number, and the pains it undergoes are far fewer."

"It is not so, Simonides," retorted Hiero; "I assure you far fewer pleasures fall to despots than to citizens of modest means, and many more and much greater pains."

"Incredible!" exclaimed Simonides. "Were it 9 so, how should a despot's throne be an object of desire to many, even of those who are reputed to be men of ample means? And how should all the world envy despots?"

"For this reason of course," said Hiero, "that 10 they speculate on the subject without experience of both estates. But I will try to show you that I am speaking the truth, beginning with the sense of sight. That was your first point, if I am not mistaken.

11 Πρῶτον μὲν γὰρ ἐν τοῖς διὰ τῆς ὄψεως θεάμασι
λογιζόμενος εὑρίσκω μειονεκτοῦντας τοὺς τυράννους. ἄλλα μέν γε ἐν ἄλλῃ χώρᾳ ἐστὶν
ἀξιοθέατα· ἐπὶ δὲ τούτων ἕκαστα οἱ μὲν ἰδιῶται
ἔρχονται καὶ εἰς πόλεις ἃς ἂν βούλωνται καὶ εἰς
τὰς κοινὰς πανηγύρεις, ἔνθα ἃ[1] ἀξιοθεατότατα
12 δοκεῖ ἀνθρώποις συναγείρεται.[2] οἱ δὲ τύραννοι
οὐ μάλα ἀμφὶ θεωρίας ἔχουσιν. οὔτε γὰρ
ἰέναι αὐτοῖς ἀσφαλὲς ὅπου μὴ κρείττονες τῶν
παρόντων μέλλουσιν ἔσεσθαι, οὔτε τὰ οἴκοι
κέκτηνται ἐχυρά, ὥστε ἄλλοις παρακαταθεμένους
ἀποδημεῖν. φοβερὸν γάρ, μὴ ἅμα στερηθῶσι τῆς
ἀρχῆς καὶ ἀδύνατοι γένωνται τιμωρήσασθαι τοὺς
13 ἀδικήσαντας. εἴποις οὖν ἂν ἴσως σύ, 'Αλλ' ἄρα
ἔρχεται αὐτοῖς τὰ τοιαῦτα καὶ οἴκοι μένουσι.
ναὶ μὰ Δία, ὦ Σιμωνίδη, ὀλίγα γε τῶν πολλῶν·
καὶ ταῦτα τοιαῦτα ὄντα οὕτω τίμια πωλεῖται
τοῖς τυράννοις, ὥστε οἱ ἐπιδεικνύμενοι καὶ ὁτιοῦν
ἀξιοῦσι πολλαπλάσια λαβόντες ἐν ὀλίγῳ χρόνῳ
ἀπιέναι παρὰ τοῦ τυράννου ἢ ὅσα ἐν παντὶ τῷ
βίῳ παρὰ πάντων τῶν ἄλλων ἀνθρώπων κτῶνται.
14 Καὶ ὁ Σιμωνίδης εἶπεν· 'Αλλ' εἰ τοῖς θεάμασι
μειονεκτεῖτε, διά γέ τοι τῆς ἀκοῆς πλεονεκτεῖτε.
ἐπεὶ τοῦ μὲν ἡδίστου ἀκροάματος, ἐπαίνου,
οὔποτε σπανίζετε· πάντες γὰρ οἱ παρόντες ὑμῖν
πάντα καὶ ὅσα ἂν λέγητε καὶ ὅσα ἂν ποιῆτε
ἐπαινοῦσι. τοῦ δ' αὖ χαλεπωτάτου ἀκροάματος,
λοιδορίας, ἀνήκοοί ἐστε· οὐδεὶς γὰρ ἐθέλει τύραννον κατ' ὀφθαλμοὺς κακηγορεῖν.[3]
15 Καὶ ὁ Ἱέρων εἶπε, Καὶ τί οἴει, ἔφη, τοὺς μὴ

---

[1] ἃ Lenklau : τὰ Sauppe with the MSS. and Stobaeus.

"In the first place, then, taking the objects that 11
we perceive by means of vision, I find by calculation
that in regard to sight-seeing, despots are worse off.
In every land there are things worth seeing: and in
search of these private citizens visit any city they
choose, and attend the national festivals, where all
things reputed to be most worth seeing are assembled.
But despots are not at all concerned with missions 12
to shows. For it is risky for them to go where they
will be no stronger than the crowd, and their property at home is too insecure to be left in charge
of others while they are abroad. For they fear to
lose their throne, and at the same time to be unable
to take vengeance on the authors of the wrong.
Perhaps you may say : ' But, after all, such spectacles 13
come to them even if they stay at home.' No, no,
Simonides, only one in a hundred such ; and what
there are of them are offered to despots at a price
so exorbitant that showmen who exhibit some trifle
expect to leave the court in an hour with far more
money than they get from all the rest of the world
in a lifetime."

"Ah," said Simonides, "but if you are worse off 14
in the matter of sight-seeing, the sense of hearing,
you know, gives you the advantage. Praise, the
sweetest of all sounds, is never lacking, for all your
courtiers praise everything you do and every word
you utter. Abuse, on the contrary, that most offensive
of sounds, is never in your ears, for no one likes to
speak evil of a despot in his presence."

"And what pleasure," asked Hiero, "comes, do 15

---

² συναγείρεται Lenklau : συναγείρεσθαι Sauppe with the
MSS. and Stobaeus.
³ τύραννον . . . κακηγορεῖν Cobet : Sauppe reads τυράννου
. . . κατηγορεῖν with the MSS. and Stobaeus.

λέγοντας κακῶς εὐφραίνειν, ὅταν εἰδῇ τις σαφῶς,
ὅτι οἱ σιωπῶντες οὗτοι πάντα κακὰ νοοῦσι τῷ
τυράννῳ· ἢ τοὺς ἐπαινοῦντας τί δοκεῖς εὐφραίνειν, ὅταν ὕποπτοι ὦσιν ἕνεκα τοῦ κολακεύειν
τοὺς ἐπαίνους ποιεῖσθαι;

16 Καὶ ὁ Σιμωνίδης εἶπε· Τοῦτο μὲν δὴ ναὶ μὰ
τὸν Δία ἔγωγέ σοι, Ἱέρων, πάνυ συγχωρῶ, τοὺς
ἐπαίνους παρὰ τῶν ἐλευθερωτάτων ἡδίστους εἶναι,
ἀλλ᾽, ὁρᾷς, ἐκεῖνό γε οὐκ ἂν ἔτι πείσαις ἀνθρώπων
οὐδένα, ὡς οὐχὶ δι᾽ ὧν τρεφόμεθα οἱ ἄνθρωποι,
πολὺ πλείω ὑμεῖς ἐν αὐτοῖς εὐφραίνεσθε.

17 Καὶ οἶδά γε, ἔφη, ὦ Σιμωνίδη, ὅτι τούτῳ
κρίνουσιν οἱ πλεῖστοι ἥδιον ἡμᾶς καὶ πίνειν
καὶ ἐσθίειν τῶν ἰδιωτῶν, ὅτι δοκοῦσι καὶ αὐτοὶ
ἥδιον ἂν δειπνῆσαι τὸ ἡμῖν παρατιθέμενον
δεῖπνον ἢ τὸ ἑαυτοῖς· τὸ γὰρ τὰ εἰωθότα ὑπερ-
18 βάλλον, τοῦτο παρέχει τὰς ἡδονάς. διὸ καὶ
πάντες ἄνθρωποι ἡδέως προσδέχονται τὰς ἑορτὰς
πλὴν οἱ τύραννοι· ἔκπλεω γὰρ αὐτοῖς ἀεὶ παρε-
σκευασμέναι οὐδεμίαν ἐν ταῖς ἑορταῖς ἔχουσιν αἱ
τράπεζαι αὐτῶν ἐπίδοσιν· ὥστε ταύτῃ πρῶτον
τῇ εὐφροσύνῃ τῆς ἐλπίδος μειονεκτοῦσι τῶν
19 ἰδιωτῶν. ἔπειτα δ᾽, ἔφη, ἐκεῖνο εὖ οἶδ᾽ ὅτι καὶ
σὺ ἔμπειρος εἶ, ὅτι ὅσῳ ἂν πλείω τις παραθῆται
τὰ περιττὰ τῶν ἱκανῶν, τοσούτῳ θᾶττον κόρος
ἐμπίπτει τῆς ἐδωδῆς· ὥστε καὶ τῷ χρόνῳ τῆς
ἡδονῆς μειονεκτεῖ ὁ παρατιθέμενος πολλὰ τῶν
μετρίως διαιτωμένων.

20 Ἀλλὰ ναὶ μὰ Δί᾽, ἔφη ὁ Σιμωνίδης, ὅσον ἂν
χρόνον ἡ ψυχὴ προσίηται, τοῦτον πολὺ μᾶλλον
ἥδονται οἱ ταῖς πολυτελεστέραις παρασκευαῖς
τρεφόμενοι τῶν τὰ εὐτελέστερα παρατιθεμένων.

you suppose, of this shrinking from evil words, when one knows well that all harbour evil thoughts against the despot, in spite of their silence? Or what pleasure comes of this praise, do you think, when the praises sound suspiciously like flattery?"

"Well yes," replied Simonides, "in this of course 16 I agree with you entirely, Hiero, that praise from the freest is sweetest. But this, now, you will not persuade anyone to believe, that the things which support human life do not yield you a far greater number of pleasures."

"Yes, Simonides, and I know that the reason 17 why most men judge that we have more enjoyment in eating and drinking than private citizens is this; they think that they themselves would find the dinner served at our table better eating than what they get. Anything, in fact, that is better than what they are accustomed to gives them pleasure. This is why all men look forward to the festivals, 18 except the despots. For their table is always laden with plenty, and admits of no extras on feast days. Here then is one pleasure in respect of which they are worse off than the private citizen, the pleasure of anticipation. But further, your own experience tells 19 you, I am sure, that the greater the number of superfluous dishes set before a man, the sooner a feeling of repletion comes over him; and so, as regards the duration of his pleasure too, the man who has many courses put before him is worse off than the moderate liver."

"But surely," said Simonides, "so long as the 20 appetite holds out, the man who dines at the costlier banquet has far more pleasure than he who is served with the cheaper meal."

21 Οὐκοῦν, ἔφη ὁ Ἱέρων, ὦ Σιμωνίδη, τὸν ἑκάστῳ ἡδόμενον μάλιστα, τοῦτον οἴει καὶ ἐρωτικώτατα ἔχειν τοῦ ἔργου τούτου ;

Πάνυ μὲν οὖν, ἔφη.

Ἡ οὖν ὁρᾷς τι τοὺς τυράννους ἥδιον ἐπὶ τὴν ἑαυτῶν παρασκευὴν ἰόντας ἢ τοὺς ἰδιώτας ἐπὶ τὴν ἑαυτῶν ;

Οὐ μὰ τὸν Δί', ἔφη, οὐ μὲν οὖν, ἀλλὰ καὶ ἀγλευκέστερον, ὡς πολλοῖς ἂν δόξειε.

22 Τί γάρ, ἔφη ὁ Ἱέρων, τὰ πολλὰ ταῦτα μηχανήματα κατανενόηκας, ἃ παρατίθεται τοῖς τυράννοις, ὀξέα καὶ δριμέα καὶ στρυφνὰ καὶ τὰ τούτων ἀδελφά ;

Πάνυ μὲν οὖν, ἔφη ὁ Σιμωνίδης, καὶ πάνυ γέ μοι δοκοῦντα παρὰ φύσιν εἶναι ταῦτα ἀνθρώποις.

23 Ἄλλο τι οὖν οἴει, ἔφη ὁ Ἱέρων, ταῦτα τὰ ἐδέσματα εἶναι ἢ μαλακῆς καὶ ἀσθενούσης τρυφῇ ψυχῆς ἐπιθυμήματα ; ἐπεὶ εὖ οἶδ' ἔγωγε, ὅτι οἱ ἡδέως ἐσθίοντες, καὶ σύ που οἶσθα, ὅτι οὐδὲν προσδέονται τούτων τῶν σοφισμάτων.

24 Ἀλλὰ μέντοι, ἔφη ὁ Σιμωνίδης, τῶν γε πολυτελῶν ὀσμῶν τούτων, αἷς χρίεσθε, τοὺς πλησιάζοντας οἶμαι μᾶλλον ἀπολαύειν ἢ αὐτοὺς ὑμᾶς, ὥσπερ γε καὶ τῶν ἀχαρίτων ὀσμῶν οὐκ αὐτὸς ὁ βεβρωκὼς αἰσθάνεται, ἀλλὰ μᾶλλον οἱ πλησιάζοντες.

25 Οὕτω μέντοι, ἔφη ὁ Ἱέρων, καὶ τῶν σίτων ὁ μὲν ἔχων παντοδαπὰ ἀεὶ οὐδὲν μετὰ πόθου αὐτῶν λαμβάνει· ὁ δὲ σπανίσας τινός οὗτός ἐστιν ὁ μετὰ χαρᾶς πιμπλάμενος, ὅταν αὐτῷ προφανῇ τι.

26 Κινδυνεύουσιν, ἔφη ὁ Σιμωνίδης, αἱ τῶν ἀφρο-

"Don't you think, Simonides, that the greater a 21 man's pleasure in any occupation the stronger is his devotion to it?"

"Certainly."

"Then do you notice that despots fall to their meal with any more zest than private persons to theirs?"

"No, no, of course not; I should rather say with more disgust, according to the common opinion."

"Well now," said Hiero, "have you observed all 22 those pickles and sauces that are put before despots —acid, bitter, astringent and so forth?"

"Yes, certainly; and very unnatural cates I think them for human beings."

"Don't you look on these condiments, then, as 23 mere fads of a jaded and pampered appetite? I know well enough, and I expect you know too, that hearty eaters have no need of these concoctions."

"Well, I certainly think that those costly un- 24 guents with which you anoint your bodies afford more satisfaction to those who are near you than to yourselves, just as the man who has eaten rank food is less conscious of the disagreeable smell than those who come near him."

"Quite so, and we may add that he who has all 25 sorts of food at all times has no stomach for any sort. Offer a man a dish that he seldom tastes, and he eats a bellyful with gusto."

"It seems," remarked Simonides, "as if the 26

δισίων μόνον ὑμῖν ἀπολαύσεις τοῦ τυραννεῖν τὰς
ἐπιθυμίας παρέχειν· ἐν γὰρ τούτῳ ἔξεστιν ὑμῖν
ὅ τι ἂν κάλλιστον ἴδητε τούτῳ συνεῖναι.

27 Νῦν δή, ἔφη ὁ Ἱέρων, εἴρηκας ἐν ᾧ γε, σάφ'
ἴσθι, μειονεκτοῦμεν τῶν ἰδιωτῶν. πρῶτον μὲν
γὰρ γάμος ὁ μὲν ἐκ μειζόνων δήπου καὶ πλούτῳ
καὶ δυνάμει κάλλιστος δοκεῖ εἶναι καὶ παρέχειν
τινὰ τῷ γήμαντι φιλοτιμίαν μεθ' ἡδονῆς. δεύτερος
δ' ὁ ἐκ τῶν ὁμοίων· ὁ δ' ἐκ τῶν φαυλοτέρων
28 πάνυ ἄτιμός τε καὶ ἄχρηστος νομίζεται. τῷ
τοίνυν τυράννῳ, ἂν μὴ ξένην γήμῃ, ἀνάγκη ἐκ
μειόνων γαμεῖν, ὥστε τὸ ἀγαπητὸν οὐ πάνυ αὐτῷ
παραγίγνεται. πολὺ δὲ καὶ αἱ θεραπεῖαι αἱ ἀπὸ
τῶν μέγιστον φρονουσῶν γυναικῶν εὐφραίνουσι
μάλιστα, αἱ δ' ἀπὸ τῶν δούλων παροῦσαι μὲν
οὐδέν τι ἀγαπῶνται, ἐὰν δέ τι ἐλλείπωσι, δεινὰς
ὀργὰς καὶ λύπας ἐμποιοῦσιν.

29 Ἐν δὲ τοῖς παιδικοῖς ἀφροδισίοις ἔτι αὖ πολὺ
μᾶλλον ἢ ἐν τοῖς τεκνοποιοῖς μειονεκτεῖ τῶν
εὐφροσυνῶν ὁ τύραννος. ὅτι μὲν γὰρ τὰ μετ'
ἔρωτος ἀφροδίσια πολὺ διαφερόντως εὐφραίνει,
30 πάντες δήπου ἐπιστάμεθα. ὁ δὲ ἔρως πολὺ αὖ
ἐθέλει ἥκιστα τῷ τυράννῳ ἐγγίγνεσθαι. οὐ γὰρ
τῶν ἑτοίμων ἥδεται ὁ ἔρως ἐφιέμενος, ἀλλὰ τῶν
ἐλπιζομένων. ὥσπερ οὖν οὐκ ἄν [1] τις ἄπειρος
ὢν δίψους τοῦ πιεῖν ἀπολαύοι, οὕτω καὶ ὁ
ἄπειρος ὢν ἔρωτος ἄπειρός ἐστι τῶν ἡδίστων
ἀφροδισίων.

31 Ὁ μὲν οὖν Ἱέρων οὕτως εἶπεν. ὁ δὲ Σιμωνίδης
ἐπιγελάσας, Πῶς λέγεις, ἔφη, ὦ Ἱέρων; τυράννῳ
οὐ φὴς παιδικῶν ἔρωτας ἐμφύεσθαι; πῶς μὴν

---

[1] οὐκ ἄν Stephanus: εἲ S. with the MSS. and Stobaeus.

satisfaction of the carnal appetites were the only motive that produces in you the craving for despotism. For in this matter you are free to enjoy the fairest that meets your eye."

"I assure you that we are worse off than private 27 citizens in the matter to which you now refer. First take marriage. It is commonly held that a marriage into a family of greater wealth and influence is most honourable, and is a source of pride and pleasure to the bridegroom. Next to that comes a marriage with equals. A marriage with inferiors is considered positively degrading and useless. Now unless a 28 despot marries a foreign girl, he is bound to marry beneath him; and so the thing to be desired does not come his way. And whereas it is exceedingly pleasant to receive the attentions of the proudest of ladies, the attentions of slaves are quite unappreciated when shown, and any little shortcomings produce grievous outbursts of anger and annoyance.

"In his relations with favourites, again, even much 29 more than in his relations with women, the despot is at a disadvantage. We all know, I suppose, that passion increases the sweets of love beyond measure. Passion, however, is very shy of entering the heart 30 of a despot, for passion is fain to desire not the easy prize, but the hoped-for joy. Therefore, just as a man who is a stranger to thirst can get no satisfaction out of drinking, so he who is a stranger to passion is a stranger to love's sweetest pleasures."

To this speech of Hiero's Simonides replied, 31 laughing:

"How say you, Hiero? You deny that passion springs up in a despot's heart? Then how about

XENOPHON

συ, ἔφη, ἐρᾷς Δαϊλόχου τοῦ καλλίστου ἐπικαλου-
μένου;

32 "Ὅτι μὰ τὸν Δί, ἔφη, ὦ Σιμωνίδη, οὐ τοῦ
ἑτοίμου παρ' αὐτοῦ δοκοῦντος εἶναι τυχεῖν τούτου
μάλιστα ἐπιθυμῶ, ἀλλὰ τοῦ ἥκιστα τυράννῳ
33 προσήκοντος κατεργάσασθαι. ἐγὼ γὰρ δὴ ἐρῶ
μὲν Δαϊλόχου ὧνπερ ἴσως ἀναγκάζει ἡ φύσις
ἀνθρώπου δεῖσθαι παρὰ τῶν καλῶν, τούτων δὲ
ὧν ἐρῶ τυχεῖν, μετὰ μὲν φιλίας καὶ παρὰ
βουλομένου πάνυ ἰσχυρῶς ἐπιθυμῶ τυγχάνειν,
βίᾳ δὲ λαμβάνειν παρ' αὐτοῦ ἧττον ἄν μοι δοκῶ
34 ἐπιθυμεῖν ἢ ἐμαυτὸν κακόν τι ποιεῖν. παρὰ μὲν
γὰρ πολεμίων ἀκόντων λαμβάνειν πάντων ἥδιστον
ἔγωγε νομίζω εἶναι, παρὰ δὲ παιδικῶν βουλομένων
35 ἥδισται οἶμαι αἱ χάριτές εἰσιν. εὐθὺς γὰρ παρὰ
τοῦ ἀντιφιλοῦντος ἡδεῖαι μὲν αἱ ἀντιβλέψεις,
ἡδεῖαι δὲ αἱ ἐρωτήσεις, ἡδεῖαι δὲ αἱ ἀποκρίσεις,
ἥδισται δὲ καὶ ἐπαφροδιτόταται αἱ μάχαι τε
36 καὶ ἔριδες· τὸ δὲ ἀκόντων παιδικῶν ἀπολαύειν
λεηλασίᾳ, ἔφη, ἔμοιγε δοκεῖ ἐοικέναι μᾶλλον ἢ
ἀφροδισίοις. καίτοι τῷ μὲν λῃστῇ παρέχει τινὰς
ὅμως ἡδονὰς τό τε κέρδος καὶ τὸ ἀνιᾶν τὸν
ἐχθρόν· τὸ δὲ οὗ ἂν ἐρᾷ τις τούτῳ ἥδεσθαι
ἀνιωμένῳ καὶ φιλοῦντα μισεῖσθαι καὶ ἅπτεσθαι
ἀχθομένου πῶς οὐχὶ τοῦτο ἤδη δυσχερὲς τὸ
37 πάθημα καὶ οἰκτρόν; καὶ γὰρ δὴ τῷ μὲν ἰδιώτῃ
εὐθὺς τεκμήριόν ἐστιν, ὅταν ὁ ἐρώμενός τι
ὑπουργῇ, ὅτι ὡς φιλῶν χαρίζεται, διὰ τὸ εἰδέναι,
ὅτι οὐδεμιᾶς ἀνάγκης οὔσης ὑπηρετεῖ, τῷ δὲ
τυράννῳ οὔποτ' ἔστι πιστεῦσαι, ὡς φιλεῖται.
38 ἐπιστάμεθα γὰρ τοὺς[1] διὰ φόβον ὑπηρετοῦντας
ὡς ᾗ μάλιστ' ἂν δύνωνται ἐξεικάζουσιν αὐτοὺς

14

your passion for Daïlochus, whom they call most fair ? "

" Why, Simonides, the explanation, of course, is 32 this : I desire to get from him not what I may have, apparently, for the asking, but that which a despot should be the last to take. The fact is, I desire of 33 Daïlochus just that which human nature, maybe, drives us to ask of the fair. But what I long to get, I very strongly desire to obtain by his goodwill, and with his consent ; but I think I could sooner desire to do myself an injury than to take it from him by force. For to take from an enemy against 34 his will is, I think, the greatest of all pleasures, but favours from a loved one are very pleasant, I fancy, only when he consents. For instance, if he is in 35 sympathy with you, how pleasant are his looks, how pleasant his questions and his answers ; how very pleasant and ravishing are the struggles and bicker-ings. But to take advantage of a favourite against 36 his will seems to me more like brigandage than love. Nay, your brigand finds some pleasure in his gain and in hurting his foe ; but to feel pleasure in hurting one whom you love, to be hated for your affection, to disgust him by your touch, surely that is a mortifying experience and pitiful ! The fact is, 37 a private citizen has instant proof that any act of compliance on the part of his beloved is prompted by affection, since he knows that the service rendered is due to no compulsion ; but the despot can never feel sure that he is loved. For we know that acts 38 of service prompted by fear copy as closely as

---

¹ τοὺς Dindorf : αὐτοὺς τοὺς S. : αὐτοὺς MSS.

ταῖς τῶν φιλούντων ὑπουργίαις. καὶ τοίνυν αἱ
ἐπιβουλαὶ ἐξ οὐδένων πλέονες τοῖς τυράννοις
εἰσὶν ἢ ἀπὸ τῶν μάλιστα φιλεῖν αὐτοὺς προσ-
ποιησαμένων.

II. Πρὸς ταῦτα δὲ εἶπεν ὁ Σιμωνίδης· Ἀλλὰ
ταῦτα μὲν πάνυ ἔμοιγε μικρὰ δοκεῖ εἶναι, ἃ σὺ
λέγεις. πολλοὺς γάρ, ἔφη, ἔγωγε ὁρῶ τῶν
δοκούντων ἀνδρῶν εἶναι ἑκόντας μειονεκτοῦντας
καὶ σίτων καὶ ποτῶν καὶ ὄψων καὶ ἀφροδισίων
2 γε ἀπεχομένους. ἀλλ' ἐν ἐκείνοις γε πολὺ
διαφέρετε τῶν ἰδιωτῶν, ὅτι μεγάλα μὲν ἐπινοεῖτε,
ταχὺ δὲ κατεργάζεσθε, πλεῖστα δὲ τὰ περιττὰ
ἔχετε, κέκτησθε δὲ διαφέροντας μὲν ἀρετῇ ἵππους,
διαφέροντα δὲ κάλλει ὅπλα, ὑπερέχοντα δὲ
κόσμον γυναιξί, μεγαλοπρεπεστάτας δ' οἰκίας
καὶ ταύτας κατεσκευασμένας τοῖς πλείστου
ἀξίοις, ἔτι δὲ πλήθει καὶ ἐπιστήμαις θεράποντας ἀρίστους κέκτησθε, ἱκανώτατοι δ' ἐστὲ
κακῶσαι μὲν ἐχθρούς, ὀνῆσαι δὲ φίλους.

3 Πρὸς ταῦτα δὲ ὁ Ἱέρων εἶπεν· Ἀλλὰ τὸ μὲν
πλῆθος τῶν ἀνθρώπων, ὦ Σιμωνίδη, ἐξαπατᾶσθαι
ὑπὸ τῆς τυραννίδος οὐδέν τι θαυμάζω· μάλα γὰρ
ὁ ὄχλος μοι δοκεῖ δοξάζειν ὁρῶν καὶ εὐδαίμονάς
4 τινας εἶναι καὶ ἀθλίους· ἡ δὲ τυραννὶς τὰ μὲν
δοκοῦντα πολλοῦ ἄξια κτήματα εἶναι ἀνεπτυγ-
μένα θεᾶσθαι πᾶσι παρέχεται, τὰ δὲ χαλεπὰ ἐν
ταῖς ψυχαῖς τῶν τυράννων κέκτηται ἀποκεκρυμ-
μένα, ἔνθαπερ καὶ τὸ εὐδαιμονεῖν καὶ τὸ κακο-
5 δαιμονεῖν τοῖς ἀνθρώποις ἀπόκειται. τὸ μὲν οὖν
τὸ πλῆθος περὶ τούτου λεληθέναι, ὥσπερ εἶπον,
οὐ θαυμάζω· τὸ δὲ καὶ ὑμᾶς ταῦτ' ἀγνοεῖν, οἳ διὰ
τῆς γνώμης θεᾶσθαι δοκεῖτε κάλλιον ἢ διὰ τῶν

possible the ministrations of affection. Indeed, even plots against despots as often as not are the work of those who profess the deepest affection for them."

II. To this Simonides replied : " Well, the points that you raise seem to me mere trifles. For I notice that many respected men willingly go short in the matter of meat and drink and delicacies, and deliberately abstain from sexual indulgence. But I will 2 show you where you have a great advantage over private citizens. Your objects are vast, your attainment swift : you have luxuries in abundance : you own horses unequalled in excellence, arms unmatched in beauty, superb jewelry for women, stately houses full of costly furniture : moreover you have servants many in number and excellent in accomplishments and you are rich in power to harm enemies and reward friends."

To this Hiero answered : " Well, Simonides, 3 that the multitude should be deceived by despotic power surprises me not at all, since the mob seems to guess wholly by appearances that one man is happy, another miserable. Despotism flaunts its 4 seeming precious treasures outspread before the gaze of the world : but its troubles it keeps concealed in the heart of the despot, in the place where human happiness and unhappiness are stored away. That this escapes the observation of the multitude I 5 say, I am not surprised. But what does seem surprising to me is that men like you, whose intelligence is supposed to give you a clearer view of

XENOPHON

ὀφθαλμῶν τὰ πλεῖστα τῶν πραγμάτων, τοῦτό
6 μοι δοκεῖ θαυμαστὸν εἶναι. ἐγὼ δὲ πεπειραμένος
σαφῶς οἶδα, ὦ Σιμωνίδη, καὶ λέγω σοι, ὅτι οἱ
τύραννοι τῶν μεγίστων ἀγαθῶν ἐλάχιστα μετέχουσι, τῶν δὲ μεγίστων κακῶν πλεῖστα κέκτην-
7 ται. αὐτίκα γὰρ εἰ μὲν εἰρήνη δοκεῖ μέγα
ἀγαθὸν τοῖς ἀνθρώποις εἶναι, ταύτης ἐλάχιστον
τοῖς τυράννοις μέτεστιν· εἰ δὲ πόλεμος μέγα
κακόν, τούτου πλεῖστον μέρος οἱ τύραννοι μετέ-
8 χουσιν. εὐθὺς γὰρ τοῖς μὲν ἰδιώταις, ἂν μὴ ἡ
πόλις αὐτῶν κοινὸν πόλεμον πολεμῇ, ἔξεστιν
ὅποι ἂν βούλωνται πορεύεσθαι μηδὲν φοβουμένους, μή τις αὐτοὺς ἀποκτείνῃ, οἱ δὲ τύραννοι
πάντες πανταχῇ ὡς διὰ πολεμίας πορεύονται.
αὐτοί τε γοῦν ὡπλισμένοι οἴονται ἀνάγκην εἶναι
διάγειν καὶ ἄλλους ὁπλοφόρους ἀεὶ συμπεριάγε-
9 σθαι.
Ἔπειτα δὲ οἱ μὲν ἰδιῶται, ἐὰν καὶ στρα-
τεύωνταί ποι εἰς πολεμίαν, ἀλλ᾽ οὖν ἐπειδάν
γε ἔλθωσιν οἴκαδε, ἀσφάλειαν σφίσιν ἡγοῦνται
εἶναι, οἱ δὲ τύραννοι ἐπειδὰν εἰς τὴν ἑαυτῶν
πόλιν ἀφίκωνται, τότε ἐν πλείστοις πολεμίοις
10 ἴσασιν ὄντες. ἐὰν δὲ δὴ καὶ ἄλλοι στρατεύωσιν
εἰς τὴν πόλιν κρείττονες, ἐὰν ἔξω τοῦ τείχους
ὄντες οἱ ἥττονες ἐν κινδύνῳ δοκῶσιν εἶναι, ἀλλ᾽
ἐπειδάν γε εἴσω τοῦ ἐρύματος ἔλθωσιν, ἐν
ἀσφαλείᾳ πάντες νομίζουσι καθεστάναι, ὁ δὲ
τύραννος οὐδ᾽ ἐπειδὰν εἴσω τῆς οἰκίας παρέλθῃ
ἐν ἀκινδύνῳ ἐστίν, ἀλλ᾽ ἐνταῦθα δὴ καὶ μάλιστα
11 φυλακτέον οἴεται εἶναι. ἔπειτα τοῖς μὲν ἰδιώταις
καὶ διὰ σπονδῶν καὶ δι᾽ εἰρήνης γίγνεται πολέμου
ἀνάπαυσις, τοῖς δὲ τυράννοις οὔτε εἰρήνη ποτὲ

most things than your eyes, should be equally
blind to it. But I know well enough by exper- 6
ience, Simonides, and I tell you that despots get the
smallest share of the greatest blessings, and have
most of the greatest evils. Thus, for instance, if 7
peace is held to be a great blessing to mankind,
very little of it falls to the share of despots : if war
is a great evil, of that despots receive the largest
share. To begin with, so long as their state is not 8
engaged in a war in which all take part, private
citizens are free to go wherever they choose without
fear of being killed. But all despots move everywhere as in an enemy's country; at any rate they think
they are bound to wear arms continually themselves,
and to take an armed escort about with them at all
times.

"Secondly, in the event of an expedition against 9
an enemy's country, private citizens at least think
themselves safe as soon as they have come home.
But when despots reach their own city, they know
that they are now among more enemies than ever.
Again, suppose that strangers invade their city in 10
superior force; true, the weaker are conscious of
danger while they are outside the walls; yet once
they are inside the fortress, all feel themselves
bestowed in safety. But the despot is not out of
danger even when he passes within the palace
gates; nay, it is just there that he thinks he must
walk most warily. Once again, to private citizens a 11
truce or peace brings rest from war ; but despots
are never at peace with the people subject to their

19

πρὸς τοὺς τυραννευουμένους γίγνεται οὔτε σπονδαῖς ἄν ποτε πιστεύσας ὁ τύραννος θαρρήσειε.

12 Καὶ πόλεμοι μὲν δή εἰσιν οὕς τε αἱ πόλεις
πολεμοῦσι καὶ οὓς οἱ τύραννοι πρὸς τοὺς βεβιασ-
μένους· τούτων δὴ τῶν πολέμων ὅσα μὲν ἔχει
χαλεπὰ ὁ ἐν ταῖς πόλεσι, ταῦτα καὶ ὁ τύραννος
13 ἔχει· καὶ γὰρ ἐν ὅπλοις δεῖ εἶναι ἀμφοτέρους
καὶ φυλάττεσθαι καὶ κινδυνεύειν, καὶ ἄν τι
πάθωσι κακὸν ἡττηθέντες, λυποῦνται ἐπὶ τούτοις
14 ἑκάτεροι. μέχρι μὲν δὴ τούτου ἴσοι οἱ πόλεμοι·
ἃ δὲ ἔχουσιν ἡδέα οἱ ἐν ταῖς πόλεσι πρὸς τὰς
15 πόλεις ταῦτα οὐκ ἔτι ἔχουσιν οἱ τύραννοι. αἱ
μὲν γὰρ πόλεις δήπου ὅταν κρατήσωσι μάχῃ τῶν
ἐναντίων, οὐ ῥάδιον εἰπεῖν, ὅσην μὲν ἡδονὴν
ἔχουσιν ἐν τῷ τρέψασθαι τοὺς πολεμίους, ὅσην
δ᾽ ἐν τῷ διώκειν, ὅσην δ᾽ ἐν τῷ ἀποκτείνειν τοὺς
πολεμίους, ὡς δὲ γαυροῦνται ἐπὶ τῷ ἔργῳ, ὡς δὲ
δόξαν λαμπρὰν ἀναλαμβάνουσιν, ὡς δ᾽ εὐφραί-
16 νονται τὴν πόλιν νομίζοντες ηὐξηκέναι. ἕκαστος
δέ τις προσποιεῖται καὶ τῆς βουλῆς μετεσχηκέναι
καὶ πλείστους ἀπεκτονέναι, χαλεπὸν δὲ εὑρεῖν
ὅπου οὐχὶ καὶ ἐπιψεύδονται, πλέονας φάσκοντες
ἀπεκτονέναι ἢ ὅσοι ἂν τῷ ὄντι ἀποθάνωσιν· οὕτω
17 καλόν τι αὐτοῖς δοκεῖ εἶναι τὸ πολὺ νικᾶν. ὁ δὲ
τύραννος ὅταν ὑποπτεύσῃ καὶ αἰσθανόμενος τῷ
ὄντι ἀντιπραττομένους τινὰς ἀποκτείνῃ, οἶδεν, ὅτι
οὐκ αὔξει ὅλην τὴν πόλιν, ἐπίσταταί τε, ὅτι
μειόνων ἄρξει, φαιδρός τε οὐ δύναται εἶναι οὐδὲ
μεγαλύνεται ἐπὶ τῷ ἔργῳ, ἀλλὰ καὶ μειοῖ καθ᾽
ὅσον ἂν δύνηται τὸ γεγενημένον καὶ ἀπολογεῖται

---

[1] i.e. in the wars that he wages against his subjects. The
whole of this paragraph is obscurely expressed and highly

despotism, and no truce can ever make a despot confident.

"There are, of course, wars that are waged by 12 states against one another, and wars waged by the despot against his oppressed subjects. Now the hardships incidental to these wars that fall on the citizen fall also on the despot. For both must 13 wear arms, be watchful, run risks; and the sting of a defeat is felt by both alike. So far, then, 14 both are equally affected by wars. But the joys that fall to the citizens of states at war are not experienced by despots.[1] For, you know, when states 15 defeat their foes in a battle, words fail one to describe the joy they feel in the rout of the enemy, in the pursuit, in the slaughter of the enemy. What transports of triumphant pride! What a halo of glory about them! What comfort to think that they have exalted their city! Everyone is crying: 16 'I had a share in the plan, I killed most'; and it's hard to find where they don't revel in falsehood, claiming to have killed more than all that were really slain. So glorious it seems to them to have won a great victory! But when a despot harbours sus- 17 picion, and, well aware that opposition is on foot, puts the conspirators to death, he knows that he does not exalt the city as a whole; he understands that the number of his subjects will be less; he cannot look cheerful; nor does he boast himself of his achievement; nay, he belittles the occurrence as much as possible, and explains, while he is at the work, that there is nothing

artificial; and it has been variously interpreted. The text also is uncertain.

ἅμα πράττων, ὡς οὐκ ἀδικῶν πεποίηκεν. οὕτως
18 οὐδ᾽ αὐτῷ δοκεῖ καλὰ τὰ ποιούμενα εἶναι. καὶ
ὅταν ἀποθάνωσιν οὓς ἐφοβήθη, οὐδέν τι μᾶλλον
τούτου θαρρεῖ, ἀλλὰ φυλάττεται ἔτι μᾶλλον ἢ τὸ
πρόσθεν. καὶ πόλεμον μὲν δὴ τοιοῦτον ἔχων
διατελεῖ ὁ τύραννος, ὃν ἐγὼ δηλῶ.

III. Φιλίας δ᾽ αὖ καταθέασαι ὡς κοινωνοῦσιν
οἱ τύραννοι. πρῶτον μὲν εἰ μέγα ἀγαθὸν ἀνθρώ-
2 ποις ἡ φιλία, τοῦτο ἐπισκεψώμεθα. ὃς γὰρ ἂν
φιλῆται δήπου ὑπό τινων, ἡδέως μὲν τούτων οἱ
φιλοῦντες παρόντα ὁρῶσιν, ἡδέως δ᾽ εὖ ποιοῦσι,
ποθοῦσι δέ, ἄν που ἀπῇ, ἥδιστα δὲ πάλιν
προσιόντα δέχονται, συνήδονται δ᾽ ἐπὶ τοῖς αὐτοῦ
ἀγαθοῖς, συνεπικουροῦσι δέ, ἐάν τι σφαλλόμενον
3 ὁρῶσιν. οὐ μὲν δὴ λέληθεν οὐδὲ τὰς πόλεις, ὅτι
ἡ φιλία μέγιστον ἀγαθὸν καὶ ἥδιστον ἀνθρώποις
ἐστί· μόνους γοῦν τοὺς μοιχοὺς νομίζουσι πολλαὶ τῶν πόλεων νηποινὶ ἀποκτείνειν, δῆλον ὅτι
διὰ ταῦτα ὅτι λυμαντῆρας αὐτοὺς νομίζουσι τῆς
τῶν γυναικῶν φιλίας πρὸς τοὺς ἄνδρας εἶναι.
4 ἐπεὶ ὅταν γε ἀφροδισιασθῇ κατὰ συμφοράν τινα
γυνή, οὐδὲν ἧττον τούτου ἕνεκεν τιμῶσιν αὐτὰς οἱ
ἄνδρες, ἐάνπερ ἡ φιλία δοκῇ αὐταῖς ἀκήρατος
5 διαμένειν. τοσοῦτον δέ τι ἀγαθὸν κρίνω ἔγωγε
τὸ φιλεῖσθαι εἶναι, ὥστε νομίζω τῷ ὄντι αὐτόματα
τἀγαθὰ τῷ φιλουμένῳ γίγνεσθαι καὶ παρὰ θεῶν
καὶ παρὰ ἀνθρώπων.
6 Καὶ τούτου τοίνυν τοῦ κτήματος τοιούτου ὄντος
μειονεκτοῦσιν οἱ τύραννοι πάντων μάλιστα. εἰ

---

[1] *Cyropaedia*, I. vi. 24.
[2] ἐπεὶ should be rendered "though," not "since" here,

wrong in what he has done, so far are his deeds from seeming honourable even to himself. Even 18 the death of those whom he feared does not restore him to confidence; he is yet more on his guard afterwards than before. And now I have shown you the kind of war that a despot wages continually.

III. " Turn next to friendship, and behold how despots share in it. First let us consider whether friendship is a great blessing to mankind. When a 2 man is loved by friends, I take it, they rejoice at his presence, delight to do him good, miss him when he is absent, greet him most joyfully on his return, rejoice with him in his good fortune, unite in aiding him when they see him tripping.[1] Even states are 3 not blind to the fact that friendship is a very great blessing, and very delightful to men. At any rate, many states have a law that adulterers only may be put to death with impunity, obviously for this reason, because they believe them to be destroyers of the wife's friendship with her husband; although,[2] 4 when a woman's lapse is the result of some accident, husbands do not honour their wives any less on that account, provided that wives seem to reserve their affection unblemished. In my judgment, to be 5 loved is a blessing so precious that I believe good things fall literally *of themselves* on him who is loved from gods and men alike.

" Such, then, is the nature of this possession—a 6 possession wherein despots above all other men are

for it introduces a reason why one might suppose that there would be some restriction on the right to kill an adulterer, and *not* the reason why all adulterers may be killed with impunity. Compare, for instance, Plato, *Protagoras*, 335 c. The "accident" is, of course, rape.

δὲ βούλει, ὦ Σιμωνίδη, εἰδέναι, ὅτι ἀληθῆ λέγω,
7 ὧδε ἐπίσκεψαι. βεβαιόταται μὲν γὰρ δήπου
δοκοῦσι φιλίαι εἶναι γονεῦσι πρὸς παῖδας καὶ
παισὶ πρὸς γονέας καὶ ἀδελφοῖς πρὸς ἀδελφοὺς
καὶ γυναιξὶ πρὸς ἄνδρας καὶ ἑταίροις πρὸς
8 ἑταίρους. εἰ τοίνυν ἐθέλεις κατανοεῖν, εὑρήσεις
μὲν τοὺς ἰδιώτας ὑπὸ τούτων μάλιστα φιλου-
μένους, τοὺς δὲ τυράννους πολλοὺς μὲν παῖδας
ἑαυτῶν ἀπεκτονότας, πολλοὺς δ᾿ ὑπὸ παίδων
αὐτοὺς ἀπολωλότας, πολλοὺς δὲ ἀδελφοὺς ἐν
τυραννίσιν ἀλληλοφόνους γεγενημένους, πολλοὺς
δὲ καὶ ὑπὸ γυναικῶν τῶν ἑαυτῶν τυράννους
διεφθαρμένους καὶ ὑπὸ ἑταίρων γε τῶν μάλιστα
9 δοκούντων φίλων εἶναι. οἵτινες οὖν ὑπὸ τῶν
φύσει πεφυκότων μάλιστα φιλεῖν καὶ νόμῳ
συνηναγκασμένων οὕτω μισοῦνται, πῶς ὑπ᾿ ἄλλου
γέ τινος οἴεσθαι χρὴ αὐτοὺς φιλεῖσθαι ;

IV. Ἀλλὰ μὴν καὶ πίστεως ὅστις ἐλάχιστον
μετέχει, πῶς οὐχὶ μεγάλου ἀγαθοῦ μειονεκτεῖ ;
ποία μὲν γὰρ συνουσία ἡδεῖα ἄνευ πίστεως τῆς
πρὸς ἀλλήλους, ποία δ᾿ ἀνδρὶ καὶ γυναικὶ τερπνὴ
ἄνευ πίστεως ὁμιλία, ποῖος δὲ θεράπων ἡδὺς
2 ἀπιστούμενος ; καὶ τούτου τοίνυν τοῦ πιστῶς
πρός τινας ἔχειν ἐλάχιστον μέτεστι τυράννῳ·
ὁπότε γε οὐδὲ σιτίοις καὶ ποτοῖς πιστεύων διάγει,
ἀλλὰ καὶ τούτων, πρὶν ἀπάρχεσθαι τοῖς θεοῖς,
τοὺς διακόνους πρῶτον κελεύουσιν ἀπογεύσασθαι
διὰ τὸ ἀπιστεῖν, μὴ καὶ ἐν τούτοις κακόν τι
3 φάγωσιν ἢ πίωσιν. ἀλλὰ μὴν καὶ αἱ πατρίδες
τοῖς μὲν ἄλλοις ἀνθρώποις πλείστου ἄξιαι.
πολῖται γὰρ δορυφοροῦσι μὲν ἀλλήλους ἄνευ
μισθοῦ ἐπὶ τοὺς δούλους, δορυφοροῦσι δ᾿ ἐπὶ τοὺς

stinted. If you want to know that I am speaking the truth, Simonides, consider the question in this way. The firmest friendships, I take it, are sup- 7 posed to be those that unite parents to children, children to parents, wives to husbands, comrades to comrades. Now you will find, if you will but 8 observe, that private citizens are, in fact, loved most deeply by these. But what of despots? Many have slain their own children; many have themselves been murdered by their children; many brothers, partners in despotism, have perished by each other's hand; many have been destroyed even by their own wives,[1] aye, and by comrades whom they accounted their closest friends. Seeing, then, 9 that they are so hated by those who are bound by natural ties and constrained by custom to love them most, how are we to suppose that they are loved by any other being?

IV. "Next take confidence. Surely he who has very little of that is stinted in a great blessing? What companionship is pleasant without mutual trust? What intercourse between husband and wife is delightful without confidence? What squire is pleasant if he is not trusted? Now of this con- 2 fidence in others despots enjoy the smallest share. They go in constant suspicion even of their meat and drink; they bid their servitors taste them first, before the libation is offered to the gods, because of their misgiving that they may sup poison in the dish or the bowl. Again, to all other men their 3 fatherland is very precious. For citizens ward one another without pay from their slaves and from

---

[1] See Introduction.

κακούργους ὑπὲρ τοῦ μηδένα τῶν πολιτῶν βιαίῳ
4 θανάτῳ ἀποθνήσκειν. οὕτω δὲ πόρρω προεληλύ-
θασι φυλακῆς, ὥστε πεποίηνται πολλοὶ νόμον τῷ
μιαιφόνῳ μηδὲ τὸν συνόντα καθαρεύειν· ὥστε διὰ
τὰς πατρίδας ἀσφαλῶς ἕκαστος βιοτεύει τῶν
5 πολιτῶν. τοῖς δὲ τυράννοις καὶ τοῦτο ἔμπαλιν
ἀνέστραπται. ἀντὶ γὰρ τοῦ τιμωρεῖν αὐτοῖς αἱ
πόλεις μεγάλως τιμῶσι τὸν ἀποκτείναντα τὸν
τύραννον, καὶ ἀντί γε τοῦ εἴργειν ἐκ τῶν ἱερῶν,
ὥσπερ τοὺς τῶν ἰδιωτῶν φονέας, ἀντὶ τούτου καὶ
εἰκόνας ἐν τοῖς ἱεροῖς ἱστᾶσιν αἱ πόλεις τῶν τοῦτο
ποιησάντων.
6 Εἰ δὲ σὺ οἴει, ὡς πλείω ἔχων τῶν ἰδιωτῶν κτήματα ὁ τύραννος διὰ τοῦτο καὶ πλείω ἀπ᾽ αὐτῶν
εὐφραίνεται, οὐδὲ τοῦτο οὕτως ἔχει, ὦ Σιμωνίδη,
ἀλλ᾽ ὥσπερ οἱ ἀθληταὶ οὐχ ὅταν ἰδιωτῶν γένωνται κρείττονες, τοῦτ᾽ αὐτοὺς εὐφραίνει, ἀλλ᾽ ὅταν
τῶν ἀνταγωνιστῶν ἥττους, τοῦτ᾽ αὐτοὺς ἀνιᾷ,
οὕτω καὶ ὁ τύραννος οὐχ ὅταν τῶν ἰδιωτῶν πλείω
φαίνηται ἔχων, τότ᾽ εὐφραίνεται, ἀλλ᾽ ὅταν ἑτέρων τυράννων ἐλάττω ἔχῃ, τούτῳ λυπεῖται· τούτους γὰρ ἀνταγωνιστὰς ἡγεῖται αὐτῷ τοῦ πλούτου
7 εἶναι. οὐδέ γε θᾶττόν τι γίγνεται τῷ τυράννῳ ἢ
τῷ ἰδιώτῃ ὧν ἐπιθυμεῖ. ὁ μὲν γὰρ ἰδιώτης οἰκίας ἢ
ἀγροῦ ἢ οἰκέτου ἐπιθυμεῖ, ὁ δὲ τύραννος ἢ πόλεων
ἢ χώρας πολλῆς ἢ λιμένων ἢ ἀκροπόλεων ἰσχυρῶν, ἅ ἐστι πολὺ χαλεπώτερα καὶ ἐπικινδυνότερα
κατεργάσασθαι τῶν ἰδιωτικῶν ἐπιθυμημάτων.
8 ἀλλὰ μέντοι καὶ πένητας ὄψει[1] οὕτως ὀλίγους
τῶν ἰδιωτῶν ὡς πολλοὺς τῶν τυράννων. οὐ γὰρ
τῷ ἀριθμῷ οὔτε τὰ πολλὰ κρίνεται οὔτε τὰ

evildoers, to the end that none of the citizens may perish by a violent death. They have gone so far 4 in measures of precaution that many have made a law whereby even the companion of the bloodguilty is deemed impure ; and so—thanks to the fatherland —every citizen lives in security. But for despots 5 the position is the reverse in this case too. Instead of avenging them, the cities heap honours on the slayer of the despot; and, whereas they exclude the murderers of private persons from the temples, the cities, so far from treating assassins in the same manner, actually put up statues of them in the holy places.

"If you suppose that just because he has more 6 possessions than the private citizen, the despot gets more enjoyment out of them, this is not so either, Simonides. Trained athletes feel no pleasure when they prove superior to amateurs, but they are cut to the quick when they are beaten by a rival athlete; in like manner the despot feels no pleasure when he is seen to possess more than private citizens, but is vexed when he has less than other despots; for he regards them as his rivals in wealth. Nor even 7 does the despot gain the object of his desire any quicker than the private citizen. For the private citizen desires a house or a farm or a servant; but the despot covets cities or wide territory or harbours or strong citadels, and these are far more difficult and perilous to acquire than the objects that attract the citizen. And, moreover, you will find that even 8 poverty is rarer among private citizens than among despots. For much and little are to be measured not

---

[1] ὄψει οὐχ S. with the MSS. and Stobaeus : οὐχ was removed by Bremi.

ὀλίγα,[1] ἀλλὰ πρὸς τὰς χρήσεις· ὥστε τὰ μὲν
ὑπερβάλλοντα τὰ ἱκανὰ πολλά ἐστι, τὰ δὲ τῶν
9 ἱκανῶν ἐλλείποντα ὀλίγα. τῷ οὖν τυράννῳ τὰ
πολλαπλάσια ἧττον ἱκανά ἐστιν εἰς τὰ ἀναγκαῖα
δαπανήματα ἢ τῷ ἰδιώτῃ. τοῖς μὲν γὰρ ἰδιώταις
ἔξεστι τὰς δαπάνας συντέμνειν εἰς τὰ καθ' ἡμέραν, ὅπῃ βούλονται, τοῖς δὲ τυράννοις οὐκ ἐνδέ-
χεται. αἱ γὰρ μέγισται αὐτοῖς δαπάναι καὶ
ἀναγκαιόταται εἰς τὰς τῆς ψυχῆς φυλακάς εἰσι·
τὸ δὲ τούτων συντέμνειν ὄλεθρος δοκεῖ εἶναι.
10 ἔπειτα δὲ ὅσοι μὲν δύνανται ἔχειν ἀπὸ τοῦ δικαίου
ὅσων δέονται, τί ἂν τούτους οἰκτείροι τις ὡς
πένητας; ὅσοι δ' ἀναγκάζονται δι' ἔνδειαν κακόν
τι καὶ αἰσχρὸν μηχανώμενοι ζῆν, πῶς οὐ τούτους
11 ἀθλίους ἄν τις καὶ πένητας δικαίως καλοίη; οἱ
τύραννοι τοίνυν ἀναγκάζονται πλεῖστα συλᾶν
ἀδίκως καὶ ἱερὰ καὶ ἀνθρώπους διὰ τὸ εἰς τὰς
ἀναγκαίας δαπάνας ἀεὶ προσδεῖσθαι χρημάτων.
ὥσπερ γὰρ πολέμου ὄντος ἀεὶ ἀναγκάζονται
στράτευμα τρέφειν ἢ ἀπολωλέναι.

V. Χαλεπὸν δ' ἐρῶ σοι καὶ ἄλλο πάθημα, ὦ
Σιμωνίδη, τῶν τυράννων. γιγνώσκουσι μὲν γὰρ
οὐδὲν ἧττον τῶν ἰδιωτῶν τοὺς ἀλκίμους[2] τε καὶ
σοφοὺς καὶ δικαίους. τούτους δ' ἀντὶ τοῦ ἄγασθαι
φοβοῦνται, τοὺς μὲν ἀνδρείους, μή τι τολμήσωσι
τῆς ἐλευθερίας ἕνεκεν, τοὺς δὲ σοφούς, μή τι
μηχανήσωνται, τοὺς δὲ δικαίους, μὴ ἐπιθυμήσῃ
2 τὸ πλῆθος ὑπ' αὐτῶν προστατεῖσθαι. ὅταν δὲ
τοὺς τοιούτους διὰ τὸν φόβον ὑπεξαιρῶνται, τίνες
ἄλλοι αὐτοῖς καταλείπονται χρῆσθαι ἀλλ' ἢ οἱ
ἄδικοί τε καὶ ἀκρατεῖς καὶ ἀνδραποδώδεις; οἱ
μὲν ἄδικοι πιστευόμενοι, διότι φοβοῦνται ὥσπερ
28

by number, but in relation to the owner's needs; so that what is more than enough is much, and what is less than enough is little. Therefore, the 9 despot with his abundance of wealth has less to meet his necessary expenses than the private citizen. For while private citizens can cut down the daily expenditure as they please, despots cannot, since the largest items in their expenses and the most essential are the sums they spend on the life-guards, and to curtail any of these means ruin. Besides, when men 10 can have all they need by honest means, why pity them as though they were poor? May not those who through want of money are driven to evil and unseemly expedients in order to live, more justly be accounted wretched and poverty-stricken? Now, 11 despots are not seldom forced into the crime of robbing temples and their fellow men through chronic want of cash to meet their necessary expenses. Living, as it were, in a perpetual state of war, they are forced to maintain an army, or they perish.

V. " Despots are oppressed by yet another trouble, Simonides, which I will tell you of. They recognize a stout-hearted, a wise or an upright man as easily as private citizens do. But instead of admiring such men, they fear them,—the brave lest they strike a bold stroke for freedom, the wise lest they hatch a plot, the upright lest the people desire them for leaders. When they get rid of such 2 men through fear, who are left for their use, save only the unrighteous, the vicious and the servile,— the unrighteous being trusted because, like the

---

[1] ὀλίγα Coppello : ἱκανά S. with the MSS. and Stobaeus.
[2] ἀλκίμους Stobaeus : κοσμίους S. with the MSS.

οἱ τύραννοι τὰς πόλεις μήποτε ἐλεύθεραι γενό-
μεναι ἐγκρατεῖς αὐτῶν γένωνται, οἱ δ' ἀκρατεῖς
τῆς εἰς τὸ παρὸν ἐξουσίας ἔνεκα, οἱ δ' ἀνδραποδώδεις διότι οὐδ' αὐτοὶ ἀξιοῦσιν ἐλεύθεροι εἶναι.
χαλεπὸν οὖν καὶ τοῦτο τὸ πάθημα ἔμοιγε δοκεῖ
εἶναι, τὸ ἄλλους μὲν ἡγεῖσθαι ἀγαθοὺς ἄνδρας,
ἄλλοις δὲ χρῆσθαι ἀναγκάζεσθαι.

3 Ἔτι δὲ φιλόπολιν μὲν ἀνάγκη καὶ τὸν τύραννον
εἶναι· ἄνευ γὰρ τῆς πόλεως οὔτ' ἂν σῴζεσθαι
δύναιτο οὔτ' ἂν εὐδαιμονεῖν· ἡ δὲ τυραννὶς ἀναγκάζει καὶ ταῖς ἑαυτῶν πατρίσιν ἐγκαλεῖν. οὔτε
γὰρ ἀλκίμους οὔτ' εὐόπλους χαίρουσι τοὺς πολίτας παρασκευάζοντες, ἀλλὰ τοὺς ξένους δεινοτέ-
ρους τῶν πολιτῶν ποιοῦντες ἥδονται μᾶλλον καὶ
4 τούτοις χρῶνται δορυφόροις. ἀλλὰ μὴν οὐδ' ἂν
εὐετηριῶν γενομένων ἀφθονία τῶν ἀγαθῶν γίγνηται, οὐδὲ τότε συγχαίρει ὁ τύραννος. ἐνδεεσ-
τέροις γὰρ οὖσι ταπεινοτέροις αὐτοῖς οἴονται
χρῆσθαι.

VI. Βούλομαι δέ σοι, ἔφη, ὦ Σιμωνίδη, κἀ-
κείνας τὰς εὐφροσύνας δηλῶσαι, ὅσαις ἐγὼ
χρώμενος, ὅτ' ἦν ἰδιώτης, νῦν ἐπειδὴ τύραννος
2 ἐγενόμην, αἰσθάνομαι στερόμενος αὐτῶν. ἐγὼ
γὰρ συνῆν μὲν ἡλικιώταις ἡδόμενος ἡδομένοις
ἐμοί, συνῆν δὲ ἐμαυτῷ, ὁπότε ἡσυχίας ἐπιθυ-
μήσαιμι, διῆγον δ' ἐν συμποσίοις πολλάκις μὲν
μέχρι τοῦ ἐπιλαθέσθαι πάντων εἴ τι χαλεπὸν ἐν
ἀνθρωπίνῳ βίῳ ἦν, πολλάκις δὲ μέχρι τοῦ ᾠδαῖς
τε καὶ θαλίαις καὶ χοροῖς τὴν ψυχὴν συγκατα-
μιγνύναι, πολλάκις δὲ μέχρι κοίτης [1] ἐπιθυμίας
3 ἐμῆς τε καὶ τῶν παρόντων. νῦν δὲ ἀπεστέρημαι
μὲν τῶν ἡδομένων ἐμοὶ διὰ τὸ δούλους ἀντὶ φίλων

despots, they fear that the cities may some day shake off the yoke and prove their masters, the vicious on account of the licence they enjoy as things are, the servile because even they themselves have no desire for freedom? This too, then, is a heavy trouble, in my opinion, to see the good in some men, and yet perforce to employ others.

"Furthermore, even a despot must needs love his 3 city, for without the city he can enjoy neither safety nor happiness. But despotism forces him to find fault even with his fatherland. For he has no pleasure in seeing that the citizens are stout-hearted and well armed; rather he delights to make the foreigners more formidable than the citizens, and these he employs as a body-guard. Again, even 4 when favourable seasons yield abundance of good things, the despot is a stranger to the general joy; for the needier the people, the humbler he thinks to find them.

VI. "But now, Simonides," he continued, "I want to show you all those delights that were mine when I was a private citizen, but which I now find are withheld from me since the day I became a despot. I communed with my fellows then : they pleased me 2 and I pleased them. I communed with myself whenever I desired rest. I passed the time in carousing, often till I forgot all the troubles of mortal life, often till my soul was absorbed in songs and revels and dances, often till the desire of sleep fell on me and all the company. But now I am cut 3 off from those who had pleasure in me, since slaves

---

[1] κοίτης Hermann : κοινῆς S. with the MSS.

ἔχειν τοὺς ἑταίρους, ἀπεστέρημαι δ' αὐτὸς τοῦ
ἡδέως ἐκείνοις ὁμιλεῖν διὰ τὸ μηδεμίαν ἐνορᾶν
εὔνοιαν ἐμοὶ παρ' αὐτῶν· μέθην δὲ καὶ ὕπνον
4 ὁμοίως ἐνέδρα φυλάττομαι. τὸ δὲ φοβεῖσθαι μὲν
ὄχλον, φοβεῖσθαι δ' ἐρημίαν, φοβεῖσθαι δὲ ἀφυ-
λαξίαν, φοβεῖσθαι δὲ καὶ αὐτοὺς τοὺς φυλάττοντας καὶ μήτ' ἀόπλους ἔχειν ἐθέλειν περὶ αὐτὸν
μήθ' ὡπλισμένους ἡδέως θεᾶσθαι πῶς οὐκ ἀργα-
5 λέον ἐστὶ πρᾶγμα; ἔτι δὲ ξένοις μὲν μᾶλλον ἢ
πολίταις πιστεύειν, βαρβάροις δὲ μᾶλλον ἢ
Ἕλλησιν, ἐπιθυμεῖν δὲ τοὺς μὲν ἐλευθέρους δούλους ἔχειν, τοὺς δὲ δούλους ἀναγκάζεσθαι ποιεῖν
ἐλευθέρους, οὐ πάντα σοι ταῦτα δοκεῖ ψυχῆς ὑπὸ
6 φόβων καταπεπληγμένης τεκμήρια εἶναι; ὅ γέ
τοι φόβος οὐ μόνον αὐτὸς ἐνὼν ταῖς ψυχαῖς
λυπηρός ἐστιν, ἀλλὰ καὶ πάντων τῶν ἡδέων
συμπαρακολουθῶν λυμεὼν γίγνεται.

7 Εἰ δὲ καὶ σὺ πολεμικῶν ἔμπειρος εἶ, ὦ Σιμωνίδη, καὶ ἤδη ποτὲ πολεμίᾳ φάλαγγι πλησίον
ἀντετάξω, ἀναμνήσθητι, ποῖον μέν τινα σῖτον
ᾑροῦ ἐν ἐκείνῳ τῷ χρόνῳ, ποῖον δέ τινα ὕπνον
8 ἐκοιμῶ. οἷα μέντοι σοὶ τότ' ἦν τὰ λυπηρά, τοιαῦτά ἐστι τὰ τῶν τυράννων καὶ ἔτι δεινότερα· οὐ
γὰρ ἐξ ἐναντίας μόνον, ἀλλὰ καὶ πάντοθεν πολεμίους ὁρᾶν νομίζουσιν οἱ τύραννοι.

9 Ταῦτα δ' ἀκούσας ὁ Σιμωνίδης ὑπολαβὼν
εἶπεν· Ὑπέρευ μοι δοκεῖς ἔνια λέγειν. ὁ γὰρ
πόλεμος φοβερὸν μέν, ἀλλ' ὅμως, ὦ Ἱέρων, ἡμεῖς
γε ὅταν ὦμεν ἐν στρατείᾳ, φύλακας προκαθιστά-
μενοι θαρραλέως δείπνου τε καὶ ὕπνου λαγχά-
νομεν.

10 Καὶ ὁ Ἱέρων ἔφη· Ναὶ μὰ Δία, ὦ Σιμωνίδη·

instead of friends are my comrades; I am cut off
from my pleasant intercourse with them, since I see
in them no sign of good-will towards me. Drink
and sleep I avoid as a snare. To fear a crowd, and 4
yet fear solitude, to fear to go unguarded, and yet
fear the very men who guard you, to recoil from
attendants unarmed and yet dislike to see them
armed—surely that is a cruel predicament! And 5
then, to trust foreigners more than citizens, strangers
more than Greeks, to long to keep free men slaves,
and yet be forced to make slaves free—do you not
think that all these are sure tokens of a soul
that is crushed with fear?[1] Fear, you know, is not 6
only painful in itself by reason of its presence in the
soul, but by haunting us even in our pleasures it
spoils them utterly.

"If, like me, you are acquainted with war, 7
Simonides, and ever had the enemy's battle-line
close in front of you, call to mind what sort of food
you ate at that time, and what sort of sleep
you slept. I tell you, the pains that despots suffer 8
are such as you suffered then. Nay, they are still
more terrible; for despots believe that they see
enemies not in front alone, but all around them."

To this Simonides made answer: "Excellent 9
words in part, I grant! War is indeed a fearsome
thing: nevertheless, Hiero, our way, when we are
on active service, is this: we post sentries to guard
us, and sup and sleep with a good courage."

Then Hiero answered: "No doubt you do, 10

[1] *Cyropaedia*, III. i. 27.

αὐτῶν μὲν γὰρ προφυλάττουσιν οἱ νόμοι, ὥστε
περὶ ἑαυτῶν φοβοῦνται καὶ ὑπὲρ ὑμῶν· οἱ δὲ
τύραννοι μισθοῦ φύλακας ἔχουσιν ὥσπερ θερισ-
11 τάς. καὶ δεῖ μὲν δήπου τοὺς φύλακας μηδὲν
οὕτω ποιεῖν δύνασθαι ὡς πιστοὺς εἶναι· πιστὸν
δὲ ἕνα πολὺ χαλεπώτερον εὑρεῖν ἢ πάνυ πολλοὺς
ἐργάτας ὁποίου βούλει ἔργου, ἄλλως τε καὶ
ὁπόταν χρημάτων μὲν ἕνεκα παρῶσιν οἱ φυλάττοντες, ἐξῇ δ' αὐτοῖς ἐν ὀλίγῳ χρόνῳ πολὺ
πλείω λαβεῖν ἀποκτείνασι τὸν τύραννον ἢ ὅσα
πολὺν χρόνον φυλάττοντες παρὰ τοῦ τυράννου
λαμβάνουσιν.

12 Ὃ δ' ἐζήλωσας ἡμᾶς, ὡς τοὺς μὲν φίλους
μάλιστα εὖ ποιεῖν δυνάμεθα, τοὺς δ' ἐχθροὺς
πάντων μάλιστα χειρούμεθα, οὐδὲ ταῦθ' οὕτως
13 ἔχει. φίλους μὲν γὰρ πῶς ἂν νομίσαις ποτὲ
εὖ ποιεῖν, ὅταν εὖ εἰδῇς, ὅτι ὁ τὰ πλεῖστα λαμβάνων παρὰ σοῦ ἥδιστ' ἂν ὡς τάχιστα ἐξ ὀφθαλμῶν σου γένοιτο ; ὅ τι γὰρ ἄν τις λάβῃ παρὰ
τυράννου, οὐδεὶς οὐδὲν ἑαυτοῦ νομίζει, πρὶν ἂν
14 ἔξω τῆς τούτου ἐπικρατείας γένηται. ἐχθροὺς
δ' αὖ πῶς ἂν φαίης μάλιστα τοῖς τυράννοις
ἐξεῖναι χειροῦσθαι, ὅταν εὖ εἰδῶσιν, ὅτι ἐχθροὶ
αὐτῶν εἰσι πάντες οἱ τυραννούμενοι, τούτους δὲ
μήτε κατακαίνειν ἅπαντας μήτε δεσμεύειν οἷόν
τε ᾖ· τίνων γὰρ ἔτι ἄρξει ; ἀλλ' εἰδότας,[1] ὅτι
ἐχθροί εἰσι, τούτους ἅμα μὲν φυλάττεσθαι δέῃ
15 καὶ χρῆσθαι δ' αὐτοῖς ἀναγκάζεσθαι ; εὖ δ' ἴσθι
καὶ τοῦτο, ὦ Σιμωνίδη, ὅτι καὶ οὓς τῶν πολιτῶν
δεδίασι, χαλεπῶς μὲν αὐτοὺς ζῶντας ὁρῶσι,
χαλεπῶς δ' ἀποκτείνουσιν. ὥσπερ γε καὶ ἵππος
εἰ ἀγαθὸς μὲν εἴη, φοβερὸς δὲ μὴ ἀνήκεστόν τι

[1] εἰδότα S.

34

Simonides! For your sentries have sentries in front of them—the laws,—and so they fear for their own skins and relieve you of fear. But despots hire their guards like harvesters. Now the chief qualification 11 required in the guards, I presume, is faithfulness. But it is far harder to find one faithful guard than hundreds of workmen for any kind of work, especially when money supplies the guards, and they have it in their power to get far more in a moment by assassinating the despot than they receive from him for years of service among his guards.

"You said that you envy us our unrivalled power 12 to confer benefits on our friends, and our unrivalled success in crushing our enemies. But that is another delusion. For how can you possibly feel that you 13 benefit friends when you know well that he who receives most from you would be delighted to get out of your sight as quickly as possible? For, no matter what a man has received from a despot, nobody regards it as his own, until he is outside the giver's dominion. Or again, how can you say 14 that despots more than others are able to crush enemies, when they know well that all who are subject to their despotism are their enemies and that it is impossible to put them all to death or imprison them—else who will be left for the despot to rule over?—and, knowing them to be their enemies, they must beware of them, and, nevertheless, must needs make use of them? And I can assure you of this, 15 Simonides: when a despot fears any citizen, he is reluctant to see him alive, and yet reluctant to put him to death. To illustrate my point, suppose that a good horse makes his master afraid that he will do him some fatal mischief: the man will feel

ποιήσῃ, χαλεπῶς μὲν ἂν τις αὐτὸν ἀποκτείναι
διὰ τὴν ἀρετήν, χαλεπῶς δὲ ζῶντι χρῷτο, εὐλα-
βούμενος, μή τι ἀνήκεστον ἐν τοῖς κινδύνοις
16 ἐργάσηται. καὶ τἆλλά γε κτήματα, ὅσα χαλεπὰ
μὲν χρήσιμα δ' ἐστίν, ὁμοίως ἅπαντα λυπεῖ μὲν
τοὺς κεκτημένους, λυπεῖ δὲ ἀπαλλαττομένους.

VII. Ἐπεὶ δὲ ταῦτα αὐτοῦ ἤκουσεν ὁ Σιμωνίδης, εἶπεν, Ἔοικεν, ἔφη, ὦ Ἱέρων, μέγα τι εἶναι
ἡ τιμή, ἧς ὀρεγόμενοι οἱ ἄνθρωποι πάντα μὲν
πόνον ὑποδύονται, πάντα δὲ κίνδυνον ὑπομένουσι.
2 καὶ ὑμεῖς, ὡς ἔοικε, τοσαῦτα πράγματα ἐχούσης,
ὁπόσα λέγεις, τῆς τυραννίδος, ὅμως προπετῶς
φέρεσθε εἰς αὐτήν, ὅπως τιμᾶσθε καὶ ὑπηρετῶσ
μὲν ὑμῖν πάντες πάντα τὰ προστασσόμενα ἀπρο-
φασίστως, περιβλέπωσι δὲ πάντες, ὑπανιστῶνται
δ' ἀπὸ τῶν θάκων ὁδῶν τε παραχωρῶσι, γεραί-
ρωσι δὲ καὶ λόγοις καὶ ἔργοις πάντες οἱ παρόντες
ἀεὶ ὑμᾶς· τοιαῦτα γὰρ δὴ ποιοῦσι τοῖς τυράννοις
οἱ ἀρχόμενοι καὶ ἄλλον ὄντιν' ἂν ἀεὶ τιμῶντες
3 τυγχάνωσι. καὶ γάρ μοι δοκεῖ, ὦ Ἱέρων, τούτῳ
διαφέρειν ἀνὴρ τῶν ἄλλων ζῴων, τῷ τιμῆς ὀρέγεσθαι. ἐπεὶ σιτίοις γε καὶ ποτοῖς καὶ ὕπνοις
καὶ ἀφροδισίοις πάντα ὁμοίως ἥδεσθαι ἔοικε τὰ
ζῷα· ἡ δὲ φιλοτιμία οὔτ' ἐν τοῖς ἀλόγοις ζῴοις
ἐμφύεται οὔτ' ἐν ἅπασιν ἀνθρώποις· οἷς δ' ἂν
ἐμφύῃ τιμῆς τε καὶ ἐπαίνου ἔρως, οὗτοί εἰσιν
ἤδη οἱ πλεῖστον μὲν τῶν βοσκημάτων διαφέροντες,
ἄνδρες δὲ καὶ οὐκέτι ἄνθρωποι μόνον νομιζόμενοι.
4 ὥστε ἐμοὶ μὲν εἰκότως δοκεῖτε ταῦτα πάντα ὑπο-
μένειν, ἃ φέρετε ἐν τῇ τυραννίδι, ἐπείπερ τιμᾶσθε
διαφερόντως τῶν ἄλλων ἀνθρώπων. καὶ γὰρ

reluctant to slaughter him on account of his good qualities, and yet his anxiety lest the animal may work some fatal mischief in a moment of danger will make him reluctant to keep him alive and use him. Yes, 16 and this is equally true of all possessions that are troublesome as well as useful : it is painful to possess them, and painful to get rid of them."

VII. These statements drew from Simonides the following reply : " A great thing, surely, Hiero, is the honour for which men strive so earnestly that they undergo any toil and endure any danger to win it ! And what if despotism brings all those troubles that 2 you tell of, yet such men as you, it seems, rush headlong into it that you may have honour, that all men may carry out your behests in all things without question, that the eyes of all may wait on you, that all may rise from their seats and make way for you, that all in your presence may glorify you by deed and word alike. (Such, in fact, is the behaviour of subjects to despots and to anyone else who happens to be their hero at the moment.) For 3 indeed it seems to me, Hiero, that in this man differs from other animals—I mean, in this craving for honour. In meat and drink and sleep and love all creatures alike seem to take pleasure ; but love of honour is rooted neither in the brute beasts nor in every human being. But they in whom is implanted a passion for honour and praise, these are they who differ most from the beasts of the field, these are accounted men and not mere human beings.[1] And 4 so, in my opinion, you have good reason for bearing all those burdens that despotism lays on you, in that you are honoured above all other men. For no

---

[1] *Cyropaedia*, i. vi. 25.

οὐδεμία ἀνθρωπίνη ἡδονὴ τοῦ θείου ἐγγυτέρω
δοκεῖ εἶναι ἢ ἡ περὶ τὰς τιμὰς εὐφροσύνη.

5   Πρὸς ταῦτα δὴ εἶπεν ὁ Ἱέρων· Ἀλλ', ὦ Σιμωνίδη, καὶ αἱ τιμαὶ τῶν τυράννων ὅμοιαι ἐμοὶ
δοκοῦσιν εἶναι οἷάπερ ἐγώ σοι τὰ ἀφροδίσια ὄντα
6 αὐτῶν ἀπέδειξα. οὔτε γὰρ αἱ μὴ ἐξ ἀντιφιλοῦν-
των ὑπουργίαι χάριτες ἡμῖν ἐδόκουν εἶναι οὔτε
τὰ ἀφροδίσια τὰ βίαια ἡδέα ἐφαίνετο. ὡσαύτως
τοίνυν οὐδὲ αἱ ὑπουργίαι αἱ παρὰ τῶν φοβου-
7 μένων τιμαί εἰσι. πῶς γὰρ ἂν φαίημεν ἢ τοὺς
βίᾳ ἐξανισταμένους θάκων διὰ τὸ τιμᾶν τοὺς
ἀδικοῦντας ἐξανίστασθαι ἢ τοὺς ὁδῶν παρα-
χωροῦντας τοῖς κρείττοσι διὰ τὸ τιμᾶν τοὺς ἀδι-
8 κοῦντας παραχωρεῖν; καὶ δῶρά γε διδόασιν οἱ
πολλοὶ τούτοις, οὓς μισοῦσι, καὶ ταῦτα ὅταν
μάλιστα φοβῶνται, μή τι κακὸν ὑπ' αὐτῶν πά-
θωσιν. ἀλλὰ ταῦτα μὲν οἶμαι δουλείας ἔργα
εἰκότως ἂν νομίζοιτο· αἱ δὲ τιμαὶ ἔμοιγε δοκοῦσιν
9 ἐκ τῶν ἐναντίων τούτοις γίγνεσθαι. ὅταν γὰρ ἄνθρωποι ἄνδρα ἡγησάμενοι εὐεργετεῖν ἱκανὸν εἶναι
καὶ ἀπολαύειν αὐτοῦ ἀγαθὰ νομίσαντες ἔπειτα
τοῦτον ἀνὰ στόμα τε ἔχωσιν ἐπαινοῦντες θεῶνταί
τ' αὐτὸν ὡς οἰκεῖον ἕκαστος ἀγαθῶν ἑκόντες τε
παραχωρῶσι τούτῳ ὁδῶν καὶ θάκων ὑπανιστῶνται φιλοῦντές τε καὶ μὴ φοβούμενοι καὶ στεφανῶσι
κοινῆς ἀρετῆς καὶ εὐεργεσίας ἕνεκα καὶ δωρεῖσθαι
ἐθέλωσιν, οἱ αὐτοὶ οὗτοι ἔμοιγε δοκοῦσι τιμᾶν
τε τοῦτον ἀληθῶς, οἳ ἂν τοιαῦτα ὑπουργήσωσι,
10 καὶ ὁ τούτων ἀξιούμενος τιμᾶσθαι τῷ ὄντι. καὶ
ἔγωγε τὸν μὲν οὕτω τιμώμενον μακαρίζω· αἰσθάνομαι γὰρ αὐτὸν οὐκ ἐπιβουλευόμενον, ἀλλὰ
φροντιζόμενον, μή τι πάθῃ, καὶ ἀφόβως καὶ

human joy seems to be more nearly akin to that of heaven than the gladness which attends upon honours."

To this Hiero replied: "Ah, Simonides, I think 5 even the honours enjoyed by despots bear a close resemblance to their courtships, as I have described them to you. The services of the indifferent 6 seemed to us not acts of grace, and favours extorted appeared to give no pleasure. And so it is with the services proffered by men in fear: they are not honours. For how can we say that men who are 7 forced to rise from their seats rise to honour their oppressors, or that men who make way for their superiors desire to honour their oppressors? And as 8 for presents, most men offer them to one whom they hate, and that too at the moment when they have cause to fear some evil at his hands. These acts, I suppose, may not unfairly be taken for acts of servility; but honours, I should say, express the very opposite feelings. For whenever men feel that some person is 9 competent to be their benefactor, and come to regard him as the fountain of blessings, so that henceforward his praise is ever on their lips, everyone of them looks on him as his peculiar blessing, they make way for him spontaneously and rise from their seats, through love and not through fear, crown him for his generosity and beneficence, and bring him freewill offerings, these same men in my opinion, honour that person truly by such services, and he who is accounted worthy of them is honoured in very deed. And, for myself, I count him a happy man who is 10 honoured thus; for I perceive that, instead of being exposed to treason, he is an object of solicitude, lest harm befall him, and he lives his life unassailed

ἀνεπιφθόνως καὶ ἀκινδύνως καὶ εὐδαιμόνως τὸν
βίον διάγοντα· ὁ δὲ τύραννος ὡς ὑπὸ πάντων
ἀνθρώπων κατακεκριμένος δι' ἀδικίαν ἀποθνήσκειν οὕτως, ὦ Σιμωνίδη, εὖ ἴσθι καὶ νύκτα καὶ
ἡμέραν διάγει.

11 Ἐπεὶ δὲ ταῦτα πάντα διήκουσεν ὁ Σιμωνίδης,
Καὶ πῶς, ἔφη, ὦ Ἱέρων, εἰ οὕτως πονηρόν ἐστι
τὸ τυραννεῖν καὶ τοῦτο σὺ ἔγνωκας, οὐκ ἀπαλ-
λάττῃ οὕτω μεγάλου κακοῦ οὔτε σὺ οὔτε ἄλλος
μὲν δὴ οὐδεὶς πώποτε ἑκὼν εἶναι τυραννίδος
ἀφεῖτο, ὅσπερ ἅπαξ ἐκτήσατο ;

12 Ὅτι, ἔφη, ὦ Σιμωνίδη, καὶ ταύτῃ ἀθλιώτατόν
ἐστιν ἡ τυραννίς· οὐδὲ γὰρ ἀπαλλαγῆναι δυνατὸν
αὐτῆς ἐστι. πῶς γὰρ ἄν τίς ποτε ἐξαρκέσειε
τύραννος ἢ χρήματα ἐκτίνων ὅσους ἀφείλετο
ἢ δεσμοὺς ἀντιπάσχοι ὅσους δὴ ἐδέσμευσεν ἢ
ὅσους κατέκανε πῶς ἂν ἱκανὰς ψυχὰς ἀντιπαρά-
13 σχοιτο ἀποθανουμένας ; ἀλλ' εἴπερ τῳ ἄλλῳ, ὦ
Σιμωνίδη, λυσιτελεῖ ἀπάγξασθαι, ἴσθι, ἔφη,
ὅτι τυράννῳ ἔγωγε εὑρίσκω μάλιστα τοῦτο λυσι-
τελοῦν ποιῆσαι. μόνῳ γὰρ αὐτῷ οὔτε ἔχειν οὔτε
καταθέσθαι τὰ κακὰ λυσιτελεῖ.

VIII. Καὶ ὁ Σιμωνίδης ὑπολαβὼν εἶπεν· Ἀλλὰ
τὸ μὲν νῦν, ὦ Ἱέρων, ἀθύμως ἔχειν σε πρὸς
τὴν τυραννίδα οὐ θαυμάζω, ἐπείπερ ἐπιθυμῶν
φιλεῖσθαι ὑπ' ἀνθρώπων ἐμποδών σοι τούτου
νομίζεις αὐτὴν εἶναι. ἐγὼ μέντοι ἔχειν μοι δοκῶ
διδάξαι σε, ὡς τὸ ἄρχειν οὐδὲν ἀποκωλύει τοῦ
φιλεῖσθαι, ἀλλὰ καὶ πλεονεκτεῖ γε τῆς ἰδιωτείας.
2 ἐπισκοποῦντες δὲ αὐτὸ εἰ οὕτως ἔχει μήπω ἐκεῖνο
σκοπῶμεν, εἰ διὰ τὸ μεῖζον δύνασθαι ὁ ἄρχων
καὶ χαρίζεσθαι πλείω δύναιτ' ἄν, ἀλλ' ἂν τὰ

by fear and malice and danger, and enjoys unbroken happiness. But what is the despot's lot? I tell you, Simonides, he lives day and night like one condemned by the judgment of all men to die for his wickedness."

When Simonides had listened to all this he asked : 11 " Pray, how comes it, Hiero, if despotism is a thing so vile, and this is your verdict, that you do not rid yourself of so great an evil, and that none other, for that matter, who has once acquired it, ever yet surrendered despotic power?"

"Simonides," said he, "this is the crowning 12 misery of despotic power, that it cannot even be got rid of. For how could any despot ever find means to repay in full all whom he has robbed, or himself serve all the terms of imprisonment that he has inflicted? Or how could he forfeit a life for every man whom he has put to death? Ah, 13 Simonides," he cried, "if it profits any man to hang himself, know what my finding is : a despot has most to gain by it, since he alone can neither keep nor lay down his troubles with profit."

VIII. "Well, Hiero," retorted Simonides, " I am not surprised that you are out of heart with despotism for the moment, since you hold that it cuts you off from gaining the affection of mankind, which you covet. Nevertheless, I think I can show you that rule so far from being a bar to popularity, actually has the advantage of a citizen's life. In 2 trying to discover whether this is so, let us for the time being pass over the question whether the ruler, because of his greater power, is able to confer more favours. Assume that the citizen and

ὅμοια ποιῶσιν ὅ τε ἰδιώτης καὶ ὁ τύραννος, ἐννόει,
πότερος μείζω ἀπὸ τῶν ἴσων κτᾶται χάριν.

Ἄρξομαι δέ σοι ἀπὸ τῶν μικροτάτων παρα-
3 δειγμάτων. ἰδὼν γὰρ πρῶτον προσειπάτω τινὰ
φιλικῶς ὅ τε ἄρχων καὶ ὁ ἰδιώτης. ἐν τούτῳ
τὴν ποτέρου πρόσρησιν μᾶλλον εὐφραίνειν τὸν
ἀκούσαντα νομίζεις; ἴθι δὴ ἐπαινεσάντων ἀμφοτέρων τὸν αὐτὸν τὸν ποτέρου δοκεῖς ἔπαινον
ἐξικνεῖσθαι μᾶλλον εἰς εὐφροσύνην; θύσας δὲ
τιμησάτω ἑκάτερος· τὴν παρὰ ποτέρου τιμὴν
4 μείζονος ἂν χάριτος δοκεῖς τυγχάνειν; κάμνοντα
θεραπευσάτωσαν ὁμοίως· οὐκοῦν τοῦτο σαφές,
ὅτι αἱ ἀπὸ τῶν δυνατωτάτων θεραπεῖαι καὶ χαρὰν
ἐμποιοῦσι μεγίστην; δότωσαν δὴ τὰ ἴσα· οὐ
καὶ ἐν τούτῳ σαφές, ὅτι αἱ ἀπὸ τῶν δυνατωτάτων ἡμίσειαι χάριτες πλέον ἢ ὅλον τὸ παρὰ τοῦ
5 ἰδιώτου δώρημα δύνανται; ἀλλ' ἔμοιγε δοκεῖ
καὶ ἐκ θεῶν τιμή τις καὶ χάρις συμπαρέπεσθαι
ἀνδρὶ ἄρχοντι. μὴ γὰρ ὅτι καλλίονα ποιεῖ ἄνδρα,
ἀλλὰ καὶ τὸν αὐτὸν τοῦτον ἥδιον θεώμεθά τε
ὅταν ἄρχῃ ἢ ὅταν ἰδιωτεύῃ διαλεγόμενοί τε ἀγαλ-
λόμεθα τοῖς προτετιμημένοις μᾶλλον ἢ τοῖς ἐκ
6 τοῦ ἴσου ἡμῖν οὖσι. καὶ μὴν παιδικά γε, ἐν οἷς
δὴ καὶ σὺ μάλιστα κατεμέμψω τὴν τυραννίδα,
ἥκιστα μὲν γῆρας ἄρχοντος δυσχεραίνει, ἥκιστα
δ' αἶσχος, πρὸς ὃν ἂν τυγχάνῃ ὁμιλῶν, τούτου
ὑπολογίζεται. αὐτὸ γὰρ τὸ τετιμῆσθαι μάλιστα
42

the despot act alike, and consider which of the two
wins the greater measure of gratitude from the same
actions.

"You shall have the most trifling examples to
begin with. First, suppose that two men greet 3
someone with a friendly remark on seeing him.
One is a ruler, the other a citizen. In this
case which greeting, do you think, is the more
delightful to the hearer? Or again, both commend
the same man. Which commendation, do you
think, is the more welcome? Suppose that each
does the honours when he offers sacrifice. Which
invitation, think you, will be accepted with the
more sincere thanks? Suppose they are equally 4
attentive to a sick man. Is it not obvious that
the attentions of the mightiest bring most comfort
to the patient? Suppose they give presents of
equal value. Is it not clear in this case too that
half the number of favours bestowed by the mightiest
count for more than the whole of the plain citizen's
gift? Nay, to my way of thinking, even the gods 5
cause a peculiar honour and favour to dance atten-
dance on a great ruler. For not only does rule
add dignity of presence to a man, but we find
more pleasure in the sight of that man when he
is a ruler than when he is a mere citizen, and we take
more pride in the conversation of those who rank
above us than in that of our equals. And 6
favourites, mark you, who were the subject of your
bitterest complaint against despotism, are not
offended by old age in a ruler, and take no account
of ugliness in the patron with whom they happen
to be associated. For high rank in itself is a most
striking embellishment to the person : it casts a

συνεπικοσμεῖ, ὥστε τὰ μὲν δυσχερῆ ἀφανίζειν,
7 τὰ δὲ καλὰ λαμπρότερα ἀναφαίνειν. ὁπότε γε
μὴν ἐκ τῶν ἴσων ὑπουργημάτων μειζόνων
χαρίτων ὑμεῖς τυγχάνετε, πῶς οὐκ ἐπειδάν γε
ὑμεῖς πολλαπλάσια μὲν διαπράττοντες ὠφελεῖν
δύνησθε, πολλαπλάσια δὲ δωρεῖσθαι ἔχητε,
ὑμᾶς καὶ πολὺ μᾶλλον φιλεῖσθαι τῶν ἰδιωτῶν
προσήκει ;
8 Καὶ ὁ Ἱέρων εὐθὺς ὑπολαβών, "Ὅτι νὴ Δί',
ἔφη, ὦ Σιμωνίδη, καὶ ἐξ ὧν ἀπεχθάνονται ἄνθρωποι, ἡμᾶς πολὺ πλείω τῶν ἰδιωτῶν ἀνάγκη
9 ἐστὶ πραγματεύεσθαι. πρακτέον μέν γε χρήματα,
εἰ μέλλομεν ἔξειν δαπανᾶν εἰς τὰ δέοντα, ἀναγ-
καστέον δὲ φυλάττειν ὅσα δεῖται φυλακῆς, κο-
λαστέον δὲ τοὺς ἀδίκους, κωλυτέον δὲ τοὺς
ὑβρίζειν βουλομένους, καὶ ὅταν γε τάχους καιρὸς
παραστῇ ἢ πεζῇ ἢ κατὰ θάλατταν ἐξορμᾶσθαι,
10 οὐκ ἐπιτρεπτέον τοῖς ῥᾳδιουργοῦσιν. ἔτι δὲ
μισθοφόρων μὲν ἀνδρὶ τυράννῳ δεῖ· τούτου δὲ
βαρύτερον φόρημα οὐδέν ἐστι τοῖς πολίταις. οὐ
γὰρ τυράννοις ἰσοτιμίας,[1] ἀλλὰ πλεονεξίας ἕνεκα
νομίζουσι τούτους τρέφεσθαι.

IX. Πρὸς ταῦτα δὴ πάλιν εἶπεν ὁ Σιμωνίδης·
Ἀλλ' ὅπως μὲν οὐ πάντων τούτων ἐπιμελητέον,
ὦ Ἱέρων, οὐ λέγω. ἐπιμέλειαι μέντοι μοι δοκοῦσιν αἱ μὲν πάνυ πρὸς ἔχθραν ἄγειν, αἱ δὲ
2 πάνυ διὰ χαρίτων εἶναι. τὸ μὲν γὰρ διδάσκειν
ἅ ἐστι βέλτιστα καὶ τὸν κάλλιστα ταῦτα
ἐξεργαζόμενον ἐπαινεῖν καὶ τιμᾶν, αὕτη μὲν

---

[1] ἰσοτιμίας of an inferior MS. is doubtless a conjecture.
S. gives ἰσοτίμους with B and a later hand in A. The

44

shade over anything repulsive in him and shows up
his best features in a high light. Moreover, inas- 7
much as equal services rendered by you rulers are
rewarded with deeper gratitude, surely, when you
have the power of doing far more for others by
your activities, and can lavish far more gifts on
them, it is natural that you should be much more
deeply loved than private citizens."

Hiero instantly rejoined : " Indeed it is not so, 8
Simonides ; for we are forced to engage far oftener
than private citizens in transactions that make men
hated. Thus, we must extort money in order to 9
find the cash to pay for what we want : we must
compel men to guard whatever needs protection :
we must punish wrongdoers ; we must check those
who would fain wax insolent ; and when a crisis arises
that calls for the immediate despatch of forces by
land and sea, we must see that there is no dilly-dally-
ing. Further, a great despot must needs have mer- 10
cenaries ; and no burden presses more heavily on
the citizens than that, since they believe that these
troops are maintained not in the interests of
equality, but for the despot's personal ends."

IX. In answer to this Simonides said : " Well,
Hiero, I do not deny that all these matters must
receive attention. But I should divide a ruler's
activities into two classes, those that lead inevitably
to unpopularity, and those that are greeted with
thanks. The duty of teaching the people what 2
things are best, and of dispensing praise and
honour to those who accomplish the same most

---

original reading in A was ἰσότιμος. The best conjecture is
still τιμῆς.

ἡ ἐπιμέλεια διὰ χαρίτων γίγνεται, τὸ δὲ τὸν
ἐνδεῶς τι ποιοῦντα λοιδορεῖν τε καὶ ἀναγκάζειν
καὶ ζημιοῦν καὶ κολάζειν, ταῦτα δὲ ἀνάγκη
3 δι' ἀπεχθείας μᾶλλον γίγνεσθαι. ἐγὼ οὖν
φημι ἀνδρὶ ἄρχοντι τὸν μὲν[1] ἀνάγκης δεόμενον
ἄλλοις προστακτέον εἶναι κολάζειν, τὸ δὲ τὰ
ἆθλα ἀποδιδόναι δι' αὑτοῦ ποιητέον. ὡς δὲ
4 ταῦτα καλῶς ἔχει, μαρτυρεῖ τὰ γιγνόμενα. καὶ
γὰρ ὅταν χοροὺς ἡμῖν βουλώμεθα ἀγωνίζεσθαι,
ἆθλα μὲν ὁ ἄρχων προτίθησιν, ἀθροίζειν δὲ
αὐτοὺς προστέτακται χορηγοῖς καὶ ἄλλοις διδάσκειν καὶ ἀνάγκην προστιθέναι τοῖς ἐνδεῶς τι
ποιοῦσιν. οὐκοῦν εὐθὺς ἐν τούτοις τὸ μὲν ἐπί-
χαρι διὰ τοῦ ἄρχοντος ἐγένετο, τὰ δ' ἀντίτυπα
5 δι' ἄλλων. τί οὖν κωλύει καὶ τἆλλα τὰ πολιτικὰ
οὕτως περαίνεσθαι; διῄρηνται μὲν γὰρ ἅπασαι αἱ
πόλεις αἱ μὲν κατὰ φυλάς, αἱ δὲ κατὰ μόρας, αἱ
δὲ κατὰ λόχους, καὶ ἄρχοντες ἐφ' ἑκάστῳ μέρει
6 ἐφεστήκασιν. οὐκοῦν εἴ τις καὶ τούτοις ὥσπερ
τοῖς χοροῖς ἆθλα προτιθείη καὶ εὐοπλίας καὶ
εὐταξίας καὶ ἱππικῆς καὶ ἀλκῆς τῆς ἐν πολέμῳ
καὶ δικαιοσύνης τῆς ἐν τοῖς συμβολαίοις, εἰκὸς καὶ
ταῦτα πάντα διὰ φιλονικίαν ἐντόνως ἀσκεῖσθαι.
7 καὶ ναὶ μὰ Δία ὁρμῷντό γ' ἂν θᾶττον ὅποι δέοι
τιμῆς ὀρεγόμενοι καὶ χρήματα θᾶττον εἰσφέροιεν,
ὁπότε τούτου καιρὸς εἴη, καὶ τὸ πάντων γε χρη-
σιμώτατον, ἥκιστα δὲ εἰθισμένον διὰ φιλονικίας
πράττεσθαι, ἡ γεωργία αὐτὴ ἂν πολὺ ἐπιδοίη,

---

[1] τὸν μὲν Thalheim : τὸ μὲν MSS. : τὸ μὲν τὸν S., after
Stephanus.

efficiently, is a form of activity that is greeted with thanks. The duty of pronouncing censure, using coercion, inflicting pains and penalties on those who come short in any respect, is one that must of necessity give rise to a certain amount of unpopularity. Therefore my sentence is that a great ruler should 3 delegate to others the task of punishing those who require to be coerced, and should reserve to himself the privilege of awarding the prizes. The excellence of this arrangement is established by daily experience. Thus, when we want to have a choral 4 competition, the ruler offers prizes, but the task of assembling the choirs is delegated to choir-masters, and others have the task of training them and coercing those who come short in any respect. Obviously, then, in this case, the pleasant part falls to the ruler, the disagreeables fall to others. Why, 5 then, should not all other public affairs be managed on this principle? For all communities are divided into parts—'tribes,' 'wards,' 'unions,' as the case may be—and every one of these parts is subject to its appointed ruler. If, then, the analogy of the 6 choruses were followed and prizes were offered to these parts for excellence of equipment, good discipline, horsemanship, courage in the field and fair dealing in business, the natural outcome would be competition, and consequently an earnest endeavour to improve in all these respects too. And 7 as a matter of course, with the prospect of reward there would be more despatch in starting for the appointed place, and greater promptitude in the payment of war taxes, whenever occasion required. Nay, agriculture itself, most useful of all occupations, but just the one in which the spirit of

47

εἴ τις ἆθλα προτιθείη κατ' ἀγροὺς ἢ κατὰ κώμας
τοῖς κάλλιστα τὴν γῆν ἐξεργαζομένοις, καὶ τοῖς
εἰς τοῦτο τῶν πολιτῶν ἐρρωμένως τρεπομένοις
8 πολλὰ ἂν ἀγαθὰ περαίνοιτο. καὶ γὰρ αἱ πρόσοδοι
αὔξοιντ' ἄν, καὶ ἡ σωφροσύνη πολὺ μᾶλλον τῇ
ἀσχολίᾳ συμπαρομαρτεῖ. καὶ μὴν κακουργίαι γε
9 ἧττον τοῖς ἐνεργοῖς ἐμφύονται. εἰ δὲ καὶ ἐμπορία
ὠφελεῖ τι πόλιν, τιμώμενος ἂν ὁ πλεῖστα τοῦτο
ποιῶν καὶ ἐμπόρους ἂν πλείους ἀγείροι. εἰ δὲ
φανερὸν γένοιτο, ὅτι καὶ ὁ πρόσοδόν τινα ἄλυπον
ἐξευρίσκων τῇ πόλει τιμήσεται, οὐδ' αὕτη ἂν ἡ
10 σκέψις ἀργοῖτο. ὡς δὲ συνελόντι εἰπεῖν, εἰ καὶ
κατὰ πάντα ἐμφανὲς εἴη, ὅτι ὁ ἀγαθόν τι εἰση-
γούμενος οὐκ ἀτίμητος ἔσται, πολλοὺς ἂν καὶ
τοῦτο ἐξορμήσειεν ἔργον ποιεῖσθαι τὸ σκοπεῖν
τι ἀγαθόν. καὶ ὅταν γε πολλοῖς περὶ τῶν ὠφε-
λίμων μέλῃ, ἀνάγκη εὑρίσκεσθαί τε μᾶλλον καὶ
ἐπιτελεῖσθαι.

11 Εἰ δὲ φοβεῖ, ὦ Ἱέρων, μὴ ἐν πολλοῖς ἄθλων
προτιθεμένων[1] πολλαὶ δαπάναι γίγνωνται, ἐν-
νόησον, ὅτι οὐκ ἔστιν ἐμπορεύματα λυσιτελέστερα ἢ ὅσα ἄνθρωποι ἄθλων ὠνοῦνται. ὁρᾷς ἐν
ἱππικοῖς καὶ γυμνικοῖς καὶ χορηγικοῖς ἀγῶσιν ὡς
μικρὰ ἆθλα μεγάλας δαπάνας καὶ πολλοὺς πόνους
καὶ πολλὰς ἐπιμελείας ἐξάγεται ἀνθρώπων ;

Χ. Καὶ ὁ Ἱέρων εἶπεν· Ἀλλὰ ταῦτα μέν, ὦ
Σιμωνίδη, καλῶς μοι δοκεῖς λέγειν· περὶ δὲ τῶν
μισθοφόρων ἔχεις τι εἰπεῖν, ὡς μὴ μισεῖσθαι δι'

---

[1] προτιθεμένων Cobit : προτεθειμένων S. with the MSS.

48

competition is conspicuous by its absence, would
make great progress if prizes were offered for the
farm or the village that can show the best
cultivation, and many good results would follow
for those citizens who threw themselves vigorously
into this occupation. For apart from the consequent 8
increase in the revenues, sobriety far more commonly
goes with industry; and remember, vices rarely
flourish among the fully employed. If commerce 9
also brings gain to a city, the award of honours for
diligence in business would attract a larger number
to a commercial career. And were it made clear
that the discovery of some way of raising revenue
without hurting anyone will also be rewarded, this
field of research too would not be unoccupied. In 1
a word, once it becomes clear in every department
that any good suggestion will not go unrewarded,
many will be encouraged by that knowledge to
apply themselves to some promising form of
investigation. And when there is a wide-spread
interest in useful subjects, an increase of discovery
and achievement is bound to come.

"In case you fear, Hiero, that the cost of offering 11
prizes for many subjects may prove heavy, you
should reflect that no commodities are cheaper
than those that are bought for a prize. Think of
the large sums that men are induced to spend on
horse-races, gymnastic and choral competitions, and
the long course of training and practice they
undergo for the sake of a paltry prize."

X. "Well, Simonides," said Hiero, "I think you
are right in saying that. But what about the
mercenaries? Can you tell me how to employ
them without incurring unpopularity? Or do you

49

αὐτούς ; ἢ λέγεις, ὡς φιλίαν κτησάμενος ἄρχων
οὐδὲν ἔτι δεήσεται δορυφόρων ;

2 Ναὶ μὰ Δία, εἶπεν ὁ Σιμωνίδης, δεήσεται μὲν οὖν.
οἶδα γάρ, ὅτι ὥσπερ ἐν ἵπποις οὕτως καὶ ἐν ἀνθρώποις τισὶν ἐγγίγνεται, ὅσῳ ἂν ἔκπλεα τὰ δέοντα
3 ἔχωσι, τοσούτῳ ὑβριστοτέροις εἶναι. τοὺς μὲν
οὖν τοιούτους μᾶλλον ἂν σωφρονίζοι ὁ ἀπὸ
τῶν δορυφόρων φόβος. τοῖς δὲ καλοῖς κἀγαθοῖς
ἀπ' οὐδενὸς ἄν μοι δοκεῖς τοσαῦτα ὠφελήματα
4 παρασχεῖν ὅσα ἀπὸ τῶν μισθοφόρων. τρέφεις
μὲν γὰρ δήπου καὶ σὺ αὐτοὺς σαυτῷ φύλακας·
ἤδη δὲ πολλοὶ καὶ δεσπόται βίᾳ ὑπὸ τῶν δούλων
ἀπέθανον. εἰ οὖν ἓν πρῶτον τοῦτ' εἴη τῶν
προστεταγμένων τοῖς μισθοφόροις, ὡς πάντων
ὄντας δορυφόρους τῶν πολιτῶν βοηθεῖν πᾶσιν,
ἄν τι τοιοῦτον αἰσθάνωνται· γίγνονται δέ που,
ὡς πάντες ἐπιστάμεθα, κακοῦργοι ἐν πόλεσιν·
εἰ οὖν καὶ τούτους φυλάττειν εἶεν τεταγμένοι,
καὶ τοῦτ' ἂν εἰδεῖεν ὑπ' αὐτῶν ὠφελούμενοι.
5 πρὸς δὲ τούτοις καὶ τοῖς ἐν τῇ χώρα ἐργάταις
καὶ κτήνεσιν οὗτοι ἂν εἰκότως καὶ θάρρος καὶ
ἀσφάλειαν δύναιντο μάλιστα παρέχειν, ὁμοίως
μὲν τοῖς σοῖς ἰδίοις, ὁμοίως δὲ τοῖς ἀνὰ τὴν
χώραν. ἱκανοί γε μὴν εἰσι καὶ σχολὴν παρέχειν
τοῖς πολίταις τῶν ἰδίων ἐπιμελεῖσθαι, τὰ ἐπί-
6 καιρα φυλάττοντες. πρὸς δὲ τούτοις καὶ πολεμίων ἐφόδους κρυφαίας καὶ ἐξαπιναίας τίνες
ἑτοιμότεροι ἢ προαισθέσθαι ἢ κωλῦσαι τῶν ἀεὶ
ἐν ὅπλοις τε ὄντων καὶ συντεταγμένων ; ἀλλὰ
μὴν καὶ ἐν στρατείᾳ τί ἐστιν ὠφελιμώτερον πολί-

say that a ruler, once he becomes popular, will have no further need of a bodyguard?"

"No, no, he will need them, of course," said 2 Simonides. "For I know that some human beings are like horses—the more they get what they want, the more unruly they are apt to become. The way 3 to manage men like that is to put the fear of the bodyguard into them. And as for the gentlemen, you can probably confer greater benefits on them by employing mercenaries than by any other means. For I presume that you maintain the force primarily 4 to protect yourself. But masters have often been murdered by their slaves. If therefore the first duty enjoined on the mercenaries were to act as the bodyguard of the whole community and render help to all, in case they got wind of any such intention—there are black sheep in every fold, as we all know—I say, if they were under orders to guard the citizens as well as the depot, the citizens would know that this is one service rendered to them by the mercenaries. Nor is this all: for 5 naturally the mercenaries would also be able to give fearlessness and security in the fullest measure to the labourers and cattle in the country, and the benefit would not be confined to your own estates, but would be felt up and down the countryside. Again, they are competent to afford the citizens 6 leisure for attending to their private affairs by guarding the vital positions. Besides, should an enemy plan a secret and sudden attack, what handier agents can be found for detecting or preventing their design than a standing force, armed and organized? Or once more, when the citizens go campaigning, what is more useful to them than mer-

ταῖς μισθοφόρων; τούτους γὰρ προπονεῖν καὶ
προκινδυνεύειν καὶ προφυλάττειν εἰκὸς ἑτοιμο-
7 τάτους εἶναι. τὰς δὲ ἀγχιτέρμονας πόλεις οὐκ
ἀνάγκη διὰ τοὺς ἀεὶ ἐν ὅπλοις ὄντας καὶ εἰρήνης
μάλιστα ἐπιθυμεῖν; οἱ γὰρ συντεταγμένοι καὶ
σώζειν τὰ τῶν φίλων μάλιστα καὶ σφάλλειν τὰ
8 τῶν πολεμίων δύναιντ' ἄν. ὅταν γε μὴν γνῶσιν
οἱ πολῖται, ὅτι οὗτοι κακὸν μὲν οὐδὲν ποιοῦσι
τὸν μηδὲν ἀδικοῦντα, τοὺς δὲ κακουργεῖν βουλομένους κωλύουσι, βοηθοῦσι δὲ τοῖς ἀδικουμένοις,
προνοοῦσι δὲ καὶ προκινδυνεύουσι τῶν πολιτῶν,
πῶς οὐκ ἀνάγκη καὶ δαπανᾶν εἰς τούτους ἥδιστα;
τρέφουσι γοῦν καὶ ἰδίᾳ ἐπὶ μείοσι τούτων φύλακας.

XI. Χρὴ δέ, ὦ Ἱέρων, οὐδ' ἀπὸ τῶν ἰδίων
κτημάτων ὀκνεῖν δαπανᾶν εἰς τὸ κοινὸν ἀγαθόν.
καὶ γὰρ ἔμοιγε δοκεῖ τὰ εἰς τὴν πόλιν ἀνα-
λούμενα μᾶλλον εἰς τὸ δέον τελεῖσθαι ἢ τὰ
2 εἰς τὸ ἴδιον ἀνδρὶ τυράννῳ. καθ' ἓν δ' ἕκαστον
σκοπῶμεν. οἰκίαν πρῶτον ὑπερβαλλούσῃ δαπάνῃ κεκαλλωπισμένην μᾶλλον ἡγῇ κόσμον ἄν
σοι παρέχειν ἢ πᾶσαν τὴν πόλιν τείχεσί τε καὶ
ναοῖς καὶ παστάσι[1] καὶ ἀγοραῖς καὶ λιμέσι
3 κατεσκευασμένην; ὅπλοις δὲ πότερον τοῖς ἐκπα-
γλοτάτοις αὐτὸς κατακεκοσμημένος δεινότερος
ἂν φαίνοιο τοῖς πολεμίοις ἢ τῆς πόλεως ὅλης
4 εὐόπλου σοι οὔσης; προσόδους δὲ ποτέρως ἂν
δοκεῖς πλείονας γίγνεσθαι, εἰ τὰ σὰ ἴδια μόνον
ἐνεργὰ ἔχοις ἢ εἰ τὰ πάντων τῶν πολιτῶν

cenaries? For these are, as a matter of course, the readiest to bear the brunt of toil and danger and watching. And must not those who possess a 7 standing force impose on border states a strong desire for peace? For nothing equals an organized body of men, whether for protecting the property of friends or for thwarting the plans of enemies. Further, when the citizens get it into their heads 8 that these troops do no harm to the innocent and hold the would-be malefactor in check, come to the rescue of the wronged, care for the citizens and shield them from danger, surely they are bound to pay the cost of them with a right good-will. At all events they keep guards in their homes for less important objects than these.

XI. "Nor should you hesitate to draw on your private property, Hiero, for the common good. For in my opinion the sums that a great despot spends on the city are more truly necessary expenses than the money he spends on himself. But let us go into 2 details. First, which do you suppose is likely to bring you more credit, to own a palace adorned with priceless objects of art, or to have the whole city garnished with walls and temples and verandahs [1] and market-places and harbours? Which will make 3 you look more terrible to the enemy, to dazzle all beholders with your own glittering panoply, or to present the whole of your people in goodly armour? Which plan, think you, will yield revenues more 4 abounding, to keep only your own capital employed, or to contrive to bring the capital of all the citizens

---

[1] παστάσι rests on the authority of Pollux: παραστάσι S. with the MSS.

XENOPHON

5 μεμηχανημένος εἴης ἐνεργὰ εἶναι ; τὸ δὲ πάντων
κάλλιστον καὶ μεγαλοπρεπέστατον νομιζόμενον
εἶναι ἐπιτήδευμα ἁρματοτροφίαν ποτέρως ἂν
δοκεῖς μᾶλλον κοσμεῖν, εἰ αὐτὸς πλεῖστα τῶν
Ἑλλήνων ἅρματα τρέφοις τε καὶ πέμποις εἰς
τὰς πανηγύρεις ἢ εἰ ἐκ τῆς σῆς πόλεως πλεῖστοι
μὲν ἱπποτρόφοι εἶεν, πλεῖστοι δ᾽ ἀγωνίζοιντο ;
νικᾶν δὲ πότερα δοκεῖς κάλλιον εἶναι ἅρματος
ἀρετῇ ἢ πόλεως, ἧς προστατεύεις, εὐδαιμονίᾳ ;
6 ἐγὼ μὲν γὰρ οὐδὲ προσήκειν φημὶ ἀνδρὶ τυράννῳ
πρὸς ἰδιώτας ἀγωνίζεσθαι. νικῶν μὲν γὰρ οὐκ
ἂν θαυμάζοιο, ἀλλὰ φθονοῖο, ὡς ἀπὸ πολλῶν
οἴκων τὰς δαπάνας ποιούμενος, νικώμενος δ᾽ ἂν
7 πάντων μάλιστα καταγελῷο. ἀλλ᾽ ἐγώ σοί
φημι, ὦ Ἱέρων, πρὸς ἄλλους προστάτας πόλεων
τὸν ἀγῶνα εἶναι, ὧν ἐὰν σὺ εὐδαιμονεστάτην
τὴν πόλιν, ἧς προστατεύεις, παρέχῃς, εὖ ἴσθι
νικῶν τῷ καλλίστῳ καὶ μεγαλοπρεπεστάτῳ ἐν
8 ἀνθρώποις ἀγωνίσματι. καὶ πρῶτον μὲν εὐθὺς
κατειργασμένος ἂν εἴης τὸ φιλεῖσθαι ὑπὸ τῶν
ἀρχομένων, οὗ δὴ σὺ ἐπιθυμῶν τυγχάνεις· ἔπειτα
δὲ τὴν σὴν νίκην οὐκ ἂν εἷς εἴη ὁ ἀνακηρύττων,
ἀλλὰ πάντες ἄνθρωποι ὑμνοῖεν ἂν τὴν σὴν ἀρετήν.
9 περίβλεπτος δὲ ὢν οὐχ ὑπὸ ἰδιωτῶν μόνον, ἀλλὰ
καὶ ὑπὸ πολλῶν πόλεων ἀγαπῷο ἂν καὶ θαυμα-
στὸς οὐκ ἰδίᾳ μόνον, ἀλλὰ καὶ δημοσίᾳ παρὰ
10 πᾶσιν ἂν εἴης, καὶ ἐξείη μὲν ἄν σοι ἕνεκεν
ἀσφαλείας, εἴ ποι βούλοιο, θεωρήσοντι πορεύεσθαι, ἐξείη δ᾽ ἂν αὐτοῦ μένοντι τοῦτο πράττειν.

54

into employment? And what about the breeding 5
of chariot horses, commonly considered the noblest
and grandest business in the world? By which
method do you think you will gain most credit for
that, if you out-do all other Greeks in the number
of teams you breed and send to the festivals, or if
the greatest number of breeders and the greatest
number of competitors are drawn from your city?
And how is the nobler victory gained, by the excellence of your team, or by the prosperity of the
city of which you are the head? Indeed my own 6
opinion is that it is not even seemly for a great despot
to compete with private citizens. For your victory
would excite envy rather than admiration, on the
ground that many estates supply the money that
you spend, and no defeat would be greeted with
so much ridicule as yours. I tell you, Hiero, 7
you have to compete with other heads of states,
and if you cause your state to surpass theirs in
prosperity, be well assured[1] that you are the victor
in the noblest and grandest competition in the
world. And in the first place you will forthwith 8
have secured just what you really want, the affection
of your subjects. Secondly, your victory will not
be proclaimed by one herald's voice, but all the
world will tell of your virtue. The observed of 9
all observers' eyes, you will be a hero, not only to
private citizens, but to many states: you will be
admired not only in your home, but in public among
all men. And you will be free to go wherever you 10
choose, so far as safety is concerned, to see the
sights, and equally free to enjoy them in your

---

[1] But εὖ ἴσθι is not right. All the MSS. have εὖ ἔσει,
which perhaps conceals εὐδαίμων ἔσει, "you will be happy,
being the victor."

ἀεὶ γὰρ ἂν παρὰ σοὶ πανήγυρις εἴη τῶν βουλομένων ἐπιδεικνύναι, εἴ τίς τι σοφὸν ἢ καλὸν ἢ
ἀγαθὸν ἔχοι, τῶν δὲ καὶ ἐπιθυμούντων ὑπηρετεῖν.
11 πᾶς δὲ ὁ μὲν παρὼν σύμμαχος ἂν εἴη σοι, ὁ δὲ
ἀπὼν ἐπιθυμοίη ἂν ἰδεῖν σε.

"Ὥστε οὐ μόνον φιλοῖο ἄν, ἀλλὰ καὶ ἐρῷο ὑπ'
ἀνθρώπων, καὶ τοὺς καλοὺς οὐ πειρᾶν, ἀλλὰ
πειρώμενον ὑπ' αὐτῶν ἀνέχεσθαι ἄν σε δέοι,
φόβον δὲ οὐκ ἂν ἔχοις, ἀλλ' ἄλλοις παρέχοις,
12 μή τι πάθῃς, ἑκόντας δὲ τοὺς πειθομένους ἔχοις
ἂν καὶ ἐθελουσίως σου προνοοῦντας θεῷο ἄν, εἰ
δέ τις κίνδυνος εἴη, οὐ συμμάχους μόνον,
ἀλλὰ καὶ προμάχους καὶ προθύμους ὁρῴης
ἄν, πολλῶν μὲν δωρεῶν ἀξιούμενος, οὐκ ἀπορῶν
δέ, ὅτῳ τούτων εὐμενεῖ μεταδώσεις, πάντας
μὲν συγχαίροντας ἔχων ἐπὶ τοῖς σοῖς ἀγαθοῖς,
πάντας δὲ πρὸ τῶν σῶν ὥσπερ τῶν ἰδίων
13 μαχομένους. θησαυρούς γε μὴν ἔχοις ἂν πάντας
τοὺς παρὰ τοῖς φίλοις πλούτους.

Ἀλλὰ θαρρῶν, ὦ Ἱέρων, πλούτιζε μὲν τοὺς
φίλους· σαυτὸν γὰρ πλουτιεῖς· αὖξε δὲ τὴν
14 πόλιν· σαυτῷ γὰρ δύναμιν περιάψεις· κτῶ δὲ
αὐτῇ συμμάχους· ...¹ νόμιζε δὲ τὴν μὲν πατρίδα
οἶκον, τοὺς δὲ πολίτας ἑταίρους, τοὺς δὲ φίλους
τέκνα σεαυτοῦ, τοὺς δὲ παῖδας ὅτιπερ τὴν
σὴν ψυχήν, καὶ τούτους πάντας πειρῶ νικᾶν εὖ
15 ποιῶν. ἐὰν γὰρ τοὺς φίλους κρατῇς εὖ ποιῶν
οὐ μή σοι δύνωνται ἀντέχειν οἱ πολέμιοι.

Κἂν ταῦτα πάντα ποιῇς, εὖ ἴσθι πάντων τῶν
ἐν ἀνθρώποις κάλλιστον καὶ μακαριώτατον κτῆμα
κεκτήσῃ. εὐδαιμονῶν γὰρ οὐ φθονηθήσῃ.

---

¹ Weiske indicates a lacuna here : S. does not.

home; for you will have a throng of aspirants before you, some eager to display something wise or beautiful or good, others longing to serve you. Everyone 11 present will be an ally, everyone absent will long to see you.

"Thus you will be not only the loved, but the adored of mankind. You will need not to court the fair, but to listen patiently to their suit. Anxiety for your welfare will fall not on yourself, but on others. You will have the willing obedience of 12 your subjects; you will mark their unsolicited care for you; and should any danger arise, you will find in them not merely allies, but champions and zealots.[1] Accounted worthy of many gifts, and at no loss for some man of goodwill with whom to share them, you will find all rejoicing in your good fortune, all fighting for your interests, as though they were their own. And all the riches in the 13 houses of your friends will be yours in fee.

"Take heart then, Hiero; enrich your friends, for so you will enrich yourself. Exalt the state, for so you will deck yourself with power. Get her allies 14 [for so you will win supporters for yourself]. Account the fatherland your estate, the citizens your comrades, friends your own children, your sons possessions dear as life. And try to surpass all these in deeds of kindness. For if you out-do your friends 15 in kindness, it is certain that your enemies will not be able to resist you.

"And if you do all these things, rest assured that you will be possessed of the fairest and most blessed possession in the world; for none will be jealous of your happiness."

[1] Or 'champions full of zeal.' The καί is not free from suspicion.

AGESILAUS

ΞΕΝΟΦΩΝΤΟΣ ΑΓΗΣΙΛΑΟΣ

I. Οἶδα μέν, ὅτι τῆς Ἀγησιλάου ἀρετῆς τε καὶ
δόξης οὐ ῥάδιον ἄξιον ἔπαινον γράψαι, ὅμως
δ᾽ ἐγχειρητέον· οὐ γὰρ ἂν καλῶς ἔχοι, εἰ ὅτι
τελέως ἀνὴρ ἀγαθὸς ἐγένετο, διὰ τοῦτο οὐδὲ
μειόνων τυγχάνοι ἐπαίνων.

2 Περὶ μὲν οὖν εὐγενείας αὐτοῦ τί ἄν τις μεῖζον
καὶ κάλλιον εἰπεῖν ἔχοι ἢ ὅτι ἔτι καὶ νῦν τοῖς
προγόνοις ὀνομαζομένοις ἀπομνημονεύεται, ὁπόσ-
τος ἀφ᾽ Ἡρακλέους ἐγένετο, καὶ τούτοις οὐκ
3 ἰδιώταις, ἀλλ᾽ ἐκ βασιλέων βασιλεῦσιν ; ἀλλὰ
μὴν οὐδὲ ταύτῃ γ᾽ ἄν τις ἔχοι καταμέμψασθαι
αὐτούς, ὡς βασιλεύουσι μέν, πόλεως δὲ τῆς
ἐπιτυχούσης· ἀλλ᾽ ὥσπερ τὸ γένος αὐτῶν τῆς
πατρίδος ἐντιμότατον, οὕτω καὶ ἡ πόλις ἐν τῇ
Ἑλλάδι ἐνδοξοτάτη· ὥστε οὐ δευτέρων πρω-
4 τεύουσιν, ἀλλ᾽· ἡγεμόνων ἡγεμονεύουσι. τῇδέ γε
μὴν καὶ κοινῇ ἄξιον ἐπαινέσαι τήν τε πατρίδα
καὶ τὸ γένος αὐτοῦ· ἥ τε γὰρ πόλις οὐδεπώποτε
φθονήσασα τοῦ προτετιμῆσθαι αὐτοὺς ἐπεχείρησε καταλῦσαι τὴν ἀρχὴν αὐτῶν οἵ τε βασιλεῖς
οὐδεπώποτε μειζόνων ὠρέχθησαν ἢ ἐφ᾽ οἷσπερ
ἐξ ἀρχῆς τὴν βασιλείαν παρέλαβον. τοιγαροῦν
ἄλλη μὲν οὐδεμία ἀρχὴ φανερά ἐστι διαγεγενη-
μένη ἀδιάσπαστος οὔτε δημοκρατία οὔτε ὀλι-

AGESILAUS

I. I KNOW how difficult it is to write an appreciation
of Agesilaus that shall be worthy of his virtue and
glory. Nevertheless the attempt must be made.
For it would not be seemly that so good a man, just
because of his perfection, should receive no tributes
of praise, however inadequate.

Now concerning his high birth what greater and 2
nobler could be said than this, that even to-day the
line of his descent from Heracles [1] is traced through
the roll of his ancestors, and those no simple citizens,
but kings and sons of kings? Nor are they open to 3
the reproach that though they were kings, they ruled
over a petty state. On the contrary, as their family
is honoured above all in their fatherland, so is their
state glorious above all in Greece ; thus they are
not first in the second rank, but leaders in a community of leaders. On one account his fatherland 4
and his family are worthy to be praised together,
for never at any time has the state been moved by
jealousy of their pre-eminence to attempt the over-
throw of their government, and never at any time
have the kings striven to obtain greater powers than
were conferred on them originally at their succession
to the throne. For this reason, while no other government—democracy, oligachy, despotism or kingdom—

---

[1] Agesilaus was twenty-fifth in line of descent from
Heracles (Herodotus, VIII. 131 ; Plutarch, *Lycurgus*, c. i ;
Agesilaus, c. i).

γαρχία οὔτε τυραννὶς οὔτε βασιλεία· αὕτη δὲ
μόνη διαμένει συνεχὴς βασιλεία.

5 ῟Ως γε μὴν καὶ πρὶν ἄρξαι ἄξιος τῆς βασιλείας
ἐδόκει εἶναι Ἀγησίλαος, τάδε τὰ σημεῖα. ἐπεὶ
γὰρ Ἆγις βασιλεὺς ὢν ἐτελεύτησεν, ἐρισάντων
περὶ τῆς ἀρχῆς Λεωτυχίδα μὲν ὡς Ἄγιδος ὄντος
υἱοῦ, Ἀγησιλάου δὲ ὡς Ἀρχιδάμου, κρίνασα ἡ
πόλις ἀνεπικλητότερον εἶναι Ἀγησίλαον καὶ τῷ
γένει καὶ τῇ ἀρετῇ τοῦτον ἐστήσατο βασιλέα.
καίτοι τὸ ἐν τῇ κρατίστῃ πόλει ὑπὸ τῶν ἀρίστων
κριθέντα τοῦ καλλίστου γέρως ἀξιωθῆναι ποίων
ἔτι τεκμηρίων προσδεῖται τῆς γε πρὶν ἄρξαι
αὐτὸν ἀρετῆς;

6 ῟Οσα γε μὴν ἐν τῇ βασιλείᾳ διεπράξατο, νῦν
ἤδη διηγήσομαι· ἀπὸ γὰρ τῶν ἔργων καὶ τοὺς
τρόπους αὐτοῦ κάλλιστα νομίζω καταδήλους
ἔσεσθαι.

Ἀγησίλαος τοίνυν ἔτι μὲν νέος ὢν ἔτυχε τῆς
βασιλείας· ἄρτι δὲ ὄντος αὐτοῦ ἐν τῇ ἀρχῇ,
ἐξηγγέλθη βασιλεὺς ὁ Περσῶν ἀθροίζων καὶ
ναυτικὸν καὶ πεζὸν πολὺ στράτευμα ὡς ἐπὶ
7 ῝Ελληνας· βουλευομένων δὲ περὶ τούτων Λακεδαιμονίων καὶ τῶν συμμάχων, Ἀγησίλαος
ὑπέστη, ἐὰν δῶσιν αὐτῷ τριάκοντα μὲν Σπαρτιατῶν, δισχιλίους δὲ νεοδαμώδεις, εἰς ἑξακισ-
χιλίους δὲ τὸ σύνταγμα τῶν συμμάχων, διαβή-
σεσθαι εἰς τὴν Ἀσίαν καὶ πειράσεσθαι εἰρήνην
ποιῆσαι, ἢ ἂν πολεμεῖν βούληται ὁ βάρβαρος,
ἀσχολίαν αὐτῷ παρέξειν στρατεύειν ἐπὶ τοὺς
8 ῝Ελληνας. εὐθὺς μὲν οὖν πολλοὶ πάνυ ἠγά-
σθησαν αὐτὸ τοῦτο τὸ ἐπιθυμῆσαι, ἐπειδὴ ὁ
Πέρσης πρόσθεν ἐπὶ τὴν Ἑλλάδα διέβη, ἀντι-

can lay claim to an unbroken existence, this kingdom alone stands fast continually.

However, there are not wanting signs that even 5 before his reign began Agesilaus was deemed worthy to be king. For on the death of King Agis there was a struggle for the throne between Leotychidas, as the son of Agis, and Agesilaus, as the son of Archidamus. The state decided in favour of Agesilaus, judging him to be the more eligible in point of birth and character alike. Surely to have been pronounced worthy of the highest privilege by the best men in the mightiest state is proof sufficient of his virtue, at least before he began to reign.

I will now give an account of the achievements 6 of his reign, for I believe that his deeds will throw the clearest light on his qualities.

Now Agesilaus was still a young man [1] when he gained the throne. He had been but a short time in power when the news leaked out that the king of the Persians was assembling a great navy and army for an attack on the Greeks. While the Lacedae- 7 monians and their allies were considering the matter, Agesilaus declared, that if they would give him thirty Spartans, two thousand newly enrolled citizens, and a contingent of six thousand allies, he would cross to Asia and try to effect a peace, or, in case the barbarian wanted to fight, would keep him so busy that he would have no time for an attack on the Greeks. His eagerness to pay back the 8 Persian in his own coin for the former invasion of Greece, his determination to wage an offensive

---

[1] He was over forty ; but see the Introduction.

διαβῆναι ἐπ' αὐτόν, τό τε αἱρεῖσθαι ἐπιόντα
μᾶλλον ἢ ὑπομένοντα μάχεσθαι αὐτῷ, καὶ τὸ
τἀκείνου δαπανῶντα βούλεσθαι μᾶλλον ἢ τὰ
τῶν Ἑλλήνων πολεμεῖν, κάλλιστον δὲ πάντων
ἐκρίνετο τὸ μὴ περὶ τῆς Ἑλλάδος, ἀλλὰ περὶ τῆς
Ἀσίας τὸν ἀγῶνα καθιστάναι.

9   Ἐπεί γε μὴν λαβὼν τὸ στράτευμα ἐξέπλευσε,
πῶς ἄν τις σαφέστερον ἐπιδείξειεν, ὡς ἐστρατή-
10 γησεν, ἢ εἰ αὐτὰ διηγήσαιτο ἃ ἔπραξεν ; ἐν
τοίνυν τῇ Ἀσίᾳ ἥδε πρώτη πρᾶξις ἐγένετο.
Τισσαφέρνης μὲν ὤμοσεν Ἀγησιλάῳ, εἰ σπεί-
σαιτο, ἕως ἔλθοιεν οὓς πέμψειε πρὸς βασιλέα
ἀγγέλους, διαπράξεσθαι αὐτῷ ἀφεθῆναι αὐτονόμους τὰς ἐν τῇ Ἀσίᾳ πόλεις Ἑλληνίδας, Ἀγησίλαος δὲ ἀντώμοσε σπονδὰς ἄξειν ἀδόλως, ὁρισά-
11 μενος τῆς πράξεως τρεῖς μῆνας. ὁ μὲν δὴ
Τισσαφέρνης ἃ ὤμοσεν εὐθὺς ἐψεύσατο· ἀντὶ
γὰρ τοῦ εἰρήνην πράττειν στράτευμα πολὺ παρὰ
βασιλέως πρὸς ᾧ πρόσθεν εἶχε μετεπέμπετο.
Ἀγησίλαος δὲ καίπερ αἰσθόμενος ταῦτα ὅμως
12 ἐνέμεινε ταῖς σπονδαῖς. ἐμοὶ οὖν τοῦτο πρῶτον
καλὸν δοκεῖ διαπράξασθαι, ὅτι Τισσαφέρνην μὲν
ἐμφανίσας ἐπίορκον ἄπιστον πᾶσιν ἐποίησεν,
ἑαυτὸν δ' ἀντεπιδείξας πρῶτον μὲν ὅρκους ἐμπε-
δοῦντα, ἔπειτα συνθήκας μὴ ψευδόμενον, πάντας
ἐποίησε καὶ Ἕλληνας καὶ βαρβάρους θαρροῦντας
συντίθεσθαι ἑαυτῷ, εἴ τι βούλοιτο.

13   Ἐπεὶ δὲ μέγα φρονήσας ὁ Τισσαφέρνης ἐπὶ τῷ
καταβάντι στρατεύματι προεῖπεν Ἀγησιλάῳ
πόλεμον, εἰ μὴ ἀπίοι ἐκ τῆς Ἀσίας, οἱ μὲν ἄλλοι
σύμμαχοι καὶ Λακεδαιμονίων οἱ παρόντες μάλα
ἀχθεσθέντες φανεροὶ ἐγένοντο, νομίζοντες μείονα
64

rather than a defensive war, and his wish to make
the enemy pay for it rather than the Greeks, were
enough to arouse an immediate and widespread
enthusiasm for his project. But what appealed most
to the imagination was the idea of entering on a
struggle not to save Greece, but to subdue Asia.

And what of his strategy after he had received 9
the army and had sailed out? A simple narrative of
his actions will assuredly convey the clearest impression of it. This, then, was his first act in Asia. 10
Tissaphernes had sworn the following oath to
Agesilaus: " If you will arrange an armistice to last
until the return of the messengers whom I will send
to the King, I will do my utmost to obtain indepen-
dence for the Greek cities in Asia" ; and Agesilaus
on his part had sworn to observe the armistice
honestly, allowing three months for the transaction.
What followed? Tissaphernes forthwith broke his 11
oath, and instead of arranging a peace, applied to the
King for a large army in addition to that which he
had before. As for Agesilaus, though well aware of
this, he none the less continued to keep the armistice.
I think, therefore, that here we have his first noble 12
achievement. By showing up Tissaphernes as a per-
jurer, he made him distrusted everywhere; and,
contrariwise, by proving himself to be a man of his
word and true to his agreements, he encouraged all,
Greeks and barbarians alike, to enter into an
agreement with him whenever he wished it.

The arrival of the new army emboldened Tissa- 13
phernes to send an ultimatum to Agesilaus, threaten-
ing war unless he withdrew from Asia; and the
allies and the Lacedaemonians present made no
concealment of their chagrin, believing that the

XENOPHON

τὴν παροῦσαν δύναμιν Ἀγησιλάῳ τῆς βασιλέως
παρασκευῆς εἶναι· Ἀγησίλαος δὲ μάλα φαιδρῷ
τῷ προσώπῳ ἀπαγγεῖλαι τῷ Τισσαφέρνει τοὺς
πρέσβεις ἐκέλευσεν, ὡς πολλὴν χάριν αὐτῷ ἔχοι,
ὅτι ἐπιορκήσας αὐτὸς μὲν πολεμίους τοὺς θεοὺς
ἐκτήσατο, τοῖς δ᾽ Ἕλλησι συμμάχους ἐποίησεν.
14 ἐκ δὲ τούτου εὐθὺς τοῖς μὲν στρατιώταις παρήγγειλε συσκευάζεσθαι ὡς εἰς στρατείαν· ταῖς
δὲ πόλεσιν, εἰς ἃς ἀνάγκη ἦν ἀφικνεῖσθαι στρα-
τευομένῳ ἐπὶ Καρίαν, προεῖπεν ἀγορὰν παρασκευάζειν. ἐπέστειλε δὲ καὶ Ἴωσι καὶ Αἰολεῦσι
καὶ Ἑλλησποντίοις πέμπειν πρὸς αὐτὸν εἰς
Ἔφεσον τοὺς συστρατευσομένους.

15   Ὁ μὲν οὖν Τισσαφέρνης, καὶ ὅτι ἱππικὸν οὐκ
εἶχεν ὁ Ἀγησίλαος, ἡ δὲ Καρία ἄφιππος ἦν,
καὶ ὅτι ἡγεῖτο αὐτὸν ὀργίζεσθαι αὐτῷ διὰ τὴν
ἀπάτην, τῷ ὄντι νομίσας ἐπὶ τὸν αὐτοῦ οἶκον εἰς
Καρίαν ὁρμήσειν αὐτὸν τὸ μὲν πεζὸν ἅπαν
διεβίβασεν ἐκεῖσε, τὸ δὲ ἱππικὸν εἰς τὸ Μαιάνδρου πεδίον περιήγαγε, νομίζων ἱκανὸς εἶναι
καταπατῆσαι τῇ ἵππῳ τοὺς Ἕλληνας πρὶν εἰς τὰ
16 δύσιππα ἀφικέσθαι. ὁ δὲ Ἀγησίλαος ἀντὶ τοῦ
ἐπὶ Καρίαν ἰέναι εὐθὺς ἀντιστρέψας ἐπὶ Φρυγίας
ἐπορεύετο· καὶ τάς τε ἐν τῇ πορείᾳ ἀπαντώσας
δυνάμεις ἀναλαμβάνων ἦγε καὶ τὰς πόλεις κατε-
στρέφετο καὶ ἐμβαλὼν ἀπροσδοκήτως παμπληθῆ
χρήματα ἔλαβε.

17   Στρατηγικὸν οὖν καὶ τοῦτο ἐδόκει διαπράξασθαι, ὅτι ἐπεὶ πόλεμος προερρήθη καὶ τὸ
ἐξαπατᾶν ὅσιόν τε καὶ δίκαιον ἐξ ἐκείνου ἐγένετο,
παῖδα ἀπέδειξε τὸν Τισσαφέρνην τῇ ἀπάτῃ.
φρονίμως δὲ καὶ τοὺς φίλους ἐνταῦθα ἔδοξε πλου-

66

strength of Agesilaus was weaker than the Persian king's armament. But Agesilaus with a beaming face bade the envoys of Tissaphernes inform their master that he was profoundly grateful to him for his perjury, by which he had gained the hostility of the gods for himself and had made them allies of the Greeks. Without a moment's delay he gave 14 the word to his troops to pack up in preparation for a campaign, and warned the cities that lay on the lines of march to Caria to have their markets ready stocked. He advised by letter the Greeks of Ionia, the Aeolid and the Hellespont, to send their contingents for the campaign to his headquarters at Ephesus.

Now Tissaphernes reflected that Agesilaus was 15 without cavalry, while Caria was a difficult country for mounted men, and he thought that Agesilaus was wroth with him on account of his deceit. Concluding, therefore, that his estate in Caria was the real object of the coming attack, he sent the whole of his infantry across to that district and took his cavalry round into the plain of the Maeander, confident that he could ride down the Greeks before they reached the country where cavalry could not operate. But 16 instead of marching on Caria, Agesilaus forthwith turned round and made for Phrygia. Picking up the various forces that met him on the route, he proceeded to reduce the cities and captured a vast quantity of booty by sudden attacks.

This achievement also was thought to be a proof 17 of sound generalship, that when war was declared and cozening in consequence became righteous and fair dealing, he showed Tissaphernes to be a child at deception. It was thought, too, that he made shrewd

67

18 τίσαι· ἐπεὶ γὰρ διὰ τὸ πολλὰ χρήματα εἰλῆφθαι
ἀντίπροικα τὰ πάντα ἐπωλεῖτο, τοῖς μὲν φίλοις
προεῖπεν ὠνεῖσθαι, εἰπὼν ὅτι καταβήσοιτο ἐπὶ
θάλατταν ἐν τάχει τὸ στράτευμα κατάγων· τοὺς
δὲ λαφυροπώλας ἐκέλευσε γραφομένους, ὁπόσου
τι πρίαιντο, προΐεσθαι τὰ χρήματα. ὥστε οὐδὲν
προτελέσαντες οἱ φίλοι αὐτοῦ οὐδὲ τὸ δημόσιον
βλάψαντες πάντες παμπληθῆ χρήματα ἔλαβον.
19 ἔτι δὲ ὁπότε αὐτόμολοι, ὡς εἰκός, πρὸς βασιλέα
ἰόντες χρήματα ἐθέλοιεν ὑφηγεῖσθαι, καὶ ταῦτα
ἐπεμέλετο ὡς διὰ τῶν φίλων ἁλίσκοιτο, ὅπως
ἅμα μὲν χρηματίζοιντο, ἅμα δὲ ἐνδοξότεροι γίγνοιντο. διὰ μὲν δὴ ταῦτα εὐθὺς πολλοὺς ἐραστὰς τῆς αὑτοῦ φιλίας ἐποιήσατο.
20 Γιγνώσκων δ' ὅτι ἡ μὲν πορθουμένη καὶ
ἐρημουμένη χώρα οὐκ ἂν δύναιτο πολὺν χρόνον
στράτευμα φέρειν, ἡ δ' οἰκουμένη μὲν σπειρομένη
δὲ ἀέναον ἂν τὴν τροφὴν παρέχοι, ἐπεμέλετο οὐ
μόνον τοῦ βίᾳ χειροῦσθαι τοὺς ἐναντίους, ἀλλὰ
21 καὶ τοῦ πρᾳότητι προσάγεσθαι. καὶ πολλάκις
μὲν προηγόρευε τοῖς στρατιώταις τοὺς ἁλισκομένους μὴ ὡς ἀδίκους τιμωρεῖσθαι, ἀλλ' ὡς
ἀνθρώπους ὄντας φυλάττειν, πολλάκις δὲ ὁπότε
μεταστρατοπεδεύοιτο, εἰ αἴσθοιτο καταλελειμ-
μένα παιδάρια μικρὰ[1] ἐμπόρων, ἃ πολλοὶ ἐπώ-
λουν διὰ τὸ νομίζειν μὴ δύνασθαι ἂν φέρειν αὐτὰ
καὶ τρέφειν, ἐπεμέλετο καὶ τούτων ὅπως συγ-
22 κομίζοιντό ποι. τοῖς δ' αὖ διὰ γῆρας καταλει-

---

[1] μικρὰ MSS. : παρὰ S. with Reuchlin.

68

use of this occasion to enrich his friends. For the 18
accumulation of plunder was so great that things were
selling for next to nothing. So he gave his friends
the word to buy, saying that he was shortly going
down to the coast with his army.[1] The auctioneers
were ordered to have a schedule made of the prices
obtained and to give delivery of the goods. Thus
without capital outlay, and without any loss to the
treasury, all his friends made a prodigious amount
of money. Further, whenever deserters offered to 19
give information where plunder might be taken,
they naturally went to the king. In such a case
he took care that the capture should be effected by
his friends, so that they might at one and the same
time make money and add to their laurels. The
immediate result was that he had many ardent
suitors for his friendship.

Recognizing that a country plundered and de- 20
populated could not long support an army, whereas
an inhabited and cultivated land would yield inexhaustible supplies, he took pains not only to crush
his enemies by force, but also to win them over by
gentleness. He would often warn his men not to 21
punish their prisoners as criminals, but to guard
them as human beings; and often when shifting
camp, if he noticed little children, the property of
merchants, left behind—many merchants offered
children for sale because they thought they would
not be able to carry and feed them[2]—he looked
after them too, and had them conveyed to some
place of refuge. Again, he arranged that prisoners 22

[1] Where the goods would be re-sold at a profit.
[2] The dealers often failed to find a buyer and consequently
abandoned these captured children.

πομένοις αἰχμαλώτοις προσέταττεν ἐπιμελεῖσθαι
αὐτῶν, ὡς μήτε ὑπὸ κυνῶν μήθ᾽ ὑπὸ λύκων
διαφθείροιντο. ὥστε οὐ μόνον οἱ πυνθανόμενοι
ταῦτα, ἀλλὰ καὶ αὐτοὶ οἱ ἁλισκόμενοι εὐμενεῖς
αὐτῷ ἐγίγνοντο. ὁπόσας δὲ πόλεις προσαγάγοιτο,
ἀφαιρῶν αὐτῶν ὅσα δοῦλοι δεσπόταις ὑπηρετοῦσι,
προσέταττεν ὅσα ἐλεύθεροι ἄρχουσι πείθονται·
καὶ τῶν κατὰ κράτος ἀναλώτων τειχέων τῇ
φιλανθρωπίᾳ ὑπὸ χεῖρα ἐποιεῖτο.

23   Ἐπεὶ μέντοι ἀνὰ τὰ πεδία οὐδὲ ἐν τῇ Φρυγίᾳ
ἐδύνατο στρατεύεσθαι διὰ τὴν Φαρναβάζου
ἱππείαν, ἔδοξεν αὐτῷ ἱππικὸν κατασκευαστέον
εἶναι, ὡς μὴ δραπετεύοντα πολεμεῖν δέοι αὐτόν.
τοὺς μὲν οὖν πλουσιωτάτους ἐκ πασῶν τῶν ἐκεῖ
24 πόλεων ἱπποτροφεῖν κατέλεξε. προεῖπε δέ, ὅστις
παρέχοιτο ἵππον καὶ ὅπλα καὶ ἄνδρα δόκιμον,
ὡς ἐξέσοιτο αὐτῷ μὴ στρατεύεσθαι· καὶ ἐποίησεν
οὕτως ἕκαστον προθύμως ταῦτα πράττειν, ὥσπερ
ἄν τις τὸν ὑπὲρ αὐτοῦ ἀποθανούμενον προθύμως
μαστεύοι. ἔταξε δὲ καὶ πόλεις, ἐξ ὧν δέοι τοὺς
ἱππέας παρασκευάζειν, νομίζων ἐκ τῶν ἱππο-
τρόφων πόλεων εὐθὺς καὶ φρονηματίας μάλιστα
ἂν ἐπὶ τῇ ἱππικῇ γενέσθαι. καὶ τοῦτ᾽ οὖν
ἀγαστῶς ἔδοξε πρᾶξαι, ὅτι κατεσκεύαστο τὸ
ἱππικὸν αὐτῷ καὶ εὐθὺς ἐρρωμένον ἦν καὶ
ἐνεργόν.

25   Ἐπειδὴ δὲ ἔαρ ὑπέφαινε, συνήγαγε πᾶν τὸ
στράτευμα εἰς Ἔφεσον· ἀσκῆσαι δὲ[1] αὐτὸ
βουλόμενος ἆθλα προὔθηκε καὶ ταῖς ἱππικαῖς
τάξεσιν, ἥτις κράτιστα ἱππεύοι, καὶ ταῖς ὁπλιτι-

---

[1] The MSS. of the *Hellenica* have δ᾽ correctly: the MSS.
have καὶ here: δὲ καὶ S.

of war who were too old to accompany the army were to be looked after, that they might not fall a prey to dogs or wolves. It thus came about that he won the goodwill not only of those who heard of these facts, but even of the prisoners themselves. In his settlement with the cities that he won over, he invariably excused them from all servile duties and required only such obedience as freemen owe to their rulers; and by his clemency he made himself master of fortresses impregnable to assault.

However, since a campaign in the plains was im- 23 possible even in Phrygia, owing to Pharnabazus' cavalry, he decided that he must raise a mounted force, if he was to avoid continually running away from the enemy. He therefore enrolled the wealthiest men in all the cities thereabouts as breeders of horses, and issued a proclamation that 24 anyone who supplied a horse and arms and an efficient man should be exempt from personal service. In this way he brought it about that every one of them carried out these requirements with the zeal of a man in quest of someone to die in his stead. He also specified cities that were to furnish contingents of cavalry, feeling sure that from the horse-breeding cities riders proud of their horsemanship would be forthcoming. This again was considered an admirable stroke on his part, that no sooner had he raised his cavalry than it became a powerful body ready for action.

At the first sign of spring [1] he collected the whole 25 of his forces at Ephesus. With a view to their training he offered prizes for the cavalry squadron that rode best, and for the company of heavy in-

[1] 395 B.C.

XENOPHON

καῖς, ἥτις ἄριστα σωμάτων ἔχοι· καὶ πελτασταῖς
δὲ καὶ τοξόταις ἆθλα προὔθηκεν, οἵτινες κράτιστοι
τὰ προσήκοντα ἔργα φαίνοιντο. ἐκ τούτου δὲ
παρῆν ὁρᾶν τὰ μὲν γυμνάσια μεστὰ τῶν ἀνδρῶν
γυμναζομένων, τὸν δὲ ἱππόδρομον ἱππέων ἱππα-
ζομένων, τοὺς δὲ ἀκοντιστὰς καὶ τοὺς τοξότας
26 ἐπὶ στόχον ἱέντας. ἀξίαν δὲ καὶ ὅλην τὴν πόλιν,
ἐν ᾗ ἦν, θέας ἐποίησεν. ἥ τε γὰρ ἀγορὰ μεστὴ
ἦν παντοδαπῶν καὶ ὅπλων καὶ ἵππων ὠνίων οἵ
τε χαλκοτύποι καὶ οἱ τέκτονες καὶ οἱ σιδηρεῖς
καὶ οἱ σκυτεῖς καὶ οἱ γραφεῖς πάντες πολεμικὰ
ὅπλα κατεσκεύαζον· ὥστε τὴν πόλιν ὄντως ἂν
27 ἡγήσω πολέμου ἐργαστήριον εἶναι. ἐπερρώσθη
δ᾽ ἄν τις κἀκεῖνο ἰδών, Ἀγησίλαον μὲν πρῶτον,
ἔπειτα δὲ καὶ τοὺς ἄλλους στρατιώτας ἐστε-
φανωμένους τε, ὅπου ἀπὸ τῶν γυμνασίων ἴοιεν,
καὶ ἀνατιθέντας τοὺς στεφάνους τῇ Ἀρτέμιδι.
ὅπου γὰρ ἄνδρες θεοὺς μὲν σέβοιεν, πολεμικὰ
δὲ ἀσκοῖεν, πειθαρχίαν δὲ μελετῷεν, πῶς οὐκ
εἰκὸς ἐνταῦθα πάντα μεστὰ ἐλπίδων ἀγαθῶν
28 εἶναι; ἡγούμενος δὲ καὶ τὸ καταφρονεῖν τῶν
πολεμίων ῥώμην τινὰ ἐμβαλεῖν πρὸς τὸ μάχεσθαι
προεῖπε τοῖς κήρυξι τοὺς ὑπὸ τῶν λῃστῶν ἁλισκομένους βαρβάρους γυμνοὺς πωλεῖν. ὁρῶντες
οὖν οἱ στρατιῶται λευκοὺς μὲν διὰ τὸ μηδέποτε
ἐκδύεσθαι, πίονας δὲ καὶ ἀπόνους διὰ τὸ ἀεὶ ἐπ᾽
ὀχημάτων εἶναι ἐνόμισαν μηδὲν διοίσειν τὸν
πόλεμον ἢ εἰ γυναιξὶ δέοι μάχεσθαι.

Προεῖπε δὲ καὶ τοῦτο τοῖς στρατιώταις, ὡς
εὐθὺς ἡγήσοιτο τὴν συντομωτάτην ἐπὶ τὰ κράτιστα τῆς χώρας, ὅπως αὐτόθεν αὐτῷ τὰ σώματα
καὶ τὴν γνώμην παρασκευάζοιντο ὡς ἀγωνιού-

fantry that reached the highest level of physical fitness. He also offered prizes to the targeteers and
the archers who showed the greatest efficiency in their
particular duties. Thereupon one might see every
gymnasium crowded with the men exercising, the
racecourse thronged with cavalrymen riding, and the
javelin-men and archers shooting at the mark.
Indeed he made the whole city in which he was 26
quartered a sight to see. For the market was full
of arms and horses of all sorts on sale, and the
coppersmiths, carpenters, workers in iron, cobblers,
and painters were all busy making weapons of war,
so that you might have thought that the city was 27
really a war factory. And an inspiring sight it
would have been to watch Agesilaus and all his
soldiers behind him returning garlanded from the
gymnasium and dedicating their garlands to
Artemis. For where men reverence the gods, train
themselves in warfare and practise obedience,
there you surely find high hopes abounding. More- 28
over, believing that contempt for the enemy would
kindle the fighting spirit, he gave instructions to
his heralds that the barbarians captured in the raids
should be exposed for sale naked. So when his
soldiers saw them white because they never stripped,
and fat and lazy through constant riding in
carriages, they believed that the war would be
exactly like fighting with women.

He also gave notice to the troops that he would
immediately lead them by the shortest route to the
most fertile parts of the country, so that he might
at once find them preparing themselves in body and

29 μένοι. ὁ μέντοι Τισσαφέρνης ταῦτα μὲν ἐνόμισε
λέγειν αὐτὸν πάλιν βουλόμενον ἐξαπατῆσαι, εἰς
Καρίαν δὲ νῦν τῷ ὄντι ἐμβαλεῖν. τό τε οὖν
πεζὸν καθάπερ τὸ πρόσθεν εἰς Καρίαν διεβίβασε
καὶ τὸ ἱππικὸν εἰς τὸ Μαιάνδρου πεδίον κατέστησεν. ὁ δὲ Ἀγησίλαος οὐκ ἐψεύσατο, ἀλλ᾽
ὥσπερ προεῖπεν, εὐθὺς εἰς [1] τὸν Σαρδιανὸν τόπον
ἐχώρησε, καὶ τρεῖς μὲν ἡμέρας δι᾽ ἐρημίας
πολεμίων πορευόμενος πολλὰ τὰ ἐπιτήδεια τῇ
στρατιᾷ παρεῖχε· τῇ δὲ τετάρτῃ ἡμέρᾳ ἧκον οἱ
30 τῶν πολεμίων ἱππεῖς. καὶ τῷ μὲν ἄρχοντι
τῶν σκευοφόρων εἶπεν ὁ ἡγεμὼν διαβάντι τὸν
Πακτωλὸν ποταμὸν στρατοπεδεύεσθαι· αὐτοὶ
δὲ κατιδόντες τοὺς τῶν Ἑλλήνων ἀκολούθους
ἐσπαρμένους καθ᾽ ἁρπαγὴν πολλοὺς αὐτῶν
ἀπέκτειναν. αἰσθόμενος δὲ ὁ Ἀγησίλαος βοηθεῖν
ἐκέλευσε τοὺς ἱππέας. οἱ δ᾽ αὖ Πέρσαι ὡς εἶδον
τὴν βοήθειαν, ἠθροίσθησαν καὶ ἀντιπαρετάξαντο
31 παμπληθέσι τῶν ἱππέων τάξεσιν. ἔνθα δὴ ὁ
Ἀγησίλαος γιγνώσκων, ὅτι τοῖς μὲν πολεμίοις
οὔπω παρείη τὸ πεζόν, αὐτῷ δὲ οὐδὲν ἀπείη
τῶν παρεσκευασμένων, καιρὸν ἡγήσατο μάχην
συνάψαι, εἰ δύναιτο. σφαγιασάμενος οὖν τὴν
μὲν φάλαγγα εὐθὺς ἦγεν ἐπὶ τοὺς ἀντιτεταγμένους
ἱππέας, ἐκ δὲ τῶν ὁπλιτῶν ἐκέλευσε τὰ δέκα ἀφ᾽
ἥβης θεῖν ὁμόσε αὐτοῖς, τοῖς δὲ πελτασταῖς
εἶπε δρόμῳ ὑφηγεῖσθαι· παρήγγειλε δὲ καὶ τοῖς
ἱππεῦσιν ἐμβάλλειν, ὡς αὐτοῦ τε καὶ παντὸς
32 τοῦ στρατεύματος ἑπομένου. τοὺς μὲν δὴ ἱππέας
ἐδέξαντο οἱ ἀγαθοὶ τῶν Περσῶν· ἐπειδὴ δὲ ἅμα
πάντα τὰ δεινὰ παρῆν ἐπ᾽ αὐτούς, ἐνέκλιναν καὶ

---

[1] εἰς is added from *Hellenica* III, iv. 21 : S. adds ἐπί.

mind for the coming struggle.   Tissaphernes, how- 29
ever, believed that in saying this he meant to
deceive him again, and that now he would really
invade Caria.   Accordingly he sent his infantry
across into Caria as before, and stationed his
cavalry in the plain of the Maeander.   But
Agesilaus did not play false: in accordance with
his notice he marched straight to the neighbour-
hood of Sardis; and for three days his route lay
through a country bare of enemies, so that he
supplied his army with abundance of provisions.
On the fourth day the enemy's cavalry came up. 30
Their leader told the officer in command of the
baggage-train to cross the river Pactolus and encamp.
The cavalry, meantime, catching sight of the Greek
camp-followers plundering in scattered bands, killed
a large number of them.   On noticing this, Agesilaus
ordered his cavalry to go to their help.   The Persians
in turn, seeing the supports coming, gathered in a
mass and confronted them with the full strength
of their horse.   Then Agesilaus, realising that the 31
enemy's infantry was not yet up, while he had all
his resources on the spot, thought the moment was
come to join battle if he could.   Therefore, after
offering sacrifice, he led forward the battle line
immediately against the opposing cavalry, the heavy
infantrymen of ten years service having orders to
run to close quarters with the enemy, while the
targeteers were to lead the advance at the double.
He also sent word to the cavalry to attack in the
knowledge that he himself was following with the
whole army.   The charge of the cavalry was met by 32
the flower of the Persians: but as soon as the full
weight of the attack fell on them, they swayed, and

75

οἱ μὲν αὐτῶν εὐθὺς ἐν τῷ ποταμῷ ἔπεσον, οἱ δὲ
ἄλλοι ἔφευγον. οἱ δὲ Ἕλληνες ἑπόμενοι αἱροῦσι
καὶ τὸ στρατόπεδον αὐτῶν. καὶ οἱ μὲν πελτασταὶ
ὥσπερ εἰκὸς ἐφ᾽ ἁρπαγὴν ἐτρέποντο· ὁ δὲ
Ἀγησίλαος ἔχων κύκλῳ πάντα καὶ φίλια καὶ
πολέμια περιεστρατοπεδεύσατο.

33 Ὡς δὲ ἤκουσε τοὺς πολεμίους ταράττεσθαι
διὰ τὸ αἰτιᾶσθαι ἀλλήλους τοῦ γεγενημένου,
εὐθὺς ἦγεν ἐπὶ Σάρδεις. κἀκεῖ ἅμα μὲν ἔκαιε
καὶ ἐπόρθει τὰ περὶ τὸ ἄστυ, ἅμα δὲ καὶ
κηρύγματι ἐδήλου τοὺς μὲν ἐλευθερίας δεομένους
ὡς πρὸς σύμμαχον αὐτὸν παρεῖναι· εἰ δέ τινες
τὴν Ἀσίαν ἑαυτῶν ποιοῦνται, πρὸς τοὺς ἐλευ-
θεροῦντας διακρινουμένους[1] ἐν ὅπλοις παρεῖναι.

34 ἐπεὶ μέντοι οὐδεὶς ἀντεξήει, ἀδεῶς δὴ τὸ ἀπὸ
τούτου ἐστρατεύετο, τοὺς μὲν πρόσθεν προσκυνεῖν
Ἕλληνας ἀναγκαζομένους ὁρῶν τιμωμένους ὑφ᾽
ὧν ὑβρίζοντο, τοὺς δ᾽ ἀξιοῦντας καὶ τὰς τῶν
θεῶν τιμὰς καρποῦσθαι, τούτους ποιήσας μηδ᾽
ἀντιβλέπειν τοῖς Ἕλλησι δύνασθαι καὶ τὴν μὲν
τῶν φίλων χώραν ἀδήωτον παρέχων, τὴν δὲ τῶν
πολεμίων οὕτω καρπούμενος, ὥστε ἐν δυοῖν ἐτοῖν
πλέον τῶν ἑκατὸν ταλάντων τῷ θεῷ ἐν Δελφοῖς
δεκάτην ἀποθῦσαι.

35 Ὁ μέντοι Περσῶν βασιλεὺς νομίσας Τισσαφέρνην αἴτιον εἶναι τοῦ κακῶς φέρεσθαι τὰ
ἑαυτοῦ Τιθραύστην καταπέμψας ἀπέτεμεν αὐτοῦ
τὴν κεφαλήν. μετὰ δὲ τοῦτο τὰ μὲν τῶν
βαρβάρων ἔτι ἀθυμότερα ἐγένετο, τὰ δὲ Ἀγησι-

[1] The text as corrected by Reiske and Schneider: τὸ
ἐλευθεροῦν διακρινομένους S.: τῷ ἐλευθεροῦν τοὺς (or τους)
διακρινομένους MSS.

some were cut down immediately in the river, while the rest fled. The Greeks followed up their success and captured their camp. The targeteers naturally fell to pillaging; but Agesilaus drew the lines of his camp round so as to enclose the property of all, friends and foes alike.[1]

On hearing that there was confusion among the 33 enemy, because everyone put the blame for what had happened on his neighbour, he advanced forthwith on Sardis. There he began burning and pillaging the suburbs, and meantime issued a proclamation calling on those who wanted freedom to join his standard, and challenging any who claimed a right to Asia to seek a decision between themselves and the liberators by an appeal to arms. As no one 34 came out to oppose him, he prosecuted the campaign henceforward in complete confidence: he beheld the Greeks, compelled erstwhile to cringe, now honoured by their oppressors; caused those who arrogantly claimed for themselves the honours paid to the gods to shrink even from looking the Greeks in the face; rendered the country of his friends inviolate, and stripped the enemy's country so thoroughly that in two years he consecrated to the god at Delphi more than two hundred talents as tithe.

But the Persian king, believing that Tissaphernes 35 was responsible for the bad turn in his affairs, sent down Tithraustes and beheaded Tissaphernes. After this the outlook became still more hopeless for the barbarians, while Agesilaus received large accessions

---

[1] *i.e.* he intrenched.

λάου πολὺ ἐρρωμενέστερα. ἀπὸ πάντων γὰρ
τῶν ἐθνῶν ἐπρεσβεύοντο περὶ φιλίας, πολλοὶ
δὲ καὶ ἀφίσταντο πρὸς αὐτὸν ὀρεγόμενοι τῆς
ἐλευθερίας, ὥστε οὐκέτι Ἑλλήνων μόνον, ἀλλὰ
καὶ βαρβάρων πολλῶν ἡγεμὼν ἦν ὁ Ἀγησίλαος.

36 Ἄξιόν γε μὴν καὶ ἐντεῦθεν ὑπερβαλλόντως
ἄγασθαι αὐτοῦ, ὅστις ἄρχων μὲν παμπόλλων
ἐν τῇ ἠπείρῳ πόλεων, ἄρχων δὲ καὶ νήσων, ἐπεὶ
καὶ τὸ ναυτικὸν προσῆψεν αὐτῷ ἡ πόλις, αὐξα-
νόμενος δὲ καὶ εὐκλείᾳ καὶ δυνάμει, παρὸν δ᾽
αὐτῷ πολλοῖς καὶ ἀγαθοῖς χρῆσθαι ὅ τι ἐβούλετο,
πρὸς δὲ τούτοις τὸ μέγιστον, ἐπινοῶν καὶ ἐλπίζων
καταλύσειν τὴν ἐπὶ τὴν Ἑλλάδα στρατεύσασαν
πρότερον ἀρχὴν ὅμως ὑπ᾽ οὐδενὸς τούτων ἐκρατήθη,
ἀλλ᾽ ἐπειδὴ ἦλθεν αὐτῷ ἀπὸ τῶν οἴκοι τελῶν
βοηθεῖν τῇ πατρίδι, ἐπείθετο τῇ πόλει οὐδὲν
διαφερόντως ἢ εἰ ἐν τῷ ἐφορείῳ ἔτυχεν ἑστηκὼς
μόνος παρὰ τοὺς πέντε, μάλα ἔνδηλον ποιῶν,
ὡς οὔτε ἂν πᾶσαν τὴν γῆν δέξαιτο ἀντὶ τῆς
πατρίδος οὔτε τοὺς ἐπικτήτους ἀντὶ τῶν ἀρχαίων
φίλων οὔτε αἰσχρὰ καὶ ἀκίνδυνα κέρδη μᾶλλον ἢ
μετὰ κινδύνων τὰ καλὰ καὶ δίκαια.

37 Ὅσον γε μὴν χρόνον ἐπὶ τῇ ἀρχῇ ἔμεινε, πῶς
οὐκ ἀξιεπαίνου βασιλέως καὶ τοῦτ᾽ ἔργον ἐπε-
δείξατο, ὅστις παραλαβὼν πάσας πόλεις, ἐφ᾽ ἃς
ἄρξων ἐξέπλευσε, στασιαζούσας διὰ τὸ τὰς
πολιτείας κινηθῆναι, ἐπεὶ Ἀθηναῖοι τῆς ἀρχῆς
ἔληξαν, ἐποίησεν ὥστ᾽ ἄνευ φυγῆς καὶ θανάτων,
ἕως αὐτὸς παρῆν, ὁμονόως πολιτευομένας καὶ
38 εὐδαίμονας τὰς πόλεις διατελέσαι; τοιγαροῦν οἱ

---

[1] In the market at Sparta. The Five Ephors sat there
daily, and it was in their power to censure the kings.

of strength.   For all the nations of the empire sent
embassies seeking his friendship, and the desire for
freedom caused many to revolt to him, so that not
Greeks alone, but many barbarians also now acknowledged the leadership of Agesilaus.

His conduct at this juncture also merits unstinted 36
admiration.   Though ruler of countless cities on the
mainland, and master of islands—for the state had
now added the fleet to his command—becoming
daily more famous and more powerful ; placed in a
position to make what use he would of his many
opportunities ; and   designing   and   expecting   to
crown his achievements by dissolving the empire
that had attacked Greece in the past : he suppressed
all thought of these things, and as soon as he
received a request from the home government to
come to the aid of his fatherland, he obeyed the
call of the state, just as though he were standing
in the Ephors' palace[1] alone before the Five, thus
showing clearly that he would not take the whole
earth in exchange for his fatherland, nor new-found
friends for old, and that he scorned to choose base
and secure gains rather than that which was right
and honourable, even though it was dangerous.

Throughout the time that he remained in his 37
command, another achievement of his showed beyond
question how admirable was his skill in kingcraft.
Having found all the cities that he had gone out
to govern rent by faction in consequence of the
political disturbances that followed on the collapse
of the Athenian empire, he brought it about by the
influence of his presence that the communities lived
in unbroken harmony and prosperity without re-
course to banishment or executions.   Therefore the 38

ἐν τῇ Ἀσίᾳ Ἕλληνες οὐχ ὡς ἄρχοντος μόνον,
ἀλλὰ καὶ ὡς πατρὸς καὶ ἑταίρου ἀπιόντος αὐτοῦ
ἐλυποῦντο. καὶ τέλος ἐδήλωσαν, ὅτι οὐ πλαστὴν
τὴν φιλίαν παρείχοντο. ἐθελούσιοι γοῦν αὐτῷ
συνεβοήθησαν τῇ Λακεδαίμονι, καὶ ταῦτα εἰδότες,
ὅτι οὐ χείροσιν ἑαυτῶν δεήσοι μάχεσθαι. τῶν
μὲν δὴ ἐν τῇ Ἀσίᾳ πράξεων τοῦτο τέλος
ἐγένετο.

II. Διαβὰς δὲ τὸν Ἑλλήσποντον ἐπορεύετο
διὰ τῶν αὐτῶν ἐθνῶν ὧνπερ ὁ Πέρσης τῷ
παμπληθεῖ στόλῳ· καὶ ἣν ἐνιαυσίαν ὁδὸν ὁ
βάρβαρος ἐποιήσατο, ταύτην μεῖον ἢ ἐν μηνὶ
κατήνυσεν ὁ Ἀγησίλαος. οὐ γὰρ ὡς ὑστερήσειε
2 τῆς πατρίδος προεθυμεῖτο. ἐπεὶ δὲ ἐξαμείψας
Μακεδονίαν εἰς Θετταλίαν ἀφίκετο, Λαρισαῖοι μὲν
καὶ Κραννώνιοι καὶ Σκοτουσσαῖοι καὶ Φαρσάλιοι
σύμμαχοι ὄντες Βοιωτοῖς καὶ πάντες δὲ Θετταλοὶ
πλὴν ὅσοι αὐτῶν φυγάδες τότε ὄντες ἐτύγχανον,
ἐκακούργουν οὗτοι ἐφεπόμενοι. ὁ δὲ τέως μὲν
ἦγεν ἐν πλαισίῳ τὸ στράτευμα, τοὺς ἡμίσεις μὲν
ἔμπροσθεν, τοὺς ἡμίσεις δὲ ἐπ᾽ οὐρὰν ἔχων τῶν
ἱππέων· ἐπεὶ δ᾽ ἐκώλυον τῆς πορείας αὐτὸν οἱ
Θετταλοὶ ἐπιτιθέμενοι τοῖς ὄπισθεν, παραπέμπει
ἐπ᾽ οὐρὰν καὶ τὸ ἀπὸ τοῦ προηγουμένου στρα-
3 τεύματος ἱππικὸν πλὴν τῶν περὶ αὐτόν. ὡς δὲ
παρετάξαντο ἀλλήλοις, οἱ μὲν Θετταλοί, νομίσαντες οὐκ ἐν καλῷ εἶναι πρὸς τοὺς ὁπλίτας
ἱππομαχεῖν, στρέψαντες βάδην ἀπεχώρουν· οἱ δὲ
μάλα σωφρόνως ἐφείποντο. γνοὺς δὲ ὁ Ἀγησίλαος ἃ ἑκάτεροι ἡμάρτανον παραπέμπει τοὺς
ἀμφ᾽ αὐτὸν μάλ᾽ εὐρώστους ἱππέας καὶ κελεύει
τοῖς τε ἄλλοις παραγγέλλειν καὶ αὐτοὺς διώκειν

Greeks in Asia mourned his departure as though they were bidding farewell not merely to a ruler, but to a father or a comrade. And at the end they showed that their affection was unfeigned. At any rate they went with him voluntarily to aid Sparta, knowing as they did that they must meet an enemy not inferior to themselves. This then was the end of his activities in Asia.

II. After crossing the Hellespont, he passed through the very same tribes as the Persian king with his mighty host; and the distance that had been traversed by the barbarian in a year was covered by Agesilaus in less than a month. For he had no intention of arriving too late to aid his fatherland. When he had passed through Macedonia and reached 2 Thessaly, the people of Larisa, Crannon, Scotussa and Pharsalus, who were allies of the Boeotians, all the Thessalians, in fact, except those who happened to be in exile at the time, followed at his heels and kept molesting him. For a time he led the army in a hollow square, with one half of the cavalry in front and the other half in the rear; but finding his progress hampered by Thessalian attacks on his rearguard, he sent round all the cavalry from the vanguard to the rear, except his own escort. When 3 the two forces faced one another in line of battle, the Thessalians, believing it inexpedient to engage heavy infantry with cavalry, wheeled round and slowly retired, their enemy following very cautiously. Agesilaus, noticing the errors into which both sides were falling, now sent round his own escort of stalwart horsemen, with orders to bid the others to charge at full speed, and to do the same themselves,

κατὰ κράτος καὶ μηκέτι δοῦναι αὐτοῖς ἀναστροφήν.
οἱ δὲ Θετταλοὶ ὡς εἶδον παρὰ δόξαν ἐλαύνοντας,
οἱ μὲν αὐτῶν οὐδ' ἀνέστρεψαν, οἱ δὲ καὶ ἀνα-
στρέφειν πειρώμενοι πλαγίους ἔχοντες τοὺς ἵππους
4 ἡλίσκοντο.   Πολύχαρμος μέντοι ὁ Φαρσάλιος
ἱππαρχῶν ἀνέστρεψέ τε καὶ μαχόμενος σὺν τοῖς
ἀμφ' αὑτὸν ἀποθνήσκει. ὡς δὲ τοῦτο ἐγένετο,
φυγὴ γίγνεται ἐξαισία· ὥσθ' οἱ μὲν ἀπέθνησκον
αὐτῶν, οἱ δὲ καὶ ζῶντες ἡλίσκοντο. ἔστησαν δ'
οὖν οὐ πρόσθεν, πρὶν ἢ ἐπὶ τῷ ὄρει τῷ Ναρθακίῳ
5 ἐγένοντο. καὶ τότε μὲν δὴ ὁ Ἀγησίλαος τρόπαιόν
τε ἐστήσατο μεταξὺ Πραντὸς καὶ Ναρθακίου·
καὶ αὐτοῦ κατέμεινε μάλα ἡδόμενος τῷ ἔργῳ, ὅτι
τοὺς μέγιστον φρονοῦντας ἐφ' ἱππικῇ ἐνενικήκει
σὺν ᾧ αὐτὸς ἐμηχανήσατο ἱππικῷ.

Τῇ δ' ὑστεραίᾳ ὑπερβάλλων τὰ Ἀχαϊκὰ τῆς
Φθίας ὄρη τὴν λοιπὴν ἤδη πᾶσαν διὰ φιλίας
6 ἐπορεύθη εἰς τὰ Βοιωτῶν ὅρια. ἐνταῦθα δὴ
ἀντιτεταγμένους εὑρὼν Θηβαίους, Ἀθηναίους,
Ἀργείους, Κορινθίους, Αἰνιᾶνας, Εὐβοέας καὶ
Λοκροὺς ἀμφοτέρους οὐδὲν ἐμέλλησεν, ἀλλ' ἐκ
τοῦ φανεροῦ ἀντιπαρέταττε, Λακεδαιμονίων μὲν
ἔχων μόραν καὶ ἥμισυ, τῶν δ' αὐτόθεν συμμάχων
Φωκέας καὶ Ὀρχομενίους μόνους τό τ' ἄλλο
7 στράτευμα, ὅπερ ἠγάγετο αὐτός. καὶ οὐ τοῦτο
λέξων ἔρχομαι, ὡς πολὺ μὲν ἐλάττους, πολὺ δὲ
χείρονας ἔχων ὅμως συνέβαλεν· εἰ γὰρ ταῦτα
λέγοιμι, Ἀγησίλαόν τ' ἄν μοι δοκῶ ἄφρονα
ἀποφαίνειν καὶ ἐμαυτὸν μῶρον, εἰ ἐπαινοίην τὸν
περὶ τῶν μεγίστων εἰκῇ κινδυνεύοντα· ἀλλὰ
μᾶλλον τάδ' αὐτοῦ ἄγαμαι, ὅτι πλῆθός τε οὐδὲν

and not to give the enemy a chance of rallying. As
for the Thessalians, on seeing the unexpected charge
they either did not rally at all, or were captured in
the attempt to do so with their horses broadside to
the enemy. Polycharmus the Pharsalian, commander 4
of the cavalry, did indeed turn, and fell fighting
along with those about him. Hereupon ensued a
wild flight, so that some of the enemy were killed
and some were taken prisoners : at any rate they
never halted until they reached Mt. Narthacium.
On that day Agesilaus set up a trophy between 5
Pras and Narthacium, and here for the moment he
paused, mightily pleased with his exploit, since he
had defeated an enemy inordinately proud of his
horsemanship with the cavalry that he had himself
created.

On the morrow he crossed the Achaean mountains
in Phthia, and now his route led him through friendly
country till he reached the borders of Boeotia.
Here he found arrayed against him the Thebans, 6
Athenians, Argives, Corinthians, Aenianians, Euboeans,
and both the Locrian tribes. Without a moment's
delay, in full view of the enemy, he drew up his army
for battle. In addition to the army that he had
brought with him he had a regiment and a half
of Lacedaemonians, and of the local allies only the
Phocians and Orchomenians. Now I am not going 7
to say that his forces were far inferior in numbers
and in quality, and that nevertheless he accepted
battle. That statement, I think, would but show a
want of common sense in Agesilaus and my own
folly in praising a leader who wantonly jeopardised
interests of vital moment. On the contrary—and
this is what I do admire him for—he brought into

μεῖον ἢ τὸ τῶν πολεμίων παρεσκευάσατο ὥπλισέ
τε οὕτως, ὡς ἅπαντα μὲν χαλκόν, ἅπαντα δὲ
8 φοινικᾶ φαίνεσθαι· ἐπεμελήθη δ', ὅπως οἱ στρατιῶται τοὺς πόνους δυνήσοιντο ὑποφέρειν· ἐνέ-
πλησε δὲ καὶ φρονήματος τὰς ψυχὰς αὐτῶν, ὡς
ἱκανοὶ εἶεν πρὸς οὕστινας δέοι μάχεσθαι· ἔτι
δὲ φιλονικίαν ἐνέβαλε πρὸς ἀλλήλους τοῖς μετ'
αὐτοῦ, ὅπως ἕκαστοι αὐτῶν ἄριστοι φαίνοιντο.
ἐλπίδων γε μὴν πάντας ἐνέπλησεν, ὡς πᾶσι
πολλὰ κἀγαθὰ ἔσοιτο, εἰ ἄνδρες ἀγαθοὶ γίγνοιντο,
νομίζων ἐκ τῶν τοιούτων ἀνθρώπους προθυμό-
τατα τοῖς πολεμίοις μάχεσθαι. καὶ μέντοι οὐκ
ἐψεύσθη.

9   Διηγήσομαι δὲ καὶ τὴν μάχην· καὶ γὰρ ἐγένετο
οἵαπερ οὐκ ἄλλη τῶν ἐφ' ἡμῶν. συνῆεσαν μὲν
γὰρ εἰς τὸ κατὰ Κορώνειαν πεδίον οἱ μὲν σὺν
Ἀγησιλάῳ ἀπὸ τοῦ Κηφισοῦ, οἱ δὲ σὺν τοῖς
Θηβαίοις ἀπὸ τοῦ Ἑλικῶνος. ἑώρων δὲ τάς τε
φάλαγγας ἀλλήλων μάλα ἰσομάχους, σχεδὸν δὲ
καὶ οἱ ἱππεῖς ἦσαν ἑκατέρων ἰσοπληθεῖς. εἶχε
δὲ ὁ Ἀγησίλαος μὲν τὸ δεξιὸν τοῦ μεθ' ἑαυτοῦ,
Ὀρχομένιοι δὲ ἔσχατοι ἦσαν αὐτῷ τοῦ εὐωνύμου.
οἱ δ' αὖ Θηβαῖοι αὐτοὶ μὲν δεξιοὶ ἦσαν, Ἀργεῖοι
10 δ' αὐτοῖς τὸ εὐώνυμον εἶχον. συνιόντων δὲ τέως
μὲν σιγὴ πολλὴ ἦν ἀπ' ἀμφοτέρων· ἡνίκα δὲ
ἀπεῖχον ἀλλήλων ὅσον στάδιον, ἀλαλάξαντες οἱ
Θηβαῖοι δρόμῳ ὁμόσε ἐφέροντο. ὡς δὲ τριῶν
ἔτι πλέθρων ἐν μέσῳ ὄντων ἀντεξέδραμον ἀπὸ
τῆς Ἀγησιλάου φάλαγγος ὧν Ἡριππίδας ἐξε-
11 νάγει (ἦσαν δ' οὗτοι τῶν τε ἐξ οἴκου αὐτῷ
συστρατευσαμένων καὶ τῶν Κυρείων τινές)[1] καὶ
Ἴωνες δὲ καὶ Αἰολεῖς καὶ Ἑλλησπόντιοι ἐχόμενοι.

the field an army not a whit inferior to the enemy's; he so armed it that it looked one solid mass of bronze and scarlet; he took care to render his men 8 capable of meeting all calls on their endurance; he filled their hearts with confidence that they were able to withstand any and every enemy; he inspired them all with an eager determination to out-do one another in valour; and lastly he filled all with anticipation that many good things would befall them, if only they proved good men. For he believed that men so prepared fight with all their might; nor in point of fact did he deceive himself.

I will describe the battle, for there has been none 9 like it in our time. The two armies met in the plain of Coronea, Agesilaus advancing from the Cephisus, the Thebans and their allies from Helicon. Their eyes told them that the opposing lines of battle were exactly matched in strength, and the number of cavalry on both sides was about the same. Agesilaus was on the right wing of his army and had the Orchomenians on his extreme left. On the other side the Thebans themselves were on the right wing and the Argives held the left. As they 10 approached both sides for a time maintained complete silence, but when they were about a furlong apart, the Thebans raised the battle-cry and rushed forward at the double. The distance between them was still about one hundred yards when the mercenary troops under Herippidas, consisting of the 11 men who had gone with Agesilaus from home and some of the Cyreians, dashed out in turn from their main body, closely followed by Ionians, Aeolians and

---

[1] The parenthesis is due to Lippelt: S., with the MSS., has a full stop after ἐξενάγει, and no break after τινές.

XENOPHON

καὶ πάντες οὗτοι τῶν συνεκδραμόντων τε ἐγένοντο
καὶ εἰς δόρυ ἀφικόμενοι ἐτρέψαντο τὸ καθ' ἑαυ-
τούς. Ἀργεῖοι μέντοι οὐκ ἐδέξαντο τοὺς ἀμφ'
Ἀγησίλαον, ἀλλ' ἔφυγον ἐπὶ τὸν Ἑλικῶνα.
κἀνταῦθα οἱ μέν τινες τῶν ξένων ἐστεφάνουν
ἤδη τὸν Ἀγησίλαον, ἀγγέλλει δέ τις αὐτῷ, ὅτι
Θηβαῖοι τοὺς Ὀρχομενίους διακόψαντες ἐν τοῖς
σκευοφόροις εἰσί. καὶ ὁ μὲν εὐθὺς ἐξελίξας τὴν
φάλαγγα ἦγεν ἐπ' αὐτούς· οἱ δ' αὖ Θηβαῖοι ὡς
εἶδον τοὺς συμμάχους πρὸς τῷ Ἑλικῶνι πεφευ-
γότας, διαπεσεῖν βουλόμενοι πρὸς τοὺς ἑαυτῶν
ἐχώρουν ἐρρωμένως.

12 Ἐνταῦθα δὴ Ἀγησίλαον ἀνδρεῖον μὲν ἔξεστιν
εἰπεῖν ἀναμφιλόγως, οὐ μέντοι εἵλετό γε τὰ
ἀσφαλέστατα· ἐξὸν γὰρ αὐτῷ παρέντι τοὺς δια-
πίπτοντας ἑπομένῳ χειροῦσθαι τοὺς ὄπισθεν οὐκ
ἐποίησε τοῦτο, ἀλλ' ἀντιμέτωπος συνέρραξε τοῖς
Θηβαίοις. καὶ συμβαλόντες τὰς ἀσπίδας ἐω-
θοῦντο, ἐμάχοντο, ἀπέκτεινον, ἀπέθνησκον. καὶ
κραυγὴ μὲν οὐδεμία παρῆν, οὐ μὴν οὐδὲ σιγή,
φωνὴ δέ τις ἦν τοιαύτη, οἵαν ὀργή τε καὶ μάχη
παράσχοιτ' ἄν. τέλος δὲ τῶν Θηβαίων οἱ μὲν
διαπίπτουσι πρὸς τὸν Ἑλικῶνα, πολλοὶ δ' ἀπο-
χωροῦντες ἀπέθανον.

13 Ἐπειδὴ δὲ ἡ μὲν νίκη σὺν Ἀγησιλάῳ ἐγένετο,
τετρωμένος δ' αὐτὸς προσηνέχθη πρὸς τὴν φάλαγγα, προσελάσαντές τινες τῶν ἱππέων λέγου-
σιν αὐτῷ, ὅτι τῶν πολεμίων ὀγδοήκοντα σὺν
τοῖς ὅπλοις ὑπὸ τῷ ναῷ εἰσι, καὶ ἠρώτων, τί χρὴ
ποιεῖν. ὁ δὲ καίπερ πολλὰ τραύματα ἔχων
πάντοσε καὶ παντοίοις ὅπλοις ὅμως οὐκ ἐπε-

Hellespontines. All these took part in the dash, and coming within spear-thrust put to flight the force in front of them. As for the Argives, they fled towards Helicon without awaiting the attack of Agesilaus. And now some of the mercenaries were in the act of crowning Agesilaus with a wreath, when a man reported to him that the Thebans had cut their way through the Orchomenians and were among the baggage train. So he immediately wheeled his main body and advanced against them; and the Thebans in their turn, seeing that their allies had sought refuge at the foot of Mt. Helicon, and wanting to break through and join their friends, made a strong move forward.

At this juncture one may say without fear of 12 contradiction that Agesilaus showed courage; but the course that he adopted was not the safest. For he might have allowed the men who were trying to break through to pass, and then have followed them and annihilated those in the rear. Instead of doing that he made a furious frontal attack on the Thebans. Thrusting shield against shield, they shoved and fought and killed and fell. There was no shouting, nor was there silence, but the strange noise that wrath and battle together will produce. In the end some of the Thebans broke through and reached Helicon, but many fell during the retreat.

The victory lay with Agesilaus; but he himself 13 had been carried wounded to his battle-line, when some horsemen rode up, and told him that eighty of the enemy retaining their arms had taken cover in the temple, and they asked what they should do. Though wounded in every part of his body with every sort of weapon, he did not

λάθετο τοῦ θείου, ἀλλ' ἐᾶν τε ἀπιέναι ὅποι
βούλοιντο ἐκέλευε καὶ ἀδικεῖν οὐκ εἴα καὶ προ-
πέμψαι ἐπέταξε τοὺς ἀμφ' αὐτὸν ἱππεῖς, ἔστε ἐν
τῷ ἀσφαλεῖ ἐγένοντο.

14 Ἐπεί γε μὴν ἔληξεν ἡ μάχη, παρῆν δὴ θεάσασθαι, ἔνθα συνέπεσον ἀλλήλοις, τὴν μὲν γῆν
αἵματι πεφυρμένην, νεκροὺς δὲ κειμένους φιλίους
καὶ πολεμίους μετ' ἀλλήλων, ἀσπίδας δὲ διατε-
θρυμμένας, δόρατα συντεθραυσμένα, ἐγχειρίδια
γυμνὰ κολεῶν, τὰ μὲν χαμαί, τὰ δ' ἐν σώματι,[1]
15 τὰ δ' ἔτι μετὰ χεῖρας. τότε μὲν οὖν, καὶ γὰρ ἦν
ἤδη ὀψέ, συνελκύσαντες τοὺς τῶν πολεμίων
νεκροὺς εἴσω φάλαγγος ἐδειπνοποιήσαντο καὶ
ἐκοιμήθησαν· πρωὶ δὲ Γῦλιν τὸν πολέμαρχον
παρατάξαι τε ἐκέλευσε τὸ στράτευμα καὶ τρόπαιον ἵστασθαι καὶ στεφανοῦσθαι πάντας τῷ
θεῷ καὶ τοὺς αὐλητὰς πάντας αὐλεῖν.

16 Καὶ οἱ μὲν ταῦτ' ἐποίουν· οἱ δὲ Θηβαῖοι
ἔπεμψαν κήρυκα, ὑποσπόνδους τοὺς νεκροὺς
αἰτοῦντες θάψαι. καὶ οὕτως δὴ αἵ τε σπονδαὶ
γίγνονται καὶ ὁ Ἀγησίλαος οἴκαδε ἀπεχώρει,
ἑλόμενος ἀντὶ τοῦ μέγιστος εἶναι ἐν τῇ Ἀσίᾳ
οἴκοι τὰ νόμιμα μὲν ἄρχειν, τὰ νόμιμα δὲ
ἄρχεσθαι.

17 Ἐκ δὲ τούτου κατανοήσας τοὺς Ἀργείους τὰ
μὲν οἴκοι καρπουμένους, Κόρινθον δὲ προσειλη-
φότας, ἡδομένους δὲ τῷ πολέμῳ στρατεύει ἐπ'
αὐτούς· καὶ δῃώσας πᾶσαν αὐτῶν τὴν χώραν

---

[1] σώματι MSS. : σώμασι S.

forget his duty towards the gods, but gave orders that these men should be suffered to go whithersoever they wished, and would not suffer them to be harmed, and charged his escort of cavalry to conduct them to a place of safety.

Now that the fighting was at an end, a weird 14 spectacle met the eye, as one surveyed the scene of the conflict—the earth stained with blood, friend and foe lying dead side by side, shields smashed to pieces, spears snapped in two, daggers bared of their sheaths, some on the ground, some embedded in the bodies, some yet gripped by the hand. Then, 15 as the day was far spent, having dragged the enemy's dead [1] within their battle line, they supped and slept. Early next morning Agesilaus ordered Gylis, the polemarch, to draw up the army in battle order and to set up a trophy, and to command every man to wear a wreath in honour of the god [2] and all the flute-players to play.

Now while they were carrying out these orders the 16 Thebans sent a herald, asking leave to bury their dead under protection of a truce. And so a truce was made, and Agesilaus left for home, choosing, instead of supreme power in Asia, to rule and to be ruled at home according to the constitution.

Some time afterwards, finding that the Argives 17 were enjoying the fruits of their land, that they had appropriated Corinth and were finding the war a pleasant occupation, he made an expedition against them. He first laid waste all their territory, then

---

[1] In order that the Thebans might not recover them. But some think τῶν πολεμίων corrupt.

[2] Apollo.

εὐθὺς ἐκεῖθεν ὑπερβαλὼν κατὰ τὰ στενὰ εἰς
Κόρινθον αἱρεῖ τὰ ἐπὶ τὸ Λέχαιον τείνοντα τείχη·
καὶ ἀναπετάσας τῆς Πελοποννήσου τὰς πύλας
οὕτως οἴκαδε ἀπελθὼν εἰς τὰ Ὑακίνθια, ὅπου
ἐτάχθη ὑπὸ τοῦ χοροποιοῦ, τὸν παιᾶνα τῷ θεῷ
συνεπετέλει.

18   Ἐκ τούτου δὲ αἰσθανόμενος τοὺς Κορινθίους
πάντα μὲν τὰ κτήνη ἐν τῷ Πειραίῳ σωζομένους,
πᾶν δὲ τὸ Πείραιον σπείροντας καὶ καρπουμένους,
μέγιστον δὲ ἡγησάμενος, ὅτι Βοιωτοὶ ταύτῃ ἐκ
Κρεύσιος ὁρμώμενοι εὐπετῶς τοῖς Κορινθίοις
παρεγίγνοντο, στρατεύει ἐπὶ τὸ Πείραιον. ἰδὼν
δὲ ὑπὸ πολλῶν φυλαττόμενον, ὡς ἐνδιδομένης
τῆς πόλεως, ἐξ ἀρίστου μετεστρατοπεδεύσατο
19   πρὸς τὸ ἄστυ· αἰσθόμενος δὲ ὑπὸ νύκτα βεβοη-
θηκότας ἐκ τοῦ Πειραίου εἰς τὴν πόλιν πασ-
συδίᾳ, ὑποστρέψας ἅμα τῇ ἡμέρᾳ αἱρεῖ τὸ
Πείραιον ἔρημον εὑρὼν φυλακῆς καὶ τά τε ἄλλα
τὰ ἐνόντα λαμβάνει καὶ τὰ τείχη, ἃ ἐνετετεί-
χιστο. ταῦτα δὲ ποιήσας οἴκαδε ἀπεχώρησε.

20   Μετὰ δὲ ταῦτα προθύμων ὄντων τῶν Ἀχαιῶν
εἰς τὴν συμμαχίαν καὶ δεομένων συστρατεύειν
αὐτοῖς εἰς Ἀκαρνανίαν . . .[1] καὶ ἐπιθεμένων ἐν
στενοῖς τῶν Ἀκαρνάνων καταλαβὼν τοῖς ψιλοῖς
τὰ ὑπὲρ κεφαλῆς αὐτῶν μάχην συνάπτει καὶ

---

[1] There is no indication of a gap in S.

---

[1] The MSS. of *Hellenica*, IV. iv. 19 give κατὰ Τεγέαν in the
corresponding passage ; this is corrected to κατὰ Τενέαν " by
way of Tenea," which is probably the right reading here.

crossed to Corinth by the pass¹ and captured the walls leading to Lechaeum. Having thus unbarred the gates of Peloponnese, he returned home for the festival of Hyacinthus² and joined in singing the paean in honour of the god,³ taking the place assigned to him by the choirmaster.

After a time, discovering that the Corinthians 18 were keeping all their cattle safe in Peiraeum, and sowing and reaping the crops throughout that district, and—what he thought most serious—that the Boeotians were finding this route convenient for sending support to the Corinthians, with Creusis as their base, he marched against Peiraeum. Seeing that it was strongly guarded, he moved his camp after the morning meal to a position before the capital, as though the city was about to surrender. But becoming aware that supports had been hurriedly 19 poured into the city during the night from Peiraeum, he turned about at daybreak and captured Peiraeum, finding it undefended, and everything in it, along with the fortresses that stood there, fell into his hands. Having done this, he returned home.

After these events, the Achaeans, who were zealous 20 advocates of the alliance, begged him to join them in an expedition against Acarnania. . . .⁴ And when the Acarnanians attacked him in a mountain pass he seized the heights above their heads with his light infantry,⁵ fought an engagement and, after inflicting

---

² Celebrated annually at Amyclae, early in the summer.

³ Apollo, who had accidentally killed Hyacinthus.

⁴ Something seems to be lost here, probably a passage that ended with the words συστρατεύει αὐτοῖς εἰς ᾿Ακαρνανίαν.

⁵ The words τοῖς ψιλοῖς are probably a correction by X.; he says the heights were taken by the heavy infantry in *Hellenica*, IV. vi. 11.

XENOPHON

πολλοὺς ἀποκτείνας αὐτῶν τρόπαιον ἐστήσατο
καὶ οὐ πρότερον ἔληξε, πρὶν Ἀχαιοῖς μὲν φίλους
ἐποίησεν Ἀκαρνᾶνας καὶ Αἰτωλοὺς καὶ Ἀργείους, ἑαυτῷ δὲ καὶ συμμάχους.

21 Ἐπειδὴ δὲ εἰρήνης ἐπιθυμήσαντες οἱ πολέμιοι
ἐπρεσβεύοντο, Ἀγησίλαος ἀντεῖπε τῇ εἰρήνῃ, ἕως
τοὺς διὰ Λακεδαιμονίους φυγόντας Κορινθίων καὶ
Θηβαίων ἠνάγκασε τὰς πόλεις οἴκαδε καταδέ-
ξασθαι. ὕστερον δ᾽ αὖ καὶ Φλειασίων τοὺς
διὰ Λακεδαιμονίους φυγόντας κατήγαγεν, αὐτὸς
στρατευσάμενος ἐπὶ Φλειοῦντα. εἰ δέ τις ἄλλῃ
πῃ ταῦτα μέμφεται, ἀλλ᾽ οὖν φιλεταιρίᾳ γε
22 πραχθέντα φανερά ἐστι. καὶ γὰρ ἐπεὶ τοὺς ἐν
Θήβαις τῶν Λακεδαιμονίων κατέκανον οἱ ἐναντίοι,
βοηθῶν αὖ τούτοις στρατεύει ἐπὶ τὰς Θήβας.
εὑρὼν δὲ ἀποτεταφρευμένα καὶ ἀπεσταυρωμένα
ἅπαντα, ὑπερβὰς τὰς Κυνὸς κεφαλὰς ἐδῄου τὴν
χώραν μέχρι τοῦ ἄστεος, παρέχων καὶ ἐν πεδίῳ
καὶ ἀνὰ τὰ ὄρη μάχεσθαι Θηβαίοις, εἰ βούλοιντο.
ἐστράτευσε δὲ καὶ τῷ ἐπιόντι ἔτει πάλιν ἐπὶ
Θήβας· καὶ ὑπερβὰς τὰ κατὰ Σκῶλον σταυ-
ρώματα καὶ τάφρους ἐδῄωσε τὰ λοιπὰ τῆς
Βοιωτίας.

23 Τὰ μὲν δὴ μέχρι τούτου κοινῇ αὐτός τε καὶ ἡ
πόλις εὐτύχει· ὅσα γε μὴν μετὰ τοῦτο σφάλματα
ἐγένοντο οὐδεὶς ἂν εἴποι ὡς Ἀγησιλάου ἡγουμένου
ἐπράχθη. ἐπεὶ δ᾽ αὖ τῆς ἐν Λεύκτροις συμφορᾶς
γεγενημένης κατακαίνουσι τοὺς ἐν Τεγέᾳ φίλους
καὶ ξένους αὐτοῦ οἱ ἀντίπαλοι σὺν Μαντινεῦσι,
συνεστηκότων ἤδη Βοιωτῶν τε πάντων καὶ Ἀρκά-

severe losses on them, set up a trophy; nor did
he cease until he had induced the Acarnanians,
Aetolians and Argives to enter into friendship with
the Achaeans and alliance with himself.

When the enemy sent embassies desiring peace, 21
Agesilaus opposed the peace until he forced Corinth 387 B.C.
and Thebes to restore to their homes the citizens Peace of
who had been exiled on account of their sympathy cidas.
with the Lacedaemonians. And again later, having 381 B.C.
led an expedition in person against Phleius, he also
restored the Phleiasian exiles who had suffered in
the same cause. Possibly some may censure these
actions on other grounds, but at least it is obvious
that they were prompted by a spirit of true comrade-
ship. It was in the same spirit that he subsequently 22
made an expedition against Thebes, to relieve the 377 B.C.
Lacedaemonians in that city when their opponents
had taken to murdering them. Finding the city protected on all sides by a trench and stockade, he
crossed the Pass of Cynoscephalae, and laid waste
the country up to the city walls, offering battle to
the Thebans both on the plain and on the hills,
if they chose to fight. In the following year he
made another expedition against Thebes, and, after
crossing the stockade and trenches at Scolus, laid
waste the rest of Boeotia.

Up to this time he and his city enjoyed unbroken 23
success; and though the following years brought a
series of troubles, it cannot be said that they were
incurred under the leadership of Agesilaus. On
the other hand, after the disaster at Leuctra,
when his adversaries in league with the Mantineans
were murdering his friends and acquaintances in
Tegea, and a coalition of all Boeotia, Arcadia and Elis

δων καὶ Ἠλείων, στρατεύει σὺν μόνῃ τῇ Λακεδαιμονίων δυνάμει, πολλῶν νομιζόντων οὐδ᾽ ἂν
ἐξελθεῖν Λακεδαιμονίους πολλοῦ χρόνου ἐκ τῆς
αὑτῶν. δῃώσας δὲ τὴν χώραν τῶν κατακανόντων
τοὺς φίλους οὕτως αὖ οἴκαδε ἀπεχώρησεν.

24 Ἀπό γε μὴν τούτου ἐπὶ τὴν Λακεδαίμονα στρα-
τευσαμένων Ἀρκάδων τε πάντων καὶ Ἀργείων
καὶ Ἠλείων καὶ Βοιωτῶν καὶ σὺν αὐτοῖς Φωκέων
καὶ Λοκρῶν ἀμφοτέρων καὶ Θετταλῶν καὶ Αἰνειά-
νων καὶ Ἀκαρνάνων καὶ Εὐβοέων, πρὸς δὲ τούτοις
ἀφεστηκότων μὲν τῶν δούλων, πολλῶν δὲ περι-
οικίδων πόλεων, καὶ αὐτῶν Σπαρτιατῶν οὐ μειόνων
ἀπολωλότων ἐν τῇ ἐν Λεύκτροις μάχῃ ἢ λειπο-
μένων, ὅμως διεφύλαξε τὴν πόλιν, καὶ ταῦτα
ἀτείχιστον οὖσαν, ὅπου μὲν ἐν παντὶ πλέον ἂν
εἶχον οἱ πολέμιοι, οὐκ ἐξάγων ἐνταῦθα, ὅπου δὲ
οἱ πολῖται πλέον ἕξειν ἔμελλον, εὐρώστως παρα-
τεταγμένος, νομίζων εἰς μὲν τὸ πλατὺ ἐξιὼν πάντοθεν ἂν περιέχεσθαι, ἐν δὲ τοῖς στενοῖς καὶ
ὑπερδεξίοις τόποις ὑπομένων τῷ παντὶ κρατεῖν ἄν.

25 Ἐπεί γε μὴν ἀπεχώρησε τὸ στράτευμα, πῶς
οὐκ ἂν φαίη τις αὐτὸν εὐγνωμόνως χρῆσθαι
ἑαυτῷ; ὡς γὰρ τοῦ στρατεύεσθαι αὐτὸν καὶ
πεζῇ καὶ ἐφ᾽ ἵππων ἀπεῖργεν ἤδη τὸ γῆρας,
χρημάτων δὲ ἑώρα τὴν πόλιν δεομένην, εἰ μέλλοι
σύμμαχόν τινα ἕξειν, ἐπὶ τὸ πορίζειν ταῦτα
ἑαυτὸν ἔταξε. καὶ ὅσα μὲν ἐδύνατο οἴκοι μένων
ἐμηχανᾶτο, ἃ δὲ καιρὸς ἦν οὐκ ὤκνει μετιέναι
οὐδ᾽ ᾐσχύνετο, εἰ μέλλοι τὴν πόλιν ὠφελήσειν,

had been formed, he took the field with the 370 B.C.
Lacedaemonian forces only, thus disappointing the
general expectation that the Lacedaemonians would
not even go outside their own borders for a long time
to come. It was not until he had laid waste the
country of those who had murdered his friends that
he returned home once more.

After this Sparta was attacked by all the Arcadians, 24
Argives, Eleians and Boeotians, who had the support
of the Phocians, both the Locrian peoples, the
Thessalians, Aenianians, Acarnanians and Euboeans.
In addition the slaves and many of the outlander
communities were in revolt, and at least as many of
the Spartan nobles had fallen in the battle of Leuctra
as survived. He kept the city safe notwithstanding,
and that though it was without walls, not going out
into the open where the advantage would have lain
wholly with the enemy, and keeping his army strongly
posted where the citizens would have the advantage;
for he believed that he would be surrounded on all
sides if he came out into the plain, but that if he
made a stand in the defiles and the heights, he
would be master of the situation.

After the retirement of the enemy, none will deny 25
that his conduct was marked by good sense. The
marching and riding incidental to active service
were no longer possible to a man of his years, but
he saw that the state must have money if she was
to gain an ally anywhere. So he applied himself
to the business of raising money. At home he did
all that ingenuity could suggest; and, if he saw any
prospect of serving the state abroad, shrank from no
measures that circumstances called for, and he was
not ashamed to go out, not as a general, but as an

95

26 πρεσβευτὴς ἐκπορευομενος ἀντὶ στρατηγοῦ. ὅμως
δὲ καὶ ἐν τῇ πρεσβείᾳ μεγάλου στρατηγοῦ ἔργα
διεπράξατο. Αὐτοφραδάτης τε γὰρ πολιορκῶν
ἐν Ἄσσῳ Ἀριοβαρζάνην σύμμαχον ὄντα δείσας
Ἀγησίλαον φεύγων ᾤχετο· Κότυς δ᾽ αὖ Σηστὸν
πολιορκῶν Ἀριοβαρζάνου ἔτι οὖσαν λύσας καὶ
οὗτος τὴν πολιορκίαν ἀπηλλάγη· ὥστ᾽ οὐκ ἂν
ἀλόγως καὶ ἀπὸ τῆς πρεσβείας τρόπαιον τῶν
πολεμίων ἑστήκει αὐτῷ. Μαύσωλός γε μὴν κατὰ
θάλατταν ἑκατὸν ναυσὶ πολιορκῶν ἀμφότερα τὰ
χωρία ταῦτα οὐκέτι δείσας, ἀλλὰ πεισθεὶς ἀπέ-
27 πλευσεν οἴκαδε. κἀνταῦθα οὖν ἄξια θαύματος
διεπράξατο· οἵ τε γὰρ εὖ πεπονθέναι νομίζοντες
ὑπ᾽ αὐτοῦ καὶ οἱ φεύγοντες αὐτὸν χρήματα
ἀμφότεροι ἔδοσαν. Ταχύς γε μὴν καὶ Μαύσωλος,
διὰ τὴν πρόσθεν Ἀγησιλάου ξενίαν συμβαλό-
μενος καὶ οὗτος χρήματα τῇ Λακεδαίμονι,
ἀπέπεμψαν αὐτὸν οἴκαδε προπομπὴν δόντες
μεγαλοπρεπῆ.

28 Ἐκ δὲ τούτου ἤδη μὲν ἔτη ἐγεγόνει ἀμφὶ τὰ
ὀγδοήκοντα· κατανενοηκὼς δὲ τὸν Αἰγυπτίων
βασιλέα ἐπιθυμοῦντα τῷ Πέρσῃ πολεμεῖν καὶ
πολλοὺς μὲν πεζούς, πολλοὺς δὲ ἱππέας, πολλὰ
δὲ χρήματα ἔχοντα ἄσμενος ἤκουσεν, ὅτι μετεπέμπετο αὐτόν, καὶ ταῦτα ἡγεμονίαν ὑπισχνού-
29 μενος. ἐνόμιζε γὰρ τῇ αὐτῇ ὁρμῇ τῷ μὲν
Αἰγυπτίῳ χάριν ἀποδώσειν ἀνθ᾽ ὧν εὐεργετήκει
τὴν Λακεδαίμονα, τοὺς δ᾽ ἐν τῇ Ἀσίᾳ Ἕλληνας
πάλιν ἐλευθερώσειν, τῷ δὲ Πέρσῃ δίκην ἐπιθήσειν
καὶ τῶν πρόσθεν καὶ ὅτι νῦν σύμμαχος εἶναι
30 φάσκων ἐπέταττε Μεσσήνην ἀφιέναι. ἐπεὶ μέντοι
ὁ μεταπεμψάμενος οὐκ ἀπεδίδου τὴν ἡγεμονίαν

envoy. And even as an envoy he accomplished 26
work worthy of a great general. For instance,
Autophradates laying siege to Ariobarzanes, an ally
of Sparta, at Assos, took to his heels from fear of
Agesilaus. Cotys for his part, besieging Sestos, while
it was still in the hands of Ariobarzanes, broke up the
siege and made off. With good reason, therefore,
might the victorious envoy have set up a trophy once
again to record these bloodless successes. Again, 27
Mausolus, laying siege to both these places with a
fleet of a hundred vessels, was induced, not indeed
by fear, but by persuasion, to sail for home. In this
affair too his success was admirable ; for those who
considered that they were under an obligation to him
and those who fled before him, both paid. Yet again,
Tachos and Mausolus (another of those who contributed money to Sparta, owing to his old ties of
hospitality with Agesilaus), sent him home with a
magnificent escort.

Subsequently, when he was now about eighty 28
years of age, he became aware that the king of
Egypt was bent on war with Persia, and was possessed
of large forces of infantry and cavalry and plenty
of money. He was delighted when a summons
for help reached him from the Egyptian king, who
actually promised him the chief command. For he 29
believed that at one stroke he would repay the
Egyptian for his good offices to Sparta, would again
set free the Greeks in Asia, and would chastise the
Persian for his former hostility, and for demanding
now, when he professed to be an ally of Sparta, that
her claim to Messene should be given up. However, 30
when this suitor for his assistance failed to give him

αὐτῷ, ὁ μὲν Ἀγησίλαος ὡς τὸ μέγιστον ἐξηπατη-
μένος ἐφρόντιζε, τί δεῖ ποιεῖν. ἐκ τούτου δὲ
πρῶτον μὲν οἱ δίχα στρατευόμενοι τῶν Αἰγυπτίων
ἀφίστανται τοῦ βασιλέως, ἔπειτα δὲ καὶ οἱ ἄλλοι
πάντες ἀπέλιπον αὐτόν. καὶ αὐτὸς μὲν δείσας
ἀπεχώρησε φυγῇ εἰς Σιδῶνα τῆς Φοινίκης, οἱ δ'
Αἰγύπτιοι στασιάζοντες διττοὺς βασιλέας αἱροῦν-
31 ται. ἐνταῦθα δὴ Ἀγησίλαος γνούς, ὅτι εἰ μὲν
μηδετέρῳ συλλήψοιτο, μισθὸν οὐδέτερος λύσει
τοῖς Ἕλλησιν, ἀγορὰν δὲ οὐδέτερος παρέξει,
ὁπότερός τ' ἂν κρατήσῃ, οὗτος ἐχθρὸς ἔσται·
εἰ δὲ τῷ ἑτέρῳ συλλήψοιτο, οὗτός γε εὖ παθὼν
ὡς τὸ εἰκὸς φίλος ἔσοιτο, οὕτω δὴ κρίνας, ὁπότερος
φιλέλλην μᾶλλον ἐδόκει εἶναι, στρατευσάμενος
μετὰ τούτου τὸν μὲν μισέλληνα μάχῃ νικήσας
χειροῦται, τὸν δ' ἕτερον συγκαθίστησι· καὶ φίλον
ποιήσας τῇ Λακεδαίμονι καὶ χρήματα πολλὰ
προσλαβὼν οὕτως ἀποπλεῖ οἴκαδε καίπερ μέσου
χειμῶνος ὄντος, σπεύδων, ὡς μὴ ἀργὸς ἡ πόλις
εἰς τὸ ἐπιὸν θέρος πρὸς τοὺς πολεμίους γένοιτο.

III. Καὶ ταῦτα μὲν δὴ εἴρηται ὅσα τῶν ἐκείνου
ἔργων μετὰ πλείστων μαρτύρων ἐπράχθη. τὰ
γὰρ τοιαῦτα οὐ τεκμηρίων προσδεῖται, ἀλλ'
ἀναμνῆσαι μόνον ἀρκεῖ καὶ εὐθὺς πιστεύεται.
νῦν δὲ τὴν ἐν τῇ ψυχῇ αὐτοῦ ἀρετὴν πειράσομαι
δηλοῦν, δι' ἣν ταῦτα ἔπραττε καὶ πάντων τῶν
καλῶν ἤρα καὶ πάντα τὰ αἰσχρὰ ἐξεδίωκεν.

2 Ἀγησίλαος γὰρ τὰ μὲν θεῖα οὕτως ἐσέβετο,
ὡς καὶ οἱ πολέμιοι τοὺς ἐκείνου ὅρκους καὶ τὰς

the command Agesilaus felt that he had been grossly
deceived, and was in doubt what he ought to do.   At
this juncture first a portion of the Egyptian troops,
operating as a separate army, revolted from the king,
and then the rest of his forces deserted him.   The
king left Egypt and fled in terror to Sidon in Phoenicia,
while the Egyptians split up into two parties, and each
chose its own king.   Agesilaus now realised that if 31
he helped neither king, neither of them would pay
the Greeks their wages, neither would provide a
market, and the conqueror, whichever he proved to
be, would be hostile, but if he co-operated with one
of them, that one, being under an obligation to him,
would in all probability adopt a friendly attitude.
Accordingly, having decided which of them showed the
stronger signs of being a friend to the Greeks, he
took the field with him.   He inflicted a crushing
defeat on the enemy of the Greeks, and helped to
establish his rival;   and so having made him
the friend of Sparta, and having received a
great sum of money in addition, he sailed home, 362 B.C.
though it was mid-winter, with all haste, in order
that the state might be in a position to take action
against her enemies in the coming summer.

III. Such, then, is the record of my hero's deeds,
so far as they were done before a crowd of witnesses.
Actions like these need no proofs ; the mere mention
of them is enough and they command belief immediately.   But now I will attempt to show the virtue
that was in his soul, the virtue through which he
wrought those deeds and loved all that is honourable
and put away all that is base.

Agesilaus had such reverence for religion, that 2
even his enemies considered his oaths and his

XENOPHON

ἐκείνου σπονδὰς πιστοτέρας ἐνόμιζον ἢ τὴν ἑαυτῶν
φιλίαν· οἳ καὶ πρὸς ἀλλήλους ἔστιν ὅτε μὲν ὤκνουν
εἰς ταὐτὸν ἰέναι, Ἀγησιλάῳ δὲ αὐτοὺς ἐγχείριζον.
ὅπως δὲ μή τις ἀπιστῇ, καὶ ὀνομάσαι βούλομαι
3 τοὺς ἐπιφανεστάτους αὐτῶν. Σπιθριδάτης μέν
γε ὁ Πέρσης εἰδώς, ὅτι Φαρνάβαζος γῆμαι μὲν
τὴν βασιλέως ἔπραττε θυγατέρα, τὴν δ᾽ αὐτοῦ
ἄνευ γάμου λαβεῖν ἐβούλετο, ὕβριν νομίσας
τοῦτο Ἀγησιλάῳ ἑαυτὸν καὶ τὴν γυναῖκα καὶ
4 τὰ τέκνα καὶ τὴν δύναμιν ἐνεχείρισε. Κότυς δὲ
ὁ τῶν Παφλαγόνων ἄρχων βασιλεῖ μὲν οὐχ
ὑπήκουσε δεξιὰν πέμποντι, φοβούμενος, μὴ
ληφθεὶς ἢ χρήματα πολλὰ ἀποτίσειεν ἢ καὶ
ἀποθάνοι, Ἀγησιλάου δὲ καὶ οὗτος ταῖς σπονδαῖς
πιστεύσας εἰς τὸ στρατόπεδόν τε ἦλθε καὶ συμμαχίαν ποιησάμενος εἵλετο σὺν Ἀγησιλάῳ στρατεύεσθαι, χιλίους μὲν ἱππέας, δισχιλίους δὲ
5 πελτοφόρους ἔχων. ἀφίκετο δὲ καὶ Φαρνάβαζος
Ἀγησιλάῳ εἰς λόγους καὶ διωμολόγησεν, εἰ μὴ
αὐτὸς πάσης τῆς στρατιᾶς στρατηγὸς καταστα.
θείη, ἀποστήσεσθαι βασιλέως· ἢν μέντοι ἐγὼ
γένωμαι στρατηγός, ἔφη, πολεμήσω σοι, ὦ
Ἀγησίλαε, ὡς ἂν ἐγὼ δύνωμαι κράτιστα. καὶ
ταῦτα λέγων ἐπίστευε μηδὲν ἂν παράσπονδον
παθεῖν. οὕτω μέγα καὶ καλὸν κτῆμα τοῖς τε
ἄλλοις ἅπασι καὶ ἀνδρὶ δὴ στρατηγῷ τὸ ὅσιόν
τε καὶ πιστὸν εἶναί τε καὶ ὄντα ἐγνῶσθαι. καὶ
περὶ μὲν εὐσεβείας ταῦτα.

---

[1] The text here is quite uncertain: there is a gap in the
manuscripts after φιλίαν.

treaties more to be relied on than their own friendship with one another: for there were times when they shrank from meeting together,[1] and yet would place themselves in the power of Agesilaus. And lest anyone should think this statement incredible, I wish to name the most famous among them. Spithridates the Persian, for example, knew that 3 Pharnabazus was negotiating for a marriage with the Great King's daughter, and intended to take his, Spithridates', daughter as a concubine. Regarding this as an outrage, he delivered himself, his wife, his children and all that he had into Agesilaus' hands. Cotys, ruler of the Paphlagonians, who had disobeyed 4 the command of the Great King, though it was accompanied with the symbol of friendship,[2] feared that he would be seized and either be fined heavily or even put to death; but he too, trusting in the armistice with Agesilaus, came to his camp and having entered into alliance elected to take the field at Agesilaus' side with a thousand horse and two thousand targeteers. And Pharnabazus too came 5 and parleyed with Agesilaus, and made agreement with him that if he were not himself appointed the Persian general, he would revolt from the Great King. "But," he said, "if I become general, I shall make war on you, Agesilaus, with all my might." He used this language in full confidence that nothing contrary to the terms of the armistice would happen to him. So great and so noble a treasure has every man, and above all a general, who is upright and trustworthy and is known to be so. So much, then, for the virtue of Piety.

[2] The "right hand," often mentioned as a pledge of good faith or friendship.

IV. Περί γε μὴν τῆς εἰς χρήματα δικαιοσύνης ποῖα ἄν τις μείζω τεκμήρια ἔχοι τῶνδε; ὑπὸ γὰρ Ἀγησιλάου στέρεσθαι μὲν οὐδεὶς οὐδὲν πώποτε ἐνεκάλεσεν, εὖ δὲ πεπονθέναι πολλοὶ πολλὰ ὡμολόγουν. ὅτῳ δὲ ἡδὺ τὰ αὑτοῦ διδόναι ἐπ' ὠφελείᾳ ἀνθρώπων, πῶς ἂν οὗτος ἐθέλοι τὰ ἀλλότρια ἀποστερεῖν ἐφ' ᾧ κακόδοξος εἶναι; εἰ γὰρ χρημάτων ἐπιθυμοίη, πολὺ ἀπραγμονέστερον τὰ αὑτοῦ φυλάττειν ἢ τὰ μὴ προσήκοντα λαμβά-
2 νειν. ὃς δὲ δὴ καὶ χάριτας ἀποστερεῖν μὴ ἐθέλοι, ὧν οὐκ εἰσὶ δίκαι πρὸς τὸν μὴ ἀποδιδόντα, πῶς ἅ γε καὶ νόμος κωλύει ἐθέλοι ἂν ἀποστερεῖν; Ἀγησίλαος δὲ οὐ μόνον τὸ μὴ ἀποδιδόναι χάριτας ἄδικον ἔκρινεν, ἀλλὰ καὶ τὸ μὴ πολὺ μείζους τὸν
3 μείζω δυνάμενον. τά γε μὴν τῆς πόλεως κλέπτειν πῇ ἄν τις αὐτὸν εἰκότως αἰτιάσαιτο, ὃς καὶ τὰς αὐτῷ χάριτας ὀφειλομένας τῇ πατρίδι καρποῦσθαι παρεδίδου; τὸ δ' ὁπότε βούλοιτο εὖ ποιεῖν ἢ πόλιν ἢ φίλους χρήμασι, δύνασθαι παρ' ἑτέρων λαμβάνοντα ὠφελεῖν, οὐ καὶ τοῦτο μέγα τεκμή-
4 ριον ἐγκρατείας χρημάτων; εἰ γὰρ ἐπώλει τὰς χάριτας ἢ μισθοῦ εὐεργέτει, οὐδεὶς ἂν οὐδὲν ὀφείλειν αὐτῷ ἐνόμισεν· ἀλλ' οἱ προῖκα εὖ πεπονθότες, οὗτοι ἀεὶ ἡδέως ὑπηρετοῦσι τῷ εὐεργέτῃ καὶ διότι εὖ ἔπαθον καὶ διότι προεπιστεύθησαν ἄξιοι εἶναι παρακαταθήκην χάριτος φυλάττειν.
5 Ὅστις δ' ᾑρεῖτο καὶ σὺν τῷ γενναίῳ μειονεκτεῖν ἢ σὺν τῷ ἀδίκῳ πλέον ἔχειν, πῶς οὗτος οὐκ ἂν

---

[1] Symposium, viii. 36.

IV. Next comes his Justice in money matters. Of this what proofs can be more convincing than the following? No man ever made any complaint that he had been defrauded by Agesilaus : but many acknowledged that they had received many benefits from him. One who delighted to give away his own for the good of others could not possibly be minded to defraud others at the price of disgrace. For if he had coveted money it would have cost him far less trouble to keep his own than to take what did not belong to him. A man who would not leave unpaid 2 debts of gratitude, which are not recoverable in the courts, cannot have been minded to commit thefts that are forbidden by law. And Agesilaus held it wrong not only to repudiate a debt of gratitude, but, having greater means, not to render in return a much greater kindness. Again, with what show of 3 reason could embezzlement of public property be charged against a man who bestowed on his fatherland the rewards due to himself? And is it not a striking proof of his freedom from avarice that he was able to get money from others, whenever he wanted, for the purpose of rendering financial assistance to the state or his friends? For had he been 4 in the habit of selling his favours or taking payment for his benefactions, no one would have felt that he owed him anything. It is the recipient of unbought, gratuitous benefits who is always glad to oblige his benefactor in return for the kindness he has received and in acknowledgment of the trust reposed in him as a worthy and faithful guardian of a favour.[1]

Further, is it not certain that the man who by a 5 noble instinct refused to take more and preferred to take less than his just share was far beyond the reach

πολυ τὴν αἰσχροκέρδειαν ἀποφεύγοι; ἐκεῖνος
τοίνυν κριθεὶς ὑπὸ τῆς πόλεως ἅπαντα ἔχειν τὰ
Ἄγιδος τὰ ἡμίσεα τοῖς ἀπὸ μητρὸς αὐτῷ ὁμογό-
νοις μετέδωκεν, ὅτι πενομένους αὐτοὺς ἑώρα. ὡς
δὲ ταῦτα ἀληθῆ, πᾶσα μάρτυς ἡ τῶν Λακεδαι-
6 μονίων πόλις. διδόντος δ' αὐτῷ πάμπολλα δῶρα
Τιθραύστου, εἰ ἀπέλθοι ἐκ τῆς χώρας, ἀπεκρίνατο
ὁ Ἀγησίλαος· Ὦ Τιθραύστα, νομίζεται παρ'
ἡμῖν τῷ ἄρχοντι κάλλιον εἶναι τὴν στρατιὰν ἢ
ἑαυτὸν πλουτίζειν καὶ παρὰ τῶν πολεμίων λάφυρα
μᾶλλον πειρᾶσθαι ἢ δῶρα λαμβάνειν.

V. Ἀλλὰ μὴν καὶ ὅσαι γε ἡδοναὶ πολλῶν
κρατοῦσιν ἀνθρώπων, ποίας οὐδέ τις Ἀγησίλαον
ἡττηθέντα; ὃς μέθης μὲν ἀποσχέσθαι ὁμοίως
ᾤετο χρῆναι καὶ μανίας,[1] σίτων δ' ὑπὲρ καιρὸν
ὁμοίως καὶ ἀργίας. διμοιρίαν γε μὴν λαμβάνων
ἐν ταῖς θοίναις οὐχ ὅπως ἀμφοτέραις ἐχρῆτο,
ἀλλὰ διαπέμπων οὐδετέραν αὐτῷ κατέλειπε,
νομίζων βασιλεῖ τοῦτο διπλασιασθῆναι οὐχὶ
πλησμονῆς ἕνεκα, ἀλλ' ὅπως ἔχοι καὶ τούτῳ
2 τιμᾶν εἴ τινα βούλοιτο. οὐ μὴν ὕπνῳ γε δεσπότῃ
ἀλλ' ἀρχομένῳ ὑπὸ τῶν πράξεων ἐχρῆτο καὶ
εὐνήν γε εἰ μὴ τῶν συνόντων φαυλοτάτην ἔχοι,
αἰδούμενος οὐκ ἄδηλος ἦν· ἡγεῖτο γὰρ ἄρχοντι
προσήκειν οὐ μαλακίᾳ, ἀλλὰ καρτερίᾳ τῶν ἰδιωτῶν περιεῖναι.

3 Τάδε μέντοι πλεονεκτῶν οὐκ ἠσχύνετο, ἐν μὲν
τῷ θέρει τοῦ ἡλίου, ἐν δὲ τῷ χειμῶνι τοῦ ψύχους·
καὶ μὴν εἴ ποτε μοχθῆσαι στρατιᾷ συμβαίη,

---

[1] μανίας and ἀργίας are adopted from the text of Athenaeus,
who refers to this passage (p. 613 c). The MSS. of the

of covetousness? Now when the state pronounced
him sole heir to the property of Agis, he gave half
of it to his mother's kinsfolk, because he saw that
they were in want; and all Lacedaemon bears wit-
ness that my statement is true.   On receiving from 6
Tithraustes an offer of gifts unnumbered if only
he would leave his country, Agesilaus answered:
"Among us, Tithraustes, a ruler's honour requires
him to enrich his army rather than himself, and to
take spoils rather than gifts from the enemy."

V. Again, among all the pleasures that prove too
strong for many men, who can mention one to which
Agesilaus yielded? Drunkenness, he thought, should
be avoided like madness, overeating like idleness.[1]
Moreover, he received a double ration at the public
meals, but instead of consuming both portions himself,
he distributed both and left neither for himself,
holding that the purpose of this double allowance to
the king was not to provide him with a heavy meal,
but to give him the opportunity of honouring whomsoever he would.   As for sleep,[2] it was not his master, 2
but the servant of his activities; and unless he
occupied the humblest bed among his comrades, he
could not conceal his shame: for he thought that a
ruler's superiority over ordinary men should be shown
not by weakness but by endurance.

There were things, to be sure, of which he was 3
not ashamed to take more than his share—for instance, the summer's heat and the winter's cold:[3]
and whenever his army was faced with a hard task,

Agesilaus have λαιμαργίας, "gluttony," and ἁμαρτίας,
"error."

[2] *Lac. Pol.*, xv. 4 ; *Cyropaedia*, VIII. ii. 4.
[3] *Cyropaedia*, I. iv. 25.

ἑκὼν ἐπόνει παρὰ τοὺς ἄλλους, νομίζων πάντα
τὰ τοιαῦτα παραμυθίαν εἶναι τοῖς στρατιώταις.
ὡς δὲ συνελόντι εἰπεῖν, Ἀγησίλαος πονῶν μὲν
ἠγάλλετο, ῥᾳστώνην δὲ πάμπαν οὐ προσίετο.

4 Περί γε μὴν ἀφροδισίων ἐγκρατείας αὐτοῦ ἆρ᾽
οὐχὶ εἰ μή του ἄλλου ἀλλὰ θαύματος ἕνεκα
ἄξιον μνησθῆναι; τὸ μὲν γὰρ ὧν μὴ ἐπεθύμησεν
ἀπέχεσθαι ἀνθρώπινον ἄν τις φαίη εἶναι· τὸ δὲ
Μεγαβάτου τοῦ Σπιθριδάτου παιδὸς ἐρασθέντα,
ὥσπερ ἂν τοῦ καλλίστου ἡ σφοδροτάτη φύσις
ἐρασθείη, ἔπειτα ἡνίκα, ἐπιχωρίου ὄντος τοῖς
Πέρσαις φιλεῖν οὓς ἂν τιμῶσιν, ἐπεχείρησε καὶ
ὁ Μεγαβάτης φιλῆσαι τὸν Ἀγησίλαον, διαμά-
χεσθαι ἀνὰ κράτος τὸ μὴ φιληθῆναι, ἆρ᾽ οὐ
τοῦτό γε ἤδη τὸ σωφρόνημα καὶ λίαν γεννικόν;
5 ἐπεὶ δὲ ὥσπερ ἀτιμασθῆναι νομίσας ὁ Μεγαβάτης
τοῦ λοιποῦ οὐκέτι φιλεῖν ἐπειρᾶτο, προσφέρει
τινὶ λόγον τῶν ἑταίρων ὁ Ἀγησίλαος πείθειν
τὸν Μεγαβάτην πάλιν τιμᾶν ἑαυτόν. ἐρομένου
δὲ τοῦ ἑταίρου, ἢν πεισθῇ ὁ Μεγαβάτης, εἰ
φιλήσει, ἐνταῦθα διασιωπήσας ὁ Ἀγησίλαος
εἶπεν· Οὐ τὼ σιώ, οὐδ᾽ εἰ μέλλοιμί γε αὐτίκα
μάλα κάλλιστός τε καὶ ἰσχυρότατος καὶ τάχιστος
ἀνθρώπων ἔσεσθαι· μάχεσθαί γε μέντοι πάλιν
τὴν αὐτὴν μάχην ὄμνυμι πάντας θεοὺς ἦ μὴν
μᾶλλον βούλεσθαι ἢ πάντα μοι ὅσα ὁρῶ χρυσᾶ
6 γενέσθαι. καὶ ὅ τι μὲν δὴ ὑπολαμβάνουσί τινες
ταῦτα, οὐκ ἀγνοῶ· ἐγὼ μέντοι δοκῶ εἰδέναι, ὅτι
πολὺ πλέονες τῶν πολεμίων ἢ τῶν τοιούτων
δύνανται κρατεῖν. ἀλλὰ ταῦτα μὲν ὀλίγων
εἰδότων πολλοῖς ἔξεστιν ἀπιστεῖν· τὰ δὲ πάντες
ἐπιστάμεθα, ὅτι ἥκιστα μὲν οἱ ἐπιφανέστατοι

he toiled willingly beyond all others, believing
that all such actions were an encouragement to the
men. Not to labour the point, Agesilaus gloried
in hard work, and showed a strong distaste for
indolence.

His habitual control of his affections surely deserves 4
a tribute of admiration, if worthy of mention on no
other ground. That he should keep at arms' length
those whose intimacy he did not desire may be
thought only human. But he loved Megabates, the
handsome son of Spithridates, with all the intensity
of an ardent nature. Now it is the custom [1] among
the Persians to bestow a kiss on those whom they
honour. Yet when Megabates attempted to kiss
him, Agesilaus resisted his advances with all his
might—an act of punctilious moderation surely!
Megabates, feeling himself slighted, tried no more 5
to kiss him, and Agesilaus approached one of his
companions with a request that he would persuade
Megabates to show him honour once again. "Will
you kiss him," asked his companion, "if Megabates
yields?" After a deep silence, Agesilaus gave his
reply : "By the twin gods, no, not if I were straight-
way to be the fairest and strongest and fleetest man
on earth! By all the gods I swear that I would
rather fight that same battle over again than that
everything I see should turn into gold." What 6
opinion some hold in regard to these matters I know
well enough ; but for my part I am persuaded that
many more men can gain the mastery over their
enemies than over impulses such as these. [2] No doubt
when these things are known to few, many have a
right to be sceptical : but we all know this, that the

---

[1] *Cyropaedia*, I. iv. 27.   [2] *Anabasis*, II. vi. 28.

τῶν ἀνθρώπων λανθάνουσιν ὅ τι ἂν ποιῶσιν·
Ἀγησίλαον δέ τι πράξαντα μὲν τοιοῦτον οὔτε
ἰδὼν πώποτε οὐδεὶς ἀνήγγειλεν οὔτε εἰκάζων
7 πιστὰ ἂν ἔδοξε λέγειν. καὶ γὰρ εἰς οἰκίαν μὲν
οὐδεμίαν ἰδίᾳ ἐν ἀποδημίᾳ κατήγετο, ἀεὶ δὲ ἦν
ἢ ἐν ἱερῷ, ἔνθα δὴ ἀδύνατον τὰ τοιαῦτα πράττειν,
ἢ ἐν φανερῷ, μάρτυρας τοὺς πάντων ὀφθαλμοὺς
τῆς σωφροσύνης ποιούμενος. εἰ δ᾽ ἐγὼ ταῦτα
ψεύδομαι ἀντία τῆς Ἑλλάδος ἐπισταμένης, ἐκεῖνον
μὲν οὐδὲν ἐπαινῶ, ἐμαυτὸν δὲ ψέγω.

VI. Ἀνδρείας γε μὴν οὐκ ἀφανῆ τεκμήριά μοι
δοκεῖ παρασχέσθαι ὑφιστάμενος μὲν ἀεὶ πολεμεῖν
πρὸς τοὺς ἰσχυροτάτους τῶν ἐχθρῶν τῇ τε πόλει
καὶ τῇ Ἑλλάδι, ἐν δὲ τοῖς πρὸς τούτους ἀγῶσι
2 πρῶτον ἑαυτὸν τάττων. ἔνθα γε μὴν ἠθέλησαν
αὐτῷ οἱ πολέμιοι μάχην συνάψαι, οὐ φόβῳ
τρεψάμενος νίκης ἔτυχεν, ἀλλὰ μάχῃ ἀντιτύπῳ
κρατήσας τρόπαιον ἐστήσατο, ἀθάνατα μὲν τῆς
ἑαυτοῦ ἀρετῆς μνημεῖα καταλιπών, σαφῆ δὲ καὶ
αὐτὸς σημεῖα ἀπενεγκάμενος τοῦ θυμῷ μάχεσθαι·
ὥστ᾽ οὐκ ἀκούοντας, ἀλλ᾽ ὁρῶντας ἐξῆν αὐτοῦ
3 τὴν ψυχὴν δοκιμάζειν. τρόπαια μὴν Ἀγησιλάου
οὐχ ὅσα ἐστήσατο, ἀλλ᾽ ὅσα ἐστρατεύσατο δίκαιον νομίζειν. μεῖον μὲν γὰρ οὐδὲν ἐκράτει, ὅτε
οὐκ ἤθελον αὐτῷ οἱ πολέμιοι μάχεσθαι, ἀκινδυνότερον δὲ καὶ συμφορώτερον τῇ τε πόλει καὶ
τοῖς συμμάχοις· καὶ ἐν τοῖς ἀγῶσι δὲ οὐδὲν
ἧττον τοὺς ἀκονιτὶ ἢ τοὺς διὰ μάχης νικῶντας
στεφανοῦσι.

---

[1] *Memorabilia*, I. i. 11.
[2] The reference is not general, but definitely to the battle
of Coronea; see c. ii, § 11-13.

greater a man's fame, the fiercer is the light that
beats on all his actions; [1] we know too that no one
ever reported that he had seen Agesilaus do any
such thing, and that no scandal based on conjecture
would have gained credence; for it was not his 7
habit, when abroad, to lodge apart in a private
house, but he was always either in a temple, where
conduct of this sort is, of course, impossible, or else
in a public place where all men's eyes became
witnesses of his rectitude.   If I speak this falsely
against the knowledge of the Greek world, I am in
no way praising my hero ; but I am censuring myself.

VI. As for Courage, he seems to me to have
afforded clear proofs of that by always engaging
himself to fight against the strongest enemies of his
state and of Greece, and by always placing himself
in the forefront of the struggle.   When the enemy 2
were willing to join battle with him, [2] it was not by
their panic flight that he won victory, but it was after
overcoming them in stubborn fighting that he set up
a trophy, leaving behind him imperishable memorials
of his own valour, and bearing in his own body
visible tokens of the fury of his fighting, so that not
by hearsay but by the evidence of their own eyes
men could judge what manner of man he was.   In 3
truth the trophies of Agesilaus are not to be counted
by telling how many he set up ; the number of his
campaigns is the number of them.   His mastery
was in no way less complete when the enemy were
unwilling to accept battle, but it was gained at less
risk and with more profit to the state and to the
allies.   So in the Great Games the unchallenged
champion is crowned no less than he who has
fought to conquer.

XENOPHON

4 Τήν γε μὴν σοφίαν αὐτοῦ ποῖαι τῶν ἐκείνου πράξεων οὐκ ἐπιδεικνύουσιν; ὃς τῇ μὲν πατρίδι οὕτως ἐχρῆτο, ὥστε μάλιστα πειθόμενος [1] ἑταίροις δὲ πρόθυμος ὢν ἀπροφασίστους τοὺς φίλους ἐκέκτητο· τοὺς δέ γε στρατιώτας ἅμα πειθομένους καὶ φιλοῦντας αὐτὸν παρεῖχε. καίτοι πῶς ἂν ἰσχυροτέρα γένοιτο φάλαγξ ἢ διὰ τὸ μὲν πείθεσθαι εὔτακτος οὖσα, διὰ δὲ τὸ φιλεῖν 5 τὸν ἄρχοντα πιστῶς παροῦσα; τοὺς γε μὴν πολεμίους εἶχε ψέγειν μὲν οὐ δυναμένους, μισεῖν δὲ ἀναγκαζομένους. τοὺς γὰρ συμμάχους ἀεὶ πλέον ἔχειν αὐτῶν ἐμηχανᾶτο, ἐξαπατῶν μὲν ὅπου καιρὸς εἴη, φθάνων δὲ ὅπου τάχους δέοι, λήθων δὲ ὅπου τοῦτο συμφέροι, πάντα δὲ τἀναντία πρὸς τοὺς πολεμίους ἢ πρὸς τοὺς φίλους 6 ἐπιτηδεύων. καὶ γὰρ νυκτὶ μὲν ὅσαπερ ἡμέρα ἐχρῆτο, ἡμέρα δὲ ὅσαπερ νυκτί, πολλάκις ἄδηλος γιγνόμενος ὅπου τε εἴη καὶ ὅποι ἴοι καὶ ὅ τι ποιήσοι. ὥστε καὶ τὰ ἐχυρὰ ἀνώχυρα τοῖς ἐχθροῖς καθίστη, τὰ μὲν παριών, τὰ δὲ ὑπερ- 7 βαίνων, τὰ δὲ κλέπτων. ὁπότε γε μὴν πορεύοιτο εἰδώς, ὅτι ἐξείη τοῖς πολεμίοις μάχεσθαι, εἰ βούλοιντο, συντεταγμένον μὲν οὕτως ἦγε τὸ στράτευμα, ὡς ἂν ἐπικουρεῖν μάλιστα ἑαυτῷ δύναιτο, ἡσύχως δ᾽, ὥσπερ ἂν παρθένος ἡ σωφρο- νεστάτη προβαίνοι, νομίζων ἐν τῷ τοιούτῳ τό τε ἀτρεμὲς καὶ ἀνεκπληκτότατον καὶ ἀθορυβητότατον καὶ ἀναμαρτητότατον καὶ δυσεπιβουλευτότατον εἶναι.

---

[1] Something is wanting here: many supply ἴσχυε πλεῖστον from Plutarch, *Ages.* c. 4—φησὶν ὁ Ξ. ὅτι πάντα τῇ πατρίδι πειθόμενος ἴσχυε πλεῖστον.

Of his Wisdom I find the evidence in every 4
one of his deeds. Towards his fatherland he
behaved in such a manner that, being entirely
obedient to her, he won the obedience of the
citizens, and by his zeal for his comrades he
held the unquestioning devotion of his friends : and
as for his troops, he gained at once their obedience
and their affection. Surely nothing is wanting to
the strength of that battle-line in which obedience
results in perfect discipline, and affection for the
general produces faithful promptitude. As for the 5
enemy, though they were forced to hate, he gave
them no chance to disparage him. For he contrived
that his allies always had the better of them, by
the use of deception when occasion offered, by
anticipating their action if speed was necessary,
by hiding when it suited his purpose, and by
practising all the opposite methods when dealing with
enemies to those which he applied when dealing with
friends. Night, for example, was to him as day, and 6
day as night,[1] for he often veiled his movements so
completely that none could guess where he was,
whither he was going, or what he meant to do.
Thus he made even strong positions untenable to the
enemy, turning one, scaling another, snatching a
third by stealth. On the march, whenever he knew 7
that the enemy could bring him to an engagement if
they chose, he would lead his army in close order,
alert and ready to defend himself, moving on as
quietly as a modest maiden, since he held that this
was the best means of maintaining calm, of avoiding
panic, confusion, and blundering, and of guarding
against a surprise attack.

---

[1] *Hellenica*, VI. i. 15 ; *Lac. Pol.*, V. 7 ; *Cyropaedia* I. v. 12.

XENOPHON

8 Τοιγαροῦν τοιαῦτα ποιῶν τοῖς μὲν πολεμίοις δεινὸς ἦν, τοῖς δὲ φίλοις θάρρος καὶ ῥώμην ἐνεποίει. ὥστε ἀκαταφρόνητος μὲν ὑπὸ τῶν ἐχθρῶν διετέλεσεν, ἀζήμιος δ᾽ ὑπὸ τῶν πολιτῶν, ἄμεμπτος δ᾽ ὑπὸ τῶν φίλων, πολυεραστότατος δὲ καὶ πολυεπαινετώτατος ὑπὸ πάντων ἀνθρώπων.

VII. Ὥς γε μὴν φιλόπολις ἦν, καθ᾽ ἓν μὲν ἕκαστον μακρὸν ἂν εἴη γράφειν· οἴομαι γὰρ οὐδὲν εἶναι τῶν πεπραγμένων αὐτῷ, ὅ τι οὐκ εἰς τοῦτο συντείνει. ὡς δ᾽ ἐν βραχεῖ εἰπεῖν, ἅπαντες ἐπιστάμεθα, ὅτι Ἀγησίλαος ὅπου ᾤετο τὴν πατρίδα τι ὠφελήσειν, οὐ πόνων ὑφίετο, οὐ κινδύνων ἀφίστατο, οὐ χρημάτων ἐφείδετο, οὐ σῶμα, οὐ γῆρας προὐφασίζετο, ἀλλὰ καὶ βασιλέως ἀγαθοῦ τοῦτο ἔργον ἐνόμιζε, τὸ τοὺς ἀρχομένους ὡς 2 πλεῖστα ἀγαθὰ ποιεῖν. ἐν τοῖς μεγίστοις δὲ ὠφελήμασι τῆς πατρίδος καὶ τόδε ἐγὼ τίθημι αὐτοῦ, ὅτι δυνατώτατος ὢν ἐν τῇ πόλει φανερὸς ἦν μάλιστα τοῖς νόμοις λατρεύων. τίς γὰρ ἂν ἠθέλησεν ἀπειθεῖν ὁρῶν τὸν βασιλέα πειθόμενον; τίς δ᾽ ἂν ἡγούμενος μειονεκτεῖν νεώτερόν τι ἐπεχείρησε ποιεῖν εἰδὼς τὸν βασιλέα νομίμως 3 καὶ τὸ κρατεῖσθαι φέροντα; ὃς καὶ πρὸς τοὺς διαφόρους ἐν τῇ πόλει ὥσπερ πατὴρ πρὸς παῖδας προσεφέρετο. ἐλοιδορεῖτο μὲν γὰρ ἐπὶ τοῖς ἁμαρτήμασιν, ἐτίμα δ᾽ εἴ τι καλὸν πράττοιεν, παρίστατο δ᾽ εἴ τις συμφορὰ συμβαίνοι, ἐχθρὸν μὲν οὐδένα ἡγούμενος πολίτην, ἐπαινεῖν δὲ πάντας ἐθέλων, σώζεσθαι δὲ πάντας κέρδος νομίζων, ζημίαν δὲ τιθείς, εἰ καὶ ὁ μικροῦ ἄξιος ἀπόλοιτο· εἰ δ᾽ ἐν τοῖς νόμοις ἠρεμοῦντες διαμένοιεν, δῆλος

112

And so, by using such methods, he was formidable 8 to his enemies, and inspired his friends with strength and confidence. Thus he was never despised by his foes, never brought to account by the citizens, never blamed by his friends, but throughout his career he was praised and idolised by all the world.

VII. Of his Patriotism it would be a long task to write in complete detail, for there is no single action of his, I think, that does not illustrate that quality. To speak briefly, we all know that when Agesilaus thought he would be serving his fatherland he never shirked toil, never shrank from danger, never spared money, never excused himself on the score of bodily weakness or old age;[1] but believed that it is the duty of a good king to do as much good as possible to his subjects. Among the greatest services he 2 rendered to his fatherland I reckon the fact that, though the most powerful man in the state, he was clearly a devoted servant of the laws. For who would be minded to disobey when he saw the king obeying? Who would turn revolutionist, thinking himself defrauded of his due, when he knew that the king was ready to yield in accordance with the laws? Here was a man whose behaviour to his 3 political opponents was that of a father to his children: though he would chide them for their errors he honoured them when they did a good deed, and stood by them when any disaster befell them, deeming no citizen an enemy, willing to praise all, counting the safety of all a gain, and reckoning the destruction even of a man of little worth as a loss. He clearly reckoned that if the citizens should continue to live in peaceful sub-

[1] *Memorabilia*, iii. ii.

ἦν εὐδαίμονα μὲν ἀεὶ ἔσεσθαι τὴν πατρίδα
λογιζόμενος, ἰσχυρὰν δὲ τότε, ὅταν οἱ Ἕλληνες
σωφρονῶσιν.

4 Εἴ γε μὴν αὖ καλὸν Ἕλληνα ὄντα φιλέλληνα
εἶναι, τίνα τις οἶδεν ἄλλον στρατηγὸν ἢ πόλιν
οὐκ ἐθέλοντα αἱρεῖν, ὅταν οἴηται πορθήσειν, ἢ
συμφορὰν νομίζοντα τὸ νικᾶν ἐν τῷ πρὸς Ἕλληνας
5 πολέμῳ; ἐκεῖνος τοίνυν, ἀγγελίας μὲν ἐλθούσης
αὐτῷ, ὡς ἐν τῇ ἐν Κορίνθῳ μάχῃ ὀκτὼ μὲν
Λακεδαιμονίων, ἐγγὺς δὲ μύριοι τῶν ἀντιπάλων
τεθναῖεν, οὐκ ἐφησθεὶς φανερὸς ἐγένετο, ἀλλ'
εἶπεν ἄρα· Φεῦ σου,[1] ὦ Ἑλλάς, ὁπότε οἱ νῦν
τεθνηκότες ἱκανοὶ ἦσαν ζῶντες νικᾶν μαχόμενοι
6 πάντας τοὺς βαρβάρους. Κορινθίων γε μὴν τῶν
φευγόντων λεγόντων, ὅτι ἐνδίδοιτο αὐτοῖς ἡ πόλις,
καὶ μηχανὰς ἐπιδεικνύντων, αἷς πάντως ἤλπιζον
ἂν[2] ἑλεῖν τὰ τείχη, οὐκ ἤθελε προσβάλλειν,
λέγων, ὅτι οὐκ ἀνδραποδίζεσθαι δέοι Ἑλληνίδας
πόλεις, ἀλλὰ σωφρονίζειν. εἰ δὲ τοὺς ἁμαρτάνοντας, ἔφη, ἡμῶν αὐτῶν ἀφανιοῦμεν, ὁρᾶν χρή, μὴ
οὐδ' ἕξομεν μεθ' ὅτου τῶν βαρβάρων κρατήσομεν.
7 Εἰ δ' αὖ καλὸν καὶ μισοπέρσην εἶναι, ὅτι καὶ
ὁ πάλαι ἐξεστράτευσεν ὡς δουλωσόμενος τὴν
Ἑλλάδα καὶ ὁ νῦν συμμαχεῖ μὲν τούτοις, μεθ'
ὁποτέρων ἂν οἴηται μείζω βλάψειν, δωρεῖται δ'
ἐκείνοις, οὓς ἂν νομίζῃ λαβόντας πλεῖστα κακὰ
τοὺς Ἕλληνας ποιήσειν, εἰρήνην δὲ συμπράττει,
ἐξ ἧς ἂν ἡγῆται μάλιστα ἡμᾶς ἀλλήλοις πολε-
μήσειν· ὁρῶσι μὲν οὖν ἅπαντες ταῦτα· ἐπεμελήθη
δέ τις ἄλλως πώποτε πλὴν Ἀγησίλαος, ἢ ὅπως

---

[1] σου is added from Priscian 2 p. 188 : it is not in S.'s text.

mission to the laws, the fatherland would always prosper and that she would be strong when the Greeks were prudent.

Again, if it is honourable in one who is a Greek 4 to be a friend to the Greeks, what other general has the world seen unwilling to take a city when he thought that it would be sacked, or who looked on victory in a war against Greeks as a disaster? Now 5 when a report reached Agesilaus that eight Lacedaemonians and near ten thousand of the enemy had fallen at the battle of Corinth, instead of showing pleasure, he actually exclaimed : " Alas for thee, Hellas ! those who now lie dead were enough to defeat all the barbarians in battle had they lived !" And when the Corinthian exiles told him that the 6 city was about to be surrendered to them and pointed to the engines with which they were confident of taking the walls, he would not make an assault, declaring that Greek cities ought not to be enslaved, but chastened. " And if," he added, " we are going to annihilate the erring members of our own race, let us beware lest we lack men to help in the conquest of the barbarians."

Or again, if it is honourable to hate the Persian 7 because in old days he set out to enslave Greece, and now allies himself with that side which offers him the prospect of working the greater mischief, makes gifts to those who, as he believes, will injure the Greeks most in return, negotiates the peace that he thinks most certain to produce war among us— well, everyone can see these things, but who except Agesilaus has ever striven either to bring about

---

¹ ἂν is added by Richards : it is not in S.'s text.

φῦλόν τι ἀποστήσεται τοῦ Πέρσου ἢ ὅπως τὸ
ἀποστὰν μὴ ἀπόληται ἢ τὸ παράπαν ὡς καὶ
βασιλεὺς κακὰ ἔχων μὴ δυνήσεται τοῖς Ἕλλησι
πράγματα παρέχειν; ὃς καὶ πολεμούσης τῆς
πατρίδος πρὸς Ἕλληνας ὅμως τοῦ κοινοῦ ἀγαθοῦ
τῇ Ἑλλάδι οὐκ ἠμέλησεν, ἀλλ' ἐξέπλευσεν ὅ τι
δύναιτο κακὸν ποιήσων τὸν βάρβαρον.

VIII. Ἀλλὰ μὴν ἄξιόν γε αὐτοῦ καὶ τὸ εὔχαρι
μὴ σιωπᾶσθαι· ᾧ γε ὑπαρχούσης μὲν τιμῆς, πα-
ρούσης δὲ δυνάμεως, πρὸς δὲ τούτοις βασιλείας,
καὶ ταύτης οὐκ ἐπιβουλευομένης ἀλλ' ἀγαπω-
μένης, τὸ μὲν μεγάλαυχον οὐκ ἂν εἶδέ τις, τὸ
δὲ φιλόστοργον καὶ θεραπευτικὸν τῶν φίλων καὶ
2 μὴ ζητῶν κατενόησεν ἄν. καὶ μὴν μετεῖχε μὲν
ἥδιστα παιδικῶν λόγων, συνεσπούδαζε δὲ πᾶν
ὅ τι δέοι φίλοις. διὰ δὲ τὸ εὔελπις καὶ εὔθυμος
καὶ ἀεὶ ἱλαρὸς εἶναι πολλοὺς ἐποίει μὴ τοῦ
διαπράξασθαί τι μόνον ἕνεκα πλησιάζειν, ἀλλὰ
καὶ τοῦ ἥδιον διημερεύειν. ἥκιστα δ' ὢν οἷος
μεγαληγορεῖν ὅμως τῶν ἐπαινούντων αὐτοὺς οὐ
βαρέως ἤκουεν, ἡγούμενος βλάπτειν οὐδὲν αὐτούς,
3 ὑπισχνεῖσθαι δὲ ἄνδρας ἀγαθοὺς ἔσεσθαι. ἀλλὰ
μὴν καὶ τῇ μεγαλογνωμοσύνῃ γε ὡς εὐκαίρως
ἐχρῆτο, οὐ παραλειπτέον. ἐκεῖνος γάρ, ὅτ' ἦλθεν
αὐτῷ ἐπιστολὴ παρὰ βασιλέως, ἣν ὁ μετὰ Καλλέα
τοῦ Λακεδαιμονίου Πέρσης ἤνεγκε, περὶ ξενίας τε
καὶ φιλίας αὐτοῦ, ταύτην μὲν οὐκ ἐδέξατο, τῷ δὲ
φέροντι εἶπεν ἀπαγγεῖλαι βασιλεῖ, ὡς ἰδίᾳ μὲν
πρὸς αὐτὸν οὐδὲν δέοι ἐπιστολὰς πέμπειν, ἢν δὲ

the revolt of a tribe from the Persian, or to save a revolting tribe from destruction, or by some means or other to involve the Great King in trouble so that he will be unable to annoy the Greeks? Nay, when his fatherland was actually at war with Greeks, he did not neglect the common good of Greece, but went out with a fleet to do what harm he could to the barbarian.

VIII. Another quality that should not go unrecorded is his urbanity. For although he held honour in fee, and had power at his beck, and to these added sovereignty—sovereignty not plotted against but regarded with affection—yet no traces of arrogance could have been detected in him, whereas signs of a fatherly affection and readiness to serve his friends, even if unsought, were evident. He 2 delighted, moreover, to take his part in light talk, yet he showed an eager sympathy with friends in all their serious concerns. Thanks to his optimism, good humour, and cheerfulness he was a centre of attraction to many, who came not merely for purposes of business, but to pass the day more pleasantly. Little inclined to boastfulness himself, he heard without annoyance the self-praise of others, thinking that, by indulging in it, they did no harm and gave earnest of high endeavour. On the other hand, 3 one must not omit a reference to the dignity that he showed on appropriate occasions. Thus, when the Persian envoy who came with Calleas, the Lacedaemonian, handed him a letter from the Great King containing offers of friendship and hospitality, he declined to accept it. "Tell his Majesty," he said to the bearer, "that there is no need for him to send me private letters, but, if he

φίλος τῇ Λακεδαίμονι καὶ τῇ Ἑλλάδι εὔνους ὢν
φαίνηται, ὅτι καὶ αὐτὸς φίλος ἀνὰ κράτος αὐτῷ
ἔσοιτο· ἢν μέντοι, ἔφη, ἐπιβουλεύων ἁλίσκηται,
μηδ' ἂν πάνυ πολλὰς ἐπιστολὰς δέχωμαι, φίλον

4 ἕξειν με οἴεσθω. ἐγὼ οὖν καὶ τοῦτο ἐπαινῶ
Ἀγησιλάου, τὸ πρὸς τὸ ἀρέσκειν τοῖς Ἕλλησιν
ὑπεριδεῖν τὴν βασιλέως ξενίαν. ἄγαμαι δὲ κἀκεῖνο, ὅτι οὐχ ὁπότερος πλείω τε χρήματα ἔχοι
καὶ πλειόνων ἄρχοι, τούτῳ ἡγήσατο μεῖζον
φρονητέον εἶναι, ἀλλ' ὁπότερος αὐτός τε ἀμείνων
εἴη καὶ ἀμεινόνων ἡγοῖτο.

5 Ἐπαινῶ δὲ κἀκεῖνο τῆς προνοίας αὐτοῦ, ὅτι
νομίζων ἀγαθὸν τῇ Ἑλλάδι ἀφίστασθαι τοῦ
βασιλέως ὡς πλείστους σατράπας οὐκ ἐκρατήθη
οὔθ' ὑπὸ δώρων οὔθ' ὑπὸ τῆς βασιλέως ῥώμης
ἐθελῆσαι ξενωθῆναι αὐτῷ, ἀλλ' ἐφυλάξατο μὴ
ἄπιστος γενέσθαι τοῖς ἀφίστασθαι βουλομένοις.

6 Ἐκεῖνό γε μὴν αὐτοῦ τίς οὐκ ἂν ἀγασθείη;
ὁ μὲν γὰρ Πέρσης νομίζων, ἢν χρήματα πλεῖστα
ἔχῃ, πάνθ' ὑφ' ἑαυτῷ ποιήσεσθαι, διὰ τοῦτο πᾶν
μὲν τὸ ἐν ἀνθρώποις χρυσίον, πᾶν δὲ τὸ ἀργύριον,
πάντα δὲ τὰ πολυτελέστατα ἐπειρᾶτο πρὸς
ἑαυτὸν ἀθροίζειν. ὁ δὲ οὕτως ἀντεσκευάσατο
τὸν οἶκον, ὥστε τούτων μηδενὸς προσδεῖσθαι.

7 εἰ δέ τις ταῦτα ἀπιστεῖ, ἰδέτω μέν, οἷα οἰκία
ἤρκει αὐτῷ, θεασάσθω δὲ τὰς θύρας αὐτοῦ·
εἰκάσειε γὰρ ἄν τις ἔτι ταύτας ἐκείνας εἶναι,
ὥσπερ Ἀριστόδημος ὁ Ἡρακλέους, ὅτε κατῆλθε,

---

1 Aristodemus was great-grandson of Hyllus, son of
Heracles. Xenophon follows the Lacedaemonian account,
according to which Aristodemus himself was leader at the
time when the Lacedaemonians obtained Sparta (Herodotus,

gives proof of friendship for Lacedaemon, and good-will towards Greece, I on my part will be his friend with all my heart. But if he is found plotting against them, let him not hope to have a friend in me, however many letters I may receive." In this 4 contempt for the king's hospitality, as nothing in comparison with the approval of the Greeks, I find one more reason for praising Agesilaus. Admirable too was his opinion that it is not for the ruler with the deeper coffers and the longer roll of subjects to set himself above his rival, but for him who is the better leader of the better people.

Again, an instance of his foresight that I find 5 worthy of praise is this: believing it to be good for Greece that as many satraps as possible should revolt from the king, he was not prevailed on either by gifts or by the king's power to accept his hospitality, but was careful not to give cause to those who wanted to revolt for mistrusting him.

There is yet another side of his character that 6 everyone must admire. It was the belief of the Persian king that by possessing himself of colossal wealth, he would put all things in subjection to himself. In this belief he tried to engross all the gold, all the silver and all the most costly things in the world. Agesilaus, on the contrary, adopted such a simple style in his home that he needed none of these things. If anyone doubts this, let him 7 mark what sort of a house contented him, and in particular, let him look at the doors: one might imagine that they were the very doors that Aristo-demus, the descendant of Heracles[1] set up with his

vi, 52). His sons, Eurysthenes and Procles, became the first joint-kings.

λαβὼν ἐπεστήσατο· πειράσθω δὲ θεάσασθαι τὴν
ἔνδον κατασκευήν, ἐννοησάτω δέ, ὡς ἐθοίναζεν
ἐν ταῖς θυσίαις, ἀκουσάτω δέ, ὡς ἐπὶ πολιτικοῦ
καννάθρου κατῄει εἰς Ἀμύκλας ἡ θυγάτηρ αὐτοῦ.
8 τοιγαροῦν οὕτως ἐφαρμόσας τὰς δαπάνας ταῖς
προσόδοις οὐδὲν ἠναγκάζετο χρημάτων ἕνεκα
ἄδικον πράττειν. καίτοι καλὸν μὲν δοκεῖ εἶναι
τείχη ἀνάλωτα κτᾶσθαι ὑπὸ πολεμίων· πολὺ
μέντοι ἔγωγε κάλλιον κρίνω τὸ τὴν αὑτοῦ ψυχὴν
ἀνάλωτον κατασκευάσαι καὶ ὑπὸ χρημάτων καὶ
ὑπὸ ἡδονῶν καὶ ὑπὸ φόβου.

IX. Ἀλλὰ μὴν ἐρῶ γε, ὡς καὶ τὸν τρόπον
ὑπεστήσατο τῇ τοῦ Πέρσου ἀλαζονείᾳ. πρῶτον
μὲν γὰρ ὁ μὲν τῷ σπανίως ὁρᾶσθαι ἐσεμνύνετο,
Ἀγησίλαος δὲ τῷ ἀεὶ ἐμφανὴς εἶναι ἠγάλλετο,
νομίζων αἰσχρουργίᾳ μὲν τὸ ἀφανίζεσθαι πρέπειν,
τῷ δὲ εἰς κάλλος βίῳ τὸ φῶς μᾶλλον κόσμον
2 παρέχειν. ἔπειτα δὲ ὁ μὲν τῷ δυσπρόσοδος εἶναι
ἐσεμνύνετο, ὁ δὲ τῷ πᾶσιν εὐπρόσοδος εἶναι
ἔχαιρε· καὶ ὁ μὲν ἡβρύνετο τῷ βραδέως δια-
πράττειν, ὁ δὲ τότε μάλιστα ἔχαιρεν, ὁπότε
τάχιστα τυχόντας ὧν δέοιντο ἀποπέμποι.
3 Ἀλλὰ μὴν καὶ τὴν εὐπάθειαν ὅσῳ ῥάονα
καὶ εὐπορωτέραν Ἀγησίλαος ἐπετήδευσεν, ἄξιον
κατανοῆσαι. τῷ μὲν γὰρ Πέρσῃ πᾶσαν γῆν
περιέρχονται μαστεύοντες, τί ἂν ἡδέως πίοι,
μυρίοι δὲ τεχνῶνται, τί ἂν ἡδέως φάγοι· ὅπως
γε μὴν καταδάρθοι, οὐδ᾽ ἂν εἴποι τις ὅσα πραγματεύονται. Ἀγησίλαος δὲ διὰ τὸ φιλόπονος

own hands in the days of his home-coming. Let him try to picture the scene within; note how he entertained on days of sacrifice, hear how his daughter used to go down to Amyclae [1] in a public car. And 8 so, thanks to this nice adjustment of his expenditure to his income, he was never compelled to commit an act of injustice for the sake of money. Doubtless it is thought noble to build oneself fortresses impregnable to an enemy: but in my judgment it is far nobler to fortify one's own soul against all the assaults of lucre, of pleasure, and of fear.

IX. I will next point out the contrast between his behaviour and the imposture of the Persian king. In the first place the Persian thought his dignity required that he should be seldom seen: Agesilaus delighted to be constantly visible, believing that, whereas secrecy was becoming to an ugly career, the light shed lustre on a life of noble purpose. In the 2 second place, the one prided himself on being difficult of approach: the other was glad to make himself accessible to all. And the one affected tardiness in negotiation: the other was best pleased when he could dismiss his suitors quickly with their requests granted.

In the matter of personal comfort, moreover, it is 3 worth noticing how much simpler and how much more easily satisfied were the tastes of Agesilaus. The Persian king has vintners scouring every land to find some drink that will tickle his palate; an army of cooks contrives dishes for his delight; and the trouble his lackeys take that he may sleep is indescribable. But Agesilaus, thanks to his love of

---

[1] To the feast of Hyacinthus; see c. ii. 17.

εἶναι πᾶν μὲν τὸ παρὸν ἡδέως ἔπινε, πᾶν δὲ τὸ
συντυχὸν ἡδέως ἤσθιεν· εἰς δὲ τὸ ἀσμένως
4 κοιμηθῆναι πᾶς τόπος ἱκανὸς ἦν αὐτῷ. καὶ
ταῦτα οὐ μόνον πράττων ἔχαιρεν, ἀλλὰ καὶ
ἐνθυμούμενος ἠγάλλετο, ὅτι αὐτὸς μὲν ἐν μέσαις
ταῖς εὐφροσύναις ἀναστρέφοιτο, τὸν δὲ βάρβαρον
ἑώρα, εἰ μέλλοι ἀλύπως βιώσεσθαι, συνελκυστέον
αὐτῷ ἀπὸ περάτων τῆς γῆς τὰ τέρψοντα.
5 εὔφραινε δὲ αὐτὸν καὶ τάδε, ὅτι αὐτὸς μὲν ᾔδει
τῇ τῶν θεῶν κατασκευῇ δυνάμενος ἀλύπως
χρῆσθαι, τὸν δὲ ἑώρα φεύγοντα μὲν θάλπη,
φεύγοντα δὲ ψύχη δι’ ἀσθένειαν ψυχῆς, οὐκ
ἀνδρῶν ἀγαθῶν, ἀλλὰ θηρίων τῶν ἀσθενεστάτων
βίον μιμούμενον.
6 Ἐκεῖνό γε μὴν πῶς οὐ καλὸν καὶ μεγαλόγνωμον,
τὸ αὐτὸν μὲν ἀνδρὸς ἔργοις καὶ κτήμασι κοσμεῖν
τὸν ἑαυτοῦ οἶκον, κύνας τε πολλοὺς θηρευτὰς
καὶ ἵππους πολεμιστηρίους τρέφοντα, Κυνίσκαν
δὲ ἀδελφὴν οὖσαν πεῖσαι ἁρματοτροφεῖν καὶ
ἐπιδεῖξαι νικώσης αὐτῆς, ὅτι τὸ θρέμμα τοῦτο
οὐκ ἀνδραγαθίας, ἀλλὰ πλούτου ἐπίδειγμά ἐστι.
7 τόδε γε μὴν πῶς οὐ σαφῶς πρὸς τὸ γενναῖον
ἔγνω, ὅτι ἅρματι μὲν νικήσας τοὺς ἰδιώτας οὐδὲν
ὀνομαστότερος ἂν γένοιτο, εἰ δὲ φίλην μὲν πάντων
μάλιστα τὴν πόλιν ἔχοι, πλείστους δὲ φίλους
καὶ ἀρίστους ἀνὰ πᾶσαν τὴν γῆν κεκτῇτο, νικῴη
δὲ τὴν μὲν πατρίδα καὶ τοὺς ἑταίρους εὐεργετῶν,
τοὺς δὲ ἀντιπάλους τιμωρούμενος, ὅτι ὄντως ἂν
εἴη νικηφόρος τῶν καλλίστων καὶ μεγαλοπρε-
πεστάτων ἀγωνισμάτων καὶ ὀνομαστότατος καὶ
ζῶν καὶ τελευτήσας γένοιτ’ ἄν;
X. Ἐγὼ μὲν οὖν τὰ τοιαῦτα ἐπαινῶ Ἀγησίλαον.

toil, enjoyed any drink that was at hand and any
food that came his way; and any place was good
enough to give him soft repose.   Nor was he happy 4
only in this behaviour : he was also proud to reflect
that, while he was surrounded with good cheer, he
saw the barbarian constrained to draw from the ends
of the world the material for his enjoyment, if he
would live without discomfort.   And it cheered 5
his heart to know that he could accommodate
himself to the divine ordering of the world, whereas
he saw his rival shunning heat and shunning
cold through weakness of character, imitating the
life, not of brave men, but of the weakest of the
brutes.

Surely, too, he did what was seemly and dignified 6
when he adorned his own estate with works and
possessions worthy of a man, keeping many hounds
and war horses, but persuaded his sister Cynisca to
breed chariot horses, and showed by her victory that
such a stud marks the owner as a person of wealth,
but not necessarily of merit.[1]   How clearly his true 7
nobility comes out in his opinion that a victory in
the chariot race over private citizens would add
not a whit to his renown ; but if he held the first
place in the affection of the people, gained the most
friends and best all over the world, outstripped all
others in serving his fatherland and his comrades
and in punishing his adversaries, then he would be
victor in the noblest and most splendid contests, and
would gain high renown both in life and after
death.

X. Such, then, are the qualities for which I praise

---

[1] *Hiero*, xi. 5.

ταῦτα γὰρ οὐχ ὥσπερ εἰ θησαυρῷ τις ἐντύχοι,
πλουσιώτερος μὲν ἂν εἴη, οἰκονομικώτερος δ᾿
οὐδὲν ἄν, καὶ εἰ νόσου δὲ πολεμίοις ἐμπεσούσης
κρατήσειεν, εὐτυχέστερος μὲν ἂν εἴη, στρατηγι-
κώτερος δὲ οὐδὲν ἄν· ὁ δὲ καρτερίᾳ μὲν πρωτεύων,
ἔνθα πονεῖν καιρός, ἀλκῇ δέ, ὅπου ἀνδρείας ἀγών,
γνώμῃ δέ, ὅπου βουλῆς ἔργον, οὗτος ἔμοιγε δοκεῖ
δικαίως ἀνὴρ ἀγαθὸς παντελῶς ἂν νομίζεσθαι.
2 εἰ δὲ καλὸν εὕρημα ἀνθρώποις στάθμη καὶ κανὼν
πρὸς τὸ ἀγαθὰ ἐργάζεσθαι, καλὸν ἄν μοι δοκεῖ
ἡ Ἀγησιλάου ἀρετὴ παράδειγμα γενέσθαι τοῖς
ἀνδραγαθίαν ἀσκεῖν βουλομένοις. τίς γὰρ ἂν
ἢ θεοσεβῆ μιμούμενος ἀνόσιος γένοιτο ἢ δίκαιον
ἄδικος ἢ σώφρονα ὑβριστὴς ἢ ἐγκρατῆ ἀκρατής;
καὶ γὰρ δὴ οὐχ οὕτως ἐπὶ τῷ ἄλλων βασιλεύειν
ὡς ἐπὶ τῷ ἑαυτοῦ ἄρχειν ἐμεγαλύνετο οὐδ᾿ ἐπὶ
τῷ πρὸς τοὺς πολεμίους, ἀλλ᾿ ἐπὶ τῷ πρὸς πᾶσαν
ἀρετὴν ἡγεῖσθαι τοῖς πολίταις.
3 Ἀλλὰ γὰρ μὴ ὅτι τετελευτηκὼς ἐπαινεῖται,
τούτου ἕνεκα θρῆνόν τις τοῦτον τὸν λόγον νομισάτω, ἀλλὰ πολὺ μᾶλλον ἐγκώμιον. πρῶτον
μὲν γὰρ ἅπερ ζῶν ἤκουε, ταῦτα καὶ νῦν λέγεται
περὶ αὐτοῦ. ἔπειτα δὲ τί καὶ πλέον θρήνου
ἄπεστιν ἢ βίος τε εὐκλεὴς καὶ θάνατος ὡραῖος;
ἐγκωμίων δὲ τί ἀξιώτερον ἢ νῖκαί τε αἱ κάλλισται
4 καὶ ἔργα τὰ πλείστου ἄξια; δικαίως δ᾿ ἂν
ἐκεῖνός γε μακαρίζοιτο, ὃς εὐθὺς μὲν ἐκ παιδὸς
ἐρασθεὶς τοῦ εὐκλεὴς γενέσθαι ἔτυχε τούτου
μάλιστα τῶν καθ᾿ ἑαυτόν· φιλοτιμότατος δὲ

---

[1] The reference is to the ceremonial hymns sung at or
after funerals, which of course contained much that would
not have been said or sung in the hero's life-time.

Agesilaus. These are the marks that distinguish him, say, from the man who, lighting on a treasure, becomes wealthier but not wiser in business, or from the man who wins victory through an outbreak of sickness among the enemy, and adds to his success but not to his knowledge of strategy. The man who is foremost in endurance when the hour comes for toil, in valour when the contest calls for courage, in wisdom when the need is for counsel—he is the man, I think, who may fairly be regarded as the perfect embodiment of goodness. If line and rule 2 are a noble discovery of man as aids to the production of good work, I think that the virtue of Agesilaus may well stand as a noble example for those to follow who wish to make moral goodness a habit. For who that imitates a pious, a just, a sober, a self-controlled man, can come to be unrighteous, unjust, violent, wanton? In point of fact, Agesilaus prided himself less on reigning over others than on ruling himself, less on leading the people against their enemies than on guiding them to all virtue.

However, let it not be thought, because one whose 3 life is ended is the theme of my praise, that these words are meant for a funeral dirge.[1] They are far more truly the language of eulogy. In the first place the words now applied to him are the very same that he heard in his lifetime. And, in the second place, what theme is less appropriate to a dirge than a life of fame and a death well-timed? What more worthy of eulogies than victories most glorious and deeds of sovereign worth? Justly may 4 the man be counted blessed who was in love with glory from early youth and won more of it than any man of his age; who, being by nature very covetous

πεφυκὼς ἀήττητος διετέλεσεν, ἐπεὶ βασιλεὺς ἐγέ-
νετο· ἀφικόμενος δὲ ἐπὶ τὸ μήκιστον ἀνθρωπίνου
αἰῶνος ἀναμάρτητος ἐτελεύτησε καὶ περὶ τούτους,
ὧν ἡγεῖτο, καὶ πρὸς ἐκείνους, οἷς ἐπολέμει.

XI. Βούλομαι δὲ καὶ ἐν κεφαλαίοις ἐπανελθεῖν
τὴν ἀρετὴν αὐτοῦ, ὡς ἂν ὁ ἔπαινος εὐμνημονε-
στέρως ἔχῃ.

Ἀγησίλαος ἱερὰ μὲν καὶ τὰ ἐν τοῖς πολεμίοις
ἐσέβετο, ἡγούμενος τοὺς θεοὺς οὐχ ἧττον ἐν τῇ
πολεμίᾳ χρῆναι ἢ ἐν τῇ φιλίᾳ συμμάχους
ποιεῖσθαι.

Ἱκέτας δὲ θεῶν οὐδὲ ἐχθροὺς ἐβιάζετο, νομίζων
ἄλογον εἶναι τοὺς μὲν ἐξ ἱερῶν κλέπτοντας
ἱεροσύλους καλεῖν, τοὺς δὲ βωμῶν ἱκέτας ἀπο-
σπῶντας εὐσεβεῖς ἡγεῖσθαι.

2 Ἐκεῖνός γε μὴν ὑμνῶν οὔποτ' ἔληγεν, ὡς τοὺς
θεοὺς οἴοιτο οὐδὲν ἧττον ὁσίοις ἔργοις ἢ ἁγνοῖς
ἱεροῖς ἥδεσθαι.

Ἀλλὰ μὴν καὶ ὁπότε εὐτυχοίη, οὐκ ἀνθρώπων
ὑπερεφρόνει, ἀλλὰ θεοῖς χάριν ᾔδει. καὶ θαρρῶν
πλείονα ἔθυεν ἢ ὀκνῶν ηὔχετο.

Εἴθιστο δὲ φοβούμενος μὲν ἱλαρὸς φαίνεσθαι,
εὐτυχῶν δὲ πρᾷος εἶναι.

3 Τῶν γε μὴν φίλων οὐ τοὺς δυνατωτάτους,
ἀλλὰ τοὺς προθυμοτάτους μάλιστα ἠσπάζετο.

Ἐμίσει δὲ οὐκ εἴ τις κακῶς πάσχων ἠμύνετο,
ἀλλ' εἴ τις εὐεργετούμενος ἀχάριστος φαίνοιτο.

Ἔχαιρε δὲ τοὺς μὲν αἰσχροκερδεῖς πένητας
ὁρῶν, τοὺς δὲ δικαίους πλουσίους ποιῶν, βουλόμενος τὴν δικαιοσύνην τῆς ἀδικίας κερδαλεωτέραν
καθιστάναι.

of honour, never once knew defeat from the day
that he became a king; who, after living to the
utmost limit of human life, died without one blunder
to his account, either concerning the men whom he
led or in dealing with those on whom he made
war.

XI. I propose to go through the story of his virtue
again, and to summarize it, in order that the praise
of it may be more easily remembered.

Agesilaus reverenced holy places even when they
belonged to an enemy, thinking that he ought to
make allies of the gods no less in hostile than in
friendly countries.

To suppliants of the gods, even if his foes, he did
no violence, believing it unreasonable to call robbers
of temples sacrilegious and yet to consider those who
dragged suppliants from altars pious men.

My hero never failed to dwell on his opinion 2
that the gods have pleasure in righteous deeds no
less than in holy temples.

In the hour of success he was not puffed up with
pride, but gave thanks to the gods. He offered
more sacrifices when confident than prayers when in
doubt.

He was wont to look cheerful when in fear, and
to be humble when successful.

Of his friends he welcomed most heartily not the 3
most powerful, but the most devoted.

He hated not the man who defended himself
when injured, but such as showed no gratitude for
a favour.

He rejoiced to see the avaricious poor and to
enrich the upright, desiring to render right more
profitable than wrong.

XENOPHON

4 Ἤσκει δὲ ἐξομιλεῖν μὲν παντοδαποῖς, χρῆσθαι
δὲ τοῖς ἀγαθοῖς.

Ὁπότε δὲ ψεγόντων ἢ ἐπαινούντων τινὰς
ἀκούοι, οὐχ ἧττον ᾤετο καταμανθάνειν τοὺς τῶν
λεγόντων τρόπους ἢ περὶ ὧν λέγοιεν.

Καὶ τοὺς μὲν ὑπὸ φίλων ἐξαπατωμένους οὐκ
ἔψεγε, τοὺς δὲ ὑπὸ πολεμίων πάμπαν κατε-
μέμφετο καὶ τὸ μὲν ἀπιστοῦντας ἐξαπατᾶν σοφὸν
ἔκρινε, τὸ δὲ πιστεύοντας ἀνόσιον.

5 Ἐπαινούμενος δὲ ἔχαιρεν ὑπὸ τῶν καὶ ψέγειν
ἐθελόντων τὰ μὴ ἀρεστὰ καὶ τῶν παρρησιαζομένων
οὐδένα ἤχθραινε, τοὺς δὲ κρυψίνους ὥσπερ
ἐνέδρας ἐφυλάττετο.

Τούς γε μὴν διαβόλους μᾶλλον ἢ τοὺς κλέπτας
ἐμίσει, μείζω ζημίαν ἡγούμενος φίλων ἢ χρημάτων
6 στερίσκεσθαι. καὶ τὰς μὲν τῶν ἰδιωτῶν ἁμαρτίας
πράως ἔφερε, τὰς δὲ τῶν ἀρχόντων μεγάλας ἦγε,
κρίνων τοὺς μὲν ὀλίγα, τοὺς δὲ πολλὰ κακῶς
διατιθέναι.

Τῇ δὲ βασιλείᾳ προσήκειν ἐνόμιζεν οὐ ῥᾳδι-
ουργίαν, ἀλλὰ καλοκἀγαθίαν.

7 Καὶ τοῦ μὲν σώματος εἰκόνα στήσασθαι ἀπέσ-
χετο, πολλῶν αὐτῷ τοῦτο δωρεῖσθαι θελόντων,
τῆς δὲ ψυχῆς οὐδέποτε ἐπαύετο μνημεῖα διαπο-
νούμενος, ἡγούμενος τὸ μὲν ἀνδριαντοποιῶν, τὸ
δὲ αὐτοῦ ἔργον εἶναι καὶ τὸ μὲν πλουσίων, τὸ δὲ
τῶν ἀγαθῶν.

8 Χρήμασί γε μὴν οὐ μόνον δικαίως, ἀλλὰ καὶ
ἐλευθερίως ἐχρῆτο, τῷ μὲν δικαίῳ ἀρκεῖν ἡγούμενος τὸ ἐᾶν τὰ ἀλλότρια, τῷ δὲ ἐλευθερίῳ καὶ
τῶν ἑαυτοῦ προσωφελητέον εἶναι.

It was his habit to associate with all sorts and con- 4
ditions of men, but to be intimate with the good.

Whenever he heard men praise or blame others,
he thought that he gained as much insight into
the character of the critics as of the persons they
criticized.

If friends proved deceivers he forebore to blame
their victims, but he heaped reproaches on those who
let an enemy deceive them; and he pronounced
deception clever or wicked according as it was
practised on the suspicious or the confiding.

The praise of those who were prepared to censure 5
faults they disapproved was pleasing to him, and he
never resented candour, but avoided dissimulation
like a snare.

Slanderers he hated more than thieves, deeming
loss of friends graver than loss of money. The mis- 6
takes of private persons he judged leniently, because
few interests suffer by their incompetence; but the
errors of rulers he treated as serious, since they lead
to many troubles.

Kingship, he held, demands not indolence, but
manly virtue.

He would not allow a statue of himself to be set 7
up, though many wanted to give him one, but on
memorials of his mind he laboured unceasingly,
thinking the one to be the sculptor's work, the
other his own, the one appropriate to the rich, the
other to the good.

In the use of money he was not only just but 8
generous, thinking that a just man may be content
to leave other men's money alone, but the generous
man is required also to spend his own in the
service of others.

Ἀεὶ δὲ δεισιδαίμων ἦν, νομίζων τοὺς μὲν καλῶς ζῶντας οὔπω εὐδαίμονας, τοὺς δὲ εὐκλεῶς τετελευτηκότας ἤδη μακαρίους.

9 Μείζω δὲ συμφορὰν ἔκρινε τὸ γιγνώσκοντα ἢ ἀγνοοῦντα ἀμελεῖν τῶν ἀγαθῶν.

Δόξης δὲ οὐδεμιᾶς ἤρα, ἧς οὐκ ἐξεπόνει τὰ ἴδια.

Μετ᾽ ὀλίγων δέ μοι ἐδόκει ἀνθρώπων οὐ καρτερίαν τὴν ἀρετήν, ἀλλ᾽ εὐπάθειαν νομίζειν· ἐπαινούμενος γοῦν ἔχαιρε μᾶλλον ἢ χρήματα κτώμενος.

Ἀλλὰ μὴν ἀνδρείαν γε τὸ πλέον μετ᾽ εὐβουλίας ἢ μετὰ κινδύνων ἐπεδείκνυτο καὶ σοφίαν ἔργῳ μᾶλλον ἢ λόγοις ἤσκει.

10 Πρᾳότατός γε μὴν φίλοις ὢν ἐχθροῖς φοβερώτατος ἦν· καὶ πόνοις μάλιστα ἀντέχων ἑταίροις ἥδιστα ὑπεῖκε, καλῶν ἔργων μᾶλλον ἢ τῶν καλῶν σωμάτων ἐπιθυμῶν.

Ἔν γε μὴν ταῖς εὐπραξίαις σωφρονεῖν ἐπιστάμενος ἐν τοῖς δεινοῖς εὐθαρσὴς ἐδύνατο εἶναι.

11 Καὶ τὸ εὔχαρι οὐ σκώμμασιν, ἀλλὰ τρόπῳ ἐπετήδευε καὶ τῷ μεγαλόφρονι οὐ σὺν ὕβρει, ἀλλὰ σὺν γνώμῃ ἐχρῆτο· τῶν γοῦν ὑπεραύχων καταφρονῶν τῶν μετρίων ταπεινότερος ἦν. καὶ γὰρ ἐκαλλωπίζετο τῇ μὲν ἀμφὶ τὸ σῶμα φαυλότητι, τῷ δ᾽ ἀμφὶ τὸ στράτευμα κόσμῳ, τῷ δ᾽ αὐτὸς μὲν ὡς ἐλαχίστων δεῖσθαι, τοὺς δὲ φίλους 12 ὡς πλεῖστα ὠφελεῖν. πρὸς δὲ τούτοις βαρύτατος μὲν ἀνταγωνιστὴς ἦν, κουφότατος δὲ κρατήσας, ἐχθροῖς μὲν δυσεξαπάτητος, φίλοις δὲ εὐπαραπειστότατος.

He was ever god-fearing, believing that they who are living life well are not yet happy, but only they who have died gloriously are blessed.

He held it a greater calamity to neglect that 9 which is good knowingly than in ignorance.

No fame attracted him unless he did the right work to achieve it.

He seemed to me one of the few men who count virtue not a task to be endured but a comfort to be enjoyed. At any rate praise gave him more pleasure than money.

Courage, as he displayed it, was joined with prudence rather than boldness, and wisdom he cultivated more by action than in words.

Very gentle with friends, he was very formidable 10 to enemies; and while he resisted fatigue obstinately, he yielded most readily to a comrade, though fair deeds appealed more to his heart than fair faces.

To moderation in times of prosperity he added confidence in the midst of danger.

His urbanity found its habitual expression not in 11 jokes but in his manner; and when on his dignity, he was never arrogant, but always reasonable; at least, if he showed his contempt for the haughty, he was humbler than the average man. For he prided himself on the simplicity of his own dress and the splendid equipment of his army, on a strict limitation of his own needs and a boundless generosity to his friends. Added to this, he was the bitterest of 12 adversaries, but the mildest of conquerors; wary with enemies, but very compliant to friends.

Ἀεὶ δὲ τιθεὶς τὰ τῶν φίλων ἀσφαλῶς ἀεὶ
ἀμαυροῦν τὰ τῶν πολεμίων ἔργον εἶχεν.

13 Ἐκεῖνον οἱ μὲν συγγενεῖς φιλοκηδεμόνα ἐκά-
λουν, οἱ δὲ χρώμενοι ἀπροφάσιστον, οἱ δ᾽
ὑπουργήσαντές τι μνήμονα, οἱ δ᾽ ἀδικούμενοι
ἐπίκουρον, οἵ γε μὴν συγκινδυνεύοντες μετὰ
θεοὺς σωτῆρα.

14 Δοκεῖ δ᾽ ἔμοιγε καὶ τόδε μόνος ἀνθρώπων
ἐπιδεῖξαι, ὅτι ἡ μὲν τοῦ σώματος ἰσχὺς γηράσκει,
ἡ δὲ τῆς ψυχῆς ῥώμη τῶν ἀγαθῶν ἀνδρῶν
ἀγήρατός ἐστιν. ἐκεῖνος γοῦν οὐκ ἀπεῖπε μεγάλης
καὶ καλῆς ἐφιέμενος δόξης,[1] εἰ καὶ μὴ τὸ σῶμα
φέρειν ἠδύνατο τὴν τῆς ψυχῆς αὐτοῦ ῥώμην.

15 τοιγαροῦν ποίας οὐ νεότητος κρεῖττον τὸ ἐκείνου
γῆρας ἐφάνη; τίς μὲν γὰρ τοῖς ἐχθροῖς ἀκμάζων
οὕτω φοβερὸς ἦν ὡς Ἀγησίλαος τὸ μήκιστον
τοῦ αἰῶνος ἔχων; τίνος δ᾽ ἐκποδὼν γενομένου
μᾶλλον ἥσθησαν οἱ πολέμιοι ἢ Ἀγησιλάου
καίπερ γηραιοῦ τελευτήσαντος; τίς δὲ συμμάχοις
θάρρος παρέσχεν ὅσον Ἀγησίλαος καίπερ ἤδη
πρὸς τῷ στόματι τοῦ βίου ὤν; τίνα δὲ νέον οἱ
φίλοι πλέον ἐπόθησαν ἢ Ἀγησίλαον γηραιὸν

16 ἀποθανόντα; οὕτω δὲ τελέως ὁ ἀνὴρ τῇ πατρίδι
ὠφέλιμος ὢν διεγένετο, ὡς καὶ τετελευτηκὼς ἤδη
ἔτι μεγαλείως ὠφελῶν τὴν πόλιν εἰς τὴν ἀίδιον
οἴκησιν κατηγάγετο, μνημεῖα μὲν τῆς ἑαυτοῦ
ἀρετῆς ἀνὰ πᾶσαν τὴν γῆν κτησάμενος, τῆς δὲ
βασιλικῆς ταφῆς ἐν τῇ πατρίδι τυχών.

---

[1] The text is corrupt. δόξης εἰ καὶ μὴ is wanting in A,
which has μεγάλην καὶ καλήν.

While ever ensuring security to his own side, he ever made it his business to bring to nought the designs of his enemy.

By his relatives he was described as "devoted to 13 his family," by his intimates as "an unfailing friend,"[1] by those who served him as "unforgetful," by the oppressed as "a champion," by his comrades in danger as "a saviour second to the gods."

In one respect, I think, he was unique. He 14 proved that, though the bodily strength decays, the vigour of good men's souls is ageless. At any rate, he never wearied in the pursuit of great and noble glory so long as his body could support the vigour of his soul. What man's youth, then, did not 15 seem weaker than his old age? For who in his prime was so formidable to his foes as Agesilaus at the very limit of human life? Whose removal brought such welcome relief to the enemy as the death of Agesilaus, despite his years? Who gave such confidence to allies as Agesilaus, though now on the threshold of death? What young man was more regretted by his friends than Agesilaus, though he died full of years? So complete was the record of 16 his service to his fatherland that it did not end even when he died: he was still a bountiful benefactor of the state when he was brought home to be laid in his eternal resting-place, and, having raised up monuments of his virtue throughout the world, was buried with royal ceremony in his own land.[2]

---

[1] *Hellenica,* **v. v.** 45.
[2] The reference is to the money which Agesilaus had obtained in Egypt, and which was brought to the city with his body. For the burial see *Const. of the Lac.*, end.

CONSTITUTION OF THE
LACEDAEMONIANS

ΞΕΝΟΦΩΝΤΟΣ ΛΑΚΕΔΑΙΜΟΝΙΩΝ ΠΟΛΙΤΕΙΑ

I. Ἀλλ' ἐγὼ ἐννοήσας ποτέ, ὡς ἡ Σπάρτη τῶν ὀλιγανθρωποτάτων πόλεων οὖσα δυνατωτάτη τε καὶ ὀνομαστοτάτη ἐν τῇ Ἑλλάδι ἐφάνη, ἐθαύμασα, ὅτῳ ποτὲ τρόπῳ τοῦτ' ἐγένετο· ἐπεὶ μέντοι κατενόησα τὰ ἐπιτηδεύματα τῶν Σπαρτιατῶν, οὐκέτι ἐθαύμαζον.

2 Λυκοῦργον μέντοι τὸν θέντα αὐτοῖς τοὺς νόμους, οἷς πειθόμενοι ηὐδαιμόνησαν, τοῦτον καὶ θαυμάζω καὶ εἰς τὰ ἔσχατα σοφὸν ἡγοῦμαι. ἐκεῖνος γὰρ οὐ μιμησάμενος τὰς ἄλλας πόλεις, ἀλλὰ καὶ ἐναντία γνοὺς ταῖς πλείσταις προέχουσαν εὐδαιμονίᾳ τὴν πατρίδα ἐπέδειξεν.

3 Αὐτίκα γὰρ περὶ τεκνοποιίας, ἵνα ἐξ ἀρχῆς ἄρξωμαι, οἱ μὲν ἄλλοι τὰς μελλούσας τίκτειν καὶ καλῶς δοκούσας κόρας παιδεύεσθαι καὶ σίτῳ ᾗ ἀνυστὸν μετριωτάτῳ τρέφουσι καὶ ὄψῳ ᾗ δυνατὸν μικροτάτῳ· οἴνου γε μὴν ἢ πάμπαν ἀπεχομένας ἢ ὑδαρεῖ χρωμένας διάγουσιν· ὥσπερ δὲ οἱ πολλοὶ τῶν τὰς τέχνας ἐχόντων ἑδραῖοί εἰσιν, οὕτω καὶ τὰς κόρας οἱ ἄλλοι Ἕλληνες ἠρεμιζούσας ἐριουργεῖν ἀξιοῦσι. τὰς μὲν οὖν οὕτω τρεφομένας πῶς χρὴ προσδοκῆσαι μεγαλεῖον ἄν τι γεννῆσαι;

136

CONSTITUTION OF THE LACEDAEMONIANS

I. It occurred to me one day that Sparta, though among the most thinly populated of states, was evidently the most powerful and most celebrated city in Greece; and I fell to wondering how this could have happened. But when I considered the institutions of the Spartans, I wondered no longer.

Lycurgus, who gave them the laws that they **2** obey, and to which they owe their prosperity, I do regard with wonder; and I think that he reached the utmost limit of wisdom. For it was not by imitating other states, but by devising a system utterly different from that of most others, that he made his country pre-eminently prosperous.

First, to begin at the beginning, I will take the **3** begetting of children.[1] In other states the girls who are destined to become mothers and are brought up in the approved fashion, live on the very plainest fare, with a most meagre allowance of delicacies. Wine is either withheld altogether, or, if allowed them, is diluted with water. The rest of the Greeks expect their girls to imitate the sedentary life that is typical of handicraftsmen—to keep quiet and do wool-work. How, then, is it to be expected that women so brought up will bear fine children?

---

[1] The prose *Constitution of the Lacedaemonians* by Critias began with the same point. See Introduction III.

4 Ὁ δὲ Λυκοῦργος ἐσθῆτας μὲν καὶ δούλας παρέχειν ἱκανὰς ἡγήσατο εἶναι, ταῖς δ᾽ ἐλευθέραις μέγιστον νομίσας εἶναι τὴν τεκνοποιίαν πρῶτον μὲν σωμασκεῖν ἔταξεν οὐδὲν ἧττον τὸ θῆλυ τοῦ ἄρρενος φύλου· ἔπειτα δὲ δρόμου καὶ ἰσχύος, ὥσπερ καὶ τοῖς ἀνδράσιν, οὕτω καὶ ταῖς θηλείαις ἀγῶνας πρὸς ἀλλήλας ἐποίησε, νομίζων ἐξ ἀμφοτέρων ἰσχυρῶν καὶ τὰ ἔκγονα ἐρρωμενέστερα γίγνεσθαι.

5 Ἐπεί γε μὴν γυνὴ πρὸς ἄνδρα ἔλθοι, ὁρῶν τοὺς ἄλλους τὸν πρῶτον τοῦ χρόνου ἀμέτρως ταῖς γυναιξὶ συνόντας, καὶ τούτου τἀναντία ἔγνω· ἔθηκε γὰρ αἰδεῖσθαι μὲν εἰσιόντα ὀφθῆναι, αἰδεῖσθαι δ᾽ ἐξιόντα. οὕτω δὲ συνόντων ποθεινοτέρως μὲν ἀνάγκη σφῶν αὐτῶν ἔχειν, ἐρρωμενέστερα δὲ γίγνεσθαι, εἴ τι βλάστοι, οὕτω μᾶλλον ἢ εἰ 6 διάκοροι ἀλλήλων εἶεν. πρὸς δὲ τούτοις καὶ ἀποπαύσας τοῦ ὁπότε βούλοιντο ἕκαστοι γυναῖκα ἄγεσθαι ἔταξεν ἐν ἀκμαῖς τῶν σωμάτων τοὺς γάμους ποιεῖσθαι, καὶ τοῦτο συμφέρον τῇ εὐγονίᾳ 7 νομίζων. εἴ γε μέντοι συμβαίη γεραιῷ νέαν ἔχειν, ὁρῶν τοὺς τηλικούτους φυλάττοντας μάλιστα τὰς γυναῖκας τἀναντία καὶ τούτου ἐνόμισε· τῷ γὰρ πρεσβύτῃ ἐποίησεν, ὁποίου ἀνδρὸς σῶμά τε καὶ ψυχὴν ἀγασθείη, τοῦτον ἐπαγομένῳ 8 τεκνοποιήσασθαι. εἰ δέ τις αὖ γυναικὶ μὲν συνοικεῖν μὴ βούλοιτο, τέκνων δὲ ἀξιολόγων ἐπιθυμοίη, καὶ τούτῳ νόμον ἐποίησεν, ἥντινα

138

But Lycurgus thought the labour of slave women 4
sufficient to supply clothing. He believed mother-
hood to be the most important function of freeborn
woman. Therefore, in the first place, he insisted
on physical training for the female no less than for
the male sex: moreover, he instituted races and
trials of strength for women competitors as for
men, believing that if both parents are strong they
produce more vigorous offspring.

He noticed, too, that, during the time immediately 5
succeeding marriage, it was usual elsewhere for the
husband to have unlimited intercourse with his wife.
The rule that he adopted was the opposite of this: for
he laid it down that the husband should be ashamed
to be seen entering his wife's room or leaving it.
With this restriction on intercourse the desire of
the one for the other must necessarily be increased,
and their offspring was bound to be more vigorous
than if they were surfeited with one another. In 6
addition to this, he withdrew from men the right to
take a wife whenever they chose, and insisted on
their marrying in the prime of their manhood, believing that this too promoted the production of fine
children. It might happen, however, that an old 7
man had a young wife; and he observed that old
men keep a very jealous watch over their young wives.
To meet these cases he instituted an entirely different
system by requiring the elderly husband to introduce
into his house some man whose physical and moral
qualities he admired, in order to beget children.
On the other hand, in case a man did not want to 8
cohabit with his wife and nevertheless desired
children of whom he could be proud, he made it
lawful for him to choose a woman who was the

139

εὔτεκνον καὶ γενναίαν ὁρῴη, πείσαντα τὸν ἔχοντα
ἐκ ταύτης τεκνοποιεῖσθαι.

9 Καὶ πολλὰ μὲν τοιαῦτα συνεχώρει· αἵ τε γὰρ
γυναῖκες διττοὺς οἴκους βούλονται κατέχειν οἵ τε
ἄνδρες ἀδελφοὺς τοῖς παισὶ προσλαμβάνειν, οἳ
τοῦ μὲν γένους καὶ τῆς δυνάμεως κοινωνοῦσι, τῶν
δὲ χρημάτων οὐκ ἀντιποιοῦνται.

10 Περὶ μὲν δὴ τεκνοποιίας οὕτω τἀναντία ᾿γνοὺς
τοῖς ἄλλοις εἴ τι διαφέροντας καὶ κατὰ μέγεθος
καὶ κατ᾿ ἰσχὺν ἄνδρας τῇ Σπάρτῃ ἀπετέλεσεν, ὁ
βουλόμενος ἐπισκοπείτω.

II. Ἐγὼ μέντοι, ἐπεὶ καὶ περὶ γενέσεως
ἐξήγημαι, βούλομαι καὶ τὴν παιδείαν ἑκατέρων
σαφηνίσαι.

Τῶν μὲν τοίνυν ἄλλων Ἑλλήνων οἱ φάσκοντες
κάλλιστα τοὺς υἱεῖς παιδεύειν, ἐπειδὰν τάχιστα
αὐτοῖς οἱ παῖδες τὰ λεγόμενα συνιῶσιν, εὐθὺς μὲν
ἐπ᾿ αὐτοῖς παιδαγωγοὺς θεράποντας ἐφιστᾶσιν,
εὐθὺς δὲ πέμπουσιν εἰς διδασκάλων μαθησο-
μένους καὶ γράμματα καὶ μουσικὴν καὶ τὰ ἐν
παλαίστρᾳ. πρὸς δὲ τούτοις τῶν παίδων πόδας
μὲν ὑποδήμασιν ἁπαλύνουσι, σώματα δὲ ἱματίων
μεταβολαῖς διαθρύπτουσι· σίτου γε μὴν αὐτοῖς
γαστέρα μέτρον νομίζουσιν.

2 Ὁ δὲ Λυκοῦργος ἀντὶ μὲν τοῦ ἰδίᾳ ἕκαστον
παιδαγωγοὺς δούλους ἐφιστάναι ἄνδρα ἐπέστησε
κρατεῖν αὐτῶν ἐξ ὧνπερ αἱ μέγισται ἀρχαὶ

---

[1] i.e. at Sparta.

mother of a fine family and of high birth, and if
he obtained her husband's consent, to make her the
mother of his children.

He gave his sanction to many similar arrangements. 9
For the wives [1] want to take charge of two households,
and the husbands want to get brothers for their sons,
brothers who are members of the family and share in
its influence, but claim no part of the money.

Thus his regulations with regard to the begetting 10
of children were in sharp contrast with those of
other states. Whether he succeeded in populating
Sparta with a race of men remarkable for their size
and strength anyone who chooses may judge for
himself.

II. Having dealt with the subject of birth, I wish
next to explain the educational system of Lycurgus,
and how it differs from other systems.

In the other Greek states parents who profess to
give their sons the best education place their boys
under the care and control of a moral tutor [2] as soon
as they can understand what is said to them, and
send them to a school to learn letters, music and the
exercises of the wrestling-ground. Moreover, they
soften the children's feet by giving them sandals,
and pamper their bodies with changes of clothing;
and it is customary to allow them as much food as
they can eat.

Lycurgus, on the contrary, instead of leaving each 2
father to appoint a slave to act as tutor, gave the
duty of controlling the boys to a member of the
class from which the highest offices are filled, in

[2] I have adopted for παιδαγωγός the term used at Oxford
for a person who has charge of, but does not teach, an under-
graduate.

καθίστανται, ὃς δὴ καὶ παιδονόμος καλεῖται.
τοῦτον δὲ κύριον ἐποίησε καὶ ἀθροίζειν τοὺς
παῖδας καὶ ἐπισκοποῦντα, εἴ τις ῥᾳδιουργοίη,
ἰσχυρῶς κολάζειν. ἔδωκε δ᾽ αὐτῷ καὶ τῶν
ἡβώντων μαστιγοφόρους, ὅπως τιμωροῖεν ὅτε
δέοι· ὥστε πολλὴν μὲν αἰδῶ, πολλὴν δὲ πειθὼ
3 ἐκεῖ συμπαρεῖναι. ἀντί γε μὴν τοῦ ἀπαλύνειν
τοὺς πόδας ὑποδήμασιν ἔταξεν ἀνυποδησίᾳ κρα-
τύνειν, νομίζων, εἰ τοῦτ᾽ ἀσκήσειαν, πολὺ μὲν
ῥᾷον ἂν ὀρθιάδε βαίνειν, ἀσφαλέστερον δὲ πρανῆ
καταβαίνειν, καὶ πηδῆσαι δὲ καὶ ἀναθορεῖν καὶ
δραμεῖν θᾶττον τὸν¹ ἀνυπόδητον, εἰ ἠσκηκὼς εἴη
4 τοὺς πόδας, ἢ τὸν ὑποδεδεμένον. καὶ ἀντί γε
τοῦ ἱματίοις διαθρύπτεσθαι ἐνόμισεν ἑνὶ ἱματίῳ
δι᾽ ἔτους προσεθίζεσθαι, νομίζων οὕτως καὶ πρὸς
ψύχη καὶ πρὸς θάλπη ἄμεινον ἂν παρεσκευάσθαι.
5 σῖτόν γε μὴν ἔταξε τοσοῦτον ἔχοντα συμβολεύειν
τὸν εἴρενα, ὡς ὑπὸ πλησμονῆς μὲν μήποτε βαρύ-
νεσθαι, τοῦ δὲ ἐνδεεστέρως διάγειν μὴ ἀπείρως
ἔχειν, νομίζων τοὺς οὕτω παιδευομένους μᾶλλον
μὲν ἂν δύνασθαι, εἰ δεήσειεν, ἀσιτήσαντας ἐπιπο-
νῆσαι, μᾶλλον δ᾽ ἄν, εἰ παραγγελθείη, ἀπὸ τοῦ
αὐτοῦ σίτου πλείω χρόνον ἐπιταθῆναι, ἧττον δ᾽
ἂν ὄψου δεῖσθαι, εὐχερέστερον δὲ πρὸς πᾶν ἔχειν
6 βρῶμα καὶ ὑγιεινοτέρως δ᾽ ἂν διάγειν, καὶ εἰς

¹ τὸν, wanting in the MSS. and in S., is twice supplied
by Cobet.

---

¹ συμβολεύειν is the conjecture of F. Portus for συμβουλεύειν,
and εἴρενα that of Schneider for ἄρρενα. The prefect took his
meals with the class of which he had charge. But Stobaeus'
text runs σῖτόν γε μὴν τοσοῦτον ἔχειν (for which read ἐσθίειν)

fact to the " Warden" as he is called. He gave this person authority to gather the boys together, to take charge of them and to punish them severely in case of misconduct. He also assigned to him a staff of youths provided with whips to chastise them when necessary; and the result is that modesty and obedience are inseparable companions at Sparta. 3 Instead of softening the boys' feet with sandals he required them to harden their feet by going without shoes. He believed that if this habit were cultivated it would enable them to climb hills more easily and descend steep inclines with less danger, and that a youth who had accustomed himself to go barefoot would leap and jump and run more nimbly than a boy in sandals. And instead of 4 letting them be pampered in the matter of clothing, he introduced the custom of wearing one garment throughout the year, believing that they would thus be better prepared to face changes of heat and cold. As to the food, he required 5 the prefect to bring with him [1] such a moderate amount of it that the boys would never suffer from repletion, and would know what it was to go with their hunger unsatisfied; for he believed that those who underwent this training would be better able to continue working on an empty stomach, if necessary, and would be capable of carrying on longer without extra food, if the word of command were given to do so: they would want fewer delicacies and would accommodate themselves more readily to anything put before them, and at the same time would enjoy better health. He also thought that a diet which 6

συνεβούλευεν ὡς, " he recommended them to eat so moderately that they "; and this is probably right.

μῆκος ἂν αὐξάνεσθαι τὴν ῥαδινὰ τὰ σώματα
ποιοῦσαν τροφὴν μᾶλλον συλλαμβάνειν ἡγήσατο
ἢ τὴν διαπλατύνουσαν τῷ σίτῳ.

Ὡς δὲ μὴ ὑπὸ λιμοῦ ἄγαν αὖ πιέζοιντο, ἀπρα-
γμόνως μὲν αὐτοῖς οὐκ ἔδωκε λαμβάνειν ὧν ἂν
προσδέωνται, κλέπτειν δ᾽ ἐφῆκεν ἔστιν ἃ τῷ λιμῷ
7 ἐπικουροῦντας. καὶ ὡς μὲν οὐκ ἀπορῶν ὅ τι δοίη
ἐφῆκεν αὐτοῖς γε μηχανᾶσθαι τὴν τροφήν, οὐδένα
οἶμαι τοῦτο ἀγνοεῖν· δῆλον δ᾽ ὅτι τὸν μέλλοντα
κλωπεύειν καὶ νυκτὸς ἀγρυπνεῖν δεῖ καὶ μεθ᾽
ἡμέραν ἀπατᾶν καὶ ἐνεδρεύειν, καὶ κατασκόπους
δὲ ἑτοιμάζειν τὸν μέλλοντά τι λήψεσθαι. ταῦτα
οὖν δὴ πάντα δῆλον ὅτι μηχανικωτέρους τῶν
ἐπιτηδείων βουλόμενος τοὺς παῖδας ποιεῖν καὶ
πολεμικωτέρους οὕτως ἐπαίδευσεν.

8 Εἴποι δ᾽ ἂν οὖν τις, τί δῆτα, εἴπερ τὸ κλέπτειν
ἀγαθὸν ἐνόμιζε, πολλὰς πληγὰς ἐπέβαλε τῷ
ἁλισκομένῳ; ὅτι, φημὶ ἐγώ, καὶ τἆλλα, ὅσα
ἄνθρωποι διδάσκουσι, κολάζουσι τὸν μὴ καλῶς
ὑπηρετοῦντα. κἀκεῖνοι οὖν τοὺς ἁλισκομένους
9 ὡς κακῶς κλέπτοντας τιμωροῦνται. καὶ ὡς
πλείστους δὴ ἁρπάσαι τυροὺς [παρ᾽ Ὀρθίας]
καλὸν θεὶς μαστιγοῦν τούτους ἄλλοις ἐπέταξε,
τοῦτο δὴ δηλῶσαι καὶ ἐν τούτῳ βουλόμενος, ὅτι
ἔστιν ὀλίγον χρόνον ἀλγήσαντα πολὺν χρόνον
εὐδοκιμοῦντα εὐφραίνεσθαι. δηλοῦται δὲ ἐν

---

[1] *Anabasis*, IV. vi. 14.
[2] At this altar the annual scourging of Spartan boys and
youths took place, according to Plutarch and Pausanias; but

made their bodies slim would do more to increase
their height than one that consisted of flesh-forming
food.

On the other hand, lest they should feel too much
the pinch of hunger,[1] while not giving them the opportunity of taking what they wanted without trouble
he allowed them to alleviate their hunger by stealing
something. It was not on account of a difficulty in 7
providing for them that he encouraged them to get
their food by their own cunning. No one, I suppose,
can fail to see that. Obviously a man who intends
to take to thieving must spend sleepless nights and
play the deceiver and lie in ambush by day, and
moreover, if he means to make a capture, he must
have spies ready. There can be no doubt then, that
all this education was planned by him in order to
make the boys more resourceful in getting supplies,
and better fighting men.

Someone may ask: But why, if he believed 8
stealing to be a fine thing, did he have the boy who
was caught beaten with many stripes? I reply:
Because in all cases men punish a learner for not
carrying out properly whatever he is taught to do.
So the Spartans chastise those who get caught for
stealing badly. He made it a point of honour to 9
steal as many cheeses as possible [from the altar of
Artemis Orthia],[2] but appointed others to scourge
the thieves, meaning to show thereby that by
enduring pain for a short time one may win
lasting fame and felicity. It is shown herein that

this custom seems to have no connexion with that of punishing those who were caught thieving. It is not improbable
that the whole of this sentence is an interpolation; if not,
the text is corrupt beyond restoration.

τούτῳ, ὅτι καὶ ὅπου τάχους δεῖ ὁ βλακεύων
ἐλάχιστα μὲν ὠφελεῖται, πλεῖστα δὲ πράγματα
λαμβάνει.

10 Ὅπως δὲ μηδ' εἰ ὁ παιδονόμος ἀπέλθοι, ἔρημοί
ποτε οἱ παῖδες εἶεν ἄρχοντος, ἐποίησε τὸν ἀεὶ
παρόντα τῶν πολιτῶν κύριον εἶναι καὶ ἐπιτάττειν
τοῖς παισὶν ὅ τι ἀγαθὸν δοκοίη εἶναι καὶ κολάζειν,
εἴ τι ἁμαρτάνοιεν. τοῦτο δὲ ποιήσας διέπραξε
καὶ αἰδημονεστέρους εἶναι τοὺς παῖδας· οὐδὲν
γὰρ οὕτως αἰδοῦνται οὔτε παῖδες οὔτε ἄνδρες
11 ὡς τοὺς ἄρχοντας. ὡς δὲ καὶ εἴ ποτε μηδεὶς
τύχοι ἀνὴρ παρών, μηδ' ὡς ἔρημοι οἱ παῖδες
ἄρχοντος εἶεν, ἔθηκε τῆς ἴλης ἑκάστης τὸν
τορώτατον τῶν εἰρένων ἄρχειν· ὥστε οὐδέποτε
ἐκεῖ οἱ παῖδες ἔρημοι ἄρχοντός εἰσι.

12 Λεκτέον δέ μοι δοκεῖ εἶναι καὶ περὶ τῶν
παιδικῶν ἐρώτων· ἔστι γάρ τι καὶ τοῦτο πρὸς
παιδείαν. οἱ μὲν τοίνυν ἄλλοι Ἕλληνες ἢ ὥσπερ
Βοιωτοὶ ἀνὴρ καὶ παῖς συζυγέντες ὁμιλοῦσιν ἢ
ὥσπερ Ἠλεῖοι διὰ χαρίτων τῇ ὥρᾳ χρῶνται· εἰσὶ
δὲ καὶ οἳ παντάπασι τοῦ διαλέγεσθαι τοὺς
ἐραστὰς εἴργουσιν ἀπὸ τῶν παίδων.

13 Ὁ δὲ Λυκοῦργος ἐναντία καὶ τούτοις πᾶσι γνοὺς
εἰ μέν τις αὐτὸς ὢν οἷον δεῖ ἀγασθεὶς ψυχὴν παιδὸς πειρῷτο ἄμεμπτον φίλον ἀποτελέσασθαι καὶ
συνεῖναι, ἐπήνει καὶ καλλίστην παιδείαν ταύτην
ἐνόμιζεν· εἰ δέ τις παιδὸς σώματος ὀρεγόμενος
φανείη, αἴσχιστον τοῦτο θεὶς ἐποίησεν ἐν Λακεδαίμονι μηδὲν ἧττον ἐραστὰς παιδικῶν ἀπέχεσθαι
ἢ γονεῖς παίδων καὶ[1] ἀδελφοὶ ἀδελφῶν εἰς
ἀφροδίσια ἀπέχονται.

[1] ἢ καὶ S. with the MSS. : ἢ was removed by Schäfer.

where there is need of swiftness, the slothful, as usual, gets little profit and many troubles.

In order that the boys might never lack a ruler 10 even when the Warden was away, he gave authority to any citizen who chanced to be present to require them to do anything that he thought right, and to punish them for any misconduct. This had the effect of making the boys more respectful; in fact boys and men alike respect their rulers above everything. And that a ruler might not be lacking to 11 the boys even when no grown man happened to be present, he selected the keenest of the prefects, and gave to each the command of a division. And so at Sparta the boys are never without a ruler.

I think I ought to say something also about intimacy 12 with boys, since this matter also has a bearing on education. In other Greek states, for instance among the Boeotians, man and boy live together, like married people;[1] elsewhere, among the Eleians, for example, consent is won by means of favours. Some, on the other hand, entirely forbid suitors to talk with boys.

The customs instituted by Lycurgus were opposed 13 to all of these. If someone, being himself an honest man, admired a boy's soul and tried to make of him an ideal friend without reproach and to associate with him, he approved, and believed in the excellence of this kind of training. But if it was clear that the attraction lay in the boy's outward beauty, he banned the connexion as an abomination; and thus he purged the relationship of all impurity, so that in Lacedaemon it resembled parental and brotherly love.

[1] *Symposium*, viii. 34.

14 Τὸ μέντοι ταῦτα ἀπιστεῖσθαι ὑπό τινων οὐ
θαυμάζω· ἐν πολλαῖς γὰρ τῶν πόλεων οἱ
νόμοι οὐκ ἐναντιοῦνται ταῖς πρὸς τοὺς παῖδας
ἐπιθυμίαις.

Ἡ μὲν δὴ παιδεία εἴρηται ἥ τε Λακωνικὴ καὶ
ἡ τῶν ἄλλων Ἑλλήνων· ἐξ ὁποτέρας δ᾽ αὐτῶν
καὶ εὐπειθέστεροι καὶ αἰδημονέστεροι καὶ ὧν δεῖ
ἐγκρατέστεροι ἄνδρες ἀποτελοῦνται, ὁ βουλόμενος
καὶ ταῦτα ἐπισκοπείσθω.

III. Ὅταν γε μὴν ἐκ παίδων εἰς τὸ μειρα-
κιοῦσθαι ἐκβαίνωσι, τηνικαῦτα οἱ μὲν ἄλλοι
παύουσι μὲν ἀπὸ παιδαγωγῶν, παύουσι δὲ ἀπὸ
διδασκάλων, ἄρχουσι δὲ οὐδένες ἔτι αὐτῶν, ἀλλ᾽
αὐτονόμους ἀφιᾶσιν· ὁ δὲ Λυκοῦργος καὶ τούτων
2 τἀναντία ἔγνω. καταμαθὼν γὰρ τοῖς τηλικούτοις
μέγιστον μὲν φρόνημα ἐμφυόμενον, μάλιστα δὲ
ὕβριν ἐπιπολάζουσαν, ἰσχυροτάτας δὲ ἐπιθυμίας
τῶν ἡδονῶν παρισταμένας, τηνικαῦτα πλείστους
μὲν πόνους αὐτοῖς ἐπέβαλε, πλείστην δὲ ἀσχολίαν
3 ἐμηχανήσατο. ἐπιθεὶς δὲ καὶ εἴ τις ταῦτα φύγοι,
μηδενὸς ἔτι τῶν καλῶν τυγχάνειν, ἐποίησε μὴ
μόνον τοὺς ἐκ δημοσίου ἀλλὰ καὶ τοὺς κηδομένους
ἑκάστων ἐπιμελεῖσθαι, ὡς μὴ ἀποδειλιάσαντες
ἀδόκιμοι παντάπασιν ἐν τῇ πόλει γένοιντο.

4 Πρὸς δὲ τούτοις τὸ αἰδεῖσθαι ἰσχυρῶς ἐμ-
φυσιῶσαι βουλόμενος αὐτοῖς καὶ ἐν ταῖς ὁδοῖς
ἐπέταξεν ἐντὸς μὲν τοῦ ἱματίου τὼ χεῖρε ἔχειν,
σιγῇ δὲ πορεύεσθαι, περιβλέπειν δὲ μηδαμοῖ,
ἀλλ᾽ αὐτὰ τὰ πρὸ τῶν ποδῶν ὁρᾶν. ἔνθα δὴ
καὶ δῆλον γεγένηται, ὅτι τὸ ἄρρεν φῦλον καὶ
εἰς τὸ σωφρονεῖν ἰσχυρότερόν ἐστι τῆς θηλείας
5 φύσεως. ἐκείνων γοῦν ἧττον μὲν ἂν φωνὴν

I am not surprised, however, that people refuse 14 to believe this. For in many states the laws are not opposed to the indulgence of these appetites.

I have now dealt with the Spartan system of education, and that of the other Greek states. Which system turns out men more obedient, more respectful, and more strictly temperate, anyone who chooses may once more judge for himself.

III. When a boy ceases to be a child, and begins to be a lad, others release him from his moral tutor and his schoolmaster: he is then no longer under a ruler and is allowed to go his own way. Here again Lycurgus introduced a wholly different system. For he observed that at this time of life 2 self-will makes strong root in a boy's mind, a tendency to insolence manifests itself, and a keen appetite for pleasure in different forms takes possession of him. At this stage, therefore, he imposed on him a ceaseless round of work, and contrived a constant round of occupation. The penalty for shirking 3 the duties was exclusion from all future honours. He thus caused not only the public authorities, but their relations also to take pains that the lads did not incur the contempt of their fellow citizens by flinching from their tasks.

Moreover, wishing modesty to be firmly rooted 4 in them, he required them to keep their hands under their cloaks, to walk in silence, not to look about them, but to fix their eyes on the ground. The effect of this rule has been to prove that even in the matter of decorum the male is stronger than the female sex. At any rate you would expect a 5

ἀκούσαις ἢ τῶν λιθίνων, ἧττον δ' ἂν ὄμματα
μεταστρέψαις ἢ τῶν χαλκῶν, αἰδημονεστέρους
δ' ἂν αὐτοὺς ἡγήσαιο καὶ αὐτῶν τῶν ἐν τοῖς
θαλάμοις¹ παρθένων. καὶ ἐπειδὰν εἰς τὸ φιλίτιόν
γε ἀφίκωνται, ἀγαπητὸν αὐτῶν καὶ τὸ ἐρωτηθὲν
ἀκοῦσαι.

Καὶ τῶν μὲν αὖ παιδίσκων οὕτως ἐπεμελήθη.

IV. Περί γε μὴν τῶν ἡβώντων πολὺ μάλιστα
ἐσπούδασε, νομίζων τούτους, εἰ γένοιντο οἵους
δεῖ, πλεῖστον ῥέπειν ἐπὶ τὸ ἀγαθὸν τῇ πόλει.
2 ὁρῶν οὖν, οἷς ἂν μάλιστα φιλονεικία ἐγγένηται,
τούτων καὶ χοροὺς ἀξιακροατοτάτους γιγνομένους
καὶ γυμνικοὺς ἀγῶνας ἀξιοθεατοτάτους, ἐνόμιζεν,
εἰ καὶ τοὺς ἡβῶντας συμβάλλοι εἰς ἔριν περὶ
ἀρετῆς, οὕτως ἂν καὶ τούτους ἐπὶ πλεῖστον
ἀφικνεῖσθαι ἀνδραγαθίας. ὡς οὖν τούτους αὖ
συνέβαλεν, ἐξηγήσομαι.

3 Αἱροῦνται τοίνυν αὐτῶν οἱ ἔφοροι ἐκ τῶν ἀκμαζόντων τρεῖς ἄνδρας· οὗτοι δὲ ἱππαγρέται καλοῦνται. τούτων δ' ἕκαστος ἄνδρας ἑκατὸν
καταλέγει, διασαφηνίζων, ὅτου ἕνεκα τοὺς μὲν
4 προτιμᾷ, τοὺς δὲ ἀποδοκιμάζει. οἱ οὖν μὴ τυγ-
χάνοντες τῶν καλῶν πολεμοῦσι τοῖς τε ἀποστεί-
λασιν αὐτοὺς καὶ τοῖς αἱρεθεῖσιν ἀνθ' αὐτῶν,
καὶ παραφυλάττουσιν ἀλλήλους, ἐάν τι παρὰ τὰ
καλὰ νομιζόμενα ῥᾳδιουργῶσι.

5 Καὶ αὕτη δὴ γίγνεται ἡ θεοφιλεστάτη τε καὶ

---

¹ Longinus and Stobaeus quote this with ὀφθαλμοῖς, "eyes,"
in place of θαλάμοις, "bridal chambers"; and the former cen-
sures the use of παρθένων for κορῶν, meaning "pupils" of the
eye.

² *Cyropaedia*, II. i. 22.

stone image to utter a sound sooner than those
lads; you would sooner attract the attention of a
bronze figure; you might think them more modest
even than a young bride in the bridal chamber.[1]
When they have taken their place at a public meal,
you must be content if you can get an answer to
a question.

Such was the care that he bestowed on the
growing lads.

IV. For those who had reached the prime of life
he showed by far the deepest solicitude. For he
believed that if these were of the right stamp they
must exercise a powerful influence for good on the
state. He saw that where the spirit of rivalry[2] is 2
strongest among the people, there the choruses are
most worth hearing and the athletic contests afford
the finest spectacle. He believed, therefore, that
if he could match the young men together in a
strife of valour, they too would reach a high level
of manly excellence.[3] I will proceed to explain,
therefore, how he instituted matches between the
young men.

The Ephors, then, pick out three of the very best 3
among them. These three are called Commanders of
the Guard. Each of them enrols a hundred others,
stating his reasons for preferring one and rejecting
another. The result is that those who fail to win 4
the honour are at war both with those who sent
them away and with their successful rivals; and they
are on the watch for any lapse from the code of
honour.

Here then you find that kind of strife that is 5

[3] *Cyropaedia*, VII. ii. 26.

πολιτικωτάτη ἔρις, ἐν ᾗ ἀποδέδεικται μὲν ἃ δεῖ
ποιεῖν τὸν ἀγαθόν, χωρὶς δ' ἑκάτεροι ἀσκοῦσιν,
ὅπως ἀεὶ κράτιστοι ἔσονται, ἐὰν δέ τι δέῃ, καθ'
6 ἕνα ἀρήξουσι τῇ πόλει παντὶ σθένει. ἀνάγκη
δ' αὐτοῖς καὶ εὐεξίας ἐπιμελεῖσθαι. καὶ γὰρ
πυκτεύουσι διὰ τὴν ἔριν ὅπου ἂν συμβάλωσι·
διαλύειν μέντοι τοὺς μαχομένους πᾶς ὁ παρα-
γενόμενος κύριος. ἢν δέ τις ἀπειθῇ τῷ διαλύοντι,
ἄγει αὐτὸν ὁ παιδονόμος ἐπὶ τοὺς ἐφόρους· οἱ δὲ
ζημιοῦσι μεγαλείως, καθιστάναι βουλόμενοι εἰς
τὸ μήποτε ὀργὴν τοῦ μὴ πείθεσθαι τοῖς νόμοις
κρατῆσαι.

7   Τοῖς γε μὴν τὴν ἡβητικὴν ἡλικίαν πεπερα-
κόσιν, ἐξ ὧν ἤδη καὶ αἱ μέγισται ἀρχαὶ καθίστανται, οἱ μὲν ἄλλοι Ἕλληνες ἀφελόντες αὐτῶν
τὸ ἰσχύος ἔτι ἐπιμελεῖσθαι στρατεύεσθαι ὅμως
αὐτοῖς ἐπιτάττουσιν, ὁ δὲ Λυκοῦργος τοῖς τηλικούτοις νόμιμον ἐποίησε κάλλιστον εἶναι τὸ θηρᾶν,
εἰ μή τι δημόσιον κωλύοι, ὅπως δύναιντο καὶ
οὗτοι μηδὲν ἧττον τῶν ἡβώντων στρατιωτικοὺς
πόνους ὑποφέρειν.

V. Ἃ μὲν οὖν ἑκάστῃ ἡλικίᾳ ἐνομοθέτησεν ὁ
Λυκοῦργος ἐπιτηδεύματα, σχεδὸν εἴρηται· οἵαν
δὲ καὶ πᾶσι δίαιταν κατεσκεύασε, νῦν πειράσομαι
διηγεῖσθαι.

2   Λυκοῦργος τοίνυν παραλαβὼν τοὺς Σπαρτιάτας
ὥσπερ τοὺς ἄλλους Ἕλληνας οἴκοι σκηνοῦντας,
γνοὺς ἐν τούτοις πλεῖστα ῥᾳδιουργεῖσθαι εἰς τὸ
φανερὸν ἐξήγαγε τὰ συσκήνια,[2] οὕτως ἡγούμενος

---

[1] *Horsemanship*, ii. 1.
[2] Lit. "moved the Syskania out into the open." See
Introduction III.

dearest to the gods, and in the highest sense
political—the strife that sets the standard of a
brave man's conduct; and in which either party
exerts itself to the end that it may never fall below
its best, and that, when the time comes, every
member of it may support the state with all his
might.[1] And they are bound, too, to keep themselves 6
fit, for one effect of the strife is that they spar whenever they meet; but anyone present has a right to
part the combatants. If anyone refuses to obey the
mediator the Warden takes him to the Ephors; and
they fine him heavily, in order to make him realize
that he must never yield to a sudden impulse to
disobey the laws.

To come to those who have passed the time of 7
youth, and are now eligible to hold the great offices
of state. While absolving these from the duty of
bestowing further attention on their bodily strength,
the other Greeks require them to continue serving
in the army. But Lycurgus established the principle
that for citizens of that age, hunting was the noblest
occupation, except when some public duty prevented, in order that they might be able to stand
the fatigues of soldiering as well as the younger men.

V. I have given a fairly complete account of
the institutions of Lycurgus so far as they apply
to the successive stages of life. I will now try to
describe the system that he established for all
alike.

Lycurgus found the Spartans boarding at home 2
like the other Greeks, and came to the conclusion
that the custom was responsible for a great deal of
misconduct. He therefore established the public
messes outside in the open,[2] thinking that this

XENOPHON

ἥκιστ᾽ ἂν παραβαίνεσθαι τὰ προσταττόμενα.
3 καὶ σῖτόν γε¹ ἔταξεν αὐτοῖς, ὡς μήτε ὑπερπλη-
ροῦσθαι μήτε ἐνδεεῖς γίγνεσθαι. πολλὰ δὲ καὶ
παράλογα γίγνεται ἀπὸ τῶν ἀγρευομένων· οἱ δὲ
πλούσιοι ἔστιν ὅτε καὶ ἄρτον ἀντιπαραβάλλουσιν·
ὥστε οὔτε ἔρημός ποτε ἡ τράπεζα βρωτῶν γίγνεται, ἔστ᾽ ἂν διασκηνῶσιν, οὔτε πολυδάπανος.
4 καὶ μὴν τοῦ πότου ἀποπαύσας τὰς² ἀναγκαίας
πόσεις, αἳ σφάλλουσι μὲν σώματα, σφάλλουσι
δὲ γνώμας, ἐφῆκεν ὁπότε διψῴη ἕκαστος πίνειν,
οὕτω νομίζων ἀβλαβέστατόν τε καὶ ἥδιστον
ποτὸν γίγνεσθαι.

Οὕτω γε μὴν συσκηνούντων πῶς ἄν τις ἢ ὑπὸ
λιχνείας ἢ οἰνοφλυγίας ἢ αὑτὸν ἢ οἶκον διαφθεί-
5 ρειε; καὶ γὰρ δὴ ἐν μὲν ταῖς ἄλλαις πόλεσιν ὡς
τὸ πολὺ οἱ ἥλικες ἀλλήλοις σύνεισι, μεθ᾽ ὧνπερ
καὶ ἐλαχίστη αἰδὼς παραγίγνεται· ὁ δὲ Λυκοῦργος
ἐν τῇ Σπάρτῃ ἀνέμιξε παιδεύεσθαι τὰ πολλὰ
τοὺς νεωτέρους ὑπὸ τῆς τῶν γεραιτέρων ἐμπειρίας.
6 καὶ γὰρ δὴ ἐπιχώριον ἐν τοῖς φιλιτίοις λέγεσθαι
ὅ τι ἂν καλῶς τις ἐν τῇ πόλει ποιήσῃ· ὥστ᾽ ἐκεῖ
ἥκιστα μὲν ὕβριν, ἥκιστα δὲ παροινίαν, ἥκιστα
7 δὲ αἰσχρουργίαν καὶ αἰσχρολογίαν ἐγγίγνεσθαι.
ἀγαθά γε μὴν ἀπεργάζεται καὶ τάδε ἡ ἔξω
σίτησις· περιπατεῖν τε γὰρ ἀναγκάζονται ἐν τῇ
οἴκαδε ἀφόδῳ καὶ μὴν τὸ ὑπὸ οἴνου μὴ σφάλλεσθαι ἐπιμελεῖσθαι, εἰδότες, ὅτι οὐκ ἔνθαπερ

¹ γε Stephanus: τε S. with the MSS.
² τὰς Madvig: τὰς οὐκ S. with the MSS.

¹ At the public meals each had his own cup: there was no
passing of cups along as at Athens and elsewhere. Critias in
Athenaeus, x. 432 D and xi. 463 E.

154

would reduce disregard of orders to a minimum.
The amount of food he allowed was just enough to 3
prevent them from getting either too much or too
little to eat. But many extras are supplied from the
spoils of the chase; and for these rich men sometimes substitute wheaten bread. Consequently the
board is never bare until the company breaks up,
and never extravagantly furnished. Another of his 4
reforms was the abolition of compulsory drinking,[1]
which is the undoing alike of body of mind. But
he allowed everyone to drink when he was thirsty,
believing that drink is then most harmless and most
welcome.

Now what opportunity did these public messes
give a man to ruin himself or his estate by gluttony
or wine-bibbing? Note that in other states the 5
company usually consists of men of the same age,
where modesty is apt to be conspicuous by its absence
from the board. But Lycurgus introduced mixed
companies[2] at Sparta, so that the experience of the
elders might contribute largely to the education of
the juniors. In point of fact, by the custom of the 6
country the conversation at the public meals turns
on the great deeds wrought in the state, and so there
is little room for insolence or drunken uproar, for
unseemly conduct or indecent talk. And the system 7
of feeding in the open has other good results. They
must needs walk home after the meal, and, of course,
must take good care not to stumble under the
influence of drink (for they know that they will not

---

[2] Something appears to be lost after ἀνέμιξε. Schneider
suggested ἀνέμιξε τὰς ἡλικίας ὥστε, "mixed the ages, so
that."

ἐδείπνουν καταμενοῦσι· καὶ τῇ ὄρφνῃ ὅσα ἡμέρα
χρηστέον· οὐδὲ γὰρ ὑπὸ φανοῦ τὸν ἔτι ἔμφρουρον
ἔξεστι πορεύεσθαι.

8 Καταμαθὼν γε μὴν ὁ Λυκοῦργος καὶ ὅτι ἀπὸ
τῶν αὐτῶν σίτων οἱ μὲν διαπονούμενοι εὔχροί τε
καὶ εὔσαρκοι καὶ εὔρωστοί εἰσιν, οἱ δ' ἄπονοι
πεφυσημένοι τε καὶ αἰσχροὶ καὶ ἀσθενεῖς ἀνα-
φαίνονται, οὐδὲ τούτου ἠμέλησεν, ἀλλ' ἐννοῶν,
ὅτι καὶ ὅταν αὐτός τις τῇ ἑαυτοῦ γνώμῃ φιλο-
πονῇ, ἀρκούντως τὸ σῶμα ἔχων ἀναφαίνεται,
ἐπέταξε τὸν ἀεὶ πρεσβύτατον ἐν τῷ γυμνασίῳ
ἑκάστῳ[1] ἐπιμελεῖσθαι ὡς μὴ πόνους αὐτοῖς[2]
9 ἐλάττους τῶν σιτίων γίγνεσθαι. καὶ ἐμοὶ μὲν
οὐδ' ἐν τούτῳ σφαλῆναι δοκεῖ. οὐκ ἂν οὖν
ῥᾳδίως γέ τις εὕροι Σπαρτιατῶν οὔτε ὑγιεινο-
τέρους οὔτε τοῖς σώμασι χρησιμωτέρους· ὁμοίως
γὰρ ἀπό τε τῶν σκελῶν καὶ ἀπὸ χειρῶν καὶ ἀπὸ
τραχήλου γυμνάζονται.

VI. Ἐναντία γε μὴν ἔγνω καὶ τάδε τοῖς
πλείστοις. ἐν μὲν γὰρ ταῖς ἄλλαις πόλεσι τῶν
ἑαυτοῦ ἕκαστος καὶ παίδων καὶ οἰκετῶν καὶ
χρημάτων ἄρχουσιν· ὁ δὲ Λυκοῦργος κατασκευάσαι βουλόμενος, ὡς ἂν μηδὲν βλάπτοντες
ἀπολαύοιέν τι οἱ πολῖται ἀλλήλων ἀγαθῶν, ἐποίησε παίδων ἕκαστον ὁμοίως τῶν ἑαυτοῦ καὶ τῶν
2 ἀλλοτρίων ἄρχειν. ὅταν δέ τις εἰδῇ, ὅτι οὗτοι
πατέρες εἰσὶ τῶν παίδων, ὧν αὐτὸς ἄρχει, ἀνάγκη
οὕτως ἄρχειν, ὥσπερ ἂν καὶ τῶν ἑαυτοῦ ἄρχεσθαι
βούλοιτο. ἢν δέ τις παῖς ποτε πληγὰς λαβὼν
ὑπ' ἄλλου κατείπῃ πρὸς τὸν πατέρα, αἰσχρόν

---

[1] ἑκάστῳ MSS. : S. reads ἑκάστων with Hermann.

stay on at the table); and they must do in the dark what they do in the day. Indeed, those who are still in the army are not even allowed a torch to guide them.

Lycurgus had also observed the effects of the 8 same rations on the hard worker and the idler; that the former has a fresh colour, firm flesh and plenty of vigour, while the latter looks puffy, ugly and weak. He saw the importance of this; and reflecting that even a man who works hard of his own will because it is his duty to do so, looks in pretty good condition, he required the senior for the time being in every gymnasium to take care that the tasks set should be not too small for the rations allowed. And I think 9 that in this matter too he succeeded. So it would not be easy to find healthier or handier men than the Spartans. For their exercises train the legs, arms and neck equally.

VI. In the following respects, again, his institutions differ from the ordinary type. In most states every man has control of his own children, servants and goods. Lycurgus wanted to secure that the citizens should get some advantage from one another without doing any harm. He therefore gave every father authority over other men's children as well as over his own. When a man knows that fathers 2 have this power, he is bound to rule the children over whom he exercises authority as he would wish his own to be ruled.[1] If a boy tells his own father when he has been whipped by another father, it is

---

[1] The text of this sentence is open to suspicion. οὗτοι πατέρες can hardly be sound.

---

[2] The text as altered by Hug.; πόνους is highly probable: the MSS. have ὡς μήποτε αὐτοὶ ἐλάττους, and S. merely omits αὐτοί, but this is not satisfactory.

ἐστι μὴ οὐκ ἄλλας πληγὰς ἐμβάλλειν τῷ υἱεῖ.
οὕτω πιστεύουσιν ἀλλήλοις μηδὲν αἰσχρὸν προστάττειν τοῖς παισίν.

3 Ἐποίησε δὲ καὶ οἰκέταις, εἴ τις δεηθείη, χρῆσθαι
καὶ τοῖς ἀλλοτρίοις. καὶ κυνῶν δὲ θηρευτικῶν
συνῆψε κοινωνίαν· ὥστε οἱ μὲν δεόμενοι παρακαλοῦσιν ἐπὶ θήραν, ὁ δὲ μὴ αὐτὸς σχολάζων ἡδέως
ἐκπέμπει. καὶ ἵπποις δὲ ὡσαύτως χρῶνται· ὁ
γὰρ ἀσθενήσας ἢ δεηθεὶς ὀχήματος ἢ ταχύ ποι
βουληθεὶς ἀφικέσθαι, ἤν που ἴδῃ ἵππον ὄντα,
λαβὼν καὶ χρησάμενος καλῶς ἀποκαθίστησιν.

4 Οὐ μὴν οὐδ᾽ ἐκεῖνό γε παρὰ τοῖς ἄλλοις εἰθισμένον ἐποίησεν ἐπιτηδεύεσθαι. ὅπου γὰρ ἂν ὑπὸ
θήρας ὀψισθέντες δεηθῶσι τῶν ἐπιτηδείων, ἢν μὴ
συνεσκευασμένοι τύχωσι, καὶ ἐνταῦθα ἔθηκε τοὺς
μὲν πεπαμένους καταλείπειν τὰ πεποιημένα, τοὺς
δὲ δεομένους ἀνοίξαντας τὰ σήμαντα, λαβόντας
ὅσων ἂν δέωνται, σημηναμένους καταλιπεῖν. τοιγαροῦν οὕτως μεταδιδόντες ἀλλήλοις καὶ οἱ τὰ
μικρὰ ἔχοντες μετέχουσι πάντων τῶν ἐν τῇ
χώρᾳ, ὁπόταν τινὸς δεηθῶσιν.

VII. Ἐναντία γε μὴν καὶ τάδε τοῖς ἄλλοις
Ἕλλησι κατέστησεν ὁ Λυκοῦργος ἐν τῇ Σπάρτῃ
νόμιμα. ἐν μὲν γὰρ δήπου ταῖς ἄλλαις πόλεσι
πάντες χρηματίζονται ὅσον δύνανται· ὁ μὲν γὰρ
γεωργεῖ, ὁ δὲ ναυκληρεῖ, ὁ δ᾽ ἐμπορεύεται, οἱ δὲ
2 καὶ ἀπὸ τεχνῶν τρέφονται· ἐν δὲ τῇ Σπάρτῃ ὁ
Λυκοῦργος τοῖς ἐλευθέροις τῶν μὲν ἀμφὶ χρη-
ματισμὸν ἀπεῖπε μηδενὸς ἅπτεσθαι, ὅσα δὲ ἐλευ-

---

[1] *i.e.* so much of it as remained over.

a disgrace if the parent does not give his son another whipping. So completely do they trust one another not to give any improper orders to the children.

He also gave the power of using other men's 3 servants in case of necessity; and made sporting dogs common property to this extent, that any who want them invite their master, and if he is engaged himself he is glad to send the hounds. A similar plan of borrowing is applied to horses also; thus a man who falls ill or wants a carriage or wishes to get to some place quickly, if he sees a horse anywhere, takes and uses it carefully and duly restores it.

There is yet another among the customs instituted 4 by him which is not found in other communities. It was intended to meet the needs of parties belated in the hunting-field with nothing ready to eat. He made a rule that those who had plenty should leave behind the prepared food,[1] and that those who needed food should break the seals, take as much as they wanted, seal up the rest and leave it behind. The result of this method of going shares with one another is that even those who have but little receive a share of all that the country yields whenever they want anything.

VII. Nor does this exhaust the list of the customs established by Lycurgus at Sparta that are contrary to those of the other Greeks. In other states, I suppose, all men make as much money as they can. One is a farmer, another a ship-owner, another a merchant, and others live by different handicrafts. But at Sparta Lycurgus forbade freeborn citizens to 2 have anything to do with business affairs. He insisted

θερίαν ταῖς πόλεσι παρασκευάζει, ταῦτα ἔταξε
3 μόνα ἔργα αὐτῶν νομίζειν. καὶ γὰρ δὴ τί πλοῦτος
ἐκεῖ γε σπουδαστέος, ἔνθα ἴσα μὲν φέρειν εἰς τὰ
ἐπιτήδεια, ὁμοίως δὲ διαιτᾶσθαι τάξας ἐποίησε
μὴ ἡδυπαθείας ἕνεκα χρημάτων ὀρέγεσθαι; ἀλλὰ
μὴν οὐδ' ἱματίων γε ἕνεκα χρηματιστέον· οὐ γὰρ
ἐσθῆτος πολυτελείᾳ, ἀλλὰ σώματος εὐεξίᾳ κοσ-
4 μοῦνται. οὐδὲ μὴν τοῦ γε εἰς τοὺς συσκήνους[1]
ἔχειν δαπανᾶν χρήματα ἀθροιστέον, ἐπεὶ τὸ τῷ
σώματι πονοῦντα ὠφελεῖν τοὺς συνόντας εὐδοξότερον ἐποίησεν ἢ τὸ δαπανῶντα,[2] ἐπιδείξας τὸ
μὲν ψυχῆς, τὸ δὲ πλούτου ἔργον.
5   Τό γε μὴν ἐξ ἀδίκων χρηματίζεσθαι καὶ ἐν
τοῖς τοιούτοις διεκώλυσε. πρῶτον μὲν γὰρ νό-
μισμα τοιοῦτον κατεστήσατο, ὃ δεκάμνων[3] μόνον
ἂν εἰς οἰκίαν εἰσελθὸν οὔτε δεσπότας οὔτε οἰκέτας
λάθοι· καὶ γὰρ χώρας μεγάλης καὶ ἁμάξης ἀγω-
6 γῆς δέοιτ' ἄν. χρυσίον γε μὴν καὶ ἀργύριον
ἐρευνᾶται, καὶ ἄν τί που φανῇ, ὁ ἔχων ζημιοῦται.
τί οὖν ἂν ἐκεῖ χρηματισμὸς σπουδάζοιτο, ἔνθα ἡ
κτῆσις πλείους λύπας ἢ ἡ χρῆσις εὐφροσύνας
παρέχει;

VIII. Ἀλλὰ γὰρ ὅτι μὲν ἐν Σπάρτῃ μάλιστα
πείθονται ταῖς ἀρχαῖς τε καὶ τοῖς νόμοις, ἴσμεν
ἅπαντες. ἐγὼ μέντοι οὐδ' ἐγχειρῆσαι οἶμαι πρότερον τὸν Λυκοῦργον ταύτην τὴν εὐταξίαν[4]

---

[1] ἕνεκα, which S. adds after συσκήνους with the MSS., was removed by Weiske.

[2] δαπανῶντα Morus: δαπανῶντας S. with the MSS.

[3] δεκάμνων Dindorf: δέκα μνῶν S. with the MSS.

[4] εὐταξίαν Dindorf: εὐεξίαν S. with the MSS.

---

[1] *Agesilaus*, ix. 6.

on their regarding as their own concern only those
activities that make for civic freedom. Indeed, 3
how should wealth be a serious object there, when
he insisted on equal contributions to the food supply
and on the same standard of living for all, and thus
cut off the attraction of money for indulgence' sake?
Why, there is not even any need of money to spend
on cloaks: for their adornment is due not to the
price of their clothes, but to the excellent condition
of their bodies. Nor yet is there any reason for 4
amassing money in order to spend it on one's mess-
mates; for he made it more respectable to help
one's fellows by toiling with the body than by
spending money,[1] pointing out that toil is an employment of the soul, spending an employment of
wealth.

By other enactments he rendered it impossible to 5
make money in unfair ways. In the first place the
system of coinage that he established was of such a
kind that even a sum of ten minae [2] could not be
brought into a house without the master and the
servants being aware of it: the money would fill a
large space and need a wagon to draw it. Moreover, 6
there is a right of search for gold and silver, and, in
the event of discovery, the possessor is fined. Why,
then, should money-making be a preoccupation in a
state where the pains of its possession are more than
the pleasures of its enjoyment?

VIII. To continue: we all know that obedience
to the magistrates and the laws is found in the
highest degree in Sparta. For my part, however,
I think that Lycurgus did not so much as attempt

---

[2] Some £40.

XENOPHON

καθιστάναι, πρὶν ὁμογνώμονας ἐποιήσατο τοὺς
2 κρατίστους τῶν ἐν τῇ πόλει. τεκμαίρομαι δὲ
ταῦτα, ὅτι ἐν μὲν ταῖς ἄλλαις πόλεσιν οἱ
δυνατώτεροι οὐδὲ βούλονται δοκεῖν τὰς ἀρχὰς
φοβεῖσθαι, ἀλλὰ νομίζουσι τοῦτο ἀνελεύθερον
εἶναι. ἐν δὲ τῇ Σπάρτῃ οἱ κράτιστοι καὶ ὑπέρχονται μάλιστα τὰς ἀρχὰς καὶ τῷ ταπεινοὶ εἶναι
μεγαλύνονται καὶ τῷ ὅταν καλῶνται τρέχοντες
ἀλλὰ μὴ βαδίζοντες ὑπακούειν, νομίζοντες, ἢν
αὐτοὶ κατάρχωσι τοῦ σφόδρα πείθεσθαι, ἕψεσθαι
καὶ τοὺς ἄλλους· ὅπερ καὶ γεγένηται.
3   Εἰκὸς δὲ καὶ τὴν τῆς ἐφορείας δύναμιν τοὺς
αὐτοὺς τούτους συγκατασκευάσαι, ἐπείπερ ἔγνω-
σαν τὸ πείθεσθαι μέγιστον ἀγαθὸν εἶναι καὶ ἐν
πόλει καὶ ἐν στρατιᾷ καὶ ἐν οἴκῳ· ὅσῳ γὰρ μείζω
δύναμιν ἔχοι[1] ἡ ἀρχή, τοσούτῳ μᾶλλον ἡγή-
σαντο αὐτὴν καὶ καταπλήξειν τοὺς πολίτας τοῦ
4 ὑπακούειν. ἔφοροι οὖν ἱκανοὶ μέν εἰσι ζημιοῦν
ὃν ἂν βούλωνται, κύριοι δ' ἐκπράττειν παραχρῆμα,
κύριοι δὲ καὶ ἄρχοντας μεταξὺ καταπαῦσαι[2] καὶ
εἶρξαί γε καὶ περὶ τῆς ψυχῆς εἰς ἀγῶνα καταστῆσαι. τοσαύτην δὲ ἔχοντες δύναμιν οὐχ
ὥσπερ αἱ ἄλλαι πόλεις ἐῶσι τοὺς αἱρεθέντας ἀεὶ
ἄρχειν τὸ ἔτος ὅπως ἂν βούλωνται, ἀλλ' ὥσπερ
οἱ τύραννοι καὶ οἱ ἐν τοῖς γυμνικοῖς ἀγῶσιν
ἐπιστάται, ἤν τινα αἰσθάνωνται παρανομοῦντά
τι, εὐθὺς παραχρῆμα κολάζουσι.
5   Πολλῶν δὲ καὶ ἄλλων ὄντων μηχανημάτων
καλῶν τῷ Λυκούργῳ εἰς τὸ πείθεσθαι τοῖς νόμοις

[1] ἔχοι Dindorf: ἔχει S. with MSS.
[2] καταπαῦσαι Stobaeus: καὶ καταπαῦσαι S. with the MSS.

to introduce this habit of discipline until he had secured agreement among the most important men in the state. I base my inference on the following 2 facts. In other states the most powerful citizens do not even wish it to be thought that they fear the magistrates: they believe such fear to be a badge of slavery. But at Sparta the most important men show the utmost deference to the magistrates: they pride themselves on their humility, on running instead of walking to answer any call, in the belief that, if they lead, the rest will follow along the path of eager obedience. And so it has proved.

It is probable also that these same citizens helped 3 to set up the office of Ephor, having come to the conclusion that obedience is a very great blessing whether in a state or an army or a household. For they thought that the greater the power of these magistrates the more they would impress the minds of the citizens.[1] Accordingly, the Ephors are com- 4 petent to fine whom they choose, and have authority to enact immediate payment: they have authority also to deprive the magistrates of office, and even to imprison and prefer a capital charge against them. Possessing such wide power they do not, like other states, leave persons elected to office to rule as they like throughout the year, but in common with despots and the presidents of the games, they no sooner see anyone breaking the law than they punish the offender.

Among many excellent plans contrived by Lycur- 5 gus for encouraging willing obedience to the laws

---

[1] τοῦ ὑπακούειν is omitted in the translation. It can hardly be right; Schneider removed it, and Cobet proposed εἰς τὸ ὑπακούειν, "so as to make them obedient."

ἐθέλειν τοὺς πολίτας, ἐν τοῖς καλλίστοις καὶ
τοῦτό μοι δοκεῖ εἶναι, ὅτι οὐ πρότερον ἀπέδωκε τῷ
πλήθει τοὺς νόμους, πρὶν ἐλθὼν σὺν τοῖς κρατίσ-
τοις εἰς Δελφοὺς ἐπήρετο τὸν θεόν, εἰ λῷον καὶ
ἄμεινον εἴη τῇ Σπάρτῃ πειθομένῃ οἷς αὐτὸς ἔθηκε
νόμοις. ἐπεὶ δ᾽ ἀνεῖλε τῷ παντὶ ἄμεινον εἶναι,
τότε ἀπέδωκεν, οὐ μόνον ἄνομον ἀλλὰ καὶ ἀνόσιον
θεὶς τὸ πυθοχρήστοις νόμοις μὴ πείθεσθαι.

IX. Ἄξιον δὲ τοῦ Λυκούργου καὶ τόδε ἀγασθῆναι, τὸ κατεργάσασθαι ἐν τῇ πόλει αἱρετώ-
τερον εἶναι τὸν καλὸν θάνατον ἀντὶ τοῦ αἰσχροῦ
βίου· καὶ γὰρ δὴ ἐπισκοπῶν τις ἂν εὕροι μείους
ἀποθνῄσκοντας τούτων ἢ τῶν ἐκ τοῦ φοβεροῦ
2 ἀποχωρεῖν αἱρουμένων. ὡς τἀληθὲς εἰπεῖν καὶ
ἕπεται τῇ ἀρετῇ τὸ[1] σῴζεσθαι εἰς τὸν πλείω
χρόνον μᾶλλον ἢ τῇ κακίᾳ· καὶ γὰρ ῥᾴων καὶ
ἡδίων καὶ εὐπορωτέρα καὶ ἰσχυροτέρα. δῆλον
δὲ ὅτι καὶ εὔκλεια μάλιστα ἕπεται τῇ ἀρετῇ· καὶ
γὰρ συμμαχεῖν πως πάντες τοῖς ἀγαθοῖς βούλονται.

3 Ἧι μέντοι ὥστε ταῦτα γίγνεσθαι ἐμηχανήσατο,
καὶ τοῦτο καλὸν μὴ παραλιπεῖν. ἐκεῖνος τοίνυν
σαφῶς παρεσκεύασε τοῖς μὲν ἀγαθοῖς εὐδαιμονίαν,
4 τοῖς δὲ κακοῖς κακοδαιμονίαν. ἐν μὲν γὰρ ταῖς
ἄλλαις πόλεσιν ὁπόταν τις κακὸς γένηται, ἐπί-
κλησιν μόνον ἔχει κακὸς εἶναι, ἀγοράζει δὲ ἐν τῷ
αὐτῷ ὁ κακὸς τἀγαθῷ καὶ κάθηται καὶ γυμνά-
ζεται, ἐὰν βούληται· ἐν δὲ τῇ Λακεδαίμονι πᾶς

---

[1] τὸ added by Morus : S. omits with the MSS.

[1] Herodotus i. 65.

among the citizens, I think one of the most excellent
was this : before delivering his laws to the people
he paid a visit to Delphi,[1] accompanied by the most
important citizens, and inquired of the god whether
it was desirable and better for Sparta that she
should obey the laws that he himself had framed.
Only when the god answered that it was better in
every way did he deliver them, after enacting that
to refuse obedience to laws given by the Pythian god
was not only unlawful, but wicked.

IX. The following achievement of Lycurgus,
again, deserves admiration. He caused his people
to choose an honourable death in preference to a
disgraceful life. And, in fact, one would find on
consideration that they actually lose a smaller proportion of their men than those who prefer to retire
from the danger zone. To tell the truth, escape 2
from premature death more generally goes with
valour than with cowardice : for valour is actually
easier and pleasanter and more resourceful and
mightier.[2] And obviously glory adheres to the
side of valour, for all men want to ally themselves
somehow with the brave.

However, it is proper not to pass over the means 3
by which he contrived to bring about this result.
Clearly, what he did was to ensure that the brave
should have happiness, and the coward misery. For 4
in other states when a man proves a coward, the only
consequence is that he is called a coward. He goes
to the same market as the brave man, sits beside
him, attends the same gymnasium, if he chooses.
But in Lacedaemon everyone would be ashamed to

[2] The sentiment is taken from Tyrtaeus.

μὲν ἄν τις αἰσχυνθείη τὸν κακὸν σύσκηνον παρα
λαβεῖν, πᾶς δ' ἂν ἐν παλαίσματι συγγυμναστήν.
5 πολλάκις δ' ὁ τοιοῦτος καὶ διαιρουμένων τοὺς
ἀντισφαιριοῦντας ἀχώριστος περιγίγνεται καὶ ἐν
χοροῖς δ' εἰς τὰς ἐπονειδίστους χώρας ἀπελαύ-
νεται, καὶ μὴν ἐν ὁδοῖς παραχωρητέον αὐτῷ καὶ
ἐν θάκοις καὶ τοῖς νεωτέροις ὑπαναστατέον, καὶ
τὰς μὲν προσηκούσας κόρας οἴκοι θρεπτέον καὶ
ταύταις τῆς ἀνανδρείας[1] αἰτίαν ὑφεκτέον, γυναι-
κὸς δὲ κενὴν ἑστίαν περιοπτέον[2] καὶ ἅμα τούτου
ζημίαν ἀποτιστέον, λιπαρὸν δὲ οὐ πλανητέον
οὐδὲ μιμητέον τοὺς ἀνεγκλήτους, ἢ πληγὰς ὑπὸ
6 τῶν ἀμεινόνων ληπτέον. ἐγὼ μὲν δὴ τοιαύτης
τοῖς κακοῖς ἀτιμίας ἐπικειμένης οὐδὲν θαυμάζω
τὸ προαιρεῖσθαι ἐκεῖ θάνατον ἀντὶ τοῦ οὕτως
ἀτίμου τε καὶ ἐπονειδίστου βίου.

X. Καλῶς δέ μοι δοκεῖ ὁ Λυκοῦργος νομοθε-
τῆσαι καὶ ᾗ μέχρι γήρως ἀσκοῖτ' ἂν ἀρετή. ἐπὶ
γὰρ τῷ τέρματι τοῦ βίου τὴν κρίσιν τῆς γεροντίας προσθεὶς ἐποίησε μηδὲ ἐν τῷ γήρᾳ ἀμελεῖ-
2 σθαι τὴν καλοκἀγαθίαν. ἀξιάγαστον δ' αὐτοῦ καὶ
τὸ ἐπικουρῆσαι τῷ τῶν ἀγαθῶν γήρᾳ· θεὶς γὰρ
τοὺς γέροντας κυρίους τοῦ περὶ τῆς ψυχῆς ἀγῶ-
νος διέπραξεν ἐντιμότερον εἶναι τὸ γῆρας τῆς
3 τῶν ἀκμαζόντων ῥώμης. εἰκότως δέ τοι καὶ
σπουδάζεται οὗτος ὁ ἀγὼν μάλιστα τῶν ἀνθρώπων. καλοὶ μὲν γὰρ καὶ οἱ γυμνικοί· ἀλλ'
οὗτοι μὲν σωμάτων εἰσίν· ὁ δὲ περὶ τῆς γεροντίας
ἀγὼν ψυχῶν ἀγαθῶν κρίσιν παρέχει. ὅσῳ οὖν
κρείττων ψυχὴ σώματος, τοσούτῳ καὶ οἱ ἀγῶνες

---

[1] ἀνδρείας S. with the better MSS.

have a coward with him at the mess or to be matched
with him in a wrestling bout. Often when sides are 5
picked for a game of ball he is the odd man left out:
in the chorus he is banished to the ignominious
place; in the streets he is bound to make way;
when he occupies a seat he must needs give it up,
even to a junior; he must support his spinster
relatives at home and must explain to them why they
are old maids: he must make the best of a fireside
without a wife, and yet pay forfeit for that: he may not
stroll about with a cheerful countenance, nor behave
as though he were a man of unsullied fame, or else
he must submit to be beaten by his betters. Small 6
wonder, I think, that where such a load of dishonour
is laid on the coward, death seems preferable to a
life so dishonoured, so ignominious.

X. The law by which Lycurgus encouraged the
practice of virtue up to old age is another excellent
measure in my opinion. By requiring men to face the
ordeal of election to the Council of Elders near the
end of life, he prevented neglect of high principles
even in old age. Worthy of admiration also is the pro- 2
tection that he afforded to the old age of good men.
For the enactment by which he made the Elders
judges in trials on the capital charge caused old age to
be held in greater honour than the full vigour of manhood. And surely it is natural that of all contests 3
in the world this should excite the greatest zeal.
For noble as are the contests in the Games, they
are merely tests of bodily powers. But the contest
for the Council judges souls whether they be good.
As much then, as the soul surpasses the body, so

---

¹ περιοπτέον Dindorf: οὐ περιοπτέον S. with the MSS.

οἱ τῶν ψυχῶν ἢ οἱ τῶν σωμάτων ἀξιοσπουδασ-
τότεροι.

4 Τόδε γε μὴν τοῦ Λυκούργου πῶς οὐ μεγάλως
ἄξιον ἀγασθῆναι ; ὃς ἐπειδὴ κατέμαθεν, ὅτι ὅπου[1]
οἱ βουλόμενοι ἐπιμελοῦνται[2] τῆς ἀρετῆς οὐχ
ἱκανοί εἰσι τὰς πατρίδας αὔξειν, ἐκεῖνος ἐν τῇ
Σπάρτῃ ἠνάγκασε δημοσίᾳ πάντας πάσας ἀσκεῖν
τὰς ἀρετάς. ὥσπερ οὖν ἰδιῶται ἰδιωτῶν διαφέρουσιν ἀρετῇ οἱ ἀσκοῦντες τῶν ἀμελούντων,
οὕτως καὶ ἡ Σπάρτη εἰκότως πασῶν τῶν πόλεων
ἀρετῇ διαφέρει, μόνη δημοσίᾳ ἐπιτηδεύουσα τὴν
5 καλοκἀγαθίαν. οὐ γὰρ κἀκεῖνο καλόν, τὸ τῶν
ἄλλων πόλεων κολαζουσῶν, ἤν τίς τι ἕτερος
ἕτερον ἀδικῇ, ἐκεῖνον ζημίας μὴ ἐλάττους ἐπιθεῖναι, εἴ τις φανερὸς εἴη ἀμελῶν τοῦ ὡς βέλτισ-
6 τος εἶναι ; ἐνόμιζε γάρ, ὡς ἔοικεν, ὑπὸ μὲν τῶν
ἀνδραποδιζομένων τινὰς ἢ ἀποστερούντων τι ἢ
κλεπτόντων τοὺς βλαπτομένους μόνον ἀδικεῖσθαι,
ὑπὸ δὲ τῶν κακῶν καὶ ἀνάνδρων ὅλας τὰς πόλεις
προδίδοσθαι. ὥστε εἰκότως ἔμοιγε δοκεῖ τούτοις
μεγίστας ζημίας ἐπιθεῖναι.

7 Ἐπέθηκε δὲ καὶ τὴν ἀνυπόστατον ἀνάγκην
ἀσκεῖν ἅπασαν πολιτικὴν ἀρετήν. τοῖς μὲν γὰρ
τὰ νόμιμα ἐκτελοῦσιν ὁμοίως ἅπασι τὴν πόλιν
οἰκείαν ἐποίησε καὶ οὐδὲν ὑπελογίσατο οὔτε
σωμάτων οὔτε χρημάτων ἀσθένειαν· εἰ δέ τις
ἀποδειλιάσειε τοῦ τὰ νόμιμα διαπονεῖσθαι, τοῦτον ἐκεῖνος ἀπέδειξε μηδὲ νομίζεσθαι ἔτι τῶν
ὁμοίων εἶναι.

8 Ἀλλὰ γὰρ ὅτι μὲν παλαιότατοι οὗτοι οἱ νόμοι

---

[1] ὅτι ἔστιν ὅπου S. with Morus.

much more worthy are the contests of the soul to kindle zeal than those of the body.

Again, the following surely entitles the work of 4 Lycurgus to high admiration. He observed that where the cult of virtue is left to voluntary effort, the virtuous are not strong enough to increase the fame of their fatherland. So he compelled all men at Sparta to practise all the virtues in public life. And therefore, just as private individuals differ from one another in virtue according as they practise or neglect it, so Sparta, as a matter of course, surpasses all other states in virtue, because she alone makes a public duty of gentlemanly conduct. For 5 was not this too a noble rule of his, that whereas other states punish only for wrong done to one's neighbour, he inflicted penalties no less severe on any who openly neglected to live as good a life as possible? For he believed, it seems, that enslave- 6 ment, fraud, robbery, are crimes that injure only the victims of them; but the wicked man and the coward are traitors to the whole body politic. And so he had good reason, I think, for visiting their offences with the heaviest penalties.

And he laid on the people the duty of practising the 7 whole virtue of a citizen as a necessity irresistible. For to all who satisfied the requirements of his code he gave equal rights of citizenship, without regard to bodily infirmity or want of money. But the coward who shrank from the task of observing the rules of his code he caused to be no more reckoned among the peers.

Now that these laws are of high antiquity there 8

---

¹ ἐπιμελοῦνται Haase : ἐπιμελεῖσθαι S. with the MSS.

XENOPHON

εἰσί, σαφές· ὁ γὰρ Λυκοῦργος κατὰ τοὺς Ἡρα-
κλείδας λέγεται γενέσθαι· οὕτω δὲ παλαιοὶ ὄντες
ἔτι καὶ νῦν τοῖς ἄλλοις καινότατοί εἰσι· καὶ γὰρ
τὸ πάντων θαυμαστότατον ἐπαινοῦσι μὲν πάντες
τὰ τοιαῦτα ἐπιτηδεύματα, μιμεῖσθαι δὲ αὐτὰ
οὐδεμία πόλις ἐθέλει.

XI. Καὶ ταῦτα μὲν δὴ κοινὰ ἀγαθὰ καὶ ἐν
εἰρήνῃ καὶ ἐν πολέμῳ· εἰ δέ τις βούλεται κατα-
μαθεῖν, ὅ τι καὶ εἰς τὰς στρατείας βέλτιον τῶν
ἄλλων ἐμηχανήσατο, ἔξεστι καὶ τούτων ἀκούειν.

2 Πρῶτον μὲν τοίνυν οἱ ἔφοροι προκηρύττουσι
τὰ ἔτη, εἰς ἃ δεῖ στρατεύεσθαι καὶ ἱππεῦσι καὶ
ὁπλίταις, ἔπειτα δὲ καὶ τοῖς χειροτέχναις· ὥστε
ὅσοισπερ ἐπὶ πόλεως χρῶνται ἄνθρωποι, πάντων
τούτων καὶ ἐπὶ στρατιᾶς οἱ Λακεδαιμόνιοι εὐ-
ποροῦσι· καὶ ὅσα δὲ ὀργάνων ἡ στρατιὰ κοινῇ
δεηθείη ἄν, ἁπάντων τὰ μὲν ἁμάξῃ προστέτακται
παρέχειν, τὰ δὲ ὑποζυγίῳ· οὕτω γὰρ ἥκιστ' ἂν
τὸ ἐκλεῖπον διαλάθοι.

3 Εἴς γε μὴν τὸν ἐν τοῖς ὅπλοις ἀγῶνα τοιάδ'
ἐμηχανήσατο, στολὴν μὲν ἔχειν φοινικίδα καὶ
χαλκῆν ἀσπίδα, ταύτην νομίζων ἥκιστα μὲν
γυναικείᾳ κοινωνεῖν, πολεμικωτάτην δ' εἶναι· καὶ
γὰρ τάχιστα λαμπρύνεται καὶ σχολαιότατα
ῥυπαίνεται. ἐφῆκε δὲ καὶ κομᾶν τοῖς ὑπὲρ τὴν
ἡβητικὴν ἡλικίαν, νομίζων οὕτω καὶ μείζους ἂν
καὶ ἐλευθεριωτέρους καὶ γοργοτέρους φαίνεσθαι.

4 Οὕτω γε μὴν κατεσκευασμένων μόρας μὲν
διεῖλεν ἓξ καὶ ἱππέων καὶ ὁπλιτῶν. ἑκάστη δὲ

---

[1] The words καὶ χαλκῆν ἀσπίδα should probably come before
καὶ γὰρ τάχιστα. There is also a suspicion that some words

can be no doubt : for Lycurgus is said to have lived in the days of the Heracleidae. Nevertheless, in spite of their antiquity, they are wholly strange to others even at this day. Indeed, it is most astonishing that all men praise such institutions, but no state chooses to imitate them.

XI. The blessings that I have enumerated so far were shared by all alike in peace and in war. But if anyone wishes to discover in what respect Lycurgus' organisation of the army on active service was better than other systems, here is the information that he seeks.

The Ephors issue a proclamation stating the age- 2 limit fixed for the levy, first for the cavalry and infantry, and then for the handicraftsmen. Thus the Lacedaemonians are well supplied in the field with all things that are found useful in civil life. All the implements that an army may require in common are ordered to be assembled, some in carts, some on baggage animals ; thus anything missing is not at all likely to be overlooked.

In the equipment that he devised for the troops 3 in battle he included a red cloak, because he believed this garment to have least resemblance to women's clothing and to be most suitable for war, and a brass shield, because it is very soon polished and tarnishes very slowly.[1] He also permitted men who were past their first youth to wear long hair, believing that it would make them look taller, more dignified and more terrifying.

The men so equipped were divided into six 4 regiments of cavalry and infantry. The officers of

referring to other details of the equipment have dropped out.

τῶι πολιτικῶν μορῶν ἔχει πολέμαρχον ἕνα,
λοχαγοὺς τέτταρας, πεντηκοντῆρας ὀκτώ, ἐνω-
μοτάρχους ἑκκαίδεκα. ἐκ δὲ τούτων τῶν μορῶν
διὰ παρεγγυήσεως καθίστανται τότε μὲν εἰς
. . . [1] ἐνωμοτίας, τότε δὲ εἰς τρεῖς, τότε δὲ εἰς ἕξ.

5 Ὁ δὲ οἱ πλεῖστοι οἴονται, πολυπλοκωτάτην
εἶναι τὴν ἐν ὅπλοις Λακωνικὴν τάξιν, τὸ ἐναντιώ-
τατον ὑπειλήφασι τοῦ ὄντος· εἰσὶ μὲν γὰρ ἐν τῇ
Λακωνικῇ τάξει οἱ πρωτοστάται ἄρχοντες καὶ ὁ
στίχος ἕκαστος πάντ᾽ ἔχων ὅσα δεῖ παρέχεσθαι.
6 οὕτω δὲ ῥᾴδιον ταύτην τὴν τάξιν μαθεῖν, ὡς ὅστις
τοὺς ἀνθρώπους δύναται γιγνώσκειν, οὐδεὶς ἂν
ἁμάρτοι· τοῖς μὲν γὰρ ἡγεῖσθαι δέδοται, τοῖς δὲ
ἕπεσθαι τέτακται. αἱ δὲ παραγωγαὶ ὥσπερ ὑπὸ
κήρυκος ὑπὸ τοῦ ἐνωμοτάρχου λόγῳ δηλοῦνται,
αἷς ἀραιαί τε καὶ βαθύτεραι αἱ φάλαγγες γίγνον-
7 ται· ὧν δὴ οὐδ᾽ ὅπως τι οὖν χαλεπὸν μαθεῖν. τὸ
μέντοι κἂν ταραχθῶσι μετὰ τοῦ παρατυχόντος
ὁμοίως μάχεσθαι, ταύτην τὴν τάξιν οὐκέτι ῥᾴδιόν
ἐστι μαθεῖν πλὴν τοῖς ὑπὸ τῶν τοῦ Λυκούργου
νόμων πεπαιδευμένοις.

8 Εὐπορώτατα δὲ καὶ ἐκεῖνα Λακεδαιμόνιοι
ποιοῦσι τὰ τοῖς ὁπλομάχοις πάνυ δοκοῦντα
χαλεπὰ εἶναι· ὅταν μὲν γὰρ ἐπὶ κέρως πορεύωνται, κατ᾽ οὐρὰν δήπου ἐνωμοτία ἐνωμοτίᾳ ἕπεται·
ἐὰν δ᾽ ἐν τῷ τοιούτῳ ἐκ τοῦ ἐναντίου πολεμία
φάλαγξ ἐπιφανῇ, τῷ ἐνωμοτάρχῃ παρεγγυᾶται εἰς

[1] No gap is indicated in S.

---

[1] Or, reading ὁπλιτικῶν with Stobaeus, "regiment of
heavy infantry."
[2] On account of *Hellenica* VII. iv. 20 and v. 10 it is thought
that δύο, "two," should be read for τέτταρας (δ').

each citizen [1] regiment comprise one colonel, four [2] captains, eight first lieutenants and sixteen second lieutenants. These regiments at the word of command form sections [3] sometimes (two), sometimes three, and sometimes six abreast.

The prevalent opinion that the Laconian infantry 5 formation is very complicated is the very reverse of the truth. In the Laconian formation the front rank men are all officers, and each file has all that it requires to make it efficient.[4] The formation is so 6 easy to understand that no one who knows man from man can possibly go wrong. For some have the privilege of leading; and the rest are under orders to follow. Orders to wheel from column into line of battle are given verbally by the second lieutenant acting as a herald, and the line is formed either thin or deep, by wheeling. Nothing whatever in these movements is difficult to understand. To be sure, 7 the secret of carrying on in a battle with any troops at hand when the line gets into confusion is not so easy to grasp, except for soldiers trained under the laws of Lycurgus.

The Lacedaemonians also carry out with perfect 8 ease manœuvres that instructors in tactics think very difficult. Thus, when they march in column, every section of course follows in the rear of the section in front of it. Suppose that at such a time an enemy in order of battle suddenly makes his appearance in front: the word is passed to the

---

[3] A number, ἕνα, "in single file," or δύο, "two," must have fallen out before ἐνωμοτίας.

[4] The exact meaning is not clear and the text is possibly corrupt. Weiske suggested πάντα παρέχει, "acts exactly as it should."

μέτωπον παρ᾽ ἀσπίδα καθίστασθαι, καὶ διὰ παντὸς οὕτως, ἔστ᾽ ἂν ἡ φάλαγξ ἐναντία καταστῇ.
ἢν γε μὴν οὕτως ἐχόντων ἐκ τοῦ ὄπισθεν οἱ πολέμιοι ἐπιφανῶσιν, ἐξελίττεται ἕκαστος ὁ στίχος,
ἵνα οἱ κράτιστοι ἐναντίοι ἀεὶ τοῖς πολεμίοις ὦσιν.
9 ὅτι δὲ ὁ ἄρχων εὐώνυμος γίγνεται, οὐδ᾽ ἐν τούτῳ
μειονεκτεῖν ἡγοῦνται, ἀλλ᾽ ἔστιν ὅτε καὶ πλεονεκτεῖν. εἰ γάρ τινες κυκλοῦσθαι ἐπιχειροῖεν, οὐκ
ἂν κατὰ τὰ γυμνά, ἀλλὰ κατὰ τὰ ὡπλισμένα
περιβάλλοιεν ἄν. ἢν δέ ποτε ἕνεκά τινος δοκῇ
συμφέρειν τὸν ἡγεμόνα δεξιὸν κέρας ἔχειν, στρέψαντες τὸ ἄγημα ἐπὶ κέρας ἐξελίττουσι τὴν
φάλαγγα, ἔστ᾽ ἂν ὁ μὲν ἡγεμὼν δεξιὸς ᾖ, ἡ δὲ
10 οὐρὰ εὐώνυμος γένηται. ἢν δ᾽ αὖ ἐκ τῶν δεξιῶν
πολεμίων τάξις ἐπιφαίνηται ἐπὶ κέρως πορευομένων, οὐδὲν ἄλλο πραγματεύονται ἢ τὸν λόχον
ἕκαστον ὥσπερ τριήρη ἀντίπρωρον τοῖς ἐναντίοις
στρέφουσι, καὶ οὕτως αὖ γίγνεται ὁ κατ᾽ οὐρὰν
λόχος παρὰ δόρυ. ἢν γε μὴν κατὰ τὰ εὐώνυμα
πολέμιοι προσίωσιν, οὐδὲ τοῦτο ἐῶσιν, ἀλλ᾽ ἀπω-
θοῦσιν ἢ ἐναντίους ἀντιπάλοις τοὺς λόχους στρέ-
φουσι· καὶ οὕτως αὖ ὁ κατ᾽ οὐρὰν λόχος παρ᾽
ἀσπίδα καθίσταται.

XII. Ἐρῶ δὲ καὶ ᾗ στρατοπεδεύεσθαι ἐνόμισε
χρῆναι Λυκοῦργος.

Διὰ μὲν γὰρ τὸ τὰς γωνίας τοῦ τετραγώνου

---

[1] *i. e.* this was the regular plan, because each of two
battle lines advancing to meet one another always tended to
converge to the right. See Thucydides, v. 71.

second lieutenant to deploy into line to the left, and so throughout the column until the battle-line stands facing the enemy. Or again, if the enemy appears in the rear while they are in this formation, each file counter-marches, in order that the best men may always be face to face with the enemy. True, the leader is then on the left, but instead of 9 thinking this a disadvantage, they regard it as a positive advantage at times. For should the enemy attempt a flanking movement he would try to encircle them, not on the exposed but on the protected side.[1] If, however, it seems better for any reason that the leader should be on the right wing, the left wing wheels, and the army counter-marches by ranks until the leader is on the right, and the rear of the column on the left. If, on the other hand, an enemy 10 force appears on the right when they are marching in column, all that they have to do is to order each company to wheel to the right so as to front the enemy like a man-of-war, and thus again the company at the rear of the column is on the right. If again an enemy approaches on the left, they do not allow that either, but either push him back[2] or wheel their companies to the left to face him, and thus the rear of the column finds itself on the left.

XII. I will now explain the method of encampment approved by Lycurgus.

Seeing that the angles of a square are useless, he

[2] This can only mean that if the Lacedaemonians are in battle-order the whole phalanx turns to the left to meet the attack : wheeling by companies to the left would only be necessary when the army marching in column was threatened on the left. But ἀλλὰ προθέουσιν found in C ("but either run forward") is almost certainly the right reading.

ἀχρήστους εἶναι εἰς κύκλον ἐστρατοπεδεύσατο,
εἰ μὴ ὄρος ἀσφαλὲς εἴη ἢ τεῖχος ἢ ποταμὸν
2 ὄπισθεν ἔχοιεν. φυλακάς γε μὴν ἐποίησε
μεθημερινὰς τὰς μὲν παρὰ τὰ ὅπλα εἴσω
βλεπούσας· οὐ γὰρ πολεμίων ἕνεκα ἀλλὰ φίλων
αὗται καθίστανται· τούς γε μὴν πολεμίους
ἱππεῖς φυλάττουσιν ἀπὸ χωρίων ὧν ἂν ἐκ
3 πλείστου προορῷεν. εἰ δέ τις προσίοι[1] νύκτωρ
ἔξω τῆς φάλαγγος ἐνόμισεν ὑπὸ Σκιριτῶν προ-
φυλάττεσθαι· νῦν δ' ἤδη καὶ ὑπὸ ξένων ἢν
4 τύχωσιν[2] αὐτῶν τινες συμπαρόντες. τὸ δὲ
ἔχοντας τὰ δόρατα ἀεὶ περιιέναι, εὖ καὶ τοῦτο
δεῖ εἰδέναι ὅτι τοῦ αὐτοῦ ἕνεκά ἐστιν οὗπερ
καὶ τοὺς δούλους εἴργουσιν ἀπὸ τῶν ὅπλων.
καὶ τοὺς ἐπὶ τὰ ἀναγκαῖα ἀπιόντας οὐ δεῖ
θαυμάζειν ὅτι οὔτε ἀλλήλων οὔτε τῶν ὅπλων
πλέον ἢ ὅσον μὴ λυπεῖν ἀλλήλους ἀπέρχονται·
καὶ γὰρ ταῦτα ἀσφαλείας ἕνεκα ποιοῦσι.
5 Μεταστρατοπεδεύονταί γε μὴν πυκνὰ καὶ τοῦ
σίνεσθαι τοὺς πολεμίους ἕνεκα καὶ τοῦ ὠφελεῖν
τοὺς φίλους.

Καὶ γυμνάζεσθαι δὲ προαγορεύεται ὑπὸ τοῦ
νόμου ἅπασι Λακεδαιμονίοις, ἔωσπερ ἂν στρατεύ-
ωνται· ὥστε μεγαλοπρεπεστέρους μὲν αὐτοὺς ἐφ'
ἑαυτοῖς γίγνεσθαι, ἐλευθεριωτέρους δὲ τῶν ἄλλων
φαίνεσθαι. δεῖ δὲ οὔτε περίπατον οὔτε δρόμον
μάσσω ποιεῖσθαι ἢ ὅσον ἂν ἡ μόρα ἐφήκῃ, ὅπως
6 μηδεὶς τῶν αὐτοῦ ὅπλων πόρρω γίγνηται. μετὰ
δὲ τὰ γυμνάσια καθίζειν μὲν ὁ πρῶτος πολέ-

---

[1] προσίοι Madvig: προΐοι S. with the MSS. S. places a
comma after φάλαγγος.

introduced the circular form of camp, except where there was a secure hill or wall, or a river afforded protection in the rear. He caused sentries to be 2 posted by day facing inwards along the place where the arms were kept, for the object of these is to keep an eye not on the enemy but on their friends. The enemy is watched by cavalry from positions that command the widest outlook. To meet the 3 case of a hostile approach at night, he assigned the duty of acting as sentries outside the lines to the Sciritae. In these days the duty is shared by foreigners, if any happen to be present in the camp. The rule that patrols invariably carry their spears, 4 has the same purpose, undoubtedly, as the exclusion of slaves from the place of arms. Nor is it surprising that sentries who withdraw for necessary purposes only go so far away from one another and from the arms as not to cause inconvenience. Safety is the first object of this rule also.

The camp is frequently shifted with the double 5 object of annoying their enemies and of helping their friends.

Moreover the law requires all Lacedaemonians to practise gymnastics regularly throughout the campaign; and the result is that they take more pride in themselves and have a more dignified appearance than other men. Neither walk nor race-course may exceed in length the space covered by the regiment, so that no one may get far away from his own arms. After the exercises the senior 6 colonel gives the order by herald to sit down—this

---

² ἢν τύχωσιν is added by Ruehl: S. reads αὐτῶν εἴ τινες with Hermann.

μαρχος κηρύττει· ἔστι δὲ τοῦτο ὥσπερ ἐξέτασις·
ἐκ τούτου δὲ ἀριστοποιεῖσθαι καὶ ταχὺ τὸν πρό-
σκοπον ὑπολύεσθαι· ἐκ τούτου δ' αὖ διατριβαὶ
καὶ ἀναπαύσεις πρὸ τῶν ἑσπερινῶν γυμνασίων.
7 μετά γε μὴν ταῦτα δειπνοποιεῖσθαι κηρύττεται,
καὶ ἐπειδὰν ᾄσωσιν εἰς τοὺς θεοὺς οἷς ἂν κεκαλλιε-
ρηκότες ὦσιν, ἐπὶ τῶν ὅπλων ἀναπαύεσθαι.

Ὅτι δὲ πολλὰ γράφω, οὐ δεῖ θαυμάζειν·
ἥκιστα γὰρ Λακεδαιμονίοις εὕροι ἄν τις παρα-
λελειμμένα ἐν τοῖς στρατιωτικοῖς ὅσα δεῖ
ἐπιμελείας.

XIII. Διηγήσομαι δὲ καὶ ἣν ἐπὶ στρατιᾶς ὁ
Λυκοῦργος βασιλεῖ δύναμιν καὶ τιμὴν παρεσκεύασε. πρῶτον μὲν γὰρ ἐπὶ φρουρᾶς τρέφει
ἡ πόλις βασιλέα καὶ τοὺς σὺν αὐτῷ· συσκηνοῦσι
δὲ αὐτῷ οἱ πολέμαρχοι, ὅπως ἀεὶ συνόντες μᾶλλον
καὶ κοινοβουλῶσιν, ἤν τι δέωνται· συσκηνοῦσι
δὲ καὶ ἄλλοι τρεῖς ἄνδρες τῶν ὁμοίων· οὗτοι
τούτοις ἐπιμελοῦνται πάντων τῶν ἐπιτηδείων,
ὡς μηδεμία ἀσχολία ᾖ αὐτοῖς τῶν πολεμικῶν
ἐπιμελεῖσθαι.

2 Ἐπαναλήψομαι δέ, ὡς ἐξορμᾶται σὺν στρατιᾷ
ὁ βασιλεύς. θύει μὲν γὰρ πρῶτον οἴκοι ὢν Διὶ
ἀγήτορι καὶ τοῖς σὺν αὐτῷ· ἢν δὲ ἐνταῦθα
καλλιερήσῃ, λαβὼν ὁ πυρφόρος πῦρ ἀπὸ τοῦ
βωμοῦ προηγεῖται ἐπὶ τὰ ὅρια τῆς χώρας· ὁ δὲ
3 βασιλεὺς ἐκεῖ αὖ θύεται Διὶ καὶ Ἀθηνᾷ. ὅταν
δὲ ἀμφοῖν τούτοιν τοῖν θεοῖν καλλιερηθῇ, τότε

---

¹ Or, if we read οἱ σὺν αὐτῷ with Haase, "he and his
staff." By "the associated gods" we should understand

is their method of inspection—and next to take breakfast and to relieve the outposts quickly. After this
there are amusements and recreations until the
evening exercises. These being finished, the herald 7
gives the order to take the evening meal, and, as soon
as they have sung to the praise of the gods to whom
they have sacrificed with good omens, to rest by
the arms.

Let not the length to which I run occasion surprise, for it is almost impossible to find any detail in
military matters requiring attention that is overlooked by the Lacedaemonians.

XIII. I will also give an account of the power
and honour that Lycurgus conferred on the King in
the field. In the first place, while on military service
the King and his staff are maintained by the state.
The colonels mess with the King, in order that constant intercourse may give better opportunities for
taking counsel together in case of need. Three of
the peers also attend the King's mess. These three
take entire charge of the commissariat for the King
and his staff, so that these may devote all their time
to affairs of war.

But I will go back to the beginning, and explain 2
how the King sets out with an army. First he offers
up sacrifice at home to Zeus the Leader and to
the gods associated with him.[1] If the sacrifice
appears propitious, the Fire-bearer takes fire
from the altar and leads the way to the borders of
the land. There the King offers sacrifice again to
Zeus and Athena. Only when the sacrifice proves 3
acceptable to both these deities does he cross the

Castor and Pollux, the Dioscuri. In the Oxford text I gave
τοῖν σιοῖν, " the twin gods."

179

διαβαίνει τὰ ὅρια τῆς χώρας· καὶ τὸ πῦρ μὲν
ἀπὸ τούτων τῶν ἱερῶν προηγεῖται οὔποτε ἀπο-
σβεννύμενον, σφάγια δὲ παντοῖα ἔπεται. ἀεὶ δὲ
ὅταν θύηται, ἄρχεται μὲν τούτου τοῦ ἔργου ἔτι
κνεφαῖος, προλαμβάνειν βουλόμενος τὴν τοῦ θεοῦ
4 εὔνοιαν. πάρεισι δὲ περὶ τὴν θυσίαν πολέμαρχοι,
λοχαγοί, πεντηκοντῆρες, ξένων στρατίαρχοι,
στρατοῦ σκευοφορικοῦ ἄρχοντες, καὶ τῶν ἀπὸ
5 τῶν πόλεων δὲ στρατηγῶν ὁ βουλόμενος· πάρεισι
δὲ καὶ τῶν ἐφόρων δύο, οἳ πολυπραγμονοῦσι μὲν
οὐδέν, ἢν μὴ ὁ βασιλεὺς προσκαλῇ· ὁρῶντες δὲ
ὅ τι ποιεῖ ἕκαστος πάντας σωφρονίζουσιν, ὡς
τὸ εἰκός. ὅταν δὲ τελεσθῇ τὰ ἱερά, ὁ βασιλεὺς
προσκαλέσας πάντας παραγγέλλει τὰ ποιητέα.
ὥστε ὁρῶν ταῦτα ἡγήσαιο ἂν τοὺς μὲν ἄλλους
αὐτοσχεδιαστὰς εἶναι τῶν στρατιωτικῶν, Λακεδαιμονίους δὲ μόνους τῷ ὄντι τεχνίτας τῶν
πολεμικῶν.
6 Ἐπειδάν γε μὴν ἡγῆται βασιλεύς, ἢν μὲν
μηδεὶς ἐναντίος φαίνηται, οὐδεὶς αὐτοῦ πρόσθεν
πορεύεται πλὴν Σκιρῖται καὶ οἱ προερευνώμενοι
ἱππεῖς· ἢν δέ ποτε μάχην οἴωνται ἔσεσθαι, λαβὼν
τὸ ἄγημα τῆς πρώτης μόρας ὁ βασιλεὺς ἄγει
στρέψας ἐπὶ δόρυ, ἔστ᾽ ἂν γένηται ἐν μέσῳ δυοῖν
7 μόραιν καὶ δυοῖν πολεμάρχοιν. οὓς δὲ δεῖ ἐπὶ
τούτοις τετάχθαι, ὁ πρεσβύτατος τῶν περὶ
δαμοσίαν συντάττει· εἰσὶ δὲ οὗτοι ὅσοι ἂν
σύσκηνοι ὦσι τῶν ὁμοίων, καὶ μάντεις καὶ ἰατροὶ
καὶ αὐληταὶ καὶ[1] οἱ τοῦ στρατοῦ ἄρχοντες, καὶ
ἐθελούσιοι ἤν τινες παρῶσιν. ὥστε τῶν δεομένων
γίγνεσθαι οὐδὲν ἀπορεῖται· οὐδὲν γὰρ ἀπρό-
σκεπτόν ἐστι.

borders of the land. And the fire from these sacrifices leads the way and is never quenched, and animals
for sacrifice of every sort follow. At all times when
he offers sacrifice, the King begins the work before
dawn of day, wishing to forestall the goodwill of the
god. And at the sacrifice are assembled colonels, 4
captains, lieutenants, commandants of foreign contingents, commanders of the baggage train, and, in
addition, any general from the states who chooses to
be present. There are also present two of the 5
Ephors, who interfere in nothing except by the
King's request, but keep an eye on the proceedings,
and see that all behave with a decorum suitable to
the occasion. When the sacrifices are ended, the
King summons all and delivers the orders of the day.
And so, could you watch the scene, you would think
all other men mere improvisors in soldiering and the
Lacedaemonians the only artists in warfare.

When the King leads, provided that no enemy 6
appears, no one precedes him except the Sciritae
and the mounted vedettes. But if ever they think
there will be fighting, he takes the lead of the first
regiment and wheels to the right, until he is between
two regiments and two colonels. The troops that 7
are to support these are marshalled by the senior
member of the King's staff. The staff consists of
all peers who are members of the royal mess, seers,
doctors, fluteplayers, commanding officers and any
volunteers who happen to be present. Thus nothing
that has to be done causes any difficulty, for everything is duly provided for.

---

[1] καὶ added by Zeune: S. omits with the MSS.

8 Μάλα δὲ καὶ τάδε ὠφέλιμα, ὡς ἐμοὶ δοκεῖ, ἐμηχανήσατο Λυκοῦργος εἰς τὸν ἐν ὅπλοις ἀγῶνα. ὅταν γὰρ ὁρώντων ἤδη τῶν πολεμίων χίμαιρα σφαγιάζηται, αὐλεῖν τε πάντας τοὺς παρόντας αὐλητὰς νόμος καὶ μηδένα Λακεδαιμονίων ἀστεφάνωτον εἶναι· καὶ ὅπλα δὲ λαμπρύνεσθαι προαγορεύεται. ἔξεστι δὲ τῷ νέῳ καὶ κεκριμένῳ[1] εἰς μάχην συνιέναι καὶ φαιδρὸν εἶναι καὶ εὐδόκιμον.

9 καὶ παρακελεύονται δὲ τῷ ἐνωμοτάρχῃ· οὐδ' ἀκούεται γὰρ εἰς ἑκάστην πᾶσαν τὴν ἐνωμοτίαν ἀφ' ἑκάστου ἐνωμοτάρχου ἔξω· ὅπως δὲ καλῶς γίγνηται, πολεμάρχῳ δεῖ μέλειν.

10 Ὅταν γε μὴν καιρὸς δοκῇ εἶναι στρατοπεδεύεσθαι, τούτου μὲν κύριος βασιλεὺς καὶ τοῦ δεῖξαί γε, ὅπου δεῖ· τὸ μέντοι πρεσβείας ἀποπέμπεσθαι καὶ φιλίας καὶ πολεμίας, τοῦτ' οὐ[2] βασιλέως. καὶ ἄρχονται μὲν πάντες ἀπὸ βασιλέως, ὅταν

11 βούλωνται πρᾶξαί τι. ἢν δ' οὖν δίκης δεόμενός τις ἔλθῃ, πρὸς ἑλλανοδίκας τοῦτον ὁ βασιλεὺς ἀποπέμπει, ἢν δὲ χρημάτων, πρὸς ταμίας, ἢν δὲ ληΐδα ἄγων, πρὸς λαφυροπώλας. οὕτω δὲ πραττομένων βασιλεῖ οὐδὲν ἄλλο ἔργον καταλείπεται ἐπὶ φρουρᾶς ἢ ἱερεῖ μὲν τὰ πρὸς τοὺς θεοὺς εἶναι, στρατηγῷ δὲ τὰ πρὸς τοὺς ἀνθρώπους.

XIV. Εἰ δέ τίς με ἔροιτο, εἰ καὶ νῦν ἔτι μοι

---

[1] κεκριμένῳ is somehow wrong. Weiske proposed καὶ κόμην διακεκριμένῳ after Plutarch, *Lyc.* 22. εὐδόκιμον also comes in oddly as the text stands. Probably some words are lost either before φαιδρὸν or after εὐδόκιμον.
[2] οὐ Weiske: αὖ S. with the MSS.

The following arrangements [1] made by Lycurgus 8
with a view to the actual fighting are also, in my
opinion, very useful. When a goat is sacrificed, the
enemy being near enough to see, custom ordains
that all the fluteplayers present are to play and
every Lacedaemonian is to wear a wreath. An order
is also given to polish arms. It is also the privilege
of the young warrior to comb his hair (?) before
entering battle, to look cheerful and earn a good
report. Moreover, the men shout words of encourage- 9
ment to the subaltern, for it is impossible for each
subaltern to make his voice travel along the whole
of his section to the far end.[2] The colonel is
responsible for seeing that all is done properly.

When the time for encamping seems to have 10
arrived, the decision rests with the King, who also
indicates the proper place. On the other hand
the dispatch of embassies whether to friends or
enemies is not the King's affair. All who have any
business to transact deal in the first instance with
the King. Suitors for justice are remitted by the 11
King to the Court of Hellanodicae, applications for
money to the treasurers; and if anyone brings booty,
he is sent to the auctioneers. With this routine the
only duties left to the King on active service are to
act as priest in matters of religion and as general in
his dealings with the men.

XIV. Should anyone ask me whether I think

---

[1] This paragraph is an afterthought, supplementing c. xi.
3–4.
[2] When two or more sections are abreast (c. xi. 4), the
men take up and repeat the exhortations of the subaltern
posted at the end of the line, and pass them along to the next
subaltern, and so on. These detached notes are not clearly
expressed.

δοκοῦσιν οἱ Λυκούργου νόμοι ἀκίνητοι διαμένειν,
2 τοῦτο μὰ Δί᾿ οὐκ ἂν ἔτι θρασέως εἴποιμι. οἶδα
γὰρ πρότερον μὲν Λακεδαιμονίους αἱρουμένους
οἴκοι τὰ μέτρια ἔχοντας ἀλλήλοις συνεῖναι μᾶλλον
ἢ ἁρμόζοντας ἐν ταῖς πόλεσι καὶ κολακευομένους
3 διαφθείρεσθαι. καὶ πρόσθεν μὲν οἶδα αὐτοὺς
φοβουμένους χρυσίον ἔχοντας φαίνεσθαι· νῦν δ᾿
ἔστιν οὓς καὶ καλλωπιζομένους ἐπὶ τῷ κεκτῆσθαι.
4 ἐπίσταμαι δὲ καὶ πρόσθεν τούτου ἕνεκα ξενηλα-
σίας γιγνομένας καὶ ἀποδημεῖν οὐκ ἐξόν, ὅπως
μὴ ῥᾳδιουργίας οἱ πολῖται ἀπὸ τῶν ξένων ἐμπί-
πλαιντο· νῦν δ᾿ ἐπίσταμαι τοὺς δοκοῦντας
πρώτους εἶναι ἐσπουδακότας, ὡς μηδέποτε
5 παύωνται ἁρμόζοντες ἐπὶ ξένης. καὶ ἦν μὲν
ὅτε ἐπεμελοῦντο, ὅπως ἄξιοι εἶεν ἡγεῖσθαι· νῦν
δὲ πολὺ μᾶλλον πραγματεύονται, ὅπως ἄρξουσιν
6 ἢ ὅπως ἄξιοι τούτου ἔσονται. τοιγαροῦν οἱ
Ἕλληνες πρότερον μὲν ἰόντες εἰς Λακεδαίμονα
ἐδέοντο αὐτῶν ἡγεῖσθαι ἐπὶ τοὺς δοκοῦντας
ἀδικεῖν· νῦν δὲ πολλοὶ παρακαλοῦσιν ἀλλήλους
7 ἐπὶ τὸ διακωλύειν ἄρξαι πάλιν αὐτούς. οὐδὲν
μέντοι δεῖ θαυμάζειν τούτων τῶν ἐπιψόγων αὐτοῖς
γιγνομένων, ἐπειδὴ φανεροί εἰσιν οὔτε τῷ θεῷ
πειθόμενοι οὔτε τοῖς Λυκούργου νόμοις.

XV. Βούλομαι δὲ καὶ ἃς βασιλεῖ πρὸς τὴν
πόλιν συνθήκας ὁ Λυκοῦργος ἐποίησε διηγήσα-
σθαι· μόνη γὰρ δὴ αὕτη ἀρχὴ διατελεῖ οἵαπερ
ἐξ ἀρχῆς κατεστάθη· τὰς δὲ ἄλλας πολιτείας
184

that the laws of Lycurgus still remain unchanged at this day, I certainly could not say that with any confidence whatever.[1] For I know that formerly the 2 Lacedaemonians preferred to live together at home with moderate fortunes rather than expose themselves to the corrupting influences of flattery as governors of dependent states. And I know too 3 that in former days they were afraid to be found in possession of gold; whereas nowadays there are some who even boast of their possessions. There 4 were alien acts in former days, and to live abroad was illegal; and I have no doubt that the purpose of these regulations was to keep the citizens from being demoralized by contact with foreigners; and now I have no doubt that the fixed ambition of those who are thought to be first among them is to live to their dying day as governors in a foreign land. There was a time when they would fain be worthy of 5 leadership; but now they strive far more earnestly to exercise rule than to be worthy of it. Therefore in 6 times past the Greeks would come to Lacedaemon and beg her to lead them against reputed wrong-doers; but now many are calling on one another to prevent a revival of Lacedaemonian supremacy. Yet we need not wonder if these reproaches are 7 levelled at them, since it is manifest that they obey neither their god nor the laws of Lycurgus.

XV. I wish also to give an account of the compact made by Lycurgus between King and state. For this is the only government that continues exactly as it was originally established, whereas

---

[1] οὐκ . . ἔτι probably does not correspond to "no longer" here. On this chapter see Introduction.

εὕροι ἄν τις μετακεκινημένας καὶ ἔτι καὶ νῦν
μετακινουμένας.

2 Ἔθηκε γὰρ θύειν μὲν βασιλέα πρὸ τῆς πόλεως
τὰ δημόσια ἅπαντα, ὡς ἀπὸ θεοῦ ὄντα, καὶ
στρατιὰν ὅποι ἂν ἡ πόλις ἐκπέμπῃ ἡγεῖσθαι.
3 ἔδωκε δὲ καὶ γέρα ἀπὸ τῶν θυομένων λαμβάνειν
καὶ γῆν τε ἐν πολλαῖς τῶν περιοίκων πόλεων
ἀπέδειξεν ἐξαίρετον τοσαύτην, ὥστε μήτ᾽ ἐνδεῖσθαι
4 τῶν μετρίων μήτε πλούτῳ ὑπερφέρειν. ὅπως
δὲ καὶ οἱ βασιλεῖς ἔξω σκηνοῖεν, σκηνὴν αὐτοῖς
δημοσίαν ἀπέδειξε, καὶ διμοιρίᾳ γε ἐπὶ τῷ δείπνῳ
ἐτίμησεν, οὐχ ἵνα διπλάσια καταφάγοιεν, ἀλλ᾽ ἵνα
καὶ ἀπὸ τοῦδε τιμῆσαι ἔχοιεν εἴ τινα βούλοιντο.
5 ἔδωκε δ᾽ αὖ καὶ συσκήνους δύο ἑκατέρῳ προσ-
ελέσθαι, οἳ δὴ καὶ Πύθιοι καλοῦνται. ἔδωκε
δὲ καὶ πασῶν τῶν συῶν ἀπὸ τόκου χοῖρον
λαμβάνειν, ὡς μήποτε ἀπορήσαι βασιλεὺς ἱερῶν,
ἤν τι δεηθῇ θεοῖς συμβουλεύσασθαι.

6 Καὶ πρὸς τῇ οἰκίᾳ δὲ λίμνη ὕδατος ἀφθονίαν
παρέχει· ὅτι δὲ καὶ τοῦτο πρὸς πολλὰ χρήσιμον,
οἱ μὴ ἔχοντες αὐτὸ μᾶλλον γιγνώσκουσι. καὶ
ἕδρας δὲ πάντες ὑπανίστανται βασιλεῖ πλὴν οὐκ
7 ἔφοροι ἀπὸ τῶν ἐφορικῶν δίφρων. καὶ ὅρκους
δὲ ἀλλήλοις κατὰ μῆνα ποιοῦνται, ἔφοροι μὲν
ὑπὲρ τῆς πόλεως, βασιλεὺς δ᾽ ὑπὲρ ἑαυτοῦ. ὁ
δὲ ὅρκος ἐστὶ τῷ μὲν βασιλεῖ κατὰ τοὺς τῆς
πόλεως κειμένους νόμους βασιλεύσειν, τῇ δὲ
πόλει ἐμπεδορκοῦντος ἐκείνου ἀστυφέλικτον τὴν
βασιλείαν παρέξειν.

8 Αὗται μὲν οὖν αἱ τιμαὶ οἴκοι[1] ζῶντι βασιλεῖ
δέδονται, οὐδέν τι πολὺ ὑπερφέρουσαι τῶν ἰδι-

[1] S., following Cobet, regards οἴκοι as spurious.

other constitutions will be found to have undergone and still to be undergoing modifications.

He ordained that the King shall offer all the 2 public sacrifices on behalf of the state, in virtue of his divine descent, and that, whatever may be the destination to which the state sends out an army, he shall be its leader. He also gave him the right to 3 receive certain parts of the beasts sacrificed, and assigned to him enough choice land in many of the outlanders' cities to ensure him a reasonable competence without excessive riches. In order that even 4 the kings should mess in public, he assigned to them a public mess tent; he also honoured them with a double portion at the meal, not that they might eat enough for two, but that they might have the wherewithal to honour anyone whom they chose. He also allowed each King to choose two mess- 5 mates, who are called Pythii. Further, he granted them to take of every litter of pigs a porker, that a King may never want victims, in case he wishes to seek counsel of the gods.

A lake near the house supplies abundance of water; 6 and how useful that is for many purposes none know so well as those who are without it. Further, all rise from their seats when the King appears; only the Ephors do not rise from their official chairs. And 7 they exchange oaths monthly, the Ephors on behalf of the state, the King for himself. And this is the King's oath: "I will reign according to the established laws of the state." And this the oath of the state: "While you abide by your oath, we will keep the kingship unshaken."

These then are the honours that are bestowed on 8 the King at home during his lifetime; and they do

ωτικῶν· οὐ γὰρ ἐβουλήθη οὔτε τοῖς βασιλεῦσι
τυραννικὸν φρόνημα παραστῆσαι οὔτε τοῖς πολί-
9 ταις φθόνον ἐμποιῆσαι τῆς δυνάμεως. αἳ δὲ
τελευτήσαντι τιμαὶ βασιλεῖ δέδονται, τῇ δὲ
βούλονται δηλοῦν οἱ Λυκούργου νόμοι, ὅτι οὐχ
ὡς ἀνθρώπους, ἀλλ᾽ ὡς ἥρωας τοὺς Λακεδαιμονίων
βασιλεῖς προτετιμήκασιν.

---

[1] Herodotus (vi. 58) gives details of these honours. The
elaborate funeral obsequies were attended by a great con-
course of men and women from all parts of Laconia. A
man and a woman in every family were compelled to go into

not greatly exceed those of private persons. For it was not the wish of Lycurgus to put into the Kings' hearts despotic pride, nor to implant in the mind of the citizens envy of their power. As for the 9 honours assigned to the King at his death, the intention of the laws of Lycurgus herein is to show that they have preferred the Kings of the Lacedaemonians in honour not as mere men, but as demigods.[1]

mourning. If a king died on foreign service his body was embalmed and brought home if possible; if not, an image of him, as in the case of Agesilaus, was buried.

WAYS AND MEANS

ΞΕΝΟΦΩΝΤΟΣ ΠΟΡΟΙ

I. Ἐγὼ μὲν τοῦτο ἀεί ποτε νομίζω, ὁποῖοί τινες ἂν οἱ προστάται ὦσι, τοιαύτας καὶ τὰς πολιτείας γίγνεσθαι. ἐπεὶ δὲ τῶν Ἀθήνησι προεστηκότων ἐλέγοντό τινες ὡς γιγνώσκουσι μὲν τὸ δίκαιον οὐδενὸς ἧττον τῶν ἄλλων ἀνθρώπων, διὰ δὲ τὴν τοῦ πλήθους πενίαν ἀναγκάζεσθαι ἔφασαν ἀδικώτεροι εἶναι περὶ τὰς πόλεις, ἐκ τούτου ἐπεχείρησα σκοπεῖν, εἴ πη δύναιντ' ἂν οἱ πολῖται διατρέφεσθαι ἐκ τῆς ἑαυτῶν, ὅθενπερ καὶ δικαιότατον, νομίζων, εἰ τοῦτο γένοιτο, ἅμα τῇ τε πενίᾳ αὐτῶν ἐπικεκουρῆσθαι ἂν καὶ τῷ ὑπόπτους τοῖς Ἕλλησιν εἶναι.

2 Σκοποῦντι δή μοι ἃ ἐπενόησα τοῦτο μὲν εὐθὺς ἀνεφαίνετο, ὅτι ἡ χώρα πέφυκεν οἵα πλείστας προσόδους παρέχεσθαι. ὅπως δὲ γνωσθῇ, ὅτι ἀληθὲς τοῦτο λέγω, πρῶτον διηγήσομαι τὴν φύσιν τῆς Ἀττικῆς.

3 Οὐκοῦν τὸ μὲν τὰς ὥρας ἐνθάδε πραοτάτας εἶναι καὶ αὐτὰ τὰ γιγνόμενα μαρτυρεῖ· ἃ γοῦν πολλαχοῦ οὐδὲ βλαστάνειν δύναιτ' ἄν, ἐνθάδε καρποφορεῖ. ὥσπερ δὲ ἡ γῆ, οὕτω καὶ ἡ περὶ τὴν χώραν θάλαττα παμφορωτάτη ἐστί. καὶ μὴν ὅσαπερ οἱ θεοὶ ἐν ταῖς ὥραις ἀγαθὰ παρέχουσι, καὶ ταῦτα πάντα ἐνταῦθα πρωιαίτατα

4 μὲν ἄρχεται, ὀψιαίτατα δὲ λήγει. οὐ μόνον δὲ κρατεῖ τοῖς ἐπ' ἐνιαυτὸν θάλλουσί τε καὶ γηράσκουσιν, ἀλλὰ καὶ ἀΐδια ἀγαθὰ ἔχει ἡ

WAYS AND MEANS

I. For my part I have always held that the constitution of a state reflects the character of the leading politicians.[1] But some of the leading men at Athens have stated that they recognize justice as clearly as other men; " but," they have said, " owing to the poverty of the masses, we are forced to be somewhat unjust in our treatment of the cities." This set me thinking whether by any means the citizens might obtain food entirely from their own soil, which would certainly be the fairest way. I felt that, were this so, they would be relieved of their poverty, and also of the suspicion with which they are regarded by the Greek world.

Now as I thought over my ideas, one thing 2 seemed clear at once, that the country is by its nature capable of furnishing an ample revenue. To drive home the truth of this statement I will first describe the natural properties of Attica.

The extreme mildness of the seasons here is shown 3 by the actual products. At any rate, plants that will not even grow in many countries bear fruit here. Not less productive than the land is the sea around the coasts. Notice too that the good things which the gods send in their season all come in earlier here and go out later than elsewhere. And the pre- 4 eminence of the land is not only in the things that bloom and wither annually : she has other good things

---

[1] See Introduction.

χώρα. πέφυκε μὲν γὰρ λίθος ἐν αὐτῇ ἄφθονος,
ἐξ οὗ κάλλιστοι μὲν ναοί, κάλλιστοι δὲ βωμοὶ
γίγνονται, εὐπρεπέστατα δὲ θεοῖς ἀγάλματα·
πολλοὶ δ' αὐτοῦ καὶ Ἕλληνες καὶ βάρβαροι
5 προσδέονται. ἔστι δὲ καὶ γῆ ἣ σπειρομένη μὲν
οὐ φέρει καρπόν, ὀρυττομένη δὲ πολλαπλασίους
τρέφει ἢ εἰ σῖτον ἔφερε. καὶ μὴν ὑπάργυρός
ἐστι σαφῶς θείᾳ μοίρᾳ· πολλῶν γοῦν πόλεων
παροικουσῶν καὶ κατὰ γῆν καὶ κατὰ θάλατταν
εἰς οὐδεμίαν τούτων οὐδὲ μικρὰ φλὲψ ἀργυρίτιδος διήκει.

6 Οὐκ ἂν ἀλόγως δέ τις οἰηθείη τῆς Ἑλλάδος
καὶ πάσης δὲ τῆς οἰκουμένης ἀμφὶ τὰ μέσα
οἰκεῖσθαι[1] τὴν πόλιν. ὅσῳ γὰρ ἄν τινες πλεῖον
ἀπέχωσιν αὐτῆς, τοσούτῳ χαλεπωτέροις ἢ ψύ-
χεσιν ἢ θάλπεσιν ἐντυγχάνουσιν· ὁπόσοι τ' ἂν
αὖ βουληθῶσιν ἀπ' ἐσχάτων τῆς Ἑλλάδος ἐπ'
ἔσχατα ἀφικέσθαι, πάντες οὗτοι ὥσπερ κύκλου
τόρνον τὰς Ἀθήνας ἢ παραπλέουσιν ἢ παρέρ-
7 χονται. καὶ μὴν οὐ περίρρυτός γε οὖσα ὅμως
ὥσπερ νῆσος πᾶσιν ἀνέμοις προσάγεταί τε ὧν
δεῖται καὶ ἀποπέμπεται ἃ βούλεται· ἀμφιθά-
λαττος γάρ ἐστι. καὶ κατὰ γῆν δὲ πολλὰ
8 δέχεται ἐμπόρια·[2] ἤπειρος γάρ ἐστιν. ἔτι δὲ
ταῖς μὲν πλείσταις πόλεσι βάρβαροι προσοι-
κοῦντες πράγματα παρέχουσιν· Ἀθηναίοις δὲ
γειτονεύουσιν αἳ καὶ αὐταὶ πλεῖστον ἀπέχουσι
τῶν βαρβάρων.

II. Τούτων μὲν οὖν ἁπάντων, ὥσπερ εἶπον,
νομίζω αὐτὴν τὴν χώραν αἰτίαν εἶναι. εἰ δὲ
πρὸς τοῖς αὐτοφυέσιν ἀγαθοῖς πρῶτον μὲν τῶν
μετοίκων ἐπιμέλεια γένοιτο· αὕτη γὰρ ἡ πρόσοδος

that last for ever. Nature has put in her abundance
of stone, from which are fashioned lovely temples
and lovely altars, and goodly statues for the gods.
Many Greeks and barbarians alike have need of it.
Again, there is land that yields no fruit if sown, and 5
yet, when quarried, feeds many times the number it
could support if it grew corn. And recollect, there
is silver in the soil, the gift, beyond doubt, of divine
providence: at any rate, many as are the states near
to her by land and sea, into none of them does even
a thin vein of silver ore extend.

One might reasonably suppose that the city lies 6
at the centre of Greece, nay of the whole inhabited
world. For the further we go from her, the more
intense is the heat or cold we meet with; and every
traveller who would cross from one to the other end
of Greece passes Athens as the centre of a circle,
whether he goes by water or by road. Then too, 7
though she is not wholly sea-girt, all the winds of
heaven bring to her the goods she needs and bear
away her exports, as if she were an island; for she lies
between two seas: and she has a vast land trade as
well; for she is of the mainland. Further, on the 8
borders of most states dwell barbarians who trouble
them: but the neighbouring states of Athens are
themselves remote from the barbarians.

II. All these advantages, as I have said, are, I
believe, due to the country itself. But instead of
limiting ourselves to the blessings that may be called
indigenous, suppose that, in the first place, we studied
the interests of the resident aliens. For in them we

---

[1] οἰκεῖσθαι papyrus fragment: ᾠκῆσθαι MSS.: ᾠκίσθαι S.,
Dindorf.

[2] ἐμπορίᾳ Schanz with M: ἐμπόρια S.: ἐμπορεῖα AC.

τῶν καλλίστων ἔμοιγε δοκεῖ εἶναι, ἐπείπερ
αὐτοὺς τρέφοντες καὶ πολλὰ ὠφελοῦντες τὰς
πόλεις οὐ λαμβάνουσι μισθόν, ἀλλὰ μετοίκιον
2 προσφέρουσιν· ἐπιμέλειά γε μὴν ἥδ' ἂν ἀρκεῖν
μοι δοκεῖ, εἰ ἀφέλοιμεν μὲν ὅσα μηδὲν ὠφελοῦντα
τὴν πόλιν ἀτιμίας τι[1] δοκεῖ τοῖς μετοίκοις παρέχειν, ἀφέλοιμεν δὲ καὶ τὸ συστρατεύεσθαι ὁπλίτας
μετοίκους τοῖς ἀστοῖς. μέγας μὲν γὰρ ὁ κίνδυνος
αὐτῶν, μέγα δὲ καὶ τὸ ἀπὸ τῶν τεχνῶν καὶ τῶν
3 οἰκείων[2] ἀπιέναι. ἀλλὰ μὴν καὶ ἡ πόλις γ' ἂν
ὠφεληθείη, εἰ οἱ πολῖται μετ' ἀλλήλων στρατεύ-
οιντο μᾶλλον ἢ εἰ συντάττοιντο αὐτοῖς, ὥσπερ
νῦν, Λυδοὶ καὶ Φρύγες καὶ Σύροι καὶ ἄλλοι
παντοδαποὶ βάρβαροι· πολλοὶ γὰρ τοιοῦτοι τῶν
4 μετοίκων. πρὸς δὲ τῷ ἀγαθῷ τῷ τούτους τοῦ[3]
συντάττεσθαι ἀφεθῆναι καὶ κόσμος ἂν τῇ πόλει
εἴη, εἰ δοκοῖεν Ἀθηναῖοι εἰς τὰς μάχας αὐτοῖς
μᾶλλον πιστεύειν ἢ ἀλλοδαποῖς.

5 Καὶ μεταδιδόντες δ' ἂν μοι δοκοῦμεν τοῖς
μετοίκοις τῶν τ' ἄλλων ὧν καλὸν μεταδιδόναι
καὶ τοῦ ἱππικοῦ εὐνουστέρους ἂν ποιεῖσθαι καὶ
ἅμα ἰσχυροτέραν ἂν καὶ μείζω τὴν πόλιν
ἀποδεικνύναι.

6 Εἶτα ἐπειδὴ καὶ πολλὰ οἰκιῶν ἔρημά ἐστιν
ἐντὸς τῶν τειχῶν,[4] καὶ οἰκόπεδα εἰ ἡ πόλις διδοίη
οἰκοδομησαμένοις ἐγκεκτῆσθαι οἳ ἂν αἰτούμενοι

---

[1] τι added by Weiske : S. omits with the MSS.
[2] οἰκείων Dindorf : οἰκιῶν S. with the MSS.
[3] τοῦ Schneider : ἐκ τοῦ S. with the MSS.
[4] Punctuation as corrected by Brinkmann. S. has the
comma after οἰκόπεδα.

---

[1] The MSS. have τῶν τέκνων, "their children."

have one of the very best sources of revenue, in my opinion, inasmuch as they are self-supporting and, so far from receiving payment for the many services they render to states, they contribute by paying a special tax. I think that we should study their 2 interests sufficiently, if we relieved them of the duties that seem to impose a certain measure of disability on the resident alien without conferring any benefit on the state, and also of the obligation to serve in the infantry along with the citizens. Apart from the personal risk, it is no small thing to leave their trades[1] and their private affairs.[2] The state itself too would gain if the citizens served 3 in the ranks together, and no longer found themselves in the same company with Lydians, Phrygians, Syrians, and barbarians of all sorts, of whom a large part of our alien population consists. In addition to 4 the advantage of dispensing with the services of these men, it would be an ornament to the state that the Athenians should be thought to rely on themselves rather than on the help of foreigners in fighting their battles.

If, moreover, we granted the resident aliens the 5 right to serve in the cavalry and various other privileges which it is proper to grant them, I think that we should find their loyalty increase and at the same time should add to the strength and greatness of the state.

Then again, since there are many vacant sites for 6 houses within the walls, if the state allowed approved applicants to erect houses on these and

---

[2] τῶν οἰκιῶν, "their houses," may possibly be right in spite of what is said below in § 6.

ἄξιοι δοκῶσιν εἶναι, πολὺ ἂν οἴομαι καὶ διὰ ταῦτα πλείους τε καὶ βελτίους ὀρέγεσθαι τῆς Ἀθήνησιν οἰκήσεως.

7 Καὶ εἰ μετοικοφύλακάς γε ὥσπερ ὀρφανοφύλακας ἀρχὴν καθισταῖμεν καὶ τούτοις τιμή τις ἐπείη, οἵτινες πλείστους [1] μετοίκους ἀποδείξειαν, καὶ τοῦτο εὐνουστέρους ἂν τοὺς μετοίκους ποιοίη καί, ὡς τὸ εἰκός, πάντες ἂν οἱ ἀπόλιδες τῆς Ἀθήνηθεν μετοικίας ὀρέγοιντο καὶ τὰς προσόδους ἂν αὔξοιεν,

III. Ὡς γε μὴν καὶ ἐμπορεύεσθαι ἡδίστη τε καὶ κερδαλεωτάτη ἡ πόλις, νῦν ταῦτα λέξω.

Πρῶτον μὲν γὰρ δήπου ναυσὶ καλλίστας καὶ ἀσφαλεστάτας ὑποδοχὰς ἔχει, ὅπου γ᾽ ἔστιν εἰσορμισθέντας ἀδεῶς [2] ἕνεκα χειμῶνος ἀναπαύε-
2 σθαι. ἀλλὰ μὴν καὶ τοῖς ἐμπόροις ἐν μὲν ταῖς πλείσταις τῶν πόλεων ἀντιφορτίζεσθαί τι ἀνάγκη· νομίσμασι γὰρ οὐ χρησίμοις ἔξω χρῶνται· ἐν δὲ ταῖς Ἀθήναις πλεῖστα μὲν ἔστιν ἀντεξάγειν ὧν ἂν δέωνται ἄνθρωποι, ἢν δὲ μὴ βούλωνται ἀντιφορτίζεσθαι, καὶ [3] ἀργύριον ἐξάγοντες καλὴν ἐμπορίαν ἐξάγουσιν. ὅπου γὰρ ἂν πωλῶσιν αὐτό, πανταχοῦ πλεῖον τοῦ ἀρχαίου λαμβάνουσιν.

3 Εἰ δὲ καὶ τῇ τοῦ ἐμπορίου ἀρχῇ ἆθλα προτιθείη τις, ὅστις δικαιότατα καὶ τάχιστα διαιροίη τὰ ἀμφίλογα, ὡς μὴ ἀποκωλύεσθαι ἀποπλεῖν τὸν βουλόμενον, πολὺ ἂν καὶ διὰ ταῦτα πλείους τε καὶ ἥδιον ἐμπορεύοιντο.

---

[1] πλείστους Cobet : πλείους S. with the MSS.
[2] ἀδεῶς Cobet : ἡδέως S. with the MSS.
[3] καὶ Deventer : καὶ οἱ S. with the MSS.

granted them the freehold of the land, I think that we should find a larger and better class of persons desiring to live at Athens.

And if we appointed a board of Guardians of 7 Aliens analogous to the Guardians of Orphans, and some kind of distinction were earmarked for guardians whose list of resident aliens was longest, that too would add to the loyalty of the aliens, and probably all without a city would covet the right of settling in Athens, and would increase our revenues.

III. I shall now say something of the unrivalled amenities and advantages of our city as a commercial centre.

In the first place, I presume, she possesses the finest and safest accommodation for shipping, since vessels can anchor here and ride safe at their moorings in spite of bad weather. Moreover, at 2 most other ports merchants are compelled to ship a return cargo, because the local currency has no circulation in other states ; but at Athens they have the opportunity of exchanging their cargo and exporting very many classes of goods that are in demand, or, if they do not want to ship a return cargo of goods, it is sound business to export silver ; for, wherever they sell it, they are sure to make a profit on the capital invested.

If prizes were offered to the magistrates of the 3 market[1] for just and prompt settlement of disputes, so that sailings were not delayed, the effect would be that a far larger number of merchants would trade with us and with much greater satisfaction.

---

[1] The market at the Peiraeus. The functions of the Board alluded to are unknown, apart from what is implied in the text.

4 ἀγαθὸν δὲ καὶ καλὸν καὶ προεδρίαις τιμᾶσθαι
ἐμπόρους καὶ ναυκλήρους καὶ ἐπὶ ξένιά γ' ἔστιν
ὅτε καλεῖσθαι, οἳ ἂν δοκῶσιν ἀξιολόγοις καὶ
πλοίοις καὶ ἐμπορεύμασιν ὠφελεῖν τὴν πόλιν.
ταῦτα γὰρ τιμώμενοι οὐ μόνον τοῦ κέρδους ἀλλὰ
καὶ τῆς τιμῆς ἕνεκεν ὡς πρὸς φίλους ἐπισπεύδοιεν
ἄν.

5 Ὅσῳ γε μὴν πλείονες εἰσοικίζοιντό τε καὶ
ἀφικνοῖντο, δῆλον ὅτι τοσούτῳ ἂν πλεῖον καὶ
εἰσάγοιτο καὶ ἐκπέμποιτο καὶ πωλοῖτο καὶ
μισθοφοροῖτο καὶ τελεσφοροίη.

6 Εἰς μὲν οὖν τὰς τοιαύτας αὐξήσεις τῶν
προσόδων οὐδὲ προδαπανῆσαι [1] δεῖ οὐδὲν ἀλλ'
ἢ ψηφίσματά τε φιλάνθρωπα καὶ ἐπιμελείας.
ὅσαι δ' ἂν ἄλλαι δοκοῦσί μοι πρόσοδοι γίγνεσθαι, γιγνώσκω ὅτι ἀφορμῆς δεήσει εἰς αὐτάς.

7 οὐ μέντοι δύσελπίς εἰμι τὸ μὴ οὐχὶ προθύμως
ἂν τοὺς πολίτας εἰς τὰ τοιαῦτα εἰσφέρειν,
ἐνθυμούμενος, ὡς πολλὰ μὲν εἰσήνεγκεν ἡ πόλις,
ὅτε Ἀρκάσιν ἐβοήθει ἐπὶ Λυσιστράτου ἡγου-

8 μένου, πολλὰ δὲ ἐπὶ Ἡγησίλεω. ἐπίσταμαι δὲ
καὶ τριήρεις πολλάκις ἐκπεμπομένας σὺν πολλῇ
δαπάνῃ [2] τούτου μὲν ἀδήλου ὄντος, εἴτε βέλτιον
εἴτε κάκιον ἔσται, ἐκείνου δὲ δῆλον, ὅτι οὐδέποτε
ἀπολήψονται ἃ ἂν εἰσενέγκωσιν οὐδὲ μεθέξουσιν

9 ὧν ἂν εἰσενέγκωσι. κτῆσιν δὲ ἀπ' οὐδενὸς ἂν οὕτω
καλὴν κτήσαιντο ὥσπερ ἀφ' οὗ ἂν προτελέσωσιν
εἰς τὴν ἀφορμήν· ᾧ μὲν γὰρ ἂν δέκα μναῖ εἰσφορὰ

---

[1] προδαπανῆσαι inferior MSS.: προσδαπανῆσαι S. with A:
δαπανῆσαι M.
[2] S. adds καὶ ταύτας γενομένας with the MSS. Schneider
conjectures καὶ ταῦτα γενόμενα: Bake κατεσκευασμένας.

It would also be an excellent plan to reserve front 4
seats in the theatre for merchants and shipowners,
and to offer them hospitality occasionally, when the
high quality of their ships and merchandise entitles
them to be considered benefactors of the state.
With the prospect of these honours before them
they would look on us as friends and hasten to visit
us to win the honour as well as the profit.

The rise in the number of residents and visitors 5
would of course lead to a corresponding expansion
of our imports and exports, of sales, rents and
customs.

Now such additions to our revenues as these need 6
cost us nothing whatever beyond benevolent legislation and measures of control. Other methods of
raising revenue that I have in mind will require
capital, no doubt. Nevertheless I venture to hope 7
that the citizens would contribute eagerly towards
such objects, when I recall the large sums contributed by the state when Lysistratus was in command and troops were sent to aid the Arcadians,[1]
and again in the time of Hegesileos.[2] I am also 8
aware that large expenditure is frequently incurred
to send warships abroad, though none can tell
whether the venture will be for better or worse, and
the only thing certain is that the subscribers will
never see their money back nor even enjoy any
part of what they contribute. But no investment 9
can yield them so fine a return as the money
advanced by them to form the capital fund. For every
subscriber of ten *minae*, drawing three *obols* a day,

---

[1] 366 B.C.
[2] 361 B.C. Hegesileos commanded at the battle of
Mantinea.

γένηται, ὥσπερ ναυτικὸν σχεδὸν ἐπίπεμπτον
αὐτῷ γίγνεται, τριώβολον τῆς ἡμέρας λαμβά-
νοντι· ᾧ δέ γ᾽ ἂν πέντε μναῖ, πλεῖον ἢ ἐπίτριτον.

10 οἱ δέ γε πλεῖστοι Ἀθηναίων πλείονα λήψονται
κατ᾽ ἐνιαυτὸν ἢ ὅσα ἂν εἰσενέγκωσιν. οἱ γὰρ
μνᾶν προτελέσαντες ἐγγὺς δυοῖν μναῖν πρός δον
ἕξουσι, καὶ ταῦτα ἐν πόλει, ὃ δοκεῖ τῶν ἀνθρωπίνων ἀσφαλέστατόν τε καὶ πολυχρονιώτατον
εἶναι.

11 Οἶμαι δὲ ἔγωγε, εἰ μέλλοιεν ἀναγραφήσεσθαι
εὐεργέται εἰς τὸν ἅπαντα χρόνον, καὶ ξένους ἂν
πολλοὺς εἰσενεγκεῖν, ἔστι δὲ ἃς ἂν καὶ πόλεις
τῆς ἀναγραφῆς ὀρεγομένας. ἐλπίζω δὲ καὶ
βασιλέας ἄν τινας καὶ τυράννους καὶ σατράπας
ἐπιθυμῆσαι μετασχεῖν ταύτης τῆς χάριτος.

12 Ὁπότε γε μὴν ἀφορμὴ ὑπάρχοι, καλὸν μὲν
καὶ ἀγαθὸν ναυκλήροις οἰκοδομεῖν καταγώγια
περὶ λιμένας πρὸς τοῖς ὑπάρχουσι, καλὸν δὲ καὶ
ἐμπόροις προσήκοντας τόπους ἐπὶ[1] ὠνῇ τε καὶ
πράσει καὶ τοῖς εἰσαφικνουμένοις δὲ δημόσια

13 καταγώγια. εἰ δὲ καὶ τοῖς ἀγοραίοις οἰκήσεις
τε καὶ πωλητήρια κατασκευασθείη καὶ ἐν Πει-
ραιεῖ καὶ ἐν τῷ ἄστει, ἅμα τ᾽ ἂν κόσμος εἴη τῇ
πόλει καὶ πολλαὶ ἂν ἀπὸ τούτων πρόσοδοι
γίγνοιντο.

14 Ἀγαθὸν δέ μοι δοκεῖ εἶναι πειραθῆναι, εἰ καὶ
ὥσπερ τριήρεις δημοσίας ἡ πόλις κέκτηται,
οὕτω καὶ ὁλκάδας δημοσίας δυνατὸν ἂν γένοιτο
κτήσασθαι καὶ ταύτας ἐκμισθοῦν ἐπ᾽ ἐγγυητῶν
ὥσπερ καὶ τἆλλα δημόσια. εἰ γὰρ καὶ τοῦτο

---

[1] προσήκοντας τόπους ἐπὶ Bergk: ἐπὶ προσήκοντας τόπους
S. with the MSS.

gets nearly twenty per cent.—as much as he would get on bottomry;[1] and every subscriber of five *minae* gets more than a third of his capital back in interest. But most of the Athenians will get over 10 a hundred per cent. in a year, for those who advance one *mina* will draw an income of nearly two *minae*, guaranteed by the state, which is to all appearances the safest and most durable of human institutions.

I think, too, that if their names were to be 11 recorded in the roll of benefactors for all time, many foreigners also would subscribe, and a certain number of states would be attracted by the prospect of enrolment. I believe that even kings and despots and oriental governors would desire to share in this reward.

When funds were sufficient, it would be a fine 12 plan to build more lodging-houses for shipowners near the harbours, and convenient places of exchange for merchants, also hotels to accommodate visitors. Again, if houses and shops were put up both in the 13 Peiraeus and in the city for retail traders, they would be an ornament to the state, and at the same time the source of a considerable revenue.

Moreover, I think it would be a good plan to 14 take a hint from the state ownership of public warships, and to see whether it be possible to acquire a fleet of public merchant vessels and to lease them under securities, like our other public property.

---

[1] 3 *obols* a day are to be paid by the state to every citizen, *i. e.* 180 *drachmae* a year, or nearly 2 *minae*, which is nearly 20 per cent. on 10 *minae*, and exactly 36 per cent. on half that sum.

οἷόν τε ὃν φανείη, πολλὴ ἂν καὶ ἀπὸ τούτων
πρόσοδος γίγνοιτο.

IV. Τά γε μὴν ἀργύρεια εἰ κατασκευασθείη
ὡς δεῖ, πάμπολλα ἂν νομίζω χρήματα ἐξ αὐτῶν
καὶ ἄνευ τῶν ἄλλων προσόδων προσιέναι. βούλομαι δὲ καὶ τοῖς μὴ εἰδόσι τὴν τούτων δύναμιν
δηλῶσαι· ταύτην γὰρ γνόντες καὶ ὅπως χρῆσθαι
δεῖ αὐτοῖς ἄμεινον ἂν βουλεύοισθε.

2 Οὐκοῦν ὅτι μὲν πάνυ παλαιὰ ἐνεργά ἐστι,
πᾶσι σαφές· οὐδεὶς γοῦν οὐδὲ πειρᾶται λέγειν,
ἀπὸ ποίου χρόνου ἐπεχειρήθη. οὕτω δὲ πάλαι
ὀρυττομένης τε καὶ ἐκφορουμένης τῆς ἀργυρίτιδος
κατανοήσατε, τί μέρος οἱ ἐκβεβλημένοι σωροὶ
3 τῶν αὐτοφυῶν τε καὶ ὑπαργύρων λόφων. οὐδὲ
μὴν ὁ ἀργυρώδης τόπος εἰς μεῖόν τι συστελλό-
μενος, ἀλλ᾽ ἀεὶ ἐπὶ πλεῖον ἐκτεινόμενος φανερός
ἐστιν.

Ἐν ᾧ γε μὴν χρόνῳ οἱ πλεῖστοι ἄνθρωποι
ἐγένοντο ἐν αὐτοῖς, οὐδεὶς πώποτε ἔργου ἠπό-
ρησέν, ἀλλ᾽ ἀεὶ τὰ ἔργα τῶν ἐργαζομένων περιῆν.
4 καὶ νῦν δὲ οἱ κεκτημένοι ἐν τοῖς μετάλλοις
ἀνδράποδα οὐδεὶς τοῦ πλήθους ἀφαιρεῖ, ἀλλ᾽
ἀεὶ προσκτᾶται ὁπόσα ἂν πλεῖστα δύνηται. καὶ
γὰρ δὴ ὅταν μὲν ὀλίγοι ὀρύττωσι καὶ ζητῶσιν,
ὀλίγα οἶμαι καὶ τὰ χρήματα εὑρίσκεται· ὅταν
δὲ πολλοί, πολλαπλασία ἡ ἀργυρῖτις ἀναφαίνεται. ὥστε ἐν μόνῳ τούτῳ ὧν ἐγὼ οἶδα ἔργων
οὐδὲ φθονεῖ οὐδεὶς τοῖς ἐπικατασκευαζομένοις.[1]

5 Ἔτι δὲ οἱ μὲν ἀγροὺς κεκτημένοι πάντες

---

[1] ἐπικατασκευαζομένοις Cobet: ἐπισκευαζομένοις S. with the
MSS.

For if this proved to be practicable, these vessels would yield another large revenue.

IV. As for the silver mines, I believe that if a proper system of working were introduced, a vast amount of money would be obtained from them apart from our other sources of revenue. I want to point out the possibilities of these mines to those who do not know. For, once you realize their possibilities, you will be in a better position to consider how the mines should be managed.

Now, we all agree that the mines have been 2 worked for many generations. At any rate, no one even attempts to date the beginning of mining operations. And yet, although digging and the removal of the silver ore have been carried on for so long a time, note how small is the size of the dumps compared with the virgin and silver-laden hills. And it is continually being found that, so 3 far from shrinking, the silver-yielding area extends further and further.

Well, so long as the maximum number of workmen was employed in them, no one ever wanted a job ; in fact, there were always more jobs than the labourers could deal with. And even at the present day no 4 owner of slaves employed in the mines reduces the number of his men ; on the contrary, every master obtains as many more as he can. The fact is, I imagine, that when there are few diggers and searchers, the amount of metal recovered is small, and when there are many, the total of ore discovered is multiplied. Hence of all the industries with which I am acquainted this is the only one in which expansion of business excites no jealousy.

Further than this, every farmer can tell just how 5

ἔχοιεν ἂν εἰπεῖν, ὁπόσα ζεύγη ἀρκεῖ εἰς τὸ χωρίον
καὶ ὁπόσοι ἐργάται· ἢν δ' ἐπὶ πλεῖον τῶν ἱκανῶν
ἐμβάλλῃ τις, ζημίαν λογίζονται· ἐν δὲ τοῖς
ἀργυρείοις ἔργοις πάντες δή φασιν ἐνδεῖσθαι
6 ἐργατῶν. καὶ γὰρ οὐδ' ὥσπερ ὅταν πολλοὶ
χαλκοτύποι γένωνται, ἀξίων γενομένων τῶν
χαλκευτικῶν ἔργων, καταλύονται οἱ χαλκοτύποι, καὶ οἱ σιδηρεῖς γε ὡσαύτως· καὶ ὅταν γε
πολὺς σῖτος καὶ οἶνος γένηται, ἀξίων ὄντων
τῶν καρπῶν, ἀλυσιτελεῖς αἱ γεωργίαι γίγνονται,
ὥστε πολλοὶ ἀφιέμενοι τοῦ τὴν γῆν ἐργάζεσθαι
ἐπ' ἐμπορίας καὶ καπηλείας καὶ τοκισμοὺς
τρέπονται· ἀργυρῖτις δὲ ὅσῳ ἂν πλείων φαίνηται καὶ ἀργύριον πλεῖον γίγνηται, τοσούτῳ
7 πλείονες ἐπὶ τὸ ἔργον τοῦτο ἔρχονται. καὶ γὰρ
δὴ ἔπιπλα μέν, ἐπειδὰν ἱκανά τις κτήσηται τῇ
οἰκίᾳ, οὐ μάλα ἔτι προσωνοῦνται· ἀργύριον δὲ
οὐδείς πω οὕτω πολὺ ἐκτήσατο, ὥστε μὴ ἔτι
προσδεῖσθαι· ἀλλ' ἤν τισι γένηται παμπληθές,
τὸ περιττεῦον κατορύττοντες οὐδὲν ἧττον ἥδονται
ἢ χρώμενοι αὐτῷ.
8   Καὶ μὴν ὅταν γε εὖ πράττωσιν αἱ πόλεις,
ἰσχυρῶς οἱ ἄνθρωποι ἀργυρίου δέονται. οἱ μὲν
γὰρ ἄνδρες ἀμφὶ ὅπλα τε καλὰ καὶ ἵππους
ἀγαθοὺς καὶ οἰκίας καὶ κατασκευὰς μεγαλοπρεπεῖς βούλονται δαπανᾶν, αἱ δὲ γυναῖκες εἰς
ἐσθῆτα πολυτελῆ καὶ χρυσοῦν κόσμον τρέπονται.
9 ὅταν τε αὖ νοσήσωσι πόλεις ἢ ἀφορίαις καρπῶν
ἢ πολέμῳ, ἔτι καὶ πολὺ μᾶλλον ἀργοῦ τῆς γῆς
γιγνομένης καὶ εἰς ἐπιτήδεια καὶ εἰς ἐπικούρους
νομίσματος δέονται.
10   Εἰ δέ τις φήσειε καὶ χρυσίον μηδὲν ἧττον χρήσι-

many yoke of oxen are enough for the farm and
how many labourers. To put more on the land than
the requisite number is counted loss. In mining
undertakings, on the contrary, everyone tells you
that he is short of labour. Mining, in fact, is quite 6
different from other industries. An increase in the
number of coppersmiths, for example, produces a fall
in the price of copper work, and the coppersmiths retire from business. The same thing happens in the
iron trade. Again, when corn and wine are abundant,
the crops are cheap, and the profit derived from
growing them disappears, so that many give up farming
and set up as merchants or shopkeepers or money-
lenders. But an increase in the amount of the silver
ore discovered and of the metal won is accompanied
by an increase in the number of persons who take up
this industry. Neither is silver like furniture, of 7
which a man never buys more when once he has got
enough for his house. No one ever yet possessed so
much silver as to want no more ; if a man finds himself
with a huge amount of it, he takes as much pleasure
in burying the surplus as in using it.

Mark too that, whenever states are prosperous, 8
silver is in strong demand. The men will spend
money on fine arms and good horses and magnificent
houses and establishments, and the women go in for
expensive clothes and gold jewelry. If, on the other 9
hand, the body politic is diseased owing to failure
of the harvest or to war, the land goes out of cultivation and there is a much more insistent demand for
cash to pay for food and mercenaries.

If anyone says that gold is quite as useful as 10

XENOPHON

μον εἶναι ἢ ἀργύριον, τούτῳ¹ μὲν οὐκ ἀντιλέγω,
ἐκεῖνο μέντοι οἶδα, ὅτι καὶ χρυσίον ὅταν πολὺ
παραφανῇ, αὐτὸ μὲν ἀτιμότερον γίγνεται, τὸ δὲ
ἀργύριον τιμιώτερον ποιεῖ.

11 Ταῦτα μὲν οὖν ἐδήλωσα τούτου ἕνεκα, ὅπως
θαρροῦντες μὲν ὅτι πλείστους ἀνθρώπους ἐπὶ τὰ
ἀργύρεια ἄγωμεν,θαρροῦντες δὲ κατασκευαζώμεθα
ἐν αὐτοῖς, ὡς οὔτε ἐπιλειψούσης ποτὲ ἀργυρίτιδος
12 οὔτε τοῦ ἀργυρίου ἀτίμου ποτὲ ἐσομένου. δοκεῖ
δέ μοι καὶ ἡ πόλις προτέρα ἐμοῦ ταῦτα ἐγνωκέναι·
παρέχει γοῦν ἐπὶ ἰσοτελείᾳ καὶ τῶν ξένων τῷ
βουλομένῳ ἐργάζεσθαι ἐν τοῖς μετάλλοις.

13 Ἵνα δὲ καὶ σαφέστερον περὶ τῆς τροφῆς εἴπω,
νῦν διηγήσομαι, ὡς κατασκευασθέντα τὰ ἀργύρεια
ὠφελιμώτατ' ἂν εἴη τῇ πόλει. ἀπ' αὐτῶν μὲν οὖν
ἔγωγε ἀφ' ὧν μέλλω λέγειν οὐδέν τι ἀξιῶ θαυμάζε-
σθαι ὡς δυσεύρετόν τι ἐξευρηκώς· τὰ μὲν γὰρ ὧν
λέξω καὶ νῦν ἔτι πάντες ὁρῶμεν, τὰ δὲ παροιχό-
μενα παρὰ τῶν πατέρων² κατὰ ταὐτὰ ἀκούομεν·³
14 τῆς μέντοι πόλεως πάνυ ἄξιον θαυμάσαι τὸ αἰσθα-
νομένην πολλοὺς πλουτιζομένους ἐξ αὐτῆς ἰδιώτας
μὴ μιμεῖσθαι τούτους. πάλαι μὲν γὰρ δήπου οἷς
μεμέληκεν ἀκηκόαμεν,ὅτι Νικίας ποτὲ ὁ Νικηράτου
ἐκτήσατο ἐν τοῖς ἀργυρείοις χιλίους ἀνθρώπους,
οὓς ἐκεῖνος Σωσίᾳ τῷ Θρᾳκὶ ἐξεμίσθωσεν ἐφ' ᾧ
ὀβολὸν μὲν ἀτελῆ ἑκάστου τῆς ἡμέρας ἀποδιδόναι,
15 τὸν δ' ἀριθμὸν ἴσους ἀεὶ παρέχειν.⁴ ἐγένετο δὲ
καὶ Ἱππονίκῳ ἑξακόσια ἀνδράποδα κατὰ τὸν
αὐτὸν τρόπον τοῦτον ἐκδεδομένα, ἃ προσέφερε μνᾶν

¹ τούτῳ Heindorf : τοῦτο S. with the MSS.
² παρὰ τῶν πατέρων Wilamowitz : πάντων MSS. : τῶν πραγμάτων S. with the Aldine.

208

silver, I am not going to contradict him; but I know this, that when gold is plentiful, silver rises and gold falls in value.

With these facts before us, we need not hesitate 11 to bring as much labour as we can get into the mines and carry on work in them, feeling confident that the ore will never give out and that silver will never lose its value. I think, indeed, that the 12 state has anticipated me in this discovery; at any rate she throws open the mining industry to foreigners on the same terms as are granted to citizens.

To make myself clearer on the subject of alimony, 13 I will now explain how the mines may be worked with the greatest advantage to the state. Not that I expect to surprise you by what I am going to say, as if I had found the solution of a difficult problem. For some things that I shall mention are still to be seen by anyone at the present day, and as for conditions in the past, our fathers have told us that they were similar. But what may well excite 14 surprise is that the state, being aware that many private individuals are making money out of her, does not imitate them. Those of us who have given thought to the matter have heard long ago, I imagine, that Nicias son of Niceratus, once owned a thousand men in the mines, and let them out to Socias the Thracian, on condition that Sosias paid him an *obol* a day per man net and filled all vacancies as they occurred. Hipponicus, again, had 15 six hundred slaves let out on the same terms and

---

³ ταὐτὰ ἂν M. : ταὐτὰ αὖ S. with other MSS.
⁴ παρέχειν Lenklau : παρεῖχεν S. with the MSS.

ἀτελῆ τῆς ἡμέρας· Φιλημονίδη δὲ τριακόσια ἃ[1]
ἡμιμναῖον· ἄλλοις δέ γε ὡς οἴομαι δύναμις ἑκά-
16 στοις ὑπῆρχεν. ἀτὰρ τί τὰ παλαιὰ δεῖ λέγειν; καὶ
γὰρ νῦν πολλοί εἰσιν ἐν τοῖς ἀργυρείοις ἄνθρωποι
17 οὕτως ἐκδεδομένοι. περαινομένων γε μὴν ὧν λέγω,
τοῦτ᾽ ἂν μόνον καινὸν γένοιτο, εἰ ὥσπερ οἱ ἰδιῶται
κτησάμενοι ἀνδράποδα πρόσοδον ἀέναον κατε-
σκευασμένοι εἰσίν, οὕτω καὶ ἡ πόλις κτῷτο
δημόσια ἀνδράποδα, ἕως γίγνοιτο τρία ἑκάστῳ
18 Ἀθηναίων. εἰ δὲ δυνατὰ λέγομεν, καθ᾽ ἓν ἕκαστον
αὐτῶν σκοπῶν ὁ βουλόμενος κρινέτω.

Οὐκοῦν τιμὴν μὲν ἀνθρώπων εὔδηλον ὅτι
μᾶλλον ἂν τὸ δημόσιον δύναιτο ἢ οἱ ἰδιῶται παρα-
σκευάσασθαι. τῇ γε μὴν βουλῇ ῥᾴδιον καὶ κηρῦ-
ξαι ἄγειν τὸν βουλόμενον ἀνδράποδα καὶ τὰ
19 προσαχθέντα πρίασθαι. ἐπειδὰν δὲ ὠνηθῇ, τί ἂν
ἧττον μισθοῖτό τις παρὰ τοῦ δημοσίου ἢ παρὰ
τοῦ ἰδιώτου, ἐπὶ τοῖς αὐτοῖς μέλλων ἕξειν;
μισθοῦνται γοῦν καὶ τεμένη[2] καὶ οἰκίας καὶ τέλη
ὠνοῦνται παρὰ τῆς πόλεως.

20 Ὅπως γε μὴν τὰ ὠνηθέντα σῴζηται, τῷ δημοσίῳ
ἔστι λαμβάνειν ἐγγύους παρὰ τῶν μισθουμένων,
ὥσπερ καὶ παρὰ τῶν ὠνουμένων τὰ τέλη. ἀλλὰ
μὴν καὶ ἀδικῆσαί γε ῥᾷον τῷ τέλος πριαμένῳ ἢ
21 τῷ ἀνδράποδα μισθουμένῳ. ἀργύριον μὲν γὰρ

---

[1] ἃ added by Hager : S. omits with the MSS.
[2] After τεμένη S. adds with the MSS. καὶ ἱερά, which was
removed by Bake.

---

[1] The MSS. add καὶ ἱερά, "and temples," for which καὶ
ἱερεῖα (victims for sacrifice) has been conjectured. But (1)
μισθοῦνται is not "contract to supply," and (2) it appears

received a rent of a *mina* a day net. Philemonides had three hundred, and received half a *mina*. There were others too, owning numbers in proportion, I presume, to their capital. But why dwell on the past? At this day there are many men in the mines let out in this way. Were my proposals adopted, the only innovation would be, that just as private individuals have built up a permanent income by becoming slave owners, so the state would become possessed of public slaves, until there were three for every citizen. Whether my plan is workable, let anyone who chooses judge for himself by examining it in detail.

So let us take first the cost of the men. Clearly the treasury is in a better position to provide the money than private individuals. Moreover the Council can easily issue a notice inviting all and sundry to bring slaves, and can buy those that are brought to it. When once they are purchased, why should there be more hesitation about hiring from the treasury than from a private person, the terms offered being the same? At any rate men hire consecrated lands[1] and houses, and farm taxes under the state.

The treasury can insure the slaves purchased by requiring some of the lessees to become guarantors, as it does in the case of the tax-farmers. In fact a tax-farmer can swindle the state more easily than a lessee of slaves. For how are you to detect

16

17

18

19

20

21

that the sacrifices were, in point of fact, paid for out of the rents received for the τεμένη, and the victims were *not* supplied by individuals on contract. Aristotle, *Ath. Pol.* c. 47, writing of the leases of state property, says nothing about victims.

211

πῶς καὶ φωράσειεν ἄν τις τὸ δημόσιον ἐξαγόμενον,
ὁμοίου τοῦ ἰδίου ὄντος αὐτῷ; ἀνδράποδα δὲ
σεσημασμένα τῷ δημοσίῳ σημάντρῳ καὶ προκει-
μένης ζημίας τῷ τε πωλοῦντι καὶ τῷ ἐξάγοντι, πῶς
ἄν τις ταῦτα κλέψειεν;

Οὐκοῦν μέχρι μὲν τούτου δυνατὸν φανεῖται τῇ
πόλει εἶναι τὸ ἀνθρώπους καὶ κτήσασθαι καὶ
22 φυλάξαι. εἰ δ' αὖ τις τοῦτ' ἐνθυμεῖται, πῶς
ἐπειδὰν πολλοὶ ἐργάται γένωνται, πολλοὶ φανοῦνται καὶ οἱ μισθωσόμενοι, ἐκεῖνο κατανοήσας
θαρρείτω, ὅτι πολλοὶ μὲν τῶν κατεσκευασμένων
προσμισθώσονται τοὺς δημοσίους, πολλὰ γάρ ἐστι
τὰ ὑπάρχοντα, πολλοὶ δ' εἰσὶ καὶ αὐτῶν τῶν ἐν
τοῖς ἔργοις γηρασκόντες,[1] πολλοὶ δὲ καὶ ἄλλοι
Ἀθηναῖοί τε καὶ ξένοι, οἳ τῷ σώματι μὲν οὔτε
βούλοιντ' ἂν οὔτε δύναιντ' ἂν ἐργάζεσθαι, τῇ δὲ
γνώμῃ ἐπιμελούμενοι ἡδέως ἂν τὰ ἐπιτήδεια
πορίζοιντο.

23 Ἢν γε μέντοι τὸ πρῶτον συστῇ διακόσια καὶ
χίλια ἀνδράποδα, εἰκὸς ἤδη ἀπ' αὐτῆς τῆς προσόδου
ἐν ἔτεσι πέντε ἢ ἐξ μὴ μεῖον ἂν τῶν[2] ἑξακισχιλίων
γενέσθαι. ἀπό γε μὴν τούτου τοῦ ἀριθμοῦ ἢν
ὀβολὸν ἕκαστος ἀτελῆ τῆς ἡμέρας φέρῃ, ἡ μὲν
24 πρόσοδος ἑξήκοντα τάλαντα τοῦ ἐνιαυτοῦ. ἀπὸ
δὲ τούτων ἢν εἰς ἄλλα ἀνδράποδα τιθῆται εἴκοσι,
τοῖς τετταράκοντα ἤδη ἐξέσται τῇ πόλει χρῆσθαι
εἰς ἄλλο ὅ τι ἂν δέῃ. ὅταν δέ γε μύρια ἀναπλη-
ρωθῇ, ἑκατὸν τάλαντα ἡ πρόσοδος ἔσται.

25 Ὅτι δὲ δέξεται πολλαπλάσια τούτων, μαρτυρή-
σαιεν ἄν μοι εἴ τινες ἔτι εἰσὶ τῶν μεμνημένων,
ὅσον τὸ τέλος εὕρισκε τῶν ἀνδραπόδων πρὸ τῶν

[1] γηράσκοντες Dindorf: γηρασκόντων S. with the MSS.

the export of public money? Money looks the
same whether it is private property or belongs to
the state. But how is a man to steal slaves when
they are branded with the public mark and it is a
penal offence to sell or export them?

So far, then, it appears to be possible for the state
to acquire and to keep men. But, one may ask, when 22
labour is abundant, how will a sufficient number
of persons be found to hire it? Well, if anyone feels
doubtful about that, let him comfort himself with
the thought that many men in the business will
hire the state slaves as additional hands, since they
have abundance of capital, and that among those
now working in the mines many are growing old.
Moreover there are many others, both Athenians
and foreigners, who have neither will nor strength
to work with their own hands, but would be glad to
to make a living by becoming managers.

Assume, however, that the total number of slaves 23
to begin with is twelve hundred. By using the
revenue derived from these the number might in
all probability be raised to six thousand at the least
in the course of five or six years. Further, if each
man brings in a clear *obol* a day, the annual revenue
derived from that number of men is sixty *talents*.
Out of this sum, if twenty *talents* are invested in 24
additional slaves, the state will have forty *talents*
available for any other necessary purpose. And
when a total of ten thousand men is reached, the
revenue will be a hundred *talents*.

But the state will receive far more than that, as 25
anyone will testify who is old enough to remember
how much the charge for slave labour brought in

---

¹ ἂν τῶν Wilamowitz : αὐτῇ S. with the MSS.

XENOPHON

ἐν Δεκελείᾳ. μαρτυρεῖ δὲ κἀκεῖνο, ὅτι εἰργασμένων ἀνθρώπων ἐν τοῖς ἀργυρείοις ἐν τῷ παντὶ
χρόνῳ ἀναριθμήτων νῦν οὐδὲν διαφέρει τὰ ἀργύρεια ἢ οἷα[1] οἱ πρόγονοι ἡμῶν ὄντα ἐμνημόνευον
26 αὐτά. καὶ τὰ νῦν δὲ γιγνόμενα πάντα μαρτυρεῖ,
ὅτι οὐκ ἄν ποτε πλείω ἀνδράποδα ἐκεῖ γένοιτο ἢ
ὅσων ἂν τὰ ἔργα δέηται. οὔτε γὰρ βάθους πέρας
27 οὔτε ὑπονόμων οἱ ὀρύττοντες εὑρίσκουσι. καὶ
μὴν καινοτομεῖν γε οὐδὲν ἧττον ἔξεστι νῦν ἢ
πρότερον. οὐ τοίνυν οὐδ' εἰπεῖν ἂν ἔχοι εἰδὼς
οὐδείς, πότερον ἐν τοῖς κατατετμημένοις πλείων
ἀργυρῖτις ἢ ἐν τοῖς ἀτμήτοις ἐστί.

28 Τί δῆτα, φαίη ἄν τις, οὐ καὶ νῦν, ὥσπερ ἔμπροσθεν, πολλοὶ καινοτομοῦσιν; ὅτι πενέστεροι
μέν εἰσιν οἱ περὶ τὰ μέταλλα· νεωστὶ γὰρ πάλιν
κατασκευάζονται· κίνδυνος δὲ μέγας τῷ καινοτο-
29 μοῦντι. ὁ μὲν γὰρ εὑρὼν ἀγαθὴν ἐργασίαν
πλούσιος γίγνεται· ὁ δὲ μὴ εὑρὼν πάντα ἀπόλ-
λυσιν, ὅσα ἂν δαπανήσῃ. εἰς τοῦτον οὖν τὸν
κίνδυνον οὐ μάλα πως ἐθέλουσιν οἱ νῦν ἰέναι.

30 Ἐγὼ μέντοι ἔχειν μοι δοκῶ καὶ περὶ τούτου
συμβουλεῦσαι, ὡς ἂν ἀσφαλέστατα καινοτομοῖτο.
εἰσὶ μὲν γὰρ δήπου Ἀθηναίων δέκα φυλαί· εἰ δ' ἡ
πόλις δοίη ἑκάστῃ αὐτῶν ἴσα ἀνδράποδα, αἱ δὲ
κοινωσάμεναι τὴν τύχην καινοτομοῖεν, οὕτως ἄν,
31 εἰ μία εὕροι, πάσαις ἂν λυσιτελὲς ἀποδείξειεν, εἰ
δὲ δύο ἢ τρεῖς ἢ τέτταρες ἢ αἱ ἡμίσειαι εὕροιεν,

---

[1] οἷα Hertlein and others : & S. with the MSS.

214

before the trouble at Decelea.[1] And there is another proof. During the history of the mines an infinite number of men has worked in them; and yet the condition of the mines to-day is exactly the same as it was in the time of our ancestors, and their memory ran not to the contrary. And present 26 conditions all lead to the conclusion that the number of slaves employed there can never be greater than the works need. For the miners find no limit to shaft or gallery. And, mark you, it is as 27 possible now to open new veins as in former times. Nor can one say with any certainty whether the ore is more plentiful in the area already under work or in the unexplored tracts.

Then why, it may be asked, are fewer new cuttings 28 made nowadays than formerly? Simply because those interested in the mines are poorer. For operations have only lately been resumed, and a man who makes a new cutting incurs a serious risk. If he strikes good stuff he makes a fortune; but if he is 29 disappointed, he loses the money he has spent. Therefore people nowadays are very chary of taking such a risk.

However, I think I can meet this difficulty too, 30 and suggest a plan that will make the opening of new cuttings a perfectly safe undertaking. The Athenians, of course, are divided into ten tribes. Now assume that the state were to offer each tribe an equal number of slaves, and that when new cuttings were made, the tribes were to pool their luck. The result would be that if one tribe found silver, 31 the discovery would be profitable to all; and if two,

---

[1] In 413 B.C., when great numbers of slaves deserted, and labour in the mines dwindled.

XENOPHON

δῆλον ὅτι λυσιτελέστερα ἂν τὰ ἔργα ταῦτα
γίγνοιτο.

Τό γε μὴν πάσας ἀποτυχεῖν οὐδενὶ τῶν παρελη-
32 λυθότων ἔοικός. οἶόν τε δὴ οὕτως καὶ ἰδιώτας συν-
ισταμένους καὶ κοινουμένους τὴν τύχην ἀσφαλέστερον κινδυνεύειν. μηδὲν μέντοι τοῦτο φοβεῖσθε,
ὡς ἢ τὸ δημόσιον οὕτω κατασκευαζόμενον παραλυ-
πήσει τοὺς ἰδιώτας ἢ οἱ ἰδιῶται τὸ δημόσιον· ἀλλ'
ὥσπερ σύμμαχοι ὅσῳ ἂν πλείους συνιῶσιν, ἰσχυ-
ροτέρους ἀλλήλους ποιοῦσιν, οὕτω καὶ ἐν τοῖς
ἀργυρείοις ὅσῳπερ ἂν πλείους ἐργάζωνται, τόσῳ
πλείονα τἀγαθὰ εὑρήσουσί τε καὶ ἐκφορήσουσι.[1]

33 Καὶ ἐμοὶ μὲν δὴ εἴρηται, ὡς ἂν ἡγοῦμαι κατα-
σκευασθείσης τῆς πόλεως ἱκανὴν ἂν πᾶσιν Ἀθη-
34 ναίοις τροφὴν ἀπὸ κοινοῦ γενέσθαι. εἰ δέ τινες
λογιζόμενοι παμπόλλης ἂν δεῖν ἀφορμῆς εἰς
ταῦτα πάντα οὐχ ἡγοῦνται ἱκανὰ ἄν ποτε χρήματα
35 εἰσενεχθῆναι, μηδὲ οὕτως ἀθυμούντων. οὐ γὰρ
οὕτως ἔχει, ὡς ἀνάγκη ἅμα πάντα ταῦτα
γίγνεσθαι, ἢ μηδὲν ὄφελος αὐτῶν εἶναι· ἀλλ'
ὁπόσα ἂν ἢ οἰκοδομηθῇ ἢ ναυπηγηθῇ ἢ ἀνδράποδα
36 ὠνηθῇ, εὐθὺς ταῦτα ἐν ὠφελείᾳ ἔσται. ἀλλὰ
μὴν καὶ τῇδέ γε συμφορώτερον τὸ κατὰ μέρος ἢ
τὸ ἅμα πάντα πράττεσθαι. οἰκοδομοῦντες μὲν
γὰρ ἀθρόοι πολυτελέστερον ἂν καὶ κάκιον ἢ
κατὰ μέρος ἀποτελοῖμεν· ἀνδράποδα δὲ παμπληθῆ
ζητοῦντες ἀναγκαζοίμεθ' ἂν καὶ χείρω καὶ τιμιώ-
τερα ὠνεῖσθαι.

[1] ἐκφορήσουσι Cobet: φορήσουσι S. with the MSS.
216

three, four, or half the tribes found, the profits from these works would obviously be greater.

Nothing that has happened in the past makes it probable that all would fail to find. Of course, 32 private individuals also are able to combine on this principle and pool their fortunes in order to diminish the risk. Nevertheless there is no reason to fear that a public company formed on this plan will conflict with the interests of private persons, or be hampered by them. No, just as every new adhesion to a confederacy brings an increase of strength to all its members, so the greater the number of persons operating in the mines, the more treasure they will discover and unearth.

I have now explained what regulations I think 33 should be introduced into the state in order that every Athenian may receive sufficient maintenance at the public expense. Some may imagine that 34 enough money would never be subscribed to provide the huge amount of capital necessary, according to their calculations, to finance all these schemes. But even so they need not despair. For it is not 35 essential that the plan should be carried out in all its details in order that any advantage may come of it. No, whatever the number of houses built, or of ships constructed, or of slaves purchased, they will immediately prove a paying concern. In 36 fact in one respect it will be even more profitable to proceed gradually than to do everything at once. For if everybody begins building, we shall pay more for worse work than if we carry out the undertaking gradually; and if we try to find an enormous number of slaves, we shall be forced to buy inferior men at a high price.

217

37 Κατά γε μὴν τὸ δυνατὸν περαίνοντες τὰ μὲν
καλῶς γνωσθέντα καὶ αὖθις ἂν ἡμῖν γενέσθαι
οἰόμεθα·[1] εἰ δέ τι ἁμαρτηθείη, ἀπεχοίμεθα ἂν
38 αὐτοῦ. ἔτι δὲ πάντων ἅμα γιγνομένων, ἡμᾶς ἂν
ἅπαντα δέοι ἐκπορίζεσθαι· εἰ δὲ τὰ μὲν περαίνοιτο,
τὰ δὲ μέλλοι, ἡ ὑπάρξασα[2] πρόσοδος τὸ ἐπιτήδειον συγκατασκευάζοι ἄν.

39 Ὁ δὲ ἴσως φοβερώτατον δοκεῖ πᾶσιν εἶναι, μὴ
εἰ ἄγαν πολλὰ κτήσαιτο ἡ πόλις ἀνδράποδα,
ὑπεργεμισθείη ἂν τὰ ἔργα, καὶ τούτου τοῦ φόβου
ἀπηλλαγμένοι ἂν εἴημεν, εἰ μὴ πλείονας ἀνθρώπους ἢ ὅσους αὐτὰ τὰ ἔργα προσαιτοίη κατ'
ἐνιαυτὸν ἐμβάλοιμεν.

40 Οὕτως ἔμοιγε δοκεῖ, ᾗπερ ῥᾷστον, ταύτῃ καὶ
ἄριστον εἶναι ταῦτα πράττειν· εἰ δ' αὖ διὰ τὰς ἐν
τῷ νῦν πολέμῳ γεγενημένας εἰσφορὰς νομίζετ' ἂν
μηδ' ὁτιοῦν δύνασθαι εἰσενεγκεῖν, ὑμεῖς δ' ὅσα μὲν
πρὸ τῆς εἰρήνης χρήματα εὕρισκε τὰ τέλη, ἀπὸ
τοσούτων καὶ τὸ ἐπιὸν ἔτος διοικεῖτε τὴν πόλιν·
ὅσα δ' ἂν ἐφευρίσκῃ διὰ τὸ εἰρήνην τε εἶναι καὶ
διὰ τὸ θεραπεύεσθαι μετοίκους καὶ ἐμπόρους καὶ
διὰ τὸ πλειόνων συναγειρομένων ἀνθρώπων πλείω
εἰσάγεσθαι καὶ ἐξάγεσθαι καὶ διὰ τὸ τὰ ἐλλιμένια[3]
καὶ τὰς ἀγορὰς αὐξάνεσθαι, ταῦτα λαμβάνοντες
κατασκευάσασθε, ὡς ἂν πλεῖσται πρόσοδοι
γίγνοιντο.

41 Εἰ δέ τινες αὖ φοβοῦνται, μὴ ματαία ἂν γένοιτο
αὕτη ἡ κατασκευή, εἰ πόλεμος ἐγερθείη, ἐννοη-

---

[1] The text is corrupt. The MSS. have ἡμῖν οἰόμεθα or
οἰοίμεθα, and γενέσθαι is a conjectural and unsatisfactory
addition.
[2] ὑπάρξασα MSS. : ὑπάρξουσα S.

By proceeding as our means allow, we can repeat 37
whatever is well conceived and avoid the repetition
of mistakes. Besides, were the whole scheme put in 38
hand at once, we should have to find the whole of
the money; but if some parts were proceeded with
and others postponed, the income realised would
help to provide the amount still required.

Possibly the gravest fear in everyone's mind is 39
that the works may become overcrowded if the state
acquires too many slaves. But we can rid ourselves
of that fear by not putting more men in year by
year than the works themselves require.

Accordingly I hold that this, which is the easiest 40
way, is also the best way of doing these things. On
the other hand, if you think that the burdens imposed during the late war [1] make it impossible for you
to contribute anything at all—well, keep down the
cost of administration during the next year to the
amount that the taxes yielded before the peace;
and invest the balances over and above that amount,
which you will get with peace, with considerate
treatment of resident aliens and merchants, with the
growth of imports and exports due to concentration
of a larger population, and with the expansion of
harbour and market dues, so that the investment
will bring in the largest revenue.[2]

Or again, if any fear that this scheme would 41
prove worthless in the event of war breaking out, they

[1] The allusion is to the "War of the Allies" who had
revolted from Athens. It lasted from 357 to 355 B.C. See
Introduction.

[2] *i.e.* invest the balances in the mines, and use the revenue
obtained to carry out my scheme.

---

[3] τὰ ἐλλιμένια Bergk: ἐν λιμένι S. with the MSS.

σάντων, ὅτι τούτων γιγνομένων πολὺ φοβερώτερος
42 ὁ πόλεμος τοῖς ἐπιφέρουσιν ἢ τῇ πόλει. τί γὰρ
δὴ εἰς πόλεμον κτῆμα χρησιμώτερον ἀνθρώπων ;
πολλὰς μὲν γὰρ ναῦς πληροῦν ἱκανοὶ ἂν εἶεν
δημοσίᾳ· πολλοὶ δ' ἂν καὶ πεζοὶ δημοσίᾳ δύναιντ'
ἂν βαρεῖς εἶναι τοῖς πολεμίοις, εἴ τις αὐτοὺς
θεραπεύοι.

43   Λογίζομαι δ' ἔγωγε καὶ πολέμου γιγνομένου
οἷόν τ' εἶναι μὴ ἐκλείπεσθαι τὰ ἀργύρεια. ἔστι
μὲν γὰρ δήπου περὶ τὰ μέταλλα ἐν τῇ πρὸς
μεσημβρίαν [1] τεῖχος ἐν Ἀναφλύστῳ, ἔστι δ' ἐν
τῇ πρὸς ἄρκτον τεῖχος ἐν Θορικῷ· ἀπέχει δὲ
ταῦτα ἀπ' ἀλλήλων ἀμφὶ τὰ ἑξήκοντα στάδια.
44 εἰ οὖν καὶ ἐν μέσῳ τούτων γένοιτο ἐπὶ τῷ ὑψη-
λοτάτῳ Βήσης τρίτον ἔρυμα, συνήκοι τ' ἂν τὰ ἔργα
εἰς ἓν ἐξ ἁπάντων τῶν τειχῶν, καὶ εἴ τι αἰσθάνοιτο
πολεμικόν, βραχὺ ἂν εἴη ἑκάστῳ εἰς τὸ ἀσφαλὲς
45 ἀποχωρῆσαι. εἰ δὲ καὶ ἔλθοιεν πλείους πολέμιοι,
δῆλον ὅτι εἰ μὲν σῖτον ἢ οἶνον ἢ πρόβατα ἔξω
εὕροιεν, ἀφέλοιντ' ἂν ταῦτα· ἀργυρίτιδος δὲ κρα-
τήσαντες τί ἂν μᾶλλον ἢ λίθοις ἔχοιεν χρῆσθαι ;
46 πῶς δὲ καὶ ὁρμήσειαν ἄν ποτε πολέμιοι πρὸς τὰ
μέταλλα ; ἀπέχει μὲν γὰρ δήπου τῶν ἀργυρείων
ἡ ἐγγύτατα πόλις Μέγαρα πολὺ πλεῖον τῶν
πεντακοσίων σταδίων· ἀπέχει δὲ ἡ μετὰ ταῦτα
πλησιαίτατα Θῆβαι πολὺ πλεῖον τῶν ἑξακοσίων.
47 ἢν οὖν πορεύωνται ἐντεῦθέν ποθεν ἐπὶ τὰ ἀργύρεια,

----

[1] S. with the MSS. adds θαλάττῃ which Bergk saw to be
spurious.

should observe that, with this system at work, war becomes far more formidable to the aggressors than to the city. For what instrument is more service- 42 able for war than men? We should have enough of them to supply crews to many ships of the state; and many men available for service in the ranks as infantry could press the enemy hard, if they were treated with consideration.[1]

But I reckon that, even in the event of war, the 43 mines need not be abandoned. There are, of course, two fortresses in the mining district, one at Anaphlystus on the south side, the other at Thoricus on the north. The distance between them is about seven miles and a half. Now suppose that we had a third 44 stronghold between them on the highest point of Besa. The works[2] would then be linked up by all the fortresses, and at the first intimation of a hostile movement, every man would have but a short distance to go in order to reach safety. In case an enemy 45 came in force, he would, no doubt, seize any corn or wine or cattle that he found outside; but the silver ore, when he had got it, would be of as much use to him as a heap of stones. And how could an 46 enemy ever go for the mines? The distance between Megara, the nearest city, and the silver mines, is of course much more than five hundred furlongs; and Thebes, which is next in proximity, lies at a distance of much more than six hundred furlongs from them. Let us assume, then, that an 47 enemy is marching on the mines from some such point.

---

[1] Observe that Xenophon alludes here not to the resident aliens, but to the state-owned slaves in the mines.

[2] Or, as some understand, "the workmen would gather from all the fortresses into one."

παριέναι αὐτοὺς δεήσει τὴν πόλιν· κἂν μὲν ὦσιν
ὀλίγοι, εἰκὸς αὐτοὺς ἀπόλλυσθαι καὶ ὑπὸ ἱππέων
καὶ ὑπὸ περιπόλων. πολλῇ γε μὴν δυνάμει
πορεύεσθαι ἐξερημοῦντας τὰ ἑαυτῶν χαλεπόν·
πολὺ γὰρ ἐγγύτερον ἂν εἴη ταῖς πόλεσιν αὐτῶν
τὸ τῶν Ἀθηναίων ἄστυ ἢ αὐτοὶ πρὸς τοῖς πετάλ-
48 λοις ὄντες. εἰ δὲ καὶ ἔλθοιεν, πῶς ἂν καὶ δύναιντο
μένειν μὴ ἔχοντες τὰ ἐπιτήδεια ; ἐπισιτίζεσθαί γε
μὴν μέρει μὲν κίνδυνος καὶ περὶ τῶν μετιόντων
καὶ περὶ ὧν ἀγωνίζονται· πάντες δὲ ἀεὶ μετιόντες
πολιορκοῖντ' ἂν μᾶλλον ἢ πολιορκοῖεν.

49 Οὐ τοίνυν μόνον ἡ ἀπὸ τῶν ἀνδραπόδων ἀποφορὰ[1] τὴν διατροφὴν τῇ πόλει αὔξοι ἄν, ἀλλὰ
πολυανθρωπίας περὶ τὰ μέταλλα ἀθροιζομένης
καὶ ἀπ' ἀγορᾶς τῆς ἐκεῖ οὔσης καὶ ἀπ' οἰκιῶν
περὶ τἀργύρεια δημοσίων καὶ ἀπὸ καμίνων καὶ
ἀπὸ τῶν ἄλλων ἁπάντων πρόσοδοι ἂν πολλαὶ
50 γίγνοιντο. ἰσχυρῶς γὰρ ἂν καὶ αὕτη πολυάν-
θρωπος γένοιτο πόλις, εἰ οὕτω κατασκευασθείη·
καὶ οἵ γε χῶροι οὐδὲν ἂν εἶεν μείονος ἄξιοι τοῖς
κεκτημένοις ἐνταῦθα ἢ τοῖς περὶ τὸ ἄστυ.

51 Πραχθέντων γε μὴν ὧν εἴρηκα σύμφημι ἐγὼ οὐ
μόνον ἂν χρήμασιν εὐπορωτέραν τὴν πόλιν εἶναι,
ἀλλὰ καὶ εὐπειθεστέραν καὶ εὐτακτοτέραν καὶ
52 εὐπολεμωτέραν γενέσθαι. οἵ τε γὰρ ταχθέντες
γυμνάζεσθαι πολὺ ἂν ἐπιμελέστερον τοῦτο πράτ-

---

[1] ἀποφορὰ Schneider : εἰσφορὰ S. with the MSS.

He is bound to pass Athens; and if his numbers are small, he is likely to be destroyed by our cavalry and patrols. On the other hand, to march on them with a large force, leaving his own property unprotected, is no easy matter; for when he arrived at the mines the city of Athens would be much nearer to his own states than he himself would be. But even supposing that he should come, how is he to 48 stay without supplies? And to send part of their forces in search of food may mean destruction to the foraging party and failure to achieve the ends for which he is contending; or if the whole force is continually foraging it will find itself blockaded instead of blockading.

However, the rent derived from the slaves would 49 not be the only source of relief to the community. With the concentration of a large population in the mining district, abundant revenue would be derived from the local market, from state-owned houses near the silver mines, from furnaces and all the other sources. For a densely populated city would grow 50 up there, if it were organised on this plan; yes, and building sites would become as valuable there as they are in our suburbs.

If the plans that I have put forward are carried 51 out, I agree[1] that, apart from the improvement in our financial position, we shall become a people more obedient, better disciplined, and more efficient in war.[2] For the classes undergoing physical 52 training will take more pains in the gymnasium when

---

[1] σύμφημι must mean "agree." If the text is right, one naturally asks "With whom?" Isocrates, Eubulus, or both? See Introduction.

[2] *Lac. Pol.* viii. 1.

τοιεν[1] ἐν τοῖς γυμνασίοις τὴν τροφὴν ἀπολαμβά-
νοντες πλείω ἢ ἐν ταῖς λαμπάσι γυμνασιαρχού-
μενοι· οἵ τε φρουρεῖν ἐν τοῖς φρουρίοις οἵ τε
πελτάζειν καὶ περιπολεῖν τὴν χώραν πάντα ταῦτα
μᾶλλον ἂν πράττοιεν, ἐφ' ἑκάστοις τῶν ἔργων τῆς
τροφῆς ἀποδιδομένης.

V. Εἰ δὲ σαφὲς δοκεῖ εἶναι, ὡς εἰ μέλλουσι
πᾶσαι αἱ πρόσοδοι ἐκ πόλεως προσιέναι, εἰρήνην
δεῖ ὑπάρχειν, ἆρ' οὐκ ἄξιον καὶ εἰρηνοφύλακας
καθιστάναι; πολὺ γὰρ ἂν καὶ αὕτη αἱρεθεῖσα ἡ
ἀρχὴ προσφιλεστέραν καὶ πυκνοτέραν εἰσ-
αφικνεῖσθαι πᾶσιν ἀνθρώποις ποιήσειε τὴν πόλιν.
2 εἰ δέ τινες οὕτω γιγνώσκουσιν, ὡς ἐὰν ἡ πόλις
εἰρήνην ἄγουσα διατελῇ, ἀδυνατωτέρα τε καὶ
ἀδοξοτέρα καὶ ἧττον ὀνομαστὴ ἐν τῇ Ἑλλάδι
ἔσται, καὶ οὗτοί γε ὡς ἐμοὶ δοκεῖ[2] παραλόγως
σκοποῦσιν. εὐδαιμονέσταται μὲν γὰρ δήπου
πόλεις λέγονται, αἱ ἂν πλεῖστον χρόνον ἐν εἰρήνῃ
διατελῶσι· πασῶν δὲ πόλεων Ἀθῆναι μάλιστα
3 πεφύκασιν ἐν εἰρήνῃ αὔξεσθαι. τίνες γὰρ ἡσυχίαν
ἀγούσης τῆς πόλεως οὐ προσδέοιντ' ἂν αὐτῆς
ἀρξάμενοι ἀπὸ ναυκλήρων καὶ ἐμπόρων; οὐχ οἱ
πολύσιτοι, οὐχ οἱ πολύοινοι,[3] τί δὲ οἱ πολυέλαιοι,
τί δὲ οἱ πολυπρόβατοι, οἱ δὲ γνώμῃ καὶ ἀργυρίῳ
4 δυνάμενοι χρηματίζεσθαι, καὶ μὴν χειροτέχναι τε
καὶ σοφισταὶ καὶ φιλόσοφοι, οἱ δὲ ποιηταί, οἱ δὲ
τὰ τούτων μεταχειριζόμενοι, οἱ δὲ ἀξιοθεάτων ἢ
ἀξιακούστων ἱερῶν ἢ ὁσίων ἐπιθυμοῦντες; ἀλλὰ
μὴν καὶ οἱ δεόμενοι πολλὰ ταχὺ ἀποδίδοσθαι ἢ

---

[1] τοῦτο πράττοιεν or πράττοιεν MSS.: πράττοιεν τὰ S. with
Lenklau.

they receive their maintenance in full than they take under the superintendents of the torch races;[1] and the classes on garrison duty in a fortress, or serving as targeteers, or patrolling the country will show greater alacrity in carrying out all these duties when the maintenance is duly supplied for the work done.

V. If it seems clear that the state cannot obtain a full revenue from all sources unless she has peace, is it not worth while to set up a board of guardians of peace? Were such a board constituted, it would help to increase the popularity of the city and to make it more attractive and more densely thronged with visitors from all parts. If any are inclined 2 to think that a lasting peace for our city will involve a loss of her power and glory and fame in Greece, they too, in my opinion, are out in their calculations. For I presume that those states are reckoned the happiest that enjoy the longest period of unbroken peace; and of all states Athens is by nature most suited to flourish in peace. For if 3 the state is tranquil, what class of men will not need her? Shipowners and merchants will head the list. Then there will be those rich in corn and wine and oil and cattle; men possessed of brains and money to invest; craftsmen and professors and 4 philosophers; poets and the people who make use of their works; those to whom anything sacred or secular appeals that is worth seeing or hearing. Besides, where will those who want to buy or sell

---

[1] The superintendents paid for the upkeep of the competitors training for public competitions. In difficult times they could not supply full rations.

---

[2] ἐμοὶ δοκεῖ Castalio : ἐμῇ δόξῃ S. with the MSS.
[3] S. retains οὐχ οἱ ἡδύοινοι after πολύοινοι with the MSS.

πρίασθαι ποῦ[1] τούτων μᾶλλον ἂν τύχοιεν ἢ[2]
Ἀθήνησιν;

5 Εἰ δὲ πρὸς ταῦτα μὲν οὐδεὶς ἀντιλέγει, τὴν δὲ
ἡγεμονίαν βουλόμενοί τινες ἀναλαβεῖν τὴν πόλιν[3]
ταύτην διὰ πολέμου μᾶλλον ἢ δι' εἰρήνης ἡγοῦνται
ἂν καταπραχθῆναι, ἐννοησάτωσαν πρῶτον μὲν τὰ
Μηδικά, πότερον βιαζόμενοι ἢ εὐεργετοῦντες τοὺς
Ἕλληνας ἡγεμονίας τε τοῦ ναυτικοῦ καὶ ἑλληνο-
6 ταμίας ἐτύχομεν. ἔτι δὲ ἐπεὶ ὠμῶς ἄγαν δόξασα
προστατεύειν ἡ πόλις ἐστερήθη τῆς ἀρχῆς, οὐ καὶ
τότε, ἐπεὶ τοῦ ἀδικεῖν ἀπεσχόμεθα, πάλιν ὑπὸ
τῶν νησιωτῶν ἑκόντων προστάται τοῦ ναυτικοῦ
7 ἐγενόμεθα; οὐκοῦν καὶ Θηβαῖοι εὐεργετούμενοι
ἡγεμονεύειν αὐτῶν ἔδωκαν Ἀθηναίοις; ἀλλὰ μὴν
καὶ Λακεδαιμόνιοι οὐ βιασθέντες ὑφ' ἡμῶν, ἀλλ'
εὖ πάσχοντες ἐπέτρεψαν Ἀθηναίοις περὶ τῆς
8 ἡγεμονίας θέσθαι ὅπως βούλοιντο. νῦν δέ γε διὰ
τὴν ἐν τῇ Ἑλλάδι ταραχὴν παραπεπτωκέναι μοι
δοκεῖ τῇ πόλει ὥστε καὶ ἄνευ πόνων καὶ ἄνευ
κινδύνων καὶ ἄνευ δαπάνης ἀνακτᾶσθαι τοὺς
Ἕλληνας. ἔστι μὲν γὰρ πειρᾶσθαι διαλλάττειν
τὰς πολεμούσας πρὸς ἀλλήλας πόλεις, ἔστι δὲ
συναλλάττειν, εἴ τινες ἐν αὐταῖς στασιάζουσιν.
9 εἰ δὲ καὶ ὅπως τὸ ἐν Δελφοῖς ἱερὸν αὐτόνομον
ὥσπερ πρόσθεν γένοιτο, φανεροὶ εἴητε ἐπιμελούμενοι, μὴ συμπολεμοῦντες, ἀλλὰ πρεσβεύοντες
ἀνὰ τὴν Ἑλλάδα, ἐγὼ μὲν οὐδὲν ἂν οἶμαι θαυμαστὸν εἶναι, εἰ καὶ πάντας τοὺς Ἕλληνας ὁμογνώ-
μονάς τε καὶ συνόρκους καὶ συμμάχους λάβοιτε

---

[1] ποῦ C: ἢ οὐ S. with the other MSS.
[2] ἢ C: S. omits with the other MSS.

many things quickly meet with better success in their efforts than at Athens?

No one, I dare say, contests this; but there are 5 some who wish the state to recover her ascendancy, and they may think that it is more likely to be won by war than by peace. Let such, in the first place, call to mind the Persian Wars. Was it by coercing the Greeks or by rendering services to them that we became leaders of the fleet and treasurers of the league funds? Further, after the state had been stripped of 6 her empire through seeming to exercise her authority with excessive harshness, did not the islanders even then restore to us the presidency of the fleet by their own free will, when we refrained from acts of injustice? And again, did not the Thebans place 7 themselves under the leadership of the Athenians in return for our good offices? Yet once again, it was not the effect of coercion on our part, but of generous treatment, that the Lacedaemonians permitted the Athenians to arrange the leadership as they chose. And now, owing to the confusion 8 prevalent in Greece, an opportunity, I think, has fallen to the state to win back the Greeks without trouble, without danger, and without expense. For she has it in her power to try to reconcile the warring states, she has it in her power to compose the factions contending in their midst. And were 9 it apparent that you are striving to make the Delphic shrine independent, as it used to be, not by joining in war, but by sending embassies up and down Greece, I for my part should not be in the least surprised if you found the Greeks all of one mind, banded together by oath and united in alliance

---

⁸ τὴν πόλιν Hartman : τῇ πόλει S. with the MSS.

ἐπ᾽ ἐκείνους, οἵτινες ἐκλιπόντων Φωκέων τὸ ἱερὸν
10 καταλαμβάνειν πειρῶντο.¹ εἰ δὲ καὶ ὅπως ἀνὰ
πᾶσαν γῆν καὶ θάλατταν εἰρήνη ἔσται, φανεροὶ
εἴητε ἐπιμελόμενοι, ἐγὼ μὲν οἶμαι πάντας ἂν
εὔχεσθαι μετὰ τὰς ἑαυτῶν πατρίδας Ἀθήνας
μάλιστα σώζεσθαι.

11 Εἰ δέ τις αὖ εἰς χρήματα κερδαλεώτερον
νομίζει εἶναι τῇ πόλει πόλεμον ἢ εἰρήνην, ἐγὼ
μὲν οὐκ οἶδα, πῶς ἂν ἄμεινον ταῦτα κριθείη ἢ
εἴ τις τὰ προγεγενημένα ἐπανασκοποίη ² τῇ πόλει
12 πῶς ἀποβέβηκεν. εὑρήσει γὰρ τό τε παλαιὸν ἐν
εἰρήνῃ μὲν πάνυ πολλὰ χρήματα εἰς τὴν πόλιν
ἀνενεχθέντα, ἐν πολέμῳ δὲ ταῦτα πάντα κατα-
δαπανηθέντα· γνώσεται δέ, ἢν σκοπῇ, καὶ ἐν τῷ
νῦν χρόνῳ διὰ μὲν τὸν πόλεμον καὶ τῶν προσόδων
πολλὰς ἐκλιπούσας καὶ τὰς εἰσελθούσας εἰς
παντοδαπὰ ³ καταδαπανηθείσας· ἐπεὶ δὲ εἰρήνη
κατὰ θάλατταν γεγένηται, ηὐξημένας τε τὰς
προσόδους καὶ ταύταις ἐξὸν τοῖς πολίταις
χρῆσθαι ὅ τι βούλοιντο.

13 Εἰ δέ τις με ἐπερωτῴη, Ἦ καὶ ἄν τις ἀδικῇ
τὴν πόλιν, λέγεις, ὡς χρὴ καὶ πρὸς τοῦτον
εἰρήνην ἄγειν; οὐκ ἂν φαίην· ἀλλὰ μᾶλλον
λέγω, ὅτι πολὺ θᾶττον ἂν τιμωροίμεθα αὐτούς,
εἰ μηδένα ὑπάρχοιμεν ἀδικοῦντες· ⁴ οὐδένα γὰρ
ἂν ἔχοιεν σύμμαχον.

VI. Ἀλλ᾽ εἴ γε μὴν τῶν εἰρημένων ἀδύνατον
μὲν μηδέν ἐστι μηδὲ χαλεπόν, πραττομένων δὲ

---

¹ πειρῶντο Madvig : ἐπειρῶντο S. with the MSS.
² ἐπανασκοποίη Dindorf : ἔτι ἀνασκοποίη S. with the MSS.
³ παντοδαπὰ Lenklau : παντοδαπὰ πολλὰ S. with the MSS.

against any that attempted to seize the shrine in the event of the Phocians abandoning it. Were you to show also that you are striving for peace in every land and on every sea, I do think that, next to the safety of their own country, all men would put the safety of Athens first in their prayers. 10

If, on the other hand, any one supposes that financially war is more profitable to the state than peace, I really do not know how the truth of this can be tested better than by considering once more what has been the experience of our state in the past. He will find that in old days a very great amount of money was paid into the treasury in time of peace, and that the whole of it was spent in time of war; he will conclude on consideration that in our own time the effect of the late war on our revenues was that many of them ceased, while those that came in were exhausted by the multitude of expenses; whereas the cessation of war by sea has been followed by a rise in the revenues, and has allowed the citizens to devote them to any purpose they choose. 11 12

But some one may ask me, Do you mean to say that, even if she is wronged, the state should remain at peace with the offender? No, certainly not; but I do say that our vengeance would follow far more swiftly on our enemies if we provoked nobody by wrong-doing; for then they would look in vain for an ally. 13

VI. Well now, surely, if none of these proposals is impossible or even difficult, if by carrying them into

---

[4] ὑπάρχοιμεν ἀδικοῦντες Cobet: παρέχοιμεν ἀδικοῦντα S. with the MSS.

XENOPHON

αὐτῶν προσφιλέστεροι μὲν τοῖς Ἕλλησι γενη-
σόμεθα, ἀσφαλέστερον δὲ οἰκήσομεν, εὐκλεέστεροι
δὲ ἐσόμεθα καὶ ὁ μὲν δῆμος τροφῆς εὐπορήσει, οἱ
δὲ πλούσιοι τῆς εἰς τὸν πόλεμον δαπάνης ἀπαλ-
λαγήσονται, περιουσίας δὲ πολλῆς γενομένης
μεγαλοπρεπέστερον μὲν ἔτι ἢ νῦν ἑορτὰς ἄξομεν,
ἱερὰ δ᾽ ἐπισκευάσομεν, τείχη δὲ καὶ νεώρια
ἀνορθώσομεν, ἱερεῦσι δὲ καὶ βουλῇ καὶ ἀρχαῖς
καὶ ἱππεῦσι τὰ πάτρια ἀποδώσομεν, πῶς οὐκ
ἄξιον ὡς τάχιστα τούτοις ἐγχειρεῖν, ἵνα ἔτι ἐφ᾽
ἡμῶν ἐπίδωμεν τὴν πόλιν μετ᾽ ἀσφαλείας εὐδαι-
μονοῦσαν ;

2 Εἴ γε μὴν ταῦτα δόξειεν ὑμῖν πράττειν,
συμβουλεύσαιμ᾽ ἂν ἔγωγε πέμψαντας καὶ εἰς
Δωδώνην καὶ εἰς Δελφοὺς ἐπερέσθαι τοὺς θεούς,
εἰ λῷον καὶ ἄμεινον εἴη ἂν τῇ πόλει οὕτω κατα-
σκευαζομένῃ καὶ αὐτίκα καὶ εἰς τὸν ἔπειτα
3 χρόνον. εἰ δὲ ταῦτα συναινοῖεν, τότ᾽ ἂν αὖ
φαίην χρῆναι ἐπερωτᾶν, τίνας θεῶν προσποιού-
μενοι ταῦτα κάλλιστα καὶ ἄριστα πράττοιμεν
ἄν· οὓς δ᾽ ἀνέλοιεν θεούς, τούτοις εἰκὸς καλ-
λιερήσαντας ἄρχεσθαι τοῦ ἔργου. σὺν γὰρ θεῷ
πραττομένων εἰκὸς καὶ τὰς πράξεις προϊέναι ἐπὶ
τὸ λῷον καὶ ἄμεινον ἀεὶ τῇ πόλει.

effect we shall be regarded with more affection by the Greeks, shall live in greater security, and be more glorious; if the people will be maintained in comfort and the rich no more burdened with the expenses of war; if with a large surplus in hand we shall celebrate our festivals with even more splendour than at present, shall restore the temples, and repair the walls and docks, and shall give back to priests, councillors, magistrates, knights their ancient privileges; surely, I say, our proper course is to proceed with this scheme forthwith, that already in our generation we may come to see our city secure and prosperous.

Furthermore, if you decide to go forward with the 2 plan, I should advise you to send to Dodona and Delphi, and inquire of the gods whether such a design is fraught with weal for the state both now and in days to come. And should they consent to 3 it, then I would say that we ought to ask them further, which of the gods we must propitiate in order that we may prosper in our handiwork. Then, when we have offered an acceptable sacrifice to the gods named in their reply, it behoves us to begin the work. For with heaven to help us in what we do, it is likely that our undertakings will go forward continually to the greater weal of the state.

THE CAVALRY COMMANDER

ΞΕΝΟΦΩΝΤΟΣ ΙΠΠΑΡΧΙΚΟΣ

I. Πρῶτον μὲν θύοντα χρὴ αἰτεῖσθαι θεοὺς
ταῦτα διδόναι καὶ νοεῖν καὶ λέγειν καὶ πράττειν,
ἀφ' ὧν θεοῖς μὲν κεχαρισμενώτατα ἄρξειας ἄν,
σαυτῷ δὲ καὶ φίλοις καὶ τῇ πόλει προσφιλέστατα
2 καὶ εὐκλεέστατα καὶ πολυωφελέστατα. θεῶν δ'
ἵλεων ὄντων ἀναβιβαστέον μέν σοι ἱππέας, καὶ
ὅπως ἀναπληρῶται ὁ κατὰ τὸν νόμον ἀριθμὸς
καὶ ὅπως τὸ ὂν ἱππικὸν μὴ μειῶται. εἰ δὲ μὴ
προσαναβήσονται ἱππεῖς, μείονες ἀεὶ ἔσονται·
ἀνάγκη γὰρ τοὺς μὲν γήρᾳ ἀπαγορεύειν, τοὺς δὲ
καὶ ἄλλως ἐκλείπειν.
3 Πληρουμένου γε μὴν τοῦ ἱππικοῦ ἐπιμελητέον
μέν, ὅπως τρέφωνται οἱ ἵπποι, ὡς ἂν δύνωνται
πόνους ὑποφέρειν· οἱ γὰρ ἥττους τῶν πόνων
οὔτε αἱρεῖν οὔτε ἀποφεύγειν δύναιντο ἄν. ἐπιμελητέον δέ, ὅπως εὔχρηστοι ὦσιν· οἱ γὰρ αὖ
ἀπειθεῖς τοῖς πολεμίοις μᾶλλον ἢ τοῖς φίλοις
4 συμμαχοῦσι. καὶ οἱ λακτίζοντες δὲ ἀναβεβα-
μένοι ἵπποι ἐκποδὼν ποιητέοι· οἱ γὰρ τοιοῦτοι
πολλάκις πλείω κακὰ ἢ οἱ πολέμιοι ποιοῦσι.
δεῖ δὲ καὶ τῶν ποδῶν ἐπιμελεῖσθαι, ὅπως δύνωνται καὶ ἐν τραχείᾳ χώρᾳ ἱππεύειν, εἰδότα,[1] ὅτι
ὅπου ἂν ἀλγῶσιν ἐλαυνόμενοι, ἐνταῦθα οὐ χρή-
σιμοί εἰσι.

[1] εἰδότα BM : εἰδότας S. with other MSS.

THE CAVALRY COMMANDER

I. The first duty is to sacrifice to the gods and pray them to grant you the thoughts, words and deeds likely to render your command most pleasing to the gods and to bring yourself, your friends and your city the fullest measure of affection and glory and advantage. Having gained the goodwill of the 2 gods, you have then to recruit a sufficient number of mounted men that you may bring the number up to the total required by the law,[1] and also may prevent any decrease in the cavalry establishment. Unless additional recruits are enrolled in the force, the number will constantly dwindle, for some men are bound to retire through old age and others to drop off for various reasons.

While the ranks are filling up, you must see that 3 the horses get enough food to stand hard work, since horses unfit for their work can neither overtake nor escape. You must see that they are docile, because disobedient animals assist the enemy more than their own side. And horses that 4 kick when mounted must be got rid of, for such brutes often do more mischief than the enemy. You must also look after their feet, so that they can be ridden on rough ground, for you know that wherever galloping is painful to them, they are useless.

[1] 1,000; but, as we shall see, the number had fallen to something like 650 at the time Xenophon wrote.

XENOPHON

5 Τῶν γε μὴν ἵππων ὑπαρχόντων οἵων δεῖ τοὺς
ἱππέας αὖ ἀσκητέον, πρῶτον μὲν ὅπως ἐπὶ τοὺς
ἵππους ἀναπηδᾶν δύνωνται· πολλοῖς γὰρ ἤδη ἡ
σωτηρία παρὰ τοῦτο ἐγένετο· δεύτερον δὲ ὅπως
ἐν παντοίοις χωρίοις ἱππάζεσθαι δυνήσονται· καὶ
γὰρ οἱ πόλεμοι ἄλλοτε ἐν ἀλλοίοις τόποις γίγνον-
6 ται. ὅταν δὲ ἤδη ἔποχοι ὦσι, δεῖ αὖ σκοπεῖσθαι,
ὅπως ἀκοντιοῦσί τε ὡς πλεῖστοι ἀπὸ τῶν ἵππων
καὶ τἆλλα δυνήσονται ποιεῖν ἃ δεῖ τοὺς ἱππικούς.

Μετὰ ταῦτα ὁπλιστέον καὶ ἵππους καὶ ἱππέας,
ὡς αὐτοὶ μὲν ἥκιστα τιτρώσκοιντ᾽ ἄν, βλάπτειν
7 δὲ τοὺς πολεμίους μάλιστα δύναιντ᾽ ἄν. ἐκ τούτων παρασκευαστέον, ὅπως εὐπειθεῖς οἱ ἄνδρες
ὦσιν· ἄνευ γὰρ τούτου οὔθ᾽ ἵππων ἀγαθῶν οὔτε
ἱππέων ἐπόχων οὔτε ὅπλων καλῶν ὄφελος οὐδέν.

Προστατεύειν μὲν οὖν τούτων πάντων ὅπως
8 καλῶς γίγνηται τὸν ἵππαρχον εἰκός ἐστιν. ἐπεὶ
δὲ καὶ ἡ πόλις χαλεπὸν ἡγησαμένη ταῦτα πάντα
τὸν ἵππαρχον μόνον ὄντα κατεργάζεσθαι προσαι-
ρεῖται μὲν αὐτῷ συνεργοὺς φυλάρχους, προσέ-
ταξε δὲ τῇ βουλῇ συνεπιμελεῖσθαι τοῦ ἱππικοῦ,
ἀγαθόν μοι δοκεῖ εἶναι τοὺς μὲν φυλάρχους
παρασκευάζειν συνεπιθυμεῖν σοι τῶν καλῶν τῷ
ἱππικῷ, ἐν δὲ τῇ βουλῇ ἔχειν ῥήτορας ἐπιτηδείους, ὅπως λέγοντες φοβῶσί τε τοὺς ἱππέας,

---

[1] A difficult feat, since the Greek rider had no stirrups.
[2] When attacking infantry in line the cavalry never
charged home; but only approached near enough to throw

Having made sure that the horses are in good 5
condition, the next business is to train the men.
First they must learn to mount from the spring,[1]
since many before now have owed their lives to that.
Secondly, they must practise riding over all sorts
of ground, since any kind of country may become
the area of war. As soon as they have acquired a 6
firm seat, your next task is to take steps that as
many as possible shall be able to throw the javelin
when mounted [2] and shall become efficient in all
the details of horsemanship.

After that both horses and men must be armed,
so that, while they are themselves thoroughly protected against wounds, they may have the means of
inflicting the greatest loss on the enemy. Then you 7
must contrive to make the men obedient : otherwise
neither good horses nor a firm seat nor fine armour
are of any use.

For ensuring efficiency in all these matters the
cavalry commander, as a matter of course, is the
principal authority. But, at the same time, the state 8
thinks it difficult for the cavalry commander to carry
out all these duties single-handed ; therefore, it also
elects colonels of regiments to assist him ; and it
has charged the Council with the duty of taking
a share in the management of the cavalry. I think
it well, then, that you should encourage the colonels
to be as eager as yourself for the efficiency of the
cavalry, and should have suitable spokesmen in the
Council, that their speeches may alarm the men—
they will do better under the influence of fear—and

the javelin with effect. Hence the importance attached to
an accomplishment by no means easy to perform without
stirrups. See especially the next treatise, c. xii.

βελτίονες γὰρ ἂν εἶεν φοβούμενοι, καταπραΰνωσί
τε τὴν βουλήν, ἤν τι παρὰ καιρὸν χαλεπαίνῃ.

9   Ταῦτα μὲν οὖν ὑπομνήματα ὧν δεῖ σε ἐπιμε-
λεῖσθαι· ὡς δ' ἂν ἕκαστα τούτων βέλτιστα
περαίνοιτο, τοῦτο δὴ πειράσομαι λέγειν.

Τοὺς μὲν τοίνυν ἱππέας δῆλον ὅτι καθιστάναι
δεῖ κατὰ τὸν νόμον τοὺς δυνατωτάτους καὶ χρήμασι καὶ σώμασιν ἢ εἰσάγοντα εἰς δικαστήριον ἢ
10 πείθοντα. ἐγὼ δὲ οἶμαι εἰς μὲν τὸ δικαστήριον
τούτους εἰσακτέον εἶναι, οὓς μὴ εἰσάγων ἄν τις
διὰ κέρδος δοκοίη τοῦτο ποιεῖν· καὶ γὰρ τοῖς
ἧττον δυναμένοις εὐθὺς ἂν εἴη ἀποστροφή, εἰ μὴ
11 τοὺς δυνατωτάτους πρώτους ἀναγκάζοις. ἔστι
δὲ καὶ οὓς ἄν μοι δοκεῖ τις νέους μὲν τὰ ἐν
ἱππικῇ λαμπρὰ λέγων εἰς ἐπιθυμίαν καθιστάναι
τοῦ ἱππεύειν, τοὺς δὲ κυρίους αὐτῶν ἧττον
ἀντιτείνοντας ἔχειν, τάδε διδάσκων, ὡς ἀναγκασθήσονται μὲν ἱπποτροφεῖν, ἢν μὴ ὑπὸ σοῦ, ὑπ'
12 ἄλλου, διὰ τὰ χρήματα· ἢν δὲ ἐπὶ σοῦ ἀναβῶσιν,
ὡς ἀποστρέψεις μὲν τοὺς παῖδας αὐτῶν τῶν
πολυτελῶν τε καὶ μανικῶν ἱππωνειῶν, ἐπιμε-
λήσει δέ, ὡς ἂν ταχὺ ἱππικοὶ γίγνοιντο. λέγοντα
δὲ οὕτω καὶ ποιεῖν ταῦτα πειρατέον.

13 Τούς γε μὴν ὄντας ἱππέας ἡ βουλὴ ἄν μοι
δοκεῖ προειποῦσα, ὡς τὸ λοιπὸν δεήσει διπλάσια
ἱππάζεσθαι καὶ ὡς τὸν μὴ δυνάμενον ἵππον
ἀκολουθεῖν ἀποδοκιμάσει, ἐπιτεῖναι ἂν τρέφειν
τε ἄμεινον καὶ ἐπιμελεῖσθαι μᾶλλον τῶν ἵππων.
238

may also appease the wrath of the Council, in case it shows indignation at the wrong time.

Here, then, you have brief notes on the matters 9 that demand your attention. I will now try to explain how these duties may best be carried out in detail.

As for the men, you must obviously raise them as required by the law, from among those who are most highly qualified by wealth and bodily vigour, either by obtaining an order of the court or by the use of persuasion. The cases that should be brought 10 before the court, I think, are those of men who otherwise might be suspected of having bribed you not to apply for a judgment. For the smaller men will at once have a ground for escaping, unless you first compel the most highly qualified to serve. I think, too, that, by dwelling on the 11 brilliancy of horsemanship, you might fire some of the young men with ambition to serve in the cavalry, and that you might overcome the opposition of their guardians by informing them that they will be required to keep horses by someone, if not by you, on account of their wealth; whereas, if their 12 boys join up during your command, you will put an end to their extravagance in buying expensive horses, and see that they soon make good riders. And you must try to suit your actions to your words.

As for the existing cavalry, I think that the 13 Council should give notice that in future double the amount of exercise will be required, and that any horse unable to keep up will be rejected. This warning would put the screw on the men and make them feed their horses better and take more care of

239

XENOPHON

14 καὶ τοὺς βιαίους δ' ἵππους ἀγαθόν μοι δοκεῖ
εἶναι προρρηθῆναι ὅτι ἀποδοκιμασθήσονται.
αὕτη γὰρ ἡ ἀπειλὴ πωλεύειν [1] ἂν τοὺς τοιούτους
μᾶλλον παρορμήσειε καὶ ἱππωνεῖν σωφρονέ-
15 στερον. ἀγαθὸν δὲ καὶ τοὺς ἐν ταῖς ἱππασίαις
λακτίζοντας ἵππους προρρηθῆναι ὅτι ἀποδοκι-
μασθήσονται· οὐδὲ γὰρ συντάττειν τοὺς τοιούτους δυνατόν, ἀλλ' ἀνάγκη κἄν ποι ἐπὶ πολεμίους
δέῃ ἐλαύνειν, ὑστάτους αὐτοὺς ἕπεσθαι, ὥστε
διὰ τὴν τοῦ ἵππου κακουργίαν ἄχρηστος καὶ ὁ
ἱππεὺς καθίσταται.
16 Ὡς δ' ἂν καὶ οἱ πόδες εἶεν τῶν ἵππων κράτιστοι, εἰ μέν τις ἔχει ῥᾴω καὶ εὐτελεστέραν
ἄσκησιν, ἐκείνη ἔστω· εἰ δὲ μή, ἐγώ φημι χρῆναι
πεῖραν ἔχων χύδην καταβαλόντα λίθους τοὺς ἐκ
τῆς ὁδοῦ ὅσον μναιαίους καὶ πλείον καὶ μεῖον ἐν
τούτοις τὸν ἵππον ψήχειν καὶ ἐνιστάναι, ὅταν
ἀπὸ τῆς φάτνης ἀποβῇ. βαδίζων γὰρ ἐν τοῖς
λίθοις οὔποτε ὁ ἵππος παύσεται οὔθ' ὅταν ψήχη-
ται οὔθ' ὅταν μυωπίζηται. ὁ δὲ πειραθεὶς τά
τε ἄλλα, ἃ λέγω, πιστεύσει καὶ στρογγύλους
τοὺς πόδας τῶν ἵππων ὄψεται.
17 Ὁπότε γε μὴν οἱ ἵπποι εἰσὶν οἵους δεῖ, ὡς ἂν αὐτοὶ
οἱ ἱππεῖς ἄριστοι γίγνοιντο, τοῦτο διηγήσομαι.
Τὸ μὲν τοίνυν τοὺς νέους αὐτῶν ἀναπηδᾶν ἐπὶ
τοὺς ἵππους πείθοιμεν ἂν αὐτοὺς μανθάνειν· τὸν
διδάξοντα δὲ παρασχὼν ἐπαίνου δικαίως ἂν
τυγχάνοις. τούς γε μὴν πρεσβυτέρους τὸν Περσικὸν τρόπον ἀναβάλλεσθαι ὑπ' ἄλλων προσε-
θίσας καὶ τούτους ὠφελήσαις ἄν.

---

[1] πωλεύειν Rühl: πωλεῖν S. with the MSS.

240

them. I think it would be well, too, if notice were 14
given that vicious horses would be rejected. Under
the stimulus of this threat men would break in such
animals more thoroughly and would be more careful
in buying horses. Again, it would be well to give 15
notice that horses found kicking at exercise will be
rejected. For it is impossible even to keep such
animals in line ; in a charge against an enemy they are
bound to lag behind, and the consequence is, that
through the bad behaviour of his horse, the man
himself becomes useless.

For getting horses' feet into the best condition,[1] 16
if anyone has an easier and cheaper method
than mine, by all means adopt it. If not, I hold—
and I speak from experience—that the right way
is to throw down some stones from the road,
averaging about a pound in weight, and to curry
the horse on these and to make him stand on them
whenever he goes out of the stable. For the horse
will constantly use his feet on the stones when he is
cleaned and when he is worried by flies. Try it, and
you will find your horses' feet round, and will believe
in the rest of my rules.

Assuming that the horses are in good condition, 17
I will explain how to make the men themselves
thoroughly efficient.

We would persuade the young recruits to learn
for themselves how to mount from the spring ;
but if you provide an instructor, you will receive
well-merited praise. The way to help the older
men is to accustom them to get a leg-up in the
Persian fashion.

[1] Horse-shoes being unknown ; cf. the following treatise,
c. iv.

18 Ὅπως γε μὴν ἐν παντοδαποῖς χωρίοις ἔποχοι
οἱ ἱππεῖς δυνήσονται εἶναι, τὸ μὲν πυκνὰ ἐξάγειν
μὴ πολέμου ὄντος ἴσως ὀχληρόν· συγκαλέσαντα
δὲ χρὴ τοὺς ἱππέας συμβουλεῦσαι αὐτοῖς μελετᾶν, καὶ ὅταν εἰς χώραν ἐλαύνωσι καὶ ὅταν
ἄλλοσέ ποι, ἐκβιβάζοντας τῶν ὁδῶν καὶ ταχὺ
ἐλαύνοντας ἐν τόποις παντοδαποῖς. τοῦτο γὰρ
ὠφελεῖ μὲν παραπλησίως τῷ ἐξάγειν, ὄχλον δ᾽
19 οὐχ ὅμοιον παρέχει. ἐπιτήδειον δὲ ὑπομιμνή-
σκειν, ὅτι καὶ ἡ πόλις ἀνέχεται δαπανῶσα εἰς
τὸ ἱππικὸν ἐγγὺς τετταράκοντα τάλαντα τοῦ
ἐνιαυτοῦ, ὡς ἢν πόλεμος γίγνηται, μὴ ζητεῖν δέῃ
ἱππικόν, ἀλλ᾽ ἐξ ἑτοίμου ἔχῃ παρεσκευασμένῳ
χρῆσθαι. ταῦτα γὰρ ἐνθυμουμένους εἰκὸς καὶ
τοὺς ἱππέας μᾶλλον ἀσκεῖν τὴν ἱππικήν, ὅπως
ἢν πόλεμος ἐγείρηται, μὴ ἀμελετήτους ὄντας
ἀγωνίζεσθαι δέῃ περί τε τῆς πόλεως καὶ περὶ
20 εὐκλείας καὶ περὶ τῆς ψυχῆς. ἀγαθὸν δὲ καὶ
τοῦτο προειπεῖν τοῖς ἱππεῦσιν, ὅτι ἐξάξεις καὶ
σύ ποτε αὐτοὺς καὶ διὰ παντοίων χωρίων ἡγήσει.
καὶ ἐν ταῖς μελέταις δὲ τῆς ἀνθιππασίας καλὸν
ἐξάγειν ἄλλοτε εἰς ἀλλοῖον τόπον· καὶ γὰρ τοῖς
ἱππεῦσι καὶ τοῖς ἵπποις βέλτιον.

21 Ἀκοντίζειν γε μὴν ἀπὸ τῶν ἵππων ὧδ᾽ ἂν
πλεῖστοί μοι δοκοῦσι μελετᾶν, εἰ τοῦτ᾽ αὖ προεί-
ποις τοῖς φυλάρχοις, ὅτι αὐτοὺς δεήσει ἡγου-
μένους τοῖς τῆς φυλῆς ἀκοντισταῖς ἐλαύνειν ἐπὶ
τὸ ἀκόντιον. φιλοτιμοῖντο γὰρ ἄν, ᾗ εἰκός, ὡς

To ensure that the men have a firm seat, what- 18
ever the nature of the ground, it is, perhaps, too
much trouble to have them out frequently when
there is no war going on ; but you should call the men
together, and recommend them to practise turning
off the roads and galloping over all sorts of ground
when they are riding to quarters or any other place.
For this does as much good as taking them out, and
it is less tedious. It is useful to remind them that 19
the state supports an expenditure of nearly forty
talents [1] a year in order that she may not have to
look about for cavalry in the event of war, but
may have it ready for immediate use. For with this
thought in their minds the men are likely to take
more pains with their horsemanship, so that when war
breaks out they may not have to fight untrained for
the state, for glory and for life. It is well also to 20
give notice to the men that you intend to take
them out yourself some day, and lead them over
country of all kinds. And during the manœuvres
that precede the sham fight it is proper to take
them out to a different piece of country at different
times : this is better for both men and horses.

As for throwing the javelin on horseback,[2] I think 21
that the greatest number will practise that if you
add a warning to the colonels that they will be required
to ride to javelin exercise themselves at the head
of the marksmen of the regiment. Thus, in all
probability, everyone of them will be eager to turn

[1] Say £9,500, a large sum in those times. The pay is, of
course, alluded to. The expenditure would amount *daily*
to nearly 666 *drachmae*. The cavalryman's normal pay was
a *drachma* a day. Hence it looks as if the number of the
cavalry in 365 B.C. had fallen to about 650.
[2] At a suspended shield.

πλείστους ἕκαστος ἀποδεῖξαι ἀκοντιστὰς τῇ πόλει.

22 Ἀλλὰ μὴν καὶ τοῦ καλῶς γε ὁπλισθῆναι τοὺς ἱππέας οἱ φύλαρχοι ἄν μοι δοκοῦσι μέγιστον συλλαμβάνειν, εἰ πεισθείησαν, ὅτι πολὺ ἐστι πρὸς τῆς πόλεως εὐδοξότερον τῇ τῆς φυλῆς λαμπρότητι κεκοσμῆσθαι ἢ μόνον τῇ ἑαυτῶν

23 στολῇ. εἰκὸς δὲ μὴ δυσπείστους εἶναι αὐτοὺς τὰ τοιαῦτα, οἵ γε φυλαρχεῖν ἐπεθύμησαν δόξης καὶ τιμῆς ὀρεγόμενοι, δυνατοὶ δ' εἰσὶ κατὰ τὰ ἐν τῷ νόμῳ ὁπλίσαι καὶ ἄνευ τοῦ αὐτοὶ δαπανᾶν τῷ μισθῷ ἐπαναγκάζοντες κατὰ τὸν νόμον ὁπλίζεσθαι.

24 Εἴς γε μὴν τὸ εὐπειθεῖς εἶναι τοὺς ἀρχομένους μέγα μὲν τὸ[1] λόγῳ διδάσκειν, ὅσα ἀγαθὰ ἔνι ἐν τῷ πειθαρχεῖν, μέγα δὲ καὶ τὸ ἔργῳ[2] πλεονεκτεῖν μὲν ποιεῖν τοὺς εὐτάκτους, μειονεκτεῖν δὲ ἐν πᾶσι τοὺς ἀτακτοῦντας.

25 Ἰσχυροτάτη δέ μοι δοκεῖ εἶναι παρόρμησις τῶν φυλάρχων εἰς τὸ φιλοτιμεῖσθαι αὐτοὺς καλῶς παρεσκευασμένης[3] ἕκαστον τῆς φυλῆς ἡγεῖσθαι, εἰ τοὺς ἀμφὶ σὲ προδρόμους κοσμήσαις μὲν ὅπλοις ὡς κάλλιστα, ἀκοντίζειν δὲ μελετᾶν ἐξαναγκάσαις ὡς μάλιστα, εἰσηγοῖο δὲ αὐτοῖς ἐπὶ τὸ ἀκόντιον αὐτὸς εὖ μάλα μεμελετηκώς.

26 εἰ δὲ καὶ ἆθλά τις δύναιτο προτιθέναι ταῖς

[1] τὸ Schneider : τὸ καὶ S. with the MSS.

[2] S. with the MSS. adds κατὰ τὸν νόμον, which was removed by Weiske.

[3] παρεσκευασμένης Weiske : παρεσκευασμένους S. with the MSS.

---

[1] The reference is first to the "establishment money"

out as many marksmen as possible for the service of the state.

Towards the proper arming of the men, I think 22 that the greatest amount of assistance will be obtained from the colonels, if they are persuaded that from the point of view of the state the brilliance of the regiment is a far more glorious ornament to them than the brightness of their own accoutrements only. It is likely that they will not 23 be hard to persuade in such matters, considering that honour and glory were the attractions that the colonelcy held out to them, and they can arm the men in accordance with the regulations laid down in the law without incurring expense themselves, afterwards compelling the men to spend their pay on their arms, as the law ordains.[1]

To make the men who are under your command 24 obedient, it is important to impress on them by word of mouth the many advantages of obedience to authority, and no less important to see that good discipline brings gain and insubordination loss in every respect.

The best way of inducing every colonel to take pride 25 in commanding a well equipped regiment, I think, is to arm your company of couriers as well as you can, to demand of them constant practice in the use of the javelin, and to instruct them in it after making yourself proficient. And if 26 you could offer prizes to the regiments for skill in

for horse and equipment, due to recruits when they had passed the examination by the Council. There is another allusion to it in c. ix. 5. This sum is independent of the pay ; and it is probable that on leaving the service the cavalryman had to refund it.

XENOPHON

φυλαῖς πάντων ὁπόσα ἀγαθὰ νομίζουσιν ἀσκεῖσθαι ἐν ταῖς θέαις ὑπὸ τοῦ ἱππικοῦ, τοῦτο πάντας
οἶμαι Ἀθηναίους γε μάλιστ' ἂν προτρέπειν εἰς
φιλονεικίαν. δῆλον δὲ τοῦτο καὶ ἐν τοῖς χοροῖς
ὡς μικρῶν ἄθλων ἕνεκα πολλοὶ μὲν πόνοι, μεγάλαι
δὲ δαπάναι τελοῦνται. τοὺς μέντοι κριτὰς τοιούτους δεῖ εὑρίσκειν, παρ' οἷς νικῶντες μάλιστ'
ἂν ἀγάλλοιντο.

II. Ἢν δὲ δή σοι ταῦτα πάντα ἐξησκημένοι
ὦσιν οἱ ἱππεῖς, δεῖ δήπου καὶ τάξιν τινὰ ἐπίστασθαι αὐτούς, ἐξ ἧς καλλίστας μὲν θεοῖς
πομπὰς πέμψουσι, κάλλιστα δὲ ἱππάσονται,
ἄριστα δὲ μαχοῦνται, ἢν δέῃ, ῥᾷστα δὲ καὶ
ἀταρακτότατα ὁδοὺς πορεύσονται καὶ διαβάσεις
περάσουσιν. ᾗ τοίνυν χρώμενοι τάξει δοκοῦσιν
ἄν μοι ταῦτα κάλλιστα διαπράττεσθαι, ταύτην
νῦν ἤδη πειράσομαι δηλοῦν.

2   Οὐκοῦν ὑπὸ μὲν τῆς πόλεως ὑπάρχουσι
διῃρημέναι φυλαὶ δέκα. τούτων δ' ἐγώ φημι
χρῆναι πρῶτον μὲν δεκαδάρχους σὺν τῇ τῶν
φυλάρχων ἑκάστου γνώμῃ καταστῆσαι ἐκ τῶν
ἀκμαζόντων τε καὶ φιλοτιμοτάτων καλόν τι
ποιεῖν καὶ ἀκούειν· καὶ τούτους μὲν πρωτοστάτας
3 δεῖ εἶναι. μετὰ δὲ τούτους ἴσους χρὴ τούτοις
ἀριθμὸν ἐκ τῶν πρεσβυτάτων τε καὶ φρονιμωτά-
των ἑλέσθαι, οἵτινες τελευταῖοι τῶν δεκάδων
ἔσονται. εἰ γὰρ δεῖ καὶ ἀπεικάσαι, οὕτω καὶ
σίδηρος μάλιστα διατέμνει σίδηρον, ὅταν τό τε
ἡγούμενον τοῦ τομέως ἐρρωμένον ᾖ καὶ τὸ
ἐπελαυνόμενον ἱκανόν.

4   Τούς γε μὴν ἐν μέσῳ τῶν πρώτων καὶ τῶν

246

all the feats that the public expects the cavalry to perform at the spectacles, I think this would appeal strongly to the spirit of emulation in every Athenian. For evidence of this I may refer to the choruses, in which many labours and heavy expenses are the price paid for trifling rewards. Only you must find judges whose suffrage will shed lustre on a victory.

II. When your men are well trained in all these points, they must, of course, understand some plan of formation, that in which they will show to greatest advantage in the sacred processions and at manœuvres, fight, if need be, with the greatest courage, and move along roads and cross rivers with perfect ease in unbroken order. So I will now try to explain the formation that I think will give the best results in these various circumstances.

Now the state has divided the cavalry into ten 2 separate regiments. I hold that within these you should, to begin with, appoint file-leaders [1] after consulting each of the colonels, choosing sturdy men, who are bent on winning fame by some brilliant deed. These should form the front rank. Next 3 you should choose an equal number of the oldest and most sensible to form the rear rank. To use an illustration, steel has most power to cut through steel when its edge is keen and its back reliable.

To fill the ranks between the front and rear, 4 the file-leaders should choose the men to form the

---

[1] "Decadarchs," commanding a file of ten ($\delta\epsilon\kappa\dot{a}s$). X. had in mind the organisation of the Spartan infantry; cp. *Constitution of the Lac.* xi. 5.

---

[1] $\delta\epsilon\kappa\alpha$ added here by Pierleoni : S. omits with the MSS.

τελευταίων, εἰ οἱ δεκάδαρχοι ἐπιστάτας ἕλοιντο
καὶ οἱ ἄλλοι ἐφέλοιντο, οὕτως εἰκὸς ἑκάστῳ
πιστότατον τὸν ἐπιστάτην εἶναι.

5 Τὸν μέντοι ἀφηγούμενον ἐκ παντὸς τρόπου
δεῖ ἱκανὸν ἄνδρα καθιστάναι. ἀγαθὸς γὰρ ὤν,
εἴτε ποτὲ δέοι ἐπὶ πολεμίους ἐλαύνειν, ἐγκελεύων
ῥώμην ἂν ἐμβάλλοι τοῖς ἔμπροσθεν, εἴτ' αὖ
καὶ ἀποχωρεῖν καιρὸς συμβαίνοι, φρονίμως
ἀφηγούμενος μᾶλλον ἄν, ὡς τὸ εἰκός, σώζοι
τοὺς φυλέτας.

6 Οἱ μέντοι δεκάδαρχοι ἄρτιοι ὄντες πλείω ἴσα
μέρη παρέχοιεν ἂν διαιρεῖν ἢ εἰ περιττοὶ εἶεν.

Αὕτη δέ μοι ἡ τάξις ἀρέσκει διὰ τάδε, ὅτι
πρῶτον μὲν οἱ πρωτοστάται πάντες ἄρχοντες
γίγνονται, οἱ δ' αὐτοὶ ἄνδρες, ὅταν ἄρχωσι,
μᾶλλόν πως οἴονται ἑαυτοῖς προσήκειν τι καλὸν
ποιεῖν ἢ ὅταν ἰδιῶται ὦσιν· ἔπειτα δὲ καὶ ὅταν
πρακτέον τι ᾖ, τὸ παραγγέλλειν μὴ ἰδιώταις,
ἀλλ' ἄρχουσι πολὺ ἀνυτικώτερον.

7 Τεταγμένων γε μὴν οὕτως χρή, ὥσπερ καὶ
τοῖς φυλάρχοις προαγορεύεται ἡ χώρα ὑπὸ τοῦ
ἱππάρχου, ἐν ᾗ ἑκάστῳ ἐλατέον, οὕτω καὶ τοῖς
δεκαδάρχοις παρηγγέλθαι ὑπὸ τῶν φυλάρχων
ὅπῃ[1] πορευτέον ἑκάστῳ. οὕτω γὰρ προειρη-
μένων πολὺ εὐτακτοτέρως ἔχοι ἢ ἂν εἰ ὥσπερ
ἐκ θεάτρου ὡς ἂν τύχωσιν ἀπιόντες λυποῦσιν
8 ἀλλήλους. καὶ μάχεσθαι δὲ μᾶλλον ἐθέλουσιν
οἵ τε πρῶτοι, ἤν τι ἐκ τοῦ πρόσθεν προσπίπτῃ,

[1] ὅπῃ Diels: ὅπως S. with the MSS.

second line, and these in turn the men to form the third, and so on throughout. In this way every man will naturally have complete confidence in the man behind him.

You must be very careful to appoint a competent 5 man as leader in the rear.[1] For if he is a good man, his cheers will always hearten the ranks in front of him in case it becomes necessary to charge; or, should the moment come to retreat, his prudent leadership will, in all probability, do much for the safety of his regiment.

An even number of file-leaders has this advantage 6 over an odd, that it is possible to divide the regiment into a larger number of equal parts.

The reasons why I like this formation are these. In the first place, all the men in the front rank are officers; and the obligation to distinguish themselves appeals more strongly to men when they are officers than when they are privates. Secondly, when anything has to be done, the word of command is much more effective if it is passed to officers rather than to privates.

Let us assume that this formation has been 7 adopted: every file-leader must know his position in the line of march by word passed along by the colonel, just as every colonel is informed by the commander of his proper place in the charge. For when these instructions are given there will be much better order than if the men hamper one another like a crowd leaving the theatre. And in the event of a frontal 8 attack, the men in the van are far more willing to

---

[1] *i.e.* the last man of each file (cf. § 3), who in some cases would have to act as leader. In the Spartan infantry he was the man with the longest service in the file.

οἳ ἂν εἰδῶσιν, ὅτι αὕτη ἡ χώρα αὐτῶν· καὶ οἱ
τελευταῖοι, ἤν τι ὄπισθεν ἐπιφαίνηται, ἐπιστά-
9 μενοι, ὅτι αἰσχρὸν λιπεῖν τὴν τάξιν. ἄτακτοι
δ' ὄντες ἀλλήλους μὲν τάραττουσι καὶ ἐν
στεναῖς ὁδοῖς καὶ ἐν διαβάσεσι, τοῖς δὲ πολεμίοις οὐδεὶς ἑκὼν αὐτὸν τάττει μάχεσθαι.

Καὶ ταῦτα μὲν δὴ πάντα ὑπάρχειν δεῖ
ἐκπεπονημένα πᾶσι τοῖς ἱππεῦσιν, εἰ μέλλουσιν
ἀπροφάσιστοι ἔσεσθαι συνεργοὶ τῷ ἡγουμένῳ.

III. Τῶνδέ γε μὴν αὐτῷ ἤδη μέλειν δεῖ τῷ
ἱππάρχῳ· πρῶτον μὲν ὅπως καλλιερήσει τοῖς
θεοῖς ὑπὲρ τοῦ ἱππικοῦ, ἔπειτα ὅπως τὰς
πομπὰς ἐν ταῖς ἑορταῖς ἀξιοθεάτους ποιήσει,
ἔτι δὲ καὶ τἆλλα ὅσα ἐπιδεικνύναι δεῖ τῇ πόλει
ὅπως ᾗ δυνατὸν κάλλιστα ἐπιδείξει, τά τε ἐν
Ἀκαδημείᾳ καὶ τὰ ἐν Λυκείῳ καὶ τὰ Φαληροῖ
καὶ τὰ ἐν τῷ ἱπποδρόμῳ.

Καὶ ταῦτα μὲν ἄλλα ὑπομνήματα· ὡς δὲ
τούτων ἕκαστα κάλλιστα ἂν πράττοιτο, νῦν
αὐτὰ ταῦτα [1] λέξω.

2 Τὰς μὲν οὖν πομπὰς οἶμαι ἂν καὶ τοῖς
θεοῖς κεχαρισμενωτάτας καὶ τοῖς θεαταῖς εἶναι,
εἰ ὅσων ἱερὰ καὶ ἀγάλματα ἐν τῇ ἀγορᾷ ἐστι,
ταῦτα ἀρξάμενοι ἀπὸ τῶν Ἑρμῶν κύκλῳ [2]
περιελαύνοιεν τιμῶντες τοὺς θεούς. καὶ ἐν τοῖς

---

[1] ταῦτα is omitted by S. with ML.
[2] S. with the MSS. adds περὶ τὴν ἀγορὰν καὶ τὰ ἱερὰ which
was removed by Herwerden.

---

[1] Nothing in the sequel refers to manœuvres at Phalerum ;
accordingly it has been proposed to omit καὶ τὰ Φαληροῖ as
spurious. The Hippodrome was probably in the N.W.

fight when they know that this is their station; so is the rear-rank in the event of a surprise attack in the rear, when the men there understand that it is disgraceful to leave their post. But if no order is 9 kept there is confusion whenever the roads are narrow or rivers are being crossed; and when an action is fought no one voluntarily takes his post in the fighting line.

All these preliminaries must be thoroughly mastered by all the cavalry, if they are to give their leader unflinching support.

III. Now we come to duties that the cavalry commander must perform himself. First, he must sacrifice to propitiate the gods on behalf of the cavalry; secondly, he must make the processions during the festivals worth seeing; further, he must conduct all the other obligatory displays before the people with as much splendour as possible, that is to say, the reviews in the Academy, in the Lyceum, at Phalerum, and in the Hippodrome.[1]

These again are only brief notes; and I will now explain exactly how the details of these various functions may be carried out with most splendour.

As for the processions, I think they would be most 2 acceptable both to the gods and to the spectators if they included a gala ride in the market place. The starting point would be the Herms[2]; and the cavalry would ride round saluting the gods at their shrines

district of the Piraeus. This treatise gives the only information that we possess about these functions.

[2] The Herms stood in two rows between the "Stoa Basileios" and the "Poicile." The Eleusinium, probably lay at the western foot of the Acropolis. See Frazer, *Pausanias* vol. ii., p. 121 and p. 131. Some think the site was at the east foot.

Διονυσίοις δὲ οἱ χοροὶ προσεπιχαρίζονται ἄλλοις τε θεοῖς καὶ τοῖς δώδεκα χορεύοντες.

Ἐπειδὰν δὲ πάλιν πρὸς τοὺς Ἑρμαῖς γένωνται περιεληλακότες, ἐντεῦθεν καλόν μοι δοκεῖ εἶναι κατὰ φυλὰς εἰς τάχος ἀνιέναι τοὺς ἵππους μέχρι

3 τοῦ Ἐλευσινίου. οὐδὲ δόρατα μὴν παραλείψω ὡς ἥκιστα ἂν ἀλλήλοις ἐπαλλάττοιτο. δεῖ γὰρ μεταξὺ τοῖν ὤτοιν τοῦ ἵππου ἕκαστον σχεῖν, εἰ μέλλει φοβερά τε καὶ εὐκρινῆ ἔσεσθαι καὶ ἅμα πολλὰ φανεῖσθαι.

4 Ἐπειδὰν δὲ τῆς εἰς τάχος διελάσεως λήξωσι, τὴν ἄλλην ἤδη καλὸν σχέδην εἰς τὰ ἱερά, ᾗπερ καὶ πρόσθεν, διελαύνειν. καὶ οὕτως ὅσα ἔστιν ἤδη ἐν ἵππῳ ἀναβεβαμένῳ, πάντα ἐπιδεδειγμένα ἔσται καὶ τοῖς θεοῖς καὶ τοῖς ἀνθρώποις.

5 Καὶ ὅτι μὲν ταῦτα οὐκ εἰθισμένοι ποιεῖν οἱ ἱππεῖς εἰσιν, οἶδα· γιγνώσκω δέ, ὅτι ἀγαθὰ καὶ καλὰ καὶ τοῖς θεαταῖς ἡδέα ἔσται. αἰσθάνομαι δὲ καὶ ἄλλα ἀγωνίσματα τοὺς ἱππέας κεκαινουργηκότας, ἐπειδὴ οἱ ἵππαρχοι ἱκανοὶ ἐγένοντο πεῖσαι ἃ ἠβουλήθησαν.

6 Ὅταν γε μὴν πρὸ τοῦ ἀκοντισμοῦ διελαύνωσιν ἐν Λυκείῳ, καλὸν ἑκατέρας τὰς πέντε φυλὰς ἐπὶ μετώπου ἐλαύνειν ὥσπερ εἰς μάχην ἡγουμένου τοῦ ἱππάρχου καὶ τῶν φυλάρχων ἐν τοιαύτῃ τάξει, ἀφ' ἧς πληρώσεται τοῦ δρόμου τὸ πλάτος.

7 ἐπειδὰν δ' ὑπερβάλωσι τὸ κεφάλαιον τοῦ ἀντιπροσώπου θεάτρου, χρήσιμον ἂν οἴομαι φανῆναι καὶ εἰ καθ' ὁπόσους μέτριον εἰς τὸ κάταντες

---

[1] The Greek text is unreliable here.
[2] The Theatre of Dionysus, facing them as they come westwards from the Lyceum.

and statues. So at the Great Dionysia the dance of the choruses forms part of the homage offered to the Twelve and to other gods.

When the circuit is completed and the cavalcade is again near the Herms, the next thing to do, I think, is to gallop at top speed by regiments as far as the Eleusinium. I will add a word on the 3 position in which the lances should be held to prevent crossing. Every man should point his lance between his horse's ears, if the weapons are to look fearsome, stand out distinctly, and at the same time to convey the impression of numbers.

The gallop finished and the goal reached, the right 4 plan is to ride back to the temples by the same route, but at a slow pace : thus every effect that can be obtained from a horse with a man on his back [1] will be included in the display, to the satisfaction of gods and men alike.

I know that our cavalrymen are not accustomed to 5 these movements: but I am sure that they are desirable and beautiful, and will delight the spectators. I am aware, too, that the cavalry have exhibited other novel feats of skill in days when the cavalry commanders had sufficient influence to get their wishes carried out.

During the parade at the Lyceum, before the 6 javelin-throwing, the right way is to ride in two divisions in line of battle, each division consisting of five regiments with its commander at the head and the colonels ; and the line should be so extended that the whole breadth of the course will be covered. As soon as they reach the highest point looking 7 down on the Theatre opposite,[2] I think it would clearly be useful if you displayed your men's ability

δυναμένους ταχὺ ἐλαύνειν ἐπιδείξαις τοὺς ἱππέας.
8 οὐ μέντοι ἀγνοῶ, ὅτι ἢν μὲν πιστεύωσι δυνήσεσθαι ταχὺ ἐλαύνειν, πάνυ ἂν ἡδέως ἐπιδείξαιντο·
ἢν δὲ ἀμελέτητοι ὦσιν, ὁρᾶν χρή, ὅπως μὴ οἱ
πολέμιοι αὐτοὺς τοῦτο δρᾶν ἀναγκάσουσιν.
9   Ἔν γε μὴν ταῖς δοκιμασίαις ἡ μὲν τάξις
εὕρηται, μεθ᾽ ἧς ἂν κάλλιστα ἱππάζοιντο. ἢν
δ᾽ ὁ ἡγούμενος, ἥνπερ ἔχῃ δυνατὸν ἵππον, ἐν τῷ
ἔξωθεν ἀεὶ στίχῳ περιφέρηται, οὕτως αὐτὸς μὲν
ἀεὶ ταχὺ ἐλᾷ καὶ οἱ σὺν αὐτῷ ἔξωθεν γιγνόμενοι
πάλιν αὖ ταχὺ ἐλῶσιν· ὥστε ἡ μὲν βουλὴ ἀεὶ
τὸ ταχὺ ἐλαυνόμενον θεάσεται, οἱ δὲ ἵπποι οὐκ
ἀπεροῦσιν ἐν μέρει ἀναπαυόμενοι.
10   Ὅταν γε μὴν ἐν τῷ ἱπποδρόμῳ ἡ ἐπίδειξις
ᾖ, καλὸν μὲν οὕτω πρῶτον τάξασθαι, ὡς ἂν ἐπὶ
μετώπου ἐμπλήσαντες ἵππων τὸν ἱππόδρομον
11 ἐξελάσειαν τοὺς ἐκ τοῦ μέσου ἀνθρώπους. καλὸν
δ᾽, ἐπεὶ αἱ φυλαὶ ἐν τῇ ἀνθιππασίᾳ φεύγουσί τε
ἀλλήλας καὶ διώκουσι ταχέως, ὅταν οἱ ἵππαρχοι
ἡγῶνται ταῖς πέντε φυλαῖς, ἑκατέρας διελαύνειν
τὰς φυλὰς δι᾽ ἀλλήλων. ταύτης γὰρ τῆς θέας
τό τε ἀντιμετώπους προσελαύνειν ἀλλήλοις
γοργὸν τό τε διελάσαντας τὸν ἱππόδρομον
ἀντίους πάλιν στῆναι ἀλλήλοις σεμνὸν καὶ
τὸ ἀπὸ σάλπιγγος αὖ τὸ δεύτερον θᾶττον ἐπε-
12 λαύνειν καλόν. στάντας δὲ ἤδη τὸ τρίτον αὖ
ἀπὸ τῆς σάλπιγγος χρὴ τάχιστα ἀλλήλοις

---

[1] The allusion is not to the inspection of recruits by the
Council, but to the manœuvres enumerated in c. iii. 1.   The
formation is that proposed in c. ii.
[2] As it is not known precisely what evolutions took place

to gallop downhill in fairly large companies. To be 8
sure, I know well enough that, if they feel confident
of their ability to gallop, they will welcome the
opportunity of showing off their skill: but you
must see that they are not short of practice, or
the enemy will compel them to do it against their
will.

The formation that would add most to the beauty 9
of the exercises at the inspections [1] has already been
explained. Provided his horse is strong enough, the
leader should ride round with the file that is on the
outside every time. He will be galloping all the
time himself, and the file whose turn it is to be on
the outside with him will also be galloping. Thus
the eyes of the Council will always be on the
galloping file, and the horses will get a breathing
space, resting by turns. [2]

When the Hippodrome is the scene of the display, 10
the right plan would be that the men should first be
drawn up on a front broad enough to fill the
Hippodrome with horses and drive out the people
standing there. In the sham fight when the 11
regiments pursue and fly from one another at the
gallop in two squadrons of five regiments, each side
led by its commander, the regiments should ride
through one another. How formidable they will look
when they charge front to front; how imposing when,
after sweeping across the Hippodrome, they stand
facing one another again; how splendid, when the
trumpet sounds and they charge once more at a
quicker pace! After the halt, the trumpet should 12
sound once more, and they should charge yet a

at the displays, it is impossible to make out what changes
Xenophon proposes.

XENOPHON

ἐπελαύνειν καὶ διελάσαντας εἰς κατάλυσιν ἤδη
ἐπὶ φάλαγγος ἅπαντας καταστάντας, ὥσπερ
13 εἰώθατε, πρὸς τὴν βουλὴν προσελαύνειν. ταῦτά
μοι δοκεῖ πολεμικώτερά τε φαίνεσθαι ἂν καὶ
καινότερα. τὸ δὲ βραδύτερον μὲν τῶν φυλάρχων
ἐλαύνειν, τὸν δ' αὐτὸν τρόπον ἐκείνοις ἱππεύειν
οὐκ ἄξιον ἱππαρχίας.
14   Ὅταν γε μὴν ἐν τῷ ἐπικρότῳ ἐν Ἀκαδημείᾳ
ἱππεύειν δέῃ, ἔχω τάδε παραινέσαι· εἰς μὲν τὸ
μὴ ἀποκρούεσθαι ἀπὸ [1] τῶν ἵππων ὑπτίους
ἀναπεπτωκότας ἐλαύνειν, εἰς δὲ τὸ μὴ πίπτειν
τοὺς ἵππους ὑπολαμβάνειν ἐν ταῖς ἀναστροφαῖς.
τὰ μέντοι ὀρθὰ ταχὺ ἐλαύνειν χρή· οὕτω γὰρ τὸ
ἀσφαλὲς καὶ τὸ καλὸν θεάσεται ἡ βουλή.
     IV. Ἔν γε μὴν ταῖς πορείας ἀεὶ δεῖ τὸν ἵππαρ-
χον προνοεῖν, ὅπως ἀναπαύῃ μὲν τῶν ἵππων τὰς
ἕδρας, ἀναπαύῃ δὲ τοὺς ἱππέας τῷ [2] βαδίζειν,
μέτριον μὲν ὀχοῦντα, μέτριον δὲ πεζοποροῦντα.
τοῦ δὲ μετρίου ἐννοῶν οὐκ ἂν ἁμαρτάνοις·
αὐτὸς γὰρ μέτρον ἕκαστος τοῦ μὴ λαθεῖν
ὑπερπονοῦντας.
2   Ὅταν μέντοι ἀδήλου ὄντος, εἰ πολεμίοις
ἐντεύξει, πορεύῃ ποι, κατὰ μέρος χρὴ τὰς φυλὰς
ἀναπαύειν. χαλεπὸν γάρ, εἰ πᾶσι καταβεβη-
κόσι πλησιάσειαν οἱ πολέμιοι.
3   Καὶ ἢν μέν γε διὰ στενῶν ὁδῶν ἐλαύνῃς,
ἀπὸ παραγγέλσεως εἰς κέρας ἡγητέον· ἢν δὲ
πλατείαις ἐπιτυγχάνῃς ὁδοῖς, ἀπὸ παραγγέλσεως αὖ πλατυντέον τῆς φυλῆς ἑκάστης τὸ

───
[1] ἀπὸ B: ποτε S. with the other MSS.
[2] τῷ Herwerden: τοῦ S. with the MSS.

third time at top speed; and when they have crossed, they should all range themselves in battle line preparatory to being dismissed, and ride up to the Council, just as you are accustomed to do. I 13 think that these manœuvres would look more like war and would have the charm of novelty. It is unworthy of his high rank that a cavalry commander should gallop at a slower pace than the colonels, and ride in the same way as they do.

When the ride is to take place in the Academy on 14 the hard ground, I have the following recommendations to make. To avoid being thrown the riders should throw the body back in charging, and collect their horses when wheeling, to keep them from falling. In the straight, however, they should gallop. The Council will thus watch a safe as well as a beautiful performance.

IV. During a march the cavalry commander must always think ahead, in order that he may rest the horses' backs and relieve the men by walking, giving moderate spells of alternate riding and marching. You can't misjudge what is a moderate spell, since every man is himself the measure [1] that will show you when they are getting tired.

But when it is uncertain whether you will en- 2 counter an enemy on your way to any place, you must give the regiments a rest in turn. For it would be a bad job if all the men were dismounted when the enemy is close at hand.

If you are riding along narrow roads, the order 3 must be given to form column; but when you find yourself on broad roads, the order must be given to

---

[1] Perhaps a reference to the theory of Protagoras, "Man is the measure of all things."

μέτωπον· ὅταν γε μὴν εἰς πεδίον ἀφικνῆσθε,
ἐπὶ φάλαγγος πάσας τὰς φυλὰς ἀκτέον.[1] ἀγαθὸν γὰρ καὶ μελέτης ἕνεκα ταῦτα ποιεῖν καὶ
τοῦ[2] ἥδιον διαπερᾶν τὰς ὁδοὺς ποικίλλοντας
ἱππικαῖς τάξεσι τὰς πορείας.

4 Ὅταν μέντοι ἔξω τῶν ὁδῶν διὰ δυσχωρίας
ἐλαύνητε, μάλα χρήσιμον καὶ ἐν πολεμίᾳ καὶ
ἐν φιλίᾳ προελαύνειν τῆς φυλῆς ἑκάστης τῶν
ὑπηρετῶν οἵτινες, ἢν ἀπόροις νάπαις ἐντυγ-
χάνωσι, παριόντες ἐπὶ τὰ εὔπορα δηλώσουσι
τοῖς ἱππεῦσιν, ἢ χρὴ τὴν ἔλασιν ποιεῖσθαι, ὡς
μὴ ὅλαι αἱ τάξεις πλανῶνται.

5 Ἢν δὲ δι᾽ ἐπικινδύνων[3] ἐλαύνητέ που, φρονίμου ἱππάρχου τὸ τῶν προόδων ἄλλους προόδους
διερευνωμένους προηγεῖσθαι· τὸ γὰρ ὡς ἐκ
πλείστου προαισθάνεσθαι πολεμίων χρήσιμον
καὶ πρὸς τὸ ἐπιθέσθαι καὶ πρὸς τὸ φυλάξασθαι·
καὶ τὸ ἀναμένειν δὲ ἐπὶ ταῖς διαβάσεσιν, ὡς
μὴ κατακόπτωσι τοὺς ἵππους οἱ τελευταῖοι τὸν
ἡγεμόνα διώκοντες. ἴσασι μὲν οὖν ταῦτα σχεδὸν
πάντες, καρτερεῖν δ᾽ ἐπιμελόμενοι οὐ πολλοὶ
ἐθέλουσι.

6 Προσήκει δὲ ἱππάρχῳ ἔτι ἐν εἰρήνῃ ἐπιμελεῖσθαι, ὅπως ἐμπείρως ἕξει τῆς τε πολεμίας καὶ
τῆς φιλίας χώρας· ἢν δ᾽ ἄρα αὐτὸς ἀπείρως
ἔχῃ, τῶν ἄλλων γε δὴ τοὺς ἐπιστημονεστάτους
ἑκάστων τόπων παραλαμβάνειν. πολὺ[4] γὰρ
διαφέρει ἡγούμενος ὁ[5] εἰδὼς τὰς ὁδοὺς τοῦ μὴ
εἰδότος, καὶ ἐπιβουλεύων δὲ πολεμίοις ὁ εἰδὼς
τοὺς τόπους τοῦ μὴ εἰδότος πολὺ διαφέρει.

---

[1] ἀκτέον added by Zeune.
[2] τοῦ Richards : τοῦτο S. with the MSS.

every regiment to extend front. When you reach
open ground, all the regiments must be in line of
battle. Incidentally these changes of order are good
for practice, and help the men to get over the
ground more pleasantly by varying the march with
cavalry manœuvres.

When riding on difficult ground away from roads, 4
whether in hostile or friendly country, it is very
useful to have some of the aides-de-camp in advance
of each regiment, that they may find a way round
into the open in case they come across pathless
woodland, and show the men what line they should
follow, so that whole companies may not go astray.

If your route lies in dangerous country, a prudent 5
commander will have a second advanced guard ahead
of his scouts for reconnaissance purposes. For it is
useful both for attack and defence to discover an
enemy as far off as possible. It is useful also to halt
at the passage of a river, that the rear guard may not
wear out their horses in chasing their leader. These
rules, no doubt, are familiar to nearly everybody;
but few will take the trouble to observe them.

A cavalry commander should be at pains even in 6
time of peace to acquaint himself with hostile and
friendly country alike. In case he is without personal
experience, he should at least consult the men in
the force who have the best knowledge of various
localities. For the leader who knows the roads has a
great advantage over one who does not. In making
plans against the enemy, too, a knowledge of the
district makes a great difference.

---

³ δι' ἐπικινδύνων B : ἐπὶ κινδύνων S. with the other MSS.

⁴ πολὺ Dindorf : πάνυ S. with the MSS.

⁵ ἡγούμενος ὁ Dindorf : ὁ ἡγούμενος S. with the MSS.

7 Καὶ κατασκόπων δὲ πρὶν πόλεμον εἶναι δεῖ
μεμεληκέναι, ὅπως ἔσονται καὶ ἐκ πόλεων ἀμφοτέ-
ροις φιλίων καὶ ἐξ ἐμπόρων· πᾶσαι γὰρ αἱ πόλεις
τοὺς εἰσάγοντάς τι ἀεὶ ὡς εὐμενεῖς δέχονται· καὶ
8 ψευδαυτόμολοι δ' ἔστιν ὅτε χρήσιμον. οὐ μέντοι
τοῖς γε κατασκόποις δεῖ ποτε πιστεύοντα φυλακῆς ἀμελεῖν, ἀλλ' ἀεὶ οὕτως κατεσκευάσθαι
χρή, ὥσπερ ἢν ἥξοντες εἰσηγγελμένοι ὦσιν οἱ
πολέμιοι. καὶ γὰρ ἢν πάνυ πιστοὶ ὦσιν οἱ κατά-
σκοποι, χαλεπὸν ἐν καιρῷ ἀπαγγέλλειν· πολλὰ
γὰρ ἐν πολέμῳ τὰ ἐμπόδια ἐμπίπτει.

9 Τάς γε μὴν ἐξαγωγὰς τοῦ ἱππικοῦ ἧττον ἂν
οἱ πολέμιοι αἰσθάνοιντο, εἰ ἀπὸ παραγγέλσεως
γίγνοιντο μᾶλλον ἢ εἰ ἀπὸ κήρυκος ἢ ἀπὸ
προγραφῆς. ἀγαθὸν οὖν καὶ πρὸς τὸ[1] διὰ
παραγγέλσεως ἐξάγειν τὸ δεκαδάρχους καθιστάναι
καὶ ἐπὶ[2] τοῖς δεκαδάρχοις πεμπαδάρχους, ἵν' ὡς
ἐλαχίστοις ἕκαστος παραγγέλλῃ· καὶ τὸ μέτωπον
δὲ οὕτω μηκύνοιεν ἂν τῆς τάξεως ἀταράκτως οἱ
πεμπάδαρχοι παράγοντες, ὁπότε τούτου καιρὸς εἴη.

10 Ὅταν γε μὴν προφυλάττειν δέῃ, ἐγὼ μὲν ἀεὶ
ἐπαινῶ τὰς κρυπτὰς σκοπάς τε καὶ φυλακάς·
οὕτω γὰρ ἅμα μὲν τῶν φίλων φυλακαὶ γίγνονται,
ἅμα δὲ τοῖς πολεμίοις ἐνέδραι κατασκευάζονται,
11 καὶ αὐτοὶ μὲν δυσεπιβουλευτότεροί εἰσιν ἀφανεῖς
ὄντες, τοῖς δὲ πολεμίοις φοβερώτεροι. τὸ γὰρ
εἰδέναι μέν, ὅτι εἰσί που φυλακαί, ὅπου δ' εἰσὶ
καὶ ὁπόσαι μὴ εἰδέναι, τοῦτο θαρρεῖν μὲν κωλύει
τοὺς πολεμίους, ὑποπτεύειν δὲ ἀναγκάζει πάντα

[1] τὸ B : τῷ S. with the other MSS.
[2] ἐπὶ added by Schneider : καὶ τοῖς B : καὶ τοῖς τε the other
MSS. : καὶ τοῖς δὲ S.

You must also have taken steps to enlist the 7
services of spies before the outbreak of war. Some
of these should be citizens of neutral states, and
some merchants, since all states invariably welcome
the importer of merchandise. Sham deserters,
too, have their use on occasions. Still, you must 8
never neglect to post guards through reliance on
spies; on the contrary, your precautions must at all
times be as complete as when you have information
that the enemy is approaching. For even if the
spies are entirely reliable, it is difficult to report at
the critical moment, since many things happen in
war to hinder them.

The advance of cavalry is less likely to be detected 9
by the enemy if orders are not given by a herald or
in writing beforehand, but passed along. Accordingly,
for this purpose, too, that the order to advance may
be given by word of mouth, it is well to post file-
leaders, and half file-leaders[1] behind them, so that
each may pass the word to as few men as possible.
Thus, too, the half file-leaders will wheel and extend
the line without confusion, whenever there is
occasion to do so.

When it is necessary to keep a look out, I am all 10
in favour of the plan of having hidden outposts and
guards. For these serve at once as guards to protect
your friends and snares to trap the enemy. And the 11
men, being unseen, are more secure themselves and
at the same time more formidable to the enemy.
For the enemy, conscious that there are outposts
somewhere, but ignorant of their whereabouts and
their strength, feels nervous and is forced to suspect

[1] These form the sixth rank.

XENOPHON

τὰ χωρία· αἱ δὲ φανεραὶ φυλακαὶ δῆλα παρέ-
12 χουσι[1] καὶ τὰ δεινὰ καὶ τὰ εὐθαρσῆ. ἔτι δὲ
τῷ μὲν κρυπτὰς ἔχοντι φυλακὰς ἐξέσται μὲν
φανεροῖς ὀλίγοις ἔμπροσθεν τῶν κρυπτῶν φυλάτ-
τοντα πειρᾶσθαι τοὺς πολεμίους εἰς ἐνέδρας
ὑπάγειν. ἀγρευτικὸν δὲ καὶ ὄπισθεν τῶν κρυπτῶν
ἄλλοις φανεροῖς ἔστιν ὅτε φυλάττειν· καὶ τοῦτο
γὰρ ἐξαπατητικὸν τῶν πολεμίων ὁμοίως τῷ
πρόσθεν εἰρημένῳ.

13 Ἀλλὰ μὴν φρονίμου γε ἄρχοντος καὶ τὸ μήποτε
κινδυνεύειν ἑκόντα, πλὴν ὅπου ἂν πρόδηλον ᾖ,
ὅτι πλέον ἕξει τῶν πολεμίων· τὸ δὲ ὑπηρετεῖν
τὰ ἥδιστα τοῖς πολεμίοις προδοσία τῶν συμμάχων δικαίως ἂν μᾶλλον ἢ ἀνδρεία κρίνοιτο.

14 σῶφρον δὲ καὶ τὸ ἐκεῖσε ὁρμᾶν, ὅπου ἂν ἀσθενῆ
τὰ τῶν πολεμίων ᾖ, κἂν πρόσω ὄντα τυγχάνῃ.
τὸ γὰρ σφόδρα πονῆσαι ἀκινδυνότερον ἢ πρὸς

15 τοὺς κρείττους ἀγωνίζεσθαι. ἢν δέ πῃ εἰς μέσον
φιλίων τειχέων εἰσίωσιν οἱ πολέμιοι, κἂν πολὺ
κρείττους ὄντες, καλὸν μὲν ἐντεῦθεν ἐπιχειρεῖν
ὁποτέρωθι ἂν λελήθῃς παρών, καλὸν δὲ καὶ ἅμα
ἀμφοτέρωθεν. ὅταν γὰρ οἱ ἕτεροι ἀποχωρῶσιν,
οἱ ἐκ τοῦ ἐπὶ θάτερα ἐλαύνοντες ταράττοιεν μὲν
ἂν τοὺς πολεμίους, σώζοιεν δ' ἂν τοὺς φίλους.

16 Καὶ τὸ μὲν διὰ κατασκόπων πειρᾶσθαι εἰδέναι
τὰ τῶν πολεμίων πάλαι εἴρηται ὡς ἀγαθόν ἐστιν.
ἐγὼ δὲ πάντων ἄριστον νομίζω εἶναι τὸ αὐτὸν
πειρᾶσθαι, ἢν ᾖ ποθεν ἐξ ἀσφαλοῦς, θεώμενον

17 τοὺς πολεμίους ἀθρεῖν, ἤν τι ἁμαρτάνωσι. καὶ
τὸ μὲν κλαπῆναι δυνατὸν πέμπειν χρὴ τοὺς
ἐπιτηδείους κλέψοντας, τὸ δ' ἁρπασθῆναι ἐγχω-

---

[1] παρέχουσι Rühl: ἔχουσι S. with the MSS.

every possible position; whereas visible outposts show them where danger lies and where all is safe. Besides, if you conceal your outposts, you will have 12 the chance of luring the enemy into an ambush by placing a few guards in the open to screen the hidden men. Occasionally, too, a cunning trap may be laid by posting a second body of exposed guards behind the men in hiding; for this plan may prove as deceptive to the enemy as the one just referred to.

A prudent commander will never take risks un- 13 necessarily, except when it is clear beforehand that he will have the advantage of the enemy. To play into the enemy's hand may fairly be considered treachery to one's allies rather than courage. Another sound principle is to go for any position 14 where the enemy is weak, even if it is a long way off, since hard work is less dangerous than a struggle against superior forces. But if the enemy places 15 himself somewhere between yourself and fortresses friendly to you, then it is proper to attack him, even if he is greatly superior, on that side where your presence is unsuspected, or on both flanks at once, for when one part of your force is retiring, a charge on the opposite flank will flurry the enemy and rescue your friends.

It is an old maxim that, in attempting to discover 16 what the enemy is about, it is well to employ spies. But the best plan of all, in my opinion, is for the commander himself to watch the enemy from some safe coign of vantage, if possible, and take notice of his mistakes. And when anything can be filched by 17 cunning, you should send likely men to steal it; and when anything may be seized you should despatch

ροῦν ἐφιέναι τοὺς ἁρπάσοντας. ἢν δὲ πορευομένων ποι τῶν πολεμίων ἀπαρτᾶταί τι ἀσθενέστερον τῆς αὐτοῦ δυνάμεως ἢ θαρροῦν ἀποσκε-
δαννύηται, οὐδὲ ταῦτα χρὴ λανθάνειν· ἀεὶ μέντοι
τῷ ἰσχυροτέρῳ τὸ ἀσθενέστερον θηρᾶν.

18   Δυνατὸν δὲ προσέχοντι τὸν νοῦν ταῦτα καταμανθάνειν, ἐπεὶ καὶ τὰ βραχυγνωμονέστερα ἀνθρώπου
θηρία οἵ τε ἴκτινοι δύνανται ὃ ἂν ἀφύλακτον ᾖ
ἀφαρπάσαντες εἰς τὸ ἀσφαλὲς ἀποχωρεῖν πρὶν
ληφθῆναι καὶ οἱ λύκοι δὲ τά τε ἐρημούμενα
φυλακῆς ἀγρεύουσι καὶ τὰ ἐν τοῖς δυσοράτοις
19 κλέπτουσι, κἂν μεταθέων γέ τις ἐπιγίγνηται
κύων, ἢν μὲν ἥττων ᾖ, τούτῳ ἐπιτίθεται· ἢν δὲ
κρείττων, ἀποσπάσας [1] ὅ τι ἂν ἔχῃ ἀποχωρεῖ.
ὅταν δέ γε φυλακῆς καταφρονήσωσι λύκοι,
τάξαντες ἑαυτῶν τοὺς μὲν ἀπελαύνειν τὴν
φυλακήν, τοὺς δὲ ἁρπάζειν, οὕτω τὰ ἐπιτήδεια
20 πορίζονται. θηρίων γε μὴν δυναμένων τὰ τοιαῦτα
φρονίμως ληίζεσθαι, πῶς οὐκ ἄνθρωπόν γε ὄντα
εἰκὸς σοφώτερον τούτων φαίνεσθαι, ἃ καὶ αὐτὰ
τέχνῃ ὑπ' ἀνθρώπου ἁλίσκεται;

    V. Κἀκεῖνό γε μὴν εἰδέναι ἱππικοῦ ἀνδρός, ἐκ
πόσου ἂν ἵππος πεζὸν ἕλοι καὶ ἐξ ὁπόσου βραδεῖς
ἂν ἵπποι ταχεῖς ἀποφύγοιεν. ἱππαρχικὸν δὲ καὶ
χωρία γιγνώσκειν, ἔνθα πεζοὶ κρείττους ἱππέων
2 καὶ ἔνθα πεζῶν κρείττους ἱππεῖς. χρὴ δὲ μηχανη-
τικὸν εἶναι καὶ τοῦ πολλοὺς μὲν φαίνεσθαι τοὺς
ὀλίγους ἱππέας, πάλιν δ' ὀλίγους τοὺς πολλοὺς
καὶ τοῦ δοκεῖν παρόντα μὲν ἀπεῖναι, ἀπόντα δὲ
παρεῖναι καὶ τοῦ μὴ τὰ τῶν πολεμίων μόνον
κλέπτειν ἐπίστασθαι, ἀλλὰ καὶ τοὺς ἑαυτοῦ

---

[1] ἀποσπάσας Courier: ἀποσφάξας S. with the MSS.

troops to seize it. If the enemy is marching on some
objective and a part of his force weaker than your
own separates from the main body or straggles carelessly, the chance must not be missed; the
hunter, however, must always be stronger than the
hunted.

You can see the point of this if you consider. 18
Even wild creatures less intelligent than man,
such as hawks, will grab unguarded plunder and
get away into a place of safety before they can
be caught: wolves, again, prey on anything left
unprotected and steal things lying in holes and
corners; and if a dog does pursue and overtake him, 19
the wolf, if stronger than the dog, attacks him; or
if weaker, snatches away the prize and makes off.
Moreover, when a pack of wolves feels no fear of
a convoy, they arrange themselves so that some shall
drive off the convoy, and others seize the plunder;
and thus they get their food. Well, if wild beasts 20
show such sagacity, surely any man may be expected
to show more wisdom than creatures that are themselves taken by the skill of man.

V. Every horseman should know at what distance
a horse can overtake a man on foot, and how much
start a slow horse needs to escape from a fast one.
A cavalry commander should also be able to judge of
the ground where infantry has an advantage over
cavalry and where cavalry has an advantage over
infantry. He must also have sufficient ingenuity to 2
make a small company of horse look large, and
conversely, to make a large one look small; to seem
to be absent when present, and present when absent;
to know how to deceive, not merely how to steal
the enemy's possessions, but also how to conceal

ἱππέας ἅμα κλέπτοντα ἐξ ἀπροσδοκήτου τοῖς
3 πολεμίοις ἐπιτίθεσθαι. ἀγαθὸν δὲ μηχάνημα καὶ
τὸ δύνασθαι, ὅταν μὲν τὰ ἑαυτοῦ ἀσθενῶς ἔχῃ,
φόβον παρασκευάζειν τοῖς πολεμίοις, ὡς μὴ
ἐπίθωνται· ὅταν δ' ἐρρωμένως, θάρρος αὐτοῖς
ἐμποιεῖν, ὡς ἐγχειρῶσιν. οὕτω γὰρ αὐτὸς μὲν
ἂν ἥκιστα κακῶς πάσχοις, τοὺς δὲ πολεμίους
μάλιστ' ἂν ἁμαρτάνοντας λαμβάνοις.
4   Ὅπως δὲ μὴ προστάττειν δοκῶ ἀδύνατα,
γράψω καὶ ὡς ἂν γίγνοιτο τὰ δοκοῦντα αὐτῶν
χαλεπώτατα εἶναι.

Τὸ μὲν τοίνυν μὴ σφάλλεσθαι ἐγχειροῦντα
διώκειν ἢ ἀποχωρεῖν ἐμπειρία ποιεῖ ἵππων
δυνάμεως. πῶς δ' ἂν ἐμπείρως ἔχοις; εἰ προσέχοις [1] τὸν νοῦν ἐν ταῖς μετὰ φιλίας ἀνθιπ-
πασίαις οἷοι [2] ἀποβαίνουσιν ἐκ τῶν διώξεών τε
καὶ φυγῶν.

5   Ὅταν μέντοι βούλῃ τοὺς ἱππέας πολλοὺς
φαίνεσθαι, ἓν μὲν πρῶτον ὑπαρχέτω, ἤνπερ
ἐγχωρῇ, μὴ ἐγγὺς τῶν πολεμίων ἐγχειρεῖν ἐξα-
πατᾶν· καὶ γὰρ ἀσφαλέστερον τὸ πρόσω καὶ
ἀπατητικώτερον. ἔπειτα δὲ χρὴ εἰδέναι, ὅτι
ἀθρόοι μὲν ἵπποι πολλοὶ φαίνονται διὰ τὸ
μέγεθος τοῦ ζῴου, διασπειρόμενοι δ' εὐαρίθμητοι
6 γίγνονται. ἔτι δ' ἂν πλεῖόν σοι τὸ ἱππικὸν τοῦ
ὄντος φαίνοιτο, εἰ τοὺς ἱπποκόμους εἰς τοὺς
ἱππέας ἐνισταίης μάλιστα μὲν δόρατα, εἰ δὲ μή,
ὅμοια δόρασιν ἔχοντας, ἤν τε ἑστηκὸς ἐπιδεικνύῃς
τὸ ἱππικὸν ἤν τε παράγῃς· ἀνάγκη γὰρ τὸν
ὄγκον τῆς τάξεως οὕτω μείζω τε καὶ πυκνότερον
φαίνεσθαι.

7   Ἢν δ' αὖ τοὺς πολλοὺς ὀλίγους βούλῃ [3] δοκεῖν

his own force and fall on the enemy unexpectedly. Another neat ruse is to create a scare among the 3 enemy when your own position is precarious, so that he may not attack, and to put him in good heart, when it is strong, so that he may make an attempt. Thus you are least likely to come to harm yourself and most likely to catch the enemy tripping.

That I may not seem to demand impossibilities, I 4 will add a solution of the problems that seem most puzzling.

Success in an attempt to pursue or retreat depends on experience of horses and their powers. But how are you to get this experience? By watching the friendly encounters of the sham fights and noticing what condition the horses are in after the pursuits and flights.

When your object is to make the number of your 5 cavalry look large, first take it for an axiom, if possible, not to attempt the ruse when you are near the enemy: for distance gives safety and increases the illusion. Secondly you must know that horses look many when crowded, owing to the animals' size, but are easily counted when scattered. Another way of 6 exaggerating the apparent strength of your force is to arm the grooms with lances or even imitation lances, and put them between the cavalrymen, whether you display the cavalry at the halt or wheel it into line. Thus the bulk of the company is bound to look denser and more massive.

On the other hand, if your object is to make a 7

---

[1] ἔχοις and προσέχοις Krüger: ἔχοι and προσέχοι S. with the MSS.

[2] οἶοι Lenklau: οἶα S. with the Aldine ed. : οἶαι MSS.

[3] βούλῃ B: S. omits with the other MSS.

εἶναι, ἢν μέν σοι χωρία ὑπάρχῃ οἷα συγκρύ-
πτειν, δῆλον ὅτι τοὺς μὲν ἐν τῷ φανερῷ ἔχων,
τοὺς δ' εἰς τὸ ἄδηλον ἀποκρύπτων κλέπτοις ἂν
τοὺς ἱππέας· ἢν δὲ πᾶν καταφανὲς ᾖ τὸ χωρίον,
δεκάδας χρὴ στοιχούσας ποιήσαντα διαλειπούσας
παράγειν· καὶ τοὺς μὲν πρὸς τῶν πολεμίων
ἱππέας ἑκάστης δεκάδος ὀρθὰ τὰ δόρατα ἔχειν,
τοὺς δ' ἄλλους ταπεινὰ καὶ μὴ ὑπερφανῆ.

8 Φοβεῖν γε μὴν τοὺς πολεμίους καὶ ψευδενέδρας
οἷόν τε καὶ ψευδοβοηθείας καὶ ψευδαγγελίας
ποιοῦντα. θαρροῦσι δὲ μάλιστα πολέμιοι, ὅταν
ὄντα[1] τοῖς ἐναντίοις πράγματα καὶ ἀσχολίας
πυνθάνωνται.

9 Τούτων δὲ γεγραμμένων μηχανᾶσθαι αὐτὸν
χρὴ πρὸς τὸ παρὸν ἀεὶ ἀπατᾶν· ὄντως γὰρ οὐδὲν
10 κερδαλεώτερον ἐν πολέμῳ ἀπάτης· ὁπότε γὰρ[2]
καὶ οἱ παῖδες ὅταν παίζωσι ποσίνδα, δύνανται
ἀπατᾶν προΐσχοντες ὥστε ὀλίγους τ' ἔχοντες
πολλοὺς δοκεῖν ἔχειν καὶ πολλοὺς προέχοντες
ὀλίγους φαίνεσθαι ἔχειν, πῶς οὐκ ἄνδρες γε τῷ
ἐξαπατᾶν προσέχοντες τὸν νοῦν δύναιντ' ἂν
11 τοιαῦτα μηχανᾶσθαι; καὶ ἐνθυμούμενος δ' ἂν
τὰ ἐν τοῖς πολέμοις πλεονεκτήματα εὕροι ἄν τις
τὰ πλεῖστα καὶ μέγιστα σὺν ἀπάτῃ γεγενημένα.
ὧν ἕνεκα ἢ οὐκ ἐγχειρητέον ἄρχειν ἢ τοῦτο σὺν
τῇ ἄλλῃ παρασκευῇ καὶ παρὰ θεῶν αἰτητέον
δύνασθαι ποιεῖν καὶ αὐτῷ μηχανητέον.

12 Οἷς δὲ θάλαττα πρόσεστιν, ἀπατητικὸν καὶ τὸ
πλοῖα παρασκευαζόμενον πεζῇ τι πρᾶξαι καὶ τὸ

---

[1] ὄντα added by Madvig.
[2] γὰρ Ribitt : γε S. with the MSS.

large number look small, then, assuming that your ground affords cover, you can obviously conceal your cavalry by having part in the open and part hidden. If, however, the whole of the ground is exposed, you must form the files into rows and wheel, leaving a gap between each two rows [1]; and the men in each file who are next the enemy must hold their lances upright, while the rest keep theirs low down out of sight.

The means to employ for scaring the enemy are 8 false ambuscades, false reliefs and false information. An enemy's confidence is greatest when he is told that the other side is in difficulties and is preoccupied.

But given these instructions, a man must himself 9 invent a ruse to meet every emergency as it occurs. For there is really nothing more profitable in war than deception. Even children are successful deceivers 10 when they play " Guess the number " ; they will hold up a counter or two and make believe that they have got a fist-full, and seem to hold up few when they are holding many; so surely men can play similar tricks when they are intent on deceiving in earnest. And on thinking over the successes gained in war 11 you will find that most of them, and these the greatest, have been won with the aid of deception. For these reasons either you should not essay to command, or you should pray to heaven that your equipment may include this qualification, and you should contrive on your own part to possess it.

For those near the sea two effective ruses are, 12 to strike on land while fitting out ships, and to

[1] The enemy will not know (a) the number of files when posted one behind another, nor (b) the depth of the line when the files have wheeled.

πεζῇ προσποιούμενον ἐπιβουλεύειν κατὰ θάλατταν ἐπιχειρῆσαι.

13 Ἱππαρχικὸν δὲ καὶ τὸ διδάσκειν τὴν πόλιν, ὡς ἀσθενὲς τὸ πεζῶν ἔρημον ἱππικὸν πρὸς τὸ ἀμίππους πεζοὺς ἔχον. ἱππαρχικὸν δὲ καὶ τὸ λαβόντα πεζοὺς αὐτοῖς χρῆσθαι· ἔστι δὲ πεζοὺς οὐ μόνον ἐντός,[1] ἀλλὰ καὶ ὄπισθεν ἱππέων[2] ἀποκρύψασθαι· πολὺ γὰρ μείζων ὁ ἱππεὺς τοῦ πεζοῦ.

14 Ταῦτα δὲ πάντα ἐγὼ καὶ ὅσα πρὸς τούτοις τις μηχανήσεται ἢ βίᾳ ἢ τέχνῃ αἱρεῖν τοὺς ἐναντίους βουλόμενος σὺν τῷ θεῷ πράττειν συμβουλεύω, ἵνα καὶ ἡ τύχη[3] συνεπαινῇ θεῶν ἵλεων ὄντων.

15 Ἔστι δ' ὅτε πάνυ ἀπατητικὸν καὶ τὸ λίαν φυλακτικὸν προσποιήσασθαι εἶναι καὶ μηδαμῶς φιλοκίνδυνον· τοῦτο γὰρ τοὺς πολεμίους πολλάκις προάγεται ἀφυλακτοῦντας μᾶλλον ἁμαρτάνειν. ἢν δ' ἅπαξ δόξῃ τις φιλοκίνδυνος εἶναι, ἔξεστι καὶ ἡσυχίαν ἔχοντα, προσποιούμενον δὲ πράξειν τι πράγματα τοῖς πολεμίοις παρέχειν.

VI. Ἀλλὰ γὰρ οὐδὲν ἄν τις δύναιτο πλάσαι οἷον βούλεται, εἰ μὴ ἐξ ὧν γε πλάττοιτο παρεσκευασμένα εἴη ὡς πείθεσθαι τῇ τοῦ χειροτέχνου γνώμῃ· οὐδέ γ' ἂν ἐξ ἀνδρῶν, εἰ μὴ σὺν θεῷ οὕτω παρεσκευασμένοι ἔσονται, ὡς φιλικῶς τε ἔχειν πρὸς τὸν ἄρχοντα καὶ φρονιμώτερον σφῶν αὐτὸν ἡγεῖσθαι περὶ τῶν πρὸς τοὺς πολεμίους ἀγώνων.

2 Εὐνοϊκῶς μὲν οὖν ἔχειν καὶ ἐκ τῶνδε εἰκὸς τοὺς ἀρχομένους, ὅταν φιλοφρόνως τε ἔχῃ πρὸς

---

[1] ἐντός Herwerden : ἐν τούτοις S. with the MSS.
[2] ἱππέων Dindorf : ἵππων S. with the MSS.

attack by sea while ostensibly planning a land attack.

Another duty of a cavalry commander is to 13 demonstrate to the city the weakness of cavalry destitute of infantry as compared with cavalry that has infantry attached to it. Further, having got his infantry, a cavalry commander should make use of it. A mounted man being much higher than a man on foot, infantry may be hidden away not only among the cavalry but in the rear as well.

For the practical application of these devices and 14 any others you may contrive for the undoing of your foes by force or craft, I counsel you to work with God, so that, the gods being propitious, fortune too may favour you.

Another ruse that proves highly effective at times 15 is to feign excess of caution and reluctance to take risks. For this pretence often lures the enemy into making a more fatal blunder through want of caution. Or once come to be thought venture-some, and you can give the enemy trouble by merely sitting still and pretending that you are on the point of doing something.

VI. However, no man can mould anything to his mind unless the stuff in which he proposes to work lies ready to obey the artist's will. No more can you make anything of men, unless, by God's help, they are ready to regard their commander with friendly feelings and to think him wiser than themselves in the conduct of operations against the enemy.

Now the feeling of loyalty will naturally be 2 fostered when the commander is kind to his men,

---

¹ ἡ τύχη Courier: τὴν τύχην S. with the MSS.

αὐτοὺς καὶ προνοῶν φαίνεται, ὅπως τε σῖτον
ἔξουσι καὶ ὅπως ἀσφαλῶς μὲν ἀποχωρήσουσι,
3 πεφυλαγμένως δὲ ἀναπαύσονται. ἐν δὲ ταῖς
φρουραῖς χρὴ καὶ χιλοῦ καὶ σκηνῶν καὶ ὑδάτων
καὶ φρυγάνων [1] καὶ τῶν ἄλλων ἐπιτηδείων φανερὸν εἶναι ἐπιμελούμενον καὶ προνοοῦντά τε καὶ
ἀγρυπνοῦντα ἕνεκα τῶν ἀρχομένων. καὶ ὅταν
γε πλέον ἔχῃ τι, τὸ μεταδοῦναι κερδαλέον τῷ
προεστηκότι.

4 Ἥκιστα δ' ἂν καταφρονοῖεν ἄρχοντος, ὡς μὲν
συνελόντι εἰπεῖν, εἰ ὁπόσα ἐκείνοις παραινοίη,
αὐτὸς ταῦτα βέλτιον ἐκείνων φαίνοιτο ποιῶν.
5 ἀρξάμενον οὖν δεῖ ἀπὸ τοῦ ἀναβαίνειν ἐπὶ τοὺς
ἵππους πάντα τὰ ἐν ἱππικῇ μελετᾶν, ὅπως ὁρῶσι
τὸν ἄρχοντα δυνάμενον ἐπὶ τοῦ ἵππου καὶ τάφρους ἀσφαλῶς περᾶν καὶ τειχία ὑπερακρίζειν
καὶ ἀπ' ὄχθων καταίρειν καὶ ἀκοντίζειν ἱκανῶς·
πάντα γὰρ ταῦτα προκόπτει τι εἰς τὸ μὴ κατα-
6 φρονεῖσθαι. ἢν δὲ δὴ καὶ τάττειν [2] γνῶσιν ἐπι-
στάμενόν τε καὶ δυνάμενον παρασκευάζειν, ὡς
ἂν πλέον ἔχοιεν τῶν πολεμίων, πρὸς δὲ τούτοις
κἀκεῖνο λάβωσιν εἰς τὴν γνώμην, ὡς οὔτ' ἂν
εἰκῇ οὔτ' ἄνευ θεῶν οὔτε παρὰ τὰ ἱερὰ ἡγήσαιτ'
ἂν ἐπὶ πολεμίους, πάντα ταῦτα πιθανωτέρους τῷ
ἄρχοντι τοὺς ἀρχομένους ποιεῖ.

VII. Παντὶ μὲν οὖν προσήκει ἄρχοντι φρονίμῳ
εἶναι· πολὺ μέντοι τὸν Ἀθηναίων ἵππαρχον διαφέρειν δεῖ καὶ τῷ τοὺς θεοὺς θεραπεύειν καὶ τῷ
πολεμικὸν εἶναι, ᾧ γε ὑπάρχουσι μὲν ὅμοροι
ἀντίπαλοι ἱππεῖς τε παραπλήσιοι τὸ πλῆθος καὶ
2 ὁπλῖται πολλοί. κἂν μὲν εἰς τὴν πολεμίαν
ἐμβάλλειν ἐπιχειρῇ ἄνευ τῆς ἄλλης πόλεως, πρὸς

and obviously takes care that they have victuals, and that they are safe in retreat and well protected when at rest. In the garrisons he must show an 3 interest in fodder, tents, water, firewood, and all other supplies: he must show that he thinks ahead and keeps his eyes open for the sake of his men. And when he is doing well the chief's best policy is to give them a share in his good things.

To put it shortly, a commander is least likely to 4 incur the contempt of his men if he shows himself more capable than they of doing whatever he requires of them. He must therefore practise every 5 detail of horsemanship—mounting and the rest,—that they may see their commander able to take a ditch without a spill, clear a wall, leap down from a bank and throw a javelin skilfully. For all these feats are so many stepping stones to their respect. If they 6 know him also to be a master of tactics and able to put them in the way of getting the better of the enemy; and if besides, they are certain that he will never lead them against an enemy recklessly or without the gods' approval or in defiance of the sacrifices, all these conditions increase the men's readiness to obey their commander.

VII. Every commander, then, should have intelligence. The Athenian cavalry commander, however, should excel greatly both in the observance of his duty to the gods and in the qualities of a warrior, seeing that he has on his borders rivals in the shape of cavalry as numerous as his and large forces of infantry.[1] And if 2 he attempts to invade the enemy's country without

---

[1] The Thebans are meant.

[1] φρυγάνων Madvig: φυλακῶν S. with the MSS.
[2] τάττειν B: πραττειν S. with the other MSS.

ἀμφοτέρους τούτους μόνοις ἂν τοῖς ἱππεῦσι δια-
κινδυνεύοι. ἢν δ' οἱ πολέμιοι εἰς τὴν Ἀθηναίων
χώραν ἐμβάλλωσι, πρῶτον μὲν οὐκ ἂν ἄλλως
ἔλθοιεν εἰ μὴ σὺν ἄλλοις τε ἱππεῦσι πρὸς τοῖς
ἑαυτῶν καὶ πρὸς τούτοις ὁπλίταις ὁπόσοις ἂν
οἴωνται πάντας Ἀθηναίους μὴ ἱκανοὺς εἶναι
3 μάχεσθαι. πρὸς οὖν τοσούτους πολεμίους ἢν
μὲν ἡ πόλις πᾶσα ἐπεξίῃ ἀρήξουσα τῇ χώρᾳ,
ἐλπίδες καλαί. ἱππεῖς τε γὰρ σὺν θεῷ ἀμείνους,
ἤν τις αὐτῶν ἐπιμελῆται ὡς δεῖ, ὁπλῖταί τε οὐ
μείους ἔσονται καὶ τὰ σώματα τοίνυν οὐ χείρω
ἔχοντες καὶ τὰς ψυχὰς φιλοτιμότεροι, ἢν ὀρθῶς
ἀσκηθῶσι σὺν θεῷ. καὶ μὴν ἐπί γε τοῖς προγόνοις οὐ μεῖον Ἀθηναῖοι ἢ Βοιωτοὶ φρονοῦσιν.
4 ἢν δὲ ἡ μὲν πόλις τρέπηται ἐπὶ τὰ ναυτικὰ καὶ
ἀρκῇ αὐτῇ τὰ τείχη διασώζειν, ὥσπερ καὶ ὁπότε
Λακεδαιμόνιοι σὺν ἅπασι τοῖς Ἕλλησιν ἐνέβαλον,
τοὺς δὲ ἱππέας ἀξιώσῃ[1] τά τε ἐκτὸς τοῦ τείχους
διασώζειν καὶ αὐτοὺς μόνους διακινδυνεύειν πρὸς
πάντας τοὺς ἐναντίους, ἐνταῦθα δὴ θεῶν μὲν
οἶμαι πρῶτον συμμάχων ἰσχυρῶν δεῖ, ἔπειτα δὲ
καὶ τὸν ἵππαρχον προσήκει ἀποτετελεσμένον
ἄνδρα εἶναι. καὶ γὰρ φρονήσεως δεῖ πολλῆς
πρὸς τοὺς πολὺ πλείους καὶ τόλμης, ὁπότε καιρὸς
παραπέσοι.
5 Δεῖ δέ, ὡς ἐμοὶ δοκεῖ, καὶ πονεῖν αὐτὸν ἱκανὸν
εἶναι. πρὸς μὲν γὰρ τὸ παρὸν στράτευμα δια-
κινδυνεύων, ᾧ μηδὲ ὅλη ἡ πόλις θέλοι ἀντικαθί-

---

[1] ἀξιώσῃ Dindorf : ἀξιώσειε S. with the MSS.

---

[1] In the Peloponnesian War.
[2] I have translated πονεῖν, but it is certainly not what X.

the other armed forces of the state, he will have to take his chance with the cavalry only against both arms. Or if the enemy invades Athenian territory, in the first place, he will certainly not fail to bring with him other cavalry besides his own and infantry in addition, whose numbers he reckons to be more than a match for all the Athenians put together. Now pro- 3 vided that the whole of the city's levies turn out against such a host in defence of their country, the prospects are good. For our cavalrymen, God helping, will be the better, if proper care is taken of them, and our heavy infantry will not be inferior in numbers, and I may add, they will be in as good condition and will show the keener spirit, if only, with God's help, they are trained on the right lines. And, remember, the Athenians are quite as proud of their ancestry as the Boeotians. But if the city falls back on her 4 navy, and is content to keep her walls intact, as in the days when the Lacedaemonians invaded us with all the Greeks to help them,[1] and if she expects her cavalry to protect all that lies outside the walls, and to take its chance unaided against her foes,— why then, I suppose, we need first the strong arm of the gods to aid us, and in the second place it is essential that our cavalry commander should be masterly. For much sagacity is called for in coping with a greatly superior force, and abundance of courage when the call comes.

I take it, he must also be able to stand hard work.[2] 5 For if he should elect to take his chance against the army confronting him—an army that not even the whole state is prepared to stand up to—it is evident

wrote. The sequel demands the sense " he must be a man of sound judgment, αὐτὸν (with B) προνοεῖν."

στασθαι, δῆλον ὅτι πάσχοι ἂν ὅ τι οἱ κρείττους
6 βούλοιντο, ποιεῖν δὲ οὐδὲν ἂν ἱκανὸς εἴη. εἰ δὲ
φυλάττοι μὲν τὰ ἔξω τείχους τοσούτοις, ὅσοι
σκοπεύειν τε τοὺς πολεμίους ἱκανοὶ ἔσονται καὶ
ἀναχωρίζειν εἰς τὸ ἀσφαλὲς τὰ δεόμενα ὡς ἐκ
πλείστου· ἱκανοὶ δὲ καὶ προορᾶν οὐδὲν ἧττον οἱ
ὀλίγοι τῶν πολλῶν καὶ φυλάττειν τοίνυν καὶ
ἀναχωρίζειν τὰ φίλια οὐκ ἀκαιρότεροι οἱ μήτε
7 αὑτοῖς μήτε τοῖς ἵπποις πιστεύοντες· ὁ γὰρ
φόβος δεινὸς δοκεῖ συμφύλαξ εἶναι· τοὺς μὲν
φύλακας ἐκ τούτων ἄν τις ποιῶν ἴσως ὀρθῶς
βουλεύοιτο· τοὺς δὲ περιττοὺς τῆς φυλακῆς εἰ
μέν τις στρατιὰν ἔχειν ἡγήσεται, ὀλίγη αὐτῷ
φανεῖται· τοῦ παντὸς γὰρ ἐνδεήσεται ὥστε ἐκ
τοῦ ἐμφανοῦς διακινδυνεύειν. ἢν δὲ ὡς λῃσταῖς
αὐτοῖς χρῆται, πάνυ ἂν ὡς τὸ εἰκὸς ἱκανὴν τοῦτο
8 πράττειν ἔχοι δύναμιν. δεῖ δέ, ὡς ἐμοὶ δοκεῖ,
τοὺς παρεσκευασμένους ἀεὶ ἔχοντα ὡς ποιεῖν τι
μὴ καταφανῆ ὄντα φυλάττειν, ἤν τι ἁμαρτάνῃ
9 τὸ τῶν πολεμίων στράτευμα. φιλοῦσι δέ πως
στρατιῶται ὅσῳ ἂν πλείους ὦσι, τοσούτῳ πλείω
ἁμαρτάνειν. ἢ γὰρ ἐπὶ τὰ ἐπιτήδεια ἐπιμελείᾳ
σκεδάννυνται ἢ πορευομένων ἀταξίᾳ οἱ μὲν προ-
έρχονται, οἱ δ᾽ ὑπολείπονται πλέον τοῦ καιροῦ.
10 τὰ οὖν τοιαῦτα ἁμαρτήματα οὐ χρὴ παριέναι
ἀκόλαστα· εἰ δὲ μή, ὅλη ἡ χώρα στρατόπεδον
ἔσται· ἐκεῖνο καλῶς προνοοῦντα, ἢν ποιήσῃ τι,
φθάσαι ἀποχωρήσαντα πρὶν τὸ πολὺ βοηθοῦν
ἐπιγενέσθαι.
11   Πολλάκις δὲ πορευόμενον στράτευμα καὶ εἰς
ὁδοὺς ἔρχεται, ἐν αἷς οὐδὲν πλεῖον οἱ πολλοὶ τῶν
ὀλίγων δύνανται. καὶ ἐν διαβάσεσί γε ἔστι τῷ

that he would be entirely at the mercy of the stronger
and incapable of doing anything. But should he 6
guard whatever lies outside the walls with a force that
will be just sufficient to keep an eye on the enemy
and to remove into safety from as great a distance as
possible property that needs saving,—and a large force
is not necessary for this: a small force can keep a
look-out as well as a large one, and when it comes to
guarding and removing the property of friends, men
who have no confidence in themselves or their horses
will meet the case, because Fear, it seems, is a 7
formidable member of a guard—well, it may perhaps
be a sound plan to draw on these men for his guards.
But if he imagines that the number remaining over
and above the guard constitutes an army, he will
find it too small; for it will be utterly inadequate to
risk a conflict in the open. Let him use these men
as raiders, and he will probably have a force quite
sufficient for this purpose. His business, it seems to 8
me, is to watch for any blunder on the enemy's part
without showing himself, keeping men constantly on
the alert and ready to strike. It happens that, the 9
greater is the number of soldiers, the more they are
apt to blunder. Either they scatter deliberately in
search of provisions, or they are so careless of order
on the march that some get too far ahead, while
others lag too far behind. So he must not let such 10
blunders go unpunished, or the whole country will
be occupied; only he must take good care to retire
the moment he has struck, without giving time for
the main supports to arrive on the scene.

An army on the march often comes to roads where 11
large numbers have no advantage over small. In
crossing rivers, again, a man with his wits about

προσέχοντι τὸν νοῦν ἀσφαλῶς ἐφεπομένῳ ταμιεύ-
σασθαι, ὥστε ὁπόσοις ἂν βούληται τῶν πολεμίων
12 ἐπιτίθεσθαι. ἔστι δ' ὅτε καλὸν καὶ στρατοπε-
δευομένοις καὶ ἀριστῶσι καὶ δειπνοποιουμένοις
ἐπιχειρεῖν καὶ ἐκ κοίτης γε ἀνισταμένοις. ἐν
πᾶσι γὰρ τούτοις ἄοπλοι στρατιῶται γίγνονται,
μείονα μὲν χρόνον οἱ ὁπλῖται, πλείονα δὲ οἱ
13 ἱππεῖς. σκοποῖς μέντοι καὶ προφυλακαῖς οὐδέποτε δεῖ παύεσθαι ἐπιβουλεύοντα. οὗτοι γὰρ
αὖ ὀλίγοι μὲν ἀεὶ καθίστανται, πολὺ δὲ τοῦ
14 ἰσχυροῦ ἐνίοτε ἀποστατοῦσιν. ὅταν δὲ τὰ τοιαῦτα
ἤδη καλῶς φυλάττωνται οἱ πολέμιοι, καλόν ἐστι
σὺν θεῷ λαθόντα ἐλθεῖν εἰς τὴν πολεμίαν με-
μελετηκότα, πόσοι τε ἑκασταχοῦ καὶ ποῦ τῆς
χώρας προφυλάττουσιν. οὐδεμία γὰρ οὕτω καλὴ
15 λεία ὡς φυλακαί, ἢν κρατηθῶσι. καὶ εὐεξα-
πάτητοι δ' εἰσὶν οἱ φύλακες· διώκουσι γὰρ ὅ τι
ἂν ὀλίγον ἴδωσι, νομίζοντές σφισι τοῦτο προσ-
τετάχθαι. τὰς μέντοι ἀποχωρήσεις σκοπεῖν δεῖ
ὅπως μὴ ἐναντίαι τοῖς βοηθοῦσιν ἔσονται.

VIII. Τοὺς μέντοι μέλλοντας δυνήσεσθαι ἀσφαλῶς τὸ πολὺ κρεῖττον στράτευμα κακουργεῖν
σαφῶς δεῖ τοσοῦτον διαφέρειν, ὥστε αὐτοὺς μὲν
ἀσκητὰς φαίνεσθαι τῶν πολεμικῶν ἐν ἱππικῇ
2 ἔργων, τοὺς δὲ πολεμίους ἰδιώτας. τοῦτο δ' ἂν
εἴη πρῶτον μὲν εἰ οἱ ληΐζεσθαι μέλλοντες ἐκπεπονημένοι εἶεν τῇ ἐλάσει, ὥστε δύνασθαι στρατιωτικοὺς πόνους ὑποφέρειν. οἱ γὰρ πρὸς ταῦτα
ἀμελῶς ἔχοντες καὶ ἵπποι καὶ ἄνδρες εἰκότως ἂν
3 ὥσπερ γυναῖκες πρὸς ἄνδρας ἀγωνίζοιντο. οἱ δέ
γε δεδιδαγμένοι τε καὶ εἰθισμένοι τάφρους διαπηδᾶν καὶ τειχία ὑπεραίρειν καὶ ἐπ' ὄχθους

him may dog the enemy's steps without danger and
regulate according to his will the number of the
enemy that he chooses to attack.   Sometimes it 12
is proper to tackle the enemy while his troops are
at breakfast or supper or when they are turning out of
bed.   For at all these moments soldiers are without
arms, infantry for a shorter and cavalry for a longer
time.   Pickets and outposts, however, should be the 13
mark of incessant plots, these being invariably weak
in numbers and sometimes remote from their main
force.   But when the enemy has learned to take 14
due precautions against such attacks, it is proper, with
God's help, to enter his country stealthily after
ascertaining his strength at various points and the
position of his outposts.   For no booty that you can
capture is so fine as a patrol.   Besides, patrols 15
are easily deceived, for they pursue a handful of
men at sight, believing that to be their special
duty.   You must see, however, that your line of
retreat does not lead you straight into the enemy's
supports.

VIII. It is clear, however, that no troops will be
able to inflict loss on a much stronger army with
impunity, unless they are so superior in the practical
application of horsemanship to war that they show
like experts contending with amateurs.   This super- 2
iority can be attained first and foremost if your
marauding bands are so thoroughly drilled in riding
that they can stand the hard work of a campaign.
For both horses and men that are carelessly trained
in this respect will naturally be like women
struggling with men.   On the contrary, those that are 3
taught and accustomed to jump ditches, leap walls,

ἀνάλλεσθαι καὶ ἀφ' ὑψηλῶν ἀσφαλῶς κατιέναι
καὶ τὰ κατάντη ταχὺ ἐλαύνεσθαι, οὗτοι δ' αὖ
τοσοῦτον διαφέροιεν ἂν τῶν ἀμελετήτων ταῦτα
ὅσονπερ πτηνοὶ πεζῶν· οἱ δέ γε αὖ τοὺς πόδας
ἐκπεπονημένοι τῶι ἀτριβάστων πρὸς τραχέα
ὅσονπερ ὑγιεῖς χωλῶν· καὶ οἵ γε τῶν τόπων
ἔμπειροι πρὸς τοὺς ἀπείρους τοσοῦτον ἐν ταῖς
προελάσεσι καὶ ἀποχωρήσεσι διαφέροιεν ἂν
ὅσονπερ οἱ ὁρῶντες τῶν τυφλῶν.

4   Καὶ τοῦτο δὲ χρὴ εἰδέναι, ὅτι οἱ εὐωχούμενοι
ἵπποι, ἐκπεπονημένοι δὲ ὥστε μὴ ἀποπνίγεσθαι
ἐν τοῖς πόνοις εὖ παρεσκευασμένοι εἰσί. χρὴ δέ,
ἐπείπερ χαλινοὶ καὶ ἐφίππια ἐξ ἱμάντων ἠρτη-
μένα ἐστί, [1] μήποτε τὸν ἵππαρχον τούτων ἔρημον
εἶναι· μικρᾷ γὰρ δαπάνῃ τοὺς ἀποροῦντας
χρησίμους ἂν παρέχοιτο.

5   Εἰ δέ τις νομίζοι [2] πολλὰ ἔχειν ἂν [3] πράγματα,
εἰ οὕτω δεήσει ἀσκεῖν τὴν ἱππικήν, ἐνθυμηθήτω,
ὅτι οἱ εἰς τοὺς γυμνικοὺς ἀγῶνας ἀσκοῦντες πολὺ
πλείω πράγματα καὶ χαλεπώτερα ἔχουσιν ἢ οἱ
6 τὴν ἱππικὴν τὰ μάλιστα μελετῶντες. καὶ γὰρ
τῶν μὲν γυμνικῶν ἀσκημάτων τὰ πολλὰ σὺν
ἱδρῶτι ἐκπονοῦνται, τῆς δὲ ἱππικῆς τὰ πλεῖστα
μεθ' ἡδονῆς. ὅπερ γὰρ εὔξαιτ' ἄν τις πτηνὸς
γενέσθαι, οὐκ ἔστιν ὅ τι μᾶλλον τῶν ἀνθρωπίνων
7 ἔργων ἔοικεν αὐτῷ. καὶ μὴν τό γ' ἐν πολέμῳ
νικᾶν πολλῷ ἐνδοξότερον [4] ἢ πυγμῇ· μετέχει
μὲν γάρ τι καὶ ἡ πόλις ταύτης τῆς δόξης· ὡς δὲ
τὰ πολλὰ ἐπὶ τῇ τοῦ πολέμου νίκῃ καὶ εὐδαι-

---

1 ἐστί Courier : ἐστὶ χρήσιμα S. with the MSS.
2 νομίζοι BM ; νομίζει S. with other MSS.
3 ἂν B : S. omits with the other MSS.
4 ἐνδοξότερον B : εὐδοξότερον S. with the other MSS.

spring up banks, leap down from heights without a spill, and gallop down steep places, will be as superior to the men and horses that lack this training as birds to beasts. Moreover, those that have their feet well hardened will differ on rough ground from the tender-footed as widely as the sound from the lame. And those that are familiar with the locality, compared with those to whom it is unfamiliar, will differ in the advance and retreat as much as men with eyes differ from the blind.

It should also be realised that horses, to be well 4 fettled, must be well fed and thoroughly exercised, so as to do their work without suffering from heaves. And since bits and saddle-cloths are fastened with straps, a cavalry leader must never be short of them, for at a trifling expense he will make men in difficulties efficient.

In case anyone feels that his troubles will be 5 endless if his duty requires him to practise horsemanship in this way, let him reflect that men in training for gymnastic contests face troubles far more numerous and exacting than the most strenuous votaries of horsemanship. For most gymnastic 6 exercises are carried out with sweat and drudgery, but nearly all equestrian exercises are pleasant work.[1] For if it is true that any man would like to fly, no action of man bears a closer resemblance to flying. And, remember, it is far more glorious to win a victory 7 in war than in a boxing match, because, whereas the state as well as the victor has a considerable share in this glory,[2] for a victory in war the gods generally

[1] *Cyropaedia* IV. iii. 15.
[2] He does not express himself clearly, but by "this glory" he means "the glory of a victory whether won in war or in the games."

μονία οἱ θεοὶ τὰς πόλεις στεφανοῦσιν. ὥστ᾽ οὐκ
οἶδ᾽ ἔγωγε, τί προσήκει ἀλλ᾽ ἄττα μᾶλλον ἀσκεῖ-
8 σθαι ἢ τὰ πολεμικά. ἐννοεῖν δὲ χρή, ὅτι καὶ οἱ
κατὰ θάλατταν λῃσταὶ διὰ τὸ πονεῖν ἠσκηκέναι
δύνανται ζῆν καὶ ἀπὸ τῶν πολὺ κρειττόνων.
προσήκει γε μὴν καὶ κατὰ γῆν οὐ τοῖς καρπου-
μένοις τὰ ἑαυτῶν, ἀλλὰ τοῖς στερισκομένοις τῆς
τροφῆς λῄζεσθαι. ἢ γὰρ ἐργαστέον ἢ ἀπὸ τῶν
εἰργασμένων θρεπτέον· ἄλλως δ᾽ οὐ ῥᾴδιον οὔτε
βιοτεύειν οὔτε εἰρήνης τυχεῖν.

9 Μεμνῆσθαι δὲ κἀκεῖνο χρή, μήποτε ἐπὶ τοὺς
κρείττους ἐλαύνειν ὄπισθεν ἵπποις δύσβατον
ποιούμενον· οὐ γὰρ ὅμοιον φεύγοντι καὶ διώκοντι
σφαλῆναι.

10 Ἔτι δὲ βούλομαι ὑπομνῆσαι καὶ τόδε φυλάττεσθαι. εἰσὶ γάρ τινες, οἳ ὅταν μὲν ἴωσιν ἐπὶ τούτους, ὧν ἂν οἴωνται κρείττους εἶναι, παντάπασιν
ἀσθενεῖ δυνάμει ἔρχονται, ὥστε πολλάκις ἔπαθον
ἃ ᾤοντο ποιήσειν· ὅταν δ᾽ ἐπὶ τούτους, ὧν ἂν
σαφῶς ἐπίστωνται ἥττους ὄντες, πᾶσαν ὅσην ἂν
11 ἔχωσι δύναμιν ἄγουσιν. ἐγὼ δέ φημι χρῆναι
τἀναντία τούτων ποιεῖν· ὅταν μὲν κρατήσειν
οἰόμενος ἄγῃ, μὴ φείδεσθαι τῆς δυνάμεως, ὅσην
ἂν ἔχῃ. τὸ γὰρ πολὺ νικᾶν οὐδενὶ πώποτε μετα-
12 μέλειαν παρέσχεν. ὅταν δὲ τοῖς πολὺ κρείττοσιν
ἐπιχειρῇ καὶ προγιγνώσκῃ, ὅτι ποιήσαντα ὅ τι
ἂν δύνηται φευκτέον ἐστίν, εἰς τὰ τοιαῦτά φημι
πολὺ κρεῖττον εἶναι ὀλίγους ἢ πάντας προσάγειν,
τοὺς μέντοι ἀπειλεγμένους καὶ ἵππους καὶ ἄνδρας
τοὺς κρατίστους. τοιοῦτοι γὰρ ὄντες καὶ ποιῆσαι

---

[1] *Hellenica* VI. v. 51.

crown states with happiness as well. For my
part, therefore, I know not why any art should
be more assiduously cultivated than the arts of war.
It should be noticed that a long apprenticeship to 8
toil enables sea-pirates to live at the expense of
much stronger folk. On land, too, pillage, though
not for those who reap what they have sown, is the
natural resource of men who are deprived of food.
For either men must work or they must eat the fruits
of other men's labour : else it is a problem how to live
and to obtain peace.

If you charge a superior force, you must remember 9
never to leave behind you ground difficult for horses.
For a fall in retreat and a fall in pursuit are very
different things.

I want to add a word of warning against another 10
error. Some men, when they suppose themselves
to be stronger than the enemy whom they are going
to attack, take an utterly inadequate force with them.[1]
The consequence is that they are apt to incur the
loss they expected to inflict. Or, when they know
themselves to be weaker than the enemy, they
use all their available strength in the attack.
The right procedure, in my opinion, is just the 11
opposite : when the commander expects to win, he
should not hesitate to use the whole of his strength :
for an overwhelming victory never yet was followed by remorse. But when he tries conclusions 12
with a much stronger force, knowing beforehand
that he is bound to retreat when he has done his
best, I hold that it is far better in such a case to
throw a small part of his strength into the attack
than the whole of it ; only horses and men alike
should be his very best. For such a force will be

ἄν τι καὶ ὑποχωρῆσαι ἀσφαλέστερον ἂν δύναιντο.
13 ὅταν δὲ πρὸς τοὺς κρείττους πάντας προσαγαγὼν
ἀποχωρεῖν βούληται, ἀνάγκη τοὺς μὲν ἐπὶ τῶν
βραδυτάτων ἵππων ἁλίσκεσθαι, τοὺς δὲ καὶ δι'
ἀφιππίαν [1] πίπτειν, τοὺς δὲ καὶ διὰ δυσχωρίας
ἀπολαμβάνεσθαι· καὶ γὰρ πολὺν τόπον χαλεπὸν
14 εὑρεῖν οἷον ἄν τις εὔξαιτο. ὑπό γε μὴν τοῦ
πλήθους καὶ συμπίπτοιεν ἂν καὶ ἐμποδίζοντες
πολλὰ ἂν ἀλλήλους κακουργοῖεν. οἱ δ' ἀγαθοὶ
ἵπποι καὶ ἱππεῖς δυνατοὶ καὶ ἐξ αὐτῶν [2] διαφεύ-
γειν, ἄλλως τε ἂν καὶ μηχανᾶταί τις τοῖς
διώκουσι φόβον ἀπὸ τῶν περιττῶν ἱππέων.
15 σύμφορον δ' εἰς τοῦτο καὶ αἱ ψευδενέδραι· χρήσιμον δὲ κἀκεῖνο, τὸ εὑρίσκειν πόθεν ἂν οἱ φίλοι
ἐξ ἀσφαλοῦς ἐπιφαινόμενοι βραδυτέρους τοὺς
16 διώκοντας παρέχοιεν. ἀλλὰ μὴν καὶ τόδε δῆλον,
ὡς πόνοις καὶ τάχει οἱ ὀλίγοι τῶν πολλῶν πολὺ
μᾶλλον ἢ οἱ πολλοὶ τῶν ὀλίγων περιγίγνοιντ' ἄν.
καὶ οὐ λέγω, ὡς διὰ τὸ ὀλίγοι εἶναι καὶ πονεῖν
μᾶλλον δυνήσονται καὶ θάττους ἔσονται, ἀλλ'
ὅτι ῥᾷον εὑρεῖν ὀλίγους ἢ πολλοὺς τοὺς καὶ
τῶν ἵππων ἐπιμελησομένους ὡς δεῖ καὶ αὐτοὺς
φρονίμως μελετήσοντας τὴν ἱππικήν.
17 Ἂν δέ ποτε συμβαίνῃ ἀγωνίζεσθαι πρὸς παραπλησίους ἱππέας, ἐγὼ μὲν οἶμαι οὐκ ἂν χεῖρον
εἶναι, εἴ τις δύο τάξεις ἐκ τῆς φυλῆς ποιήσειε καὶ
τῆς μὲν ὁ φύλαρχος ἡγοῖτο, τῆς δὲ ἄλλης ὅστις
18 ἄριστος δοκοίη εἶναι, οὗτος δὲ τέως μὲν ἕποιτο
κατ' οὐρὰν τῆς μετὰ τοῦ φυλάρχου τάξεως, ἐπεὶ
δ' ἐγγὺς ἤδη εἶεν οἱ ἀντίπαλοι, ἀπὸ παραγ-

---

[1] ἀφιππίαν is a correction in B: ἀφιππείαν S. with the MSS.

able to achieve something and to retreat with less
risk. But when he has thrown the whole of his 13
strength into an attack on a stronger force, and wants
to retire, the men on the slowest mounts are bound
to be taken prisoners; others to be thrown through
lack of horsemanship; and others to be cut off
owing to inequalities in the ground, since it is hard
to find a wide expanse of country entirely to your
liking. Moreover, owing to their numbers they 14
will collide and hinder and hurt one another frequently. But good horses and men will contrive
to escape, especially if you manage to scare the
pursuers by using your reserves. Sham ambuscades, 15
too, are helpful for this purpose. It is also useful to
discover on what quarter your friends may suddenly
reveal themselves in a safe position and make
the pursuit slower. Then again it is obvious that in 16
point of endurance and speed the advantage is much
more likely to rest with a small than with a large force.
I do not mean that mere paucity of numbers will
increase the men's powers of endurance and add
to their speed; but it is easier to find few men than
many who will take proper care of their horses and
will practise the art of horsemanship intelligently on
their own account.

Should it happen at any time that the cavalry 17
forces engaged are about equal, I think it would be
a good plan to split each regiment into two divisions,
putting one under the command of the colonel, and
the other under the best man available. The latter 18
would follow in the rear of the colonel's division for
a time; but presently, when the adversary is near,

γέλσεως παρελαύνοι ἐπὶ τοὺς πολεμίους. οὕτω
γὰρ οἶμαι καὶ ἐκπληκτικωτέρους τοῖς ἐχθροῖς ἂν
19 εἶναι καὶ δυσμαχωτέρους. εἰ δὲ πεζοὺς ἔχοιεν
ἑκάτεροι, καὶ οὗτοι ἀποκεκρυμμένοι ὄπισθεν τῶν
ἱππέων, ἐξαπίνης δὲ παραφαινόμενοι καὶ ὁμόσε
ἰόντες δοκοῦσιν ἄν μοι τὴν νίκην πολὺ μᾶλλον
κατεργάζεσθαι. ὁρῶ γὰρ τὰ παράδοξα ἢν μὲν
ἀγαθὰ ἦν, μᾶλλον εὐφραίνοντα τοὺς ἀνθρώπους,
20 ἢν δὲ δεινά, μᾶλλον ἐκπλήττοντα. ταῦτα δὲ
γνοίη ἄν τις μάλιστα ἐνθυμούμενος, ὡς οἵ τε
ἐνέδραις ἐμπίπτοντες ἐκπλήττονται, καὶ ἐὰν
πολὺ πλείους ὦσι· καὶ ὅταν πολέμιοι ἀλλήλοις
ἀντικάθωνται, ὡς πολὺ ταῖς πρώταις ἡμέραις
φοβερώτατα ἔχουσιν.

21 Ἀλλὰ τὸ μὲν διατάξαι ταῦτα οὐ χαλεπόν· τὸ
δ᾽ εὑρεῖν τοὺς φρονίμως καὶ πιστῶς καὶ προθύμως
καὶ εὐψύχως παρελῶντας ἐπὶ τοὺς πολεμίους,
22 τοῦτο ἤδη ἀγαθοῦ ἱππάρχου. δεῖ γὰρ καὶ
λέγειν αὐτὸν ἱκανὸν εἶναι καὶ ποιεῖν τοιαῦτα, ἀφ᾽
ὧν οἱ ἀρχόμενοι γνώσονται ἀγαθὸν εἶναι τό τε
πείθεσθαι καὶ τὸ ἔπεσθαι καὶ τὸ ὁμόσε ἐλαύνειν
τοῖς πολεμίοις καὶ ἐπιθυμήσουσι τοῦ καλόν τι
ἀκούειν καὶ δυνήσονται ἃ ἂν γνῶσιν ἐγκαρτερεῖν.

23 Ἐὰν δέ ποτε αὖ ἢ φαλάγγων ἀντιτεταγμένων
ἢ χωρίων ἑκατέροις ὑπαρχόντων ἐν τῷ μέσῳ τοῖς
ἱππεῦσιν ἀναστροφαί τε καὶ διώξεις καὶ ἀποχωρήσεις γίγνωνται, εἰώθασι μὲν ὡς τὰ πολλὰ ἐκ
τῶν τοιούτων ὁρμᾶν μὲν¹ βραδέως ἀμφότεροι,
24 τὸ δ᾽ ἐν μέσῳ τάχιστα ἐλαύνειν. ἢν δέ τις οὕτω
προδείξας ἔπειτα² ἐκ τῶν ἀναστροφῶν ταχέως

---

¹ S. reads ὁρμᾶν μὲν ἐκ τῶν ἀναστροφῶν with the MSS. : ἐκ
τῶν ἀναστροφῶν is rightly removed by Rühl.

he would wheel on receiving the order and charge.
This plan, I think, would make the blow delivered
by the regiment more stunning and more difficult to
parry. Both divisions should have an infantry con- 19
tingent; and if the infantry, hidden away behind the
cavalry, came out suddenly and went for the enemy,
I think they would prove an important factor in
making the victory more decisive; for I have noticed
that a surprise cheers men up if it is pleasant,
but stuns them if it is alarming. Anyone will 20
recognise the truth of this who reflects that, however
great their advantage in numbers, men are dazed
when they fall into an ambuscade, and that two
hostile armies confronting each other are scared out
of their wits for the first few days.

There is no difficulty in adopting these tactics; 21
but only a good cavalry commander can find men
who will show intelligence, reliability and courage in
wheeling to charge the enemy. For the commander 22
must be capable both by his words and action of
making the men under him realize that it is good to
obey, to back up their leader, and to charge home;
of firing them with a desire to win commendation;
and of enabling them to carry out their intentions
with persistence.

Suppose now that the cavalry are busy in the 23
no-man's-land that separates two battle lines drawn
up face to face or two strategic positions, wheeling,
pursuing and retreating. After such manœuvres
both sides usually start off at a slow pace, but gallop
at full speed in the unoccupied ground. But if a 24
commander first feints in this manner, and then after

---

² ἔπειτα Hartman: ἔπειτα δ' S. with the MSS.

τε διώκῃ καὶ ταχέως ἀποχωρῇ, βλάπτειν τ' ἂν
μάλιστα τοὺς πολεμίους δύναιτο καὶ ὡς τὸ εἰκὸς
ἀσφαλέστατ' ἂν διάγοι, ταχὺ μὲν διώκων ἐν ᾧ
ἂν ἐγγὺς ᾖ τοῦ ἑαυτοῦ ἰσχυροῦ, ταχὺ δὲ ἀπο-
25 χωρῶν ἀπὸ τῶν τοῖς πολεμίοις ἰσχυρῶν. εἰ δὲ
καὶ λαθεῖν δύναιτο ἀπὸ τῆς τάξεως ἑκάστης
καταλιπὼν ἢ τέτταρας ἢ πέντε τῶν κρατίστων
ἵππων τε καὶ ἀνδρῶν, πολὺ ἂν προέχοιεν εἰς τὸ
ἐπαναστρεφομένοις τοῖς πολεμίοις ἐμπίπτειν.

IX. Ταῦτα δὲ ἀναγιγνώσκειν μὲν καὶ ὀλιγάκις
ἀρκεῖ, ἐννοεῖν[1] δὲ τὸ παρατυγχάνον αὐτῷ ἀεὶ[2]
δεῖ καὶ πρὸς τὸ παριστάμενον σκοποῦντα τὸ
συμφέρον ἐκπονεῖν. γράψαι δὲ πάντα, ὁπόσα
δεῖ ποιεῖν, οὐδὲν μᾶλλον οἷόν τέ ἐστιν ἢ τὰ μέλ-
2 λοντα πάντα εἰδέναι. πάντων δὲ τῶν ὑπομνη-
μάτων ἔμοιγε δοκεῖ κράτιστον εἶναι τὸ ὅσα ἂν
γνῷ ἀγαθὰ εἶναι ἐπιμελεῖσθαι ὡς ἂν πραχθῇ.
ὀρθῶς δὲ γιγνωσκόμενα οὐ φέρει καρπὸν οὔτε ἐν
γεωργίᾳ οὔτ' ἐν ναυκληρίᾳ οὔτ' ἐν ἀρχῇ, ἢν μή
τις ἐπιμελῆται ὡς ἂν ταῦτα σὺν τοῖς θεοῖς[3]
ἐκπεραίνηται.[4]

3 Φημὶ δ' ἐγὼ[5] καὶ τὸ πᾶν ἱππικὸν ὧδ' ἂν
πολὺ θᾶττον ἐκπληρωθῆναι εἰς τοὺς χιλίους ἱππέας καὶ πολὺ ῥᾷον τοῖς πολίταις, εἰ διακοσίους
ἱππεῖς ξένους καταστήσαιντο· δοκοῦσι γὰρ ἄν

[1] ἐννοεῖν Madvig: ποιεῖν S. with the MSS.
[2] αὐτῷ ἀεὶ BM: ἀεὶ αὐτῷ S. with other MSS.
[3] The MSS. have no σὺν τοῖς θεοῖς here, but have ταῦτα σὺν
τοῖς θεοῖς in the next sentence—see next note but one. S.
follows the text of the MSS.: the correction is by Madvig.
[4] ἐκπεραίνηται B: περαίνηται S. with the other MSS.
[5] ἐγὼ ταῦτα S. with the MSS.: ταῦτα was removed by
Lenklau.

wheeling, pursues and retreats at the gallop he will
be able to inflict the greatest loss on the enemy, and
will probably come through with the least harm,
by pursuing at the gallop so long as he is near his
own defence, and retreating at the gallop from the
enemy's defences. If, moreover, he can secretly 25
leave behind him four or five of the best horses and
men in each division, they will be at a great
advantage in falling on the enemy as he is turning
to renew the charge.

IX. To read these suggestions a few times is
enough ; but it is always necessary for the commander to hit on the right thing at the right
moment, to think of the present situation and to
carry out what is expedient in view of it. To write
out all that he ought to do is no more possible than
to know everything that is going to happen. The 2
most important of all my hints, I think, is this:
Whatever you decide to be best, see that it gets done.
Whether you are a farmer,[1] a skipper or a commander, sound decisions bear no fruit unless you see
to it that, with heaven's help,[2] they are duly carried
out.

Further, I am of opinion that the full complement 3
of a thousand cavalry would be raised much more
quickly and in a manner much less burdensome
to the citizens if they established a force of two
hundred foreign cavalry.[3] For I believe that the

[1] *Oeconomicus* xi. 8.
[2] This expression undoubtedly comes here ; compare
especially the maxim "Act with god" (§ 8), and the end
of the *Ways and Means*.
[3] The 200 mercenaries would be included in the total of
1000.

μοι οὗτοι προσγενόμενοι καὶ εὐπειστότερον ἂν
πᾶν τὸ ἱππικὸν ποιῆσαι καὶ φιλοτιμότερον πρὸς
4 ἀλλήλους περὶ ἀνδραγαθίας. οἶδα δ' ἔγωγε καὶ
Λακεδαιμονίοις ἱππικὸν ἀρξάμενον εὐδοκιμεῖν,
ἐπεὶ ξένους ἱππέας προσέλαβον. καὶ ἐν ταῖς
ἄλλαις δὲ πόλεσι πανταχοῦ τὰ ξενικὰ ὁρῶ
εὐδοκιμοῦντα· ἡ γὰρ χρεία μεγάλην προθυμίαν
5 συμβάλλεται. εἰς δὲ τιμὴν τῶν ἵππων νομίζω
ἂν αὐτοῖς χρήματα ὑπάρξαι καὶ παρὰ τῶν
σφόδρα ἀπεχομένων μὴ ἱππεύειν, ὅτι καὶ οἷς
καθίστησι τὸ ἱππικὸν ἐθέλουσι τελεῖν ἀργύριον
ὡς μὴ ἱππεύειν, καὶ παρὰ πλουσίων μέν,[1] ἀδυ-
νάτων δὲ τοῖς σώμασιν· οἶμαι δὲ καὶ παρ'
6 ὀρφανῶν τῶν δυνατοὺς οἴκους ἐχόντων. νομίζω
δὲ καὶ μετοίκων φιλοτιμεῖσθαι ἄν τινας εἰς
ἱππικὸν[2] καθισταμένους· ὁρῶ γὰρ καὶ τῶν
ἄλλων ὁπόσων ἂν καλῶν ὄντων μεταδιδῶσιν
αὐτοῖς οἱ πολῖται, φιλοτίμως ἐνίους ἐθέλοντας τὸ
7 προσταχθὲν διαπράττεσθαι. δοκεῖ δ' ἄν μοι καὶ
πεζὸν σὺν τοῖς ἵπποις ἐνεργότατον εἶναι, εἰ
συσταθείη ἐξ ἀνδρῶν τῶν ἐναντιωτάτων τοῖς
πολεμίοις.

Ταῦτα δὲ πάντα θεῶν συνεθελόντων γένοιτ' ἄν.
8 εἰ δέ τις τοῦτο θαυμάζει, ὅτι πολλάκις γέγραπται
τὸ σὺν θεῷ πράττειν, εὖ ἴστω, ὅτι ἢν πολλάκις
κινδυνεύῃ, ἧττον τοῦτο θαυμάσεται καὶ ἤν γε
κατανοῇ, ὅτι ὅταν πόλεμος ᾖ, ἐπιβουλεύουσι μὲν

---

[1] μὲν Dindorf : γε S. with the MSS.
[2] ἱππικὸν Bake : ἱππικὴν S. with the MSS.

presence of these men would improve the discipline of the whole force and would foster rivalry in the display of efficiency. I know that the fame of the 4 Lacedaemonian horse dates from the introduction of foreign cavalry: and in the other states everywhere I notice that the foreign contingents enjoy a high reputation; for need helps to produce great eagerness. To defray the cost of their horses,[1] I 5 believe that money would be forthcoming from those who strongly object to serve in the cavalry—since even men actually enrolled [2] are willing to pay in order to get out of the service—from rich men who are physically unfit, and also, I think, from orphans [3] possessed of large estates. I believe also that some 6 of the resident aliens would be proud to be enrolled in the cavalry. For I notice that, whenever the citizens give them a share in any other honourable duty, some are willing enough to take pride in doing the part assigned to them. I fancy, too, that infantry 7 attached to the cavalry will be most effective if it consists of persons who are very bitter against the enemy.

All these things are feasible provided the gods give their consent. If anyone is surprised at my frequent 8 repetition of the exhortation to work with God, I can assure him that his surprise will diminish, if he is often in peril, and if he considers that in time

---

[1] The mercenaries would not receive "establishment" money.

[2] οἶς καθίστησι is not right; but the translation gives the approximate sense of what Xenophon must have written.

[3] Orphans were exempt from state burdens until a year after attaining their majority. The meaning seems to be that during this period of exemption they might fairly be asked to contribute to such a fund.

XENOPHON

ἀλλήλοις οἱ ἐναντίοι, ὀλιγάκις δὲ ἴσασι, πῶς ἔχει
9 τὰ ἐπιβουλευόμενα. τὰ οὖν τοιαῦτα οὐδ' ὅτῳ
συμβουλεύσαιτ' ἄν τις οἷόν τε εὑρεῖν πλὴν θεῶν·
οὗτοι δὲ πάντα ἴσασι καὶ προσημαίνουσιν ᾧ ἂν
ἐθέλωσι καὶ ἐν ἱεροῖς καὶ ἐν οἰωνοῖς καὶ ἐν
φήμαις καὶ ἐν ὀνείρασιν. εἰκὸς δὲ μᾶλλον
ἐθέλειν αὐτοὺς συμβουλεύειν τούτοις, οἳ ἂν μὴ
μόνον ὅταν δέωνται ἐπερωτῶσι, τί χρὴ ποιεῖν,
ἀλλὰ καὶ ἐν ταῖς εὐτυχίαις θεραπεύωσιν ὅ τι ἂν
δύνωνται τοὺς θεούς.

of war foemen plot and counterplot, but seldom know what will come of their plots. Therefore 9 there is none other that can give counsel in such a case but the gods. They know all things, and warn whomsoever they will in sacrifices, in omens, in voices, and in dreams.[1] And we may suppose that they are more ready to counsel those who not only ask what they ought to do in the hour of need, but also serve the gods in the days of their prosperity with all their might.

[1] *Memorabilia* I. i. 3.

ON THE ART
OF HORSEMANSHIP

ΞΕΝΟΦΩΝΤΟΣ ΠΕΡΙ ΙΠΠΙΚΗΣ

I. Ἐπειδὴ διὰ τὸ συμβῆναι ἡμῖν πολὺν χρόνον ἱππεύειν οἰόμεθα ἔμπειροι ἱππικῆς γεγενῆσθαι, βουλόμεθα καὶ τοῖς νεωτέροις τῶν φίλων δηλῶσαι, ᾗ ἂν νομίζομεν αὐτοὺς ὀρθότατα ἵπποις προσφέρεσθαι. συνέγραψε μὲν οὖν καὶ Σίμων περὶ ἱππικῆς, ὃς καὶ τὸν κατὰ τὸ Ἀθήνησιν Ἐλευσίνιον ἵππον χαλκοῦν ἀνέθηκε καὶ ἐν τῷ βάθρῳ τὰ ἑαυτοῦ ἔργα ἐξετύπωσεν· ἡμεῖς γε μέντοι ὅσοις συνετύχομεν ταὐτὰ γνόντες ἐκείνῳ, οὐκ ἐξαλείφομεν ἐκ τῶν ἡμετέρων, ἀλλὰ πολὺ ἥδιον παραδώσομεν αὐτὰ τοῖς φίλοις, νομίζοντες ἀξιοπιστότεροι εἶναι, ὅτι κἀκεῖνος κατὰ ταὐτὰ ἡμῖν ἔγνω ἱππικὸς ὤν· καὶ ὅσα δὴ παρέλιπεν, ἡμεῖς πειρασόμεθα δηλῶσαι.

Πρῶτον δὲ γράψομεν, ὡς ἄν τις ἥκιστα ἐξαπατῷτο ἐν ἱππωνείᾳ.

Τοῦ μὲν τοίνυν ἔτι ἀδαμάστου πώλου δῆλον ὅτι τὸ σῶμα δεῖ δοκιμάζειν· τῆς γὰρ ψυχῆς οὐ πάνυ σαφῆ τεκμήρια παρέχεται ὁ μήπω ἀναβαινόμενος.

2 Τοῦ γε μὴν σώματος πρῶτόν φαμεν χρῆναι τοὺς πόδας σκοπεῖν. ὥσπερ γὰρ οἰκίας οὐδὲν

---

[1] A considerable fragment of this work survives in a MS. in Emmanuel College, Cambridge. The most recent editions are those of Oder and Rühl. The "cavalry commander"

ON THE ART
OF HORSEMANSHIP

I. INASMUCH as we have had a long experience of
cavalry, and consequently claim familiarity with
the art of horsemanship, we wish to explain to
our younger friends what we believe to be the
correct method of dealing with horses. True there
is already a treatise on horsemanship by Simon,[1]
who also dedicated the bronze horse in the
Eleusinium at Athens and recorded his own feats in
relief on the pedestal. Nevertheless, we shall not
erase from our work the conclusions that happen to
coincide with his, but shall offer them to our friends
with far greater pleasure, in the belief that they are
more worthy of acceptance because so expert a
horseman held the same opinions as we ourselves :
moreover, we shall try to explain all the points that
he has omitted.

First we will give directions how best to avoid being
cheated in buying a horse.

For judging an unbroken colt, the only criterion,
obviously, is the body, for no clear signs of temper
are to be detected in an animal that has not yet had
a man on his back.

In examining his body, we say you must first look 2
at his feet. For, just as a house is bound to be worth-

named Simon referred to in Aristophanes' *Knights* 242, is
just a member of the chorus, but the name probably recalls
the author.

ὄφελος ἂν εἴη, εἰ τὰ ἄνω πάνυ καλὰ ἔχοι μὴ
ὑποκειμένων οἵων δεῖ θεμελίων, οὕτω καὶ ἵππου
πολεμιστηρίου οὐδὲν ἂν ὄφελος εἴη, οὐδ' εἰ τἆλλα
πάντα ἀγαθὰ ἔχοι, κακόπους δ' εἴη· οὐδενὶ γὰρ
ἂν δύναιτο τῶν ἀγαθῶν χρῆσθαι.

3 Πόδας δ' ἄν τις δοκιμάζοι πρῶτον μὲν τοὺς
ὄνυχας σκοπῶν· οἱ γὰρ παχεῖς πολὺ τῶν λεπτῶν
διαφέρουσιν εἰς εὐποδίαν· ἔπειτα οὐδὲ τοῦτο δεῖ
λανθάνειν, πότερον αἱ ὁπλαί εἰσιν ὑψηλαὶ ἢ
ταπειναὶ καὶ ἔμπροσθεν καὶ ὄπισθεν ἢ χαμηλαί.
αἱ μὲν γὰρ ὑψηλαὶ πόρρω ἀπὸ τοῦ δαπέδου
ἔχουσι τὴν χελιδόνα καλουμένην, αἱ δὲ ταπειναὶ
ὁμοίως βαίνουσι τῷ τε ἰσχυροτάτῳ καὶ τῷ
μαλακωτάτῳ τοῦ ποδός, ὥσπερ οἱ βλαισοὶ τῶν
ἀνθρώπων· καὶ τῷ ψόφῳ δέ φησι Σίμων δήλους
εἶναι τοὺς εὔποδας, καλῶς λέγων· ὥσπερ γὰρ
κύμβαλον ψοφεῖ πρὸς τῷ δαπέδῳ ἡ κοίλη ὁπλή.

4 Ἐπεὶ δὲ ἠρξάμεθα ἐντεῦθεν, ταύτῃ καὶ ἀνα-
βησόμεθα πρὸς τὸ ἄλλο σῶμα.

Δεῖ τοίνυν καὶ τὰ ἀνωτέρω μὲν τῶν ὁπλῶν
κατωτέρω δὲ τῶν κυνηπόδων ὀστᾶ μήτε ἄγαν
ὀρθὰ εἶναι ὥσπερ αἰγός· ἀντιτυπώτερα γὰρ ὄντα
κόπτει τε τὸν ἀναβάτην καὶ παραπίμπραται
μᾶλλον τὰ τοιαῦτα σκέλη· οὐδὲ μὴν ἄγαν ταπεινὰ
τὰ ὀστᾶ δεῖ εἶναι· ψιλοῖντο γὰρ ἂν καὶ ἑλκοῖντο οἱ
κυνήποδες εἴτ' ἐν βώλοις εἴτ' ἐν λίθοις ἐλαύνοιτο
ὁ ἵππος.

5 Τῶν γε μὴν κνημῶν τὰ ὀστᾶ παχέα χρὴ εἶναι·
ταῦτα γάρ ἐστι στήριγγες τοῦ ὤματος· οὐ

---

[1] " M. Bourgelat, in his preface to the second volume of *Les
Elemens Hippiatriques* reprehends this remark as trifling and
false ; and if our author is to be understood literally, the

less if the foundations are unsound, however well the upper parts may look, so a war-horse will be quite useless, even though all his other points are good, if he has bad feet; for in that case he will be unable to use any of his good points.

When testing the feet first look to the hoofs. For [3] it makes a great difference in the quality of the feet if they are thick rather than thin. Next you must not fail to notice whether the hoofs are high both in front and behind, or low. For high hoofs have the frog, as it is called, well off the ground; but flat hoofs tread with the strongest and weakest part of the foot simultaneously, like a bow-legged man. Moreover, Simon says that the ring, too, is a clear test of good feet: and he is right; for a hollow hoof rings like a cymbal in striking the ground.[1]

Having begun here, we will proceed upwards by [4] successive steps to the rest of the body.

The bones (of the pastern) above the hoofs and below the fetlocks should not be too upright, like a goat's: such legs give too hard a tread, jar the rider, and are more liable to inflammation. Nor yet should the bones be too low,[2] else the fetlocks are likely to become bare and sore when the horse is ridden over clods or stones.

The bones of the shanks should be thick,[3] since [5] these are the pillars of the body; but not thick with

criticism is certainly just."—Berenger i, 221. Yet it is unlikely that Simon and X. were both mistaken.

[2] "The pasterns (of the hackney) should neither be too oblique, which bespeaks weakness: nor too straight, which wears the horse out and is unpleasant to the rider."—Blair in Loudon's *Agriculture*.

[3] "Wide" would be a more suitable word.

μέντοι φλεψί γε οὐδὲ σαρξὶ παχέα· εἰ δὲ μή,
ὅταν ἐν σκληροῖς ἐλαύνηται, ἀνάγκη αἵματος
ταῦτα πληροῦσθαι καὶ κρισσοὺς γίγνεσθαι καὶ
παχύνεσθαι μὲν τὰ σκέλη, ἀφίστασθαι δὲ τὸ
δέρμα. χαλῶντος δὲ τούτου πολλάκις καὶ ἡ
περόνη ἀποστᾶσα χωλὸν ἀπέδειξε τὸν ἵππον.

6 Τά γε μὴν γόνατα ἢ βαδίζων ὁ πῶλος ὑγρῶς
κάμπτῃ, εἰκάζοις ἂν καὶ ἱππεύοντα ὑγρὰ ἕξειν τὰ
σκέλη· πάντες γὰρ προϊόντος τοῦ χρόνου ὑγρο-
τέρως κάμπτουσιν ἐν τοῖς γόνασι. τὰ δὲ ὑγρὰ
δικαίως εὐδοκιμεῖ· ἀπταιστότερον γὰρ καὶ ἀκο-
πώτερον τὸν ἵππον τῶν σκληρῶν σκελῶν
παρέχει.

7 Μηροί γε μέντοι οἱ ὑπὸ ταῖς ὠμοπλάταις ἢν
παχεῖς ὦσιν, ἰσχυρότεροί τε καὶ εὐπρεπέστεροι
ὥσπερ ἀνδρὸς φαίνονται.

Καὶ μὴν στέρνα πλατύτερα ὄντα καὶ πρὸς
κάλλος καὶ πρὸς ἰσχὺν καὶ πρὸς τὸ μὴ ἐπαλλὰξ
ἀλλὰ διὰ πολλοῦ τὰ σκέλη φέρειν εὐφυέστερα.

8 Ἀπό γε μὴν τοῦ στέρνου ὁ μὲν αὐχὴν αὐτοῦ μὴ
ὥσπερ κάπρου προπετὴς πεφύκοι, ἀλλ᾽ ὥσπερ
ἀλεκτρυόνος ὀρθὸς πρὸς τὴν κορυφὴν ἥκοι, λαγα-
ρὸς δὲ εἴη τὰ κατὰ τὴν συγκαμπήν, ἡ δὲ κεφαλὴ
ὀστώδης οὖσα μικρὰν σιαγόνα ἔχοι. οὕτως ὁ μὲν
τράχηλος πρὸ τοῦ ἀναβάτου ἂν εἴη, τὸ δὲ ὄμμα
τὰ πρὸ τῶν ποδῶν ὁρῷη. καὶ βιάζεσθαι δὲ ἥκιστ᾽
ἂν δύναιτο ὁ τοιοῦτος σχῆμα ἔχων καὶ εἰ πάνυ
θυμοειδὴς εἴη· οὐ γὰρ ἐγκάμπτοντες, ἀλλ᾽ ἐκτεί-
νοντες τὸν τράχηλον καὶ τὴν κεφαλὴν βιάζεσθαι
οἱ ἵπποι ἐπιχειροῦσι.

---

[1] The Greek word means the fibula in man, but the fibula,
of course, is no part of the shank in the horse. Morgan

veins nor with flesh, else when the horse is ridden over hard ground, these parts are bound to become charged with blood and varicose; the legs will swell, and the skin will fall away, and when this gets loose the pin,[1] too, is apt to give way and lame the horse.

If the colt's knees are supple when bending as he 6 walks, you may guess that his legs will be supple when he is ridden too, for all horses acquire greater suppleness at the knee as time goes on. Supple knees are rightly approved, since they render the horse less likely to stumble and tire than stiff legs.

The arms below the shoulders,[2] as in man, are 7 stronger and better looking if they are thick.

A chest of some width is better formed both for appearance and for strength, and for carrying the legs well apart without crossing.

His neck should not hang downwards from the 8 chest like a boar's, but stand straight up to the crest, like a cock's;[3] but it should be flexible at the bend; and the head should be bony, with a small cheek. Thus the neck will protect the rider, and the eye see what lies before the feet.[4] Besides, a horse of such a mould will have least power of running away, be he never so high-spirited, for horses do not arch the neck and head, but stretch them out when they try to run away.

rightly says that X. writes throughout of the horse as he appears outwardly, and not of the skeleton (with which he was unacquainted), and that the allusion is to the back sinew of the shin.

[2] The forearm, not the true arm, which X. includes in the chest.

[3] The horse should not be "cock-throttled."

[4] He will not be a "star-gazer."

9 Σκοπεῖν δὲ χρὴ καὶ εἰ ἀμφότεραι μαλακαὶ αἱ γνάθοι ἢ σκληραὶ ἢ ἡ ἑτέρα. ἑτερόγναθοι γὰρ ὡς τὰ πολλὰ οἱ μὴ ὁμοίας τὰς γνάθους ἔχοντες γίγνονται.

Καὶ μὴν τὸ ἐξόφθαλμον εἶναι ἐγρηγορὸς μᾶλλον φαίνεται τοῦ κοιλοφθάλμου, καὶ ἐπὶ πλεῖον δ᾽ ἂν
10 ὁ τοιοῦτος ὁρῴη. καὶ μυκτῆρές γε οἱ ἀναπεπταμένοι τῶν συμπεπτωκότων εὐπνοώτεροί τε ἅμα εἰσὶ καὶ γοργότερον τὸν ἵππον ἀποδεικνύουσι. καὶ γὰρ ὅταν ὀργίζηται ἵππος ἵππῳ ἢ ἐν ἱππασίᾳ θυμῶται, εὐρύνει μᾶλλον τοὺς μυκτῆρας.

11 Καὶ μὴν κορυφὴ μὲν μείζων, ὦτα δὲ μικρότερα ἱππωδεστέραν τὴν κεφαλὴν ἀποφαίνει.

Ἡ δ᾽ αὖ ὑψηλὴ ἀκρωμία τῷ τε ἀναβάτῃ ἀσφαλεστέραν τὴν ἕδραν καὶ τοῖς ὤμοις[1] ἰσχυροτέραν τὴν πρόσφυσιν παρέχεται.

Ῥάχις γε μὴν ἡ διπλῆ τῆς ἁπλῆς καὶ ἐγκαθῆσθαι μαλακωτέρα καὶ ἰδεῖν ἡδίων.

12 Καὶ πλευρὰ δὲ ἡ βαθυτέρα καὶ πρὸς τὴν γαστέρα ὀγκωδεστέρα ἅμα εὐεδρότερόν τε καὶ ἰσχυρότερον καὶ εὐχιλότερον ὡς ἐπὶ τὸ πολὺ τὸν ἵππον παρέχεται.

Ὀσφῦς γε μὴν ὅσῳ ἂν πλατυτέρα καὶ βραχυτέρα ᾖ, τοσούτῳ ῥᾷον μὲν ὁ ἵππος τὰ πρόσθεν αἴρεται, ῥᾷον δὲ τὰ ὄπισθεν προσάγεται· καὶ ὁ κενεὼν δὲ οὕτω μικρότατος φαίνεται, ὅσπερ μέγας ὢν μέρος μέν τι καὶ αἰσχύνει, μέρος δέ τι καὶ ἀσθενέστερον καὶ δυσφορώτερον αὐτὸν τὸν ἵππον παρέχεται.

13 Τά γε μὴν ἰσχία πλατέα μὲν εἶναι χρὴ καὶ εὔσαρκα, ἵνα ἀκόλουθα ᾖ ταῖς πλευραῖς καὶ τοῖς στέρνοις· ἢν δὲ πάντα στερεὰ ᾖ, κουφότερα ἂν τὰ

---

[1] ὤμοις Schneider: ὤμοις καὶ τῷ σώματι S. with the MSS.

You should notice, too, whether both jaws are soft 9 or hard, or only one ; for horses with unequal jaws are generally unequally sensitive in the mouth.

A prominent eye looks more alert than one that is hollow, and, apart from that, it gives the horse a greater range of vision. And wide open nostrils 10 afford room for freer breathing than close ones, and at the same time make the horse look fiercer, for whenever a horse is angry with another or gets excited under his rider, he dilates his nostrils.

A fairly large crest and fairly small ears give the 11 more characteristic shape to a horse's head.

High withers offer the rider a safer seat and a stronger grip on the shoulders.

The double back [1] is both softer to sit on than the single and more pleasing to the eye.

The deeper the flanks and the more swelling 12 toward the belly, the firmer is the seat and the stronger, and as a rule, the better feeder is the horse.

The broader and shorter the loins, the more easily the horse lifts his fore quarters and the more easily he brings up his hind quarters. And, apart from that, the belly looks smallest so, and if it is big it disfigures the horse to some extent, and also makes him to some extent both weaker and clumsier.

The haunches must be broad and fleshy, that 13 they may be in right proportion to the flanks and chest, and if they are firm all over, they will

---

[1] "That was before the days of saddles, and horsemen had a tender interest in the double back—the characteristic back of dappled horses."—Pocock, *Horses*, p. 118. "Duplex agitur per lumbos spina," says Virgil (*Georg.* iii. 87).

πρὸς τὸν δρόμον εἴη καὶ ὀξύτερον μᾶλλον ἂν[1] τὸν
ἵππον παρέχοιτο.

14 Μηρούς γε μὴν τοὺς ὑπὸ τῇ οὐρᾷ ἢν ἅμα
πλατείᾳ τῇ γραμμῇ διωρισμένους ἔχῃ, οὕτω καὶ
τὰ ὄπισθεν σκέλη διὰ πολλοῦ ὑποθήσει· τοῦτο
δὲ ποιῶν ἅμα γοργοτέραν τε καὶ ἰσχυροτέραν ἕξει
τὴν ὑπόβασίν τε καὶ ἱππασίαν καὶ ἅπαντα
βελτίων ἔσται ἑαυτοῦ.[2] τεκμήραιο δ' ἂν καὶ ἀπ'
ἀνθρώπων. ὅταν γάρ τι ἀπὸ τῆς γῆς ἄρασθαι
βούλωνται, διαβαίνοντες πάντες μᾶλλον ἢ συμ-
βεβηκότες ἐπιχειροῦσιν αἴρεσθαι.

15 Τούς γε μὴν ὄρχεις δεῖ μὴ μεγάλους τὸν ἵππον
ἔχειν, ὃ οὐκ ἔστι πώλου κατιδεῖν.

Περί γε μὴν τῶν κάτωθεν ἀστραγάλων ἢ
κνημῶν καὶ κυνηπόδων καὶ ὁπλῶν τὰ αὐτὰ
λέγομεν ἅπερ περὶ τῶν ἔμπροσθεν.

16 Γράψαι δὲ βούλομαι καὶ ἐξ ὧν ἂν περὶ μεγέ-
θους ἥκιστα ἀποτυγχάνοι τις. ὅτου γὰρ ἂν ὦσιν
αἱ κνῆμαι εὐθὺς γιγνομένου ὑψηλόταται, οὗτος
μέγιστος γίγνεται. προϊόντος γὰρ τοῦ χρόνου
πάντων τῶν τετραπόδων αἱ μὲν κνῆμαι εἰς
μέγεθος οὐ μάλα αὔξονται, πρὸς δὲ ταύτας ὡς ἂν
συμμέτρως ἔχῃ συναύξεται καὶ τὸ ἄλλο σῶμα.

17 Εἶδος μὲν δὴ πώλου οὕτω δοκιμάζοντες μάλιστ'
ἂν ἡμῖν δοκοῦσι τυγχάνειν εὔποδος καὶ ἰσχυροῦ
καὶ εὐσάρκου καὶ εὐσχήμονος καὶ εὐμεγέθους. εἰ
δέ τινες αὐξανόμενοι μεταβάλλουσιν, ὅμως οὕτω

---

[1] ἂν Dindorf: αὐτὸν τὸν A : αὐτὸν B : αὖ S. with M.
[2] βελτίων ἔσται ἑαυτοῦ A: βελτίω ἔσται ἑαυτῶν S. with the
other MSS.

---

[1] He must not be "cat-hammed" (Berenger), which means
that the hocks will be turned inwards. Such horses are

be lighter for running and will make the horse speedier.

If the gap that separates the hams under the tail 14 is broad,[1] he will also extend his hind legs well apart under his belly; and by doing that he will be more fiery and stronger when he throws himself on his haunches and when he is ridden, and will make the best of himself in all ways. One can infer this from the action of a man: for when he wants to lift anything from the ground, a man invariably tries to lift it with his legs apart rather than close together.

A horse's stones should not be big: but it is 15 impossible to observe this in a colt.

As for the parts below, the hocks, shin bones, fetlocks and hoofs, what we have said about the corresponding parts in the forelegs applies to these also.

I want also to explain how one is least likely to be 16 disappointed in the matter of size. The colt that is longest in the shanks at the time he is foaled makes the biggest horse.[2] For in all quadrupeds the shanks increase but little in size as time goes on, whereas the rest of the body grows to them, so as to be in the right proportion.

He who applies these tests to a colt's shape is 17 sure, in my opinion, to get a beast with good feet, strong, muscular, of the right look and the right size. If some change as they grow, still we may

often good trotters (Blane), but the Greek cavalry rider did not require that.

[2] "For his stature this is an infallible rule that the shinne bone . . . never increaseth, no not from the first foaling . . . insomuch that if those bones be long and large, we are ever assured that the Foale will prove a tall and large Horse." G. Markham, *Cavalerice*, 1617.

θαρροῦντες δοκιμάζοιμεν ἄν·[1] πολλῷ γὰρ πλείονες εὔχρηστοι[2] ἐξ αἰσχρῶν ἢ ἐκ τοιούτων αἰσχροὶ γίγνονται.

II. Ὅπως γε μὴν δεῖ πωλεύειν, δοκεῖ ἡμῖν μὴ γραπτέον εἶναι. τάττονται μὲν γὰρ δὴ ἐν ταῖς πόλεσιν ἱππεύειν οἱ τοῖς χρήμασί τε ἱκανώτατοι καὶ τῆς πόλεως οὐκ ἐλάχιστον μετέχοντες· πολὺ δὲ κρεῖττον τοῦ πωλοδάμνην εἶναι τῷ μὲν νέῳ εὐεξίας τε ἐπιμελεῖσθαι τῆς ἑαυτοῦ καὶ ἱππικὴν[3] ἐπισταμένῳ ἤδη ἱππάζεσθαι μελετᾶν· τῷ δὲ πρεσβυτέρῳ τοῦ τε οἴκου καὶ τῶν φίλων καὶ τῶν πολιτικῶν καὶ τῶν πολεμικῶν μᾶλλον ἢ ἀμφὶ

2 πώλευσιν διατρίβειν. ὁ μὲν δὴ ὥσπερ ἐγὼ γιγνώσκων περὶ πωλείας δῆλον ὅτι ἐκδώσει τὸν πῶλον. χρὴ μέντοι ὥσπερ τὸν παῖδα ὅταν ἐπὶ τέχνην ἐκδῷ, συγγραψάμενον ἃ δεήσει ἐπιστάμενον ἀποδοῦναι οὕτως ἐκδιδόναι. ταῦτα γὰρ ὑπομνήματα[4] ἔσται τῷ πωλοδάμνῃ ὧν δεῖ ἐπιμεληθῆναι, εἰ μέλλει τὸν μισθὸν ἀπολήψεσθαι.

3 Ὅπως μέντοι πρᾷός τε καὶ χειροήθης καὶ φιλάνθρωπος ὁ πῶλος ἐκδιδῶται τῷ πωλοδάμνῃ, ἐπιμελητέον. τὸ γὰρ τοιοῦτον οἴκοι τε τὰ πλεῖστα καὶ διὰ τοῦ ἱπποκόμου ἀποτελεῖται, ἢν ἐπίστηται τὸ μὲν πεινῆν καὶ διψῆν καὶ μυωπίζεσθαι παρασκευάζειν μετ' ἐρημίας γίγνεσθαι τῷ πώλῳ, τὸ δὲ φαγεῖν καὶ πιεῖν καὶ τῶν λυπούντων ἀπαλλάττεσθαι δι' ἀνθρώπων. τούτων γὰρ γιγνομένων ἀνάγκη μὴ μόνον φιλεῖσθαι ἀλλὰ καὶ ποθεῖσθαι

4 ὑπὸ πώλων ἀνθρώπους. καὶ ἅπτεσθαι δὲ χρὴ

---

[1] ἄν, added by Dindorf, is wanting in S.
[2] εὔχρηστοι Schneider: εὐχράστοι S. with the MSS.
[3] ἱππικὴν ἐν (sic) A: ἱππικῆς ἢ S. with the other MSS.

confidently rely on these tests, for it is far commoner for an ugly colt to make a useful horse than for a colt like this to turn out ugly.

II. We do not think it necessary to give directions[1] for breaking a colt. For in our states the cavalry are recruited from those who have ample means and take a considerable part in the government. And it is far better for a young man to get himself into condition and when he understands the art of horsemanship to practise riding than to be a horse-breaker; and an older man had far better devote himself to his estate and his friends and affairs of state and of war than spend his time in horse-breaking. So he who shares my opinion 2 about horse-breaking will, of course, send his colt out. Still he should put in writing what the horse is to know when he is returned, just as when he apprentices his son to a profession. For these articles will serve as notes to remind the horse-breaker of what he must attend to if he is to get his money.

Still, care must be taken that the colt is gentle, 3 tractable, and fond of man when he is sent to the horse-breaker. That sort of business is generally done at home through the groom, if he knows how to contrive that hunger and thirst and horseflies are associated by the colt with solitude, while eating and drinking and delivery from irritation come through man's agency. For in these circumstances a foal is bound not only to like men, but to hanker after them. One should also handle those parts in 4

[1] Or, perhaps, "to give many directions." Something is lost in the MSS., in which the μὴ (added by Courier) does not appear.

---

[4] ὑπομνήματα AB : ὑποδείγματα S. with M.

ὧν ψηλαφωμένων ὁ ἵππος μάλιστα ἥδεται·
ταῦτα δ' ἐστὶ τά τε λασιώτατα καὶ οἷς αὐτὸς
ἥκιστα δύναται ὁ ἵππος, ἤν τι λυπῇ αὐτόν,
5 ἐπικουρεῖν. προστετάχθω δὲ τῷ ἱπποκόμῳ καὶ
τὸ δι' ὄχλου διάγειν καὶ παντοδαπαῖς μὲν ὄψεσι
παντοδαποῖς δὲ ψόφοις πλησιάζειν. τούτων δὲ
ὁπόσα ἂν ὁ πῶλος φοβῆται, οὐ χαλεπαίνοντα δεῖ,
ἀλλὰ πραΰνοντα διδάσκειν, ὅτι οὐ δεινά ἐστι.

Καὶ περὶ μὲν πωλείας ἀρκεῖν μοι δοκεῖ τῷ
ἰδιώτῃ εἰπεῖν τοσαῦτα πράττειν.

III. Ὅταν γε μὴν ἱππαζόμενον ὠνῆταί τις,
ὑπομνήματα γράψομεν, ἃ δεῖ καταμανθάνειν τὸν
μέλλοντα μὴ ἐξαπατᾶσθαι ἐν ἱππωνείᾳ.

Πρῶτον μὲν τοίνυν μὴ λαθέτω αὐτόν, τίς ἡ
ἡλικία· ὁ γὰρ μηκέτι ἔχων γνώμονας οὔτ'
ἐλπίσιν εὐφραίνει οὔτε ὁμοίως εὐαπάλλακτος
γίγνεται.

2   Ὁπότε δὲ ἡ νεότης σαφής, δεῖ αὖ μὴ λαθεῖν, πῶς
μὲν εἰς τὸ στόμα δέχεται τὸν χαλινόν, πῶς δὲ
περὶ τὰ ὦτα τὴν κορυφαίαν. ταῦτα δ' ἥκιστ' ἂν
λανθάνοι, εἰ ὁρῶντος μὲν τοῦ ὠνουμένου ἐμβάλ-
λοιτο ὁ χαλινός, ὁρῶντος δ' ἐξαιροῖτο.

3   Ἔπειτα δὲ προσέχειν δεῖ τὸν νοῦν, πῶς ἐπὶ τὸν
νῶτον δέχεται τὸν ἀναβάτην. πολλοὶ γὰρ ἵπποι
χαλεπῶς προσίενται ἃ πρόδηλα αὐτοῖς ἐστιν ὅτι
προσέμενοι πονεῖν ἀναγκασθήσονται.

4   Σκεπτέον δὲ καὶ τόδε, εἰ ἀναβαθεὶς ἐθέλει ἀφ'
ἵππων ἀποχωρεῖν ἢ εἰ παρ' ἑστηκότας ἱππεύων
μὴ ἐκφέρει πρὸς τούτους. εἰσὶ δὲ καὶ οἳ διὰ

---

[1] The knowledge of the teeth as a criterion of age is
rudimentary.

which the horse likes most to be cherished, that is to say the hairiest parts and those where the horse has least power of helping himself, if anything worries him. Let the groom be under orders also to lead 5 him through crowds, and accustom him to all sorts of sights and all sorts of noises. If the colt shies at any of them, he must teach him, by quieting him and without impatience, that there is nothing to be afraid of.

I think that the directions I have given on the subject of horse-breaking are sufficient for the private person.

III. In case the intention is to buy a horse already ridden, we will write out some notes that the buyer must thoroughly master if he is not to be cheated over his purchase.

First, then, he must not fail to ascertain the age. A horse that has shed all his milk teeth does not afford much ground for pleasing expectations, and is not so easily got rid of.[1]

If he is clearly a youngster, one must notice 2 further how he receives the bit in his mouth and the headstall about his ears. This may best be noticed if the buyer sees the bridle put on and taken off again.

Next, attention must be paid to his behaviour 3 when he receives the rider on his back. For many horses will not readily accept a thing if they know beforehand that, if they accept it, they will be forced to work.

Another thing to be observed is whether when 4 mounted he is willing to leave his companions, or whether in passing standing horses he does not bolt towards them. Some too, in consequence of bad

κακὴν ἀγωγὴν πρὸς τὰς οἴκαδε ἀφόδους φεύγουσιν
ἐκ τῶν ἱππασιῶν.

5 Τούς γε μὴν ἑτερογνάθους μηνύει μὲν καὶ ἡ
πέδη καλουμένη ἱππασία, πολὺ δὲ μᾶλλον καὶ τὸ
μεταβάλλεσθαι τὴν ἱππασίαν. πολλοὶ γὰρ οὐκ
ἐγχειροῦσιν ἐκφέρειν, ἢν μὴ ἅμα συμβῇ ἥ τε
ἄδικος γνάθος καὶ ἡ πρὸς οἶκον ἐκφορά. δεῖ γε
μὴν εἰδέναι καὶ εἰ ἀφεθεὶς εἰς τάχος ἀναλαμβά-
νεται ἐν βραχεῖ καὶ εἰ ἀποστρέφεσθαι ἐθέλει.

6 ἀγαθὸν δὲ μὴ ἄπειρον εἶναι, εἰ καὶ πληγῇ ἐγερθεὶς ἐθέλει ὁμοίως πείθεσθαι. ἄχρηστον μὲν γὰρ
δήπου καὶ οἰκέτης καὶ στράτευμα ἀπειθές· ἵππος
δὲ ἀπειθὴς οὐ μόνον ἄχρηστος, ἀλλὰ πολλάκις
καὶ ὅσαπερ προδότης διαπράττεται.

7 Ἐπεὶ δὲ πολεμιστήριον ἵππον ὑπεθέμεθα
ὠνεῖσθαι, ληπτέον πεῖραν ἁπάντων, ὅσωνπερ
καὶ ὁ πόλεμος πεῖραν λαμβάνει. ἔστι δὲ
ταῦτα, τάφρους διαπηδᾶν, τειχία ὑπερβαίνειν,
ἐπ' ὄχθους ἀνορούειν, ἀπ' ὄχθων καθάλλεσθαι·
καὶ πρὸς ἄναντες δὲ καὶ κατὰ πρανοῦς καὶ πλάγια
ἐλαύνοντα πεῖραν λαμβάνειν. πάντα γὰρ ταῦτα
καὶ τὴν ψυχὴν εἰ καρτερὰ καὶ τὸ σῶμα εἰ ὑγιὲς
βασανίζει.

8 Οὐ μέντοι τὸν μὴ καλῶς πάνυ ταῦτα ποιοῦντα
ἀποδοκιμαστέον. πολλοὶ γὰρ οὐ διὰ τὸ μὴ
δύνασθαι, ἀλλὰ διὰ τὸ ἄπειροι εἶναι τούτων
ἐλλείπονται. μαθόντες δὲ καὶ ἐθισθέντες καὶ
μελετήσαντες καλῶς ἂν ταῦτα πάντα ποιοῖεν, εἰ

training run away from the riding ground to the paths that lead home.

A horse with jaws unequally sensitive is detected 5 by the exercise called the "ring," [1] but much more by changing the exercise.[2] For many do not attempt to bolt unless they have a bad mouth, and the road along which they can bolt home gives them their chance.[3] It is likewise necessary to know whether, when going at full speed he can be pulled up sharp, and whether he turns readily. And it is 6 well to make sure whether he is equally willing to obey when roused by a blow. For a disobedient servant and a disobedient army are of course useless; and a disobedient horse is not only useless, but often behaves just like a traitor.

As we have assumed that the horse to be bought 7 is designed for war, he must be tested in all the particulars in which he is tested by war. These include springing across ditches, leaping over walls, rushing up banks, jumping down from banks. One must also try him by riding up and down hill and on a slope. All these experiments prove whether his spirit is strong and his body sound.

Nevertheless, it is not necessary to reject a horse 8 that is not perfect in these trials. For many break down in these not from want of ability, but from lack of experience. With teaching, use and discipline they will perform all these exercises well,

---

[1] *i.e.* the "volte"; see note at c. vii. § 13.

[2] *i.e.* by riding on the other hand. The allusion, as Hermann saw, is not to the inverted volte.

[3] The meaning is, that if, for example, the road on the right leads home, the horse with a more sensitive right jaw will try to bolt down it.

9 γ᾽ ἄλλως ὑγιεῖς καὶ μὴ κακοὶ εἶεν. τούς γε μέντοι
ὑπόπτας φύσει φυλακτέον. οἱ γὰρ ὑπέρφοβοι
βλάπτειν μὲν τοὺς πολεμίους ἀφ᾽ ἑαυτῶν οὐκ
ἐῶσι, τὸν δὲ ἀναβάτην ἔσφηλάν τε πολλάκις καὶ
εἰς τὰ χαλεπώτατα ἐνέβαλον.

10 Δεῖ δὲ καὶ εἴ τινα χαλεπότητα ἔχοι ὁ ἵππος,
καταμανθάνειν, εἴτε πρὸς ἵππους εἴτε πρὸς
ἀνθρώπους, καὶ εἰ δυσγάργαλίς γε εἴη· πάντα γὰρ
ταῦτα χαλεπὰ τοῖς κεκτημένοις γίγνεται.

11 Τὰς δέ γε τῶν χαλινώσεων καὶ ἀναβάσεων
ἀποκωλύσεις καὶ τἆλλα δὴ [1] νεύματα πολὺ ἂν ἔτι
μᾶλλον καταμάθοι τις, εἰ πεπονηκότος ἤδη τοῦ
ἵππου πάλιν πειρῷτο ποιεῖν ταὐτὰ ὅσαπερ πρὶν
ἄρξασθαι ἱππεύειν. ὅσοι δ᾽ ἂν πεπονηκότες
ἐθέλωσι πάλιν πόνους ὑποδύεσθαι, ἱκανὰ τεκμήρια παρέχονται ταῦτα ψυχῆς καρτερᾶς.

12 Ὡς δὲ συνελόντι εἰπεῖν, ὅστις εὔπους μὲν εἴη,
πρᾶος δέ, ἀρκούντως δὲ ποδώκης, ἐθέλοι δὲ καὶ
δύναιτο πόνους ὑποφέρειν, πείθοιτο δὲ μάλιστα,
οὗτος ἂν εἰκότως ἀλυπότατός τ᾽ εἴη καὶ σωτη-
ριώτατος τῷ ἀμβάτῃ ἐν τοῖς πολεμικοῖς. οἱ δὲ ἢ
διὰ βλακείαν ἐλάσεως πολλῆς δεόμενοι ἢ διὰ
τὸ ὑπέρθυμοι εἶναι πολλῆς θωπείας τε καὶ
πραγματείας ἀσχολίαν μὲν ταῖς χερσὶ τοῦ
ἀναβάτου παρέχουσιν, ἀθυμίαν δ᾽ ἐν τοῖς κινδύνοις.

IV. Ὅταν γε μὴν ἀγασθεὶς ἵππον πρίηταί τις
καὶ οἴκαδε ἀγάγηται, καλὸν μὲν ἐν τοιούτῳ τῆς
οἰκίας τὸν σταθμὸν εἶναι, ὅπου πλειστάκις ὁ
δεσπότης ὄψεται τὸν ἵππον· ἀγαθὸν δ᾽ οὕτω
κατεσκευάσθαι τὸν ἱππῶνα, ὥστε μηδὲν μᾶλλον
οἷόν τ᾽ εἶναι τὸν τοῦ ἵππου σῖτον κλαπῆναι ἐκ

provided they are otherwise sound and not faulty. But one should beware of horses that are naturally 9 shy. For timid horses give one no chance of using them to harm the enemy, and often throw their rider and put him in a very awkward situation.

It is necessary also to find out whether the 10 horse has any vice towards horses or towards men, and whether he will not stand tickling: for all these things prove troublesome to the owner.

As regards objection to being bridled or mounted, 11 and the other reactions, there is a much better way still of detecting these, namely, by trying to do over again, after the horse has finished his work, just what one did before starting on the ride. All horses that are willing after their work to do another spell thereby give sufficient proofs of a patient temper.

To sum up : the horse that is sound in his feet, 12 gentle and fairly speedy, has the will and the strength to stand work, and, above all, is obedient, is the horse that will, as a matter of course, give least trouble and the greatest measure of safety to his rider in warfare. But those that want a lot of driving on account of their laziness, or a lot of coaxing and attention on account of their high spirit, make constant demands on the rider's hands and rob him of confidence in moments of danger.

IV. When a man has found a horse to his mind, bought him and taken him home, it is well to have the stable so situated with respect to the house that his master can see him very often ; and it is a good plan to have the stall so contrived that it will be as difficult to steal the horse's fodder out of the manger

---

[1] For δὴ νεύματα S. reads δινεύματα, a conjecture of Stephanus (δεινεύματα some inferior MSS.)

τῆς φάτνης ἢ τὸν τοῦ δεσπότου ἐκ τοῦ ταμιείου.
ὁ δὲ τούτου ἀμελῶν ἐμοὶ μὲν ἑαυτοῦ δοκεῖ ἀμε-
λεῖν· δῆλον γὰρ ὅτι ἐν τοῖς κινδύνοις τὸ αὑτοῦ
σῶμα τῷ ἵππῳ ὁ δεσπότης παρακατατίθεται.
2 ἔστι δὲ οὐ μόνον τοῦ μὴ κλέπτεσθαι ἕνεκα τὸν
σῖτον ἀγαθὸς ὁ ἐχυρὸς ἱππών, ἀλλ' ὅτι καὶ ὅταν
πῃ ἐκκομίζῃ τὸν σῖτον ὁ ἵππος, φανερὸν γίγνεται.
τούτου δ' ἄν τις αἰσθόμενος γιγνώσκοι, ὅτι ἢ
τὸ σῶμα ὑπεραιμοῦν δεῖται θεραπείας ἢ κόπου
ἐνόντος δεῖται ἀναπαύσεως ἢ κριθίασις ἢ ἄλλη
τις ἀρρωστία ὑποδύεται. ἔστι δ' ὥσπερ ἀνθρώπῳ
οὕτω καὶ ἵππῳ ἀρχόμενα πάντα εὐιατότερα ἢ ἐπειδὰν ἐνσκιρρωθῇ τε καὶ ἐξαμαρτηθῇ τὰ νοσήματα.
3 Ὥσπερ δὲ τῷ ἵππῳ σίτου τε καὶ γυμνασίων
ἐπιμελητέον, ὅπως ἂν τὸ σῶμα ἰσχύῃ, οὕτω καὶ
τοὺς πόδας ἀσκητέον. τὰ μὲν τοίνυν ὑγρά τε καὶ
λεῖα τῶν σταθμῶν λυμαίνεται καὶ ταῖς εὐφυέσιν
ὁπλαῖς. δεῖ δέ, ὡς μὲν μὴ ᾖ ὑγρά, εἶναι ἀπόρ-
ρυτα, ὡς δὲ μὴ λεῖα, λίθους ἔχοντα κατορωρυ-
γμένους προσαλλήλους παραπλησίους ὁπλαῖς τὸ
μέγεθος. τὰ γὰρ τοιαῦτα σταθμὰ καὶ ἐφεστη-
κότων ἅμα στερεοῖ τοὺς πόδας.
4 Ἔπειτά γε μὴν τῷ ἱπποκόμῳ ἐξακτέον μὲν
τὸν ἵππον ὅπου ψήξει, μεταδετέον δὲ μετὰ τὸ
ἄριστον ἀπὸ τῆς φάτνης, ἵν' ἥδιον ἐπὶ τὸ δεῖπνον
ἴῃ. ὧδε δ' ἂν αὖ ὁ ἔξω σταθμὸς βέλτιστος εἴη
καὶ τοὺς πόδας κρατύνοι, εἰ λίθων στρογγύλων
ἀμφιδόχμων ὅσον μναιαίων ἁμάξας τέτταρας καὶ

as the master's victuals from the larder. He who neglects this seems to me to neglect himself; for it is plain that in danger the master entrusts his life to his horse. But a well-secured stall is not only 2 good for preventing theft of the fodder but also because one can see when the horse spills his food. And on noticing this one may be sure that either his body is overfull of blood and needs treatment or that the horse is over-worked and wants rest, or that colic or some other ailment is coming on. It is the same with horses as with men: all distempers in the early stage are more easily cured than when they have become chronic and have been wrongly treated.

Just as the food and exercise of the horse must be 3 attended to in order that he may keep sound, so his feet must be cared for. Now damp and slippery floors ruin even well-formed hoofs. In order that they may not be damp,[1] the floors should have a slope to carry off the wet, and, that they may not be slippery, they should be paved all over with stones, each one about the size of the hoof. Such floors, indeed, have another advantage because they harden the feet of the horses standing on them.

To take the next point: the groom must lead out 4 the horse to clean him, and must loose him from the stall after the morning feed, that he may return to his evening feed with more appetite. Now the stable-yard will be of the best form and will strengthen the feet if he throws down and spreads over it four or five loads of round stones, the size of a fist, about a pound

---

[1] The text of this sentence is conjectural; and it is thought that some words are lost before τὰ γὰρ and after σταθμὰ in the next.

πέντε χύδην καταβάλλοι, περιχειλώσας σιδήρῳ,
ὡς ἂν μὴ σκεδαννύωνται· ἐπὶ γὰρ τούτων ἑστηκὼς
ὥσπερ ἐν ὁδῷ λιθώδει ἀεὶ ἂν μέρος τῆς ἡμέρας
5 πορεύοιτο. ἀνάγκη δὲ καὶ ψηχόμενον καὶ μυωπι-
ζόμενον χρῆσθαι ταῖς ὁπλαῖς καθάπερ ὅταν
βαδίζῃ. καὶ τὰς χελιδόνας δὲ τῶν ποδῶν οἱ
οὕτω κεχυμένοι λίθοι στερεοῦσιν.

Ὡς δὲ περὶ τῶν ὁπλῶν ὅπως καρτεραὶ ἔσονται,
οὕτως καὶ περὶ τῶν στομάτων ὅπως μαλακὰ
ἔσται ἐπιμελεῖσθαι δεῖ. τὰ δ' αὐτὰ ἀνθρώπου
τε σάρκα καὶ ἵππου στόμα ἁπαλύνει.

V. Ἱππικοῦ δὲ ἀνδρὸς ἡμῖν δοκεῖ εἶναι καὶ τὸν
ἱπποκόμον πεπαιδεῦσθαι ἃ δεῖ περὶ τὸν ἵππον
πράττειν.

Πρῶτον μὲν τοίνυν τῆς ἐπιφατνιδίας φορβειᾶς
ἐπίστασθαι αὐτὸν δεῖ μήποτε τὸ ἅμμα ποιεῖσθαι
ἔνθαπερ ἡ κορυφαία περιτίθεται. πολλάκις γὰρ
κνῶν ὁ ἵππος ἐπὶ τῇ φάτνῃ τὴν κεφαλήν, εἰ μὴ
ἀσινὴς ἡ φορβειὰ περὶ τὰ ὦτα ἔσται, πολλάκις
ἂν ἕλκη ποιοίη. ἑλκουμένων γε μὴν τούτων ἀνάγκη τὸν ἵππον καὶ περὶ τὸ χαλινοῦσθαι καὶ περὶ
2 τὸ ψήχεσθαι δυσκολώτερον εἶναι. ἀγαθὸν δὲ καὶ
τὸ τετάχθαι τῷ ἱπποκόμῳ καθ' ἡμέραν τὴν κόπρον
καὶ τὰ ὑποστρώματα τοῦ ἵππου ἐκφέρειν εἰς ἓν
χωρίον. τοῦτο γὰρ ποιῶν αὐτός τ' ἂν ῥᾷστα
3 ἀπαλλάττοι καὶ ἅμα τὸν ἵππον ὠφελοίη. εἰδέναι δὲ χρὴ τὸν ἱπποκόμον καὶ τὸν κημὸν περιτιθέναι τῷ ἵππῳ καὶ ὅταν ἐπὶ ψῆξιν καὶ ὅταν
ἐπὶ καλίστραν ἐξάγῃ. καὶ ἀεὶ δὲ ὅποι ἂν ἀχα-
λίνωτον ἄγῃ κημοῦν δεῖ. ὁ γὰρ κημὸς ἀναπνεῖν
μὲν οὐ κωλύει, δάκνειν δὲ οὐκ ἐᾷ· καὶ τὸ ἐπι-

in weight, and surrounds them with a border of iron
so that they may not be scattered. Standing on
these will have the same effect as if the horse
walked on a stone road for some time every day.
When he is being rubbed down and teased with 5
flies he is bound to use his hoofs in the same way
as when he walks. The frogs also are hardened
by stones scattered in this way.

The same care must be taken to make his mouth
tender as to harden his hoofs. This is done by the
same methods as are employed to soften human flesh.

V. It is a mark of a good horseman, in our opinion,
to see that his groom, like himself, is instructed in
the way in which he should treat the horse.

First then the man ought to know that he should
never make the knot in the halter at the point where
the headstall is put on. For if the halter is not easy
about the ears, the horse will often rub his head
against the manger and may often get sores in consequence. Now if there are sore places thereabouts
the horse is bound to be restive both when he is
bridled and when he is rubbed down. It is well also 2
for the groom to have orders to remove the dung and
litter daily to one and the same place. For by doing
this he will get rid of it most easily and at the same
time relieve the horse. The groom must also know 3
about putting the muzzle on the horse when he takes
him out to be groomed or to the rolling-place. In
fact he must always put the muzzle on when he leads
him anywhere without a bridle.[1] For the muzzle
prevents him from biting without hampering his
breathing; and moreover, when it is put on, it

[1] The muzzle appears on several Greek vases. The Greek
horse was given to biting.

317

βουλεύειν δὲ περικείμενος μᾶλλον ἐξαιρεῖ τῶν ἵππων.

4 Καὶ μὴν δεσμεύειν τὸν ἵππον ἄνωθεν τῆς κεφαλῆς δεῖ. πάντα γὰρ ὁπόσα ἂν δύσκολ᾽ ᾖ περὶ τὸ πρόσωπον ὁ ἵππος ἐκνεύειν πέφυκεν ἄνω. ἐκνεύων γε μὴν οὕτω δεδεμένος χαλᾷ μᾶλλον ἢ διασπᾷ τὰ δεσμά.

5 Ἐπειδὰν δὲ ψήχῃ, ἄρχεσθαι μὲν ἀπὸ τῆς κεφαλῆς καὶ τῆς χαίτης· μὴ γὰρ καθαρῶν τῶν ἄνω ὄντων μάταιον τὰ κάτω καθαίρειν. ἔπειτα δὲ κατὰ μὲν τὸ ἄλλο σῶμα πᾶσι τοῖς τῆς καθάρσεως ὀργάνοις ἀνιστάντα δεῖ τὴν τρίχα σοβεῖν τὴν κόνιν κατὰ[1] φύσιν τῆς τριχός· τῶν δ᾽ ἐν τῇ ῥάχει τριχῶν ἄλλῳ μὲν ὀργάνῳ οὐδενὶ δεῖ ἅπτεσθαι, ταῖς δὲ χερσὶ τρίβειν καὶ ἀπαλύνειν ᾗπερ φύσει κέκλινται· ἥκιστα

6 γὰρ ἂν βλάπτοι τὴν ἕδραν τοῦ ἵππου. ὕδατι δὲ καταπλύνειν τὴν κεφαλὴν χρή. ὀστώδης γὰρ οὖσα εἰ σιδήρῳ ἢ ξύλῳ καθαίροιτο, λυποίη ἂν τὸν ἵππον. καὶ τὸ προκόμιον δὲ χρὴ βρέχειν· καὶ γὰρ αὗται εὐμήκεις οὖσαι αἱ τρίχες ὁρᾶν μὲν οὐ κωλύουσι τὸν ἵππον, ἀποσοβοῦσι δὲ ἀπὸ τῶν ὀφθαλμῶν τὰ λυποῦντα. καὶ τοὺς θεοὺς δὲ οἴεσθαι χρὴ δεδωκέναι ταύτας τὰς τρίχας ἵππῳ ἀντὶ τῶν μεγάλων ὤτων, ἃ ὄνοις τε καὶ ἡμιόνοις

7 ἔδοσαν ἀλεξητήρια πρὸ τῶν ὀμμάτων. καὶ οὐρὰν δὲ καὶ χαίτην πλύνειν χρή, ἐπείπερ αὔξειν δεῖ τὰς τρίχας, τὰς μὲν ἐν τῇ οὐρᾷ, ὅπως ἐπὶ πλεῖστον ἐξικνούμενος ἀποσοβῆται ὁ ἵππος τὰ λυποῦντα, τὰς δὲ ἐν τῷ τραχήλῳ, ὅπως τῷ ἀμβάτῃ

8 ὡς ἀφθονωτάτη ἀντίληψις ᾖ. δέδοται δὲ παρὰ

_____
[1] κατὰ MSS. : οὐ κατὰ S. with Gesner.

goes far towards preventing any propensity to mischief.

He should tie up the horse at a place above the 4 head, because when anything irritates his face, the horse instinctively tries to get rid of it by tossing his head upwards; and if he is tied thus he loosens the halter instead of breaking it by tossing up his head.

In rubbing the horse down, the man should start at 5 the head and mane; for if the upper parts are not clean, it is idle to clean his lower parts. Next, going over the rest of his body, he should make the hair stand up with all the dressing instruments,[1] and get the dust out by rubbing him the way the hair lies. But he should not touch the hair on the backbone with any instrument; he should rub and smooth it down with the hands the way it naturally grows; for so he will be least likely to injure the rider's seat. He must wash the head well with 6 water, for, as it is bony, to clean it with iron or wood would hurt the horse. He must also wet the forelock, for this tuft of hair, even if pretty long, does not obstruct his sight, but drives from his eyes anything that worries them; and we must presume that the gods have given the horse this hair in lieu of the long ears that they have given to asses and mules as a protection to their eyes. He should also wash the tail and mane, for growth 7 of the tail is to be encouraged in order that the horse may be able to reach as far as possible and drive away anything that worries him, and growth of the mane in order to give the rider as good a hold as possible. Besides, the mane, forelock and tail have been 8

---

[1] The instructions are rather vague.

XENOPHON

θεῶν καὶ ἀγλαΐας ἕνεκα ἵππῳ χαίτη καὶ προ-
κόμιόν τε καὶ οὐρά. τεκμήριον δέ· αἱ γὰρ ἀγε-
λαῖαι τῶν ἵππων οὐχ ὁμοίως ὑπομένουσι τοὺς
ὄνους ἐπὶ τῇ ὀχείᾳ, ἕως ἂν κομῶσιν· οὗ ἕνεκα
καὶ ἀποκείρουσι πρὸς τὴν ὀχείαν τὰς ἵππους
ἅπαντες οἱ ὀνοβατοῦντες.

9   Τήν γε μὴν τῶν σκελῶν κατάπλυσιν ἀφαιροῦ-
μεν· ὠφελεῖ μὲν γὰρ οὐδέν, βλάπτει δὲ τὰς
ὁπλὰς ἡ καθ' ἑκάστην ἡμέραν βρέξις. καὶ τὴν
ὑπὸ γαστέρα δὲ ἄγαν κάθαρσιν μειοῦν χρή· αὕτη
γὰρ λυπεῖ μὲν μάλιστα τὸν ἵππον, ὅσῳ δ' ἂν
καθαρώτερα ταῦτα γένηται, τοσούτῳ πλείονα τὰ
10   λυποῦντα ἀθροίζει ὑπὸ τὴν γαστέρα· ἢν δὲ καὶ
πάνυ διαπονήσηταί τις ταῦτα, οὐ φθάνει τε
ἐξαγόμενος ὁ ἵππος καὶ εὐθὺς ὅμοιός ἐστι τοῖς
ἀκαθάρτοις. ταῦτα μὲν οὖν ἐᾶν χρή· ἀρκεῖ δὲ
καὶ ἡ τῶν σκελῶν ψῆξις αὐταῖς ταῖς χερσὶ
γιγνομένη.

VI. Δηλώσομεν δὲ καὶ τοῦτο, ὡς ἂν ἀβλαβέστατα μέν τις ἑαυτῷ, τῷ δ' ἵππῳ ὠφελιμώτατα
ψήχοι. ἢν μὲν γὰρ εἰς τὸ αὐτὸ βλέπων τῷ ἵππῳ
καθαίρῃ, κίνδυνος καὶ τῷ γόνατι καὶ τῇ ὁπλῇ
2   εἰς τὸ πρόσωπον πληγῆναι· ἢν δὲ ἀντία τῷ ἵππῳ
ὁρῶν καὶ ἔξω τοῦ σκέλους, ὅταν καθαίρῃ, κατὰ
τὴν ὠμοπλάτην καθίζων ἀποτρίβῃ, οὕτω πάθοι
μὲν ἂν οὐδέν, δύναιτο δ' ἂν καὶ τὴν χελιδόνα τοῦ
ἵππου θεραπεύειν ἀναπτύσσων τὴν ὁπλήν. ὡς
δ' αὕτως καὶ τὰ ὄπισθεν σκέλη καθαιρέτω.

---

[1] Several allusions to this erroneous belief of the Greeks
are collected by the commentators.

[2] The text shows that the parts washed were not

given to the horse by the gods as an ornament. A proof of this is that brood mares herding together, so long as they have fine manes,[1] are reluctant to be covered by asses; for which reason all breeders of mules cut off the manes of the mares for covering.

Washing down of the legs we disapprove of; it 9 does no good, and the hoofs are injured by being wetted every day. Excessive cleaning under the belly also should be diminished; for this worries the horse very much, and the cleaner these parts are, the more they collect under the belly things offensive to it;[2] and notwithstanding all the pains that 10 may be taken with these parts, the horse is no sooner led out than he looks much the same as an unwashed animal. So these operations should be omitted; and as for the rubbing of the legs, it is enough to do it with the bare hands.

VI. We will now show how one may rub down a horse with least danger to oneself and most advantage to the horse. If in cleaning him[3] the man faces in the same direction as the horse, he runs the risk of getting a blow in the face from his knee and his hoof. But if he faces in the opposite direction 2 to the horse and sits by the shoulder out of reach of his leg when he cleans him, and rubs him down so, then he will come to no harm, and can also attend to the horse's frog by lifting up the hoof.[4] Let him do exactly the same in cleaning the hind-legs.

thoroughly dried: indeed, efficient drying cloths were not used. See Pollux i. 185.

[3] What follows refers to cleaning the fore-legs, to which a reference has doubtless dropped out of the text.

[4] On the vase referred to in the Introduction (p. xxxiv) the groom examining his frog is crouching under the horse and facing the same way.

XENOPHON

3 εἰδέναι δὲ χρὴ τὸν περὶ τὸν ἵππον, ὅτι καὶ ταῦτα
καὶ τἆλλα πάντα, ὅσα πράττειν δεῖ, ὡς ἥκιστα
χρὴ κατὰ τὸ πρόσωπόν τε καὶ οὐρὰν ποιήσοντα
προσιέναι· ἢν γὰρ ἐπιχειρῇ ἀδικεῖν, κατ᾽ ἀμφότερα ταῦτα κρείττων ὁ ἵππος ἀνθρώπου. ἐκ
πλαγίου δ᾽ ἄν τις προσιὼν ἀβλαβέστατα μὲν
ἑαυτῷ, κάλλιστα[1] δ᾽ ἂν ἵππῳ δύναιτο χρῆσθαι.

4 Ἐπειδάν γε μὴν ἄγειν δέῃ τὸν ἵππον, τὴν μὲν
ὄπισθεν ἀγωγὴν διὰ τάδε οὐκ ἐπαινοῦμεν, ὅτι τῷ
μὲν ἄγοντι οὕτως ἥκιστα ἔστι φυλάξασθαι, τῷ
δὲ ἵππῳ οὕτως μάλιστα ἔξεστι ποιῆσαι ὅ τι ἂν

5 βούληται. τὸ δ᾽ αὖ ἔμπροσθεν μακρῷ τῷ ἀγωγεῖ
προϊόντα διδάσκειν ὑφηγεῖσθαι τὸν ἵππον διὰ
τάδε αὖ ψέγομεν. ἔξεστι μὲν γὰρ τῷ ἵππῳ καθ᾽
ὁπότερ᾽ ἂν βούληται τῶν πλαγίων κακουργεῖν,
ἔξεστι δὲ ἀναστρεφόμενον ἀντίον γίγνεσθαι τῷ

6 ἄγοντι. ἀθρόοι δὲ δὴ ἵπποι πῶς ἄν ποτε ἀλλήλων
δύναιντο ἀπέχεσθαι οὕτως ἀγόμενοι ; ἐκ πλαγίου
δὲ ἵππος ἐθισθεὶς παράγεσθαι ἥκιστα μὲν ἂν καὶ
ἵππους καὶ ἀνθρώπους δύναιτ᾽ ἂν κακουργεῖν,
κάλλιστα δ᾽ ἂν παρεσκευασμένος τῷ ἀναβάτῃ
εἴη καὶ εἴ ποτε ἐν τάχει ἀναβῆναι δεήσειεν.

7 Ἵνα δὲ ὁ ἱπποκόμος καὶ τὸν χαλινὸν ὀρθῶς
ἐμβάλῃ, πρῶτον μὲν προσίτω κατὰ τὰ ἀριστερὰ
τοῦ ἵππου· ἔπειτα τὰς μὲν ἡνίας περιβαλὼν περὶ
τὴν κεφαλὴν καταθέτω ἐπὶ τῇ ἀκρωμίᾳ, τὴν δὲ
κορυφαίαν τῇ δεξιᾷ αἰρέτω, τὸ δὲ στόμιον τῇ

8 ἀριστερᾷ προσφερέτω. κἂν μὲν δέχηται, δῆλον
ὅτι περιτιθέναι δεῖ τὸν κεκρύφαλον· ἐὰν δὲ μὴ
ὑποχάσκῃ, ἔχοντα δεῖ πρὸς τοῖς ὀδοῦσι τὸν
χαλινὸν τὸν μέγαν δάκτυλον τῆς ἀριστερᾶς χειρὸς

---

[1] κάλλιστα Herwerden : πλεῖστα S. with the MSS.

The man employed about the horse is to know that in 3
these operations and in all that he has to do he must
be very chary of approaching from the head or tail
to do his work. For if the horse attempts to show
mischief he has the man in his power in both these
directions; but if he approaches from the side he can
manage the horse with least danger to himself and
in the best manner.

When it is necessary to lead the horse, we do not 4
approve of leading him behind one for this reason,
that the man leading him is then least able to take
care of himself while the horse has the utmost
freedom to do whatever he chooses. On the other 5
hand we also disapprove of training the horse to go
in front on a long lead for the following reasons:
the horse has the power of misbehaving on either
side as he chooses, and has also the power of turning round and facing his driver. And if several 6
horses together are driven in this fashion, how can
they possibly be kept from interfering with one
another? But a horse that is accustomed to being
led from the side will have least power of doing
harm either to horses or to men, and will be in the
handiest position for the rider should he want to
mount quickly.

In order to put the bit in properly, first let the 7
groom approach on the near side of the horse.
Then let him throw the reins over the head and
drop them on the withers, and next lift the headstall
with the right hand and offer the bit with the left.
If he takes the bit, of course the bridle should be put 8
on. But if he refuses to open his mouth, the man
must hold the bit to his teeth and put the thumb of

323

εἴσω τῆς γνάθου τῷ ἵππῳ ποιῆσαι. οἱ γὰρ
πολλοὶ τούτου γιγνομένου χαλῶσι τὸ στόμα. ἢν
δὲ μηδ᾽ οὕτω δέχηται, πιεσάτω τὸ χεῖλος περὶ τῷ
κυνόδοντι· καὶ πάνυ τινὲς ὀλίγοι οὐ δέχονται
9 τοῦτο πάσχοντες. δεδιδάχθω δὲ καὶ τάδε ὁ
ἱπποκόμος, πρῶτον μὲν μήποτε ἄγειν τῆς ἡνίας
τὸν ἵππον· τοῦτο γὰρ ἑτερογνάθους ποιεῖ· ἔπειτα
δὲ ὅσον δεῖ ἀπέχειν τὸν χαλινὸν τῶν γνάθων. ὁ
μὲν γὰρ ἄγαν πρὸς αὐταῖς τυλοῖ τὸ στόμα, ὥστε
μὴ εὐαίσθητον εἶναι, ὁ δὲ ἄγαν εἰς ἄκρον τὸ
στόμα καθιέμενος ἐξουσίαν παρέχει συνδάκνοντι
10 τὸ στόμιον μὴ πείθεσθαι. χρὴ δὲ τὸν ἱπποκόμον
καὶ τὰ τοιάδε παρατηρεῖν, εἰ μὴ ῥᾳδίως τὸν
χαλινὸν ὁ ἵππος δέχεται, αἰσθανόμενος ὅτι[1] δεῖ
πονεῖν. οὕτω γὰρ δὴ μέγα ἐστὶ τὸ λαμβάνειν
ἐθέλειν τὸν ἵππον τὸν χαλινόν, ὡς ὁ μὴ δεχόμενος
11 παντάπασιν ἄχρηστος. ἢν δὲ μὴ μόνον ὅταν
πονεῖν μέλλῃ χαλινῶται, ἀλλὰ καὶ ὅταν ἐπὶ τὸν
σῖτον καὶ ὅταν ἐξ ἱππασίας εἰς οἶκον ἀπάγηται,
οὐδὲν ἂν εἴη θαυμαστόν, εἰ ἁρπάζοι[2] τὸν χαλινὸν
αὐτόματος προτεινόμενον.
12 Ἀγαθὸν δὲ τὸν ἱπποκόμον καὶ ἀναβάλλειν
ἐπίστασθαι τὸν Περσικὸν τρόπον, ὅπως αὐτός
τε ὁ δεσπότης, ἤν ποτε ἀρρωστήσῃ ἢ πρεσβύτερος
γένηται, ἔχῃ τὸν εὐπετῶς ἀναβιβάζοντα καὶ ἄλλῳ
ἤν τινι βούληται τὸν ἀναβαλοῦντα ἐπιχαρίσηται.
13 Τὸ δὲ μήποτε σὺν ὀργῇ τῷ ἵππῳ προσφέρεσθαι,
ἓν τοῦτο καὶ δίδαγμα καὶ ἔθισμα πρὸς ἵππον
ἄριστον. ἀπρονόητον γὰρ ἡ ὀργή, ὥστε πολ-

---

[1] ἱππόκομον . . . ὅτι A : the other MSS. have παραξύνθαι
for the παρατηρεῖν of AB; all but A omit μὴ . . αἰσθανόμενος,
and have τι for ὅτι: S. adds ἵππον μὴ κατὰ τοιάδε παραξύνθαι,
εἴ τι between τὸν and δεῖ.

the left hand in the horse's jaw. Most horses open the mouth when this is done. If he still resists, the man should squeeze his lip against the tusk; and very few resist when they are treated in this way. The groom should also be instructed in the following 9 points: first, never to lead the horse on the rein — that gives the horse a hard mouth on one side—and secondly, what is the correct distance from the bit to the jaws. For if it is too high up, it hardens the mouth so that it loses its sensitiveness; and if it lies too low in the mouth, it gives the horse power to take it between his teeth and refuse to obey. The 10 groom must also pay some attention to such points as the following: whether the horse will not easily take the bit when he knows that he has work to do. Willingness to receive the bit is, in fact, so important that a horse that refuses it is quite useless. But if he 11 is bridled not only when he is going to be ridden, but also when he is taken to his food and when he is led home from exercise, it would not be at all surprising if he seized the bit of his own accord when offered to him.

It is well for the groom to know how to give a leg- 12 up in the Persian fashion,[1] so that his master himself, in case he is indisposed or is getting old may have someone to put him up conveniently, and may, if he wishes, oblige his friend with a man to give him a lift-up.

The one best rule and practice in dealing with a 13 horse is never to approach him in anger; for anger is a reckless thing, so that it often makes a man do what

[1] See *Cavalry Commander*, i. 17.

---

² ἁρπάζοι A : ἁρπάζει S. with the other MSS.

XENOPHON

14 λάκις ἐξεργάζεται ὧν μεταμέλειν ἀνάγκη. καὶ
ὅταν δὲ ὑποπτεύσας τι ὁ ἵππος μὴ θέλῃ πρὸς
τοῦτο προσιέναι, διδάσκειν δεῖ, ὅτι οὐ δεινά ἐστι,
μάλιστα μὲν οὖν ἵππῳ εὐκαρδίῳ· εἰ δὲ μή, ἁπτό-
μενον αὐτὸν τοῦ δεινοῦ δοκοῦντος εἶναι καὶ τὸν
15 ἵππον πράως προσάγοντα. οἱ δὲ πληγαῖς ἀν-
αγκάζοντες ἔτι πλείω φόβον παρέχουσιν· οἴονται
γὰρ οἱ ἵπποι, ὅταν τι χαλεπὸν πάσχωσιν ἐν
τῷ τοιούτῳ, καὶ τούτου τὰ ὑποπτευόμενα αἴτια
εἶναι.

16 Ἐπειδάν γε μὴν ὁ ἱπποκόμος τὸν ἵππον παρα-
διδῷ τῷ ἀναβάτῃ, τὸ μὲν ἐπίστασθαι ὑποβιβά-
ζεσθαι τὸν ἵππον, ὥστε εὐπετὲς εἶναι ἀναβῆναι,
οὐ μεμφόμεθα· τόν γε μέντοι ἱππέα νομίζομεν
χρῆναι μελετᾶν καὶ μὴ παρέχοντος ἵππου δύνασθαι ἀναβαίνειν. ἄλλοτε μὲν γὰρ ἀλλοῖος ἵππος
παραπίπτει, ἄλλοτε δὲ ἄλλως ὁ αὐτὸς ὑπηρετεῖ.

VII. Ὅταν γε μὴν παραδέξηται τὸν ἵππον
ὡς ἀναβησόμενος, νῦν αὖ γράψομεν, ὅσα ποιῶν
ὁ ἱππεὺς καὶ ἑαυτῷ καὶ τῷ ἵππῳ ὠφελιμώτατος
ἂν ἐν τῇ ἱππικῇ εἴη.

Πρῶτον μὲν τοίνυν τὸν ῥυταγωγέα χρὴ ἐκ
τῆς ὑποχαλινιδίας ἢ ἐκ τοῦ ψαλίου ἠρτημένον
εὐτρεπῆ εἰς τὴν ἀριστερὰν χεῖρα λαβεῖν καὶ οὕτω
χαλαρόν, ὡς μήτ' ἂν[1] τῶν τριχῶν παρὰ τὰ ὦτα
λαβόμενος μέλλῃ ἀναβήσεσθαι μήτε ἂν ἀπὸ
δόρατος ἀναπηδᾷ, σπᾶν τὸν ἵππον. τῇ δεξιᾷ δὲ
τὰς ἡνίας παρὰ τὴν ἀκρωμίαν λαμβανέτω ὁμοῦ
τῇ χαίτῃ, ὅπως μηδὲ καθ' ἕνα τρόπον ἀναβαίνων

---

[1] ἂν τῶν Courier: ἂν ἀνιὼν τῶν MSS.: ἂν ἀνιμῶν τῶν
S. with Stephanus.

he must regret.[1] Moreover, when the horse is shy of 14
anything and will not come near it, you should teach
him that there is nothing to be afraid of, either with
the help of a plucky horse—which is the surest way—
or else by touching the object that looks alarming
yourself, and gently leading the horse up to it. To 15
force him with blows only increases his terror; for
when horses feel pain in such a predicament, they
think that this too is caused by the thing at
which they shy.

When the groom presents the horse to his rider, 16
we take no exception to his understanding how to
cause the horse to crouch, for convenience in mounting. We think, however, that the rider should get
used to mounting even without his horse's help.
For a rider gets a different sort of horse at different
times, and the same one does not always serve him
in the same way.

VII. We will now describe what the rider should
do when he has received his horse and is going to
mount, if he is to make the best of himself and his
horse in riding.

First, then, he must hold the leading-rein fastened
to the chin-strap or the nose-band ready in the left
hand, and so loose as not to jerk the horse whether
he means to mount by holding on to the mane near
the ears or to spring up with the help of the spear.
With his right hand let him take hold of the reins
by the withers along with the mane, so that he may

------

[1] *Hellenica*, v. iii. 7.

2 σπάσῃ τῷ χαλινῷ τὸ στόμα τοῦ ἵππου. ἐπειδὰν
δὲ ἀνακουφίσῃ ἑαυτὸν εἰς τὴν ἀνάβασιν, τῇ μὲν
ἀριστερᾷ ἀνιμάτω τὸ σῶμα, τὴν δὲ δεξιὰν ἐντεί-
νων συνεπαιρέτω ἑαυτόν· οὕτω γὰρ ἀναβαίνων
οὐδὲ ὄπισθεν αἰσχρὰν θέαν παρέξει συγκεκαμ-
μένῳ[1] τῷ σκέλει· καὶ μηδὲ τὸ γόνυ ἐπὶ τὴν
ῥάχιν τοῦ ἵππου τιθέτω, ἀλλ᾽ ὑπερβησάτω ἐπὶ
τὰς δεξιὰς πλευρὰς τὴν κνήμην. ὅταν δὲ περι-
ενέγκῃ τὸν πόδα, τότε καὶ τῶ γλουτῶ καθέτω ἐπὶ
τὸν ἵππον.

3 Ἢν δὲ τύχῃ ὁ ἱππεὺς τῇ μὲν ἀριστερᾷ ἄγων
τὸν ἵππον, τῇ δὲ δεξιᾷ τὸ δόρυ ἔχων, ἀγαθὸν
μὲν ἡμῖν δοκεῖ εἶναι τὸ καὶ ἐκ τῶν δεξιῶν μελε-
τῆσαι ἀναπηδᾶν. μαθεῖν δ᾽ οὐδὲν δεῖ ἄλλο ἢ ἃ
μὲν τότε τοῖς δεξιοῖς τοῦ σώματος ἐποίει, τοῖς
ἀριστεροῖς ποιεῖν, ἃ δὲ τότε τοῖς ἀριστεροῖς, τοῖς
4 δεξιοῖς. τούτου δ᾽ ἕνεκα καὶ ταύτην ἐπαινοῦμεν
τὴν ἀνάβασιν, ὅτι ἅμα τε ἀναβεβηκὼς ἂν εἴη
καὶ κατεσκευασμένος πάντα, εἴ τι δέοι ἐξαίφνης
πρὸς πολεμίους ἀγωνίζεσθαι.

5 Ἐπειδάν γε μὴν καθίζηται ἐάν τε ἐπὶ ψιλοῦ
ἐάν τε ἐπὶ τοῦ ἐφιππίου, οὐ τὴν ὥσπερ ἐπὶ τοῦ
δίφρου ἕδραν ἐπαινοῦμεν, ἀλλὰ τὴν ὥσπερ ὀρθὸς
ἂν διαβεβηκὼς εἴη τοῖν σκελοῖν. τοῖν τε γὰρ
μηροῖν οὕτως ἂν ἔχοιτο μᾶλλον τοῦ ἵππου, καὶ
ὀρθὸς ὢν ἐρρωμενεστέρως ἂν δύναιτο καὶ ἀκοντίσαι καὶ πατάξαι ἀπὸ τοῦ ἵππου, εἰ δέοι.

---

[1] δὲ τῷ with a colon after παρέξει and comma after σκέλει
S. The δὲ is not in AB.

---

[1] In the jockey mode. "I think that those critics are
in error who understand that X. meant that the rider

not jerk the horse's mouth with the bit in any way as he mounts. When he has made his spring in order 2 to mount, he should raise his body with his left hand, while at the same time he helps himself up by stretching out his right; for by mounting in this way he will not present an awkward appearance even from behind by bending his leg. Neither must he touch the horse's back with his knee, but throw the leg right over the off side. Having brought the foot over, he must then let his buttocks down on the horse's back.

In case the horseman happens to be leading the 3 horse with the left hand and holding his spear in the right, it is well, we think, to practise mounting on the off side also. For this purpose all that he needs to learn is to do with the left parts of the body what in the other case he did with the right, and *vice versa*. The reason why we recom- 4 mend this method of mounting also is, that no sooner is the rider mounted than he is quite ready to fight with the enemy on a sudden, if occasion requires.

When he is seated, whether on the bare back or 5 on the cloth, we would not have him sit as if he were on his chair,[1] but as though he were standing upright with his legs astride. For thus he will get a better grip of his horse with his thighs, and the erect position will enable him, if need be, to throw his spear and deliver a blow on horseback with more force.

should take the extreme 'fork' seat; for not only would such a position be very insecure upon the simple saddles of the Greeks, but it is inconsistent with the graceful and firm positions exhibited by the marbles." E. L. Anderson in *Riding* (Badminton series).

XENOPHON

6   Χρὴ δὲ καὶ χαλαρὰν ἀπὸ τοῦ γόνατος ἀφεῖσθαι
τὴν κνήμην σὺν τῷ ποδί. σκληρὸν μὲν γὰρ ἔχων
τὸ σκέλος εἰ προσκόψειέ τῳ, προσκεκλασμένος
ἂν εἴη· ὑγρὰ δὲ οὖσα ἡ κνήμη, εἴ τι καὶ προσ-
πίπτοι αὐτῇ, ὑπείκοι ἂν καὶ τὸν μηρὸν οὐδὲν
7 μετακινοίη. δεῖ δὲ τὸν ἱππέα καὶ τὸ ἄνωθεν τῶν
ἑαυτοῦ ἰσχίων σῶμα ὡς ὑγρότατον ἐθίζειν εἶναι.
οὕτω γὰρ ἂν πονεῖν[1] τέ τι μᾶλλον δύναιτο καὶ
εἰ ἕλκοι τις αὐτὸν ἢ ὠθοίη, ἧττον ἂν σφάλλοιτο.

8   Ἐπειδάν γε μὴν καθίζηται, πρῶτον μὲν ἠρεμεῖν
δεῖ διδάσκειν τὸν ἵππον, ἕως ἂν καὶ ὑποσπάσηται,
ἤν τι δέηται, καὶ ἡνίας ἰσώσηται καὶ δόρυ λάβῃ,
ὡς ἂν εὐφορώτατον εἴη. ἔπειτα δὲ ἐχέτω τὸν
ἀριστερὸν βραχίονα πρὸς ταῖς πλευραῖς· οὕτω
γὰρ εὐσταλέστατός τε ὁ ἱππεὺς ἔσται καὶ ἡ χεὶρ
9 ἐγκρατεστάτη. ἡνίας γε μὴν ἐπαινοῦμεν ὁποῖαι
ἴσαι τέ εἰσι καὶ μὴ ἀσθενεῖς μηδὲ ὀλισθηραὶ μηδὲ
παχεῖαι, ἵνα καὶ τὸ δόρυ, ὅταν δέῃ, δέχεσθαι ἡ
χεὶρ δύνηται.

10   Ὅταν δὲ προχωρεῖν σημήνῃ τῷ ἵππῳ, βάδην
μὲν ἀρχέσθω· τοῦτο γὰρ ἀταρακτότατον. ἡνιο-
χείτω δέ, ἢν μὲν κυφαγωγότερος ᾖ ὁ ἵππος,
ἀνωτέρω ταῖς χερσίν, ἢν δὲ μᾶλλον ἀνακεκυφώς,
κατωτέρω· οὕτω γὰρ ἂν μάλιστα κοσμοίη τὸ
11 σχῆμα. μετὰ δὲ ταῦτα τὸν αὐτοφυῆ διατρο-
χάζων διαχαλῴη τ' ἂν ἀλυπότατα τὸ σῶμα καὶ
εἰς τὸ ἐπιρραβδοφορεῖν ἥδιστ' ἂν ἀφικνοῖτο.
ἐπείπερ δὲ καὶ ἀπὸ τῶν ἀριστερῶν ἄρχεσθαι
εὐδοκιμώτερον, ὧδ' ἂν μάλιστα ἀπὸ τούτων
ἄρχοιτο, εἰ διατροχάζοντος μέν, ὁπότε ἐμβαίνοι

---

[1] πονεῖν A: ποιεῖν S. with the other MSS.

The lower leg including the foot must hang lax 6 and easy from the knee down. For if he keeps his leg stiff and should strike it against anything, he may break it, whereas a loose leg will recoil, whatever it encounters, without disturbing the position of the thigh at all. The rider must also accustom 7 himself to keeping his body above the hips as loose as possible, for thus he will be able to stand more fatigue and will be less liable to come off when he is pulled or pushed.

As soon as he is seated, he must teach his horse 8 to stand quiet at first, until he has shifted anything that wants arranging underneath him, gathered the reins even in his hand and grasped his spear in the most convenient manner. Then let him keep his left arm close to his side, for thus the horseman's figure will look best, and his hand will have most power. As for reins, we recommend that they be 9 of equal strength, not weak nor slippery nor thick, in order that the spear may be held in the same hand when necessary.

When he directs his horse to go forward, let him 10 begin at a walk, for this prevents any flurry. If the horse carries his head too low, let the rider hold the hands higher; if too high, lower; for in this way he will give him the most graceful carriage. After 11 this, if he breaks into his natural trot, he will relax his body in the easiest fashion and come to the gallop most readily. Since, too, the more approved method is to begin with the left,[1] one will best begin on this side, by giving the horse the signal

---

[1] The left lead comes natural to the horse. The Parthenon figures show the right lead; but the Greeks approved of many things in art that they did not practise.

τῷ δεξιῷ, τότε σημαίνοι τῷ ἵππῳ τὸ ἐπιρρα-
12 βδοφορεῖν. τὸ γὰρ ἀριστερὸν μέλλων αἴρειν ἐκ
τούτου ἂν ἄρχοιτο, καὶ ὁπότε ἐπὶ τὰ εὐώνυμα
ἀναστρέφοι, τότε καὶ τῆς ἐπισκελίσεως ἄρχοιτο.
καὶ γὰρ πέφυκεν ὁ ἵππος εἰς μὲν τὰ δεξιὰ
στρεφόμενος τοῖς δεξιοῖς ἀφηγεῖσθαι, εἰς εὐώνυμα
δὲ τοῖς ἀριστεροῖς.
13 Ἱππασίαν δ' ἐπαινοῦμεν τὴν πέδην καλουμένην·
ἐπ' ἀμφοτέρας γὰρ τὰς γνάθους στρέφεσθαι
ἐθίζει. καὶ τὸ μεταβάλλεσθαι δὲ τὴν ἱππασίαν
ἀγαθόν, ἵνα ἀμφότεραι αἱ γνάθοι καθ' ἑκάτερον
14 τῆς ἱππασίας ἰσάζωνται. ἐπαινοῦμεν δὲ καὶ τὴν
ἑτερομήκη πέδην μᾶλλον τῆς κυκλοτεροῦς. ἥδιον
μὲν γὰρ οὕτως ἂν στρέφοιτο ὁ ἵππος ἤδη πλήρης
ὢν τοῦ εὐθέος καὶ τό τε ὀρθοδρομεῖν καὶ τὸ
15 ἀποκάμπτειν ἅμα μελετῴη ἄν. δεῖ δὲ καὶ
ὑπολαμβάνειν ἐν ταῖς στροφαῖς· οὐ γὰρ ῥᾴδιον
τῷ ἵππῳ οὐδ' ἀσφαλὲς ἐν τῷ τάχει ὄντα κάμπτειν
ἐν μικρῷ, ἄλλως τε κἂν ἀπόκροτον ἢ ὀλισθηρὸν
16 ᾖ τὸ χωρίον. ὅταν γε μὴν ὑπολαμβάνῃ, ὡς
ἥκιστα μὲν χρὴ τὸν ἵππον πλαγιοῦν τῷ χαλινῷ,
ὡς ἥκιστα δ' αὐτὸν πλαγιοῦσθαι· εἰ δὲ μή, εὖ
χρὴ εἰδέναι, ὅτι μικρὰ πρόφασις ἀρκέσει κεῖσθαι
17 καὶ αὐτὸν καὶ τὸν ἵππον. ἐπειδάν γε μὴν ἐκ
τῆς στροφῆς εἰς τὸ εὐθὺς βλέπῃ ὁ ἵππος, ἐν
τούτῳ πρὸς τὸ θᾶττον αὐτὸν ὁρμάτω. δῆλον

---

[1] A remarkable proof of X's. power of observation.
When the trotting horse treads with the right fore-leg, the
hind-legs are in the position that the horse assumes when
galloping on the left lead, and the horse will strike off with
the left fore-leg.
[2] Literally "fetter." The old English term is "ring,"

to gallop while trotting, at the instant when he is treading with the right (fore) foot. As he is then 12 on the point of raising the left, he will begin with it, and, as soon as the rider turns him to the left, will immediately begin the stride. For it is natural for the horse to lead with the right when turned to the right, and with the left when turned to the left.[1]

The exercise that we recommend is the one called 13 the ring,[2] since it accustoms the horse to turn on both jaws. It is also well to change the exercise,[3] in order that both jaws may be equally practised on each side of the exercise.[4] We recommend the 14 manage[5] rather than the complete ring, for thus the horse will turn more willingly when he has gone some distance in a straight course, and one can practise the career and the turn at the same time. It is necessary to collect him at the turns; for it is 15 neither easy for the horse nor safe to turn short when going fast, especially if the ground is uneven or slippery. In collecting him the rider must slant the 16 horse as little as possible with the bit, and slant his own body as little as possible; else he may be sure that a trifling cause will be enough to bring him and his horse down. As soon as the horse 17 faces the straight after turning, push him along at

now volte. Of course the horse was exercised first in one direction, then in the other.

[3] *i.e.* ride on the other hand ; this is not part of the volte.

[4] *i.e.* may have both jaws equally sensitive on whichever hand he is ridden.

[5] I have ventured to use this term since X. means precisely what Gervase Markham calls the "manage" in the strict sense, *i.e.* two straight treads with a semicircle at either end.

γὰρ ὅτι καὶ ἐν τοῖς πολέμοις αἱ στροφαί εἰσιν
ἢ τοῦ διώκειν ἢ τοῦ ἀποχωρεῖν ἕνεκα. ἀγαθὸν

18 οὖν τὸ στραφέντα ταχύνειν μελετᾶν. ὅταν δὲ
ἱκανῶς ἤδη δοκῇ τὸ γυμνάσιον τῷ ἵππῳ ἔχειν,
ἀγαθὸν καὶ διαπαύσαντα ὁρμῆσαι ἐξαίφνης εἰς
τὸ τάχιστον καὶ ἀφ' ἵππων μέντοι, μὴ ¹ πρὸς
ἵππους· καὶ ἐκ τοῦ ταχέος αὖ ὡς ἐγγυτάτω
ἠρεμίζειν, καὶ ἐκ τοῦ ἑστάναι δὲ στρέψαντα
πάλιν ² ὁρμᾶν. πρόδηλον γὰρ ὅτι ἔσται ποτὲ
ὅτε ἑκατέρου τούτων δεήσει.

19 Ὅταν γε μὴν καταβαίνειν ἤδη καιρὸς ᾖ, μήτε
ἐν ἵπποις ποτὲ καταβαίνειν μήτε παρὰ σύστασιν
ἀνθρώπων μήτε ἔξω τῆς ἱππασίας, ἀλλ' ὅπουπερ
καὶ πονεῖν ἀναγκάζεται ὁ ἵππος, ἐνταῦθα καὶ τῆς
ῥᾳστώνης τυγχανέτω.

VIII. Ἐπειδήπερ ἔστιν ὅπου τρέχειν δεήσει
τὸν ἵππον καὶ πρανῆ καὶ ὄρθια καὶ πλάγια,
ἔστι δ' ὅπου διαπηδᾶν, ἔστι δ' ὅπου καὶ ἐκπηδᾶν,
ἔνθα δὲ καὶ καθάλλεσθαι, καὶ ταῦτα πάντα
διδάσκειν τε δεῖ καὶ μελετᾶν καὶ αὐτὸν καὶ τὸν
ἵππον· οὕτω γὰρ ἂν σωτήριοί τε εἶεν ἀλλήλοις
καὶ καθόλου ³ χρησιμώτεροι ἂν δοκοῖεν εἶναι.

2 Εἰ δέ τις διλογεῖν ἡμᾶς οἴεται, ὅτι περὶ τῶν
αὐτῶν λέγομεν νῦν τε καὶ πρόσθεν, οὐ διλογία
ταῦτά ἐστιν. ὅτε μὲν γὰρ ἐωνεῖτο, πειρᾶσθαι
ἐκελεύομεν, εἰ δύναιτο ὁ ἵππος ταῦτα ποιεῖν·
νῦν δὲ διδάσκειν φαμὲν χρῆναι τὸν ἑαυτοῦ καὶ
γράψομεν, ὡς δεῖ διδάσκειν.

---

¹ μὴ MSS.: καὶ S. with Camerarius.
² πάλιν Lenklau: δεῖ πάλιν S. with the MSS.
³ καθόλου placed here by Pollack: in the MSS. it comes
after αὐτὸν in the previous sentence: S. omits with Dindorf.

once. For of course, in war too, turns are made with a view to pursuit or retreat. It is well, therefore, to practise increasing the pace after turning. So 18 soon as the horse appears to have been exercised enough, it is well to let him rest a certain time, and then suddenly to put him to his top speed again, of course away from, not towards, other horses, and to pull him up again in the midst of his career as short as possible, and then to turn and start him again from the stand. For it is obvious that a time will come when it will be necessary to do one or the other.

When the time has come to dismount, the rider 19 must never dismount among other horses or near a group of people or outside the riding-ground; but let the place where the horse is forced to work be the place where he also receives his reward of ease.

VIII. As the horse will frequently have to gallop down hill and up hill and along a slope, and as he will have to leap over, and to leap out, and to jump down at various times, the rider must teach and practise both himself and his horse in all these things. For thus they will be able to help each other, and will be thought altogether more efficient.

If anyone thinks that we are repeating ourselves, 2 because we are referring to matters already dealt with, this is not repetition. For we recommended the purchaser to try whether the horse could do these things at the time of buying: but now we say that a man should teach his own horse; and we will show how to teach him.

3 Τὸν μὲν γὰρ παντάπασιν ἄπειρον τοῦ διαπηδᾶν λαβόντα δεῖ τοῦ ἀγωγέως καταβεβλημένου προδιαβῆναι αὐτὸν τὴν τάφρον, ἔπειτα δὲ ἐντείνειν 4 δεῖ τῷ ἀγωγεῖ, ὡς διάλληται. ἢν δὲ μὴ ἐθέλῃ, ἔχων τις μάστιγα ἢ ῥάβδον ἐμβαλέτω ὡς ἰσχυρότατα· καὶ οὕτως ὑπεραλεῖται οὐ τὸ μέτρον, ἀλλὰ πολὺ πλεῖον τοῦ καιροῦ· καὶ τὸ λοιπὸν οὐδὲν δεήσει παίειν, ἀλλ' ἢν μόνον ἴδῃ ὄπισθέν 5 τινα ἐπελθόντα, ἁλεῖται. ἐπειδὰν δὲ οὕτω διαπηδᾶν ἐθισθῇ, καὶ ἀναβεβηκὼς ἐπαγέτω τὸ μὲν πρῶτον μικράς, ἔπειτα δὲ καὶ μείζους. ὅταν δὲ μέλλῃ πηδᾶν, παισάτω αὐτὸν τῷ μύωπι. ὡσαύτως δὲ καὶ τὸ ἀναπηδᾶν καὶ τὸ καταπηδᾶν διδάσκων παισάτω τῷ μύωπι. ἀθρόῳ γὰρ τῷ σώματι ταῦτα πάντα ποιῶν καὶ ἑαυτῷ ὁ ἵππος καὶ τῷ ἀναβάτῃ ἀσφαλέστερον ποιήσει μᾶλλον ἢ ἂν ἐλλείπῃ τὰ ὄπισθεν ἢ διαπηδῶν ἢ ἀνορούων ἢ καθαλλόμενος.

6 Εἴς γε μὴν τὸ κάταντες πρῶτον χρὴ ἐν μαλακῷ χωρίῳ διδάσκειν. καὶ τελευτῶν ἐπειδὰν τοῦτο ἐθισθῇ, πολὺ ἥδιον τὸ πρανὲς τοῦ ὀρθίου δραμεῖται. ἃ δὲ φοβοῦνταί τινες μὴ ἀπορρηγνύωνται τοὺς ὤμους κατὰ τὰ πρανῆ ἐλαυνόμενοι, θαρρούντων μαθόντες, ὅτι Πέρσαι καὶ Ὀδρύσαι ἅπαντες τὰ κατάντη ἁμιλλώμενοι οὐδὲν ἧττον τῶν Ἑλλήνων ὑγιεῖς τοὺς ἵππους ἔχουσι.

7 Παρήσομεν δὲ οὐδὲ ὅπως τὸν ἀναβάτην ὑπηρετεῖν δεῖ πρὸς ἕκαστα τούτων. χρὴ γὰρ ὁρμῶντος μὲν ἐξαίφνης ἵππου προνεύειν· ἧττον γὰρ ἂν καὶ ὑποδύοι ὁ ἵππος καὶ ἀναβάλοι τὸν ἀναβάτην· ἐν μικρῷ δὲ ἀναλαμβανομένου ἀναπίπτειν. ἧττον 8 γὰρ ἂν αὐτὸς κόπτοιτο. τάφρον δὲ διαλλομένου

When a man has a raw horse quite ignorant of 3
leaping, he must get over the ditch himself first,
holding him loosely by the leading-rein, and then give
him a pull with the rein to make him leap over.
If he refuses, let someone strike him as hard as he 4
can with a whip or a stick : whereupon he will leap,
and not only the necessary distance, but much
further than was required. In future there will be
no need to beat him, for if he merely sees a man
approaching behind him, he will leap. As soon as he 5
has grown accustomed to leap in this way, let him
be mounted and tried first at narrow, and then
at wider ditches. Just as he is on the point of
springing touch him with the spur. Similarly
he should be taught to leap up and to leap down
by a touch of the spur. For if he does all these
things with his body compactly gathered, it will be
safer for the horse as well as the rider than if his
hind-quarters lag in taking a leap over, or in
springing upwards or jumping downwards.

Going down hill should first be taught on soft 6
ground ; and in the end, when the horse gets used
to this, he will canter down more readily than
up hill. If some fear that horses may put out
their shoulders by being ridden down hill, they may
take comfort when they understand that the Persians
and Odrysians all ride races down hill, and yet keep
their horses just as sound as the Greeks.

Nor will we omit to state how the rider is to 7
assist in all these movements. If the horse springs
suddenly, he should lean forward ; for so the
horse is less likely to slip away and throw the rider off.
But in pulling him up short he should lean back ;
for so he himself will be less jolted. When jumping 8

καὶ πρὸς ὄρθιον ἱεμένου καλὸν[1] χαίτης ἐπιλαμβάνεσθαι, ὡς μὴ ὁ ἵππος τῷ τε χωρίῳ ἅμα καὶ
τῷ χαλινῷ βαρύνηται. εἴς γε μὴν τὸ πρανὲς καὶ
ἑαυτὸν ὑπτιαστέον καὶ τοῦ ἵππου ἀντιληπτέον
τῷ χαλινῷ, ὡς μὴ προπετῶς εἰς τὸ κάταντες
μήτε αὐτὸς μήτε ὁ ἵππος φέρηται.

9 Ὀρθῶς δὲ ἔχει καὶ τὸ ἄλλοτε μὲν ἐν ἄλλοις
τόποις, ἄλλοτε δὲ μακρὰς ἄλλοτε δὲ βραχείας
τὰς ἱππασίας ποιεῖσθαι. ἀμισέστερα γὰρ τῷ
ἵππῳ καὶ ταῦτα τοῦ ἀεὶ ἐν τοῖς αὐτοῖς τόποις
καὶ ὁμοίως τὰς ἱππασίας ποιεῖσθαι.

10 Ἐπεὶ δὲ δεῖ ἐν παντοίοις τε χωρίοις τὸν ἵππον
ἀνὰ κράτος[2] ἐλαύνοντα ἔποχον εἶναι καὶ ἀπὸ τοῦ
ἵππου τοῖς ὅπλοις καλῶς δύνασθαι χρῆσθαι, ὅπου
μέν ἐστι χωρία ἐπιτήδεια καὶ θηρία, ἄμεμπτος ἡ
ἐν θήραις μελέτη τῆς ἱππικῆς· ὅπου δὲ ταῦτα μὴ
ὑπάρχει, ἀγαθὴ ἄσκησις καὶ ἢν δύο ἱππότα
συνθεμένω ὁ μὲν φεύγῃ ἐπὶ τοῦ ἵππου παντοῖα
χωρία καὶ τὸ δόρυ εἰς τοὔπισθεν μεταβαλόμενος
ὑποχωρῇ, ὁ δὲ διώκῃ ἐσφαιρωμένα τε ἔχων
ἀκόντια καὶ δόρυ ὡσαύτως πεπραγματευμένον·
καὶ ὅπου μὲν ἂν εἰς ἀκόντιον ἀφικνῆται, ἀκοντίζῃ
τὸν φεύγοντα τοῖς σφαιρωτοῖς· ὅπου δ᾽ ἂν εἰς
11 δόρατος πληγήν, παίῃ τὸν ἁλισκόμενον. ἀγαθὸν
δὲ κἄν ποτε συμπέσωσιν, ἑλκύσαντα ἐφ᾽ ἑαυτὸν
τὸν πολέμιον ἐξαίφνης ἀπῶσαι· τοῦτο γὰρ κατα-
βλητικόν. ὀρθῶς δὲ ἔχει καὶ τῷ ἑλκομένῳ ἐπε-

---

[1] καλὸν AB : κακὸν M : οὐ κακὸν S. with L.
[2] ἀνὰ κράτος MSS. : S. reads ἀγκράτος from Suidas.

a ditch or riding up hill it is well [1] to take hold of the mane, that the horse may not be burdened by his bridle and the difficulty of the ground at the same time. When going down a steep incline, he should throw his body back and support the horse with the bridle, that neither rider nor horse may be tossed headlong down hill.

It is correct also to exercise the horse sometimes 9 in one place, sometimes in another, and to make the exercises sometimes long and sometimes short; for this is less irksome to the horse than being exercised always in the same place and for the same length of time.

Since it is necessary that the rider should have a 10 firm seat when riding at top speed over all sorts of country, and should be able to use his weapons properly on horseback, the practice of horsemanship by hunting is to be recommended where the country is suitable and big game is to be found. Where these conditions are lacking, it is a good method of training for two riders to work together thus : one flies on his horse over all kinds of ground and retreats, reversing his spear so that it points backwards, while the other pursues, having buttons on his javelins and holding his spear in the same position, and when he gets within javelin shot, tries to hit the fugitive with the blunted weapons, and if he gets near enough to use his spear, strikes his captive with it. It is also a good plan, 11 in case of a collision between them, for one to pull his adversary towards him and suddenly push him back again, since that is the way to dismount him. The right thing for the man who is being pulled is to

[1] Of course no modern rider would approve of this.

λαύνειν τὸν ἵππον· τοῦτο γὰρ ποιῶν ὁ ἑλκόμενος
καταβάλοι ἂν μᾶλλον τὸν ἕλκοντα ἢ καταπέσοι.

12   Ἦν δέ ποτε καὶ στρατοπέδου ἀντικαθημένου
ἀνθιππεύωσιν ἀλλήλοις καὶ διώκωσι μὲν μέχρι
τῆς πολεμίας φάλαγγος τοὺς ἀντίους, φεύγωσι
δὲ μέχρι τῆς φιλίας, ἀγαθὸν καὶ ἐνταῦθα ἐπίστασθαι, ὅτι ἕως μὲν ἂν παρὰ τοὺς φίλους τις ᾖ,
καλὸν καὶ ἀσφαλὲς τὸ ἐν πρώτοις ἐπιστρέψαντα
ἀνὰ κράτος ἐπικεῖσθαι, ὅταν δ' ἐγγὺς τῶν ἐναντίων γίγνηται, ὑποχείριον τὸν ἵππον ἔχειν. οὕτω
γὰρ ἂν ὡς τὸ εἰκὸς μάλιστα δύναιτο βλάπτων
τοὺς ἐναντίους μὴ βλάπτεσθαι ὑπ' αὐτῶν.

13   Ἀνθρώποις μὲν οὖν ἄνθρωπον θεοὶ ἔδοσαν λόγῳ
διδάσκειν ἃ δεῖ ποιεῖν, ἵππον δὲ δῆλον ὅτι λόγῳ
μὲν οὐδὲν ἂν διδάξαις· ἢν δὲ ὅταν μὲν ποιήσῃ
ὡς ἂν βούλῃ, ἀντιχαρίσῃ αὐτῷ, ὅταν δὲ ἀπειθῇ,
κολάζῃς, οὕτω μάλιστα μάθοι ἂν τὸ δέον ὑπη-
14   ρετεῖν· καὶ ἔστι μὲν τοῦτο ἐν βραχεῖ εἰπεῖν, δι'
ὅλης δὲ τῆς ἱππικῆς παρακολουθεῖ. καὶ γὰρ
χαλινὸν μᾶλλον ἂν λαμβάνοι, εἰ ὁπότε δέξαιτο
ἀγαθόν τι αὐτῷ ἀποβαίνοι· καὶ διαπηδῴη δ'
ἂν καὶ ἐξάλλοιτο καὶ τἄλλα πάντα ὑπηρετοίη
ἄν, εἰ προσδοκῴη ὁπότε τὰ σημαινόμενα πράξειε
ῥᾳστώνην τινά.

IX. Καὶ τὰ μὲν δὴ εἰρημένα ταῦτά ἐστιν, ὡς
ἂν ἥκιστα μὲν ἐξαπατῷτο καὶ πῶλον καὶ ἵππον
ὠνούμενος, ἥκιστα δ' ἂν διαφθείραι χρώμενος,
μάλιστα δ' ἂν ἵππον ἀποδεικνύειν δέοι ἔχοντα
ὧν ἱππεὺς δεῖται εἰς πόλεμον. καιρὸς δ' ἴσως
γράψαι καὶ εἴ ποτε συμβαίη θυμοειδεστέρῳ
ἵππῳ τοῦ καιροῦ χρῆσθαι ἢ βλακωδεστέρῳ, ὡς
ἂν ὀρθότατα ἑκατέρῳ χρῷτο.

urge his horse forward; by doing this the pulled is more likely to unhorse the puller than to be unhorsed himself.

If at any time when an enemy's camp lies in front 12 there is a cavalry skirmish, and one side presses the pursuit right up to the enemy's line of battle, but then retreats hastily to its own main body, it is well to know in that case that so long as you are by your friends, it is proper and safe to be among the first to wheel and make for the enemy at full speed; but when you come near the enemy to keep your horse well in hand. For in this way you have the best chance of injuring the enemy without coming to harm yourself.

Now, whereas the gods have given to men the power 13 of instructing one another in their duty by word of mouth, it is obvious that you can teach a horse nothing by word of mouth. If, however, you reward him when he behaves as you wish, and punish him when he is disobedient, he will best learn to do his duty. This rule can be stated in few words, but it applies 14 to the whole art of horsemanship. He will receive the bit, for example, more willingly if something good happens to him as soon as he takes it. He will also leap over and jump out of anything, and perform all his actions duly if he can expect a rest as soon as he has done what is required of him.

IX. So far we have described how to avoid being cheated in buying a colt or a horse, how to avoid spoiling him in usage and how to impart to a horse all the qualities required by a cavalryman for war. It is time perhaps to give directions, in case one has to deal with a horse that is too spirited or too sluggish, for the correct way of managing either.

XENOPHON

2   Πρῶτον τοίνυν χρὴ τοῦτο γνῶναι, ὅτι ἐστὶ
θυμὸς ἵππῳ ὅπερ ὀργὴ ἀνθρώπῳ. ὥσπερ οὖν
καὶ ἄνθρωπον ἥκιστ' ἂν ὀργίζοι τις μήτε λέγων
χαλεπὸν μηδὲν μήτε ποιῶν, οὕτω καὶ ἵππον

3 θυμοειδῆ ὁ μὴ ἀνιῶν ἥκιστ' ἂν ἐξοργίζοι. εὐθὺς
μὲν οὖν χρὴ ἐν τῇ ἀναβάσει ἐπιμελεῖσθαι, ὡς
ἂν ἥκιστ' ἀναβαίνων λυποίη· ἐπειδὰν δ' ἀναβῇ,
ἠρεμίσαντα πλείω χρόνον ἢ τὸν ἐπιτυχόντα
οὕτω προκινεῖν αὐτὸν ὡς πραοτάτοις σημείοις.
ἔπειτα δ' ἐκ τοῦ βραδυτάτου ἀρχόμενον οὕτως
αὖ εἰς τὸ θᾶττον προάγειν, ὡς ἂν μάλιστα
λανθάνοι αὐτὸν ὁ ἵππος εἰς τὸ ταχὺ ἀφικνού-

4 μενος. ὅ τι δ' ἂν ἐξαίφνης σημήνῃ, θυμοειδῆ
ἵππον ὥσπερ ἄνθρωπον ταράττει τὰ ἐξαπίναια
καὶ ὁράματα καὶ ἀκούσματα καὶ παθήματα.
εἰδέναι δὲ χρή, ὅτι καὶ ἐν ἵππῳ τὰ ἐξαπίναια

5 τάραχον ἐξεργάζεται.[1] ἢν δὲ καὶ εἰς τὸ θᾶττον
ὁρμώμενον τοῦ καιροῦ ὑπολαμβάνειν βούλῃ τὸν
θυμοειδῆ, οὐ δεῖ ἐξαπιναίως σπᾶν, ἀλλ' ἠρεμαίως
προσάγεσθαι τῷ χαλινῷ πραΰνοντα, οὐ βιαζό-

6 μενον ἠρεμεῖν. καὶ αἵ τε μακραὶ ἐλάσεις μᾶλλον
ἢ αἱ πυκναὶ ἀποστροφαὶ πραΰνουσι τοὺς ἵππους
καὶ αἱ ἡσυχαῖαι μέν,[2] πολυχρόνιοι δὲ[3] καθέψουσι
καὶ πραΰνουσι καὶ οὐκ ἀνεγείρουσι τὸν θυμοειδῆ.

7 εἰ δέ τις οἴεται, ἢν ταχὺ καὶ πολλὰ ἐλαύνηται,
ἀπειπεῖν ποιήσας τὸν ἵππον πραΰνειν, τἀναντία
γιγνώσκει τοῦ γιγνομένου. ἐν γὰρ τοῖς τοιούτοις
ὁ θυμοειδὴς καὶ ἄγειν βίᾳ μάλιστα ἐπιχειρεῖ καὶ
σὺν τῇ ὀργῇ ὥσπερ ἄνθρωπος ὀργίλος πολλάκις
καὶ ἑαυτὸν καὶ τὸν ἀναβάτην πολλὰ ἀνήκεστα

---

[1] S. with Cobet would omit this sentence. The καὶ before
ἐν is in A only, and is therefore not in S.

342

First, then, it must be realised that spirit in a 2
horse is precisely what anger is in a man. Therefore,
just as you are least likely to make a man angry if
you neither say nor do anything disagreeable to
him, so he who abstains from annoying a spirited
horse is least likely to rouse his anger. Accordingly, 3
at the moment of mounting, the rider should take
care to worry him as little as possible; and when he
is mounted, he should let him stand still longer than
is otherwise usual, and then direct him to go by the
most gentle aids. Then let him begin at a very slow
pace and increase the speed with the same gentle
help, so that the horse will not be aware of the tran-
sition to a quicker motion. Any sudden sign disturbs 4
a spirited horse, just as sudden sights and sounds and
sensations disturb a man. It is important to realise
that a horse too is flurried by anything sudden. If 5
you want to correct a spirited horse when he is going
too fast, do not pull him suddenly, but quietly check
him with the bit, soothing him, not forcing him, to a
quiet pace. Long rides rather than frequent turn- 6
ings, calm horses; and quiet ones lasting long soothe
and calm a spirited horse and do not excite him. But 7
if anyone supposes that he will calm a horse by
frequent riding at a quick pace so as to tire him,
his opinion is the opposite of the truth. For in such
cases a spirited horse does his utmost to get the upper
hand by force, and in his excitement, like an angry
man, he often causes many irreparable injuries both

---

² μὲν is omitted by S.
³ πολυχρόνιοι δὲ Madvig: πολὺν δὲ χρόνον A: πολὺν χρόνον
S. with the other MSS.

8 ἐποίησεν. ἐπιλαμβάνειν δὲ χρὴ ἵππον θυμοειδῆ
καὶ τοῦ εἰς τὸ τάχιστον ὁρμᾶν, τοῦ δὲ δὴ παρα-
βάλλειν ἵππῳ καὶ παντάπασιν ἀπέχεσθαι· σχεδὸν γὰρ καὶ φιλονικότατοι οἱ θυμοειδέστατοι τῶν
ἵππων γίγνονται.

9 Καὶ χαλινοὶ δὲ οἱ λεῖοι ἐπιτηδειότεροι τῶν
τραχέων. ἐὰν δὲ καὶ τραχὺς ἐμβληθῇ, τῇ χαλαρότητι λείῳ δεῖ αὐτὸν ἀφομοιοῦν. ἀγαθὸν δὲ
ἐθίζειν αὐτὸν καὶ τὸ ἠρεμεῖν, μάλιστα ἐπὶ θυμοει-
δοῦς ἵππου, καὶ τὸ ὡς ἥκιστα ἄλλῳ τινὶ ἅπτεσθαι
ἢ οἷς τοῦ καθῆσθαι ἀσφαλῶς ἕνεκα ἁπτόμεθα.

10 Εἰδέναι δὲ χρή, ὅτι δίδαγμά ἐστι καὶ τὸ ποππυσμῷ μὲν πραΰνεσθαι, κλωγμῷ δὲ ἐγείρεσθαι.
καὶ εἴ τις ἐξ ἀρχῆς ἐπὶ μὲν κλωγμῷ τὰ πραέα,
ἐπὶ δὲ ποππυσμῷ τὰ χαλεπὰ προσφέροι, μάθοι
ἂν ὁ ἵππος ποππυσμῷ μὲν ἐγείρεσθαι, κλωγμῷ
11 δὲ πραΰνεσθαι. οὕτως οὖν δεῖ καὶ παρὰ κραυγὴν
καὶ παρὰ σάλπιγγα μήτ᾽ αὐτὸν φαίνεσθαι τεθο-
ρυβημένον τῷ ἵππῳ μήτε μὴν ἐκείνῳ θορυβῶδες
μηδὲν προσφέρειν, ἀλλ᾽ εἰς τὸ δυνατὸν καὶ ἀναπαύειν ἐν τῷ τοιούτῳ καὶ ἄριστα καὶ δεῖπνα, εἰ
12 συγχωροίη, προσφέρειν. κάλλιστον δὲ συμβού-
λευμα τὸ ἄγαν θυμοειδῆ ἵππον μὴ κτᾶσθαι εἰς
πολέμους.

Βλακί γε μὴν ἵππῳ ἀρκεῖν μοι δοκεῖ γράψαι
πάντα τἀναντία ποιεῖν ὅσα τῷ θυμοειδεῖ χρῆσθαι
συμβουλευόμεν.

X. Ἣν δέ τίς ποτε βουληθῇ χρῆσθαι τῷ

to himself and to his rider. One must prevent [1] a 8
high-spirited horse from going at his top speed, and
of course, entirely avoid letting him race with another
horse; for as a rule the most highly spirited horses
are also most eager for victory.

As for bits, the smooth are more suitable than the 9
rough; but if a rough one is used, it should be made
to resemble a smooth one by lightness of hand. It
is also well to accustom oneself to sit still, especially
on a spirited horse, and to touch him as little as
possible with anything other than the parts that
give us a safe seat by contact.

It should also be known that a horse can be taught 10
to be calm by a chirp with the lips and to be roused
by a cluck with the tongue. And if from the first
you use with the cluck aids to calm him, and with the
chirp aids to rouse him, the horse will learn to rouse
himself at the chirp and to calm down at the cluck.
Accordingly, if a shout is heard or a trumpet sounds, 11
you must not allow the horse to notice any sign of
alarm in you, and must on no account do anything
to him to cause him alarm, but as far as possible let
him rest in such circumstances, and, if you have the
opportunity, bring him his morning or evening meal.
But the best advice is not to get an over-spirited 12
horse for war.

As for a sluggish beast, I may be content with
the remark that in everything you must do the
opposite of what we advise for the treatment of a
high-spirited one.

X. If a man wants to make a useful war-horse

---

[1] Or, reading τότε τοῦ for τοῦ with Pollack "one must try
to stop a spirited horse even then from going at his full
speed." A has τότε for τοῦ.

χρησίμῳ εἰς πόλεμον ἵππῳ μεγαλοπρεπεστέρῳ
τε καὶ περιβλεπτοτέρῳ ἱππάζεσθαι, τοῦ μὲν
ἕλκειν τε τὸ στόμα τῷ χαλινῷ καὶ μυωπίζειν
τε καὶ μαστιγοῦν τὸν ἵππον, ἃ οἱ πολλοὶ ποιοῦντες λαμπρύνειν οἴονται, ἀπέχεσθαι δεῖ· πάντα
γὰρ τἀναντία οὗτοί γε ποιοῦσιν ὧν βούλονται.

2 τά τε γὰρ στόματα ἕλκοντες ἄνω ἀντὶ τοῦ
προορᾶν ἐκτυφλοῦσι τοὺς ἵππους καὶ μυωπίζοντες
καὶ παίοντες ἐκπλήττουσιν, ὥστε τεταράχθαι καὶ
κινδυνεύειν. ταῦτα δ᾽ ἐστὶν ἵππων ἔργα τῶν
μάλιστα ἀχθομένων ἱππασίᾳ καὶ αἰσχρὰ καὶ

3 οὐ καλὰ ποιούντων. ἐὰν δέ τις διδάξῃ τὸν ἵππον
ἐν χαλαρῷ μὲν τῷ χαλινῷ ἱππεύειν, ἄνω δὲ τὸν
αὐχένα διαίρειν, ἀπὸ δὲ τῆς κεφαλῆς κυρτοῦσθαι,
οὕτως ἂν ἀπεργάζοιτο ποιεῖν τὸν ἵππον οἷοισπερ

4 καὶ αὐτὸς ἥδεταί τε καὶ ἀγάλλεται. τεκμήριον
δὲ ὅτι τούτοις ἥδεται. ὅταν γὰρ σχηματοποιεῖσθαι θέλῃ[1] παρ᾽ ἵππους, μάλιστα δὲ ὅταν
παρὰ θηλείας, τότε αἴρει τε τὸν αὐχένα ἀνωτάτω
καὶ κυρτοῖ μάλιστα τὴν κεφαλὴν γοργούμενος
καὶ τὰ μὲν σκέλη ὑγρὰ μετεωρίζει, τὴν δὲ οὐρὰν

5 ἄνω ἀνατείνει. ὅταν οὖν τις αὐτὸν εἰς ταῦτα
προάγῃ, ἅπερ αὐτὸς σχηματοποιεῖται, ὅταν
μάλιστα καλλωπίζηται, οὕτως ἡδόμενόν τε τῇ
ἱππασίᾳ καὶ μεγαλοπρεπῆ καὶ γοργὸν καὶ περί-
βλεπτον ἀποφαίνει τὸν ἵππον. ὡς οὖν ἡγούμεθα
ταῦτ᾽ ἂν ἀπεργασθῆναι, νῦν αὖ πειρασόμεθα
διηγεῖσθαι.

6 Πρῶτον μὲν τοίνυν χρὴ οὐ μεῖον δυοῖν χαλινοῖν
κεκτῆσθαι. τούτων δὲ ἔστω ὁ μὲν λεῖος, τοὺς

---

[1] σχηματοποιεῖσθαι θέλῃ A: the rest have θέλῃ only: S.
reads λυθεὶς θέῃ with Jacobs.

look more stately and showy when ridden, he must avoid pulling his mouth with the bit, and using the spur and whip, means by which most people imagine that they show off a horse. In point of fact the results they produce are the very opposite of what they intend. For by dragging the mouth up they 2 blind their horses instead of letting them see ahead, and by spurring and whipping, flurry them so that they are startled and get into danger.[1] That is the behaviour of horses that strongly object to being ridden and that behave in an ugly and unseemly fashion. But if you teach the horse to go with a 3 slack bridle, to hold his neck up and to arch it towards the head, you will cause the horse to do the very things in which he himself delights and takes the greatest pleasure. A proof that he delights in 4 them is that whenever he himself chooses to show off before horses, and especially before mares, he raises his neck highest and arches his head most, looking fierce; he lifts his legs freely off the ground and tosses his tail up. Whenever, therefore, you 5 induce him to carry himself in the attitudes he naturally assumes when he is most anxious to display his beauty, you make him look as though he took pleasure in being ridden, and give him a noble, fierce, and attractive appearance. How we think that these effects may be produced we will now try to explain.

To begin with, you should possess two bits at 6 least.[2] One of these should be smooth and have the

---

[1] Or, reading διveύειv, which occurred to Pollack and the translator independently, "twist about," "indulge in reactions." This is much more probable.

[2] See Introduction.

τροχοὺς εὐμεγέθεις ἔχων, ὁ δὲ ἕτερος τοὺς μὲν
τροχοὺς καὶ βαρεῖς καὶ ταπεινούς, τοὺς δ' ἐχίνους
ὀξεῖς, ἵνα ὁπόταν μὲν τοῦτον λάβῃ, ἀσχάλλων
τῇ τραχύτητι διὰ τοῦτο ἀφίῃ, ὅταν δὲ τὸν λεῖον
μεταλάβῃ, τῇ μὲν λειότητι αὐτοῦ ἡσθῇ, ἃ δὲ
ὑπὸ τοῦ τραχέος παιδευθῇ, ταῦτα καὶ ἐν τῷ
7 λείῳ ποιῇ. ἢν δ' αὖ καταφρονήσας τῆς λειότητος
θαμινὰ ἀπερείδηται ἐν αὐτῷ, τούτου ἕνεκα τοὺς
τροχοὺς μεγάλους τῷ λείῳ προστίθεμεν ἵνα
χάσκειν ἀναγκαζόμενος ὑπ' αὐτῶν ἀφίῃ τὸ
στόμιον. οἷόν τε δὲ καὶ τὸν τραχὺν παντο-
δαπὸν ποιεῖν καὶ κατειλοῦντα καὶ κατατείνοντα.
8 ὁποῖοι δ' ἂν ὦσι χαλινοί, πάντες ὑγροὶ ἔστωσαν.
τὸν μὲν γὰρ σκληρόν, ὅπῃ ἂν ὁ ἵππος λάβῃ, ὅλον
ἔχει πρὸς ταῖς γνάθοις· ὥσπερ καὶ ὀβελίσκον,
9 ὁπόθεν ἄν τις λάβῃ, ὅλον αἴρει. ὁ δ' ἕτερος
ὥσπερ ἡ ἄλυσις ποιεῖ· ὃ γὰρ ἂν ἔχῃ τις αὐτοῦ,
τοῦτο μόνον ἄκαμπτον μένει, τὸ δὲ ἄλλο ἀπήρτη-
ται. τὸ δὲ φεῦγον ἐν τῷ στόματι ἀεὶ θηρεύων
ἀφίησιν ἀπὸ τῶν γνάθων τὸ στόμιον· τούτου
ἕνεκα καὶ οἱ κατὰ μέσον ἐκ τῶν ἀξόνων δακτύ-
λιοι κρεμάννυνται, ὅπως τούτους διώκων τῇ τε
γλώττῃ καὶ τοῖς ὀδοῦσιν ἀμελῇ τοῦ ἀναλαμβάνειν
πρὸς τὰς γνάθους τὸν χαλινόν.
10   Εἰ δέ τις ἀγνοεῖ, τί τὸ ὑγρὸν τοῦ χαλινοῦ καὶ
τί τὸ σκληρόν, γράψομεν καὶ τοῦτο. ὑγρὸν μὲν
γάρ ἐστιν, ὅταν οἱ ἄξονες εὐρείας καὶ λείας ἔχωσι
τὰς συμβολάς, ὥστε ῥᾳδίως κάμπτεσθαι, καὶ

---

[1] So as to mitigate the roughness of the teeth. This was
sometimes done by covering the teeth with wax (Pollux
i. 207).

discs of a good size ; the other should have the discs
heavy and low, and the teeth sharp, so that when
the horse seizes it he may drop it because he objects
to its roughness, and when he is bitted with the
smooth one instead, may welcome its smoothness
and may do on the smooth bit what he has been
trained to do with the aid of the rough one. In 7
case, however, he takes no account of it because
of its smoothness, and keeps bearing against it,
we put large discs on the smooth bit to stop
this, so that they may force him to open his mouth
and drop the bit. It is possible also to make the
rough bit adaptable by wrapping [1] it up and tighten-
ing the reins.[2] But whatever be the pattern of the 8
bits, they must all be flexible. For wherever a
horse seizes a stiff one, he holds the whole of it
against his jaws, just as you lift the whole of a spit
wherever you take hold of it. But the other kind of 9
bit acts like a chain : for only the part that you hold
remains unbent, while the rest of it hangs loose. As
the horse continually tries to seize the part that eludes
him in his mouth, he lets the bit drop from his
jaws. This is why little rings [3] are hung in the
middle on the axles, in order that the horse may
feel after them with his tongue and teeth and not
think of taking the bit up against the jaws.

In case the meaning of the terms flexible and 10
stiff as applied to a bit is not known, we will explain
this too. "Flexible" means that the axles have
broad and smooth links so that they bend easily ;

[2] See c. ix, § 9.
[3] Two sets, one hanging to each of the two links that form
the centre joint of the two axles of which the "flexible"
bit consisted. They are found in both the Berlin bits.

πάντα δὲ ὁπόσα περιτίθεται περὶ τοὺς ἄξονας,
ἢν εὐρύστομα ᾖ καὶ μὴ σύμπυκνα, ὑγρότερά
11 ἐστιν. ἢν δὲ χαλεπῶς ἕκαστα τοῦ χαλινοῦ δια-
τρέχῃ καὶ συνθέῃ, τοῦτ᾽ ἐστὶ σκληρὸν εἶναι.

Ὁποῖος δ᾽ ἄν τις ᾖ, τούτῳ τάδε γε πάντα
ταὐτὰ ποιητέον, ἥπερ γε βούληται ἀποδείξασθαι
12 τὸν ἵππον οἱονπερ εἴρηται. ἀνακρουστέον μὲν
τὸ στόμα τοῦ ἵππου οὔτε ἄγαν χαλεπῶς ὥστε
ἐκνεύειν, οὔτε ἄγαν ἡσύχως ὡς μὴ αἰσθάνεσθαι.
ἐπειδὰν δὲ ἀνακρουόμενος αἴρῃ τὸν αὐχένα, δοτέον
εὐθὺς τὸν χαλινόν. καὶ τἆλλα δὲ δεῖ, ὥσπερ οὐ
παυόμεθα λέγοντες, ἐν ᾧ ἂν καλῶς ὑπηρετῇ,
13 χαρίζεσθαι τῷ ἵππῳ. καὶ ὅταν δ᾽ αἴσθηται
ἡδόμενον τὸν ἵππον τῇ τε ὑψηλαυχενίᾳ καὶ τῇ
χαλαρότητι, ἐν τούτῳ οὐδὲν δεῖ χαλεπὸν προσφέρειν ὡς πονεῖν ἀναγκάζοντα, ἀλλὰ θωπεύειν
ὡς παύσασθαι βουλόμενον· οὕτω γὰρ μάλιστα
14 θαρρῶν πρόεισιν εἰς τὴν ταχεῖαν ἱππασίαν. ὡς
δὲ καὶ τῷ ταχὺ θεῖν ἵππος ἥδεται, τεκμήριον·
ἐκφυγὼν γὰρ οὐδεὶς βάδην πορεύεται, ἀλλὰ θεῖ.
τούτῳ γὰρ πέφυκεν ἥδεσθαι, ἢν μή τις πλείω
τοῦ καιροῦ θεῖν ἀναγκάζῃ· ὑπερβάλλον δὲ τὸν
καιρὸν οὐδὲν τῶν πάντων ἡδὺ οὔτε ἵππῳ οὔτε
ἀνθρώπῳ.

15 Ὅταν γε μὴν εἰς τὸ ἱππάζεσθαι μετὰ τοῦ
κυδροῦ ἀφιγμένος ᾖ, εἰθισμένος μὲν δήπου ἡμῖν
ἦν ἐν τῇ πρώτῃ ἱππασίᾳ ἐκ τῶν στροφῶν εἰς τὸ
θᾶττον ὁρμᾶσθαι. ἢν δέ τις τοῦτο μεμαθηκότος

---

[1] Meaning (1) the toothed cylinders, (2) the pendants to
which the reins were attached, (3) the curved or S-shaped
branches with eyes to which the bridle was fastened. It is

and if everything that goes round the axles[1] has large openings, and does not fit tight, it is more flexible. "Stiff," on the other hand, means that the [11] pieces of the bit do not run over the axles and work in combination easily.

Whatever the pattern may be, the same method of using it must be carried out in all the points that follow, assuming that you want your horse to have just the appearance I have described. The mouth [12] must neither be pulled so hard that he holds his nose in the air, nor so gently that he takes no notice. As soon as he raises his neck when you pull, give him the bit at once. Invariably, in fact, as we cannot too often repeat, you must humour your horse whenever he responds to your wishes. And when [13] you notice that high carriage of his neck and lightness of hand give him pleasure, you should not deal hardly with him as though you were forcing him to work, but coax him as when you want to stop[2]; for thus he will break into a fast pace with most confidence. There is plain proof that a horse [14] takes pleasure in going fast: for when he breaks loose a horse never goes at a walking pace, but always runs. He instinctively takes pleasure in this, provided he is not compelled to run too far for his strength. Nothing in excess is ever pleasing either to horse or man.

When your horse has progressed so far as to bear [15] himself proudly when ridden, he has, of course, already been accustomed in the early exercises to break into a quicker pace after turning.[3] Now if after

curious that we do not know the Greek terms for (2) and (3). "Let all the parts be loose" is what X. means.
[2] A has ἱππάσασθαι "to ride," for παύσασθαι.   [3] vii. 17.

αὐτοῦ ἅμα ἀντιλαμβάνηταί τε τῷ χαλινῷ καὶ
σημήνῃ τῶν ὁρμητηρίων τι, οὕτως ὑπὸ μὲν τοῦ
χαλινοῦ πιεσθείς, ὑπὸ δὲ τοῦ ὁρμᾶν σημανθῆναι
ἐγερθεὶς [1] προβάλλεται μὲν τὰ στέρνα, αἴρει δὲ
ἄνω [2] τὰ σκέλη ὀργιζόμενος, οὐ μέντοι ὑγρὰ γε·
οὐ γὰρ μάλα, ὅταν λυπῶνται, ὑγροῖς τοῖς σκέ-
16 λεσιν ἵπποι χρῶνται. ἢν δέ τις οὕτως ἀνεζω-
πυρημένῳ αὐτῷ δῷ τὸν χαλινόν, ἐνταῦθα ὑφ᾽
ἡδονῆς τῷ διὰ τὴν χαλαρότητα τοῦ στομίου
λελύσθαι νομίζειν, κυδρῷ μὲν τῷ σχήματι,
ὑγροῖν δὲ τοῖν σκελοῖν γαυριώμενος φέρεται,
παντάπασιν ἐκμιμούμενος τὸν πρὸς ἵππους καλ-
17 λωπισμόν. καὶ οἱ θεώμενοι τὸν ἵππον τοιοῦτον
ἐπικαλοῦσιν [3] ἐλευθέριόν τε καὶ ἐθελουργὸν καὶ
ἱππαστὴν καὶ θυμοειδῆ καὶ σοβαρὸν καὶ ἅμα
ἡδύν τε καὶ [4] γοργὸν ἰδεῖν.

Καὶ ταῦτα μὲν δή, ἢν τούτων τις ἐπιθυμήσῃ,
μέχρι τούτων ἡμῖν γεγράφθω.

XI. Ἢν δέ τις ἄρα βουληθῇ καὶ πομπικῷ καὶ
μετεώρῳ καὶ λαμπρῷ ἵππῳ χρήσασθαι, οὐ μάλα
μὲν τὰ τοιαῦτα ἐκ παντὸς ἵππου γίγνεται, ἀλλὰ
δεῖ ὑπάρξαι αὐτῷ καὶ τὴν ψυχὴν μεγαλόφρονα
2 καὶ τὸ σῶμα εὔρωστον. οὐ μέντοι ὅ γε οἴονταί
τινες, τὸν τὰ σκέλη ὑγρὰ ἔχοντα καὶ τὸ σῶμα
αἴρειν δυνήσεσθαι, οὐχ οὕτως ἔχει· ἀλλὰ μᾶλλον
ὃς ἂν τὴν ὀσφῦν ὑγράν τε καὶ βραχεῖαν καὶ
ἰσχυρὰν ἔχῃ, καὶ οὐ τὴν κατ᾽ οὐρὰν λέγομεν,
ἀλλ᾽ ἢ πέφυκε μεταξὺ τῶν τε πλευρῶν καὶ τῶν
ἰσχίων κατὰ τὸν κενεῶνα, οὗτος δυνήσεται πόρρω
ὑποτιθέναι τὰ ὀπίσθια σκέλη ὑπὸ τὰ ἐμπρόσθια.

---

[1] ἐγερθεὶς Weiske : ἐγείρεται καὶ S. with the MSS.

he has learnt this you pull him up with the bit and at the same time give him one of the signs to go forward, then being held back by the bit and yet roused by the signal to go forward, he throws his chest out and lifts his legs from the ground impatiently, but not with a supple motion; for when horses feel uncomfortable, the action of their legs is not at all supple. But if, when he is thus 16 excited, you give him the bit, then, mistaking the looseness of the bit for a deliverance from restraint, he bounds forward for very joy with a proud bearing and supple legs, exultant, imitating exactly in every way the graces that he displays before horses. And 17 those who watch the horse when he is like that call him well-bred, a willing worker, worth riding, mettlesome, magnificent, and declare his appearance to be at once pleasing and fiery.

And here we conclude these explanations addressed to those who want this sort of thing.

XI. But in case anyone wants to own a horse suitable for parade, with a high and showy action, such qualities are by no means to be found in every horse: but it is essential that he should have plenty of spirit and a strong body. Many suppose that an 2 animal that has supple legs will also be capable of rearing his body. That, however, is not the case: rather it is the horse with supple, short, strong loins that will be able to extend his hind-legs well under the forelegs. By "loins" we do not mean the parts about the tail, but those between the flanks and

---

² ἄνω AB : ἀνωτέρω S. with the rest.
³ ἐπικαλοῦσιν Herwerden : ἀποκαλοῦσιν S. with the MSS.
⁴ καὶ A : καὶ ἅμα S. with the rest.

3 ἦν οὖν τις ὑποτιθέντος αὐτοῦ ἀνακρούῃ τῷ
χαλινῷ, ὀκλάζει μὲν τὰ ὀπίσθια ἐν τοῖς ἀστρα-
γάλοις, αἴρει δὲ τὸ πρόσθεν σῶμα, ὥστε τοῖς ἐξ
ἐναντίας φαίνεσθαι τὴν γαστέρα καὶ τὰ αἰδοῖα.
δεῖ δὲ καὶ ὅταν ταῦτα ποιῇ, διδόναι αὐτῷ τὸν
χαλινόν, ὅπως τὰ κάλλιστα ἵππου ἑκόντα
4 ποιῆσαι [1] δοκῇ τοῖς ὁρῶσιν. εἰσὶ μέντοι οἳ καὶ
ταῦτα διδάσκουσιν οἱ μὲν ῥάβδῳ ὑπὸ τοὺς ἀστρα-
γάλους κρούοντες, οἱ δὲ καὶ βακτηρίᾳ παρατρέ-
χοντά τινα κελεύοντες ὑπὸ τὰς μηριαίας παίειν.
5 ἡμεῖς γε μέντοι τὸ κράτιστον τῶν διδασκαλιῶν
νομίζομεν, ὥσπερ ἀεὶ λέγομεν, ἢν ἐν παντὶ παρέ-
πηται τὸ ἐν ᾧ ἂν ποιήσῃ τῷ ἀναβάτῃ κατὰ
6 γνώμην τυγχάνειν ῥᾳστώνης παρ' αὐτοῦ. ἃ μὲν
γὰρ ὁ ἵππος ἀναγκαζόμενος ποιεῖ, ὥσπερ καὶ
Σίμων λέγει, οὔτ' ἐπίσταται οὔτε καλά ἐστιν,
οὐδὲν μᾶλλον ἢ εἴ τις ὀρχηστὴν μαστιγοίη καὶ
κεντρίζοι· πολὺ γὰρ ἂν πλείω ἀσχημονοίη ἢ
καλὰ ποιοίη ὁ τοιαῦτα πάσχων καὶ ἵππος καὶ
ἄνθρωπος. ἀλλὰ δεῖ ἀπὸ σημείων ἑκόντα πάντα
τὰ κάλλιστα καὶ λαμπρότατα ἐπιδείκνυσθαι.
7 ἢν δὲ καὶ ὅταν μὲν ἱππάζηται, μέχρι πολλοῦ
ἱδρῶτος ἐλαύνηται, ὅταν δὲ καλῶς μετεωρίζῃ ἑαυτόν, ταχύ τε καταβαίνηται καὶ ἀποχαλινῶται, εὖ
χρὴ εἰδέναι, ὅτι ἑκὼν εἶσιν εἰς τὸ μετεωρίζειν ἑαυτόν.
8 Ἐπὶ τῶν τοιούτων δὲ ἤδη ἱππαζόμενοι ἵππων
καὶ θεοὶ καὶ ἥρωες γράφονται, καὶ ἄνδρες οἱ
καλῶς χρώμενοι αὐτοῖς μεγαλοπρεπεῖς φαίνονται.
9 οὕτω δὲ καὶ ἔστιν ὁ μετεωρίζων ἑαυτὸν ἵππος
σφόδρα ἀγαστόν, [2] ὡς πάντων τῶν ὁρώντων καὶ

ἑκόντα ποιῆσαι Courier: ἑκών τε ποιῇ καὶ S. with the MSS.

haunches about the belly. Now, if when he is 3
planting his hind-legs under him you pull him up
with the bit, he bends the hind-legs on the hocks and
raises the fore-part of his body, so that anyone facing
him can see the belly and the sheath. When he
does that you must give him the bit that he may
appear to the onlookers to be doing willingly the
finest things that a horse can do. Some, however, 4
teach these accomplishments by striking him under
the hocks with a rod, others by telling a man to
run alongside and hit him with a stick under the gas-
kins. We, however, consider that the lesson is most 5
satisfactory if, as we have repeatedly said, the rider
invariably allows him relaxation when he has done
something according to his wishes. For what a horse 6
does under constraint, as Simon says, he does without
understanding, and with no more grace than a dancer
would show if he was whipped and goaded. Under
such treatment horse and man alike will do much
more that is ugly than graceful. No, a horse must
make the most graceful and brilliant appearance in
all respects of his own will with the help of aids.
Further, if you gallop him during a ride until he 7
sweats freely, and as soon as he prances in fine
style, quickly dismount and unbridle him, you may
be sure that he will come willingly to the prance.

This is the attitude in which artists represent the 8
horses on which gods and heroes ride, and men who
manage such horses gracefully have a magnificent
appearance. Indeed a prancing horse is a thing so 9
graceful, terrible and astonishing that it rivets the

---

² ἀγαστόν Cobet: ἢ καλὸν ἢ δεινὸν ἢ ἀγαστὸν ἢ θαυμαστὸν
AB: ἢ καλὸν ἢ θαυμαστὸν ἢ ἀγαστόν S. with the other
MSS.

νέων καὶ γεραιτέρων τὰ ὄμματα κατέχει. οὐδεὶς
γοῦν οὔτε ἀπολείπει αὐτὸν οὔτε ἀπαγορεύει θεώ-
μενος, ἔστ᾽ ἄν περ ἐπιδεικνύηται τὴν λαμπρό-
τητα.

10 Ἢν γε μήν ποτε συμβῇ τινι τῶν τοιοῦτον
ἵππον κεκτημένων ἢ φυλαρχῆσαι ἢ ἱππαρχῆσαι,
οὐ δεῖ αὐτὸν τοῦτο σπουδάζειν, ὅπως αὐτὸς μόνος
λαμπρὸς ἔσται, ἀλλὰ πολὺ μᾶλλον ὅπως ὅλον
11 τὸ ἑπόμενον ἀξιοθέατον φανεῖται. ἢν μὲν οὖν
ἡγῆται, ὡς μάλιστα ἐπαινοῦσι τοὺς τοιούτους
ἵππους, ὃς ἂν ἀνωτάτω αἰρόμενος καὶ πυκνότατα
τὸ σῶμα βραχύτατον προβαίνῃ, δῆλον ὅτι καὶ
βάδην ἔποιντ᾽ ἂν οἱ ἄλλοι ἵπποι αὐτῷ. ἐκ δὲ
ταύτης τῆς ὄψεως τί ἂν καὶ λαμπρὸν γένοιτ᾽ ἄν·
12 ἢν δὲ ἐξεγείρας τὸν ἵππον ἡγῇ μήτε τῷ ἄγαν
τάχει μήτε τῷ ἄγαν βράδει, ὡς δ᾽ εὐθυμότατοι
ἵπποι καὶ γοργότατοι καὶ[1] εὐσχημονέστατοι
γίγνονται, ἐὰν ἡγῇ αὐτοῖς οὕτως, ἀθρόος μὲν ἂν[2]
ὁ τύπος, ἀθρόον δὲ τὸ φρύαγμα καὶ τὸ φύσημα
τῶν ἵππων συμπαρέποιτο[3] ὥστε οὐ μόνον αὐτός,
ἀλλὰ καὶ πάντες οἱ[4] συμπαρεπόμενοι ἀξιοθέατοι
ἂν φαίνοιντο.

13 Ἢν γε μήν[5] τις καλῶς ἱππωνήσῃ, τρέφῃ δὲ
ὡς πόνους δύνασθαι ὑποφέρειν, ὀρθῶς δὲ χρῆται
καὶ ἐν τοῖς πρὸς πόλεμον μελετήμασι καὶ ἐν ταῖς
πρὸς ἐπίδειξιν ἱππασίαις καὶ ἐν τοῖς πολεμικοῖς
ἀγωνίσμασι, τί ἔτι ἐμποδὼν τούτῳ μὴ οὐχὶ
πλείονός τε ἀξίους ἵππους ποιεῖν ἢ οἵους[6] ἂν
παραλαμβάνῃ, καὶ εὐδοκίμους μὲν ἵππους ἔχειν,

---

[1] καὶ Weiske : καὶ πονεῖν S. with the MSS.
[2] ἄν, added by Courier, is omitted by S. with the MSS.
[3] συμπαρέποιτο AB : συμπαρέσοιτο the other MSS. : S. omits.

gaze of all beholders, young and old alike. At all
events no one leaves him or is tired of gazing at
him so long as he shows off his brilliance.

Should the owner of such a horse happen to 10
be a colonel or a general, he must not make it his
object to be the one brilliant figure,[1] but must attach
much more importance to making the whole troop
behind him worth looking at. Now if a horse is 11
leading in the manner which wins most praise for
such horses, prancing high and with his body
closely gathered, so that he moves forward with
very short steps, the rest of the horses must
obviously follow also at a walking pace. Now what
can there be really brilliant in such a sight? But 12
if you rouse your horse and lead neither too fast nor
too slow, but at the pace at which the most spirited
horses look most fiery and stately—if you lead your
men in that way, there will be such a continual
stamping, such a continual neighing and snorting of
the horses going on behind you, that not only you
yourself but all the troop behind you will be worth
watching.

If a man buys his horses well, trains them so that 13
they can stand work, and uses them properly in the
training for war, in the exhibition rides and on the
battle-fields, what is there then to hinder him from
making horses more valuable than they are when he
takes them over, and why should he not be the
owner of famous horses, and also become famous

[1] *Cavalry Commander*, i. 22.

---

⁴ οἱ A : ὅσοι S. with the other MSS.

⁵ μήν A : μέν B : μέντοι S. with the rest.

⁶ ἢ οἵους A : ἢ οὓς the other MSS. : οὓς S.

εὐδοκιμεῖν δὲ αὐτὸν ἐν τῇ ἱππικῇ, ἢν μή τι δαιμόνιον κωλύῃ ;

XII. Γράψαι δὲ βουλόμεθα καὶ ὡς δεῖ ὡπλίσθαι τὸν μέλλοντα ἐφ' ἵππου κινδυνεύειν.

Πρῶτον μὲν τοίνυν φαμὲν χρῆναι τὸν θώρακα πρὸς τὸ σῶμα πεποιῆσθαι· τὸν μὲν γὰρ [1] καλῶς ἁρμόζοντα ὅλον φέρει τὸ σῶμα, τὸν δὲ ἄγαν χαλαρὸν οἱ ὦμοι μόνοι φέρουσιν, ὅ γε μὴν λίαν 2 στενὸς δεσμός, οὐχ ὅπλον ἐστίν. ἐπεὶ δὲ καὶ ὁ αὐχήν ἐστι τῶν καιρίων, φαμὲν χρῆναι καὶ τούτῳ ἐξ αὐτοῦ τοῦ θώρακος ὅμοιον τῷ αὐχένι στέγασμα πεποιῆσθαι. τοῦτο γὰρ ἅμα κόσμον τε παρέξει καὶ ἢν οἷον δεῖ εἰργασμένον ᾖ, δέξεται ὅταν βούληται τῷ ἀναβάτῃ τὸ πρόσωπον μέχρι 3 τῆς ῥινός. κράνος γε μὴν κράτιστον εἶναι νομίζομεν τὸ βοιωτιουργές· τοῦτο γὰρ αὖ στεγάζει μάλιστα πάντα τὰ ὑπερέχοντα τοῦ θώρακος, ὁρᾶν δὲ οὐ κωλύει. ὁ δ' αὖ θώραξ οὕτως εἰργάσθω, ὡς μὴ κωλύῃ μήτε καθίζειν μήτ' ἐπικύ 4 πτειν. περὶ δὲ τὸ ἦτρον καὶ τὰ αἰδοῖα καὶ τὰ κύκλῳ αἱ πτέρυγες τοιαῦται καὶ τοσαῦται ἔστω 5 σαν, ὥστε στέγειν τὰ βέλη.[2] ἐπεὶ δὲ καὶ ἡ ἀριστερὰ χεὶρ ἤν τι πάθῃ, καταλύει τὸν ἱππέα, καὶ ταύτῃ ἐπαινοῦμεν τὸ εὑρημένον ὅπλον τὴν χεῖρα καλουμένην. τόν τε γὰρ ὦμον σκεπάζει καὶ τὸν βραχίονα καὶ τὸν πῆχυν καὶ τὸ ἐχόμενον τῶν ἡνιῶν, καὶ ἐκτείνεται δὲ καὶ συγκάμπτεται· πρὸς δὲ τούτοις καὶ τὸ διαλεῖπον τοῦ θώρακος 6 ὑπὸ τῇ μασχάλῃ καλύπτει. τήν γε μὴν δεξιὰν ἐπαίρειν δεῖ, ἤν τε ἀκοντίσαι ἤν τε πατάξαι

_____

[1] τὸν μὲν γὰρ A : τὸν μὲν the other MSS. : ὅτι τὸν μὲν S.
[2] βέλη AB : μέλη S. with the rest.

himself for his horsemanship, provided no divine power prevents?

XII. We want to explain also how a man who is to face danger on horseback should be armed.

We say, then, that in the first place his breast-plate must be made to fit his body. For the well-fitting breastplate is supported by the whole body, whereas one that is too loose is supported by the shoulders only, and one that is too tight is rather an encumbrance than a defence. And, since the 2 neck is one of the vital parts, we hold that a covering should be available for it also, standing up from the breastplate itself and shaped to the neck. For this will serve as an ornament, and at the same time, if properly made, will cover the rider's face, when he pleases, as high as the nose. For the 3 helmet we consider the Boeotian pattern the most satisfactory: for this, again, affords the best protection to all the parts that project above the breastplate without obstructing the sight. As for the pattern of the breastplate, it should be so shaped as not to prevent the wearer from sitting down or stooping. About the abdomen and middle and round that region 4 let the flaps be of such material and such a size that they will keep out missiles. And as a wound in the 5 left hand disables the rider, we also recommend the piece of armour invented for it called the "hand."[1] For it protects the shoulder, the arm, the elbow, and the fingers that hold the reins; it will also extend and fold up; and in addition it covers the gap left by the breastplate under the armpit. But the right 6 hand must be raised when the man intends to fling

---

[1] *i.e.* a gauntlet.

βουληθῇ. τοῦ μὲν οὖν θώρακος τὸ κωλῦον ταύτῃ ἀφαιρετέον· ἀντὶ δὲ τούτου πτέρυγας ἐν τοῖς γιγγλύμοις προσθετέον, ὅπως ὅταν[1] μὲν διαίρηται, ὁμοίως ἀναπτύσσωνται, ὅταν δὲ
7 καταίρηται, ἐπικλείωνται. τῷ γε μὴν βραχίονι τὸ ὥσπερ κνημὶς παρατιθέμενον βέλτιον[2] ἡμῖν δοκεῖ εἶναι ἢ συνδεθὲν ὅπλῳ. τό γε μὴν ψιλούμενον αἰρομένης τῆς δεξιᾶς στεγαστέον ἐγγὺς τοῦ θώρακος ἢ μοσχείῳ ἢ χαλκείῳ· εἰ δὲ μή, ἐν τῷ ἐπικαιροτάτῳ ἀφύλακτον ἔσται.

8 Ἐπείπερ δὲ ἤν τι πάσχῃ ὁ ἵππος, ἐν παντὶ κινδύνῳ καὶ ὁ ἀναβάτης γίγνεται, ὁπλίζειν δεῖ καὶ τὸν ἵππον προμετωπιδίῳ καὶ προστερνιδίῳ καὶ παραμηριδίοις· ταῦτα γὰρ ἅμα καὶ τῷ ἀμβάτῃ παραμηρίδια γίγνεται. πάντων δὲ μάλιστα τοῦ ἵππου τὸν κενεῶνα δεῖ σκεπάζειν· καιριώτατον γὰρ ὂν καὶ ἀφαυρότατόν ἐστι· δυνατὸν δὲ
9 σὺν[3] τῷ ἐφιππίῳ καὶ[4] αὐτὸν σκεπάσαι. χρὴ δὲ καὶ τὸ ἔποχον τοιοῦτον ἐρράφθαι, ὡς ἀσφαλέστερόν τε τὸν ἱππέα καθῆσθαι καὶ τὴν ἕδραν τοῦ ἵππου μὴ σίνεσθαι.

Καὶ τὰ μὲν δὴ ἄλλα οὕτω καὶ ὁ ἵππος καὶ ὁ
10 ἱππεὺς ὡπλισμένοι ἂν εἶεν. κνῆμαι δὲ καὶ πόδες ὑπερέχοιεν μὲν ἂν εἰκότως τῶν παραμηριδίων, ὁπλισθείη δὲ καὶ ταῦτα, εἰ ἐμβάδες[5] γένοιντο σκύτους, ἐξ οὗπερ[6] αἱ κρηπῖδες ποιοῦνται· οὕτω γὰρ ἂν ἅμα ὅπλον τε κνήμαις καὶ ποσὶν ὑπόδήματ' ἂν εἴη.

---

[1] πτέρυγας . . . προσθετέον ὅπως ὅταν A : πτέρυγες προσθεταί, ὅταν S. with the rest. He also reads ἀναπτύσσονται and ἐπικλείονται against the MSS.

[2] βέλτιον A: ἀρκεῖν βέλτιον S. with the rest.

[3] All MSS. have σύν, which S. omits.

his javelin or strike a blow. Consequently that
portion of the breastplate that hinders him in doing
that should be removed; and in place of it there
should be detachable flaps at the joints, in order
that, when the arm is elevated, they may open
correspondingly, and may close when it is lowered.
For the fore-arm it seems to us that the piece put 7
over it separately like a greave is better than one
that is bound up together with a piece of armour.[1]
The part that is left exposed when the right arm is
raised should be covered near the breastplate with
calf-skin or metal; otherwise the most vital part
will be unprotected.

Since the rider is seriously imperilled in the event 8
of his horse being wounded, the horse also should
be armed, having head, chest, and thigh pieces:
the last also serve to cover the rider's thighs. But
above all the horse's belly must be protected; for
this, which is the most vital part, is also the
weakest. It is possible to make the cloth serve
partly as a protection to it. The quilting of the 9
cloth should be such as to give the rider a safer seat
and not to gall the horse's back.

Thus horse and man alike will be armed in most
parts. But the rider's shins and feet will of course 10
be outside the thigh-pieces. These too can be
guarded if boots made of shoe-leather are worn:
there will thus be armour for the shins and covering
for the feet at the same time.

---

[1] *i.e.* with the breastplate. Schneider thought that $\tau\hat{\wp}$
should be inserted before $\ddot{\sigma}\pi\lambda\wp$.

---

[4] $\kappa\alpha\grave{\iota}$ AB : S. omits.
[5] $\grave{\epsilon}\mu\beta\acute{\alpha}\delta\epsilon\varsigma$ A : $\grave{\epsilon}\mu\beta\acute{\alpha}\tau\alpha\iota$ S. with the other MSS.
[6] $\mathrm{o}\mathring{\upsilon}\pi\epsilon\rho$ AB : $\mathrm{o}\check{\iota}\mathrm{o}\upsilon\pi\epsilon\rho$ S. with M.

11 Ὡς μὲν δὴ μὴ βλάπτεσθαι θεῶν ἵλεων ὄντων
ταῦτα ὅπλα. ὡς δὲ τοὺς ἐναντίους βλάπτειν,
μάχαιραν μὲν μᾶλλον ἢ ξίφος ἐπαινοῦμεν· ἐφ'
ὑψηλοῦ γὰρ ὄντι τῷ ἱππεῖ κοπίδος μᾶλλον ἡ

12 πληγὴ ἢ ξίφους ἀρκέσει. ἀντί γε μὴν δόρατος
καμακίνου, ἐπειδὴ καὶ ἀσθενὲς καὶ δύσφορόν
ἐστι, τὰ κρανέϊνα δύο παλτὰ μᾶλλον ἐπαινοῦμεν.
καὶ γὰρ ἐξαφεῖναι τὸ ἕτερον δυνατὸν τῷ ἐπισταμένῳ καὶ τῷ λειπομένῳ οἷόν τε χρῆσθαι καὶ εἰς
τὸ ἀντίον καὶ εἰς τὰ πλάγια καὶ εἰς τοὔπισθεν[1]
καὶ ἅμα ἰσχυρότερά τε τοῦ δόρατος καὶ εὐφορώ-
τερά ἐστιν.

13 Ἀκόντισμά γε μὴν τὸ μακρότατον ἐπαινοῦμεν·
καὶ γὰρ ἀποστρέψαι καὶ μεταλαβεῖν παλτὸν
οὕτω μᾶλλον ὁ χρόνος ἐγχωρεῖ. γράψομεν δὲ
ἐν βραχεῖ καὶ ὡς ἄν τις κράτιστα ἀκοντίζοι. ἢν
γὰρ προβαλλόμενος μὲν τὰ ἀριστερά, ἐπανάγων
δὲ τὰ δεξιά, ἐξανιστάμενος δ' ἐκ τῶν μηρῶν,
μικρὸν ἐπανακύπτουσαν τὴν λόγχην ἀφῇ, οὕτω
σφοδρότατόν τε καὶ μακρότατον οἴσεται τὸ
ἀκόντιον, εὐστοχώτατον μέντοι, ἐὰν κατὰ τὸν
σκοπὸν ἀφιεμένη ἀεὶ ὁρᾷ ἡ λόγχη.

14 Καὶ ταῦτα μὲν δὴ ἰδιώτῃ καὶ ὑπομνήματα καὶ
μαθήματα καὶ μελετήματα γεγράφθω ἡμῖν. ἃ
δὲ ἱππάρχῳ προσῆκεν εἰδέναι τε καὶ πράττειν,
ἐν ἑτέρῳ λόγῳ δεδήλωται.

---

[1] τοὔπισθεν A : τοὔμπροσθεν S. with the other MSS.

These are the defensive arms which with the 11
gracious assistance of heaven will afford protection
from harm. For harming the enemy we recommend the sabre[1] rather than the sword, because,
owing to his lofty position, the rider will find the cut
with the Persian sabre more efficacious than the
thrust with the sword. And, in place of the spear 12
with a long shaft, seeing that it is both weak and
awkward to manage, we recommend rather the
two Persian javelins of cornel wood. For the skilful
man may throw the one and can use the other in
front or on either side or behind. They are also
stronger than the spear and easier to manage.[2]

We recommend throwing the javelin at the longest 13
range possible. For this gives a man more time to
turn his horse and to grasp the other javelin. We
will also state in a few words the most effective way
of throwing the javelin. If a man, in the act of
advancing his left side, drawing back his right, and
rising from his thighs, discharges the javelin with its
point a little upwards, he will give his weapon the
strongest impetus and the furthest carrying power;
it will be most likely to hit the mark, however, if at
the moment of discharge the point is always set on
it.

These notes, instructions and exercises which we 14
have here set down are intended only for the private
person. What it belongs to a cavalry leader to know
and to do has been set forth in another book.

[1] The sabre (μάχαιρα) was used in the Lacedaemonian and
the Persian army. κοπίς is the special term for the Persian
weapon.
[2] The two Persian javelins were shorter than the Greek
spear.

ON HUNTING

ΞΕΝΟΦΩΝΤΟΣ ΚΥΝΗΓΕΤΙΚΟΣ

I. Τὸ μὲν εὕρημα θεῶν, Ἀπόλλωνος καὶ Ἀρτέ-
μιδος, ἄγραι καὶ κύνες· ἔδοσαν δὲ καὶ ἐτίμησαν
2 τούτῳ Χείρωνα διὰ δικαιότητα. ὁ δὲ λαβὼν
ἐχάρη τῷ δώρῳ καὶ ἐχρῆτο· καὶ ἐγένοντο αὐτῷ
μαθηταὶ κυνηγεσίων τε καὶ ἑτέρων καλῶν Κέφαλος, Ἀσκληπιός, Μειλανίων, Νέστωρ, Ἀμφιάραος, Πηλεύς, Τελαμών, Μελέαγρος, Θησεύς,
Ἱππόλυτος, Παλαμήδης, Ὀδυσσεύς, Μενεσθεύς,
Διομήδης, Κάστωρ, Πολυδεύκης, Μαχάων, Ποδαλείριος, Ἀντίλοχος, Αἰνείας, Ἀχιλλεύς· ὧν κατὰ
3 χρόνον ἕκαστος ὑπὸ θεῶν ἐτιμήθη. θαυμαζέτω
δὲ μηδείς, ὅτι οἱ πολλοὶ αὐτῶν ἀρέσκοντες θεοῖς
ὅμως ἐτελεύτησαν· τοῦτο μὲν γὰρ ἡ φύσις· ἀλλ᾽
οἱ ἔπαινοι αὐτῶν μεγάλοι ἐγένοντο· μηδὲ ὅτι οὐ
καὶ αἱ αὐταὶ ἡλικίαι πᾶσι τούτοις.[1] ὁ γὰρ Χείρω-
4 νος βίος πᾶσιν ἐξήρκει. Ζεὺς γὰρ καὶ Χείρων
ἀδελφοὶ πατρὸς μὲν τοῦ αὐτοῦ, μητρὸς δὲ ὁ μὲν
Ῥέας, ὁ δὲ Ναΐδος νύμφης· ὥστε ἐγεγόνει μὲν
πρότερος τούτων, ἐτελεύτησε δὲ ὕστερος ἐπεὶ[2]
Ἀχιλλέα ἐπαίδευσεν.
5 Ἐκ δὲ τῆς ἐπιμελείας τῆς[3] τῶν κυνῶν
καὶ κυνηγεσίων καὶ τῆς ἄλλης παιδείας πολὺ
διενεγκόντες κατὰ τὴν ἀρετὴν ἐθαυμάσθησαν.

---

[1] πᾶσι τούτοις A: S. omits with the rest.
[2] ὕστερος ἐπεὶ A: ὕστερον ἢ ὡς S. with M.

ON HUNTING

I. GAME and hounds are the invention of gods, of Apollo and Artemis. They bestowed it on Cheiron and honoured him therewith for his righteousness. And he, receiving it, rejoiced in the gift, and used it. And he had for pupils in venery and in other noble 2 pursuits—Cephalus, Asclepius, Meilanion, Nestor, Amphiaraus, Peleus, Telamon, Meleager, Theseus, Hippolytus, Palamedes, Odysseus, Menestheus, Diomedes, Castor, Polydeuces, Machaon, Podaleirius, Antilochus, Aeneas, Achilles, of whom each in his time was honoured by gods. Let no man marvel that 3 the more part of these, even though they pleased gods, died none the less; for that was nature's work ; but the praise of them grew mightily ;—nor yet that not all of these flourished at one time. For Cheiron's lifetime sufficed for all. For Zeus and Cheiron were 4 brethren, sons of one sire, but the mother of the one was Rhea, of the other the nymph Nais : and so, though he was born before these, he died after them, for he taught Achilles.

Through the heed they paid to hounds and 5 hunting and the rest of their scholarship they excelled greatly and were admired for their virtue.

---

§ τῆς Schneider : τῆς ἐκ S. with the MSS.

XENOPHON

6 Κέφαλος μὲν καὶ ὑπὸ θεᾶς ἡρπάσθη, Ἀσκληπιὸς
δὲ μειζόνων ἔτυχεν, ἀνιστάναι μὲν τεθνεῶτας,
νοσοῦντας δὲ ἰᾶσθαι· διὰ δὲ ταῦτα θεὸς ὡς παρ'

7 ἀνθρώποις ἀείμνηστον κλέος ἔχει. Μειλανίων δὲ
τοσοῦτον ὑπερέσχε φιλοπονίᾳ, ὥστε ὢν αὐτῷ
ἀντερασταὶ ἐγένοντο οἱ τότε[1] ἄριστοι τῶν τότε
μεγίστων γάμων μόνος ἔτυχεν Ἀταλάντης.
Νέστορος δὲ προδιελήλυθεν ἡ ἀρετὴ τῶν Ἑλλήνων

8 τὰς ἀκοάς, ὥστε εἰδόσιν ἂν λέγοιμι. Ἀμφιάραος
δὲ ὅτ' ἐπὶ Θήβας ἐστράτευσε, πλεῖστον κτησάμενος
ἔπαινον ἔτυχε παρὰ θεῶν ἀείζως[2] τιμᾶσθαι.
Πηλεὺς δ' ἐπιθυμίαν παρέσχε καὶ θεοῖς δοῦναί τε
Θέτιν αὐτῷ καὶ τὸν γάμον παρὰ Χείρωνι ὑμνῆσαι.

9 Τελαμὼν δὲ τοσοῦτος ἐγένετο, ὥστε ἐκ μὲν πόλεως
τῆς μεγίστης ἣν αὐτὸς ἐβούλετο γῆμαι Περίβοιαν
τὴν Ἀλκάθου· ὅτε δὲ ὁ πρῶτος τῶν Ἑλλήνων
ἐδίδου τὰ ἀριστεῖα Ἡρακλῆς ὁ Διός, ἐλὼν

10 Τροίαν, Ἡσιόνην αὐτῷ ἔδωκεν. Μελέαγρος δὲ
τὰς μὲν τιμὰς ἃς ἔλαβε φανεραί· πατρὸς δ' ἐν
γήρᾳ ἐπιλανθανομένου τῆς θεοῦ οὐχ αὐτοῦ
αἰτίαις ἐδυστύχησεν. Θησεὺς δὲ τοὺς μὲν τῆς
Ἑλλάδος ἐχθροὺς πάσης μόνος ἀπώλεσε· τὴν δ'
αὐτοῦ πατρίδα πολλῷ μείζω ποιήσας ἔτι καὶ νῦν

11 θαυμάζεται. Ἱππόλυτος δὲ ὑπὸ μὲν τῆς Ἀρτέ-
μιδος ἐτιμᾶτο καὶ ἐν λόγοις ἦν, σωφροσύνῃ δὲ καὶ
ὁσιότητι μακαρισθεὶς ἐτελεύτησε. Παλαμήδης
δὲ ἕως μὲν ἦν, πολὺ τῶν ἐφ' ἑαυτοῦ ὑπερέσχε
σοφίᾳ, ἀποθανὼν δὲ ἀδίκως τοσαύτης ἔτυχε
τιμωρίας ὑπὸ θεῶν, ὅσης οὐδεὶς ἄλλος ἀνθρώπων.

---

[1] This τότε is omitted by S.
[2] ἀείζως Dindorf: ἀεὶ ζῶν S. with the MSS.

368

Cephalus was carried away by a goddess.[1] Asclepius 6
won yet [2] greater preferment—to raise the dead, to
heal the sick ; and for these things he has everlasting
fame as a god among men. Meilanion was so peerless 7
in love of toil that, though the princeliest of that age
were his rival suitors for the greatest Lady of the
time, only he won Atalanta. Nestor's virtue is an old
familiar tale to Greek ears; so there is no need
for me to tell of it. Amphiaraus when he fought 8
against Thebes, gained great praise and won from the
gods the honour of immortality. Peleus stirred
a desire even in the gods to give him Thetis and to
hymn their marriage in Cheiron's home. Telamon 9
waxed so mighty that he wedded from the greatest
city the maiden of his choice, Periboea, daughter
of Alcathus : and when the first of the Greeks,
Heracles son of Zeus, distributed the prizes of valour
after taking Troy, to him he gave Hesioné. As for 10
Meleager, the honours that he won are manifest;
and it was not by his own fault that he came to sorrow
when his father in old age forgot the goddess.[3]
Theseus single-handed slew the enemies of all
Greece ; and because he enlarged greatly the borders
of his country he is admired to this day. Hippolytus 11
was honoured by Artemis and held converse with
her; and for his prudence and holiness he was
counted happy when he died. Palamedes far outstripped the men of his generation in wisdom while
he lived ; and being unjustly slain he won from the
gods such vengeance as fell to the lot of no other

---

[1] Aurora.

[2] The καὶ before ὑπὸ in the text should probably be placed
before μειζόνων.

[3] *i.e.* when his father Oeneus forgot Artemis,—a laps
which led ultimately to the death of Meleager.

ἐτελεύτησε δὲ οὐχ ὑφ' ὧν οἴονταί τινες· οὐ γὰρ ἂν
ἦν ὁ μὲν σχεδόν τι ἄριστος, ὁ δὲ ὅμοιος ἀγαθοῖς·
12 κακοὶ δὲ ἔπραξαν τὸ ἔργον. Μενεσθεὺς δὲ ἐκ
τῆς ἐπιμελείας τῆς [1] τῶν κυνηγεσίων τοσοῦτον
ὑπερέβαλε φιλοπονίᾳ, ὥστε ὁμολογεῖν τοὺς τῶν
Ἑλλήνων πρώτους ὑστέρους εἶναι τὰ εἰς τὸν
πόλεμον ἐκείνου πλὴν Νέστορος· καὶ οὗτος οὐ
13 προέχειν λέγεται, ἀλλὰ ἐρίζειν. Ὀδυσσεὺς δὲ
καὶ Διομήδης λαμπροὶ μὲν καὶ καθ' ἓν ἕκαστον,
τὸ δὲ ὅλον αἴτιοι Τροίαν ἁλῶναι. Κάστωρ δὲ
καὶ Πολυδεύκης ὅσα ἐπεδείξαντο ἐν τῇ Ἑλλάδι
τῶν παρὰ Χείρωνος διὰ τὸ ἀξίωμα τὸ ἐκ τούτων
14 ἀθάνατοί εἰσι. Μαχάων δὲ καὶ Ποδαλείριος
παιδευθέντες τὰ αὐτὰ πάντα ἐγένοντο καὶ τέχνας
καὶ λόγους καὶ πολέμους ἀγαθοί. Ἀντίλοχος
δὲ τοῦ πατρὸς ὑπεραποθανὼν τοσαύτης ἔτυχεν
εὐκλείας, ὥστε μόνος φιλοπάτωρ παρὰ τοῖς
15 Ἕλλησιν ἀναγαρευθῆναι. Αἰνείας δὲ σώσας μὲν
τοὺς πατρῴους καὶ μητρῴους θεούς, σώσας δὲ καὶ
αὐτὸν τὸν πατέρα δόξαν εὐσεβείας ἐξηνέγκατο,
ὥστε καὶ οἱ πολέμιοι μόνῳ ἐκείνῳ ὧν ἐκράτησαν
16 ἐν Τροίᾳ ἔδοσαν μὴ συληθῆναι. Ἀχιλλεὺς δ' ἐν
ταύτῃ τῇ παιδείᾳ τραφεὶς οὕτω καλὰ καὶ μεγάλα
μνημεῖα παρέδωκεν, ὥστε οὔτε λέγων οὔτε ἀκούων
περὶ ἐκείνου οὐδεὶς ἀπαγορεύει.
17 Οὗτοι τοιοῦτοι ἐγένοντο ἐκ τῆς ἐπιμελείας τῆς

---

[1] τῆς Schneider : τῆς ἐκ S. with the MSS.

[1] Odysseus and Diomedes, who, according to one account,
drowned Palamedes when he was fishing. The reference
here may be to this version. In *Memorabilia* IV. ii. 4
X. follows the commoner version that Odysseus got P. put to

mortal. But his end was not compassed by those[1] whom some imagine, else could not the one of them have been well-nigh the best, and the other the peer of the good ; but bad men did the deed. Menestheus 12 through the heed he paid to hunting, so far surpassed others in love of toil that the first of the Greeks confessed themselves his inferiors in feats of war, all save Nestor ; and he, it is said,[2] outdid not, but rivalled him. Odysseus and Diomedes were brilliant in 13 every single deed, and in short, to them was due the capture of Troy. Castor and Polydeuces, through the renown that they won by displaying in Greece the arts they learned of Cheiron, are immortal. Machaon and Podaleirius, schooled in all the self- 14 same arts, proved in crafts and reasonings and wars good men. Antilochus, by giving his life for his father,[3] won such glory that he alone was proclaimed among the Greeks as " the Devoted Son." Aeneas 15 saved the gods of his father's and his mother's family, and withal his father himself; wherefore he bore away fame for his piety, so that to him alone among all the vanquished at Troy even the enemy granted not to be despoiled. Achilles, nursed in this school- 16 ing, bequeathed to posterity memorials so great and glorious that no man wearies of telling and hearing of him.

These, whom the good love even to this day and 17

death by a false charge of treachery ; and in the *Odysseus* attributed to the rhetorician Alcidamus, Diomedes and Sthenelus are associated with Odysseus in bringing this charge. In revenge for his death his father Nauplius caused the shipwreck of the Greek fleet off the south of Euboea.

[2] In *Iliad* ii. 555.

[3] How Antilochus, son of Nestor, saved his father's life is told by Pindar in the sixth *Pythian*.

παρὰ Χείρωνος, ὧν οἱ μὲν ἀγαθοὶ ἔτι καὶ νῦν
ἐρῶσιν, οἱ δὲ κακοὶ φθονοῦσιν, ὥστ᾿ ἐν μὲν τῇ
Ἑλλάδι εἴ τῳ συμφοραὶ ἐγίγνοντο ἢ πόλει ἢ
βασιλεῖ, ἐλύοντο δι᾿ [1] αὐτούς· εἰ δὲ πρὸς τοὺς βαρβάρους πάντας πάσῃ τῇ Ἑλλάδι νεῖκος ἢ πόλεμος, διὰ τούτους οἱ Ἕλληνες ἐκράτουν, ὥστε
ἀνίκητον τὴν Ἑλλάδα παρασχεῖν.

18   Ἐγὼ μὲν οὖν παραινῶ τοῖς νέοις μὴ καταφρονεῖν κυνηγεσίων μηδὲ τῆς ἄλλης παιδείας· ἐκ
τούτων γὰρ γίγνονται τὰ εἰς τὸν πόλεμον ἀγαθοὶ
εἴς τε τὰ ἄλλα, ἐξ ὧν ἀνάγκη καλῶς νοεῖν καὶ
λέγειν καὶ πράττειν.

II. Πρῶτον μὲν οὖν χρὴ ἐλθεῖν ἐπὶ τὸ ἐπιτήδευμα τὸ τῶν κυνηγεσίων τὸν ἤδη ἐκ παιδὸς
ἀλλάττοντα τὴν ἡλικίαν, εἶτα δὲ καὶ ἐπὶ τὰ ἄλλα
παιδεύματα, τὸν μὲν ἔχοντα σκεψάμενον τὴν οὐ-
σίαν· ᾧ μὲν ἔστιν ἱκανή, ἀξίως τῆς αὑτοῦ
ὠφελείας, ᾧ δὲ μὴ ἔστιν, ἀλλ᾿ οὖν τήν γε προθυμίαν παρεχέσθω μηδὲν ἐλλείπων τῆς ἑαυτοῦ
δυνάμεως.

2   Ὅσα δὲ καὶ οἷα δεῖ παρεσκευασμένον ἐλθεῖν
ἐπ᾿ αὐτό, φράσω καὶ αὐτὰ καὶ τὴν ἐπιστήμην
ἑκάστου, ἵνα προειδὼς ἐγχερῇ τῷ ἔργῳ. καὶ
μηδεὶς αὐτὰ φαῦλα νομισάτω εἶναι· ἄνευ γὰρ δὴ
τούτων οὐκ ἂν εἴη πρᾶξις.

3   Χρὴ δὲ τὸν μὲν ἀρκυωρὸν εἶναι ἐπιθυμοῦντα τοῦ
ἔργου καὶ τὴν φωνὴν Ἕλληνα, τὴν δὲ ἡλικίαν
περὶ ἔτη εἴκοσι, τὸ δὲ εἶδος ἐλαφρόν, ἰσχυρόν,
ψυχὴν δὲ ἱκανόν, ἵνα τῶν πόνων τούτοις κρατῶν
4   χαίρῃ τῷ ἔργῳ. τὰς δὲ ἄρκυς Φασιανοῦ ἢ Καρ-

---

[1] S. omits δι᾿ with the better MSS.

the evil envy, were made so perfect through the care they learned of Cheiron that, when troubles fell upon any state or any king in Greece, they were composed through their influence; or if all Greece was at strife or at war with all the Barbarian powers, these brought victory to the Greeks, so that they made Greece invincible.

Therefore I charge the young not to despise 18 hunting or any other schooling. For these are the means by which men become good in war and in all things out of which must come excellence in thought and word and deed.

II. The first pursuit, therefore, that a young man just out of his boyhood should take up is hunting, and afterwards he should go on to the other branches of education, provided he has means. He must look to his means, and, if they are sufficient, spend as much as the benefit to himself is worth; or, if they are insufficient, at least let him supply enthusiasm, in no way coming short of his power.[1]

I will give a list and a description of the intending 2 hunter's outfit, and the explanation of each item, in order that he may understand the business before he puts his hand to it. And let no one regard these details as trivial; inasmuch as nothing can be done without them.

The net-keeper should be a man with a keen 3 interest in the business, one who speaks Greek, about twenty years old, agile and strong, and resolute, that, being well qualified to overcome his tasks, he may take pleasure in the business. The purse-nets should 4

---

[1] The text of this paragraph is open to suspicion. The words from εἶτα to ἔχοντα may be an afterthought.

χηδονίου λεπτοῦ λίνου καὶ τὰ ἐνόδια καὶ τὰ δίκτυα.

Ἔστωσαν δὲ αἱ μὲν ἄρκυς ἐννεάλινοι ἐκ τριῶν τόνων, ἕκαστος δὲ τόνος ἐκ τριῶν λίνων, τὸ δὲ μέγεθος πεντεσπίθαμοι, διπάλαιστοι δὲ τοὺς βρόχους, περικείσθωσαν[1] δὲ τοὺς περιδρόμους ἀναμμάτους,[2] ἵνα εὔτροχοι ὦσι, τὰ δ' ἐνόδια δωδεκά-
5 λινα, τὰ δὲ δίκτυα ἑκκαιδεκάλινα, τὸ δὲ μέγεθος τὰ μὲν ἐνόδια διώρυγα, τετρώρυγα, πεντώρυγα, τὰ δὲ δίκτυα δεκώρυγα, εἰκοσώρυγα, τριακον- τώρυγα· ἐὰν δὲ ᾖ μείζω, δυσμεταχείριστα ἔσται· ἀμφότερα δὲ τριακονθάμματα, καὶ τῶν βρόχων
6 τὸ διάστημα ἴσον ταῖς ἄρκυσιν. ἐν δὲ τοῖς ἀκρωλενίοις τὰ μὲν ἐνόδια ἐχέτω μαστούς, τὰ δὲ δίκτυα δακτυλίους, τοὺς δὲ περιδρόμους ἀπὸ
7 στροφείων. αἱ δὲ σχαλίδες τῶν μὲν ἀρκύων τὸ μῆκος δέκα παλαιστῶν, ἔστωσαν δὲ καὶ ἐλάττους· αἱ μὲν ἄνισοι αὐτῶν ἐν τοῖς ἑτεροκλινέσι τῶν χωρίων, ἵν' ἴσα τὰ ὕψη ἐξαίρωσιν, ἐν δὲ τοῖς ὁμαλέσιν αἱ ἴσαι· αὗται δ' εὐπερίσπαστοι τὰ ἄκρα καὶ αὗται λεῖαι· τῶν δὲ ἐνοδίων διπλά-

---

[1] περικείσθωσαν A : ὑφείσθωσαν S., a conjecture based on the other MSS

[2] οἱ περίδρομοι ἀναμμάτοι S. against the MSS.

---

[1] i.e. Colchian. Much flax and linen was exported from Colchis.

[2] The cords meant here are those that ran round the mouth of the purse, and served as a running noose to close it when the hare got in.

[3] i.e. ten meshes, so that the extreme height, if the net was fully stretched, would be five feet. Poachers now use slip-knots or nets about four feet deep with a mesh of two-and-a-half inches.

be made of fine Phasian[1] or Carthaginian flax, and
the road-nets and hayes of the same material.

Let the purse-nets be of nine threads woven in
three strands, each strand consisting of three threads.
The proper length for these nets is forty-five inches,
the proper width of the meshes six inches. The
cords that run round[2] them must be without knots,
so that they may run easily. The road-nets should 5
be of twelve threads, and the hayes of sixteen. The
length of the road-nets may be twelve, twenty-four
or thirty-feet; that of the hayes sixty, a hundred and
twenty, or a hundred and eighty feet. If they are
longer, they will be unwieldy. Both kinds should be
thirty knots[3] high, and should have meshes of the
same width as those of the purse-nets. At the elbows 6
at either end let the road-nets have slip-knots of
string and the hayes metal rings,[4] and let the
cords[5] be attached by loops. The stakes for the 7
purse-nets should be thirty inches long, but some
should be shorter. Those of unequal length are for
use on sloping ground, to make the height of
the nets equal, while those of the same length are
used on the level. These stakes must be so shaped
at the top that the nets will pull off readily and they
must be smooth.[6] The stakes for the road-nets

---

[4] The rings running down the two sides were used for
joining two nets together.

[5] *i.e.* the cords running along the top and bottom of the
nets.

[6] The author means, I think, to imply a contrast between
the stakes of the purse-nets and those of the other nets.
The second αὗται in the text can scarcely be right: possibly
καὶ αὗται λεῖαι should be omitted, or αὐταί, "they themselves," read with Dindorf.

σιαι, αἱ δὲ τῶν δικτύων τὸ μὲν μέγεθος πεντεσπίθαμοι, δικρᾶ ἔχουσαι μικρά, τὰ ἐντμήματα μὴ
βαθέα· εὐπαγεῖς δὲ πᾶσαι καὶ μὴ ἀσύμμετροι τὰ
8 πάχη πρὸς τὰ μήκη. τῷ δὲ πλήθει τῶν σχαλίδων
οἷόν τέ ἐστι χρῆσθαι πρὸς τὰ δίκτυα πολλῷ καὶ
ὀλίγῳ· ἐλάττονι μέν, ἂν σφόδρα τείνηται ἐν τῇ
9 στάσει· πλέονι δ᾽, ἂν ἡσυχῇ. ἔστω δὲ καὶ ἐν
ὅτῳ ἔσονται αἱ ἄρκυς καὶ τὰ ἐνόδια καὶ δίκτυα [1]
κυνοῦχος μόσχειος καὶ τὰ δρέπανα, ἵνα ᾖ τῆς
ὕλης τέμνοντα φράττειν τὰ δεόμενα.

III. Τὰ δὲ γένη τῶν κυνῶν ἐστι διττά, αἱ μὲν
γὰρ καστόριαι, αἱ δὲ ἀλωπεκίδες. ἔχουσι δ᾽ αἱ
μὲν καστόριαι τὴν ἐπωνυμίαν ταύτην, ὅτι Κάστωρ
ἡσθεὶς τῷ ἔργῳ μάλιστα αὐτὰς διεφύλαξεν· αἱ δ᾽
ἀλωπεκίδες, διότι ἐκ κυνῶν τε καὶ ἀλωπέκων
ἐγένοντο· ἐν πολλῷ δὲ χρόνῳ συγκέκραται αὐτῶν
2 ἡ φύσις. χείρους δὲ καὶ πλείους αἱ τοιαίδε,
μικραί, γρυπαί, χαροποί, μυωποί, ἄμορφοι,[2]
σκληραί, ἀσθενεῖς, ψιλαί, ὑψηλαί, ἀσύμμετροι,
3 ἄψυχοι, ἄρρινες, οὐκ εὔποδες. αἱ μὲν οὖν μικραὶ
πολλάκις [3] ἀποστεροῦνται τῆς ἐργασίας διὰ τὸ
μικρόν· αἱ δὲ γρυπαὶ ἄστομοι καὶ διὰ τοῦτο οὐ
κατέχουσι τὸν λαγῶ· χαροποὶ [4] δὲ καὶ μυωποὶ
χείρω τὰ ὄμματα ἔχουσιν, ἄμορφοι δὲ καὶ αἰσχραὶ
ὁρᾶσθαι· αἱ δὲ σκληραὶ τὰ εἴδη χαλεπῶς ἀπὸ
τῶν κυνηγεσίων ἀπαλλάττουσι· πονεῖν δὲ ἀδύνατοι αἱ ἀσθενεῖς καὶ αἱ ψιλαί· καὶ αἱ ὑψηλαὶ
μὲν καὶ ἀσύμμετροι ἀσύντακτα ἔχουσαι τὰ

---

[1] τὰ ἐνόδια καὶ δίκτυα A: τὰ δίκτυα ἐν ἑκατέροις S. with the rest.
[2] ἄμορφοι Rühl: αἰσχαὶ MSS.: S. omits.
[3] S. adds ἐκ τῶν κυνηγεσίων omitted in AB.
[4] μυωποὶ δὲ καὶ χαροποὶ S. with BM.

should be twice the length of these, and those
for the hayes forty-five inches long. The latter[1]
should have little forks with shallow grooves, and all
should be stout, of a thickness proportioned to
the length. The number of stakes used for the 8
hayes may be large or small ; fewer are required if
the nets are strained tight when set up, more if they
are slack. A calf-skin bag will be wanted for carry- 9
ing the purse-nets and road-nets and hayes and the
bill-hooks for cutting wood and stopping gaps where
necessary.

III. The hounds used are of two kinds, the
Castorian and the Vulpine.[2] The Castorian is so
called because Castor paid special attention to the
breed, making a hobby of the business. The Vulpine
is a hybrid between the dog and the fox : hence
the name. In the course of time the nature of the
parents has become fused. Inferior specimens (that 2
is to say, the majority) show one or more of the
following defects. They are small, hook-nosed,
grey-eyed, blinking, ungainly, stiff, weak, thin-
coated, lanky, ill-proportioned, cowardly, dull-scented,
unsound in the feet. Now small dogs often drop out 3
of the running through their want of size ; hook-nosed
dogs have no mouth and can't hold the hare ; grey-
eyed dogs and blinkers have bad sight ; ungainly dogs
look ugly ; stiff ones are in a bad way at the end of
the hunt ; no work can be got out of the weak
and the thin-coated ones ; those that are lanky and
ill-proportioned are heavy movers and carry them-

---

[1] Or perhaps he means *both* sets.

[2] Both are Laconian varieties, the Castorian being much
the larger. The Vulpine resembled a fox ; hence the
erroneous idea that it was a hybrid between dog and fox
(O. Keller, *die antike Tierwelt*, i. 121).

σώματα βαρέως διαφοιτῶσιν· αἱ ἄψυχοι δὲ λείπουσι τὰ ἔργα καὶ ἀφίστανται τὸν ἥλιον ὑπὸ τὰς σκιὰς καὶ κατακλίνονται· αἱ δὲ ἄρρινοι μόλις καὶ ὀλιγάκις αἰσθάνονται τοῦ λαγῶ· αἱ δὲ ἄποδες οὐδ' ἐὰν ὦσιν εὔψυχοι, τοὺς πόνους δύνανται ἀνέχεσθαι, ἀλλ' ἀπαγορεύουσι διὰ τὸ ἄλγος τῶν ποδῶν.

4 Εἰσὶ δὲ καὶ τῆς ἰχνεύσεως πολλοὶ τρόποι ἐκ τῶν αὐτῶν κυνῶν· αἱ μὲν γὰρ ἐπειδὰν λάβωσι τὰ ἴχνη, πορεύονται ἀσήμως, ὥστε μὴ γιγνώσκεσθαι ὅτι ἰχνεύουσιν, αἱ δὲ τὰ ὦτα μόνον διακινοῦσι, τὴν δὲ οὐρὰν ἡσυχῇ ἔχουσιν, αἱ δὲ τὰ ὦτα μὲν ἀκίνητα ἔχουσιν, ἄκρᾳ δὲ τῇ οὐρᾷ σείουσιν.

5 ἄλλαι δὲ συνάγουσι τὰ ὦτα καὶ ἐπισκυθρωπάσασαι διὰ τοῦ ἴχνους σχάσασαι τὴν οὐρὰν καὶ φράξασαι διατρέχουσι· πολλαὶ δὲ τούτων μὲν οὐδὲν ποιοῦσι, μανικῶς δὲ περιφερόμεναι ὑλακτοῦσι περὶ τὰ ἴχνη, ὅτε δὲ[1] εἰσπίπτουσιν εἰς αὐτά, ἀφρόνως καταπατοῦσι τὰς αἰσθήσεις.

6 εἰσὶ δ' αἱ κύκλοις πολλοῖς χρώμεναι καὶ πλάνοις ὑπολαμβάνουσαι ἐκ τοῦ πρόσω[2] τὰ ἴχνη παραλείπουσι τὸν λαγῶ, ὁσάκις δ' ἐπιτρέχουσι τὰ ἴχνη, εἰκάζουσι, προορώμεναι δὲ τὸν λαγῶ τρέμουσι καὶ οὐκ ἐπέρχονται, πρὶν ἴδωσιν ὑποκι-

7 νοῦντα. ὅσαι δὲ τὰ τῶν ἄλλων κυνῶν εὑρήματα ἐν ταῖς ἰχνείαις καὶ μεταδρομαῖς προθέουσι θαμινὰ σκοποῦσαι, ἑαυταῖς ἀπίστως ἔχουσι· θρασεῖαι δ' αἱ οὐκ ἐῶσι τῶν συνεργῶν τὰς σοφὰς εἰς τὸ πρόσθεν προϊέναι, ἀλλ' ἀνείργουσι θορυβοῦσαι· αἱ δὲ ἀσπαζόμεναι τὰ ψευδῆ καὶ ὑπερλαμπρυνόμεναι ἐφ' ὅτῳ ἂν τύχωσι προάγουσι συνειδυῖαι

---

[1] δὲ is omitted by S. with M.

selves anyhow; cowards leave their work and give
up and slink away from the sun into shady places
and lie down; dogs with no nose seldom scent the
hare and only with difficulty ; and those with bad feet,
even if they are plucky, can't stand the hard work,
and tire because they are foot-sore.

Moreover, hounds of the same breed vary much 4
in behaviour when tracking. Some go ahead as
soon as they find the line without giving a sign,
and there is nothing to show that they are on it.
Some move the ears only, but keep the tail still ; others
keep the ears still and wag the tip of the tail.
Others prick up the ears[1] and run frowning along 5
the track, dropping their tails and putting them between their legs. Many do none of these things, but
rush about madly round the track, and when they
happen upon it, stupidly trample out the traces, barking all the time. Others again, continually circling 6
and straying, get ahead of the line when clean off it
and pass the hare, and every time they run against
the line, begin guessing, and if they catch sight of
the hare, tremble and never go for her until they
see her stir. Hounds that run forward and frequently 7
examine the discoveries of the others when they are
casting about and pursuing have no confidence in
themselves; while those that will not let their
cleverer mates go forward, but fuss and keep them
back, are confident to a fault. Others will drive
ahead, eagerly following false lines and getting
wildly excited over anything that turns up, well know-

---

[1] The Greek hound had short ears (cf. c. iv. 1) like a fox-
terrier.

---

² πρόσθεν S. with M.

ἑαυταῖς ὅτι ἐξαπατῶσιν· αἱ δ' οὐκ εἰδυῖαι τὸ αὐτὸ
ποιοῦσι ταύταις· φαῦλαι δὲ αἱ οὐκ ἀπαλλατ-
τόμεναι ἐκ τῶν τριμμῶν τὰ ὀρθὰ οὐ γιγνώσκουσαι.

8 ὅσαι δὲ τῶν κυνῶν τὰ ἴχνη τὰ μὲν εὐναῖα
ἀγνοοῦσι, τὰ δὲ δρομαῖα ταχὺ διατρέχουσιν, οὐκ
εἰσὶ γνήσιαι· διώκουσι δὲ αἱ μὲν ἀρχόμεναι
σφόδρα, διὰ δὲ μαλακίαν ἀνιᾶσιν, αἱ δὲ ὑπο-
θέουσιν, εἶτα ἁμαρτάνουσιν, ἕτεραι δὲ ἀνοήτως
ἐμπίπτουσαι εἰς τὰς ὁδοὺς ἁμαρτάνουσι τὸ
9 ἀνήκουστον πολὺ ἔχουσαι. πολλαὶ δὲ τὰ διώγ-
ματα ἀφιεῖσαι ἐπανέρχονται διὰ τὸ μισόθηρον,
πολλαὶ δὲ διὰ τὸ φιλάνθρωπον· αἱ δ' ἐκ τῶν
ἰχνῶν κεκλαγγυῖαι ἐξαπατᾶν πειρῶνται ἀληθῆ
10 τὰ ψευδῆ ποιούμεναι. εἰσὶ δ' αἱ τοῦτο μὲν οὐ
ποιοῦσι, μεταξὺ δὲ θέουσαι ἄν ποθεν ἀκούσωσι
κραυγῆς, καταλείπουσαι τὰ αὑτῶν ἔργα ἀπρο-
νοήτως ἐπὶ τοῦτο φέρονται· μεταθέουσι γὰρ αἱ
μὲν ἀσαφῶς, αἱ δὲ πολὺ ὑπολαμβάνουσιν,
δοξάζουσαι δὲ ἑτέρως·[1] αἱ δὲ πεπλασμένως,
φθονερῶς δὲ ἄλλαι ἐκκυνοῦσι παρὰ τὸ ἴχνος διὰ
τέλους συμπεριφερόμεναι.

11 Τὰ μὲν οὖν πλεῖστα τούτων φύσει ἔχουσι,[2] τὰ
δὲ ἡγμέναι ἀνεπιστημόνως δύσχρηστοί εἰσιν· αἱ
τοιαῦται μὲν οὖν κύνες ἀποτρέψειαν ἂν τοὺς
ἐπιθυμοῦντας κυνηγεσίων. οἵας δὲ δεῖ εἶναι τοῦ
αὐτοῦ γένους τά τε εἴδη καὶ τὰ ἄλλα, φράσω.

IV. Πρῶτον μὲν οὖν χρὴ εἶναι μεγάλας, εἶτα
ἐχούσας τὰς κεφαλὰς ἐλαφράς, σιμάς, ἀρθρώδεις,
ἰνώδη τὰ κάτωθεν τῶν μετώπων, ὄμματα μετέωρα,
μέλανα, λαμπρά, μέτωπα μεγάλα καὶ πλατέα,

---

[1] ἑτέρως A : ἕτερα S. with BM.
[2] ἔχουσαι S. with M.

ing that they are playing the fool; others will do the same thing in ignorance. Those that stick to game paths and don't recognise the true line are poor tools. A hound that ignores the trail[1] and races over the 8 track of the hare on the run is ill-bred. Some, again, will pursue hotly at first, and then slack off from want of pluck; others will cut in ahead and then get astray; while others foolishly dash into roads and go astray, deaf to all recall. Many abandon the 9 pursuit and go back through their hatred of game, and many through their love of man. Others try to mislead by baying on the track, representing false lines as true ones. Some, though free from this fault, 10 leave their own work when they hear a shout from another quarter while they are running, and make for it recklessly. When pursuing some are dubious, others are full of assumptions but their notions are wrong. Then there are the skirters, some of whom merely pretend to hunt, while others out of jealousy perpetually scamper about together beside the line.

Now most of these faults are natural defects, but 11 some by which hounds are spoilt are due to unintelligent training. Anyhow such hounds may well put a keen hunter off the sport. What hounds of the same breed[2] ought to look like and what they should be in other respects I will now explain.

IV. First, then, they should be big. Next, the head should be light, flat[3] and muscular; the lower parts of the forehead sinewy; the eyes prominent, black and sparkling; the forehead broad, with a

---

[1] "The trail of the hare is the path she takes in going to her seat."—Beckford.
[2] The author's ideal harrier is clearly the Castorian.
[3] In profile.

τὰς διακρίσεις βαθείας, ὦτα μικρά,[1] λεπτά,
ψιλὰ ὄπισθεν, τραχήλους μακρούς, ὑγρούς, περιφερεῖς, στήθη πλατέα, μὴ ἄσαρκα, ἀπὸ τῶν
ὤμων τὰς ὠμοπλάτας διεστώσας μικρόν, σκέλη
τὰ πρόσθια μικρά, ὀρθά, στρογγύλα, στιφρά,
τοὺς ἀγκῶνας ὀρθούς, πλευρὰς μὴ ἐπὶ γῆν[2]
βαθείας, ἀλλ᾿ εἰς τὸ πλάγιον παρηκούσας, ὀσφῦς
σαρκώδεις, τὰ μεγέθη μεταξὺ μακρῶν καὶ βρα-
χέων, μητε ὑγρὰς λίαν μήτε σκληράς, λαγόνας
μεταξὺ μεγάλων καὶ μικρῶν, ἰσχία στρογγύλα,
ὄπισθεν σαρκώδη, ἄνωθεν δὲ μὴ συνδεδεμένα,
ἔνδοθεν δὲ προσεσταλμένα, τὰ κάτωθεν τῶν
κενεώνων λαγαρὰ καὶ αὐτοὺς τοὺς κενεῶνας, οὐρὰς
μακράς, ὀρθάς, λιγυράς, μηριαίας σκληράς, ὑποκώλια μακρά, περιφερῆ, εὐπαγῆ, σκέλη πολὺ
μείζω τὰ ὄπισθεν τῶν ἔμπροσθεν καὶ ἐπίρρικνα,
2 πόδας περιφερεῖς. καὶ ἐὰν ὦσι τοιαῦται αἱ
κύνες, ἔσονται ἰσχυραὶ τὰ εἴδη, ἐλαφραί, σύμ-
μετροι, ποδώκεις καὶ ἀπὸ τῶν προσώπων φαιδραὶ
καὶ εὔστομοι.
3   Ἰχνευέτωσαν δ᾿ ἐκ τῶν τριμμῶν ταχὺ ἀπαλλατ-
τόμεναι, τιθεῖσαι τὰς κεφαλὰς ἐπὶ γῆν λεχρίας,
ἐμμειδιῶσαι μὲν πρὸς τὰ ἴχνη, ἐπικαταβάλλουσαι
δὲ τὰ ὦτα, καὶ [3] τὰ μὲν ὄμματα πυκνὰ διακινοῦ-
σαι, ταῖς δὲ οὐραῖς διασαίνουσαι, κύκλους πολλοὺς
πρὸς τὰς εὐνὰς προΐτωσαν ὁμοῦ διὰ τοῦ ἴχνους
4 ἅπασαι. ὅταν δὲ περὶ αὐτὸν ὦσι τὸν λαγῶ,

---

[1] μακρά S., a wrong conjecture.
[2] ἐπὶ γῆν AB   ἐπίπαν S. with M.
[3] καὶ A : S. omits with the rest.

---

[1] *i.e.* not bent inwards or outwards.

deep dividing line; the ears small and thin with
little hair behind; the neck long, loose and round;
the chest broad and fairly fleshy; the shoulder-blades
slightly outstanding from the shoulders; the fore-
legs short, straight, round and firm; the elbows
straight [1]; the ribs not low down on the ground,[2] but
sloping in an oblique line; the loins fleshy, of
medium length, and neither too loose nor too hard;
the flanks of medium size; the hips round and fleshy
at the back, not close at the top, and smooth on the
inside [3]; the under part of the belly and the belly itself
slim; the tail long, straight and thin; the thighs hard;
the shanks [4] long, round and solid; the hind-legs much
longer than the fore-legs and slightly bent; the
feet round. Hounds like these will be strong in 2
appearance, agile, well-proportioned, and speedy;
and they will have a jaunty expression and a good
mouth.

When tracking they should get out of the 3
game paths quickly, hold their heads well down and
aslant, smiling when they find the scent and lower-
ing their ears; then they should all go forward together along the trail towards the form circling
frequently,[5] with eyes continually on the move and
tails wagging. As soon as they are close on the hare, 4

---

[2] So Pollux read, for he says μὴ πρὸς τὴν γῆν βαθυνομένας.
The sense is then that the ribs are not to be low on the
ground when the hound is couchant, but well tucked up
behind. ἐπίπαν βαθείας, "deep throughout," would apply to
the depth from wall to wall, and the meaning would be that
the ribs are to contract towards the flanks.

[3] i.e. without folds in the coat towards the loins.

[4] From the elbows to the feet.

[5] A particle to govern κύκλους πολλοὺς has dropped out
of the text.

XENOPHON

δῆλον ποιείτωσαν τῷ κυνηγέτῃ θᾶττον φοιτῶσαι,
μᾶλλον γνωρίζουσαι ἀπὸ τοῦ θυμοῦ, ἀπὸ τῆς
κεφαλῆς, ἀπὸ τῶν ὀμμάτων, ἀπὸ τῆς μεταλ-
λάξεως τῶν σχημάτων καὶ ἀπὸ τῶν ἀναβλεμ-
μάτων καὶ ἐμβλεμμάτων εἰς τὴν ὕλην καὶ ἀνα-
στρεμμάτων¹ τῶν ἐπὶ τὰς καθέδρας τοῦ λαγῶ καὶ
ἀπὸ τῶν εἰς τὸ πρόσθεν καὶ ὄπισθεν καὶ εἰς τὸ
πλάγιον διαρριμμάτων καὶ ἀπὸ τοῦ ἀληθῶς ἤδη
αἰωρεῖσθαι τὴν ψυχὴν καὶ ὑπερφαίρειν, ὅτι τοῦ
λαγῶ ἐγγύς εἰσι.

5 Διωκέτωσαν δὲ ἐρρωμένως καὶ μὴ ἐπανιεῖσαι
σὺν πολλῇ κλαγγῇ καὶ ὑλαγμῷ, συνεκπερῶσαι
μετὰ τοῦ λαγῶ πάντη· μεταθείτωσαν δὲ ταχὺ
καὶ λαμπρῶς, πυκνὰ μεταφερόμεναι καὶ ἐπανακλαγγάνουσαι δικαίως· πρὸς δὲ τὸν κυνηγέτην μὴ
ἐπανίτωσαν λιποῦσαι τὰ ἴχνη.

6 Μετὰ δὲ τοῦ εἴδους καὶ τοῦ ἔργου τούτου εὔψυχοι
ἔστωσαν καὶ εὔρινες καὶ εὔποδες² καὶ εὔτριχες.
εὔψυχοι μὲν οὖν ἔσονται, ἐὰν μὴ λίπωσι τὰ
κυνηγέσια, ὅταν ᾖ πνίγη· εὔρινες δέ, ἐὰν τοῦ λαγῶ
ὀσφραίνωνται ἐν τόποις ψιλοῖς, ξηροῖς, προσ-
ηλίοις τοῦ ἄστρου ἐπιόντος· εὔποδες δέ, ἐὰν τῇ
αὐτῇ ὥρᾳ μὴ καταρρηγνύωνται αὐτῶν οἱ πόδες
τὰ ὄρη θεουσῶν· εὔτριχες δέ, ἐὰν ἔχωσι λεπτὴν
7 καὶ πυκνὴν καὶ μαλακὴν τὴν τρίχα. τὰ δὲ
χρώματα οὐ χρὴ εἶναι τῶν κυνῶν οὔτε πυρρὰ
οὔτε μέλανα οὔτε λευκὰ παντελῶς· ἔστι γὰρ οὐ
γενναῖον τοῦτο, ἀλλὰ τὸ³ ἁπλοῦν καὶ θηριῶδες.
8 αἱ μὲν οὖν πυρραὶ ἔχουσαι ἔστωσαν λευκὴν τρίχα
ἐπανθοῦσαν περὶ τὰ πρόσωπα καὶ αἱ μέλαιναι, αἱ

¹ εἰς . . ἀναστρεμμάτων is omitted by S.

384

they should let the huntsman know, quickening the pace and showing more emphatic signs by their excitement, movements of the head and eyes, changes of attitude, by looking up and looking into the covert and returning again and again to the hare's form, by leaps forward, backward and to the side, displays of unaffected agitation and overpowering delight at being near the hare.

They should pursue with unremitting vigour, 5 giving tongue and barking freely, dogging the hare's steps wherever she goes. They should be fast and brilliant in the chase, frequently casting about and giving tongue in the right fashion; and they should not leave the track and go back to the huntsman.

Along with this appearance and behaviour they 6 should have pluck, keen noses, sound feet and good coats. They will be plucky if they don't leave the hunting-ground when the heat is oppressive; keen-nosed if they smell the hare on bare, parched and sunny ground in the dog days[1]; sound in the feet if at the same season their feet are not torn to bits during a run in the mountains; they will have a good coat if the hair is fine, thick and soft. The colour of the hounds should not be entirely 7 tawny, black or white; for this is not a sign of good breeding: on the contrary, unbroken colour indicates a wild strain. So the tawny and the black 8 hounds should show a patch of white about the

[1] The older commentators are probably right in understanding the allusion to be to the Dog-star, not to the Sun.

---

[2] εὔρινες καὶ εὔποδες A: εὔποδες καὶ εὔρινες S. with the rest.

[3] ἀλλὰ τὸ Radermacher: ἀλλ' S. with the MSS.

δὲ λευκαὶ πυρράν· ἐπὶ δὲ ταῖς μηριαίαις ἄκραις
τρίχας ὀρθάς, βαθείας, καὶ ἐπὶ ταῖς ὀσφύσι καὶ
ταῖς οὐραῖς κάτω, ἄνωθεν δὲ μετρίας.

9 Ἄγειν δὲ ἄμεινον τὰς κύνας εἰς τὰ ὄρη πολλάκις, τὰ δὲ ἔργα ἧττον· τὰ μὲν γὰρ ὄρη οἷόν τ᾽
ἐστὶ καὶ ἰχνεύειν καὶ μεταθεῖν καθαρῶς, τὰ δὲ
10 ἔργα οὐδέτερα διὰ τοὺς τριμμούς. ἔστι δὲ καὶ
ἄνευ τοῦ εὑρίσκειν τὸν λαγῶ ἀγαθὸν ἄγειν τὰς
κύνας εἰς τὰ τραχέα· καὶ γὰρ εὔποδες γίγνονται
καὶ τὰ σώματα διαπονοῦσαι ἐν τόποις τοιούτοις
11 ὠφελοῦνται. ἀγέσθωσαν δὲ θέρους μὲν μέχρι
μεσημβρίας, χειμῶνος δὲ δι᾽ ἡμέρας, μετοπώρου
δ᾽ ἔξω μεσημβρίας, ἐντὸς δ᾽ ἑσπέρας τὸ ἔαρ. ταῦτα
γὰρ μέτρια.

V. Τὰ δὲ ἴχνη τοῦ λαγῶ τοῦ μὲν χειμῶνος μακρά
ἐστι διὰ τὸ μῆκος τῶν νυκτῶν, τοῦ δὲ θέρους
βραχέα διὰ τὸ ἐναντίον. χειμῶνος μὲν οὖν πρωὶ
οὐκ ὄζει αὐτῶν, ὅταν πάχνη ᾖ ἢ παγετός· ἡ μὲν
γὰρ πάχνη τῇ αὑτῆς ἰσχύϊ ἀντισπάσασα τὸ θερ-
2 μὸν ἔχει ἐν αὑτῇ, ὁ δὲ παγετὸς ἐπιπήξας. καὶ αἱ
κύνες μαλκιῶσαι τὰς ῥῖνας οὐ δύνανται αἰσθάνεσθαι, ὅταν ᾖ τοιαῦτα, πρὶν ἂν ὁ ἥλιος διαλύσῃ
αὐτὰ ἢ προϊοῦσα ἡ ἡμέρα· τότε δὲ καὶ αἱ
κύνες ὀσφραίνονται καὶ αὐτὰ ἐπαναφερόμενα ὄζει.
3 ἀφανίζει δὲ καὶ ἡ πολλὴ δρόσος καταφέρουσα
αὐτά, καὶ οἱ ὄμβροι οἱ γιγνόμενοι διὰ χρόνου
ὀσμὰς ἄγοντες τῆς γῆς¹ ποιοῦσι δύσοσμον, ἕως
ἂν ψυχθῇ· χείρω δὲ καὶ τὰ νότια ποιεῖ· ὑγραί-
νοντα γὰρ διαχεῖ· τὰ δὲ βόρεια, ἐὰν ᾖ ἄλυτα,

---

¹ ἄγειν τῆς γῆς has no parallel in Greek prose : perhaps ἐκ
has fallen out or τὴν γῆν should be read.

face, and the white hounds a tawny patch. At the top of the thighs the hair should be straight and thick, and on the loins and at the lower end of the tail, but it should be moderately thick higher up.

It is advisable to take the hounds to the mountains 9 often, but less frequently to cultivated land. For in the mountains it is possible to track and follow a hare without hindrance, whereas it is impossible to do either in cultivated land owing to the game paths. It is also well to take the hounds out into rough 10 ground, whether they find a hare or not; for they get sound in the feet, and hard work in such country is good for their bodies. In summer they should be 11 out till midday, in winter at any hour of the day, in autumn at any time except midday, and before evening during the spring; for at these times the temperature is mild.

V. The scent of the hare lies long in winter owing to the length of the nights, and for a short time in summer for the opposite reason. In the winter, however, there is no scent in the early morning whenever there is a white frost or the earth is frozen hard. For both white and black frost hold heat; since the one draws it out by its own strength, and the other congeals it. The hounds' noses, too, 2 are numbed by the cold, and they cannot smell when the tracks are in such a state until the tracks thaw in the sun or as day advances. Then the dogs can smell and the scent revives. A heavy dew, 3 again, obliterates scent by carrying it downwards; and storms, occurring after a long interval, draw smells from the ground [1] and make the earth bad for scent until it dries. South winds spoil scent, because the moisture scatters it, but north winds concentrate

XENOPHON

4 συνίστησι καὶ σώζει. οἱ δὲ ὑετοὶ κατακλύζουσι
καὶ αἱ ψακάδες, καὶ ἡ σελήνη ἀμαυροῖ τῷ θερμῷ,
μάλιστα δὲ ὅταν ᾖ πανσέληνος· καὶ μανότατα
τότε· χαίροντες γὰρ τῷ φέγγει ἐπαναρριπτοῦντες
μακρὰ διαίρουσιν[1] ἀντιπαίζοντες· ταραχώδη δέ,
5 ὅταν ἀλώπεκες προδιεξέλθωσι, γίγνεται. τὸ δὲ
ἔαρ κεκραμένον τῇ ὥρᾳ καλῶς παρέχει τὰ ἴχνη
λαμπρά, πλὴν εἴ τι ἡ γῆ ἐξανθοῦσα βλάπτει τὰς
κύνας, εἰς τὸ αὐτὸ συμμιγνύουσα τῶν ἀνθῶν τὰς
ὀσμάς. λεπτὰ δὲ καὶ ἀσαφῆ τοῦ θέρους· διά-
πυρος γὰρ οὖσα ἡ γῆ ἀφανίζει τὸ θερμόν, ὃ
ἔχουσιν· ἔστι γὰρ λεπτόν· καὶ αἱ κύνες ἧττον
ὀσφραίνονται τότε διὰ τὸ ἐκλελύσθαι τὰ σώματα.
τοῦ δὲ μετοπώρου καθαρά· ὅσα γὰρ ἡ γῆ φέρει,
τὰ μὲν ἥμερα συγκεκόμισται, τὰ δὲ ἄγρια γήρᾳ
διαλέλυται· ὥστε οὐ παραλυποῦσι τῶν καρπῶν
6 αἱ ὀσμαὶ εἰς ταὐτὰ φερόμεναι. ἔστι δὲ τοῦ χειμῶνος καὶ τοῦ θέρους καὶ τοῦ μετοπώρου τὰ ἴχνη
ὀρθὰ ἐπὶ τὸ πολύ, τοῦ δ' ἦρος συμπεπλεγμένα·
τὸ γὰρ θηρίον συνδυάζεται μὲν ἀεί, μάλιστα δὲ
ταύτην τὴν ὥραν· ὥστε διὰ τοῦτο ἐξ ἀνάγκης μετ'
ἀλλήλων πλανώμενοι τοιαῦτα ποιοῦσιν.
7 Ὄζει δὲ τῶν ἰχνῶν ἐπὶ πλείω χρόνον τῶν
εὐναίων ἢ τῶν δρομαίων· τὰ μὲν γὰρ εὐναῖα ὁ
λαγὼς πορεύεται ἐφιστάμενος, τὰ δὲ δρομαῖα
ταχύ· ἡ γῆ οὖν τῶν μὲν πυκνοῦται, τῶν δὲ οὐ
πίμπλαται. ἐν δὲ τοῖς ὑλώδεσι μᾶλλον ἢ ἐν
τοῖς ψιλοῖς ὄζει· διατρέχων γὰρ καὶ ἀνακαθίζων
ἅπτεται πολλῶν.

---

[1] διαίρουσιν Radermacher : διαιροῦσιν S. with the MSS.

[1] Or "deadens the heat" if we read τὸ θερμόν with Gesner.
But the Greeks did attribute heat to the moon.

and preserve it, if it has not been previously dissolved. Heavy showers drown it, and so does light rain, and 4 the moon deadens it by its warmth,[1] especially when at the full. Scent is most irregular at that time, for the hares, enjoying the light, fling themselves high in the air and jump a long way, frolicking with one another; and it becomes confused when foxes have crossed it. Spring with its genial temperature yields 5 a clear scent, except where the ground is studded with flowers and hampers the hounds by mingling the odours of the flowers with it. In summer it is thin and faint, for the ground, being baked, obliterates what warmth it possesses, which is thin; and the hounds' noses are not so good at that season, because their bodies are relaxed. In the autumn it is unimpeded; for the cultivated crops have been harvested and the weeds have withered, so that the odours of the herbage do not cause trouble by mingling with it. In winter and summer and autumn the 6 scent lies straight in the main. In spring it is complicated; for though the animal couples at all times, it does so especially at this season;[2] so instinct prompts them to roam about together, and this is the result they produce.

The scent left by the hare in going to her form 7 lasts longer than the scent of a running hare. For on the way to the form the hare keeps stopping, whereas when on the run she goes fast; consequently the ground is packed with it in the one case, but in the other is not filled with it. In coverts it is stronger than in open ground, because she touches many objects while running about and sitting up.

[1] The " March hare."

XENOPHON

8 Κατακλίνονται δ' εἰς ἃ ἡ γῆ φύει ἢ ἔχει ἐφ'
ἑαυτῆς ὑπὸ παντί, ἐπ' αὐτῶν, ἐν αὐτοῖς, παρ'
αὐτά, ἄποθεν πολύ, μικρόν, μεταξὺ τούτων· ὁτὲ
δὲ καὶ ἐν τῇ θαλάττῃ διαρριπτῶν ἐπὶ τὸ δυνατὸν
καὶ ἐν ὕδατι, ἐάν τι ᾖ ὑπερέχον ἢ ἐμπεφυκὸς ἐν
9 τούτῳ. ὁ μὲν οὖν¹ εὐναῖος ποιούμενος εὐνὴν ἐπὶ
τὸ πολὺ ὅταν μὲν ᾖ ψύχη, ἐν εὐδιεινοῖς, ὅταν δὲ
καύματα, ἐν παλισκίοις, τὸ δὲ ἔαρ καὶ τὸ φθινό-
πωρον ἐν προσηλίοις· οἱ δὲ δρομαῖοι οὐχ οὕτω
διὰ τὸ ὑπὸ τῶν κυνῶν ἔκπληκτοι² γίγνεσθαι.
10 κατακλίνεται δὲ ὑποθεὶς τὰ ὑποκώλια ὑπὸ τὰς
λαγόνας, τὰ δὲ πρόσθεν σκέλη τὰ πλεῖστα
συνθεὶς καὶ ἐκτείνας, ἐπ' ἄκρους δὲ τοὺς πόδας
τὴν γένυν καταθείς, τὰ δὲ ὦτα ἐπιπετάσας ἐπὶ
τὰς ὠμοπλάτας, εἶτα δὲ ὑποστέγει τὰ ὑγρά· ἔχει
δὲ καὶ τὴν τρίχα στεγανήν· πυκνὴ γὰρ καὶ
11 μαλακή. καὶ ὅταν μὲν ἐγρηγόρῃ, καταμύει τὰ
βλέφαρα, ὅταν δὲ καθεύδῃ, τὰ μὲν βλέφαρα
ἀναπέπταται ἀκίνητα, οἱ δὲ ὀφθαλμοὶ ἀτρέμας
ἔχουσι· τοὺς δὲ μυκτῆρας, ὅταν μὲν εὕδῃ, κινεῖ
12 πυκνά, ὅταν δὲ μή, ἧττον. ὅταν δὲ ἡ γῆ βρύῃ,
μᾶλλον τὰ ἔργα ἢ τὰ ὄρη ἔχουσιν. ὑπομένει δὲ
πανταχοῦ ἰχνευόμενος, ἐὰν μήτι περίφοβος τῆς
νυκτὸς γένηται· παθὼν δὲ τοῦτο ὑποκινεῖ.
13 Πολύγονον δ' ἐστὶν οὕτως, ὥστε τὰ μὲν τέτοκε,

¹ οὖν should probably be omitted.
² ἔμπληκτοι S., after Schneider.

---

¹ See "The Hare," *Fur and Feather* Series, p. 38 f.
² The fluctuation between plural and singular is in the
Greek.

They find a resting-place where there is anything 8 growing or lying on the ground, underneath anything, on the top of the objects, inside, alongside, well away or quite near or fairly near; occasionally even in the sea[1] by springing on to anything she[2] can reach, or in fresh water, if there is anything sticking out or growing in it, the hare,[3] when going to her 9 form generally choosing a sheltered place for it in cold weather and a cool one in hot, but in spring and autumn a place exposed to the sun; but hares on the run do not do that, because they are scared by the hounds. When she sits, she puts the hind-legs under the 10 flanks, and most commonly keeps the fore-legs close together and extended, resting the chin on the ends of the feet, and spreading the ears over the shoulder-blades, so that[4] she covers the soft parts. The hair too, being thick and soft, serves as a protection. When 11 awake she blinks her eyelids; but when she is asleep the eyelids are wide open and motionless, and the eyes still. She moves her nostrils continually when sleeping, but less frequently when awake. When the ground is bursting with vegetation they 12 frequent the fields rather than the mountains. Wherever she may be she remains there when tracked, except when she is suddenly alarmed at night; in which case she moves off.

The animal is so prolific that at the same time she is 13

The distinction is not, as often supposed, between hares with different *habits* ("squatters," εὐναῖοι, and "roamers," δρομαῖοι—a non-existent distinction), but merely between the behaviour of all hares in different circumstances. The unusual, but not unexampled, position of the article—δ and οἱ—has misled interpreters. Blane saw the true meaning.

[4] I do not think that εἶτα δὲ can mean this, and suspect that εἶτα is wrong.

τὰ δὲ τίκτει, τὰ δὲ κυεῖ. τῶν δὲ μικρῶν λαγίων
ὄζει μᾶλλον ἢ τῶν μεγάλων· ἔτι γὰρ ὑγρομελῆ
14 ὄντα ἐπισύρεται ὅλα ἐπὶ τῆς γῆς. τὰ μὲν οὖν
λίαν νεογνὰ οἱ φιλοκυνηγέται ἀφιᾶσι τῇ θεῷ· οἱ
δὲ ἤδη ἔτειοι τάχιστα θέουσι τὸν πρῶτον δρόμον,
τοὺς δ᾽ ἄλλους οὐκ ἔτι· εἰσὶ γὰρ ἐλαφροί, ἀδύνατοι δέ.

15 Λαμβάνειν δὲ τοῦ λαγῶ τὰ ἴχνη ὑπάγοντα
τὰς κύνας ἐκ τῶν ἔργων ἄνωθεν· ὅσοι δὲ μὴ
ἔρχονται αὐτῶν εἰς τὰ ἐργάσιμα, τοὺς λειμῶνας,
τὰς νάπας, τὰ ῥεῖθρα, τοὺς λίθους, τὰ ὑλώδη·
καὶ ἐὰν ὑποκινῇ, μὴ ἀναβοᾶν, ἵνα μὴ αἱ κύνες
ἔκφρονες γιγνόμεναι χαλεπῶς τὰ ἴχνη γνωρίζωσιν.
16 εὑρισκόμενοι δὲ ὑπ᾽ αὐτῶν καὶ διωκόμενοι ἔστιν
ὅτε διαβαίνουσι τὰ ῥεύματα, καὶ ὑποκάμπτουσι
καὶ καταδύονται εἰς φάραγγας καὶ εἰς εἰλυούς·
πεφόβηνται γὰρ οὐ μόνον τὰς κύνας ἀλλὰ καὶ
τοὺς ἀετούς· ὑπερβάλλοντες γὰρ τὰ σιμὰ καὶ τὰ
ψιλὰ ἀναρπάζονται, ἕως ἂν ὦσιν ἔτειοι· τοὺς δὲ
μείζους ἐπιτρέχουσαι αἱ κύνες ἀναιροῦνται.[1]
17 Ποδωκέστατοι μὲν οὖν εἰσιν οἱ ὄρειοι, οἱ πεδινοὶ
δὲ ἧττον, βραδύτατοι δὲ οἱ ἕλειοι· οἱ δ᾽ ἐπὶ
πάντας τοὺς τόπους πλανῆται χαλεποὶ πρὸς
τοὺς δρόμους· τὰ γὰρ σύντομα ἴσασι· θέουσι γὰρ
μάλιστα μὲν τὰ ἀνάντη ἢ τὰ ὁμαλά, τὰ δὲ
ἀνώμαλα[2] ἀνομοίως, τὰ δὲ κατάντη ἥκιστα.
18 διωκόμενοι δέ εἰσι κατάδηλοι μάλιστα μὲν διὰ

---

[1] ἀναιροῦνται Richards : ἀφαιροῦνται S. with the MSS.
[2] ἀνώμαλα A : ἀνόμοια S. with the rest.

---

[1] Artemis.

rearing one litter, she produces another and she is pregnant. The scent of the little leverets is stronger than that of the big ones; for while their limbs are still soft they drag the whole body on the ground. Sports- 14 men, however, leave the very young ones to the goddess.[1] Yearlings go very fast in the first run, but then flag, being agile, but weak.

Find the hare's track by beginning with the 15 hounds in the cultivated lands and gradually working downwards.[2] To track those that do not come into cultivated land, search[3] the meadows, valleys, streams, stones and woody places. If she moves off, don't shout, or the hounds may get wild with excitement and fail to recognise the tracks. Hares when 16 found by hounds and pursued sometimes cross brooks and double back and slip into gullies or holes. The fact is they are terrified not only of the hounds, but of eagles as well; for they are apt to be snatched up while crossing hillocks and bare ground until[4] they are yearlings, and the bigger ones are run down and caught by the hounds.

The swiftest are those that frequent mountains; 17 those of the plain are not so speedy; and those of the marshes are the slowest. Those that roam over any sort of country are difficult to chase, since they know the short cuts. They run mostly uphill[5] or on the level, less frequently in uneven ground, and very seldom downhill. When being pursued they are 18

[2] The cultivated land is on the lower slopes of the mountains.

[3] There is evidently a gap in the Greek before τοὺς λειμῶνας, which has nothing to govern it.

[4] Not "so long as"; cf. § 14.

[5] *i.e.* when pursued.

γῆς κεκινημένης, ἐὰν ἔχωσιν ἔνιον ἐρύθημα, καὶ
διὰ καλάμης διὰ τὴν ἀνταύγειαν· κατάδηλοι δὲ
καὶ ἐν τοῖς τριμμοῖς καὶ ἐν ταῖς ὁδοῖς, ἐὰν ὦσιν
ἰσόπεδοι· τὸ γὰρ φανὸν τὸ ἐν αὐτοῖς ἐνὸν ἀντι-
λάμπει· ἄδηλοι δέ, ὅταν τοὺς λίθους, τὰ ὄρη, τὰ
φέλλια, τὰ δασέα ἀποχωρῶσι, διὰ τὴν ὁμόχροιαν.

19 προλαμβάνοντες δὲ τὰς κύνας ἐφίστανται καὶ
ἀνακαθίζοντες ἐπαίρουσιν αὐτοὺς καὶ ἐπακού-
ουσιν, εἴ που πλησίον κλαγγὴ ἢ ψόφος τῶν κυνῶν·

20 καὶ ὅθεν ἂν ἀκούσωσιν, ἀποτρέπονται. ὁτὲ δὲ
καὶ οὐκ ἀκούσαντες, ἀλλὰ δόξαντες ἢ πεισθέντες
ὑφ' αὑτῶν παρὰ τὰ αὐτά, διὰ τῶν αὐτῶν, ἐπαλ-
λάττοντες ἅλματα, ἐμποιοῦντες ἴχνεσιν ἴχνη,

21 ἀποχωροῦσι. καί εἰσι μακροδρομώτατοι μὲν οἱ
ἐκ τῶν ψιλῶν εὑρισκόμενοι διὰ τὸ καταφανές,
βραχυδρομώτατοι δὲ οἱ ἐκ τῶν δασέων· ἐμποδὼν
γὰρ τὸ σκοτεινόν.

22 Δύο δὲ καὶ τὰ γένη ἐστὶν αὐτῶν· οἱ μὲν γὰρ
μεγάλοι τὸ χρῶμα [1] ἐπίπερκνοι καὶ τὸ λευκὸν τὸ
ἐν τῷ μετώπῳ μέγα ἔχουσιν, οἱ δ' ἐλάττους

23 ἐπίξανθοι, μικρὸν τὸ λευκὸν ἔχοντες. τὴν δὲ
οὐρὰν οἱ μὲν κύκλῳ περιποίκιλον, οἱ δὲ παρά-
σειρον, καὶ τὰ ὄμματα οἱ μὲν ὑποχάροποι, οἱ δ'
ὑπόγλαυκοι· καὶ τὰ μέλανα τὰ περὶ τὰ ὦτα

24 ἄκρα [2] οἱ μὲν ἐπὶ πολύ, οἱ δὲ ἐπὶ μικρόν. ἔχουσι
δὲ αὐτῶν αἱ πολλαὶ τῶν νήσων τοὺς ἐλάττους,
αἵ τ' ἔρημοι καὶ οἰκούμεναι· τὸ δὲ πλῆθος πλείους

---

[1] τὸ χρῶμα AB and Pollux : S. omits with M.
[2] ἄκρα ὦτα S.

most conspicuous across ground that has been broken
up, if they have some red in their coats, or across
stubble, owing to the shadow they cast. They are
also conspicuous in game paths and on roads if these
are level, since the bright colour of their coats shows
up in the light. But when their line of retreat is
amongst stones, in the mountains, over rocky or
thickly wooded ground they cannot be seen owing to
the similarity of colouring. When they are well 19
ahead of the hounds, they will stop, and sitting up
will raise themselves and listen for the baying or the
footfall of the hounds anywhere near; and should
they hear the sound of them from any quarter, they
make off. Occasionally, even when they hear 20
no sound, some fancy or conviction prompts them
to jump hither and thither past and through the
same objects, mixing the tracks as they retreat.
The longest runners are those that are found on 21
bare land, because they are exposed to view; the
shortest, those found in thick covers, since the
darkness hinders their flight.

There are two species of hare.[1] The large are dark 22
brown, and the white patch on the forehead is large;
the smaller are chestnut, with a small white patch.
The larger have spots round the scut, the smaller at 23
the side of it. The eyes in the large species are
blue, in the small grey. The black at the tip of the
ear is broad in the one species, narrow in the other.
The smaller are found in most of the islands, both 24
desert and inhabited. They are more plentiful

[1] The common hare and a smaller variety of the same;
which is said to be "more brindled in colour" than the
larger kind. See "The Hare" in *Fur and Feather* Series,
p. 5.

XENOPHON

ἐν αὐταῖς ἢ ἐν ταῖς ἠπείροις· οὐ γάρ εἰσιν οὔτ'
ἀλώπεκες ἐν ταῖς πολλαῖς αὐτῶν, αἵτινες καὶ
αὐτοὺς καὶ τὰ τέκνα ἐπιοῦσαι ἀναιροῦνται, οὔτε
ἀετοί· τὰ μεγάλα γὰρ ὄρη ἔχουσι μᾶλλον ἢ τὰ
μικρά· ἐλάττω δ' ἐπὶ τὸ πολὺ τὰ ἐν ταῖς νήσοις.
25 κυνηγέται δὲ εἰς μὲν τὰς ἐρήμους ὀλιγάκις ἀφικ-
νοῦνται, ἐν δὲ ταῖς οἰκουμέναις ὀλίγοι εἰσὶ[1] καὶ
οὐ φιλόθηροι οἱ πολλοί· εἰς δὲ τὰς ἱερὰς τῶν
νήσων οὐδὲ διαβιβάζειν οἷόν τε κύνας. ὅταν οὖν
τῶν τε ὑπαρχόντων ὀλίγους ἐκθηρῶνται καὶ τῶν
ἐπιγιγνομένων, ἀνάγκη ἀφθόνους εἶναι.

26 Βλέπει δὲ οὐκ ὀξὺ διὰ πολλά· τά τε γὰρ
ὄμματα ἔχει ἔξω καὶ τὰ βλέφαρα ἐλλείποντα καὶ
οὐκ ἔχοντα προβολὴν ταῖς αὐγαῖς· ἡ ὄψις οὖν
27 διὰ ταῦτα ἀμαυρά, ἐσκεδασμένη. ἅμα δὲ τούτοις καὶ ἐν ὕπνῳ ὂν τὰ πολλὰ τὸ θηρίον οὐκ
ὠφελεῖται πρὸς τὸ ὁρᾶν. καὶ ἡ ποδώκεια πρὸς
τὸ ἀμβλυωπεῖν αὐτῷ πολὺ συμβάλλεται· ταχὺ
γὰρ ἑκάστου παραφέρει τὴν ὄψιν, πρὶν νοῆσαι
28 ὅ τι ἐστί. καὶ οἱ φόβοι τῶν κυνῶν, ὅταν διώκωνται, ἑπόμενοι μετὰ τούτων συνεξαιροῦνται
τὸ προνοεῖσθαι. ὥστε διὰ ταῦτα προσπίπτων
λανθάνει πρὸς πολλὰ καὶ εἰς τὰς ἄρκυς ἐμπίπτων.
29 εἰ δ' ἔφευγεν ὀρθόν, ὀλιγάκις ἂν ἔπασχε τὸ
τοιοῦτον· νῦν δὲ περιβάλλων καὶ ἀγαπῶν τοὺς
τόπους, ἐν οἷς ἐγένετο καὶ ἐτράφη, ἁλίσκεται.
κατὰ πόδας δὲ οὐ πολλάκις ὑπὸ τῶν κυνῶν διὰ
τὸ τάχος κρατεῖται· ὅσοι δὲ ἁλίσκονται, παρὰ
φύσιν τοῦ σώματος, τύχῃ δὲ χρώμενοι· οὐδὲν
γὰρ τῶν ὄντων ἰσομέγεθες τούτῳ ὅμοιόν ἐστι

---

[1] εἰσὶ Dindorf : ὄντες S. with the MSS.

396

in the islands than on the mainland, for in the
majority of these there are no foxes to attack and
carry off the hares and their young ; nor eagles, for
they haunt big mountains rather than small, and
the mountains in the islands, generally speaking,
are rather small.   Hunters seldom visit the desert 25
islands, and there are few people in the inhabited
ones, and most of them are not sportsmen ; and if an
island is consecrated, one may not even take dogs
into it.   Since, then, but few of the old hares and
the leverets that they produce are exterminated by
hunting, they are bound to be abundant.

The sight of the hare is not keen for several 26
reasons.   The eyes are prominent ; the lids are
too small and do not give protection to the pupils ;
consequently the vision is weak and blurred.   Added 27
to this, though the animal spends much time asleep,
it gets no benefit from that, so far as seeing goes.   Its
speed, too, accounts in no small degree for its dim
sight.   For it glances at an object and is past it in a
flash, before realising its nature.   And those terrors, 28
the hounds, close behind them when they are
pursued combine with these causes to rob them of
their wits.   The consequence is that the hare bumps
against many obstacles unawares and plunges into
the net.   If she ran straight, she would seldom 29
meet with this mishap.   But instead of that she
comes round and hugs the place where she was born
and bred, and so is caught.   In a fair run she is
seldom beaten by the hounds owing to her speed.
Those that are caught are beaten in spite of their
natural characteristics through meeting with an
accident.   Indeed, there is nothing in the world of
equal size to match the hare as a piece of mechanism.

πρὸς ἁρμόν·[1] σύγκειται γὰρ ἐκ τοιούτων τὸ
σῶμα.

30   Ἔχει γὰρ κεφαλὴν κούφην, μικράν, καταφερῆ,
στενὴν ἐκ τοῦ πρόσθεν, ὦτα ὑψηλά, τράχηλον
λεπτόν, περιφερῆ, οὐ σκληρόν, μῆκος ἱκανόν,
ὠμοπλάτας ὀρθάς, ἀσυνδέτους ἄνωθεν, σκέλη
τὰ ἐπ᾽ αὐτῶν ἐλαφρά, σύγκωλα, στῆθος οὐ
βαρύτονον, πλευρὰς ἐλαφράς, συμμέτρους, ὀσφῦν
περιφερῆ, κωλῆν σαρκώδη, λαγόνας ὑγράς, λα-
παρὰς ἱκανῶς, ἰσχία στρογγύλα, πλήρη κύκλῳ,
ἄνωθεν δὲ ὡς χρὴ διεστῶτα, μηροὺς μικρούς,[2]
εὐπαγεῖς, ἔξωθεν μῦς[3] ἐπιτεταμένους, ἔνδοθεν
δὲ οὐκ ὀγκώδεις, ὑποκώλια μακρά, στιφρά, πόδας
τοὺς πρόσθεν ἄκρως ὑγρούς, στενούς, ὀρθούς,
τοὺς δὲ ὄπισθεν στερεούς, πλατεῖς, πάντας τὸ
οὐδενὸς τραχέος φροντίζοντας, σκέλη τὰ ὄπισθεν
μείζω πολὺ τῶν ἔμπροσθεν καὶ ἐγκεκλιμένα
31 μικρὸν ἔξω, τρίχωμα βραχύ, κοῦφον. ἔστιν οὖν
ἀδύνατον μὴ οὐκ εἶναι ἐκ τοιούτων συνηρμοσμένον
ἰσχυρόν, ὑγρόν, ὑπερέλαφρον.

Τεκμήριον δὲ ὡς ἐλαφρόν ἐστιν· ὅταν ἀτρέμα
διαπορεύηται, πηδᾷ, βαδίζοντα δὲ οὐδεὶς ἑώρακεν
οὐδ᾽ ὄψεται, τιθεὶς εἰς τὸ ἐπέκεινα τῶν ἔμπροσθεν
ποδῶν τοὺς ὄπισθεν καὶ ἔξω, καὶ[4] θεῖ οὕτως.
32 δῆλον δὲ τοῦτο ἐν χιόνι. οὐρὰν δὲ οὐκ ἐπιτηδείαν
ἔχει πρὸς δρόμον· ἐπευθύνειν γὰρ οὐχ ἱκανὴ τὸ
σῶμα διὰ τὴν βραχύτητα· ἀλλὰ τῷ ὠτὶ ἑκατέρῳ
τοῦτο ποιεῖ, καὶ ὅταν ἀνιστῆται[5] ὑπὸ τῶν κυνῶν,

---

[1] ἁρμόν ABM : δρόμον S. with inferior MSS.
[2] μικρούς Pierleoni : μακρούς S.
[3] μῦς MSS. : μὲν S.
[4] καὶ MSS. : S. omits with Schneider.

For the various parts that make up her body are formed as follows.

The head is light, small, drooping, narrow at the 30 front; the ears are upright;[1] the neck is thin, round, not stiff, and fairly long; the shoulder-blades are straight and free at the top; the fore-legs are agile and close together; the chest is not broad; the ribs are light and symmetrical; the loins are circular; the rump is fleshy; the flanks are soft and fairly spongy; the hips are round, well filled out, and the right distance apart at the top; the thighs are small and firm, muscular on the outside and not puffy on the inside; the shanks are long and firm; the fore-feet are extremely pliant and narrow and straight and the hind-feet hard and broad; and all four are indifferent to rough ground; the hind-legs are much longer than the fore-legs, and slightly bent outwards; the coat is short and light. With such a 31 frame she cannot fail to be strong, pliant and very agile.

Here is a proof of her agility. When going quietly, she springs—no one ever saw or ever will see a hare walking—bringing the hind-feet forward in advance of the fore-feet and outside them; and that is how she runs. This is obvious when snow is on the 32 ground. The scut is of no assistance in running, for it is not able to steer the body owing to its short-ness. The hare does this by means of one of her ears; and when she is roused by the hounds she

---

[1] "The ears are upright" is not in the MSS., and is inserted from Pollux. As our author is enumerating those characteristics of the hare that make for speed, it is not quite certain that the words are his, but see § 33.

---

[5] ἀνιστῆται Pierleoni: ἁλίσκηται S. with the MSS.

καταβάλλων καὶ[1] παραβάλλων τὸ ἕτερον οὓς
πλάγιον, ὁποτέρᾳ ἂν λυπῆται, ἀπερειδόμενος
δὴ εἰς τοῦτο ὑποστρέφεται ταχύ, ἐν μικρῷ πολὺ
33 καταλιπὼν τὸ ἐπιφερόμενον. οὕτω δὲ ἐπίχαρί
ἐστι τὸ θέαμα,[2] ὥστε οὐδεὶς ὅστις οὐκ ἂν ἰδὼν
ἰχνευόμενον, εὑρισκόμενον, μεταθεόμενον, ἁλισκόμενον ἐπιλάθοιτ' ἂν εἴ του ἐρῴη.

34 Ἐν δὲ τοῖς ἔργοις κυνηγετοῦντα ἀπέχεσθαι
ὧν ὧραι φέρουσι καὶ τὰ νάματα καὶ τὰ ῥεῖθρα
ἐᾶν. τὸ γὰρ ἅπτεσθαι τούτων αἰσχρὸν καὶ
κακόν, καὶ ἵνα μὴ τῷ νόμῳ ἐναντίοι ὦσιν οἱ
ἰδόντες. καὶ ὅταν ἀναγρία ἐμπίπτῃ, ἀναλύειν
χρὴ τὰ περὶ κυνηγέσιον πάντα.

VI. Κυνῶν δὲ κόσμος δέραια, ἱμάντες, στελμο-
νίαι· ἔστω δὲ τὰ μὲν δέραια μαλακά, πλατέα,
ἵνα μὴ θραύῃ τὰς τρίχας τῶν κυνῶν, οἱ δὲ ἱμάντες
ἔχοντες ἀγκύλας τῇ χειρί, ἄλλο δὲ μηδέν· οὐ
γὰρ καλῶς τηροῦσι τὰς κύνας οἱ ἐξ αὐτῶν
εἰργασμένοι τὰ δέραια· αἱ δὲ στελμονίαι πλατεῖς
τοὺς ἱμάντας, ἵνα μὴ τρίβωσι τὰς λαγόνας αὐτῶν·
ἐγκατερραμμέναι δὲ ἐγκεντρίδες, ἵνα τὰ γένη
φυλάττωσιν.

2 Ἐξάγειν δὲ αὐτὰς οὐ χρὴ ἐπὶ τὰ κυνηγέσια,
ὅταν μὴ τὰ προσφερόμενα δέχωνται ἡδέως·
τεκμήριον δὲ τοῦτο, ὅτι οὐκ ἔρρωνται· μηδὲ ὅταν
ἄνεμος πνέῃ μέγας. διαρπάζει γὰρ τὰ ἴχνη καὶ
οὐ δύνανται ὀσφραίνεσθαι οὐδὲ αἱ ἄρκυς ἑστάναι
3 οὐδὲ τὰ δίκτυα. ὅταν δὲ τούτων μηδέτερον
κωλύῃ, ἄγειν διὰ τρίτης ἡμέρας. τὰς δὲ ἀλώ-

---

[1] καὶ Dindorf : γὰρ καὶ S. with the MSS.
[2] θέαμα Arrian, Hermogenes : θηρίον S. with the MSS.

drops one ear on the side on which she is being pressed and throws it aslant, and then bearing on this she wheels round sharply and in a moment leaves the assailant far behind. So charming is the 33 sight that to see a hare tracked, found, pursued and caught is enough to make any man forget his heart's desire.

When hunting on cultivated land avoid growing 34 crops and let pools and streams alone. It is unseemly and wrong to interfere with them, and there is a risk of encouraging those who see to set themselves against the law.[1] On days on which there is no hunting,[2] all hunting tackle should be removed.

VI. The trappings of hounds are collars, leashes, and surcingles. The collars should be soft and broad, so as not to chafe the hounds' coat. The leashes should have a noose for the hand, and nothing else; for if the collar is made in one piece with the leash, perfect control of the hounds is impossible. The straps of the surcingles should be broad, so as not to rub the flanks, and they should have little spurs sewed on to them, to keep the breed pure.

Hounds should not be taken out hunting when off 2 their feed, since this is a proof that they are ailing; nor when a strong wind is blowing, since it scatters the scent and they cannot smell, and the purse-nets will not stand in position, nor the hayes. But when 3 neither of these hindrances prevents, have the hounds out every other day. Do not let them

---

[1] Both text and meaning are doubtful here. By "the law" is probably meant the law (or custom?) that allowed hunters to hunt over growing crops. See c. xii. 5.

[2] *i.e.* during festivals.

πεκας μὴ ἐθίζειν τὰς κύνας διώκειν· διαφθορὰ
γὰρ μεγίστη καὶ ἐν τῷ δέοντι οὔποτε πάρεισιν.
4 εἰς δὲ τὰ κυνηγέσια μεταβάλλοντα ἄγειν, ἵνα
ὦσιν ἔμπειροι τῶν κυνηγεσίων, αὐτὸς [1] δὲ τῆς
χώρας. ἐξιέναι δὲ πρωΐ, ἵνα τῆς ἰχνεύσεως μὴ
ἀποστερῶνται, ὡς οἱ ὀψιζόμενοι ἀφαιροῦνται τὰς
μὲν κύνας τοῦ εὑρεῖν τὸν λαγῶ, αὐτοὺς δὲ τῆς
ὠφελείας· οὐ γὰρ ἐπιμένει τοῦ ἴχνους ἡ φύσις
λεπτὴ οὖσα πᾶσαν ὥραν.
5 Τὴν δὲ στολὴν ὁ ἀρκυωρὸς ἐξίτω ἔχων ἐπὶ
θήραν μὴ ἔχουσαν βάρος. τὰς δὲ ἄρκυς ἱστάτω
εἰς ὁδοὺς ἀμφιδρόμους,[2] τραχείας, σιμάς, λαγαράς,
σκοτεινάς, ῥοῦς, χαράδρας, χειμάρρους ἀενάους·
εἰς ταῦτα γὰρ μάλιστα φεύγει· εἰς ὅσα δὲ ἄλλα
6 ἄπειρον εἰπεῖν· τούτων δὲ παρόδους, διόδους,
καταφανεῖς, λεπτάς,[3] εἰς ὄρθρον καὶ μὴ πρωΐ,
ἵνα ἐὰν ᾖ πλησίον τὸ ἀρκυστάσιον τῶν ζητησίμων,
μὴ φοβῆται ἀκούων ὁμοῦ τὸν ψόφον (ἐὰν δὲ ᾖ
ἀπ' ἀλλήλων πολύ, ἧττον κωλύει πρωΐ) καθαρὰς
ποιούμενος [4] τὰς ἀρκυστασίας, ἵνα αὐτῶν μηδὲν
7 ἀντέχηται. πηγνύειν δὲ τὰς σχαλίδας ὑπτίας,
ὅπως ἂν ἐπαγόμεναι ἔχωσι τὸ σύντονον· ἐπὶ δὲ
ἄκρας ἴσους τοὺς βρόχους ἐπιβαλλέτω καὶ ὁμοίως

---

[1] αὐτὸς Weiske: αὐτοὶ S. with the MSS.
[2] A has εἰς ἀμφιδρόμους, the rest ἀμφιδρόμους only : S. reads
ἀμφὶ δρόμους, ὁδοὺς τραχείας. Probably some substantive has
dropped out of the MSS., but ὁδοὺς is unlikely. Perhaps
εἰς ἀμφιδρομὰς should be read ; ὁδοὺς is not in the MSS.
[3] A word to govern these accusatives must have been lost.
[4] ποιουμένους S.

---

[1] This portentous sentence is a literal presentation of the
Greek text, which, however, is rather uncertain. If the

take to pursuing foxes; for it is utter ruin, and
they are never at hand when wanted. Vary the 4
hunting-ground frequently, so that the hounds may
be familiar with the hunting-grounds and the master
with the country. Start early, and so give the
hounds a fair chance of following the scent. A late
start robs the hounds of the find and the hunters
of the prize; for the scent is by its nature too thin
to last all day.

Let the net-keeper wear light clothing when he 5
goes hunting. Let him set up the purse-nets in
winding, rough, steep, narrow, shady paths, brooks,
ravines, running watercourses (these are the places
in which the hare is most apt to take refuge: a
list of all the others would be endless), leaving un- 6
obstructed and narrow passages to and through these
places, just about daybreak, and not too early, so
that in case the line of nets be near the growth to be
searched, the hare may not be frightened by hearing
the noise close by (if the distance is considerable, it
matters less if the work is done early), seeing that the
nets stand clear so that nothing may cling to them.[1]
He must fix the stakes aslant,[2] so that when 7
pulled they may stand the strain. On the tops of
them let him put an equal number of meshes,[3] and

nets are fixed near the covert before daybreak, the hare is
likely to stir at the noise. After daybreak she will not
stir.
  [2] *i.e.* sloping towards the side from which the hare will
come. The nets, of course, hang on the other side of the
stakes.
  [3] If ἴσους means "equal in number," more than one mesh is
to be put in the groove of each stake, so that the top of the row
of nets will be puckered. Perhaps, however, "level in
height" is the sense.

XENOPHON

ἀντερειδέτω, ἐπαίρων εἰς μέσον τὸν κεκρύφαλον.
8 εἰς δὲ τὸν περίδρομον ἐναπτέτω λίθον μακρὸν
καὶ μέγαν, ἵνα ἡ ἄρκυς, ὅταν ἔχῃ τὸν λαγῶ, μὴ
ἀντιτείνῃ· στοιχιζέτω δὲ μακρά, ὑψηλά, ὅπως ἂν
μὴ ὑπερπηδᾷ.

Ἐν δὲ ταῖς ἰχνείαις μὴ ὑπερβάλλεσθαι· ἔστι
γὰρ θηρατικὸν μὲν οὔ,[1] φιλόπονον δὲ τὸ ἐκ παντὸς
τρόπου ἑλεῖν ταχύ.

9 Τὰ δὲ δίκτυα τεινέτω ἐν ἀπέδοις, ἐμβαλλέτω
δὲ τὰ ἐνόδια εἰς τὰς ὁδοὺς καὶ ἐκ τῶν τριμμῶν
εἰς τὰ συμφέροντα, καθάπτων τοὺς περιδρόμους
ἐπὶ τὴν γῆν, τὰ ἀκρωλένια συνάγων, πηγνύων
τὰς σχαλίδας μεταξὺ τῶν σαρδόνων, ἐπὶ ἄκρας
ἐπιβάλλων τοὺς ἐπιδρόμους καὶ τὰ [2] παράδρομα
10 συμφράττων. φυλαττέτω δὲ ἐκπεριιών· ἐὰν δὲ
ἐκκλίνῃ τὸν στοῖχον ἢ [3] ἄρκυς, ἀνιστάτω. διωκο-
μένου δὲ τοῦ [4] λαγῶ εἰς τὰς ἄρκυς εἰς τὸ πρόσθεν
προϊέσθω καὶ ἐπιθέων μὲν ἐκβοάτω· ἐμπεπτω-
κότος δὲ τὴν ὀργὴν τῶν κυνῶν παυέτω, μὴ ἁπτό-
μενος ἀλλὰ παραμυθούμενος· καὶ δηλούτω τῷ
κυνηγέτῃ, ὅτι ἑάλωκεν ἀναβοήσας ἢ ὅτι παρα-
δεδράμηκε παρὰ τάδε ἢ τάδε ἢ ὅτι οὐχ ἑώρακεν
ἢ οὐ κατεῖδε.

[1] οὐ A: S. omits with the rest.
[2] S. omits τὰ with BM.
[3] A has τὸν στίχον ἤ: BM στοῖχος ἤ: S. reads στοῖχος ἤ.
[4] διωκόμενον δὲ τὸν S. with BM.

---

[1] Small sticks were used for propping up the purse on the
inside, and the purse was propped higher towards the middle;
it ended in a point, so that it resembled the net on a woman's
head.
[2] See c. ii. §4. The stone serves as an anchor when the
net falls off the stakes.

set the props[1] uniformly, raising the purse towards
the centre. To the cord[2] let him attach a long, big 8
stone, so that the net may not pull away when the
hare is inside. Let him make his line long and
high,[3] so that the hare may not jump over.

When it comes to tracking the hare, he must not
be too zealous. To do everything possible to effect
a quick capture shows perseverance, but is not
hunting.[4]

Let him stretch the hayes on level ground and 9
put the road-nets[5] in roads and from game tracks
into the adjacent ground, fastening down the
(lower) cords to the ground, joining the elbows,
fixing the stakes between the selvedges,[6] putting the
ends on the top of the stakes and stopping the by-
ways. Let him mount guard, going round the nets. 10
If a purse-net is pulling its stake out of line, let
him put it up. When the hare is being chased
into the purse-nets he must run forward and shout as
he runs after her. When she is in, he must calm
the excitement of the hounds, soothing without
touching them. He must also shout to the huntsman and let him know that the hare is caught, or
that she has run past on this or that side, or that he
has not seen her, or where he caught sight of her.

---

[3] The stakes must not be too deep in the ground, or the
nets will not be high enough.

[4] These remarks read like an afterthought.

[5] The hayes and purse-nets seem to be connected in the
same series; but the road-nets seem to be independent
screens.

[6] We are to think of a series of nets joined together.
These stakes will be inserted in the top and bottom line of
meshes. The selvedge runs along the top and bottom of the
net.

11 Τὸν δὲ κυνηγέτην ἔχοντα ἐξιέναι ἠμελημένην
ἐλαφρὰν ἐσθῆτα ἐπὶ τὸ κυνηγέσιον καὶ ὑπόδεσιν,
ἐν δὲ τῇ χειρὶ ῥόπαλον, τὸν δὲ ἀρκυωρὸν ἔπεσθαι·
πρὸς δὲ τὸ κυνηγέσιον σιγῇ προσιέναι, ἵνα μὴ ὁ
λαγῶς, ἐάν που ᾖ πλησίον, ὑποκινῇ ἀκούων τῆς
12 φωνῆς. δήσαντα δ' ἐκ τῆς ὕλης τὰς κύνας
ἑκάστην χωρίς, ὅπως ἂν εὔλυτοι ὦσιν, ἱστάναι
τὰς ἄρκυς καὶ τὰ δίκτυα, ὡς εἴρηται. μετὰ δὲ
τοῦτο τὸν μὲν ἀρκυωρὸν εἶναι ἐν φυλακῇ· αὐτὸν
δὲ τὰς κύνας λαβόντα ἰέναι πρὸς τὴν ὑπαγωγὴν
13 τοῦ κυνηγεσίου. καὶ εὐξάμενον τῷ Ἀπόλλωνι
καὶ τῇ Ἀρτέμιδι τῇ Ἀγροτέρᾳ μεταδοῦναι τῆς
θήρας λῦσαι μίαν κύνα, ἥτις ἂν ᾖ σοφωτάτη
ἰχνεύειν, ἐὰν μὲν ᾖ χειμών, ἅμ' ἡλίῳ ἀνέχοντι,
ἐὰν δὲ θέρος, πρὸ ἡμέρας, τὰς δὲ ἄλλας ὥρας
14 μεταξὺ τούτων. ἐπειδὰν δὲ ἡ κύων λάβῃ τὸ
ἴχνος ὀρθὸν ἐκ τῶν ἐπηλλαγμένων, παραλῦσαι καὶ
ἑτέραν· περαινομένου δὲ τοῦ ἴχνους διαλιπόντα
μὴ πολὺ καὶ τὰς ἄλλας ἀφιέναι κατὰ μίαν καὶ
ἕπεσθαι μὴ ἐγκείμενον, ὀνομαστὶ ἑκάστην προσ-
αγορεύοντα, μὴ πολλά, ἵνα μὴ παροξύνωνται
15 πρὸ τοῦ καιροῦ. αἱ δ' ὑπὸ χαρᾶς καὶ μένους
προΐασιν ἐξίλλουσαι τὰ ἴχνη, ὡς πέφυκε, διπλᾶ,
τριπλᾶ, προφορούμεναι παρὰ τὰ αὐτά, διὰ τῶν
αὐτῶν, ἐπηλλαγμένα, περιφερῆ, ὀρθά, καμπύλα,
πυκνά, μανά, γνώριμα, ἄγνωστα, ἑαυτὰς παραθέουσαι, ταχὺ ταῖς οὐραῖς διασείουσαι καὶ ἐπικλί-
νουσαι τὰ ὦτα καὶ ἀστράπτουσαι τοῖς ὄμμασιν.
16 ἐπειδὰν δὲ περὶ τὸν λαγῶ ὦσι, δῆλον ποιήσουσι

Let the huntsman go out to the hunting ground 11
in a simple light dress and shoes, carrying a cudgel
in his hand, and let the net-keeper follow. Let
them keep silence while approaching the ground,
so that, in case the hare is near, she may not move
off on hearing voices. Having tied the hounds 12
separately to the trees so that they can easily be
slipped, let him set up the purse-nets and hayes[1]
in the manner described. After this let the net-
keeper keep guard, and let the huntsman take
the hounds and go to the place in the hunting
ground where the hare may be lurking; and after 13
registering a vow to Apollo and Artemis the Huntress
to give them a share of the spoil, let him loose one
hound, the cleverest at following a track, at sun-
rise in winter, before dawn in summer, and some
time between at other seasons. As soon as the 14
hound picks up a line from the network of tracks
that leads straight ahead, let him slip another. If
the track goes on, let him set the others going one by
one at short intervals, and follow without pressing
them, accosting each by name, but not often, that
they may not get excited too soon. They will go 15
forward full of joy and ardour, disentangling the
various tracks, double or triple—springing forward
now beside, now across the same ones—tracks inter-
laced or circular, straight or crooked, close or scattered,
clear or obscure, running past one another with tails
wagging, ears dropped and eyes flashing. As soon 16
as they are near the hare they will let the huntsman

---

[1] Neither here nor in § 26 is there any reference to the
road-nets. It is impossible to suggest a reason for this, and
perhaps the necessary words have dropped out in both places,
as might easily happen.

τῷ κυνηγέτῃ σὺν ταῖς οὐραῖς τὰ σώματα ὅλα
συνεπικραδαίνουσαι, πολεμικῶς ἐπιφερόμεναι,
φιλονίκως παραθέουσαι, συντρέχουσαι φιλοπόνως, συνιστάμεναι ταχύ, διιστάμεναι, πάλιν
ἐπιφερόμεναι· τελευτῶσαι δὲ ἀφίξονται πρὸς
τὴν εὐνὴν τοῦ λαγὼ καὶ ἐπιδραμοῦνται ἐπ᾽ αὐτόν.
17 ὁ δ᾽ ἐξαίφνης ἀνᾴξας ἐφ᾽ αὑτὸν ὑλαγμὸν ποιήσει
τῶν κυνῶν καὶ κλαγγὴν φεύγων. ἐμβοάτω¹ δὲ
αὐτῷ διωκομένῳ, ἰὼ κύνες, ἰὼ καλῶς,² σοφῶς³
γε ὦ κύνες, καλῶς γε ὦ κύνες. καὶ κυνοδρομεῖν
περιελίξαντα ὃ ἀμπέχεται περὶ τὴν χεῖρα καὶ
τὸ ῥόπαλον ἀναλαβόντα κατὰ τὸν λαγὼ καὶ μὴ
18 ὑπαντᾶν· ἄπορον γάρ. ὁ δὲ ὑποχωρῶν ταχὺ
ἐκλείπων τὴν ὄψιν πάλιν περιβάλλει ὅθεν εὑρί-
σκεται ἐπὶ τὸ πολύ. ἀναβοᾶν δ᾽ ἐκεῖνον μὲν
αὐτῷ, παισάτω παῖς·⁴ παῖε δή, παῖε δή·⁵ ὁ δέ,
ἐάν τε ἑαλωκὼς ᾖ ἐάν τε μή, δηλούτω.

Καὶ ἐὰν μὲν ἑαλωκὼς ᾖ ἐν τῷ πρώτῳ δρόμῳ,
ἀνακαλεσάμενον τὰς κύνας ζητεῖν ἄλλον· ἐὰν δὲ
μή, κυνοδρομεῖν ὡς τάχιστα καὶ μὴ ἀνιέναι,⁶ ἀλλ᾽
19 ἐκπερᾶν φιλοπόνως. καὶ ἐὰν πάλιν ἀπαντῶσι
διώκουσαι αὐτόν, ἀναβοᾶν, εὖ γε εὖ γε ὦ κύνες,
ἕπεσθε ὦ κύνες· ἐὰν δὲ πολὺ προειληφυῖαι ὦσι
καὶ μὴ οἷός τ᾽ ᾖ κυνοδρομῶν ἐπιγίγνεσθαι αὐταῖς,
ἀλλὰ διημαρτηκὼς ᾖ τῶν δρόμων ἢ καὶ πλησίον

¹ ἐμβοάτω A : ἐμβοώντων S. with BM.
² ἰὼ καλῶς Falbe : ἰὼ κακὸς BM, whence ἰὼ κακῶς S. : A
omits.
³ σοφῶς, Gesner : σαφῶς S. with the MSS.
⁴ S. gives ἐκεῖνον μέν, αὐτῷ παῖς, αὐτῷ παῖς. The text
follows A.
⁵ If παῖ δή, παῖ δή (BM) is right, παῖ is an imperative of
παίω, not vocative of παῖς.

know by the quivering of the whole body as well
as the tail, by making fierce rushes, by racing past
one another, by scampering along together persistently, massing quickly, breaking up and again rushing
forward. At length they will reach the hare's
form and will go for her. She will start up suddenly, 17
and will leave the hounds barking and baying behind
her as she makes off. Let the huntsman shout at
her as she runs, "Now, hounds, now! Well done!
Bravo, hounds! Well done, hounds!" Wrapping
his cloak round his arm and seizing his cudgel he
must follow up behind the hare and not try to head
her off, since that is useless. The hare, making off, 18
though out of sight, generally doubles back to the
place where she is found. Let him call out[1] to the
man, "Hit her, boy; hit her, hit her!" and the man
must let him know whether she is caught or not.

If she is caught in the first run, let him call in
the hounds and look for another. But if not, he
must follow up at top speed and not let her go, but
stick to it persistently. If the hounds come on 19
her again in the pursuit, let him cry, "Good, good,
hounds; after her, hounds!" If they have got so
far ahead of him that he cannot overtake them by
following up and is quite out of the running, or if he

---

[1] *i.e.* at the moment when the hare, making for the place
where she was found, comes near the nets. Something is
amiss with the text here. The "man" is, of course, the
net-keeper. He, too, has a cudgel, but the author has not
said so.

• ἀνιέναι A : ἀφιέναι S. with BM.

που φοιτώσας[1] ἢ ἐχομένας τῶν ἰχνῶν μὴ δύνηται
ἰδεῖν, πυνθάνεσθαι παραθέοντα ἅμα ὅτῳ ἂν προσ-
πελάζῃ ἀναβοῶντα, ἢ κατεῖδες ὠὴ τὰς κύνας;
20 ἐπειδὰν δὲ πύθηται ἤδη, ἐὰν μὲν ἐν τῷ ἴχνει ὦσι,
προσστάντα ἐγκελεύειν, τοὔνομα μεταβάλλοντα
ἑκάστης τῆς κυνός, ὁποσαχῇ οἷόν τ' ἂν ᾖ τοὺς
τόνους τῆς φωνῆς ποιούμενον, ὀξύ, βαρύ, μικρόν,
μέγα· πρὸς δὲ τοῖς ἄλλοις κελεύμασιν, ἐὰν ὦσιν
ἐν ὄρει αἱ μεταδρομαί, ἐπικελεύειν τόδε, εὖα[2]
κύνες, εὖα ὦ κύνες. ἐὰν δὲ μὴ πρὸς αὐτοῖς
ὦσι τοῖς ἴχνεσιν, ἀλλ' ὑπερβάλλωσι, καλεῖν
21 αὐτάς, οὐ πάλιν οὐ πάλιν ὦ κύνες· ἐπειδὰν δὲ
προσστῶσι τοῖς ἴχνεσι, περιάγειν αὐτὰς κύκλους
πολλοὺς[3] ποιούμενον· ὅπου δ' ἂν ᾖ αὐταῖς ἀμαυρὸν
τὸ ἴχνος, σημεῖον θέσθαι στοῖχον ἑαυτῷ καὶ ἀπὸ
τούτου συνείρειν, μέχρι ἂν σαφῶς γνωρίσωσιν,
22 ἐγκελεύοντα καὶ θωπεύοντα. αἱ δ' ἐπειδὰν λαμπρὰ
ᾖ τὰ ἴχνη, ἐπιρριπτοῦσαι, παραπηδῶσαι, κοινω-
νοῦσαι, ὑπολαμβάνουσαι, ἐνσημαινόμεναι, ὅρους
τιθέμεναι ἑαυταῖς γνωρίμους ταχὺ μεταθεύσονται·
ὅταν δὲ οὕτως διὰ τοῦ ἴχνους πυκνῶς διάττωσι,
μὴ κατέχοντα κυνοδρομεῖν, ἵνα μὴ ὑπὸ φιλοτιμίας
ὑπερβάλλωσι τὰ ἴχνη.
23 Ἐπειδὰν δὲ περὶ τὸν λαγὼ ὦσι καὶ τοῦτο
ἐπιδεικνύωνται σαφῶς τῷ κυνηγέτῃ, προσέχειν,
ὅπως ἂν μὴ ὑποκινῇ εἰς τὸ πρόσθεν πεφοβημένος
τὰς κύνας, αἱ δὲ διαρριπτοῦσαι τὰς οὐρὰς καὶ

---

[1] I have omitted ἢ ἐπιβοώσας here with Schneider.
[2] εὖα twice Gesner : εὖ twice S. with the MSS.
[3] πολλοὺς A : πολλοὺς πυκνοὺς BM : πολλοὺς καὶ πυκνοὺς S.
with Stephanus.

cannot see them though they are moving about somewhere near or sticking to the tracks, let him find
out by shouting as he runs past to anyone near,
"Hullo! have you seen the hounds?" As soon 20
as he has found out, let him stand near if they
are on the track, and cheer them on, running
through the hounds' names, using all the varia-
tions of tone he can produce, pitching his voice
high and low, soft and loud. Amongst other
calls, if the chase is in the mountains, let him sing
out, "Oho, hounds, oho!"[1] If they are not clinging
to the track, but are over-running, let him call them
in with, "Back, hounds, back with you!" As soon 21
as they are close on the tracks, let him cast them
round,[2] making many circles, and wherever they find
the track dim, let him stick a pole in the ground as
a mark, and beginning from this mark keep them
together until they clearly recognise the track,
encouraging and coaxing them. As soon as the track 22
is clear they will be off in hot pursuit, hurling themselves on it, jumping beside it, working together,
guessing, signalling to one another and setting
bounds for one another that they can recognise.
When they are thus scurrying in a bunch along
the track, let him follow up without pressing them,
or they may over-run the line through excess of zeal.

As soon as they are near the hare and give the 23
huntsman clear evidence of the fact, let him take care,
or in her terror of the hounds she will slip away and
be off. The hounds, wagging their tails, colliding and

---

[1] Imitating the call of the Bacchic revellers, "the Hounds
of Madness," on Mount Cithaeron.

[2] Nowadays hounds are left to make their own cast and
are only assisted when they fail to recover the line.

ἑαυταῖς ἐμπίπτουσαι καὶ πολλὰ ὑπερπηδῶσαι καὶ
ἐπανακλαγγάνουσαι, ἐπαναίρουσαι τὰς κεφαλάς,
εἰσβλέπουσαι εἰς τὸν κυνηγέτην, ἐπιγνωρίζουσαι
ἀληθῆ εἶναι ἤδη ταῦτα, ὑφ' αὑτῶν ἀναστήσουσι
24 τὸν λαγῶ καὶ ἐπίασι κεκλαγγυῖαι. ἐὰν δὲ εἰς
τὰς ἄρκυς ἐμπίπτῃ ἢ ἔξω ἢ ἐντὸς παρενεχθῇ,
καθ' ἓν ἕκαστον τούτων ὁ ἀρκυωρὸς γεγωνείτω. καὶ
ἐὰν μὲν ᾖ ἑαλωκώς, ἕτερον ἐπιζητεῖν· ἐὰν δὲ μή,
μεταθεῖν χρώμενον τοῖς αὐτοῖς ἐγκελεύμασιν.
25 Ἐπειδὰν δὲ μεταθέουσαι αἱ κύνες ἤδη ὑπόκοποι
ὦσι καὶ ᾖ ὀψὲ ἤδη τῆς ἡμέρας, τότε δεῖ τὸν
κυνηγέτην τὸν λαγῶ ἀπειρηκότα ζητεῖν, μὴ
παραλείποντα μηδὲν ὧν ἡ γῆ ἀνίησιν ἢ ἔχει
ἐφ' ἑαυτῆς, τὰς ἀναστροφὰς ποιούμενον πυκνάς,
ὅπως ἂν μὴ παραλειφθῇ· κατακλίνεται γὰρ ἐν
μικρῷ τὸ θηρίον καὶ οὐκ ἀνίσταται ὑπὸ κόπου
καὶ φόβου· τὰς κύνας ἐπαγόμενον, ἐγκελεύοντα,
παραμυθούμενον τὴν φιλάνθρωπον πολλά, τὴν
αὐθάδη ὀλίγα, τὴν μέσην μέτρια, ἕως ἂν ἢ
ἀποκτείνῃ αὐτὸν κατὰ πόδας ἢ εἰς τὰς ἄρκυς
ἐμβάλῃ.
26 Μετὰ δὲ ταῦτα ἀνελόντα τὰς ἄρκυς καὶ τὰ
δίκτυα ἀνατρίψαντα τὰς κύνας ἀπιέναι ἐκ τοῦ
κυνηγεσίου, ἐπιμείναντα, ἐὰν ᾖ θερινὴ μεσημβρία,
ὅπως ἂν τῶν κυνῶν οἱ πόδες μὴ καίωνται ἐν τῇ
πορείᾳ.
VII. Σκυλακεύειν δὲ αὐτὰς ἐπανιέντα τῶν
πόνων τοῦ χειμῶνος, ἵνα ἔχουσαι τὴν ἡσυχίαν
πρὸς τὸ ἔαρ ἐπάγωνται τὴν φύσιν γενναίαν· ὁ
γὰρ ὥρα πρὸς τὰς αὐξήσεις τῶν κυνῶν κρατίστη
αὐτή· εἰσὶ δὲ τετταρεσκαίδεκα ἡμέραι, ἐν αἷς ἡ
2 ἀνάγκη αὕτη ἔχει. ἄγειν δὲ καταπαυομένας, ἵνα

frequently jumping over one another, and baying loudly, with heads uplifted and glances at the huntsman, showing him plainly that they have the real thing now, will rouse the hare for themselves and go for her, giving tongue. If she plunges into the purse-nets 24 or bolts past them on the inside or outside, the net-keeper must in each event make it known by shouting. If she is caught, look for another; if not, continue the pursuit, using the same methods of encouragement.

As soon as the hounds are getting tired of pursuing 25 and the day is far advanced, it is time for the huntsman to search for the hare, worn out as she is, passing over nothing growing or lying on the ground, retracing his steps continually for fear of an oversight—since the animal rests in a small space and is too tired and frightened to get up,—bringing the hounds along, encouraging and exhorting the gentle frequently, the wilful sparingly, the average sort in moderation, until he kills her in a fair run or drives her into the purse-nets.

After this take up the purse-nets and[1] hayes, rub 26 down the hounds and leave the hunting-ground, after waiting, if it be an afternoon in summer, in order that the hounds' feet may not be overheated on the road.

VII. For breeding purposes, relieve the bitches of work in the winter, that the rest may help them to produce a fine litter towards spring, which is the best growing season for hounds. They are in heat for fourteen days. Mate them with good dogs near 2 the end of the period, that they may the sooner

---

[1] Where are the road-nets?

θᾶττον ἐγκύμονες γίγνωνται, πρὸς κύνας ἀγαθούς·
ἐπειδὰν δὲ ὦσιν ἐπίφοροι, μὴ ἐξάγειν ἐπὶ κυνηγέσιον ἐνδελεχῶς, ἀλλὰ διαλείπειν, ἵνα μὴ φιλο-
3 πονίᾳ διαφθείρωσι. κυοῦσι δ᾽[1] ἑξήκονθ᾽ ἡμέρας.
ἐπειδὰν δὲ γένηται τὰ σκυλάκια, ὑπὸ τῇ τεκούσῃ
ἐᾶν καὶ μὴ ὑποβάλλειν ὑφ᾽ ἑτέραν κύνα· αἱ γὰρ
θεραπεῖαι αἱ ἀλλότριαι οὐκ εἰσὶν αὔξιμοι· τὸ δὲ
τῶν μητέρων καὶ τὸ γάλα ἀγαθὸν καὶ τὸ πνεῦμα
4 καὶ αἱ περιβολαὶ φίλαι. ἐπειδὰν δὲ ἤδη πλα-
νᾶται τὰ σκυλάκια, διδόναι γάλα μέχρι ἐνιαυτοῦ
καὶ οἷς μέλλει τὸν ἅπαντα χρόνον βιώσεσθαι,
ἄλλο δὲ μηδέν· αἱ γὰρ βαρεῖαι πλησμοναὶ
τῶν σκυλακίων διαστρέφουσι τὰ[2] σκέλη, τοῖς[3]
σώμασι νόσους ἐμποιοῦσι, καὶ τὰ ἐντὸς ἄδικα
γίγνεται.
5   Τὰ δ᾽ ὀνόματα αὐταῖς τίθεσθαι βραχέα, ἵνα
εὐανάκλητα ᾖ. εἶναι δὲ χρὴ τοιάδε, Ψυχή,
Θυμός, Πόρπαξ, Στύραξ, Λόγχη, Λόχος, Φρουρά,
Φύλαξ, Τάξις, Ξίφων, Φόναξ, Φλέγων, Ἀλκή,
Τεύχων, Ὑλεύς, Μήδας, Πόρθων, Σπέρχων, Ὀργή,
Βρέμων, Ὕβρις, Θάλλων, Ῥώμη, Ἀνθεύς, Ἥβα,
Γηθεύς, Χαρά, Λεύσσων, Αὐγώ, Πολύς, Βία,
Στίχων, Σπουδή, Βρύας, Οἰνάς, Στερρός, Κραύγη,
Καίνων, Τύρβας, Σθένων, Αἰθήρ, Ἀκτίς, Αἰχμή,
Νόης, Γνώμη, Στίβων, Ὁρμή.
6   Ἄγειν δὲ τὰς σκύλακας ἐπὶ τὸ κυνηγέσιον
τὰς μὲν θηλείας ὀκταμήνους, τοὺς δὲ ἄρρενας
δεκαμήνους· πρὸς δὲ τὰ ἴχνη τὰ εὐναῖα μὴ λύειν,

---

[1] κυοῦσι δ᾽ AB : κυοῦσιν S. with M.
[2] τὰ A : S omits with BM.
[3] τοῖς added from Arrian : S. omits.

become pregnant. When they are near their time do not take them out hunting continually, but only now and then, or love of work may result in a miscarriage. The period of gestation is sixty days. After the birth of the puppies leave them with the 3 mother and do not place them under another bitch ; for nursing by a foster mother does not promote growth, whereas the mother's milk and breath do them good, and they like her caresses. As soon as the 4 puppies can get about, give them milk for a year, and the food that will form their regular diet, and nothing else. For heavy feeding warps the puppies' legs and sows the seeds of disease in the system, and their insides go wrong.

Give the hounds short names, so as to be able 5 to call to them easily. The following are the right sort : Psyche, Thymus, Porpax, Styrax, Lonché, Lochus, Phrura, Phylax, Taxis, Xiphon, Phonax, Phlegon, Alcé, Teuchon, Hyleus, Medas, Porthon, Sperchon, Orgé, Bremon, Hybris, Thallon, Rhomé, Antheus, Hebe, Getheus, Chara, Leusson, Augo, Polys, Bia, Stichon, Spudé, Bryas, Oenas, Sterrus, Craugé, Caenon, Tyrbas, Sthenon, Aether, Actis, Aechmé, Noës, Gnomé, Stibon, Hormé.[1]

Take the bitches to the hunting ground at eight 6 months, the dogs at ten. Do not slip them on the

---

[1] The names are significant of the colour, strength, spirit, sagacity or behaviour of the hounds. Hebe and Psyche are still in the list of bitches' names, and modern equivalents of several of the other names are in use, e.g. Lance (Lonché), Sentinel (Phylax), Ecstasy (Chara), Blueskin (Oenas), Crafty (Medas), Hasty (Sperchon), Vigorous (Thallon), Impetus (Hormé), Counsellor (Noës), Bustler (dog) or Hasty (bitch); cf. Sperchon. For Πολύς we should probably read Πολεύς, "Rover."

ἀλλ' ἔχοντα ὑφημμένας μακροῖς ἱμᾶσιν ἀκολουθεῖν ταῖς κυσὶν ἰχνευούσαις, ἐῶντα αὐτὰς
7 διατρέχειν τὰ ἴχνη. καὶ ἐπειδὰν ὁ λαγῶς
εὑρίσκηται, ἐὰν μὲν καλαὶ ὦσι πρὸς τὸν δρόμον
τὰ εἴδη, μὴ ἀνιέναι εὐθύς· ἐπειδὰν δὲ προλάβῃ
ὁ λαγῶς τῷ δρόμῳ, ὥστε μὴ ἐφορᾶν ἔτι αὐτόν,
8 τὰς σκύλακας ἱέναι. ἐὰν γὰρ ὁμόθεν καλὰς τὰ
εἴδη οὔσας καὶ εὐψύχους πρὸς τὸν δρόμον ἐπιλύῃ,
ὁρῶσαι τὸν λαγῶ ἐντεινόμεναι ῥήγνυνται, οὔπω
ἔχουσαι συνεστῶτα τὰ σώματα· διαφυλάττειν
9 οὖν δεῖ τοῦτο τὸν κυνηγέτην. ἐὰν δὲ αἰσχίους
ὦσι πρὸς τὸν δρόμον, οὐδὲν κωλύει ἱέναι· εὐθὺς
γὰρ δὴ ἀνέλπιστοι οὖσαι τοῦ ἑλεῖν οὐ πείσονται
τοῦτο. τὰ δὲ δρομαῖα τῶν ἰχνῶν, ἕως ἂν ἕλωσι,
μεταθεῖν ἐᾶν· ἁλισκομένου δὲ τοῦ λαγῶ διδόναι
10 αὐταῖς ἀναρρηγνύναι. ἐπειδὰν δὲ μηκέτι θέλωσι
προσμένειν [ταῖς ἄρκυσιν],[1] ἀλλ' ἀποσκεδαν-
νύωνται, ἀναλαμβάνειν, ἕως ἂν ἐθισθῶσιν εὑρίσκειν προσθέουσαι τὸν λαγῶ, μὴ οὐκ ἐν κόσμῳ
ἀεὶ τοῦτον ζητοῦσαι τελευτῶσαι γίγνωνται
ἔκκυνοι, πονηρὸν μάθημα.
11 Πρὸς δὲ ταῖς ἄρκυσι διδόναι τὰ σιτία αὐταῖς,
ἕως ἂν νέαι ὦσιν, ὅταν ἀναιρῶνται, ἵν' ἐὰν πλα-
νηθῶσιν ἐν τῷ κυνηγεσίῳ δι' ἀπειρίαν, πρὸς τοῦτο
ἐπανιοῦσαι σῴζωνται. ἀφεθήσονται δὲ τούτου,
ὅταν ἤδη τῷ θηρίῳ ἔχωσι πολεμίως, ἐπιμέλειαν δὲ

---

[1] The MSS. add τῷ ἴχνει after ἕλωσι above, but it is
rightly omitted by S. after Dindorf: here too ταῖς ἄρκυσιν
must be omitted, or changed, with Richards, to τοῖς ἴχνεσιν.

[1] But how is the hunter to know whether the hounds are
on the trail leading to the form or on the track of a running
hare?

trail that leads to the form, but keep them in long
leashes and follow the tracking hounds, letting the
youngsters run to and fro in the tracks.[1] As soon as 7
the hare is found, if they shape well for the run don't
let them go at once; but as soon as the hare has got
so far ahead in the run that they can't see her, send
them along. For if the huntsman slips good looking, 8
plucky runners close to the hare, the sight of her
will cause them to strain themselves and crack,
since their bodies are not yet firm. So he
should be very careful about this. But if they are 9
poor runners there is no reason why he should not
let them go, for as they have no hope of catching
the hare from the first, they will not meet with
this accident. On the other hand, let the youngsters follow the track of the hare on the run
until they catch her; and when she is caught,
give her to them to break up.[2] As soon as they 10
show reluctance to stick to it and begin scattering,
call them in, until they grow accustomed to keep
on till they find the hare, lest if they get into the
way of misbehaving when they seek her, they
end by becoming skirters—a vile habit.

Give them their food near the purse-nets so 11
long as they are young, while the nets are being
taken up, so that if they have gone astray in the
hunting ground, through inexperience, they may come
back safe for their meal. This will be discontinued
when they come to regard the game as an enemy;

[2] Not to eat. Some hunters object more or less strongly
to this injunction; but Beckford (*Thoughts on Hunting*),
quoted by Blane, goes so far as to say, "I think it but
reasonable to give the hounds a hare sometimes. I always
gave mine the last they killed, if I thought they deserved
her."

ποιήσονται τούτου μᾶλλον ἢ ἐκείνου φροντίζειν.
12 χρὴ δὲ καὶ ὡς τὰ πολλὰ δεομέναις[1] διδόναι τὰ
ἐπιτήδεια ταῖς κυσὶν αὐτόν· ὅταν μὲν γὰρ μὴ[2]
ἐνδεεῖς ὦσι, τούτου τὸν αἴτιον οὐκ ἴσασιν, ὅταν
δὲ ἐπιθυμοῦσαι λάβωσι, τὸν διδόντα στέργουσιν.

VIII. Ἰχνεύεσθαι δὲ τοὺς λαγῶς, ὅταν νίφῃ
ὁ θεός, ὥστε ἠφανίσθαι τὴν γῆν· εἰ δ' ἐνέσται
μελάγχιμα, δυσζήτητος ἔσται. ἔστι δέ, ὅταν
μὲν ἐπινεφῇ[3] καὶ ᾖ βόρειον, τὰ ἴχνη ἔξω πολὺν
χρόνον δῆλα· οὐ γὰρ ταχὺ συντήκεται· ἐὰν δὲ
νότιόν τε ᾖ καὶ ἥλιος ἐπιλάμπῃ, ὀλίγον χρόνον·
ταχὺ γὰρ διαχεῖται.

Ὅταν δ' ἐπινίφῃ συνεχῶς, οὐδὲν δεῖ· ἐπικα-
λύπτει γάρ· οὐδ' ἐὰν πνεῦμα ᾖ μέγα· συμφοροῦν
2 γὰρ τὴν χιόνα ἀφανίζει. κύνας μὲν οὖν οὐδὲν
δεῖ ἔχοντα ἐξιέναι ἐπὶ τὴν θήραν ταύτην· ἡ γὰρ
χιὼν καίει τῶν κυνῶν τὰς ῥῖνας, τοὺς πόδας, τὴν
ὀσμὴν τοῦ λαγῶ ἀφανίζει διὰ τὸ ὑπέρπαγες·
λαβόντα δὲ τὰ δίκτυα μετ' ἄλλου ἐλθόντα πρὸς
τὰ ὄρη παριέναι ἀπὸ τῶν ἔργων καὶ ἐπειδὰν
3 λάβῃ τὰ ἴχνη, πορεύεσθαι κατὰ ταῦτα. ἐὰν δ'
ἐπηλλαγμένα ᾖ, ἐκ τῶν αὐτῶν πάλιν εἰς τὸ
αὐτὸ ἥκοντα κύκλους ποιούμενον ἐκπεριιέναι τὰ
τοιαῦτα, ζητοῦντα ὅποι ἔξεισι. πολλὰ δὲ πλα-
νᾶται ὁ λαγῶς ἀπορούμενος ὅπου κατακλιθῇ,
ἅμα δὲ καὶ εἴθισται τεχνάζειν τῇ βαδίσει διὰ
4 τὸ διώκεσθαι ἀεὶ ἀπὸ τῶν τοιούτων. ἐπειδὰν
δὲ φανῇ τὸ ἴχνος, προϊέναι εἰς τὸ πρόσθεν. ἄξει
δὲ ἢ πρὸς σύσκιον τόπον ἢ πρὸς ἀπόκρημνον·
τὰ γὰρ πνεύματα ὑπερφορεῖ τὴν χιόνα ὑπὲρ τῶν

---

[1] δεομέναις A: S. omits with BM.
[2] μὴ added by Gesner: S. omits.

they will be too intent on that to worry about their
food. As a rule when they are hungry the master 12
should feed the hounds himself; for when they are
not hungry they do not know to whom that is due;
but when they want food and get it, they love
the giver.

VIII. Track the hare when it snows so hard that
the ground is covered; but if there are black spaces,
she will be hard to find. When it is cloudy and the
wind is in the north, the tracks lie plain on the
surface for a long time, because they melt slowly;
but only for a short time if the wind is south and
the sun shines, since they soon melt away.

But when it snows without stopping, don't
attempt it, since the tracks are covered; nor when
there is a high wind, since they are buried in the
snowdrifts it causes. On no account have the hounds 2
out with you for this kind of sport, for the snow
freezes their noses and feet, and destroys the scent
of the hare owing to the hard frost. But take the
hayes, and go with a companion to the mountains,
passing over the cultivated land, and as soon as
the tracks are found, follow them. If they are 3
complicated, go back from the same ones to the same
place and work round in circles and examine them,
trying to find where they lead. The hare roams
about uncertain where to rest, and, moreover, it is
her habit to be tricky in her movements, because
she is constantly being pursued in this manner.
As soon as the track is clear, push straight 4
ahead. It will lead either to a thickly wooded
spot or to a steep declivity. For the gusts of wind

---

[8] ἐπινεφῇ van Leeuwen: ἐπινίφῃ S. with the MSS.

XENOPHON

τοιούτων. παραλείπεται οὖν εὐνάσιμα πολλά·
5 ζητεῖ δὲ τοῦτο. ἐπειδὰν δὲ τὰ ἴχνη πρὸς τὰ
τοιαῦτα φέρῃ, μὴ προσιέναι ἐγγύς, ἵνα μὴ
ὑποκινῇ, ἀλλὰ κύκλῳ ἐκπεριιέναι· ἐλπὶς γὰρ
αὐτοῦ εἶναι. δῆλον δ᾽ ἔσται· τὰ γὰρ ἴχνη ἀπὸ
6 τῶν τοιούτων οὐδαμοῦ περάσει. ἐπειδὰν δὲ ᾖ
σαφὲς ὅτι αὐτοῦ ἐστίν, ἐὰν μενεῖ γάρ· ἕτερον
δὲ ζητεῖν, πρὶν τὰ ἴχνη ἄδηλα γενέσθαι, τῆς
ὥρας ἐνθυμούμενον, ὅπως ἂν καὶ ἑτέρους εὑρίσκῃ,
7 ἔσται ἡ λειπομένη ἱκανὴ περιστήσασθαι. ἥκοντος
δὲ τούτου περιτείνειν αὐτῶν ἑκάστῳ τὰ δίκτυα
τὸν αὐτὸν τρόπον ὅνπερ ἐν τοῖς μελαγχίμοις,
περιλαμβάνοντα ἐντὸς πρὸς ὅτῳ ἂν ᾖ, καὶ
8 ἐπειδὰν ἑστηκότα ᾖ, προσελθόντα κινεῖν. ἐὰν
δὲ ἐκκυλισθῇ ἐκ τῶν δικτύων, μεταθεῖν κατὰ τὰ
ἴχνη· ὁ δὲ ἀφίξεται πρὸς ἕτερα τοιαῦτα χωρία,
ἐὰν μὴ ἄρα ἐν αὐτῇ τῇ χιόνι πιέσῃ ἑαυτόν.
σκεψάμενον οὖν δεῖ ὅπου ἂν ᾖ περιίστασθαι.
ἐὰν δὲ μὴ ὑπομένῃ, μεταθεῖν· ἁλώσεται γὰρ καὶ
ἄνευ τῶν δικτύων· ταχὺ γὰρ ἀπαγορεύει διὰ
τὸ βάθος τῆς χιόνος καὶ διὰ τὸ κάτωθεν τῶν
ποδῶν λασίων ὄντων προσέχεσθαι αὐτῷ ὄγκον
πολύν.

IX. Ἐπὶ δὲ τοὺς νεβροὺς καὶ τὰς ἐλάφους
κύνας εἶναι Ἰνδικάς· εἰσὶ γὰρ ἰσχυραί, μεγάλαι,
ποδώκεις, οὐκ ἄψυχοι· ἔχουσαι δὲ ταῦτα ἱκαναὶ
γίγνονται πονεῖν. τοὺς μὲν οὖν νεογνοὺς τῶν

---

[1] The object is to make sure whether the track really does
end there or not. If it does, he is to go on to seek another
hare. "My father used to relate that in his student days
an old forester on his brother-in-law's estate, when he wanted
to make sure of supplying a hare for his master's visitors,

carry the snow over such places ; consequently many resting-places are left, and she looks for one of these. As soon as the tracks lead to such a place, don't go 5 near, or she will move off, but go round and explore.[1] For she is probably there, and there will be no doubt about the matter, since the tracks will nowhere run out from such places. As soon as it is evident that she is there, 6 leave her—for she will not stir—and look for another before the tracks become obscure, and take care, in case you find others, that you will have enough daylight left to surround them with nets. When the time has come, stretch the hayes round 7 each of them in the same way as in places where no snow lies, enclosing anything she may be near, and as soon as they are up, approach and start her. If she wriggles out of the hayes, run after her along 8 the tracks. She will make for other places of the same sort, unless indeed she squeezes herself into the snow itself. Wherever she may be, mark the place and surround it ; or, if she doesn't wait, continue the pursuit. For she will be caught even without the hayes ; for she soon tires owing to the depth of the snow, and because large lumps of it cling to the bottom of her hairy feet.

IX. For hunting fawns and deer [2] use Indian [3] hounds ; for they are strong, big, speedy and plucky, and these qualities render them capable of hard

would surround the hare's form in the early morning, and the hare would not leave her form for hours." A Körte (*Hermes*, 1918, p. 317).

[2] The red deer is meant. Hunting the calves immediately after their birth seems a poor game ; but no doubt they were good eating.

[3] **Thibet dogs, called by Grattius (159) Seres.**

XENOPHON

νεβρῶν τοῦ ἦρος θηρᾶν· ταύτην γὰρ τὴν ὥραν
2 γίγνονται. κατασκέψασθαι δὲ πρότερον προ-
ελθόντα εἰς τὰς ὀργάδας, οὗ εἰσιν ἔλαφοι πλεῖ-
σται· ὅπου δ' ἂν ὦσιν, ἔχοντα τὸν κυναγωγὸν
τὰς κύνας καὶ ἀκόντια πρὸ ἡμέρας ἐλθόντα εἰς
τὸν τόπον τοῦτον τὰς μὲν κύνας δῆσαι ἄποθεν
ἐκ τῆς ὕλης, ὅπως μή, ἂν ἴδωσι τὰς ἐλάφους,
3 ὑλακτῶσιν, αὐτὸν δὲ σκοπιωρεῖσθαι. ἅμα δὲ
τῇ ἡμέρᾳ ὄψεται ἀγούσας τοὺς νεβροὺς πρὸς τὸν
τόπον, οὗ ἂν μέλλῃ ἑκάστη τὸν ἑαυτῆς εὐνάσειν.
κατακλίνασαι δὲ καὶ γάλα δοῦσαι καὶ διασκε-
ψάμεναι, μὴ ὁρῶνται ὑπό τινος, φυλάττει τὸν
ἑαυτῆς ἑκάστη ἀπελθοῦσα εἰς τὸ ἀντιπέρας.
4 ἰδόντα δὲ ταῦτα τὰς μὲν κύνας λῦσαι, αὐτὸν δὲ
λαβόντα ἀκόντια προϊέναι ἐπὶ τὸν νεβρὸν τὸν
πρῶτον, ὅπου εἶδεν εὐνασθέντα, τῶν τόπων
ἐνθυμούμενον, ὅπως μὴ διαμαρτήσεται· πολὺ γὰρ
ἀλλοιοῦνται τῇ ὄψει ἐγγὺς προσιόντι ἢ οἷοι
5 πόρρωθεν ἔδοξαν εἶναι. ἐπειδὰν δὲ ἴδῃ αὐτόν,
προσιέναι ἐγγύς. ὁ δ' ἕξει ἀτρέμα πιέσας ὡς
ἐπὶ γῆν καὶ ἐάσει ἀνελέσθαι, ἐὰν μὴ ἐφυσμένος
ᾖ, βοῶν μέγα. τούτου δὲ γενομένου οὐ μενεῖ·
ταχὺ γὰρ τὸ ὑγρόν, ὃ ἔχει ἐν ἑαυτῷ, ὑπὸ τοῦ
ψυχροῦ συνιστάμενον ποιεῖ ἀποχωρεῖν αὐτόν.
6 ἁλώσεται δὲ ὑπὸ τῶν κυνῶν σὺν πόνῳ διωκό-
μενος· λαβόντα δὲ δοῦναι τῷ ἀρκυωρῷ· ὁ δὲ
βοήσεται· ἡ δ' ἔλαφος τὰ μὲν ἰδοῦσα, τὰ δ'
ἀκούσασα ἐπιδραμεῖται τῷ ἔχοντι αὐτὸν ζητοῦσα
7 ἀφελέσθαι. ἐν δὲ τούτῳ τῷ καιρῷ ἐγκελεύειν ταῖς
κυσὶ καὶ χρῆσθαι τοῖς ἀκοντίοις. κρατήσαντα
δὲ τούτου πορεύεσθαι καὶ ἐπὶ τοὺς ἄλλους καὶ
τῷ αὐτῷ εἴδει πρὸς αὐτοὺς χρῆσθαι τῆς θήρας.

work. Hunt the calves in spring, since they are born at that season. First go to the meadows and 2 reconnoitre, to discover where hinds are most plentiful. Wherever they are, let the keeper of the hounds[1] go with the hounds and javelins to this place before daybreak and tie up the dogs to trees some distance off, so that they may not catch sight of the hinds and bark, and let him watch from a coign of vantage. At daybreak he will see every dam leading 3 her fawn to the place where she means to lay it. When they have put them down, suckled them, and looked about to make sure that they are not seen, they move away into the offing and watch their calves. On seeing this, let him loose the dogs, and taking the 4 javelins approach the spot where he saw the nearest fawn laid, carefully observing the positions so as not to make a mistake, since they look quite different when approached from what they seemed to be at a distance. As soon as he sees the fawn, let him go 5 close up to it. It will keep still, squeezing its body tight against the ground, and will let itself be lifted, bleating loudly, unless it is wet through, in which case it will not stay, since the rapid condensation of the moisture in its body by the cold causes it to make off. But it will be caught by the hounds 6 if hotly pursued. Having taken it, let him give it to the net-keeper. It will cry out; and the sight and the sound between them will bring the hind running up to the holder, in her anxiety to rescue it. That is the 7 moment to set the hounds on her, and ply the javelins. Having settled this one, let him proceed to tackle the rest, hunting them in the same manner.

[1] The "Keeper of hounds" has not been mentioned in connection with hare hunting. Apparently he is the person to whom all these instructions are addressed.

8 Καὶ οἱ μὲν νέοι τῶν νεβρῶν οὕτως ἁλίσκονται·
οἱ δὲ ἤδη μεγάλοι χαλεπῶς· νέμονται γὰρ
μετὰ τῶν μητέρων καὶ ἑτέρων ἐλάφων· καὶ
ἀποχωροῦσιν, ὅταν διώκωνται, ἐν μέσαις, ὁτὲ
9 δὲ πρόσθεν, ἐν δὲ τῷ ὄπισθεν ὀλιγάκις. αἱ δ᾽
ἔλαφοι τὰς κύνας ὑπὲρ αὐτῶν ἀμυνόμεναι κατα-
πατοῦσιν· ὥστ᾽ οὐκ εὐάλωτοί εἰσιν, ἐὰν μὴ
προσμείξας τις εὐθὺς διασκεδάσῃ αὐτὰς ἀπ᾽
10 ἀλλήλων, ὥστε μονωθῆναί τινα αὐτῶν. βιασθεῖσαι
δὲ τοῦτο τὸν μὲν πρῶτον δρόμον αἱ κύνες ἀπολεί-
πονται· ἥ τε γὰρ ἀπουσία τῶν ἐλάφων ποιεῖ
αὐτὸν περίφοβον τό τε τάχος οὐδενὶ ἔοικός ἐστι
τῶν τηλικούτων νεβρῶν· δευτέρῳ δὲ καὶ τρίτῳ
δρόμῳ ταχὺ ἁλίσκονται· τὰ γὰρ σώματα αὐτῶν
διὰ τὸ ἔτι νεαρὰ εἶναι τῷ πόνῳ οὐ δύνανται
ἀντέχειν.

11 Ἵστανται δὲ καὶ ποδοστράβαι ταῖς ἐλάφοις
ἐν τοῖς ὄρεσι, περὶ τοὺς λειμῶνας καὶ τὰ ῥεῖθρα
καὶ τὰς νάπας ἐν ταῖς διόδοις καὶ τοῖς ἔργοις,
12 πρὸς ὅ τι ἂν προσίῃ. χρὴ δὲ εἶναι τὰς ποδοστράβας σμίλακος πεπλεγμένας, μὴ περιφλοίους,
ἵνα μὴ σήπωνται, τὰς δὲ στεφάνας εὐκύκλους
ἐχούσας, καὶ τοὺς ἥλους ἐναλλὰξ σιδηροῦς τε
καὶ ξυλίνους ἐγκαταπεπλεγμένους ἐν τῷ πλο-
κάνῳ· μείζους δὲ τοὺς σιδηροῦς, ὅπως ἂν οἱ μὲν
13 ξύλινοι ὑπείκωσι τῷ ποδί, οἱ δὲ πιέζωσι. τὸν
δὲ βρόχον τῆς σειρίδος τὸν ἐπὶ τὴν στεφάνην
ἐπιτεθησόμενον πεπλεγμένον σπάρτου καὶ αὐτὴν
τὴν σειρίδα· ἔστι γὰρ ἀσηπτότατον τοῦτο. ὁ δὲ
βρόχος αὐτὸς ἔστω στιφρὸς καὶ ἡ σειρίς· τὸ δὲ
ξύλον τὸ ἐξαπτόμενον ἔστω μὲν δρυὸς ἢ πρίνου,

Young fawns are caught by this method ; but big 8
ones are difficult to catch. For they graze with their
dams and other deer ; and when pursued they make
off in the midst of them, or sometimes in front, but
rarely in the rear. The hinds trample on the hounds 9
in their efforts to defend their fawns ; consequently it
is not easy to catch them, unless a man gets amongst
them at once [1] and scatters them, so that one of the
fawns is isolated. The result of this strain on the 10
hounds is that they are left behind in the first run ;
for the absence of the hinds fills the creature with
terror, and the speed of fawns at that age is without
parallel. But they are soon caught in the second or
third run, since their bodies are still too young to
stand the work.

Caltrops are set for deer in the mountains, about 11
meadows and streams and glades, in alleys and cultivated lands that they frequent. The caltrops should 12
be made of plaited yew, stripped of the bark, so as not
to rot. They should have circular crowns, and the
nails should be of iron and wood alternately, plaited
into the rim,[2] the iron nails being the longer, so that
the wooden ones will yield to the foot and the others
hurt it. The noose of the cord to be laid on the 13
crown and the cord itself should be of woven *sparto*,[3]
since this is rot-proof. The noose itself and the
cord must be strong ; and the clog attached must be
of common or evergreen oak, twenty-seven inches

---

[1] The author has omitted to explain how this is to be
done.

[2] The "rim" (an unsatisfactory rendering) is the same
thing as the "crown."

[3] Yates (Textrinum Antiquorum) considers that *sparto* is
the Spanish broom (*genista*) and not the grass (*stipa tenuissima*)
now called esparto.

μέγεθος τρισπίθαμον, περίφλοιον, πάχος παλαιστῆς.

14 Ἱστάναι δὲ τὰς ποδοστράβας διελόντα τῆς γῆς βάθος πεντεπάλαιστον, περιφερὲς δὲ τοῦτο καὶ ἄνωθεν ἴσον ταῖς στεφάναις τῶν ποδοστραβῶν, εἰς δὲ τὸ κάτω ἀμειβόμενον στενότητι· διελεῖν δὲ καὶ τῇ σειρίδι καὶ τῷ ξύλῳ τῆς γῆς ὅσον ἵζεσθαι

15 ἀμφοῖν. ποιήσαντα δὲ ταῦτα ἐπὶ μὲν τὸ βάθος τὴν ποδοστράβην ἐπιθεῖναι κατωτέρω ἰσόπεδον, περὶ δὲ τὴν στέγην[1] τὸν βρόχον τῆς σειρίδος, καὶ αὐτὴν καὶ τὸ ξύλον καθέντα εἰς τὴν χώραν τὴν ἑκατέρου, τῇ στέγῃ ἐπιθεῖναι δοκίδας ἀτρακτυλίδος μὴ ὑπερτεινούσας εἰς τὸ ἔξω, ἐπὶ δὲ

16 τούτων πέταλα λεπτά, ὧν ἂν ἡ ὥρα ᾖ. μετὰ δὲ τοῦτο τῆς γῆς ἐπιβαλεῖν ἐπ' αὐτὰ πρῶτον μὲν τὴν ἐπιπολῆς ἐξαιρεθεῖσαν ἐκ τῶν ὀρυγμάτων, ἄνωθεν δὲ γῆς στερεᾶς τῆς ἄποθεν, ἵνα ᾖ τῇ ἐλάφῳ ὅτι μάλιστα ἄδηλος ἡ στάσις· τὴν δὲ περιοῦσαν τῆς γῆς ἀποφέρειν πόρρω ἀπὸ τῆς ποδοστράβης. ἐὰν γὰρ ὀσφραίνηται νεωστὶ κεκινημένης. δυσωπεῖται· ταχὺ δὲ ποιεῖ τοῦτο.

17 ἐπισκοπεῖν δὲ ἔχοντα τὰς κύνας τὰς μὲν ἐν τοῖς ὄρεσιν ἑστώσας, μάλιστα μὲν ἕωθεν, χρὴ δὲ καὶ τῆς ἄλλης ἡμέρας, ἐν δὲ τοῖς ἔργοις πρωί. ἐν μὲν γὰρ τοῖς ὄρεσιν οὐ μόνον τῆς νυκτὸς ἁλίσκονται, ἀλλὰ καὶ μεθ' ἡμέραν διὰ τὴν ἐρημίαν· ἐν δὲ τοῖς ἔργοις τῆς νυκτὸς διὰ τὸ μεθ' ἡμέραν πεφοβῆσθαι τοὺς ἀνθρώπους.

18 Ἐπειδὰν δὲ εὕρῃ ἀνεστραμμένην τὴν ποδοστράβην, μεταθεῖν ἐπιλύσαντα τὰς κύνας καὶ ἐπικελεύσαντα κατὰ τὸν ὁλκὸν τοῦ ξύλου, σκοπούμενον ὅπου ἂν φέρηται. ἔσται δὲ οὐκ ἄδηλον

long, not stripped of the bark, and three inches
thick.

To set the caltrops make a round hole in the 14
ground fifteen inches deep, of the same size at the
top as the crowns of the traps, but tapering towards
the bottom. Make shallow drills in the ground for
the cord and the clog to lie in. Having done this lay 15
the caltrop on the hole a little below the surface, and
level, and put the noose of the cord round the top.
Having laid the cord and the clog in their places, lay
spindle-wood twigs on the top, not letting them
stick out beyond the circle, and on these any light
leaves in season. Next throw some earth on them, 16
beginning with the surface soil taken from the holes,
and on top of this some unbroken soil from a distance, in order that the position may be completely
concealed from the deer. Remove any earth remaining over to a place some distance from the caltrop ; for if the deer smells earth recently disturbed,
it shies ; and it is not slow to smell it. Accompanied 17
by the hounds, inspect the traps set in the mountains,
preferably at daybreak (but it should be done also at
other times during the day), in the cultivated lands
early. For in the mountains deer may be caught
in the daytime as well as at night owing to the
solitude ; but on cultivated land only at night,
because they are afraid of human beings in the
daytime.

On coming across a caltrop upset, slip the hounds, 18
give them a hark-forward, and follow along the
track of the clog, noticing which way it runs. That

---

¹ στέγην and (presently) στέγῃ A : στεφάνην and στεφάνῃ
S. with M.

ἐπὶ τὸ πολύ· οἵ τε γὰρ λίθοι ἔσονται κεκινημένοι
τά τ᾽ ἐπισύρματα τοῦ ξύλου καταφανῆ ἐν τοῖς
ἔργοις· ἐὰν δὲ τραχεῖς τόπους διαπερᾷ, αἱ πέτραι
ἕξουσι τὸν φλοιὸν τοῦ ξύλου ἀφηρπασμένον καὶ
κατὰ τοῦτο ῥᾷους αἱ μεταδρομαὶ ἔσονται.

19 Ἐὰν μὲν οὖν τοῦ προσθίου ποδὸς ἁλῷ, ταχὺ
ληφθήσεται· ἐν γὰρ τῷ δρόμῳ πᾶν τὸ σῶμα
τύπτει καὶ τὸ πρόσωπον· ἐὰν δὲ τοῦ ὄπισθεν,
ἐφελκόμενον τὸ ξύλον ἐμποδὼν ὅλῳ ἐστὶ τῷ
σώματι· ἐνίοτε δὲ καὶ εἰς δικρόας τῆς ὕλης
ἐμπίπτει φερόμενον, καὶ ἐὰν μὴ ἀπορρήξῃ τὴν
20 σειρίδα, καταλαμβάνεται αὐτοῦ. χρὴ δ᾽ ἐὰν
οὕτως ἕλῃ ἢ περιγενόμενος πόνῳ, μὴ προσιέναι
ἐγγύς· τοῖς γὰρ κέρασι παίει ἐὰν μὲν ᾖ ἄρρην,[1]
καὶ τοῖν ποδοῖν· ἐὰν δὲ θήλεια τοῖν ποδοῖν.
ἄποθεν οὖν ἀκοντίζειν.

Ἁλίσκονται δὲ καὶ ἄνευ ποδοστράβης διωκό-
μεναι, ὅταν ᾖ ἡ ὥρα θερινή· ἀπαγορεύουσι γὰρ
σφόδρα, ὥστε ἑστῶσαι ἀκοντίζονται· ῥιπτοῦσι
δὲ καὶ εἰς τὴν θάλατταν, ἐὰν κατέχωνται, καὶ εἰς
τὰ ὕδατα ἀπορούμεναι· ὁτὲ δὲ διὰ δύσπνοιαν
πίπτουσι.

X. Πρὸς δὲ τὸν ὗν τὸν ἄγριον κεκτῆσθαι κύνας
Ἰνδικάς, Κρητικάς, Λοκρίδας, Λακαίνας, ἄρκυς,
ἀκόντια, προβόλια, ποδοστράβας. πρῶτον μὲν
οὖν χρὴ εἶναι τὰς κύνας ἑκάστου[2] γένους μὴ τὰς
ἐπιτυχούσας, ἵνα ἕτοιμαι ὦσι πολεμεῖν τῷ θηρίῳ.
2 αἱ δὲ ἄρκυς λίνων μὲν τῶν αὐτῶν ὦνπερ αἱ τῶν
λαγῶν, ἔστωσαν δὲ πεντεκαιτετταρακοντάλινοι

---

[1] ἐὰν μὲν ᾖ ἄρρην follows πόνῳ in S. and the MSS.: Diels
saw that it belongs here: M has τοῖς ποσίν and omits ἐὰν δὲ
θήλεια τοῖν ποδοῖν by oversight; and so S.

will be clear enough for the most part : for the stones will be displaced and the trail of the clog will be obvious in the cultivated ground; and if the deer crosses rough places, there will be fragments of bark torn from the clog on the rocks, and the pursuit will be all the easier.

If the deer is caught by the fore-foot it will soon 19 be taken, as it hits every part of its body and its face with the clog during the run; or if by the hind-leg, the dragging of the clog hampers the whole body; and sometimes it dashes into forked branches of trees, and unless it breaks the cord, is caught on the spot. But, whether you catch it in this way or by 20 wearing it out, don't go near it; for it will butt, if it's a stag, and kick, and if it's a hind, it will kick. So throw javelins at it from a distance.

In the summer months they are also caught by pursuit without the aid of a caltrop; for they get dead beat, so that they are hit standing. When hard pressed, they will even plunge into the sea and into pools in their bewilderment; and occasionally they drop from want of breath.

X. For hunting the wild boar provide yourself with Indian, Cretan, Locrian and Laconian [1] hounds, boar nets, javelins, spears and caltrops. In the first place the hounds of each breed must be of high quality, that they may be qualified to fight the beast. The 2 nets must be made of the same flax as those used for hares, of forty-five threads woven in three strands,

---

[1] *i.e.* Laconian hounds of the Castorian variety; see c. iii. § 5.

---

[2] ἑκάστου from the text as quoted by Aristides : ἐκ τούτου τοῦ S. with the MSS.

ἐκ τριῶν τόνων, ἕκαστος δὲ τόνος ἐκ πεντεκαίδεκα
λίνων, ἀπὸ δὲ τοῦ κορυφαίου τὸ μέγεθος δεχάμ-
ματοι, τὸ δὲ βάθος τῶν βρόχων πυγόνος· οἱ δὲ
περίδρομοι ἡμιόλιοι τοῦ τῶν ἀρκύων πάχους· ἐπ'
ἄκροις δὲ δακτυλίους ἐχέτωσαν, ὑφείσθωσαν δ'
ὑπὸ τοὺς βρόχους, τὸ δὲ ἄκρον αὐτῶν ἐκπεράτω
ἔξω διὰ τῶν δακτυλίων· ἱκαναὶ [1] δὲ πεντεκαίδεκα.

3   Τὰ δὲ ἀκόντια ἔστω παντοδαπά, ἔχοντα τὰς
λόγχας εὐπλατεῖς καὶ ξυρήκεις, ῥάβδους δὲ
στιφράς. τὰ δὲ προβόλα πρῶτον μὲν λόγχας
ἔχοντα τὸ μὲν μέγεθος πεντεπαλαίστους, κατὰ δὲ
μέσον τὸν αὐλὸν κνώδοντας ἀποκεχαλκευμένους,
στιφρούς, καὶ τὰς ῥάβδους κρανείας δορατοπαχεῖς·
αἱ δὲ ποδοστράβαι ὅμοιαι ταῖς τῶν ἐλάφων.
συγκυνηγέται δ' ἔστωσαν· τὸ γὰρ θηρίον μόλις
καὶ ὑπὸ πολλῶν ἁλίσκεται. ὅπως δὲ δεῖ τούτων
ἑκάστῳ χρῆσθαι πρὸς θήραν, διδάξω.

4   Πρῶτον μὲν οὖν χρὴ ἐλθόντας οὗ ἂν οἴωνται [2]
ὑπάγειν τὸ κυνηγέσιον, λύσαντας μίαν τῶν
κυνῶν τῶν Λακαινῶν, τὰς δ' ἄλλας ἔχοντας δεδε-
5   μένας συμπεριιέναι τῇ κυνί. ἐπειδὰν δὲ λάβῃ
αὐτοῦ τὰ ἴχνη, ἕπεσθαι ἐξῆς τῇ ἰχνεύσει ἡγου-
μένῃ ἀκολουθοῦντας σαφῶς. [3] ἔσται δὲ καὶ τοῖς
κυνηγέταις πολλὰ δῆλα αὐτοῦ, ἐν μὲν τοῖς μαλα-

---

[1] ἱκανοὶ S. with A.
[2] εἶναι which S. and the MSS. add after οἴωνται was
removed by Pierleoni.
[3] ἀκολουθοῦντας σαφῶς A: ἀκολουθίᾳ S. with B: ἀκολου-
θίαν M.

---

[a] This means, I believe, ten meshes, so that the net would
be about 150 inches high. Otto Manns (*Über die Jagd bei den*

each strand containing fifteen threads. The height should be ten knots, counted from the top,[1] and the depths of the meshes fifteen inches. The ropes at top and bottom must be half as thick again as the nets. There must be metal rings at the elbows, and the ropes must be inserted under the meshes, and their ends must pass out through the rings.[2] Fifteen nets are sufficient.[3]

The javelins must be of every variety, the blades 3 broad and keen, and the shafts strong. The spears must have blades fifteen inches long, and stout teeth at the middle of the socket, forged in one piece but standing out; and their shafts must be of cornel wood, as thick as a military spear. The caltrops must be similar to those used in hunting deer. There must be several huntsmen, for the task of capturing the beast is no light one even for a large number of men. I will now explain how to use each portion of the outfit in hunting.

First then, when the company reach the place 4 where they suppose the game to lurk, let them slip one of the Laconian hounds, and taking the others in leash, go round the place with the hound. As 5 soon as she has found his tracks, let the field follow, one behind another, keeping exactly to the line of the track. The huntsmen also will find many evi-

Grieschen), however, thinks that the net was five feet high only, i.e. four meshes (cf. c. iv. § 5); but (1) it is hard to see how "four meshes" can be got out of "ten knots," and (2) the "bosom" (see § 7) requires a considerably greater height than five feet.

[2] The ends of the upper ropes appear to have been used for fastening the nets together.

[3] It is strange that the author does not state the length of the nets.

κοῖς τῶν χωρίων τὰ ἴχνη, ἐν δὲ τοῖς λασίοις τῆς
ὕλης κλάσματα· ὅπου δ' ἂν δένδρα ᾖ, πληγαὶ
6 τῶν ὀδόντων. ἡ δὲ κύων ἐπὶ τὸ πολὺ ἀφίξεται
τόπον ὑλώδη ἰχνεύουσα. κατακλίνεται γὰρ τὸ
θηρίον ὡς ἐπὶ τὸ πολὺ εἰς τοιαῦτα· τοῦ μὲν γὰρ
χειμῶνός ἐστιν ἀλεεινά, τοῦ δὲ θέρους ψυχεινά.
7 ἐπειδὰν δ' ἀφίκηται ἐπὶ τὴν εὐνήν, ὑλακτεῖ· ὁ δ'
οὐκ ἀνίσταται ὡς τὰ πολλά. λαβόντα οὖν τὴν
κύνα καὶ ταύτην μετὰ τῶν ἄλλων δῆσαι ἄποθεν
ἀπὸ τῆς εὐνῆς πολὺ καὶ εἰς τοὺς ὅρμους ἐμβάλ-
λεσθαι τὰς ἄρκυς, ἐπιβάλλοντα τοὺς βρόχους
ἐπὶ ἀποσχαλιδώματα τῆς ὕλης δικρᾶ· τῆς δὲ
ἄρκυος αὐτῆς μακρὸν προήκοντα κόλπον ποιεῖν,
ἀντηρίδας ἔνδοθεν ἑκατέρωθεν ὑφιστάντα κλῶνας,
ὅπως ἂν εἰς τὸν κόλπον διὰ τῶν βρόχων αἱ αὐγαὶ
τοῦ φέγγους ὡς μάλιστα ἐνέχωσιν, ἵνα προσ-
θέοντι ὡς φανότατον ᾖ τὸ ἔσω· καὶ τὸν περίδρομον ἐξάπτειν ἀπὸ δένδρου ἰσχυροῦ καὶ μὴ ἐκ
ῥάχου· συνέχονται¹ γὰρ ἐν τοῖς ψιλοῖς αἱ ῥάχοι.
ὑπὲρ δὲ ἑκάστης ἐμφράττειν τῇ ὕλῃ καὶ τὰ
δύσορμα, ἵνα εἰς τὰς ἄρκυς ποιῆται τὸν δρόμον
μὴ ἐξαλλάττων.
8   Ἐπειδὰν δὲ στῶσιν, ἐλθόντας πρὸς τὰς κύνας
λῦσαι ἁπάσας καὶ λαβόντας τὰ ἀκόντια καὶ τὰ
προβόλια προϊέναι. ἐγκελεύειν δὲ ταῖς κυσὶν
ἕνα τὸν ἐμπειρότατον, τοὺς δ' ἄλλους ἕπεσθαι
κοσμίως ἀπολείποντας ἀπ' ἀλλήλων πολύ, ὅπως
ἂν ᾖ αὐτῷ ἱκανὴ διαδρομή· ἐὰν γὰρ ὑποχωρῶν
ἐμπέσῃ εἰς πυκνούς, κίνδυνος πληγῆναι· ᾧ γὰρ
ἂν προσπέσῃ, εἰς τοῦτον τὴν ὀργὴν κατέθετο.

---

¹ The text is doubtful. I now think συγκλῶνται probable
for συνέχονται.

dences of the quarry, the tracks in soft ground, broken branches where the bushes are thick, and marks of his tusks wherever there are trees. The hound 6 following the track will, as a rule, arrive at a well-wooded spot. For the beast usually lies in such places, since they are warm in winter and cool in summer. As soon as the hound reaches the lair, she will bark. But in most cases the boar will not 7 get up. So take the hound and tie her up with the others at a good distance from the lair, and have the nets put up in the convenient anchorages, hanging the meshes on forked branches of trees. Out of the net itself make a long projecting bosom, putting sticks inside to prop it up on both sides, so that the light of day may penetrate as much as possible into the bosom through the meshes, in order that the interior may be as light as possible when the boar rushes at it. Fasten the (lower) rope to a strong tree, not to a bush, since the bushes give way at the bare stem.[1] Wherever there is a gap between a net and the ground,[2] fill in the places that afford no anchorage with wood, in order that the boar may rush into the net, and not slip out.

As soon as they are in position, let the party go to 8 the hounds and loose them all, and take the javelins and the spears and advance. Let one man, the most experienced, urge on the hounds, while the others follow in regular order, keeping well behind one another, so that the boar may have a free passage between them; for should he beat a retreat and dash into a crowd, there is a risk of being gored, since he spends his rage on anyone he encounters.

---

[2] The text is again uncertain, but the sense is clear. I incline to ὑπὸ δ' ἑκάστην.

XENOPHON

9 Ἐπειδὰν δὲ αἱ κύνες ἐγγὺς ὦσι τῆς εὐνῆς,
ἐπεισίασι· θορυβούμενος δ' ἐξαναστήσεται, καὶ
ἥτις ἂν τῶν κυνῶν προσφέρηται αὐτῷ πρὸς τὸ
πρόσωπον, ἀναρρίψει· θέων δ' ἐμπεσεῖται· ἐὰν
δὲ μή, μεταθεῖν ἀνάγκη. καὶ ἐὰν μὲν ᾖ τὸ
χωρίον καταφερές, ἐν ᾧ ἂν ἔχῃ αὐτὸν ἡ ἄρκυς,
ταχὺ ἐξαναστήσεται. ἐὰν δὲ ἄπεδον, εὐθὺς
10 ἑστήξει περὶ αὐτὸν ἔχων. ἐν τούτῳ δὲ τῷ
καιρῷ αἱ μὲν κύνες προσκείσονται· αὐτοὺς δὲ
χρὴ φυλαττομένους αὐτὸν ἀκοντίζειν καὶ λίθοις
βάλλειν, περισταμένους ὄπισθεν καὶ πολὺ ἄποθεν,
ἕως ἂν κατατείνῃ προωθῶν αὐτὸν τῆς ἄρκυος τὸν
περίδρομον. εἶτα ὅστις ἂν ᾖ τῶν παρόντων
ἐμπειρότατος καὶ ἐγκρατέστατος, προσελθόντα
11 ἐκ τοῦ πρόσθεν τῷ προβολίῳ παίειν. ἐὰν δὲ μὴ
βούληται ἀκοντιζόμενος καὶ βαλλόμενος κατα-
τεῖναι τὸν περίδρομον, ἀλλ' ἐπανιεὶς ἔχῃ πρὸς
τὸν προσιόντα περιδρομὴν ποιούμενος, ἀνάγκη,
ὅταν οὕτως ἔχῃ, λαβόντα τὸ προβόλιον προσιέναι, ἔχεσθαι δ' αὐτοῦ τῇ μὲν χειρὶ τῇ ἀριστερᾷ πρόσθεν, τῇ δ' ἑτέρᾳ ὄπισθεν· κατορθοῖ
γὰρ ἡ μὲν ἀριστερὰ αὐτό, ἡ δὲ δεξιὰ ἐπεμβάλλει·
ἔμπροσθεν δὲ ὁ ποὺς ὁ μὲν ἀριστερὸς ἑπέσθω τῇ
12 χειρὶ τῇ ὁμωνύμῳ, ὁ δὲ δεξιὸς τῇ ἑτέρᾳ· προσιόντα δὲ προβάλλεσθαι τὸ προβόλιον μὴ πολλῷ
μείζω διαβάντα ἢ ἐν πάλῃ, ἐπιστρέφοντα τὰς
πλευρὰς τὰς εὐωνύμους ἐπὶ τὴν χεῖρα τὴν εὐώνυμον, εἶτα εἰσβλέποντα εἰς τὸ ὄμμα τοῦ θηρίου,
ἐνθυμούμενον τὴν κίνησιν τὴν ἀπὸ τῆς κεφαλῆς
τῆς ἐκείνου. προσφέρειν δὲ τὸ προβόλιον φυλαττόμενον, μὴ ἐκκρούσῃ ἐκ τῶν χειρῶν τῇ κεφαλῇ
ἐκνεύσας· τῇ γὰρ ῥύμῃ τῆς ἐκκρούσεως ἔπεται.
434

As soon as the hounds are near the lair, they will 9
go for him. The noise will cause him to get up, and
he will toss any hound that attacks him in front.
He will run and plunge into the nets; or if not, you
must pursue him. If the ground where he is caught
in the net is sloping, he will quickly get up; if it is
level, he will immediately stand still, intent on himself. At this moment the hounds will press their 10
attack, and the huntsmen must fling their javelins at
him warily, and pelt him with stones, gathering round
behind and a good way off, till he shoves hard enough
to pull the rope of the net tight. Then let the most
experienced and most powerful man in the field
approach him in front and thrust his spear into him.
If, in spite of javelins and stones, he refuses to pull 11
the rope tight, but draws back, wheels round and
marks his assailant, in that case the man must
approach him spear in hand, and grasp it with the
left in front and the right behind, since the left
steadies while the right drives it. The left foot
must follow the left hand forward, and the right
foot the other hand. As he advances let him hold 12
the spear before him, with his legs not much further
apart than in wrestling, turning the left side towards
the left hand, and then watching the beast's eye
and noting the movement of the fellow's head.
Let him present the spear, taking care that the
boar doesn't knock it out of his hand with a jerk of
his head, since he follows up the impetus of the

13 παθόντα δὲ τοῦτο πίπτειν δεῖ ἐπὶ στόμα καὶ
ἔχεσθαι τῆς ὕλης κάτωθεν· τὸ γὰρ θηρίον ἐὰν
μὲν οὕτως ἔχοντι προσπέσῃ, διὰ τὴν σιμότητα
τῶν ὀδόντων τὸ σῶμα οὐ δύναται ὑπολαβεῖν·
ἐὰν δὲ μετεώρῳ, ἀνάγκη πληγῆναι. πειρᾶται
μὲν οὖν μετεωρίζειν. ἐὰν δὲ μὴ δύνηται, ἀμφιβὰς
14 πατεῖ. ἀπαλλαγὴ δὲ τούτων μία ἐστὶ μόνη,
ὅταν ἐν τῇ ἀνάγκῃ ταύτῃ ἔχηται, προσελθόντα
ἐγγὺς τῶν συγκυνηγετῶν ἕνα ἔχοντα προβόλιον
ἐρεθίζειν ὡς ἀφήσοντα· ἀφιέναι δὲ οὐ χρή, μὴ
15 τύχῃ τοῦ πεπτωκότας. ὅταν δὲ ἴδῃ τοῦτο, καταλιπὼν ὃν ἂν ἔχῃ ὑφ' αὑτῷ ἐπὶ τὸν ἐρεθίζοντα ὑπ'
ὀργῆς καὶ θυμοῦ ἐπιστρέψει. τὸν δὲ ταχὺ ἀναπηδᾶν, τὸ δὲ προβόλιον μεμνῆσθαι ἔχοντα ἀνί-
στασθαι· οὐ γὰρ καλὴ ἡ σωτηρία ἄλλως ἢ
16 κρατήσαντι. προσφέρειν δὲ πάλιν τὸν αὐτὸν
τρόπον καὶ προτεῖναι ἐντὸς τῆς ὠμοπλάτης, ᾗ ἡ
σφαγή, καὶ ἀντερείσαντα ἔχειν ἐρρωμένως· ὁ δ'
ὑπὸ τοῦ μένους πρόεισι, καὶ εἰ μὴ κωλύοιεν οἱ
κνώδοντες τῆς λόγχης, ἀφίκοιτ' ἂν διὰ τῆς
ῥάβδου προωθῶν αὐτὸν πρὸς τὸν τὸ προβόλιον
ἔχοντα.
17 Οὕτω δὲ πολλὴ ἡ δύναμίς ἐστιν αὐτοῦ, ὥστε
καὶ ἃ οὐκ ἂν οἴοιτό τις πρόσεστιν αὐτῷ· τε-
θνεῶτος γὰρ εὐθὺς ἐάν τις ἐπὶ τὸν ὀδόντα ἐπιθῇ
τρίχας, συντρέχουσιν· οὕτως εἰσὶ θερμοί· ζῶντι
δὲ διάπυροι, ὅταν ἐρεθίζηται· οὐ γὰρ ἂν τῶν
κυνῶν ἁμαρτάνων τῇ πληγῇ τοῦ σώματος ἄκρα
τὰ τριχώματα περιεπίμπρα.
18 Ὁ μὲν οὖν ἄρρην τοσαῦτα καὶ ἔτι πλείω

sudden knock. In case this accident should happen, 13
the man must fall on his face and clutch the
undergrowth beneath him, for, if the beast attacks
him in this position, he is unable to lift the man's
body owing to the upward curve of his tusks; but if
his body is off the ground, the man is certain to be
gored. Consequently the boar tries to lift him up,
and, if he cannot, he stands over and tramples on
him. For a man in this critical situation there is 14
only one escape from these disasters. One of his
fellow huntsmen must approach with a spear and
provoke the boar by making as though he would
hurl it; but he must not hurl it, or he may hit the
man on the ground. On seeing this the boar will 15
leave the man under him and turn savagely and
furiously on his tormentor. The other must jump up
instantly, remembering to keep his spear in his hand as
he rises, for safety without victory is not honourable.
He must again present the spear in the same way as 16
before, and thrust it inside the shoulder-blade where
the throat is, and push with all his might. The
enraged beast will come on, and but for the teeth of
the blade, would shove himself forward along the
shaft far enough to reach the man holding the
spear.

His strength is so great that he has some peculiar 17
properties which one would never imagine him to
possess. Thus, if you lay hairs on his tusks immediately after he is dead, they shrivel up, such is
the heat of the tusks. While he is alive they become
intensely hot whenever he is provoked, or the
surface of the hounds' coats would not be singed
when he tries to gore them and misses.

All this trouble, and even more, the male animal 18

πράγματα παρασχὼν ἁλίσκεται. ἐὰν δὲ θήλεια
ᾖ ἡ ἐμπεσοῦσα, ἐπιθέοντα παίειν φυλαττόμενον
μὴ ὠσθεὶς πέσῃ· παθόντα δὲ τοῦτο πατεῖσθαι
ἀνάγκη καὶ δάκνεσθαι. ἑκόντα οὖν οὐ χρὴ ὑποπί-
πτειν· ἐὰν δὲ ἄκων ἔλθῃ εἰς τοῦτο, διαναστάσεις
γίγνονται αἱ αὐταὶ ὥσπερ ἐπὶ τοῦ ἄρρενος·
ἐξαναστάντα δὲ δεῖ παίειν τῷ προβολίῳ, ἕως
ἂν ἀποκτείνῃ.

19   Ἁλίσκονται δὲ καὶ ὧδε. ἵστανται μὲν αὐτοῖς
αἱ ἄρκυς ἐπὶ τὰς διαβάσεις τῶν ναπῶν εἰς τοὺς
δρυμούς, τὰ ἄγκη, τὰ τραχέα, ᾗ εἰσβολαί εἰσιν
εἰς τὰς ὀργάδας καὶ τὰ ἕλη καὶ τὰ ὕδατα. ὁ δὲ
τεταγμένος ἔχων τὸ προβόλιον φυλάττει τὰς
ἄρκυς. οἱ δὲ τὰς κύνας ἐπάγουσι τοὺς τόπους
ζητοῦντες τοὺς καλλίστους· ἐπειδὰν δὲ εὑρεθῇ,
20 διώκεται. ἐὰν οὖν εἰς τὴν ἄρκυν ἐμπίπτῃ, τὸν
ἀρκυωρὸν ἀναλαβόντα τὸ προβόλιον προσιέναι
καὶ χρῆσθαι ὡς εἴρηκα· ἐὰν δὲ μὴ ἐμπέσῃ, μεταθεῖν. ἁλίσκεται δὲ καὶ ὅταν ᾖ πνίγη, διωκόμενος
ὑπὸ τῶν κυνῶν· τὸ γὰρ θηρίον καίπερ ὑπερβάλλον δυνάμει ἀπαγορεύει ὑπέρασθμον γιγνό-
21 μενον. ἀποθνήσκουσι δὲ κύνες πολλαὶ ἐν τῇ
τοιαύτῃ θήρᾳ καὶ αὐτοὶ οἱ κυνηγέται κινδυνεύουσιν, ὅταν γε[1] ἐν ταῖς μεταδρομαῖς ἀπειρηκότι
ἀναγκάζωνται προσιέναι τὰ προβόλια ἢ ἐν ὕδατι
ὄντι ἢ ἐφεστῶτι[2] πρὸς ἀποκρήμνῳ ἢ ἐκ δασέος
μὴ θέλοντι ἐξιέναι· οὐ γὰρ κωλύει αὐτὸν οὔτε
ἄρκυς οὔτε ἄλλο οὐδὲν φέρεσθαι ὁμόσε τῷ
πλησιάζοντι· ὅμως μέντοι προσιτέον, ὅταν ἔχῃ
οὕτως, καὶ ἐπιδεικτέον τὴν εὐψυχίαν, δι᾽ ἣν
22 εἵλοντο ἐκπονεῖν τὴν ἐπιθυμίαν ταύτην. χρη-
στέον δὲ τῷ προβολίῳ καὶ ταῖς προβολαῖς τοῦ

causes before he is caught. If the creature in the
toils is a sow, run up and stick her, taking care not
to be knocked down. Such an accident is bound
to result in your being trampled and bitten. So
don't fall under her, if you can help it. If you
get into that position unintentionally, the same aids
to rise that are used to assist a man under a boar
are employed. When on your feet again, you must
ply the spear until you kill her.

Another way of capturing them is as follows. 19
The nets are set up for them at the passages from
glens into oak coppices, dells and rough places, on
the outskirts of meadows, fens and sheets of water.
The keeper, spear in hand, watches the nets. The
huntsmen take the hounds and search for the likeliest
places. As soon as the boar is found, he is pursued.
If he falls into the net, the net-keeper must take 20
his spear, approach the boar, and use it as I have
explained. The boar is also captured, in hot weather,
when pursued by the hounds; for in spite of his prodigious strength, the animal tires with hard breathing. Many hounds are killed in this kind of sport, 21
and the huntsmen themselves run risks, whenever in
the course of the pursuit they are forced to approach
a boar with their spears in their hands, when he is
tired or standing in water or has posted himself by a
steep declivity or is unwilling to come out of a thicket;
for neither net nor anything else stops him from
rushing at anyone coming near him. Nevertheless
approach they must in these circumstances, and
show the pluck that led them to take up this
hobby. They must use the spear and the forward 22

---

¹ γε Pierleoni: δὲ S. with the MSS.
² ἐφεστῶτι A: ἀφεστῶτι S. with BM.

σώματος ὡς εἴρηται· εἰ γάρ τι καὶ πάσχοι, οὐκ ἂν διά γε τὸ μὴ[1] ὀρθῶς ποιεῖν πάσχοι.

Ἵστανται δὲ αἱ ποδοστράβαι αὐτοῖς ὥσπερ ταῖς[2] ἐλάφοις ἐν τοῖς αὐτοῖς τόποις, καὶ ἐπισκέψεις αἱ αὐταὶ καὶ μεταδρομαὶ καὶ αἱ πρόσοδοι καὶ αἱ χρεῖαι τοῦ προβολίου.

23 Τὰ δὲ νεογενῆ αὐτῶν ὅταν ἁλίσκηται, χαλεπῶς τοῦτο πάσχει· οὔτε γὰρ μονοῦται, ἕως ἂν μικρὰ ᾖ, ὅταν τε αἱ κύνες εὕρωσιν ἢ προΐδῃ τι, ταχὺ εἰς τὴν ὕλην ἀφανίζεται· ἕπονται δὲ ἐπὶ τὸ πολὺ ὧν ἂν ὦσιν ἄμφω, χαλεποὶ ὄντες τότε καὶ μᾶλλον μαχόμενοι ὑπὲρ ἐκείνων ἢ ὑπὲρ αὐτῶν.

XI. Λέοντες δέ, παρδάλεις, λύγκες, πάνθηρες, ἄρκτοι καὶ τἆλλα ὅσα ἐστὶ τοιαῦτα θηρία ἁλίσκεται ἐν ξέναις χώραις περὶ τὸ Πάγγαιον ὄρος καὶ τὸν Κιττὸν τὸν ὑπὲρ τῆς Μακεδονίας, τὰ δ᾿ ἐν τῷ Ὀλύμπῳ τῷ Μυσίῳ καὶ ἐν Πίνδῳ, τὰ δ᾿ ἐν τῇ Νύσῃ τῇ ὑπὲρ τῆς Συρίας καὶ πρὸς τοῖς ἄλλοις ὄρεσιν, ὅσα οἷά τ᾿ ἐστὶ τρέφειν 2 τοιαῦτα. ἁλίσκεται δὲ τὰ μὲν ἐν τοῖς ὄρεσι φαρμάκῳ διὰ δυσχωρίαν ἀκονίτικῳ. παραβάλλουσι δὲ τοῦτο οἱ θηρώμενοι συμμιγνύντες εἰς τὸ αὐτό, ὅτῳ ἂν ἕκαστον χαίρῃ, περὶ τὰ ὕδατα 3 καὶ πρὸς ὅ τι ἂν ἄλλο προσίῃ. τὰ δὲ αὐτῶν καταβαίνοντα εἰς τὸ πεδίον τῆς νυκτὸς ἀποκλεισθέντα μετὰ ἵππων καὶ ὅπλων ἁλίσκεται, εἰς 4 κίνδυνον καθιστάντα τοὺς αἱροῦντας. ἔστι δὲ οἷς αὐτῶν καὶ ὀρύγματα ποιοῦσι περιφερῆ, μεγάλα, βαθέα, ἐν μέσῳ λείποντες κίονα τῆς γῆς. ἐπὶ δὲ τούτου εἰς νύκτα ἐπέθεσαν δήσαντες αἶγα καὶ ἔφραξαν κύκλῳ τὸ ὄρυγμα ὕλῃ, ὥστε μὴ προορᾶν,

---

[1] μὴ omitted by S.

position of the body as explained; then, if a man does come to grief, it will not be through doing things the wrong way.

Caltrops are also set for them as for the deer and in the same places. The routine of inspection and pursuit, the methods of approach and the use of the spear are the same.

The young pigs are not to be caught without 23 difficulty. For they are not left alone so long as they are little, and when the hounds find them or they see something coming, they quickly vanish into the wood; and they are generally accompanied by both parents, who are fierce at such times and more ready to fight for their young than for themselves.

XI. Lions, leopards, lynxes, panthers, bears and all similar wild beasts are captured in foreign countries, about Mt. Pangaeus and Cittus beyond Macedonia, on Mysian Olympus and Pindus, on Nysa beyond Syria, and in other mountain ranges capable of supporting such animals. On the 2 mountains they are sometimes poisoned, owing to the difficulty of the ground, with aconite. Hunters put it down mixed with the animals' favourite food round pools and in other places that they frequent. Sometimes, while they are going down to the plain 3 at night, they are cut off by parties of armed and mounted men. This is a dangerous method of capturing them. Sometimes the hunters dig large, round, 4 deep holes, leaving a pillar of earth in the middle. They tie up a goat and put it on the pillar in the evening, and pile wood round the hole without leaving an entrance, so that the animals cannot see

---

² ταῖς A: τοῖς S. with BM.

εἴσοδον οὐ λείποντες. τὰ δὲ ἀκούοντα τῆς φωνῆς
ἐν τῇ νυκτὶ κύκλῳ τὸν φραγμὸν περιθέουσι
καὶ ἐπειδὰν μὴ εὑρίσκῃ δίοδον, ὑπερπηδᾷ καὶ
ἁλίσκεται.

XII. Περὶ μὲν αὐτῶν τῶν πράξεων τῶν ἐν
τοῖς κυνηγεσίοις εἴρηται. ὠφελήσονται δ' οἱ
ἐπιθυμήσαντες τούτου τοῦ ἔργου πολλά· ὑγίειάν
τε γὰρ τοῖς σώμασι παρασκευάζει καὶ ὁρᾶν καὶ
ἀκούειν μᾶλλον, γηράσκειν δὲ ἧττον, τὰ δὲ πρὸς
2 τὸν πόλεμον μάλιστα παιδεύει. πρῶτον μὲν τὰ
ὅπλα ὅταν ἔχοντες πορεύωνται ὁδοὺς χαλεπάς,
οὐκ ἀπεροῦσιν· ἀνέξονται γὰρ τοὺς πόνους διὰ
τὸ εἰθίσθαι μετὰ τούτων αἱρεῖν τὰ θηρία. ἔπειτα
εὐνάζεσθαί τε σκληρῶς δυνατοὶ ἔσονται καὶ
3 φύλακες εἶναι ἀγαθοὶ τοῦ ἐπιταττομένου. ἐν δὲ
ταῖς προσόδοις ταῖς πρὸς τοὺς πολεμίους ἅμα
οἷοί τε ἔσονται ἐπιέναι καὶ τὰ παραγγελλόμενα
ποιεῖν διὰ τὸ οὕτω καὶ αὐτοὶ αἱρεῖν τὰς ἄγρας.
τεταγμένοι δ' ἐν τῷ πρόσθεν οὐ λείψουσι τὰς
4 τάξεις διὰ τὸ καρτερεῖν δύνασθαι. ἐν φυγῇ δὲ
τῶν πολεμίων ὀρθῶς καὶ ἀσφαλῶς διώξονται τοὺς
ἐναντίους ἐν παντὶ χωρίῳ διὰ συνήθειαν. δυστυ-
χήσαντος δὲ οἰκείου στρατοπέδου ἐν χωρίοις ὑλώδεσι καὶ ἀποκρήμνοις ἢ ἄλλως[1] χαλεποῖς οἷοί τ'
ἔσονται καὶ αὐτοὶ σώζεσθαι μὴ αἰσχρῶς καὶ
ἑτέρους σώζειν· ἡ γὰρ συνήθεια τοῦ ἔργου παρέ-
5 ξει αὐτοῖς πλέον τι εἰδέναι. καὶ ἤδη τινὲς τῶν
τοιούτων, πολλοῦ ὄχλου συμμάχων τρεφθέντος,
τῇ αὐτῶν εὐεξίᾳ καὶ θράσει διὰ δυσχωρίαν
ἁμαρτόντας τοὺς πολεμίους νενικηκότας ἀναμα-

___
[1] ἄλλως Stobaeus: ἄλλοις S. with the MSS.

what lies in front. On hearing the bleating in the night, the beasts run round the barrier, and finding no opening, jump over and are caught.

XII. With the practical side of hunting I have finished. But the advantages that those who have been attracted by this pursuit will gain are many. For it makes the body healthy, improves the sight and hearing, and keeps men from growing old; and it affords the best training for war. In the first place, 2 when marching over rough roads under arms, they will not tire: accustomed to carry arms for capturing wild beasts, they will bear up under their tasks. Again, they will be capable of sleeping on a hard bed and of guarding well the place assigned to them. In an attack [1] on the enemy they will be able to go 3 for him and at the same time to carry out the orders that are passed along, because they are used to do the same things on their own account when capturing the game. If their post is in the van they will not desert it, because they can endure. In the rout 4 of the enemy they will make straight for the foe without a slip over any kind of ground, through habit. If part of their own army has met with disaster in ground rendered difficult by woods and defiles or what not, they will manage to save themselves without loss of honour and to save others. For their familiarity with the business will give them knowledge that others lack. Indeed, it has happened 5 before now, when a great host of allies has been put to flight, that a little band of such men, through their fitness and confidence, has renewed the battle and routed the victorious enemy when he has

---

[1] The word πρόσοδος in this sense is a hunters' term.

XENOPHON

χόμενοι ἐτρέψαντο· ἀεὶ γὰρ ἔστι τοῖς τὰ σώματα
καὶ τὰς ψυχὰς εὖ ἔχουσιν ἐγγὺς εἶναι τοῦ εὐτυ-
6 χῆσαι. εἰδότες δὲ καὶ οἱ πρόγονοι ἡμῶν, ὅτι
ἐντεῦθεν εὐτύχουν πρὸς τοὺς πολεμίους, ἐπιμέλειαν
τῶν νέων ἐποιήσαντο· σπανίζοντες γὰρ καρπῶν
τὸ ἐξ ἀρχῆς ἐνόμισαν ὅμως τοὺς κυνηγέτας μὴ
κωλύειν διὰ μηδενὸς[1] τῶν ἐπὶ τῇ γῇ φυομένων
7 ἀγρεύειν· πρὸς δὲ τούτῳ μὴ νυκτερεύειν ἐντὸς
πολλῶν σταδίων, ἵνα μὴ ἀφαιροῖντο τὰς θήρας
αὐτῶν οἱ ἔχοντες ταύτην τὴν τέχνην. ἑώρων γάρ,
ὅτι τῶν νεωτέρων ἡ ἡδονὴ μόνη αὕτη πλεῖστα
ἀγαθὰ παρασκευάζει. σώφρονάς τε γὰρ ποιεῖ καὶ
8 δικαίους διὰ τὸ ἐν τῇ ἀληθείᾳ παιδεύεσθαι· τά
τε ἄλλα γὰρ καὶ τὰ[2] τοῦ πολέμου διὰ τούτων[3]
εὐτυχοῦντες ᾐσθάνοντο· καὶ[4] τῶν ἄλλων εἴ τι
βούλονται ἐπιτηδεύειν καλῶν οὐδενὸς ἀποστερεῖ
ὥσπερ ἕτεραι κακαὶ ἡδοναί, ἃς οὐ χρὴ μανθάνειν.
ἐκ τῶν τοιούτων οὖν στρατιῶταί τε ἀγαθοὶ καὶ
9 στρατηγοὶ γίγνονται. ὧν γὰρ οἱ πόνοι τὰ μὲν
αἰσχρὰ καὶ ὑβριστικὰ ἐκ τῆς ψυχῆς καὶ τοῦ
σώματος ἀφαιροῦνται, ἐπιθυμίαν δ' ἀρετῆς ἐν-
ηύξησαν, οὗτοι δ' ἄριστοι· οὐ γὰρ ἂν περιίδοιεν
οὔτε τὴν πόλιν τὴν ἑαυτῶν ἀδικουμένην οὔτε τὴν
χώραν πάσχουσαν κακῶς.
10 Λέγουσι δέ τινες, ὡς οὐ χρὴ ἐρᾶν κυνηγεσίων,
ἵνα μὴ τῶν οἰκείων ἀμελῶσιν, οὐκ εἰδότες ὅτι οἱ
τὰς πόλεις καὶ τοὺς φίλους εὖ ποιοῦντες πάντες

---

[1] διὰ μηδενὸς A: διὰ τὸ μηδὲν BM: τὸ μηδὲν S.
[2] τὰ τε ἄλλα γὰρ καὶ τὰ AB: τά τε M: S. omits τά τε . .
ᾐσθάνοντο with Schneider.
[3] τούτων AB: τῶν τοιούτων S. with M.
[4] καὶ τῶν AB: τῶν τε S. with M.

blundered owing to difficulties in the ground. For
men who are sound in body and mind may
always stand on the threshold of success. It was 6
because they knew that they owed their successes
against the enemy to such qualities that our ancestors
looked after the young men. For in spite of the scarcity
of corn it was their custom from the earliest times
not to prevent hunters from hunting over any growing
crops; and, in addition, not to permit hunting at 7
night within a radius of many furlongs from the city,
so that the masters of that art might not rob the young
men of their game. In fact they saw that this is the
only one among the pleasures of the younger men that
produces a rich crop of blessings. For it makes
sober and upright men of them, because they are
trained in the school of truth [1] (and they perceived 8
that to these men they owed their success in war, as
in other matters); and it does not keep them
from any other honourable occupation they wish to
follow, like other and evil pleasures that they
ought not to learn. Of such men, therefore, are
good soldiers and good generals made. For they 9
whose toils root out whatever is base and froward
from mind and body and make desire for virtue to
flourish in their place—they are the best, since they
will not brook injustice to their own city nor injury
to its soil.

Some say that it is not right to love hunting, 10
because it may lead to neglect of one's domestic
affairs. They are not aware that all who benefit
their cities and their friends are more attentive

[1] *i.e.* a training that really builds up the character. There
is an implied contrast with the imposture of the education
given by sophists.

XENOPHON

11 τῶν οἰκείων ἐπιμελέστεροί εἰσιν. εἰ οὖν οἱ φιλοκυνηγέται παρασκευάζουσιν αὑτοὺς τῇ πατρίδι
χρησίμους εἶναι εἰς τὰ μέγιστα, οὐδ' ἂν τὰ ἴδια
πρόοιντο· σὺν γὰρ τῇ πόλει καὶ σῴζεται καὶ
ἀπόλλυται τὰ οἰκεῖα ἑκάστου· ὥστε πρὸς τοῖς
αὑτῶν καὶ τὰ τῶν ἄλλων ἰδιωτῶν οἱ τοιοῦτοι
12 σῴζουσι. πολλοὶ δὲ ὑπὸ φθόνου ἀλόγιστοι τῶν
ταῦτα λεγόντων αἱροῦνται διὰ τὴν αὑτῶν κακίαν
ἀπολέσθαι μᾶλλον ἢ ἑτέρων ἀρετῇ σῴζεσθαι· αἱ
γὰρ ἡδοναὶ αἱ πολλαὶ κακαί· ὧν ἡττώμενοι ἢ
13 λέγειν ἢ πράττειν ἐπαίρονται τὰ χείρω. εἶτα ἐκ
μὲν τῶν ματαίων λόγων ἔχθρας ἀναιροῦνται, ἐκ
δὲ τῶν κακῶν ἔργων νόσους καὶ ζημίας καὶ θανά-
τους καὶ αὑτῶν καὶ παίδων καὶ φίλων, ἀναι-
σθήτως μὲν τῶν κακῶν ἔχοντες, τῶν δὲ ἡδονῶν
πλέον τῶν ἄλλων αἰσθανόμενοι, οἷς τίς ἂν
14 χρήσαιτο εἰς πόλεως σωτηρίαν ; τούτων μέντοι
τῶν κακῶν οὐδεὶς ὅστις οὐκ ἀφέξεται ἐρασθεὶς
ὧν ἐγὼ παραινῶ· παίδευσις γὰρ καλὴ διδάσκει
χρῆσθαι νόμοις καὶ λέγειν περὶ τῶν δικαίων καὶ
15 ἀκούειν. οἱ μὲν οὖν παρασχόντες αὑτοὺς ἐπὶ τὸ
ἀεί τι μοχθεῖν τε καὶ διδάσκεσθαι αὐτοῖς μὲν
μαθήσεις καὶ μελέτας ἐπιπόνους ἔχουσι, σωτηρίαν
δὲ ταῖς ἑαυτῶν πόλεσιν· οἱ δὲ μὴ θέλοντες διὰ
τὸ ἐπίπονον διδάσκεσθαι, ἀλλὰ ἐν ἡδοναῖς ἀκαί-
16 ροις διάγειν, φύσει οὗτοι κάκιστοι. οὔτε γὰρ
νόμοις οὔτε λόγοις ἀγαθοῖς πείθονται· οὐ γὰρ
εὑρίσκουσι διὰ τὸ μὴ πονεῖν, οἷον χρὴ τὸν ἀγαθὸν
εἶναι· ὥστε οὔτε θεοσεβεῖς δύνανται εἶναι οὔτε
σοφοί· τῷ δὲ ἀπαιδεύτῳ χρώμενοι πολλὰ ἐπι-
17 τιμῶσι τοῖς πεπαιδευμένοις. διὰ μὲν οὖν τούτων

446

to their domestic affairs than other men. There- 11
fore, if keen sportsmen fit themselves to be useful
to their country in matters of vital moment,
neither will they be remiss in their private
affairs: for the state is necessarily concerned both
in the safety and in the ruin of the individual's
domestic fortunes. Consequently such men as these
save the fortunes of every other individual as well as
their own. But many of those who talk in this 12
way, blinded by jealousy, choose to be ruined
through their own evil rather than be saved by
other men's virtue. For most pleasures are evil, and
by yielding to these they are encouraged either to
say or to do what is wrong. Then by their frivolous 13
words they make enemies, and by their evil deeds
bring diseases and losses and death on themselves,
their children and their friends, being without per-
ception of the evils, but more perceptive than others of
the pleasures. Who would employ these to save a
state? From these evils, however, everyone who loves 14
that which I recommend will hold aloof, since a
good education teaches a man to observe laws,
to talk of righteousness and hear of it. Those, 15
then, who have given themselves up to continual
toil and learning hold for their own portion laborious
lessons and exercises, but they hold safety for their
cities. But if any decline to receive instruction because of the labour and prefer to live among un-
timely pleasures, they are by nature utterly evil.
For they obey neither laws nor good words, for 16
because they toil not, they do not discover what
a good man ought to be, so that they cannot be
pious or wise men; and being without education
they constantly find fault with the educated. In 17

οὐδὲν ἂν καλῶς ἔχοι· διὰ δὲ τῶν ἀμεινόνων
ἅπασαι αἱ ὠφέλειαι τοῖς ἀνθρώποις εὕρηνται·
18 ἀμείνους οὖν οἱ θέλοντες πονεῖν. καὶ τοῦτο ἐπι-
δέδεικται μεγάλῳ παραδείγματι· τῶν γὰρ παλαιο-
τέρων οἱ παρὰ Χείρωνι ὧν ἐπεμνήσθην νέοι ὄντες
ἀρξάμενοι ἀπὸ τῶν κυνηγεσίων πολλὰ καὶ καλὰ
ἔμαθον· ἐξ ὧν ἐγένετο αὐτοῖς μεγάλη ἀρετή, δι'
ἣν καὶ νῦν θαυμάζονται· ἧς ὅτι μὲν ἐρῶσι πάντες,
εὔδηλον, ὅτι δὲ διὰ πόνων ἔστι τυχεῖν αὐτῆς, οἱ
19 πολλοὶ ἀφίστανται. τὸ μὲν γὰρ κατεργάσασθαι
αὐτὴν ἄδηλον, οἱ δὲ πόνοι οἱ ἐν αὐτῇ ἐνόντες
φανεροί.

Ἴσως μὲν οὖν εἰ ἦν τὸ σῶμα αὐτῆς δῆλον,
ἧττον ἂν ἠμέλουν οἱ ἄνθρωποι ἀρετῆς εἰδότες
ὅτι ὥσπερ αὐτοῖς ἐκείνη ἐμφανής ἐστιν, οὕτω καὶ
20 αὐτοὶ ὑπ' ἐκείνης ὁρῶνται. ὅταν μὲν γάρ τις ὁρᾶται
ὑπὸ τοῦ ἐρωμένου, ἅπας ἑαυτοῦ ἐστι βελτίων καὶ
οὔτε λέγει οὔτε ποιεῖ αἰσχρὰ οὐδὲ κακά, ἵνα μὴ
21 ὀφθῇ ὑπ' ἐκείνου. ὑπὸ δὲ τῆς ἀρετῆς οὐκ οἰόμενοι
ἐπισκοπεῖσθαι πολλὰ κακὰ καὶ αἰσχρὰ ἐναντίον
ποιοῦσιν, ὅτι αὐτὴν ἐκεῖνοι οὐχ ὁρῶσιν· ἡ δὲ
πανταχοῦ πάρεστι διὰ τὸ εἶναι ἀθάνατος καὶ
τιμᾷ τοὺς περὶ αὐτὴν ἀγαθούς, τοὺς δὲ κακοὺς
22 ἀτιμάζει. εἰ οὖν εἰδεῖεν τοῦτο, ὅτι θεᾶται αὐτούς,
ἵεντο ἂν ἐπὶ τοὺς πόνους καὶ τὰς παιδεύσεις, αἷς
ἁλίσκεται μόλις, καὶ κατεργάζοιντο ἂν αὐτήν.

XIII. Θαυμάζω [1] δὲ τῶν σοφιστῶν καλουμένων

---

[1] S. regards the whole of this chapter as a spurious
addition.

---

[1] The argument, such as it is, would be better with "the
toilers," for "the better sort," and the next words would

these men's hands, therefore, nothing can prosper. All discoveries that have benefited mankind are due to the better sort.[1] Now the better sort are those who are willing to toil. And this has been proved by a great example. For among the ancients the 18 companions of Cheiron to whom I referred learnt many noble lessons in their youth, beginning with hunting; from these lessons there sprang in them great virtue, for which they are admired even to-day. That all desire Virtue is obvious, but because they must toil if they are to gain her, the many fall away. For the achievement of her is hidden in 19 obscurity, whereas the toils inseparable from her[2] are manifest.

It may be that, if her body were visible, men would be less careless of virtue, knowing that she sees them as clearly as they see her. For 20 when he is seen by his beloved every man rises above himself and shrinks from what is ugly and evil in word or deed, for fear of being seen by him. But in the presence of Virtue men do many evil and 21 ugly things, supposing that they are not regarded by her because they do not see her. Yet she is present everywhere because she is immortal, and she honours those who are good to her, but casts off the bad. Therefore, if men knew that she is watching 22 them, they would be impatient to undergo the toils and the discipline by which she is hardly to be captured, and would achieve her.

XIII. I am surprised at the sophists, as they

then be "those who are willing to toil, therefore, are the better men."

[2] αὐτῷ, "it," *i.e.* the achievement, would be an improvement.

ὅτι φασὶ μὲν ἐπ' ἀρετὴν ἄγειν οἱ πολλοὶ τοὺς
νέους, ἄγουσι δ' ἐπὶ τοὐναντίον· οὔτε γὰρ ἄνδρα
που ἑωράκαμεν, ὅντιν' οἱ νῦν σοφισταὶ ἀγαθὸν
ἐποίησαν, οὔτε γράμματα παρέχονται, ἐξ ὧν χρὴ
ἀγαθοὺς γίγνεσθαι, ἀλλὰ περὶ μὲν τῶν ματαίων
2 πολλὰ αὐτοῖς γέγραπται, ἀφ' ὧν τοῖς νέοις αἱ
μὲν ἡδοναὶ κεναί, ἀρετὴ δ' οὐκ ἔνι. διατριβὴν δ'
ἄλλως παρέχει τοῖς ἐλπίσασί τι ἐξ αὐτῶν μαθή-
σεσθαι μάτην καὶ ἑτέρων κωλύει χρησίμων καὶ
3 διδάσκει κακά. μέμφομαι οὖν αὐτοῖς τὰ μὲν
μεγάλα μειζόνως· περὶ δὲ ὧν γράφουσιν ὅτι τὰ
μὲν ῥήματα αὐτοῖς ἐζήτηται, γνῶμαι δὲ ὀρθῶς
ἔχουσαι, αἷς ἂν παιδεύοιντο οἱ νεώτεροι ἐπ'
4 ἀρετήν, οὐδαμοῦ. ἐγὼ δὲ ἰδιώτης μέν εἰμι, οἶδα
δέ, ὅτι κράτιστον μέν ἐστι παρὰ αὐτῆς τῆς φύσεως
τὸ ἀγαθὸν διδάσκεσθαι, δεύτερον δὲ παρὰ τῶν
ἀληθῶς ἀγαθόν τι ἐπισταμένων μᾶλλον ἢ ὑπὸ
5 τῶν ἐξαπατᾶν τέχνην ἐχόντων. ἴσως οὖν τοῖς
μὲν ὀνόμασιν οὐ σεσοφισμένως λέγω· οὐδὲ γὰρ
ζητῶ τοῦτο· ὧν δὲ δέονται εἰς ἀρετὴν οἱ καλῶς
πεπαιδευμένοι, ὀρθῶς ἐγνωσμένα ζητῶ λέγειν·
ὀνόματα μὲν γὰρ οὐκ ἂν παιδεύσειαν, γνῶμαι δέ,
6 εἰ καλῶς ἔχοιεν. ψέγουσι δὲ καὶ ἄλλοι πολλοὶ
τοὺς νῦν σοφιστὰς καὶ οὐ τοὺς φιλοσόφους, ὅτι ἐν
τοῖς ὀνόμασι σοφίζονται καὶ οὐκ ἐν τοῖς νοή-
μασιν.

Οὐ λανθάνει δέ με, ὅτι καλῶς καὶ ἑξῆς γεγραμμένα φήσει τις ἴσως τῶν τοιούτων οὐ καλῶς οὐδ'

are called, because, though most of them profess to
lead the young to virtue they lead them to the
very opposite. We have never seen anywhere the
man whose goodness was due to the sophists of our
generation. Neither do their contributions to literature tend to make men good : but they have written 2
many books on frivolous subjects, books that offer
the young empty pleasures, but put no virtue into
them. To read them in the hope of learning something from them is mere waste of time, and they
keep one from useful occupations and teach what is
bad. Therefore their grave faults incur my graver 3
censure. As for the style of their writings, I
complain that the language is far-fetched, and there
is no trace in them of wholesome maxims by which
the young might be trained to virtue. I am no 4
professor, but I know that the best thing is to be
taught what is good by one's own nature, and the
next best thing is to get it from those who really
know something good instead of being taught by
masters of the art of deception. I daresay that 5
I do not express myself in the language of a sophist ;
in fact, that is not my object : my object is rather to
give utterance to wholesome thoughts that will meet
the needs of readers well educated in virtue. For
words will not educate, but maxims, if well found.
Many others besides myself blame the sophists of our 6
generation—philosophers I will not call them—
because the wisdom they profess consists of words
and not of thoughts.

I am well aware that someone, perhaps one of
this set,[1] will say that what is well and methodically

---

[1] *i.e.* a sophist. But the text of what follows is open to
suspicion.

ἑξῆς [1] γεγράφθαι· ῥᾴδιον γὰρ ἔσται αὐτοῖς ταχὺ
7 μὴ ὀρθῶς μέμψασθαι· καίτοι γέγραπταί γε οὕτως,
ἵνα ὀρθῶς ἔχῃ καὶ μὴ σοφιστικοὺς ποιῇ, ἀλλὰ
σοφοὺς καὶ ἀγαθούς· οὐ γὰρ δοκεῖν αὐτὰ βούλομαι μᾶλλον ἢ εἶναι χρήσιμα, ἵνα ἀνεξέλεγκτα
8 ᾖ εἰς ἀεί. οἱ σοφισταὶ δ' ἐπὶ τῷ ἐξαπατᾶν
λέγουσι καὶ γράφουσιν ἐπὶ τῷ ἑαυτῶν κέρδει καὶ
οὐδένα οὐδὲν ὠφελοῦσιν· οὐδὲ γὰρ σοφὸς αὐτῶν
ἐγένετο οὐδεὶς οὐδ' ἔστιν, ἀλλὰ καὶ ἀρκεῖ ἑκάστῳ
σοφιστὴν κληθῆναι, ὅ ἐστιν ὄνειδος παρά γε εὖ
9 φρονοῦσι. τὰ μὲν οὖν τῶν σοφιστῶν παραγγέλ-
ματα παραινῶ φυλάττεσθαι, τὰ δὲ τῶν φιλοσόφων
ἐνθυμήματα μὴ ἀτιμάζειν· οἱ μὲν γὰρ σοφισταὶ
πλουσίους καὶ νέους θηρῶνται, οἱ δὲ φιλόσοφοι
πᾶσι κοινοὶ καὶ φίλοι· τύχας δὲ ἀνδρῶν οὔτε
τιμῶσιν οὔτε ἀτιμάζουσι.
10 Μὴ ζηλοῦν δὲ μηδὲ τοὺς ἐπὶ τὰς πλεονεξίας
εἰκῇ ἰόντας, μήτ' ἐπὶ τὰς ἰδίας μήτ' ἐπὶ τὰς
δημοσίας, ἐνθυμηθέντα, ὅτι οἱ μὲν ἄριστοι αὐτῶν [2]
γιγνώσκονται μὲν ἐπὶ τὰ βελτίω ἐπίφθονοι [3] δ' [4]
εἰσίν, οἱ δὲ κακοὶ πάσχουσί τε κακῶς καὶ γιγνώ-
11 σκονται ἐπὶ τὰ χείρω. τάς τε γὰρ τῶν ἰδιωτῶν
οὐσίας ἀφαιρούμενοι καὶ τὰ τῆς πόλεως εἰς τὰς
κοινὰς σωτηρίας ἀνωφελέστεροί εἰσι τῶν ἰδιωτῶν,
τά τε σώματα πρὸς τὸν πόλεμον κάκιστα καὶ
αἴσχιστα ἔχουσι πονεῖν οὐ δυνάμενοι. οἱ δὲ κυνηγέται εἰς τὸ κοινὸν τοῖς πολίταις καὶ τὰ σώματα
12 καὶ τὰ κτήματα καλῶς ἔχοντα παρέχουσιν. ἔρχονται δὲ οἱ μὲν ἐπὶ τὰ θηρία, οἱ δ' ἐπὶ τοὺς φίλους.

---

[1] γεγραμμένα . . . ἑξῆς is omitted by S. with M.
[2] αὐτῶν MSS. : ἀνδρῶν S.
[3] I have substituted ἐπίφθονοι for ἐπίπονοι.

written[1] is not well and methodically written—for
hasty and false censure will come easily to them.
But my aim in writing has been to produce sound 7
work that will make men not wiseacres, but wise
and good. For I wish my work not to seem useful,
but to be so, that it may stand for all time unrefuted.
The sophists talk to deceive and write for their 8
own gain, and do no good to anyone. For there is
not, and there never was, a wise man among them;
everyone of them is content to be called a sophist,
which is a term of reproach among sensible men.
So my advice is: Avoid the behests of the sophists, 9
and despise not the conclusions of the philosophers;
for the sophists hunt the rich and young, but the
philosophers are friends to all alike: but as for men's
fortunes, they neither honour nor despise them.

Envy not those either who recklessly seek their 10
own advantage whether in private or in public life[2]
—bear in mind that the best of them, though they
are favourably judged, are envied, and the bad both
fare badly and are unfavourably judged. For 11
engaged in robbing private persons of their property,
or plundering the state, they render less service
than private persons when plans for securing the
common safety are afoot,[3] and in body they are dis-
gracefully unfit for war because they are incapable
of toil. But huntsmen offer their lives and their
property in sound condition for the service of the
citizens. These attack the wild beasts, those others 12

---

[1] ἐγνωσμένα, "thought," would be a great improvement on
γεγραμμένα, "written."
[2] Professional politicians.
[3] i.e. they contrive to "save their pockets."

---

[4] δ' Kaibel: τ' S. with the MSS.

καὶ οἱ μὲν ἐπὶ τοὺς φίλους ἰόντες δύσκλειαν
ἔχουσι παρὰ πᾶσιν, οἱ δὲ κυνηγέται ἐπὶ τὰ θηρία
ἰόντες εὔκλειαν· ἑλόντες μὲν γὰρ πολέμια νικῶσι,
μὴ ἑλόντες δὲ πρῶτον μὲν ὅτι πάσης τῆς πόλεως
ἐχθροῖς ἐπιχειροῦσιν ἔπαινον ἔσχον, ἔπειτα ὅτι
οὔτ᾽ ἐπ᾽ ἀνδρὸς βλάβῃ οὔτε φιλοκερδείᾳ ἔρχονται.

13 ἔπειτα ἐξ αὐτοῦ τοῦ ἐπιχειρήματος βελτίους γίγνονται πρὸς πολλὰ καὶ σοφώτεροι δι᾽ οὗ διδάξομεν.
ἐὰν γὰρ μὴ πόνοις καὶ ἐνθυμήμασι καὶ ἐπιμελείαις
πολλαῖς ὑπερβάλλωνται, οὐκ ἂν ἕλοιεν ἄγρας.

14 τὰ γὰρ ἀντίπαλα αὐτῶν ὑπὲρ τῆς ψυχῆς ἀγωνιζό-
μενα καὶ ἐν τῇ αὐτῶν οἰκήσει ἐν ἰσχύι πολλῇ
ἐστιν· ὥστε τῷ κυνηγέτῃ μάτην οἱ πόνοι γίγνονται, ἐὰν μὴ μείζονι φιλοπονίᾳ καὶ πολλῇ συνέσει
κρατήσῃ αὐτῶν.

15 Οἱ μὲν οὖν κατὰ πόλιν βουλόμενοι πλεονεκτεῖν
μελετῶσι νικᾶν φίλους, οἱ δὲ κυνηγέται κοινοὺς
ἐχθρούς· καὶ τοὺς μὲν ἡ μελέτη αὕτη ποιεῖ πρὸς
τοὺς ἄλλους πολεμίους ἀμείνους, τοὺς δὲ πολὺ
χείρους· καὶ τοῖς μὲν ἡ ἄγρα μετὰ σωφροσύνης,

16 τοῖς δὲ μετὰ αἰσχροῦ θράσους. κακοηθείας δὲ
καὶ αἰσχροκερδείας οἱ μὲν δύνανται καταφρονεῖν,
οἱ δ᾽ οὐ δύνανται· φωνὴν δὲ οἱ μὲν εὐεπῆ ἱᾶσιν, οἱ
δ᾽ αἰσχράν· πρὸς δὲ τὰ θεῖα τοῖς μὲν οὐδὲν

17 ἐμποδὼν ἀσεβεῖν, οἱ δ᾽ εὐσεβέστατοι. λόγοι γὰρ
παλαιοὶ κατέχουσιν, ὡς καὶ θεοὶ τούτῳ τῷ ἔργῳ
χαίρουσι καὶ πράττοντες καὶ ὁρῶντες· ὥστε
ὑπάρχειν ἐνθυμουμένους τούτων θεοφιλεῖς τ᾽ εἶναι

their friends. And whereas those who attack their friends earn infamy by general consent, huntsmen by attacking the wild beasts gain a good report. For if they make a capture, they win victory over enemy forces: and if they fail, they are commended, in the first place, because they assail powers hostile to the whole community; and, secondly, because they go out neither to harm a man nor for sordid gain. Moreover, the very attempt makes 13 them better in many ways and wiser; and we will give the reason. Unless they abound in labours and inventions and precautions, they cannot capture game. For the forces contending with them, fighting 14 for their life and in their own home, are in great strength; so that the huntsman's labours are in vain, unless by greater perseverance and by much intelligence he can overcome them.

In fine, the politician whose objects are selfish 15 practises for victory over friends, the huntsman for victory over common foes. This practice makes the one a better, the other a far worse fighter against all other enemies. The one takes prudence with him for companion in the chase, the other base rashness. The one can despise malice and avarice, the other 16 cannot. The language of the one is gracious,[1] of the other ugly. As for religion, nothing checks impiety in the one, the other is conspicuous for his piety. In fact, an ancient story has it that the 17 gods delight in this business, both as followers and spectators of the chase. Therefore, reflecting on these things, the young who do what I exhort them to do will put themselves in the way of being dear

---

[1] *i.e.* kindly and pleasant; not reckless and shameless like that of the politicians.

καὶ εὐσεβεῖς τοὺς νέους τοὺς ποιοῦντας ἃ ἐγὼ
παραινῶ, οἰομένους ὑπὸ θεῶν του ὁρᾶσθαι ταῦτα.
οὗτοι δ᾽ ἂν εἶεν καὶ τοκεῦσιν ἀγαθοὶ καὶ πάσῃ τῇ
ἑαυτῶν πόλει καὶ ἑνὶ ἑκάστῳ τῶν πολιτῶν καὶ
18 φίλων. οὐ μόνον δὲ ὅσοι ἄνδρες κυνηγεσίων
ἠράσθησαν ἐγένοντο ἀγαθοί, ἀλλὰ καὶ αἱ γυναῖκες,
αἷς ἔδωκεν ἡ θεὸς ταῦτα,[1] Ἀταλάντη καὶ Πρόκρις
καὶ εἴ τις ἄλλη,

[1] Ἄρτεμις, which follows ταῦτα in the MSS., was removed
by Weiske.

to the gods and pious men, conscious that one or other of the gods is watching their deeds. These will be good to parents, good to the whole city, to every one of their friends and fellow-citizens. For all men who have loved hunting have been 18 good: and not men only, but those women also to whom the goddess[1] has given this blessing, Atalanta and Procris and others like them.

[1] Artemis.

CONSTITUTION OF THE
ATHENIANS

INTRODUCTION

I. *The Problem*

A treatise on the constitution of the Athenians, composed in a style that is tantalizingly inept, was preserved in antiquity among the works of Xenophon. At least it was attributed to that master of Greek prose as early as the first century B.C.: the critic Demetrius of Magnesia was able to pronounce the attribution false (Diog. Laer. 3. 57). Pollux in the second century and Stobaeus in the fifth knew the work as Xenophon's, and it was still under his name and embedded amid his genuine writings that the work passed to the modern age.

The judgment of Demetrius was acute; all scholars would now concur. Xenophon could never have written such prose, so repetitive and often so awkward. Not that the author, whoever he was, eschewed all elegance, but rather that he was not very good at it.[1] Moreover, his Attic was not without a slight admixture of Ionic (e.g. 2. 2, 2. 14, 2. 17). As for structure, he had worked it out carefully (the opening sentences show this), but the sequence of arguments is lacking in smoothness and clarity. If Xenophon was not the author of this piece, who was? When was it written, and how came it into the corpus of another's works?

---

[1] He does, for example, attempt a stylish word order at 1. 11 and a flourish of anaphora at 3. 2.

INTRODUCTION

The treatise is among the most enigmatic and most important of the literary texts from classical Greece. The author has never been identified, and probably cannot be; nor has any satisfactory reason ever been advanced for the appearance of the work as Xenophon's. Perhaps it was found, as some scholars like to say, among Xenophon's papers (and comparison is possible with a political treatise attributed to Herodes Atticus)[1]; perhaps the author was another person named Xenophon.[2] There is unfortunately no way of telling.

A few observations can be made about the author from the text itself, though none will prove decisive. He writes about the Athenians largely in the third person, and he alludes to Athens by αὐτόθι. Yet once in a while he numbers himself among the Athenians by the use of a first person plural: so at 1. 12 and 2. 12. He seems to envisage lively objections to his remarks from an interlocutor or correspondent, and at one point (1. 11) he refers to someone by second-singular forms in an argument suggesting that the other person is living in Sparta (or at least normally does). One fact about the author is quite clear: he is a stalwart oligarch. He disapproves vehemently of the Athenian constitution and—such is his admiration of the Athenians' cleverness in preserving it—he sees no hope of gradually subverting it; it has to be overthrown utterly or not at all. The

[1] On the περὶ πολιτείας "among the papers" of Herodes. cf. H. T. Wade-Gery, *CQ*, 39 (1945), 19 ff = *Essays in Greek History* (1958), 271 ff.

[2] E.g. the general mentioned by Thucydides at 2. 70.1 and 2. 79. 1.

firm convictions of the man and his repetitive style
have earned him in the English-speaking world the
designation "Old Oligarch".[1]

It has been suggested that the oligarch was writing
as a foreigner in Athens or as an Athenian in foreign
parts; it has been suggested that he is addressing
another oligarch or explaining Athenian ways to a
Spartan.[2] The evidence is unclear, and so is the
answer. The opening sentence of the treatise suggests
an extract from a larger work, and there seems to be
no conclusion. One would like at least to know the
historical context of the piece, and that means its
date.

Few problems have been discussed so much and so
inconclusively as the date of pseudo-Xenophon. The
issues, as they are now, take their origins from the
remarks of W. Roscher in 1842 (*Leben, Werk, und
Zeitalter des Thukydides*, p. 529). Roscher emphasized
that 2. 5 in the treatise, concerning the impossibility
of long overland marches, was falsified by the great
northward expedition of Brasidas in 424; therefore,
that year was the *terminus ante* for the composition

[1] No one seems to know the origin of this expression. I
have been assured that it antedates Gilbert Murray to
whom many (in casual conversation) ascribe it. It would
appear to have acquired a certain currency in talk or
lectures before its début in print (which may well have
been in Murray's *Ancient Greek Literature* of 1897). Nor
is the force of "old" quite clear—whether age, endearment
("dear old"), disgust ("cursed old"), or a combination of
two of these is implied. The expression has no parallel
in scholarship other than English, and it has little to
recommend it there.

[2] For a survey of views, cf. H. Frisch, *The Constitution
of the Athenians* (1942), pp. 88 ff.

of the treatise. Some scholars have tried to controvert Roscher's point,[1] but it still remains one of the more tenable arguments in the whole debate over pseudo-Xenophon. Apart from 3. 11 there are no explicit references anywhere to datable events; it is apparent from allusions to Athens' allies and the tribute that the context, is, broadly speaking, the time of the Athenian empire. But controversy subsists about a more precise date, and the following passages are frequently adduced. (The most important discussions of these passages will be found in the works of Kirchhoff, Instinsky, and Gelzer registered in part IV of this introduction.)

2. 2	Assumed to presuppose the formation of the Chalcidic League in 432.
2. 13	Assumed to presuppose the Pylos campaign.
2. 14–16	Assumed to presuppose the Spartan invasions of Attica at the beginning of the Peloponnesian War and the attendant removal of Athenian property to Euboea.
2. 18	Assumed to presuppose a legal ban on comedy such as that introduced in 440–39 or in 415.
3. 2	Assumed to refer to a war currently being fought.

None of the assumptions is necessary (cf. the notes to the translation of these texts in the following pages). It is, however, of greater moment that the whole

[1] Most recently, A. Fuks in *Scripta Hierosolymitana*, **1** (1954), 21 ff., and H. B. Mattingly in *Historia* 10 (1961) 179.

middle portion of pseudo-Xenophon's work (1. 19–2. 16) is startlingly reminiscent of Thucydides; the theme is the supreme value of sea power, and the reader will be put particularly in mind of the first speech of Pericles at the end of Thucydides' Book I. The consideration of advantages which would accrue to Athens if she were an island is perhaps the most striking common point. But there are others, although the two writers approach their similar items in very different ways. (On this J. de Romilly is excellent: "Le Pseudo-Xénophon et Thucydide", *Rev. de Phil.* 36 (1962), 225 ff.) Yet it is impossible to draw secure chronological conclusions from the Thucydidean parallels. The common source might be Pericles himself, or—more likely—current talk in Athens over a period of ten or even twenty years.

The historical events which are mentioned in 3. 11 are three in number, none of which can be dated later than 443; one of the events belongs certainly to the sixties and another probably to the fifties. (Cf. the notes on this passage.) Inasmuch as the author is here discussing the disastrous incompatibility of Athenian democracy with oligarchy in other states, the present writer has argued elsewhere that the omission of the Samian Revolt is important: *HSCP*, 71 (1966), 37–8 Together with the allusion to some (but not much) irregularity in tribute assessments, the omission of Samos is taken to indicate a *terminus ante* of 441; the first irregular assessment of tribute occurred in 443. Possibly the treatise of pseudo-Xenophon should be associated with the ostracism of Thucydides, the son of Melesias, in 443 or its immediate aftermath.

INTRODUCTION

II. *The Text*

The following text of the "Constitution of the Athenians" is based upon a new collation of the four principal manuscripts (ABCM); two of the derivative manuscripts were also collated (Mα Mβ). The establishment of the text takes into account an assessment of the manuscript C which is substantially different from that in all modern editions. I have discussed at length the nature of C and the textual problems connected with it in *HSCP*, 71 (1966), 38 ff. and offer here an epitome of what appears there.

There has never been any dispute that the principal manuscripts of pseudo-Xenophon are four in number:

A   Vaticanus 1950, fourteenth century.
B   Vaticanus 1335, late fourteenth or early fifteenth century.
C   Mutinensis 145=α. γ. 17, fifteenth century.
M   Marcianus 511=590, fourteenth century.

The other manuscripts are all derivative from M and eliminable: they are clearly described in the introduction to Kalinka's Teubner text of 1914, and a stemma for them will be found in my own article of 1966. They are as follows:

Mα   Marcianus 368=852, fifteenth century.
Mβ   Marcianus 369=1045, fifteenth century.
L   Laurentianus 55. 21, fourteenth century.
F   Laurentianus conv. suppr. 110 Flor., fifteenth century.
Par   Parisinus 2955, fifteenth century.
Per   Perusinus B 34, fifteenth century.
La   Laurentianus 55. 22, fourteenth century.
Lβ   Laurentianus 80. 13, early fifteenth century.

INTRODUCTION

It may be helpful to note here that Mα and Mβ were certainly copied directly from M, and that LFParPer all cease with the words μάλιστα ἦσαν Ἀθηναίων in 1. 16.

After Kirchhoff's important but highly idiosyncratic edition if 1874, which shot the text through with putative lacunae, the major editions are these:

H. Müller-Strübing, *Philologus* Suppl. 4 (1884).

F. Ruehl, Teubner, 1912.

E. Kalinka, Teubner, 1914.

E. C. Marchant, Oxford, 1919.

H. Frisch, Copenhagen, 1942.

The relationship of ABCM is indicated above all by the common omissions in ABC at both 1. 20 and 3. 10 of words which are to be found in M. Hence for ABC a common origin (α) which M does not have. Since B is a later manuscript than A, A cannot derive from it; and it can be seen from the agreement of BC against A at 1. 8 and of AC against B at 3. 5 that B cannot derive from A. Furthermore, at 3. 8 it will be seen that CM are found in agreement against AB. Therefore there was at least one manuscript (β) intermediate between α and AB.

It is C which is puzzling.[1] In many instances ABM are in agreement against C, yet in only one of these (3. 1) does C obviously have the right reading: πάντας C: πάντες, —ας M: πάντες AB. The correction in M was made by the first hand and both terminations were copied into Mα and Mβ. πάντας is a simple

---

[1] It has been usual for editors to give particular value to C in view of its many unique readings. With the exception of Ruehl, who felt a modicum of disquiet, all modern editors have agreed.

correction and absolutely necessary in the context; in the light of all the other disagreements of C πάντας is best considered a fortunate and easy conjecture. The variants in C, taken together, show signs of a consistent effort to improve, correct, or complete this difficult text. One suspects the hand of an interpolator. Observe, for example, the extra and balancing phrases appearing only in C at 1. 13 and at 2. 5. Or again the rhetorical amplification at 3. 3 of πλείω (as in ABM) to πολλῷ πλείω in C. Or consider the ignorance of a pedant adding the ἄν at 1. 6 in the apodosis of a present contrary-to-fact condition containing the expression ἦν ἀγαθά. A reader of the critical apparatus will easily discover in C more examples of this sort of thing. He will also discover a few absurd errors which an interpolator would not have tolerated (e.g. at 1. 19 ναυτικῇ ABM: ἀττικῇ C): hence the alterations were not made for the first time in C, and at least one lost manuscript (γ)—the interpolated one—must be postulated as intermediate between α and C.

The four manuscripts ABCM all contain two errors which clearly point to a lost uncial manuscript: 2. 9 ΚΤΑCΘΑΙ for ΙCΤΑCΘΑΙ and 3. 3 ΕΠΕΔΙΔΟCΑΝ for ΕΤΙΕΔΙΔΟCΑΝ. There are no evident minuscule confusions in common; but as the text is short and the manuscripts are late, one may be justified in assuming a minuscule archetype in which a copyist made the original misreadings of uncial. Apart from accidental coincidences (e.g. when A or B agrees with M against the other two manuscripts of the α group), the congruence of M with one or more manuscripts of the α group will reveal the reading of the archetype. C is virtually useless except on the rare occasions when it agrees with M against AB (as at 3. 8).

Here is a stemma for ABCM:

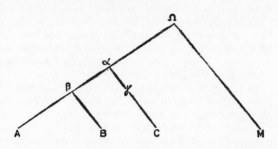

III. *The Translation*

It is disturbing and difficult at the best of times to speak with another's voice. It is particularly unsettling to try to speak with the voice of pseudo-Xenophon. The writer's prose is often rough and ugly, and perfect lucidity is not always a friend to him; he repeats himself. All of these features will inevitably appear in any reasonably faithful translation, and indeed they should. The translator has no obligation to misrepresent the author, even if to improve on him. Accordingly, the present translation has been accomplished in a style which is not the translator's own.

Pseudo-Xenophon is vexing above all in his frequent use of certain terms for the upper and lower classes: χρηστοί, βέλτιστοι, δυνάμενοι, πονηροί, δημοτικοί, etc. After several attempts I found it

impossible always to render these terms in the same
way: their tone varies within the treatise itself, and
they appear so often that identical renderings become
intolerable in an English version. It is not always
clear how far the oligarch is using these terms simply
to designate social (or economic) groups and how far
he is using them to pass favourable or unfavourable
comment. I have, therefore, varied my translations
of words of this kind.

In an effort to provide a continuous translation, I
have generally given coherent English versions of
passages containing textual cruces. These versions
represent my view of what the author said, although
my inability to determine his actual Greek at these
points will be apparent from appropriate signs in the
text on the left-hand pages and from footnotes
attached to the relevant part of the English text.

IV. *Bibliography*

E. Kalinka, in his massive commentary *Die pseudoxenophontische* Ἀθηναίων πολιτεία (1913) has provided a full bibliography of work on pseudo-
Xenophon before his own. Therefore, it may be
useful to list first only the most valuable of the
items published before 1913.

W. Roscher, *Leben, Werk, und Zeitalter des Thuky-
    dides* (1842), pp. 526 ff.
C. Wachsmuth, *Commentatio de Xenophontis qui
    fertur libello* Ἀθηναίων πολιτεία (1874).
A. Kirchhoff, "Über die Schrift vom Staate der
    Athener," *Abhandl. königl. Akad. Berlin* (1874), 1 ff.

INTRODUCTION

A. Kirchhoff, "Über die Abfassungszeit der Schrift vom Staate der Athener," *Abhandl. königl. Akad. Berlin* (1878), 1 ff.

Th. Bergk, "De libello περὶ Ἀθηναίων πολιτείας," *Hermes*, 18 (1883), 514 ff.

H. Müller-Strübing, "Ἀθηναίων πολιτεία die attische Schrift vom Staat der Athener," *Philologus* Suppl. 4 (1884), 1 ff.

What follows is a full bibliography of works concerned directly with pseudo-Xenophon and published after 1913.

E. Bruhn, "Die oligarchische Denkschrift über die Verfassung Athens als Schullektüre," *Neue Jahrb. für Pädagogik*, 48 (1921), 17 ff.

G. Stail, *Über die pseudoxenophontische Ἀθηναίων πολιτεία* (1921).

M. Kupferschmid, *Zur Erklärung der pseudo-xenophontischen Ἀθηναίων πολιτεία* (1932).

K. Münscher, "Kritische Nachlese zur pseudo-xenophontischen Ἀθηναίων πολιτεία." *Rhein. Mus.* 81 (1932), 209 ff.

H. U. Instinsky, *Die Abfassungszeit der Schrift vom Staate der Athener* (1933).

K. I. Gelzer, *Die Schrift vom Staate der Athener* (1937).

E. Rupprecht, *Die Schrift vom Staate der Athener, Interpretationen* (1939).

G. Prestel, *Die antidemokratische Strömung in Athen des 5. Jahrhunderts bis zum Tode des Perikles* (1939).

H. Diller, Review of Gelzer, *Gnomon*, 15 (1939), 113 ff.

INTRODUCTION

A. W. Gomme, "The Old Oligarch," *HSCP* Suppl. 1 (1940), 211 ff.=*More Essays in Greek History and Literature* (1962), 38 ff.

M. Volkening, *Das Bild des attischen Staates in der pseudoxenophontischen Schrift vom Staate der Athener* (1940).

H. Frisch, *The Constitution of the Athenians* (1942).

E. Rupprecht, Review of Volkening, *Gnomon*, 18 (1942), 2 ff.

W. Nestle, "Zum Rätsel der Ἀθ. πολ." *Hermes*, 78 (1943), 232 ff.

H. Fränkel, "Notes on the Closing Sections of Pseudo-Xenophon's Constitution of the Athenians," *AJP*, 68 (1947), 309 ff.

E. Hohl, "Zeit und Zweck der pseudoxenophontischen Ath. Pol.," *CP*, 45 (1950), 26 ff.

L. C. Stecchini, Ἀθηναίων πολιτεία (1950).

L. Siegel, "Zur pseudoxenophontischen Ἀθ. πολ.," *Wiener Studien*, 65 (1950/1), 156 ff.

M. F. Galiano, *Pseudo-Jenofonte; La Republica de los Atenienses* (1951).

M. Gigante, "A Pseudo-Senofonte Ἀθ. πολ. 3. 11," *Parol. del Pass.* 6 (1951), 448 ff.

M. F. Galiano, "Ps. Xen. Ath. Resp. 3. 13," *Aegyptus*, 32 (1952), 382 ff.

M. Gigante, *La Costituzione degli Ateniesi* (1953).

M. Gigante, "A Pseudo-Senofonte Ἀθ. πολ. 1. 11," *Parol. del Pass.* 9 (1954), 300 ff.

A. Fuks, "The Old Oligarch," *Scripta Hierosolymitana*, 1 (1954), 21 ff.

H. Haffter, "Die Komposition der pseudoxenophontischen Schrift vom Staat der Athener," *Navicula Chilonensis; Festschrift Jacoby* (1956), 79 ff.

INTRODUCTION

J. de Romilly, "Le Pseudo-Xénophon et Thucydide,"
　　Rev. de Phil. 36 (1962), 225 ff.

R. Renehan, "Pseudo-Xenophon Ath. Pol. 2. 12,"
　　CP, 58 (1963), 38.

G. W. Bowersock, "Pseudo-Xenophon," *HSCP*, 71
　　(1966), 33 ff.

M. Treu, "Ps.-Xenophon, Πολιτεία 'Αθηναίων," *P-W*
　　Zweite Reihe 18, IX.A.2, cols. 1928 ff. (1967).

ΞΕΝΟΦΩΝΤΟΣ ΡΗΤΟΡΟΣ
ΑΘΗΝΑΙΩΝ ΠΟΛΙΤΕΙΑ

I. Περὶ δὲ τῆς Ἀθηναίων πολιτείας, ὅτι μὲν εἵλοντο
τοῦτον τὸν τρόπον τῆς πολιτείας, οὐκ ἐπαινῶ διὰ
τόδε, ὅτι ταῦθ᾽ ἑλόμενοι εἵλοντο τοὺς πονηροὺς
ἄμεινον πράττειν ἢ τοὺς χρηστούς. διὰ μὲν οὖν
τοῦτο οὐκ ἐπαινῶ· ἐπεὶ δὲ ταῦτα ἔδοξεν οὕτως[1] αὐτοῖς,
ὡς εὖ διασῴζονται τὴν πολιτείαν καὶ τἆλλα διαπράττονται
ἃ δοκοῦσιν ἁμαρτάνειν τοῖς ἄλλοις Ἕλλησι, τοῦτ᾽
ἀποδείξω.

2 Πρῶτον μὲν οὖν τοῦτο ἐρῶ, ὅτι δίκαιοι[2] αὐτόθι καὶ
οἱ πένητες καὶ ὁ δῆμος πλέον ἔχειν[3] τῶν γενναίων καὶ
τῶν πλουσίων διὰ τόδε, ὅτι ὁ δῆμός ἐστιν ὁ ἐλαύνων
τὰς ναῦς καὶ ὁ τὴν δύναμιν περιτιθεὶς τῇ πόλει, καὶ οἱ
κυβερνῆται καὶ οἱ κελευσταὶ καὶ οἱ πεντηκόνταρχοι
καὶ οἱ πρῳρᾶται καὶ οἱ ναυπηγοί,—οὗτοί εἰσιν οἱ τὴν
δύναμιν περιτιθέντες τῇ πόλει πολὺ μᾶλλον ἢ οἱ
ὁπλῖται[4] καὶ οἱ γενναῖοι καὶ οἱ χρηστοί. ἐπειδὴ οὖν
ταῦτα οὕτως ἔχει, δοκεῖ δίκαιον εἶναι πᾶσι τῶν ἀρχῶν

Ξενοφῶντος ῥήτορος Ἀθηναίων πολιτεία ΑΜ: Ξενοφῶντος
Ἀθηναίων πολιτεία C: tit. om. B

[1] ἔδοξεν οὕτως ΑΒC: οὕτως ἔδοξεν Μ
[2] δίκαιοι Münscher: δικαίως ΑΒCΜ
[3] ἔχειν ΑΒC: ἔχει Μ
[4] ὁπλῖται Krüger: πολῖται ΑΒCΜ

THE CONSTITUTION OF
THE ATHENIANS

by Xenophon the Orator

I. And as for the fact that the Athenians have chosen the kind of constitution that they have, I do not think well of their doing this inasmuch as in making their choice they have chosen to let the worst people be better off than the good. Therefore, on this account I do not think well of their constitution. But since they have decided to have it so, I intend to point out how well they preserve their constitution and accomplish those other things for which the rest of the Greeks criticize them.[1]

First I want to say this: there the poor and the 2 people generally are right to have more than the high-born and wealthy for the reason that it is the people who man the ships and impart strength to the city; the steersmen, the boatswains, the sub-boatswains, the look-out officers, and the shipwrights—these are the ones who impart strength to the city far more than the hoplites, the high-born, and the good men. This being the case, it seems right for everyone to have a

[1] Here the author indicates the two basic topics of his treatise, and he alludes to this passage at 3. 1 when he has completed discussion of the first topic.

μετεῖναι ἔν τε τῷ κλήρῳ[1] καὶ τῇ[2] χειροτονίᾳ καὶ
3 λέγειν ἐξεῖναι τῷ βουλομένῳ τῶν πολιτῶν. ἔπειτα
ὁπόσαι μὲν σωτηρίαν φέρουσι τῶν ἀρχῶν χρησταὶ
οὖσαι καὶ μὴ χρησταὶ κίνδυνον[3] τῷ δήμῳ ἅπαντι,
τούτων μὲν τῶν ἀρχῶν οὐδὲν δεῖται ὁ δῆμος μετεῖναι
(οὔτε τῶν στρατηγιῶν[4] κλήρῳ[5] οἴονται[6] σφίσι χρῆναι
μετεῖναι οὔτε τῶν ἱππαρχιῶν)· γιγνώσκει γὰρ ὁ
δῆμος ὅτι πλείω ὠφελεῖται ἐν τῷ μὴ αὐτὸς ἄρχειν
ταύτας τὰς ἀρχάς, ἀλλ' ἐὰν τοὺς δυνατωτάτους ἄρχειν·
ὁπόσαι δ' εἰσὶν ἀρχαὶ μισθοφορίας ἕνεκα καὶ ὠφελίας
εἰς τὸν οἶκον, ταύτας ζητεῖ ὁ δῆμος ἄρχειν.
4 ἔπειτα δὲ ὃ ἔνιοι θαυμάζουσιν ὅτι πανταχοῦ πλέον
νέμουσι τοῖς πονηροῖς καὶ πένησι καὶ δημοτικοῖς ἢ τοῖς
χρηστοῖς, ἐν αὐτῷ τούτῳ φανοῦνται τὴν δημοκρατίαν
διασῴζοντες. οἱ μὲν γὰρ πένητες καὶ οἱ δημοτικοὶ[7]
καὶ οἱ χείρους εὖ πράττοντες καὶ πολλοὶ οἱ τοιοῦτοι
γιγνόμενοι τὴν δημοκρατίαν αὔξουσιν· ἐὰν δὲ εὖ
πράττωσιν οἱ πλούσιοι καὶ οἱ χρηστοί, ἰσχυρὸν τὸ
ἐναντίον σφίσιν αὐτοῖς καθιστᾶσιν οἱ δημοτικοί.
5 ἔστι δὲ πάσῃ γῇ τὸ βέλτιστον ἐναντίον τῇ δημοκρατίᾳ·
ἐν γὰρ τοῖς βελτίστοις ἔνι ἀκολασία τε ὀλιγίστη καὶ
ἀδικία, ἀκρίβεια δὲ πλείστη εἰς τὰ χρηστά, ἐν δὲ τῷ
δήμῳ ἀμαθία τε πλείστη καὶ ἀταξία καὶ πονηρία·
ἥ τε γὰρ πενία αὐτοὺς μᾶλλον ἄγει ἐπὶ τὰ αἰσχρά,
καὶ ἡ ἀπαιδευσία καὶ ἡ ἀμαθία δι' ἔνδειαν χρημάτων
⟨ἔνι⟩ ἐνίοις[8] τῶν ἀνθρώπων.

[1] τῷ κλήρῳ ABC: τῷ νῦν κλήρῳ (ὔνκ in ras.) M
[2] καὶ τῇ ABC: καὶ ἐν τῇ M
[3] κίνδυνον ABC: ἢ κίνδυνον M
[4] στρατηγιῶν M: στρατηγικῶν ABC
[5] κλήρῳ Wachsmuth: κλήρων ABM: om. C
[6] οἴονται CM: οἷόν τε AB
[7] οἱ δημοτικοί Kirchhoff: οἱ δημόται M: ἰδιῶται ABC
[8] ἔνι add. Christian

share in the magistracies, both allotted and elective, for anyone to be able to speak his mind if he wants to. Then there are those magistracies which bring safety 3 or danger to the people as a whole depending on whether or not they are well managed: of these the people claim no share (they do not think they should have an allotted share in the generalships or cavalry commands). For these people realize that there is more to be gained from their not holding these magistracies but leaving them instead in the hands of the most influential men. However, such magistracies as are salaried and domestically profitable the people are keen to hold.

Then there is a point which some find extraordinary, 4 that they everywhere assign more to the worst persons, to the poor, and to the popular types than to the good men: in this very point they will be found manifestly preserving their democracy. For the poor, the popular, and the base, inasmuch as they are well off and the likes of them are numerous, will increase the democracy; but if the wealthy, good men are well off, the men of the people create a strong opposition to themselves. And everywhere on earth the best 5 element is opposed to democracy. For among the best people there is minimal wantonness and injustice but a maximum of scrupulous care for what is good, whereas among the people there is a maximum of ignorance, disorder, and wickedness; for poverty draws them rather to disgraceful actions, and because of a lack of money some men are uneducated and ignorant.

6 εἴποι δ' ἄν τις ὡς ἐχρῆν αὐτοὺς μὴ ἐᾶν λέγειν πάντας
ἐξ ἴσης[1] μηδὲ βουλεύειν, ἀλλὰ τοὺς δεξιωτάτους καὶ
ἄνδρας ἀρίστους· οἳ δὲ καὶ ἐν τούτῳ ἄριστα βουλεύονται
ἐῶντες καὶ τοὺς πονηροὺς λέγειν. εἰ μὲν γὰρ οἱ
χρηστοὶ ἔλεγον καὶ ἐβουλεύοντο, τοῖς ὁμοίοις σφίσιν
αὐτοῖς ἦν[2] ἀγαθά, τοῖς δὲ δημοτικοῖς οὐκ ἀγαθά·
νῦν δὲ λέγων ὁ βουλόμενος ἀναστὰς ἄνθρωπος πονηρὸς
ἐξευρίσκει τὸ ἀγαθὸν αὑτῷ τε καὶ τοῖς ὁμοίοις αὑτῷ.
7 εἴποι τις ἄν, τί ἂν οὖν γνοίη ἀγαθὸν αὑτῷ ἢ τῷ δήμῳ
τοιοῦτος ἄνθρωπος; οἳ δὲ γιγνώσκουσιν ὅτι ἡ τούτου
ἀμαθία καὶ πονηρία καὶ εὔνοια μᾶλλον λυσιτελεῖ ἢ ἡ
8 τοῦ χρηστοῦ ἀρετὴ καὶ σοφία καὶ κακόνοια. εἴη μὲν
οὖν ἂν πόλις οὐκ ἀπὸ τοιούτων διαιτημάτων ἡ βελτίστη,
ἀλλ' ἡ δημοκρατία μάλιστ' ἂν σῴζοιτο οὕτως. ὁ γὰρ
δῆμος βούλεται οὔκ, εὐνομουμένης τῆς πόλεως, αὐτὸς
δουλεύειν,[3] ἀλλ' ἐλεύθερος εἶναι καὶ ἄρχειν, τῆς δὲ
κακονομίας[4] αὑτῷ ὀλίγον μέλει·[5] ὃ γὰρ σὺ νομίζεις
οὐκ εὐνομεῖσθαι, αὐτὸς ἀπὸ τούτου ἰσχύει ὁ δῆμος
9 καὶ ἐλεύθερός ἐστιν. εἰ δ' εὐνομίαν ζητεῖς, πρῶτα
μὲν ὄψει τοὺς δεξιωτάτους αὐτοῖς τοὺς νόμους τιθέντας·
ἔπειτα κολάσουσιν οἱ χρηστοὶ τοὺς πονηροὺς καὶ
βουλεύσουσιν οἱ χρηστοὶ περὶ τῆς πόλεως καὶ οὐκ
ἐάσουσι μαινομένους ἀνθρώπους βουλεύειν[6] οὐδὲ λέγειν
οὐδὲ ἐκκλησιάζειν. ἀπὸ τούτων τοίνυν τῶν ἀγαθῶν
τάχιστ' ἂν ὁ δῆμος εἰς δουλείαν καταπέσοι.
10 Τῶν δούλων δ' αὖ καὶ τῶν μετοίκων πλείστη ἐστὶν
Ἀθήνησιν ἀκολασία καὶ οὔτε πατάξαι ἔξεστιν αὐτόθι

---

[1] ἐξ ἴσης Bergk: ἐξῆς ABCM
[2] ἦν ABM: ἦν ἂν C
[3] δουλεύειν ABM: βουλεύειν C
[4] κακονομίας ABC: κακονοίας M
[5] μέλει BCM: μέλλει A
[6] βουλεύειν ABC: δουλεύειν M

Someone might say that they ought not to let every- 6 one speak on equal terms and serve on the council, but rather just the cleverest and finest. Yet their policy is also excellent in this very point of allowing even the worst people to speak. For if the good men were to speak and make policy, it would be splendid for the likes of themselves but not so for the men of the people. But, as things are, any wretch who wants to can stand up and obtain what is good for him and the likes of himself. Someone might say, "What good 7 would such a man propose for himself and the people?" But they know that this man's ignorance, baseness, and favour are more profitable than the good man's virtue, wisdom, and ill will. A city would not be the 8 best on the basis of such a way of life, but the democracy would be best preserved that way. For the people do not want a good government under which they themselves are slaves; they want to be free and to rule. Bad government is of little concern to them. What *you* consider bad government is the very source of the people's strength and freedom. If it is good govern- 9 ment you seek, you will first observe the cleverest men establishing the laws in their own interest. Then the good men will punish the bad; they will make policy for the city and not allow madmen to participate or to speak their minds or to meet in assembly. As a result of these excellent measures the people would swiftly fall into slavery.

Now among the slaves and metics[1] at Athens there is 10 the greatest uncontrolled wantonness; you can't hit

---

[1] Metics were resident aliens.

οὔτε ὑπεκστήσεταί σοι ὁ δοῦλος. οὗ δ'ἕνεκέν ἐστι
τοῦτο ἐπιχώριον, ἐγὼ φράσω· εἰ νόμος ἦν τὸν δοῦλον
ὑπὸ τοῦ ἐλευθέρου τύπτεσθαι ἢ τὸν μέτοικον ἢ τὸν
ἀπελεύθερον, πολλάκις ἂν οἰηθεὶς εἶναι τὸν Ἀθηναῖον
δοῦλον ἐπάταξεν ἄν· ἐσθῆτά τε γὰρ οὐδὲν βελτίων[1] ὁ
δῆμος αὐτόθι ἢ οἱ δοῦλοι καὶ οἱ μέτοικοι, καὶ τὰ εἴδη
11 οὐδὲν βελτίους εἰσίν. εἰ δέ τις καὶ τοῦτο θαυμάζει[2]
ὅτι ἐῶσι τοὺς δούλους τρυφᾶν αὐτόθι καὶ μεγαλοπρεπῶς
διαιτᾶσθαι ἐνίους, καὶ τοῦτο γνώμῃ φανεῖεν ἂν
ποιοῦντες. ὅπου γὰρ ναυτικὴ δύναμίς ἐστιν, ἀπὸ
χρημάτων ἀνάγκη τοῖς ἀνδραπόδοις δουλεύειν, ἵνα
†λαμβάνων μὲν πράττῃ†[3] τὰς ἀποφοράς, καὶ ἐλευθέρους
ἀφιέναι· ὅπου δ'εἰσὶ πλούσιοι δοῦλοι, οὐκέτι ἐνταῦθα
λυσιτελεῖ τὸν ἐμὸν δοῦλον σὲ δεδιέναι· ἐν δὲ τῇ
Λακεδαίμονι ὁ ἐμὸς δοῦλος σ' ἐδεδοίκει·[4] ἐὰν δὲ
δεδίῃ ὁ σὸς δοῦλος ἐμέ, κινδυνεύσει καὶ τὰ χρήματα
διδόναι τὰ ἑαυτοῦ ὥστε μὴ κινδυνεύειν περὶ ἑαυτοῦ.
12 διὰ τοῦτ' οὖν ἰσηγορίαν καὶ τοῖς δούλοις πρὸς τοὺς
ἐλευθέρους ἐποιήσαμεν, καὶ τοῖς μετοίκοις πρὸς τοὺς
ἀστούς, διότι δεῖται ἡ πόλις μετοίκων διά τε τὸ πλῆθος
τῶν τεχνῶν καὶ διὰ τὸ ναυτικόν· διὰ τοῦτο οὖν καὶ
τοῖς μετοίκοις εἰκότως τὴν ἰσηγορίαν ἐποιήσαμεν.
13 Τοὺς δὲ γυμναζομένους αὐτόθι καὶ τὴν μουσικὴν
ἐπιτηδεύοντας καταλέλυκεν ὁ δῆμος νομίζων τοῦτο
†οὐ καλὸν εἶναι, γνοὺς ὅτι οὐ† δυνατὰ[5] ταῦτά ἐστιν
ἐπιτηδεύειν. ἐν ταῖς χορηγίαις αὖ καὶ γυμνασιαρχίαις
καὶ τριηραρχίαις γιγνώσκουσιν ὅτι χορηγοῦσι μὲν οἱ

---

[1] βελτίων Brodaeus: βέλτιον ABCM
[2] θαυμίζει ABM : θαυμάζοι C
[3] λαμβάνων μὲν πράττῃ ABCM: λαμβάνωμεν ἃς πράττει (omisso τὰς) Leonclavius
[4] σ' ἐδεδοίκει Elter: σε δεδοίκει ABM: σε δέδοικεν C
[5] δυνατὰ ABM: δυνατὸς C

them there, and a slave will not stand aside for you. I shall point out why this is their native practice: if it were customary for a slave (or metic or freedman) to be struck by one who is free, you would often hit an Athenian citizen by mistake on the assumption that he was a slave. For the people there are no better dressed than the slaves and metics, nor are they any more handsome. If anyone is also startled by the fact 11 that they let the slaves live luxuriously there and some of them sumptuously, it would be clear that even this they do for a reason. For where there is a naval power, it is necessary from financial considerations to be slaves to the slaves in order to take a portion of their earnings, and it is then necessary to let them go free.[1] And where there are rich slaves, it is no longer profitable in such a place for my slave to fear you. In Sparta my slave would fear you; but if your slave fears me, there will be the chance that he will give over his money so as not to have to worry anymore. For 12 this reason we have set up equality between slaves and free men, and between metics and citizens. The city needs metics in view of the many different trades and the fleet. Accordingly, then, we have reasonably set up a similar equality also for the metics.

The people have spoiled the athletic and musical 13 activities at Athens because they thought them unfitting (they know they can't do them).[2] In the training of dramatic choruses and in providing for athletic contests and the fitting out of triremes, they

---

[1] The text of this sentence contains a corruption which makes it impossible to be sure of the sense.

[2] The text of this sentence is corrupt.

πλούσιοι, χορηγεῖται δὲ ὁ δῆμος, καὶ γυμνασιαρχοῦσι
οἱ πλούσιοι, ὁ[1] δὲ δῆμος τριηραρχεῖται καὶ γυμνασιαρ-
χεῖται. ἀξιοῖ[2] γοῦν[3] ἀργύριον λαμβάνειν ὁ δῆμος καὶ
ᾄδων καὶ τρέχων καὶ ὀρχούμενος καὶ πλέων ἐν ταῖς
ναυσίν, ἵνα αὐτός τε ἔχῃ καὶ οἱ πλούσιοι πενέστεροι
γίγνωνται· ἔν τε τοῖς δικαστηρίοις οὐ τοῦ δικαίου
αὐτοῖς μᾶλλον μέλει[4] ἢ τοῦ αὐτοῖς συμφόρου.

14 Περὶ δὲ τῶν συμμάχων—, ὅτι ἐκπλέοντες συκοφαν-
τοῦσιν, ὡς δοκοῦσι, καὶ μισοῦσι τοὺς χρηστούς,
γιγνώσκοντες ὅτι μισεῖσθαι μὲν ἀνάγκη τὸν ἄρχοντα
ὑπὸ τοῦ ἀρχομένου, εἰ δὲ ἰσχύσουσιν οἱ πλούσιοι καὶ
χρηστοὶ[5] ἐν ταῖς πόλεσιν, ὀλίγιστον χρόνον ἡ ἀρχὴ
ἔσται τοῦ δήμου τοῦ Ἀθήνησι,[6] διὰ ταῦτα οὖν[7] τοὺς
μὲν χρηστοὺς ἀτιμοῦσι[8] καὶ χρήματα ἀφαιροῦνται[9] καὶ
ἐξελαύνονται καὶ ἀποκτείνουσι, τοὺς δὲ πονηροὺς
αὔξουσιν. οἱ δὲ χρηστοὶ Ἀθηναίων τοὺς χρηστοὺς ἐν

Cf. Stob., *Anth.* 4. 1. 50 Ξενοφῶντος ἐκ τῆς Ἀθηναίων
πολιτείας ὅτι μισεῖσθαι μὲν ἀνάγκη τὸν ἄρχοντα ὑπὸ τοῦ ἀρχομένου,
εἰ δὲ ἰσχύσουσιν οἱ πλούσιοι καὶ ἰσχυροί[1] ἐν ταῖς πόλεσιν ὀλίγιστον
χρόνον ἡ ἀρχὴ ἔσται τοῦ δήμου, διὰ ταῦτα τοὺς μὲν χρηστοὺς
ἀτιμοῦσι καὶ χρήματα ἀφαιροῦνται καὶ ἐξελαύνονται[2] καὶ
ἀποκτείνουσι, τοὺς δὲ πονηροὺς αὔξουσιν.

[1] ἰσχυροί S: οἱ ἰσχυροί A   [2] ἐξελαύνονται A: ἐξελαύνουσι S

ταῖς συμμαχίσι πόλεσι σῴζουσι, γιγνώσκοντες ὅτι
σφίσιν ἀγαθόν ἐστι τοὺς βελτίστους σῴζειν ἀεὶ ἐν
15 ταῖς πόλεσιν. εἴποι δέ τις ἂν ἰσχύς ἐστιν αὕτη
Ἀθηναίων, ἐὰν οἱ σύμμαχοι δυνατοὶ ὦσι χρήματα
εἰσφέρειν· τοῖς δὲ δημοτικοῖς δοκεῖ μεῖζον ἀγαθὸν
εἶναι τὰ τῶν συμμάχων χρήματα ἕνα ἕκαστον Ἀθηναίων[10]

[1] πλούσιοι ὁ ABM: πλούσιοι καὶ τριηραρχοῦσιν ὁ C
[2] ἀξιοῖ ABM: ἀξιοῦσι C
[3] γοῦν ABC: οὖν M

know that it is the wealthy who lead the choruses but the people who are led in them, and it is the wealthy who provide for athletic contests, but the people who are presided over in the triremes and in the games. At least the people think themselves worthy of taking money for singing, running, dancing, and sailing in ships, so that they become wealthy and the wealthy poorer. And in the courts they are not so much concerned with justice as with their own advantage.

In regard to the allies: the Athenians sail out and lay information, as they are said to do; they hate the aristocrats inasmuch as they realize that the ruler is necessarily hated by the ruled and that if the rich and aristocratic men in the cities are strong, the rule of the people at Athens will last for a very short time. This is why they disfranchise the aristocrats, take away their money, expel and kill them, whereas they promote the interests of the lower class. The Athenian aristocrats protect their opposite numbers in the allied cities, since they realize that it will be to their advantage always to protect the finer people in the cities. Someone might say that the Athenians' strength consists in the allies' ability to pay tribute-money; but the rabble thinks it more advantageous for each one of the Athenians to possess the resources of the allies and for

---

⁴ μᾶλλον μέλει BC: μᾶλλον μέλλει A: μέλει μᾶλλον M
⁵ χρηστοὶ Heinrich: ἰσχυροὶ ABCM Stob.
⁶ τοῦ Ἀθήνησι ABCM: om. Stob.
⁷ σὺν ABCM: om. Stob.
⁸ ἀτιμοῦσι ABC Stob.: ἀτιμῶσι M
⁹ ἀφαιροῦνται ABC Stob.: ἀφαιρῶνται M
¹⁰ Ἀθηναίων ἔχειν ABC: ἔχειν Ἀθηναίων M

ἔχειν, ἐκείνους δὲ ὅσον ζῆν, καὶ ἐργάζεσθαι ἀδυνάτους
ὄντας ἐπιβουλεύειν.

16 Δοκεῖ δὲ ὁ δῆμος ὁ Ἀθηναίων[1] καὶ ἐν τῷδε κακῶς
βουλεύεσθαι, ὅτι τοὺς συμμάχους ἀναγκάζουσι πλεῖν
ἐπὶ δίκας Ἀθήναζε. οἱ δὲ ἀντιλογίζονται ὅσα ἐν
τούτῳ ἔνι ἀγαθὰ τῷ δήμῳ τῷ Ἀθηναίων· πρῶτον
μὲν ἀπὸ τῶν πρυτανείων τὸν μισθὸν δι᾿ ἐνιαυτοῦ
λαμβάνειν. εἶτ᾿ οἴκοι καθήμενοι ἄνευ νεῶν ἔκπλου
διοικοῦσι τὰς πόλεις τὰς συμμαχίδας, καὶ τοὺς μὲν
τοῦ δήμου σῴζουσι, τοὺς δ᾿ ἐναντίους ἀπολλύουσιν ἐν
τοῖς δικαστηρίοις· εἰ δὲ οἴκοι εἶχον ἕκαστοι τὰς
δίκας, ἅτε ἀχθόμενοι Ἀθηναίοις τούτους ἂν σφῶν
αὐτῶν ἀπώλλυσαν οἵτινες φίλοι μάλιστα ἦσαν Ἀθηναίων
17 τῷ δήμῳ. πρὸς δὲ τούτοις ὁ δῆμος τῶν Ἀθηναίων
τάδε κερδαίνει τῶν δικῶν Ἀθήνησιν οὐσῶν τοῖς
συμμάχοις· πρῶτον μὲν γὰρ ἡ ἑκατοστὴ τῇ πόλει
πλείων ἡ ἐν Πειραιεῖ· ἔπειτα εἴ τῳ συνοικία ἐστίν,
ἄμεινον[2] πράττειν· ἔπειτα εἴ τῳ ζεῦγός ἐστιν ἢ
ἀνδράποδον μισθοφοροῦν· ἔπειτα οἱ κήρυκες ἄμεινον
πράττουσι διὰ τὰς ἐπιδημίας τὰς τῶν συμμάχων.
18 πρὸς δὲ τούτοις, εἰ μὲν μὴ ἐπὶ δίκας ᾖσαν οἱ σύμμαχοι,
τοὺς ἐκπλέοντας Ἀθηναίων ἐτίμων ἂν μόνους, τούς τε
στρατηγοὺς καὶ τοὺς τριηράρχους καὶ πρέσβεις· νῦν
δ᾿ ἠνάγκασται τὸν δῆμον κολακεύειν τῶν Ἀθηναίων[3]
εἷς ἕκαστος τῶν συμμάχων, γιγνώσκων ὅτι δεῖ μὲν

[1] ὁ Ἀθηναίων M: Ἀθηναίων ABC
[2] ἄμεινον . . . ζεῦγός ἐστιν ABC: om. M
[3] τὸν Ἀθηναίων AC: τῶν Ἀθηναίων BM

---

[1] The accuracy of the author here is in dispute. For
discussion of the controversial problem of the judicial
relations of Athens and her allies, cf. G. E. M. de Ste.
Croix, "Notes on Jurisdiction in the Athenian Empire,"

the allies themselves to possess only enough for survival and to work without being able to plot defection.

Also in another point the Athenian people are thought 16 to act ill-advisedly: they force the allies to sail to Athens for judicial proceedings.[1] But they reply that the Athenian people benefit from this. First, from the deposits at law they receive their dicastic pay through the year. Then, sitting at home without going out in ships, they manage the affairs of the allied cities; in the courts they protect the democrats and ruin their opponents. If the allies were each to hold trials locally, they would, in view of their annoyance with the Athenians, ruin those of their citizens who were the leading friends of the Athenian people. In addition, the people at Athens profit in 17 the following ways when trials involving allies are held in Athens: first, the one per-cent tax in the Peiraeus brings in more for the city[2]; secondly, if anyone has lodgings to rent, he does better, and so does anyone who lets out on hire a team of animals or a slave; further, the heralds of the assembly do better when the allies are in town. In addition, were the allies not to 18 go away for judicial proceedings, they would honour only those of the Athenians who sail out from the city, namely generals, trierarchs, and ambassadors. As it is now, each one of the allies is compelled to flatter the Athenian populace from the realization that

CQ, N.S. 11 (1961), 94 ff. and 268 ff. Observe the Athenians' own account of their alleged litigiousness in the difficult passage of Thucydides at 1. 77.1.

[2] On the one per-cent tax, cf. Aristoph., *Wasps*, 658. Evidently a customs duty of some kind.

ἀφικόμενον Ἀθήναζε δίκην δοῦναι καὶ λαβεῖν οὐκ ἐν
ἄλλοις τισὶν ἀλλ' ἐν τῷ δήμῳ, ὅς ἐστι δὴ νόμος Ἀθήνησι·
καὶ ἀντιβολῆσαι ἀναγκάζεται ἐν τοῖς δικαστηρίοις καὶ
εἰσιόντος του ἐπιλαμβάνεσθαι τῆς χειρός. διὰ τοῦτο
οὖν οἱ σύμμαχοι δοῦλοι τοῦ δήμου[1] τῶν Ἀθηναίων
καθεστᾶσι μᾶλλον.

19   Πρὸς δὲ τούτοις διὰ τὴν κτῆσιν τὴν ἐν τοῖς ὑπερορίοις
καὶ διὰ τὰς ἀρχὰς τὰς εἰς τὴν ὑπερορίαν λελήθασι
μανθάνοντες ἐλαύνειν τῇ κώπῃ αὐτοί τε καὶ οἱ ἀκόλουθοι·
ἀνάγκη γὰρ ἄνθρωπον πολλάκις πλέοντα κώπην
λαβεῖν καὶ αὐτὸν καὶ τὸν οἰκέτην καὶ ὀνόματα μαθεῖν
20 τὰ ἐν τῇ ναυτικῇ.[2] καὶ κυβερνῆται ἀγαθοὶ γίγνονται
δι' ἐμπειρίαν τε τῶν πλόων[3] καὶ διὰ μελέτην·
ἐμελέτησαν[4] δὲ οἱ μὲν πλοῖον κυβερνῶντες, οἱ δὲ
ὁλκάδα οἱ δ' ἐντεῦθεν ἐπὶ τριήρεσι[5] κατέστησαν· οἱ
δὲ πολλοὶ ἐλαύνειν εὐθέως[6] οἷοί τε[7] εἰσβάντες εἰς
ναῦς[8] ἅτε ἐν παντὶ τῷ[9] βίῳ προμεμελετηκότες.[10]

II. τὸ δὲ ὁπλιτικὸν αὐτοῖς, ὃ ἥκιστα δοκεῖ εὖ ἔχειν
Ἀθήνησιν, οὕτω[11] καθέστηκεν καὶ τῶν μὲν πολεμίων
ἥττους τε σφᾶς αὐτοὺς ἡγοῦνται εἶναι καὶ ὀλείζους,[12] τῶν
δὲ συμμάχων οἳ φέρουσι τὸν φόρον καὶ κατὰ γῆν
κράτιστοί εἰσι, καὶ νομίζουσι τὸ ὁπλιτικὸν ἀρκεῖν[13] εἰ
2 τῶν συμμάχων κρείττονές εἰσι. πρὸς δὲ καὶ κατὰ

---

[1] τοῦ δήμου ABM: om. C
[2] ναυτικῇ ABM: ἀττικῇ C
[3] πλόων ABC: πλοίων M
[4] ἐμελέτησαν . . . κυβερνῶντες M: om. ABC
[5] τριήρεσι ABC: τριήρη M
[6] εὐθέως Wells: εὐθὺς ὡς ABCM
[7] οἷοί τε ABM: οἷόν τε C
[8] εἰς ναῦς seclusit Wilamowitz
[9] παντὶ τῷ ABM: τῷ παντὶ C

judicial action for anyone who comes to Athens is in the hands of none other than the populace (this indeed is the law at Athens); in the courts he is obliged to entreat whoever comes in and to grasp him by the hand. In this way the allies have become instead the slaves of the Athenian people.

Furthermore, as a result of their possessions abroad 19 and the tenure of magistracies which take them abroad, both they and their associates have imperceptibly learned to row; for of necessity a man who is often at sea takes up an oar, as does his slave, and they learn naval terminology. Both through experience of 20 voyages and through practice they become fine steersmen. Some are trained by service as steersmen on an ordinary vessel, others on a freighter, others—after such experience—on triremes. Many are able to row as soon as they board their ships, since they have been practising beforehand throughout their whole lives.

II. But the Athenian infantry, which has the reputation of being very weak, has been deliberately so constituted: they consider that they are weaker and fewer than their enemies, but they number among their allies who pay tribute those who are the strongest on land, and they think their infantry sufficient if they are stronger than their allies.

---

[10] προμεμελετηκότες M: προσμεμελετηκότες ABC
[11] οὕτω CM: οὕτως AB
[12] ὀλείζους Wilamowitz: μείζους ABCM
[13] ἀρκεῖν Courier: ἄρχειν ABCM

487

τύχην τι αὐτοῖς τοιοῦτον καθέστηκε· τοῖς μὲν κατὰ
γῆν ἀρχομένοις οἷόν τ'ἐστιν ἐκ μικρῶν πόλεων συνοι-
κισθέντας ἀθρόους μάχεσθαι· τοῖς δὲ κατὰ θάλατταν
ἀρχομένοις, ὅσοι νησιῶταί εἰσιν, οὐχ οἷόν τε συνάρασθαι
εἰς τὸ αὐτὸ τὰς πόλεις· ἡ γὰρ θάλαττα ἐν τῷ μέσῳ,
οἱ δὲ κρατοῦντες θαλασσοκράτορές εἰσιν. εἰ δ'οἷόν τε
καὶ λαθεῖν συνελθοῦσιν εἰς ταὐτὸ τοῖς νησιώταις εἰς
3 μίαν νῆσον, ἀπολοῦνται λιμῷ· ὁπόσαι δ'ἐν[1] τῇ
ἠπείρῳ εἰσὶ πόλεις ὑπὸ τῶν Ἀθηναίων ἀρχόμεναι, αἱ μὲν
μεγάλαι διὰ δέος ἄρχονται, αἱ δὲ μικραὶ πάνυ διὰ
χρείαν· οὐ γάρ ἐστι πόλις οὐδεμία ἥτις οὐ δεῖται
εἰσάγεσθαί τι ἢ ἐξάγεσθαι· ταῦτα τοίνυν οὐκ ἔσται
αὐτῇ, ἐὰν μὴ ὑπήκοος ᾖ τῶν ἀρχόντων τῆς θαλάττης.
4 ἔπειτα δὲ τοῖς ἄρχουσι τῆς θαλάττης οἷόν τ'ἐστὶ
ποιεῖν, ἅπερ τοῖς τῆς γῆς ἐνίοτε τέμνειν τὴν γῆν τῶν
κρειττόνων· παραπλεῖν γὰρ ἔξεστιν ὅπου ἂν μηδεὶς ᾖ
πολέμιος ἢ ὅπου ἂν ὀλίγοι, ἐὰν δὲ προσίωσιν, ἀναβάντα
ἀποπλεῖν· καὶ τοῦτο ποιῶν ἧττον ἀπορεῖ ἢ ὁ πεζῇ
5 παραβοηθῶν. ἔπειτα δὲ τοῖς μὲν κατὰ θάλατταν
ἄρχουσιν οἷόν τε ἀποπλεῦσαι ἀπὸ τῆς σφετέρας αὐτῶν
ὁπόσον βούλει πλοῦν, τοῖς δὲ κατὰ γῆν οὐχ οἷόν τε
ἀπὸ τῆς σφετέρας αὐτῶν ἀπελθεῖν πολλῶν ἡμερῶν
ὁδόν· βραδεῖαί τε γὰρ αἱ πορεῖαι καὶ σῖτον οὐχ οἷόν
τε ἔχειν πολλοῦ χρόνου πεζῇ ἰόντα· καὶ τὸν μὲν πεζῇ
ἰόντα δεῖ διὰ φιλίας ἰέναι ἢ νικᾶν μαχόμενον, τὸν δὲ
πλέοντα, οὗ μὲν ἂν ᾖ κρείττων, ἔξεστιν ἀποβῆναι

---

[1] δ'ἐν ABM: δὲ C

---

[1] Cf. the formation of the Chalcidic League in 432 (Thuc.
1. 58. 2), but these words need hardly be an allusion to it.
[2] Cf. Pericles in Thuc. 1. 143. 3 and the Athenian raiding
of the Peloponnesian coast (e.g. in 431, Thuc. 2. 23. 1).
But the author need not refer here to the Peloponnesian War;
in 455 Tolmides also proved the point (Thuc. 1. 108. 5).

Besides, there is the following accidental circum- 2
stance which applies to them: subject peoples on land
can combine a few cities and fight collectively,[1] but
subject peoples at sea, by virtue of being islanders,
cannot join their cities together into the same unit.
For the sea is in the midst, and those who rule it are
thalassocrats. If it is possible for islanders to combine unnoticed on a single island, they will die of
starvation. Of the Athenians' subject cities on the 3
mainland, some which are large are ruled because of
fear, and some small are ruled because of actual need;
for there is no city which does not have to import or
export, and these activities will be impossible for a city
unless it is subject to the rulers of the sea.

Moreover, the rulers of the sea can do just what 4
rulers of the land sometimes can do,—ravage the
territory of the stronger.[2] For wherever there is no
enemy (or wherever enemies are few), it is possible
to put in along the coast and—if there is an attack,—
to go on board one's ship and sail away; one who does
this is less badly off than one who comes to help with
infantry. Further, the rulers of the sea can sail away 5
from their own land to anywhere at all, whereas a
land power can take a journey of only a few days from
its own territory.[3] Progress is slow, and going on foot
one cannot carry provisions sufficient for a long time.
One who goes on foot must pass through friendly
country or else fight and win, whereas it is possible
for the seafarer to go on shore wherever he has the

---

[3] This dogma was proved false by Brasidas' march to
the north in 424 and hence was probably composed before
that year. The observation is due to W. Roscher,
Leben, Werk, und Zeitalter des Thukydides (1842), p. 529.

. . .[1] ταύτης[2] τῆς γῆς, ἀλλὰ[3] παραπλεῦσαι, ἕως ἂν ἐπὶ
6 φιλίαν χώραν ἀφίκηται ἢ ἐπὶ ἥττους αὑτοῦ. ἔπειτα
νόσους τῶν καρπῶν, αἳ ἐκ Διός εἰσιν, οἱ μὲν κατὰ
γῆν κράτιστοι χαλεπῶς φέρουσιν, οἱ δὲ κατὰ θάλατταν
ῥαδίως· οὐ γὰρ ἅμα πᾶσα γῆ νοσεῖ, ὥστε ἐκ τῆς
εὐθενούσης[4] ἀφικνεῖται τοῖς τῆς θαλάττης ἄρχουσιν.[5]
7 Εἰ δὲ δεῖ καὶ σμικροτέρων μνησθῆναι, διὰ τὴν ἀρχὴν
τῆς θαλάττης πρῶτον μὲν τρόπους εὐωχιῶν ἐξηῦρον
ἐπιμισγόμενοι ἄλλῃ ἄλλοις·[6] ὅ τι ἐν Σικελίᾳ ἡδὺ ἢ ἐν
Ἰταλίᾳ ἢ ἐν Κύπρῳ ἢ ἐν Αἰγύπτῳ ἢ ἐν Λυδίᾳ ἢ ἐν τῷ
Πόντῳ ἢ ἐν Πελοποννήσῳ ἢ ἄλλοθί που, ταῦτα πάντα
8 εἰς ἓν ἠθροίσθη[7] διὰ τὴν ἀρχὴν τῆς θαλάττης. ἔπειτα
φωνὴν πᾶσαν ἀκούοντες ἐξελέξαντο τοῦτο μὲν ἐκ τῆς,
τοῦτο δὲ ἐκ τῆς· καὶ οἱ μὲν Ἕλληνες ἰδίᾳ μᾶλλον καὶ
φωνῇ καὶ διαίτῃ καὶ σχήματι χρῶνται, Ἀθηναῖοι δὲ
κεκραμένῃ ἐξ ἁπάντων τῶν Ἑλλήνων καὶ βαρβάρων.
9 θυσίας δὲ καὶ ἱερὰ καὶ ἑορτὰς καὶ τεμένη, γνοὺς ὁ
δῆμος ὅτι οὐχ οἷόν τέ ἐστιν ἑκάστῳ τῶν πενήτων
θύειν καὶ εὐωχεῖσθαι καὶ ἵστασθαι[8] ἱερὰ καὶ πόλιν
οἰκεῖν καλὴν καὶ μεγάλην, ἐξηῦρεν ὅτῳ τρόπῳ ἔσται
ταῦτα. θύουσιν οὖν δημοσίᾳ μὲν ἡ πόλις ἱερεῖα πολλά·
ἔστι δὲ ὁ δῆμος ὁ εὐωχούμενος καὶ διαλαγχάνων τὰ
10 ἱερεῖα. καὶ γυμνάσια καὶ λουτρὰ καὶ ἀποδυτήρια τοῖς
μὲν πλουσίοις ἐστὶν ἰδίᾳ ἐνίοις, ὁ δὲ δῆμος αὐτὸς αὑτῷ

---

[1] lac. stat. Kirchhoff
[2] ταύτης ABM: ἐνταῦθα C
[3] γῆς ἀλλὰ AB: γῆς ἅλα M: γῆς οὐ δ'ἂν μὴ ᾖ μὴ ἀποβῆναι ἀλλὰ C
[4] εὐθενούσης Dindorf: εὐθηνούσης ABCM
[5] ἀφικνεῖται τοῖς . . . ἄρχουσιν ABM: τοῖς . . . ἄρχουσιν ἀφικνεῖται C
[6] ἄλλῃ ἄλλοις Kirchhoff: ἀλλήλοις ABCM
[7] ἠθροίσθη Leonclavius: ἠθροῖσθαι ABCM: ἤθροισται Kalinka
[8] ἵστασθαι Kirchhoff: κτᾶσθαι ABCM

stronger power ... this land, but to sail along the coast until he comes to a friendly region or to those weaker than himself.[1] Further, the strongest land 6 powers suffer badly from visitations of disease on the crops, but sea powers bear them easily. For the whole earth does not ail at the same time, so that from a prosperous land imports reach the rulers of the sea.

If there should be mention also of slighter matters,[2] 7 first, by virtue of their naval power, the Athenians have mingled with various peoples and discovered types of luxury. Whatever the delicacy in Sicily, Italy, Cyprus, Egypt, Lydia, Pontus, the Peloponnese, or anywhere else,—all these have been brought together into one place by virtue of naval power. Further, hearing every kind of dialect, they have 8 taken something from each; the Greeks individually tend to use their own dialect, way of life, and type of dress, but the Athenians use a mixture from all the Greeks and non-Greeks. The Athenian populace 9 realizes that it is impossible for each of the poor to offer sacrifices, to give lavish feasts, to set up shrines, and to manage a city which will be beautiful and great, and yet the populace has discovered how to have sacrifices, shrines, banquets, and temples. The city sacrifices at public expense many victims, but it is the people who enjoy the feasts and to whom the victims are allotted. Some rich persons have private gym- 10 nasia, baths, and dressing-rooms, but the people have

---

[1] There is a lacuna in this sentence.
[2] Cf. Pericles in the Funeral Oration: Thuc. 2. 38, on luxuries and delights, and on the presence in Athens of good things from everywhere.

οἰκοδομεῖται ἰδίᾳ παλαίστρας πολλάς, ἀποδυτήρια,
λουτρῶνας· καὶ πλείω τούτων ἀπολαύει ὁ ὄχλος ἢ οἱ
ὀλίγοι καὶ οἱ εὐδαίμονες.

11 Τὸν δὲ πλοῦτον μόνοι οἷοί τ᾽ εἰσὶν ἔχειν τῶν Ἑλλήνων
καὶ τῶν βαρβάρων. εἰ γάρ τις πόλις πλουτεῖ ξύλοις
ναυπηγησίμοις, ποῖ διαθήσεται, ἐὰν μὴ πείσῃ τοὺς
ἄρχοντας[1] τῆς θαλάττης; τί δ᾽ εἴ τις σιδήρῳ ἢ χαλκῷ
ἢ λίνῳ πλουτεῖ πόλις, ποῖ διαθήσεται, ἐὰν μὴ πείσῃ[2]
τοὺς ἄρχοντας[3] τῆς θαλάττης; ἐξ αὐτῶν μέντοι τούτων
καὶ δὴ νῆές μοί εἰσι, παρὰ μὲν τοῦ ξύλα, παρὰ δὲ τοῦ
σίδηρος, παρὰ δὲ τοῦ χαλκός, παρὰ δὲ τοῦ λίνου, παρὰ

12 δὲ τοῦ κηρός. πρὸς δὲ τούτοις ἄλλοσε ἄγειν οὐκ
ἐάσουσιν οἵ τινες[4] ἀντίπαλοι ἡμῖν εἰσιν ἢ οὐ χρήσονται
τῇ θαλάττῃ. καὶ ἐγὼ μὲν οὐδὲν ποιῶν ἐκ τῆς γῆς
πάντα ταῦτα ἔχω διὰ τὴν θάλατταν, ἄλλη δ᾽ οὐδεμία
πόλις δύο τούτων ἔχει· οὐδ᾽ ἐστὶ τῇ αὐτῇ ξύλα καὶ
λίνον, ἀλλ᾽ ὅπου λίνον ἐστὶ πλεῖστον, λεία χώρα καὶ
ἄξυλος·[5] οὐδὲ χαλκὸς καὶ σίδηρος ἐκ τῆς αὐτῆς πόλεως
οὐδὲ τἆλλα δύο ἢ τρία μιᾷ πόλει, ἀλλὰ τὸ μὲν τῇ, τὸ
δὲ τῇ.

13 Ἔτι δὲ πρὸς τούτοις παρὰ πᾶσαν ἤπειρόν ἐστιν ἢ
ἀκτὴ προέχουσα[6] ἢ νῆσος προκειμένη ἢ στενόπορόν τι·
ὥστε ἔξεστιν ἐνταῦθα ἐφορμοῦσι τοῖς τῆς θαλάττης
ἄρχουσι λωβᾶσθαι τοὺς τὴν ἤπειρον οἰκοῦντας.

14 Ἑνὸς δὲ ἐνδεεῖς εἰσιν· εἰ γὰρ νῆσον οἰκοῦντες

---

[1] πείσῃ τοὺς ἄρχοντας AB: πρὸς τοὺς ἄρχοντας C: πείσῃ τὸν
ἄρχοντα M
[2] ἐὰν μὴ πείσῃ ABM: εἰ μὴ πρὸς C
[3] τοὺς ἄρχοντας Kirchhoff: τὸν ἄρχοντα ABCM
[4] οἵ τινες Renehan: οἵτινες ACM: εἴ τινες B (εἴ in ras.)
[5] λεία χώρα καὶ ἄξυλος ABM: λεία καὶ ἄξυλος χώρα C
[6] προέχουσα ABM: προύχουσα C

built for their own use many wrestling-quarters, dressing-rooms, and public baths. The rabble has more enjoyment of these things than the well-to-do members of the upper class.

Wealth they alone of the Greeks and non-Greeks 11 are capable of possessing. If some city is rich in ship-timber, where will it distribute it without the consent of the rulers of the sea? Again if some city is rich in iron, copper, or flax, where will it distribute without the consent of the rulers of the sea? However, it is from these very things that I have my ships: timber from one place, iron from another, copper from another, flax from another, wax from another. In 12 addition, they will forbid export to wherever any of our enemies are, on pain of being unable to use the sea. And I, without doing anything, have all this from the land because of the sea; yet no other city has even two of these things: the same city does not have timber and flax, but wherever there is flax in abundance, the land is smooth and timberless. There is not even copper and iron from the same city, not any two or three other things in a single city, but there is one product here and another there.

Furthermore, every mainland has either a pro- 13 jecting headland or an offshore island or some strait, so that it is possible for a naval power to put in there and to injure those who dwell on the land.[1]

But there is one thing the Athenians lack.[2] If they 14

[1] Cf. Thuc. 1. 142 for a similar idea. Some have seen in this passage an allusion to the Pylos affair. That is hardly necessary.

[2] This section of pseudo-Xenophon is strikingly similar to Pericles' remarks in Thuc. 1. 143. 5.

θαλασσοκράτορες ἦσαν Ἀθηναῖοι, ὑπῆρχεν ἂν αὐτοῖς
ποιεῖν μὲν κακῶς, εἰ ἠβούλοντο,[1] πάσχειν δὲ μηδέν,
ἕως τῆς θαλάττης ἦρχον, μηδὲ τμηθῆναι τὴν ἑαυτῶν
γῆν μηδὲ προσδέχεσθαι τοὺς πολεμίους· νῦν δὲ οἱ
γεωργοῦντες καὶ οἱ πλούσιοι Ἀθηναίων ὑπέρχονται
τοὺς πολεμίους μᾶλλον, ὁ δὲ δῆμος, ἅτε εὖ εἰδὼς ὅτι
οὐδὲν τῶν σφῶν ἐμπρήσουσιν οὐδὲ τεμοῦσιν, ἀδεῶς ζῇ
15 καὶ οὐχ ὑπερχόμενος αὐτούς. πρὸς δὲ τούτοις καὶ
ἑτέρου δέους ἀπηλλαγμένοι ἂν ἦσαν, εἰ νῆσον ᾤκουν,
μηδέποτε προδοθῆναι τὴν πόλιν ὑπ᾽ ὀλίγων μηδὲ
πύλας ἀνοιχθῆναι μηδὲ πολεμίους ἐπεισπεσεῖν· πῶς
γὰρ νῆσον οἰκούντων ταῦτ᾽ ἂν[2] ἐγίγνετο; μηδ᾽ αὖ
στασιάσαι τῷ δήμῳ μηδένα,[3] εἰ νῆσον ᾤκουν· νῦν
μὲν γὰρ[4] εἰ στασιάσαιεν, ἐλπίδα ἂν ἔχοντες ἐν τοῖς
πολεμίοις στασιάσειαν ὡς κατὰ γῆν ἐπαξόμενοι· εἰ
δὲ νῆσον ᾤκουν, καὶ ταῦτα ἂν ἀδεῶς εἶχεν αὐτοῖς.[5]
16 ἐπειδὴ οὖν ἐξ ἀρχῆς οὐκ ἔτυχον οἰκήσαντες νῆσον,
νῦν τάδε ποιοῦσι· τὴν μὲν οὐσίαν ταῖς νήσοις παρατί-
θενται πιστεύοντες[6] τῇ ἀρχῇ τῇ κατὰ θάλατταν, τὴν
δὲ Ἀττικὴν γῆν περιορῶσι τεμνομένην, γιγνώσκοντες
ὅτι εἰ αὐτὴν ἐλεήσουσιν ἑτέρων ἀγαθῶν μειζόνων
στερήσονται.
17 Ἔτι δὲ συμμαχίας καὶ τοὺς ὅρκους ταῖς μὲν
ὀλιγαρχουμέναις πόλεσιν ἀνάγκη ἐμπεδοῦν· ἢν δὲ μὴ

---

[1] ἠβούλοντο ABM: ἐβούλοντο C
[2] ἂν ABC: om. M
[3] μηδένα Faltin: μηδέν ABCM
[4] γὰρ ABC: γὰρ ἂν M
[5] εἶχεν αὐτοῖς AB: ὑπῆρχεν αὐτοῖς C: αὐτοῖς εἶχεν M
[6] πιστεύοντες ABM: πιστεύσαντες C

---

[1] At the beginning of the Peloponnesian War the
Athenians certainly did move property to Euboea (Thuc.
2. 14. 1); and Attic land was ravaged by Spartans who

were thalassocrats living on an island, it would be possible for them to inflict harm, if they wished, but as long as they ruled the sea, to suffer none,—neither the ravaging of their land nor the taking on of enemies. As it is, of the Athenians the farmers and the wealthy curry favour with the enemy, whereas the people, knowing that nothing of theirs will be burnt or cut down, live without fear and refuse to fawn upon the enemy. Furthermore, if they lived on an island, 15 they would have been relieved of another fear: the city would never be betrayed by oligarchs nor would the gates be thrown open nor enemies invade. (For how would these things happen to islanders?) Besides no one would rebel against the democracy, if they lived on an island; as it is, if there were civil strife, the rebels would place their hope in bringing in the enemy by land. If they lived on an island, even this would be of no concern to them. However, since from the 16 beginning they happen not to have lived on an island, they now do the following: they place their property on islands while trusting in the naval empire and they allow their land to be ravaged, for they realize that if they concern themselves with this, they will be deprived of other greater goods.[1]

Further, for oligarchic cities it is necessary to keep 17 to alliances and oaths. If they do not abide by

were unopposed by the Athenians (Thuc. 2. 23. 1). But after the war began, it was impossible to say that the people ἀδεῶς ζῇ (cf. Thuc. 2. 65. 2); therefore, this passage is not persuasive evidence of a date of 431 or later. (One would be hard put to discover an apt moment *within* the year 431 after the land was ravaged but before the people felt discomfort.)

ἐμμένωσι ταῖς συνθήκαις ἢ ὑπό του ἀδικῇ,[1] ὀνόματα
ἀπὸ τῶν ὀλίγων οἳ συνέθεντο. ἄσσα δ᾽ ἂν ὁ δῆμος
συνθῆται, ἔξεστιν αὐτῷ, ἑνὶ ἀνατιθέντι τὴν αἰτίαν τῷ
λέγοντι καὶ τῷ ἐπιψηφίσαντι, ἀρνεῖσθαι τοῖς ἄλλοις
ὅτι οὐ παρῆν οὐδὲ ἀρέσκει οἵ γε[2] τὰ συγκείμενα
†πυνθάνονται† ἐν πλήρει τῷ δήμῳ· καὶ εἰ μὴ δόξαι
εἶναι ταῦτα, προφάσεις μυρίας ἐξηύρηκε τοῦ μὴ ποιεῖν
ὅσα ἂν μὴ βούλωνται. καὶ ἂν μέν τι κακὸν ἀναβαίνῃ
ἀπὸ ὧν ὁ δῆμος ἐβούλευσεν, αἰτιᾶται ὁ δῆμος ὡς
ὀλίγοι ἄνθρωποι αὐτῷ ἀντιπράττοντες διέφθειραν·
ἐὰν δέ τι ἀγαθόν, σφίσιν αὐτοῖς τὴν αἰτίαν ἀνατιθέασι.

18 κωμῳδεῖν δ᾽αὖ καὶ κακῶς λέγειν τὸν μὲν δῆμον οὐκ
ἐῶσιν, ἵνα μὴ αὐτοὶ ἀκούωσι κακῶς· ἰδίᾳ δὲ κελεύουσιν,
εἴ τίς τινα βούλεται, εὖ εἰδότες ὅτι οὐχὶ τοῦ δήμου
ἐστὶν οὐδὲ τοῦ πλήθους ὁ κωμῳδούμενος ὡς ἐπὶ τὸ
πολύ, ἀλλ᾽ ἢ πλούσιος ἢ γενναῖος ἢ δυνάμενος, ὀλίγοι
δέ τινες τῶν πενήτων καὶ τῶν δημοτικῶν κωμῳδοῦνται
καὶ οὐδ᾽ οὗτοι ἐὰν μὴ διὰ πολυπραγμοσύνην καὶ διὰ
τὸ ζητεῖν πλέον τι ἔχειν τοῦ δήμου, ὥστε οὐδὲ τοὺς
τοιούτους ἄχθονται κωμῳδουμένους.

19 φημὶ οὖν[3] ἔγωγε τὸν δῆμον τὸν Ἀθήνησι γιγνώσκειν
οἵτινες χρηστοί εἰσι τῶν πολιτῶν καὶ οἵτινες πονηροί,
γιγνώσκοντες δὲ τοὺς μὲν σφίσιν αὐτοῖς ἐπιτηδείους καὶ
συμφόρους φιλοῦσι, κἂν πονηροὶ ὦσι, τοὺς δὲ χρηστοὺς

---

[1] ὑπό του ἀδικῇ Frisch: ὑφ᾽ ὅτου ἀδικεῖ ABCM
[2] οἵ γε AM: εἴ γε B: εἴ γε μὴν C
[3] οὖν ABC: μὲν οὖν M

---

[1] There is a corruption in this sentence, but the sense is
clear.
[2] This passage has nothing to do with the known bans
on comedy in 440/39–437/6 or in 415: see K. I. Gelzer, *Die
Schrift vom Staate der Athener* (1937), pp. 71 and 128–132.

agreements or if injustice is done, there are the names of the few who made the agreement. But whatever agreements the populace makes can be repudiated by referring the blame to the one who spoke or took the vote, while the others declare that they were absent or did not approve of the agreement made in the full assembly.[1] If it seems advisable for their decisions not to be effective, they invent myriad excuses for not doing what they do not want to do. And if there are any bad results from the people's plans, they charge that a few persons, working against them, ruined their plans; but if there is a good result, they take the credit for themselves.

They do not permit the people to be ill spoken of 18 in comedy, so that they may not have a bad reputation[2]; but if anyone wants to attack private persons, they bid him do so, knowing perfectly well that the person so treated in comedy does not, for the most part, come from the populace and mass of people but is a person of either wealth, high birth, or influence. Some few poor and plebeian types are indeed abused in comedy but only if they have been meddling in others' affairs and trying to rise above their class, so that the people feel no vexation at seeing such persons abused in comedy.

It is *my* opinion that the people at Athens know 19 which citizens are good and which bad, but that in spite of this knowledge they cultivate those who are complaisant and useful to themselves, even if bad;

Despite Gelzer's powerful arguments, there is, however, still controversy on this matter. It should be noted that the People (Demos) is a character in Aristophanes' *Knights* (produced in 424).

μι τοῦσι μᾶλλον· οὐ γὰρ νομίζουσι τὴν ἀρετὴν αὑτοῖς πρὸς
τῷ σφετέρῳ ἀγαθῷ πεφυκέναι, ἀλλ' ἐπὶ τῷ κακῷ· καὶ
τοὐναντίον γε τούτου ἔνιοι, ὄντες ὡς ἀληθῶς τοῦ
20 δήμου, τὴν φύσιν οὐ δημοτικοί εἰσι. δημοκρατίαν δ'ἐγὼ
μὲν αὑτῷ[1] τῷ δήμῳ συγγιγνώσκω· αὑτὸν μὲν γὰρ
εὖ ποιεῖν παντὶ[2] συγγνώμη ἐστίν· ὅστις δὲ μὴ ὢν τοῦ
δήμου εἵλετο ἐν δημοκρατουμένῃ πόλει οἰκεῖν μᾶλλον
ἢ ἐν[3] ὀλιγαρχουμένῃ, ἀδικεῖν παρεσκευάσατο καὶ
ἔγνω ὅτι μᾶλλον οἷόν τε διαλαθεῖν κακῷ ὄντι ἐν
δημοκρατουμένῃ πόλει μᾶλλον[4] ἢ ἐν ὀλιγαρχουμένῃ·

Cf. Stob., *Anth.* 4. 1. 51 δημοκρατίαν δ'ἐγὼ αὐτῷ μὲν τῷ
δήμῳ συγγινώσκω, ἑαυτὸν μὲν γὰρ εὖ ποιεῖν πάντῃ συγγνώμη
ἐστίν, ὅστις δὲ μὴ ὢν τοῦ δήμου εἵλετο ἐν δημοκρατουμένῃ πόλει
οἰκεῖν μᾶλλον ἢ ὀλιγαρχουμένῃ ἀδικεῖν παρεσκευάσατο καὶ ἔγνω
ὅτι μᾶλλον οἷόν τε διαλαθεῖν κακῷ ὄντι ἐν δημοκρατουμένῃ πόλει
ἢ ἐν ὀλιγαρχουμένῃ.

III. καὶ περὶ τῆς Ἀθηναίων πολιτείας τὸν μὲν
τρόπον οὐκ ἐπαινῶ· ἐπειδήπερ[5] ἔδοξεν αὐτοῖς δημο-
κρατεῖσθαι, εὖ μοι δοκοῦσι διασῴζεσθαι τὴν δημοκρατίαν
τούτῳ τῷ τρόπῳ χρώμενοι ᾧ ἐγὼ ἐπέδειξα.

Ἔτι δὲ καὶ τάδε τινὰς ὁρῶ μεμφομένους Ἀθηναίους
ὅτι ἐνίοτε οὐκ ἔστιν αὐτόθι χρηματίσαι τῇ βουλῇ οὐδὲ
τῷ δήμῳ ἐνιαυτὸν καθημένῳ ἀνθρώπῳ· καὶ τοῦτο
Ἀθήνησι γίγνεται οὐδὲν δι' ἄλλο ἢ ⟨διότι⟩[6] διὰ τὸ
πλῆθος τῶν πραγμάτων οὐχ οἷοί τε πάντας[7] ἀποπέμπειν
2 εἰσὶ χρηματίσαντες. πῶς γὰρ ἂν καὶ οἷοί τε εἶεν,
οὕστινας πρῶτον μὲν δεῖ ἑορτάσαι ἑορτὰς ὅσας οὐδεμία
τῶν Ἑλληνίδων πόλεων (ἐν δὲ ταύταις ἧττόν τινα

1 μὲν αὑτῷ ABCM: αὐτῷ μὲν Stob.
2 παντὶ ABCM: πάντῃ Stob.
3 ἐν ante ὀλιγ. ABCM: om. Stob.
4 μᾶλλον ABCM: om. Stob.

and they tend to hate the good. For they do not think that the good are naturally virtuous for the people's benefit, but for their hurt. On the other hand, some persons are not by nature democratic although they are truly on the people's side. I 20 pardon the people themselves for their democracy. One must forgive everyone for looking after his own interests. But whoever is not a man of the people and yet prefers to live in a democratic city rather than in an oligarchic one has readied himself to do wrong and has realized that it is easier for an evil man to escape notice in a democratic city than in an oligarchic.

III. As for the constitution of the Athenians I do not praise its form; but since they have decided to have a democracy, I think they have preserved the democracy well by the means which I have indicated.[1]

I notice also that objections are raised against the Athenians because it is sometimes not possible for a person, though he sit about for a year, to negotiate with the council or the assembly. This happens at Athens for no other reason than that owing to the quantity of business they are not able to deal with all persons before sending them away. For how could they do 2 this? First of all they have to hold more festivals than any other Greek city (and when these are going on

---

[1] Cf. the opening paragraph of the treatise.

---

[5] ἐπειδήπερ ABM: ἐπειδὴ δ' C

[6] διότι add. Kirchhoff

[7] πάντας C: πάντες, -ας (superscr. man. prim.) M: πάντες AB

δυνατόν ἐστι διαπάττεσθαι τῶν τῆς πόλεως), ἔπειτα
δὲ δίκας καὶ γραφὰς καὶ εὐθύνας ἐκδικάζειν ὅσας οὐδ'
οἱ σύμπαντες ἄνθρωποι ἐκδικάζουσι, τὴν δὲ βουλὴν
βουλεύεσθαι πολλὰ μὲν περὶ τοῦ πολέμου, πολλὰ δὲ
περὶ πόρου χρημάτων, πολλὰ δὲ περὶ νόμων θέσεως,
πολλὰ δὲ περὶ τῶν κατὰ πόλιν ἀεὶ γιγνομένων, πολλὰ
δὲ καὶ τοῖς συμμάχοις, καὶ φόρον δέξασθαι καὶ νεωρίων
ἐπιμεληθῆναι καὶ ἱερῶν; ἆρα δή τι θαυμαστόν ἐστιν εἰ
τοσούτων ὑπαρχόντων[1] πραγμάτων μὴ οἷοί τ' εἰσὶ
3 πᾶσιν ἀνθρώποις χρηματίσαι; λέγουσι δέ τινες· ἢν τις
ἀργύριον ἔχων προσίῃ πρὸς βουλὴν ἢ δῆμον, χρηματιεῖ-
ται. ἐγὼ δὲ τούτοις ὁμολογήσαιμ' ἂν ἀπὸ χρημάτων
πολλὰ διαπράττεσθαι Ἀθήνησι καὶ ἔτι ἂν πλείω[2]
διαπράττεσθαι εἰ πλείους ἔτι ἐδίδοσαν[3] ἀργύριον·
τοῦτο μέντοι εὖ οἶδα διότι πᾶσι διαπρᾶξαι ἡ πόλις τῶν
δεομένων οὐχ ἱκανή, οὐδ' εἰ ὁποσονοῦν[4] χρυσίον καὶ
4 ἀργύριον διδοίη τις αὐτοῖς. δεῖ δὲ καὶ τάδε διαδικάζειν,
εἴ τις τὴν ναῦν μὴ ἐπισκευάζει ἢ κατοικοδομεῖ τι
δημόσιον· πρὸς δὲ τούτοις χορηγοῖς διαδικάσαι εἰς
Διονύσια καὶ Θαργήλια καὶ Παναθήναια καὶ Προμήθια
καὶ Ἡφαίστια ὅσα ἔτη.

καὶ τριήραρχοι καθίστανται τετρακόσιοι ἑκάστου
ἐνιαυτοῦ, καὶ τούτων τοῖς βουλομένοις διαδικάσαι ὅσα
ἔτη· πρὸς δὲ τούτοις ἀρχὰς δοκιμάσαι καὶ διαδικάσαι
καὶ ὀρφανοὺς δοκιμάσαι καὶ φύλακας δεσμωτῶν

---

[1] ὑπαρχόντων BCM: ὑπερχόντων A
[2] πλείω ABM: πολλῷ πλείω C
[3] ἔτι ἐδίδοσαν Cobet: ἐπεδίδοσαν ABCM
[4] ὁποσονοῦν ABM: ὁπόσον ἦν C

---

[1] Kirchhoff inferred wrongly from this passage that there
was a war on: *Abhandl. d. königl. Akad. Berlin* (1878), 8. Cf.

it is even less possible for any of the city's affairs to be transacted), next they have to preside over private and public trials and investigations into the conduct of magistrates to a degree beyond that of all other men, and the council has to consider many issues involving war,[1] revenues, law-making, local problems as they occur, also many issues on behalf of the allies, receipt of tribute, the care of dockyards and shrines. Is there accordingly any cause for surprise if with so much business they are unable to negotiate with all persons? But **3** some say, "If you go to the council or assembly with money, you will transact your business." I should agree with these people that many things are accomplished at Athens for money and still more would be accomplished if still more gave money. This, however, I know well, that the city has not the wherewithal to deal with everyone who asks, not even if you give them any amount of gold and silver. They have also to adjudicate cases when a man does **4** not repair his ship or builds something on public property, and in addition to settle disputes every year with chorus leaders at the Dionysia, Thargelia, Panathenaea, Promethia, and Hephaestia.

Four hundred trierarchs are appointed every year,[2] and disputes have to be settled for any of these who wish. Moreover, magistrates have to be approved and their disputes settled, orphans approved and

HSCP, 71 (1966), 34-5

[2] From the numbers of ships in Thuc. 2. 13. 8 and Aristoph. *Acharn.* 545 one would expect 300 trierarchs. Our manuscripts of Andocides 3.9 mention 400 ships, but it is clear from Aeschines' plagiarism (2. 175) of Andocides that the original reading was 300. Perhaps in pseudo-Xenophon too.

5 καταστῆσαι. ταῦτα μὲν οὖν ὅσα ἔτη. διὰ χρόνου
⟨δὲ⟩[1] διαδικάσαι δεῖ ἀστρατείας[2] καὶ ἐάν τι ἄλλο
ἐξαπιναῖον ἀδίκημα γίγνηται, ἐάν τε ὑβρίζωσί τινες
ἄηθες ὕβρισμα, ἐάν τε ἀσεβήσωσι.

πολλὰ ἔτι πάνυ[3] παραλείπω· τὸ δὲ μέγιστον
εἴρηται πλὴν αἱ τάξεις τοῦ φόρου· τοῦτο δὲ γίγνεται
6 ὡς τὰ πολλὰ δι' ἔτους πέμπτου. φέρε δὴ τοίνυν, ταῦτα
οὐκ οἴεσθαι ⟨χρὴ⟩[4] χρῆναι διαδικάζειν ἅπαντα; εἰπάτω
γάρ τις ὅ τι οὐ χρῆν αὐτόθι διαδικάζεσθαι. εἰ δ' αὖ
ὁμολογεῖν δεῖ[5] ἅπαντα χρῆναι διαδικάζειν, ἀνάγκη
δι' ἐνιαυτοῦ, ὡς οὐδὲ νῦν δι' ἐνιαυτοῦ δικάζοντες
ὑπάρχουσιν ὥστε παύειν τοὺς ἀδικοῦντας ὑπὸ τοῦ
7 πλήθους τῶν ἀνθρώπων. φέρε δή, ἀλλὰ φήσει τις
χρῆναι δικάζειν μέν, ἐλάττους δὲ δικάζειν. ἀνάγκη
τοίνυν, ἐὰν μὴ[6] ὀλίγα ποιῶνται δικαστήρια, ὀλίγοι ἐν
ἑκάστῳ ἔσονται τῷ δικαστηρίῳ, ὥστε καὶ διασκευά-
σασθαι ῥᾴδιον ἔσται πρὸς ὀλίγους δικαστὰς καὶ
συνδεκάσαι,[7] πολὺ ἧττον ⟨δὲ⟩[8] δικαίως δικάζειν.
8 πρὸς δὲ τούτοις οἴεσθαι χρὴ καὶ ἑορτὰς ἄγειν χρῆναι
Ἀθηναίους ἐν αἷς οὐχ οἷόν τε δικάζειν· καὶ ἄγουσι
μὲν ἑορτὰς διπλασίους ἢ οἱ ἄλλοι· ἀλλ' ἐγὼ μὲν
τίθημι ἴσας τῇ ὀλιγίστας[9] ἀγούσῃ πόλει. τούτων
τοίνυν τοιούτων ὄντων οὔ φημι οἷόν τ' εἶναι ἄλλως
ἔχειν τὰ πράγματα Ἀθήνησιν ἢ ὥσπερ νῦν ἔχει,
πλὴν εἰ κατὰ μικρόν τι οἷόν τε τὸ μὲν ἀφελεῖν τὸ δὲ

---

[1] δὲ add. F. Portus
[2] ἀστρατείας Brodaeus: στρατιᾶς AC: στρατιὰς M: στρατιὰ B
[3] πάνυ ABM: om. C
[4] χρὴ add. Wachsmuth
[5] ὁμολογεῖν δεῖ Leonclavius: ὁμολογεῖ δεῖν ABCM
[6] ἐὰν μὴ Lβ m₁ per coniecturam: ἐὰν μὲν ABCM
[7] συνδεκάσαι Matthiae: συνδικάσαι ABCM
[8] δὲ add. Kalinka
[9] ὀλιγίστας CM: ὀλιγούσας AB

prisoners' guards appointed. And these things happen every year. Now and again they have to deal 5 with cases of desertion and other unexpected misdeeds, whether it be an irregular act of wantonness or an act of impiety.

There are still many items which I altogether pass over. The most important have been mentioned except for the assessments of tribute. These generally occur every four years.[1] Well then, ought 6 one to think that all these cases should not be dealt with? Let someone say what should not be dealt with there. If, on the other hand, one must agree that it is all necessary, the adjudicating has to go on throughout the year, since not even now when they do adjudicate throughout the year can they stop all the wrongdoers because there are so many. All right, 7 yet someone will say that they ought to judge cases, but that fewer people should do the judging. Unless they have only a few courts, there will necessarily be few jurors in each court, so that it will be easier to adapt oneself to a few jurors and to bribe them, and easier to judge much less justly. Further, one must 8 consider that the Athenians have to hold festivals during which the courts are closed. They hold twice as many festivals as others do, but I am counting only those which have equivalents in the state holding the smallest number. Under such circumstances, therefore, I deny that it is possible for affairs at Athens to be otherwise than as they now are, except insofar as it is possible to take away a bit here and add a bit

[1] Literally in the fifth year, inclusively quinquennial like the Olympic games. The first irregular assessment occurred in 443. Cf. *HSCP* 71 (1966) 38.

προσθεῖναι, πολὺ δ'οὐχ οἷόν τε μετακινεῖν, ὥστε μὴ
9 οὐχὶ τῆς δημοκρατίας ἀφαιρεῖν τι. ὥστε μὲν γὰρ
βέλτιον ἔχειν τὴν πολιτείαν, οἷόν τε[1] πολλὰ ἐξευρεῖν·
ὥστε μέντοι ὑπάρχειν μὲν δημοκρατίαν[2] εἶναι, ἀρκούντως
δὲ τοῦτο ἐξευρεῖν ὅπως δὴ[3] βέλτιον πολιτεύσονται,
οὐ ῥάδιον, πλὴν ὅπερ ἄρτι εἶπον κατὰ μικρόν τι
προσθέντα ἢ ἀφελόντα.
10 Δοκοῦσι δὲ Ἀθηναῖοι καὶ τοῦτό μοι οὐκ ὀρθῶς
βουλεύεσθαι ὅτι τοὺς χείρους αἱροῦνται ἐν ταῖς πόλεσι
ταῖς στασιαζούσαις. οἳ δὲ τοῦτο γνώμῃ ποιοῦσιν· εἰ
μὲν γὰρ ἡροῦντο τοὺς βελτίους, ἡροῦντ' ἂν οὐχὶ τοὺς
ταὐτὰ γιγνώσκοντας σφίσιν αὐτοῖς· ἐν οὐδεμιᾷ γὰρ
πόλει τὸ βέλτιστον εὔνουν ἐστὶ τῷ δήμῳ, ἀλλὰ τὸ
κάκιστον ἐν ἑκάστῃ ἐστὶ πόλει εὔνουν τῷ δήμῳ·[4]
οἱ γὰρ ὅμοιοι τοῖς ὁμοίοις εὔνοοι[5] εἰσι· διὰ ταῦτα
οὖν Ἀθηναῖοι τὰ σφίσιν αὐτοῖς προσήκοντα αἱροῦνται.
11 ὁποσάκις δ' ἐπεχείρησαν αἱρεῖσθαι τοὺς βελτίστους,
οὐ συνήνεγκεν αὐτοῖς· ἀλλ' ἐντὸς ὀλίγου χρόνου ὁ
δῆμος ἐδουλεύσεν ὁ ἐν[6] Βοιωτοῖς· τοῦτο δὲ ὅτε
Μιλησίων εἵλοντο τοὺς βελτίστους, ἐντὸς ὀλίγου χρόνου
ἀποστάντες τὸν δῆμον κατέκοψαν· τοῦτο δὲ ὅτε
εἵλοντο Λακεδαιμονίους ἀντὶ Μεσσηνίων, ἐντὸς ὀλίγου
χρόνου Λακεδαιμόνιοι καταστρεψάμενοι Μεσσηνίους
ἐπολέμουν Ἀθηναίοις.
12 Ὑπολάβοι δέ τις ἂν ὡς οὐδεὶς ἄρα ἀδίκως ἠτίμωται
Ἀθήνησιν. ἐγὼ δὲ φημί τινας εἶναι οἳ ἀδίκως

---

[1] οἷόν τε Ma m₂ per coniecturam: οἴονται ABCM
[2] μὲν δημοκρατίαν ABC: δημοκρατίαν μὲν M
[3] δὴ scripsi: δὲ ABM: om. C
[4] ἀλλὰ ... δήμῳ M: om. ABC
[5] εὔνοοι ABC: εὖνοι M
[6] ὁ ἐν Madvig: ὁ μὲν ABM: τοῦτο μὲν C

there; a substantial change is impossible without removing some part of the democracy. It is possible 9 to discover many ways to improve the constitution; however, it is not easy to discover a means whereby the democracy may continue to exist but sufficient at the same time to provide a better polity, except—as I have just said—by adding or subtracting a little.

Also in the following point the Athenians seem to 10 me to act ill-advisedly: in cities embroiled in civil strife they take the side of the lower class. This they do deliberately; for if they preferred the upper class, they would prefer those who are contrary-minded to themselves. In no city is the superior element well disposed to the populace, but in each city it is the worst part which is well disposed to the populace. For like is well disposed to like. Accordingly the Athenians prefer those sympathetic to themselves. Whenever they have undertaken to prefer the upper 11 class, it has not turned out well for them; within a short time the people in Boeotia were enslaved[1]; similarly when they preferred the Milesian upper class, within a short time that class had revolted and cut down the people[2]; similarly when they preferred the Spartans to the Messenians, within a short time the Spartans had overthrown the Messenians and were making war on the Athenians.[3]

Someone might interject that no one has been 12 unjustly disfranchised at Athens. I say that there

[1] This presumably happened sometime in the period 456–446: cf. *HSCP*, 71 (1966), 35–6.
[2] Perhaps soon after 446: cf. *JHS*, 82 (1962), 1 ff. Formerly dated to the late fifties.
[3] An allusion to Athenian aid to Sparta in the sixties on the occasion of the Messenian Revolt.

ἠτίμωνται, ὀλίγοι μέντοι τινές. ἀλλ' οὐκ ὀλίγων δεῖ
τῶν ἐπιθησομένων τῇ δημορατίᾳ τῇ Ἀθήνησιν·
ἐπεί τοι καὶ οὕτως ἔχει, οὐ δεῖ[1] ἐνθυμεῖσθαι ἀνθρώπους
εἴ τινες[2] δικαίως ἠτίμωνται,[3] ἀλλ' εἴ τινες ἀδίκως.
13 πῶς ἂν οὖν ἀδίκως οἴοιτό τις ἂν τοὺς πολλοὺς ἠτιμῶσθαι
Ἀθήνησιν, ὅπου ὁ δῆμός ἐστιν ὁ ἄρχων τὰς ἀρχάς; ἐκ
δὲ τοῦ μὴ δικαίως ἄρχειν μηδὲ λέγειν τὰ δίκαια <μηδὲ>[4]
πράττειν, ἐκ τοιούτων ἄτιμοί εἰσιν Ἀθήνησι. ταῦτα
χρὴ λογιζόμενον μὴ νομίζειν εἶναί τι δεινὸν ἀπὸ τῶν
ἀτίμων Ἀθήνησιν.

[1] οὐ δεῖ H. Fraenkel: οὐδὲν ABCM
[2] εἴ τινες Bergk: οἵ τινες ABCM
[3] ἠτίμωνται Elmsley: τιμῶνται ABCM
[4] μηδὲ add. H. Stephanus

are some who have been unjustly disfranchised but very few indeed. To attack the democracy at Athens not a few are required. As this is so, there is no need to consider whether any persons have been justly disfranchised, only whether unjustly. Now how 13 would anyone think that many people were unjustly disfranchised at Athens, where the people are the ones who hold the offices? It is from failing to be a just magistrate or failing to say or do what is right that people are disfranchised at Athens. In view of these considerations one must not think that there is any danger at Athens from the disfranchised.

INDEX

[References are to chapter and section]

HIERO

Agriculture, prizes for, IX. 7
Bodyguard, foreign, V. 3; VI. 10
Choirs and choir-masters, IX. 4
Confidence, IV. 1
Dailochus, favourite of Hiero, I. 31
Despots, misfortunes of, I. 11, 15,
  17, 27; II. 6, 9, 12; III. 6; IV. 1,
  3, 6; V. 1, 3; VI. 5, 7, 13; VII. 5,
  12; VIII. 8; advice to, IX. 3;
  X. 2; XI.
Eating and drinking, I. 17; VI. 2
Expenditure, IV. 9; VIII. 8; XI. 1
Fatherland, IV. 1; V. 3
Favourites, I. 29; VIII. 6
Favours, VI. 12; VIII. 1
Fear, IV. 4
Festivals, I. 12; XI. 5
Friendship, III. 1
Honour, desire of, VII. 2
Horses, X. 2; horse-breeding, XI. 5
Industry, IX. 8
Marriage, I. 27
Mercenaries, VIII. 10; X. 1
Murder, III. 8; X. 4
Peace and war, II. 7
Popularity, how to win, IX. 1; XI. 1
Poverty, IV. 8
Praise and censure, I. 14; IX. 2
Prizes, IX. 3
Rank, advantages of high, VIII. 5
Revelry, VI. 1
Suspicion, IV. 1; V. 1; VI. 5
Unpopularity, IX. 1; X. 1
War, II. 7; V. 7; VI. 7

AGESILAUS

Acarnania, II. 20
Achaean mountains, II. 5

Agesilaus, descent of, I. 2; age at
  accession, I. 6; at eighty years,
  II. 28; age at death, X. 4; XI.
  15; in Asia, I. 9–38; in Thessaly,
  II. 2; at the battle of Coronea,
  II. 6–16; expedition against
  Argos and Corinth, II. 17–19;
  against Acarnania, II. 20; against
  Phleius, II. 21; against Thebes,
  II. 22; against Mantinea, II. 23;
  defends Sparta against invasion,
  II. 24; as envoy, II. 25; in
  Egypt, II. 28–31; his virtues,
  III. 1; VIII. 8; XI.; contrasted
  with the Persian king, IX. 1;
  his sister, IX. 6; daughter, VIII. 7
Agis, king, I. 5
Amyclae, VIII. 7
Archidamus, father of Agesilaus,
  I. 5
Argos, II. 17
Aristodemus, VIII. 7
Artemis of Ephesus, I. 27
Athenian empire, I. 37
Boeotians, II. 2, 18, 23
Car, the, VIII. 7; Introduction, p. x.
Caria, I. 14, 29
Cephisus, river, II. 9
Choir at Hyacinthia, II. 17
Corinth, Agesilaus before, II. 17;
  battle of, VII. 5; Corinthians,
  II. 6, 18, 21; VII. 6
Coronea, battle of, II. 9
Cynisca, daughter of Agesilaus,
  IX. 6
Cynoscephalae, pass of, II. 22
Cyreians, *i.e.* the Greeks who aided
  Cyrus against Artaxerxes, II. 11
Delphi, I. 34
Egypt, dealings of Agesilaus with,
  II. 28–31

509

INDEX

Ephesus, I. 25
Ephors, I. 36
Helicon, Mt., II. 11
Hellespont, II. 1
Heracles, I. 2; VIII. 7
Hyacinthus, festival of, II. 17
Leuctra, battle of, II. 23
Leotychidas, son of Agis, I. 5
Mantineans, II. 23
Narthacium, Mt., II. 4
Pactolus, I. 30
Peiraeum, port of Corinth, II. 18
Persian king, I. 6; IX. 1
Pharnabazus, I. 23; III. 3, 5
Phleius, II. 21
Phthia, II. 5
Prizes, I. 25
Sardis, I. 29, 33
Thebes, II. 22; Thebans, II. 6, 9-16
Thessaly and Thessalians, II. 2
Tissaphernes, satrap of Lydia, I. 10-
    17, 29, 35
Tithraustes, I. 35; iv. 6

CONSTITUTION OF THE
LACEDAEMONIANS

Aliens, expulsion of, XIV. 4
Army, XI.; levy and supplies, 2;
    equipment, 3; organisation, 4;
    formation, 5-10; encampment,
    XII. 1-5; XIII. 10; exercises and
    recreation, XII. 5-7
Artemis Orthia, confused reference
    to, II. 9
Athena, XIII. 2
Boys, education and care of, II;
    clothes, 3; diet, 5; V. 8; whip-
    ping, 8
Children, begetting of, I. 3; control
    of, II. 2; VI. 2
Choruses, IV. 2; IX. 5
Clothes, II. 3
Coinage, IV. 5
Commissariat, XIII. 1
Constitution, permanence of
    Spartan, XV. 1
Cowardice, IX. 1-5
Cowards, treatment of, IX. 4-5;
    X. 7
Delphi, visit of Lycurgus to, VIII. 5
Diet, II. 5; V. 8
Discipline, II; VIII. 1-5
Education, II.
Elders, Council of, X. 1-3

Ephors, IV. 3, 6; authority and
    privileges of, VIII, 3, 4; XV. 6, 7;
    with the army, XIII. 5
Exercise, physical, V. 8; XII. 5, 7
Fathers, authority of, VI. 2
Fire-bearer in Spartan army, XIII. 2
Governors, Spartan, XIV. 4
Gymnasia, V. 8
Hellanodicae, court of, XIII. 11
Heracleidae, X. 8
Horses, common use of, VI. 3
Hounds, common use of, VI. 3
Hunting, IV. 7; VI. 4
Kings, powers and duties of, in
    field, XIII.; in peace, XV. 2 f.;
    oath of, XV. 7; staff of, XIII. 7;
    meals of, XIII. 1; XV. 4; burial
    of, XV. 8, 9
Lads, training of, III.
Lycurgus, I. 2; his institutions,
    I.-XIII.; antiquity of his laws,
    X. 8; no longer observed, XIV.
Matches between young men, IV. 2
Men, mature, V. 7
Messes, public, V. 2-7
Modesty of lads, III. 4 f.
Money at Sparta, VII. 3-6; XIV. 2, 3
Old age, honour paid to, X. 1-2
Orthia, II. 9
Peers, X. 7; XIII. 1, 7
Pythii, XV. 4
Sacrifices, XIII. 2-5; XV. 2
Sciritae, XIII. 3, 6
Servants, common use of, VI. 3
Sexes, relations of, I. 5 f.; ii. 10 f.
Syskania, V. 2 f.; Introduction,
    p. xxiii.
Tutors, II. 10
Virtue, cult of, X. 1, 4-7
Wardens, II. 10
Youths, training of, IV.
Zeus the Leader, XIII. 2

WAYS AND MEANS

Aliens, resident, a source of revenue,
    II. 1; need of studying their
    interests, II. 2; not to serve in
    army, II. 3; but in cavalry,
    II. 4
Alimony, to be provided by state,
    IV. 13 f., 33, 52
Anaphlystus, IV. 43
Arcadians, III. 7
Athenian empire, V. 6

510

INDEX

Athens, as centre of Greek world, I. 6; as commercial centre, III. 1 f.; parts of, II. 1
Attica, natural properties of, I. 2 f.
Barbarians in Athenian army, II. 3
Benefactors of state, II. 3
Besa, IV. 44
Capital, provision of, III. 8 f.; IV. 34
Climate of Attica, I. 3
Company, project for joint stock, III. 9; for working mines, IV. 32
Contributions to state purposes, III. 7
Council, the, IV. 18
Currency, III. 2
Decelea, IV. 25
Delphi, V. 9; VI. 2
Dividends, III. 9 f.
Dodona, VI. 2
Economy, call for, IV. 40
Exports, III. 5; IV. 40
Fortresses in mining district, IV. 43 f.
Freeholds for aliens, II. 6
Gods to be consulted, VI. 2
Gold, IV. 10
Guardians of aliens and orphans, II. 7; of peace, V. 1
Hipponicus, IV. 15
Hotels to be built, III. 12
Houses for aliens, II. 6; to be built, III. 13; IV. 35
Imports, III. 5; IV. 40
Industries, IV. 6
Justice, politicians and, I. 1
Labour in mines, IV. 3 f.; 39
Lacedaemonians, V. 7
Lysistratus, III. 7
Marble in Attica, I. 4
Megara, IV. 46
Merchant ships, project for a state-owned fleet of, III. 14; IV. 35
Merchants, III. 3, 4
Mines, the silver, IV.; inexhaustible, IV. 2; profit derived from, IV. 14 f.
Mining, different from other industries, IV. 6
Nicias, IV. 14
Peace, need for and effect of, V. 1 f.
Persian wars, V. 5
Philodemus, IV. 15
Phocians, V. 9
Politicians, influence of, on constitution, I. 1

Ports of Athens, II. 1
Poverty, I. 1
Prizes to be offered, III. 3
Shipping, III. 3
Silver, in Attica, I. 5; demand for, IV. 8, 9; export of, III. 2
Slaves, to be purchased by the state, IV. 4; revenue expected from, IV. 23, 35, 49
Sosias, IV. 14
Theatre, seats in, III. 4
Thebes, IV. 46; Thebans, V. 7
Thoricus, IV. 43
Training, physical, IV. 52
War, effects of, IV. 41 f.; V. 5 f.; War of Allies, IV. 40; Persian Wars, V. 5

THE CAVALRY COMMANDER

Academy, review at the, III. 1, 14
Aides-de-camp, IV. 4
Aliens, IX. 6
Ambuscades, VIII. 15, 20
Arming of recruits, I. 6, 22, **23**
Boeotians, VII. 3
Cavalry, complement of, I. 2, 9–12; IX. 3; recruiting for, I. 2, 9 f.; training recruits for, I. 5; arming, I. 6, 22, 23; expense of, I. 19; retirement from, I. 2
Children's games, V. 10
Choruses, I. 26
Colonels, duties of, I. 8, 21, 22, 25; II. 1, 7; III. 6; VIII. 17, 18
Council, share in control of cavalry, I. 8, 13; III. 9, 12, 14
Country, knowledge of, IV. **6**
Couriers, I. 25
Deception, use of, V. 7–10
Dionysia, III. 2
Eleusinium, III. 2
Emulation, encouraging, I. 26
Enemy, dealing with, IV. 11–18; V. 2, 5–12; VII. 2 f.; VIII. 1, 9 f.
Expenses, I. 19; IX. 5
Extravagance, avoiding, I. 12
File-leaders, II. 1, 6, 7; IV. 9
Forces, strength of, VIII. 10–12
Foreign contingents in cavalry, IX. 4, 5
Formation, II. 1 f.
Galloping at review, III. 7
Games, VIII. 5 f.
Garrisons, VI. 3

INDEX

Gods, duty to, I. 10; IX. 8; sacrifice to, III. 1; saluting statues of, III. 2; help of, v. 14; VII. 4
Hawks, sagacity of, IV. 18
Herms, III. 2
Hippodrome, review in, III. 1, 10, 11
Horses, care and training of, I. 3, 4, 13–17; VIII. 4
Horsemanship in war, VIII. 1, 16
Infantry, v. 1; use of, in cavalry, v. 13; VII. 3; VIII. 19; IX. 7
Ingenuity, value of, in commander, v. 2
Inspection of cavalry, III. 9
Intelligence, need of, in commander, VII. 1
Invasion, VII. 2 f.
Javelin throwing, I. 21
Lacedaemonians, VII. 4; their cavalry, IX. 4
Lance, position of, III. 3; v. 7
Loyalty, how to secure, v. 1 f.
Lyceum, review at, III. 1, 6
Marching, duties of commander when, IV. 1 f.
Mercenaries, IX. 3
Mounting, I. 5, 17
Navy, VII. 4
Numbers, correct use of, III. 6
Obedience, I. 24; VIII. 22
Orders, how to give, IV. 9
Outposts, IV. 9, 10, 11
Pay, I. 23
Phalerum, III. 1
Pickets, enemy, VII. 13
Pirates, VIII. 8
Prizes for efficiency, I. 26
Processions, III. 1 f.
Rear-leader, II. 5
Recruits, I. 17
Regiments, I. 21, 22, 25; III. 2, 6, 11; IV. 2–4; VIII. 17
Reviews, III. 1 f.
Risk, avoidance of, IV. 13
Ruses, use of, v. 3 f., 15
Scouts, IV. 5
Seat, good, I. 6, 7, 18
Sham fights, I 20; IV. 5
Spies, IV. 7, 8, 16
Stones, throwing down, I. 16
Straps, supply of, VIII. 1
Theatre of Dionysus, III. 7
Traps for enemy, laying, IV. 11, 12
War, IV. 7 f.
Wolves, sagacity of, IV. 18

HORSEMANSHIP

Age, test of, III. 1
Ailments, IV. 2
Armour of mounted man, XII. 1 f.; of horse, XII. 8 f.
Bits and bitting, VI. 7 f.; VIII. 14; IX. 9; X. 6 f.
Boeotian helmet, XII. 3
Boots, XII. 10
Breaking, II. 1, 2, 3–5
Breastplate, pattern of, XII. 1–7
Bridling, III. 11
Buying, I. 1 f.; III. 1 f.
Cavalry recruiting, II. 1; the cavalry horse, III. 7
Cloth, the, XII. 8
Colic, IV. 2
Collecting a horse, VII. 15
Colt, buying, I. 1 f.; points of, I. 3 f.
Eleusinium, the, I. 1
Exercises, III. 5 f.; VII. 13 f.
Floor of stable, IV. 3
Fodder, IV. 1 f.
Galloping, VII. 11 f.
Gauntlet, the, XII. 5
Groom, duties of, II. 3–5; IV. 4; v. 1 f.; VI. 1 f.
Halter, v. 1, 4
Helmet, XII. 3
Hoofs, care of, IV. 4, 5
Horse, for war, III. 7; buying, III. 1 f.; how to show off, X. 1 f.; for parade, XI. 1 f; how to show off, XI. 10 f.; training, VIII. 13; high-spirited, IX. 2 f.; sluggish, IX. 12; in art, XI. 8
Horse-breaker, duties of the, II. 2
Hunting, VIII. 10
Javelin, XII. 12 f.
Jumping, VIII. 1 f.
Leading a horse, VI. 4–6
Leg, loose, VII. 6, 7
Manage, the, VII. 14
Mounting, III. 11; VI. 12 f.; VII. 1 f.; IX. 3
Muzzle, v. 3
Odrysians, VIII. 6
Persians, VIII. 6; Persian javelin, XII. 12; sabre, XII. 11
Prancing, XI. 7 f.
Pulling up, VII. 18
Rearing, XI. 1
Resting, VII. 18

INDEX

Ring, *i.e.* volte, III. 5; VII. 13
Rubbing down, V. 5; VI. 1 f.
Sabre, XII. 11
Seat, VII. 5
Shy horses, II. 5; III. 9
Simon, I. 1, 3; XI. 6
Stable, IV. 1
Stall, IV. 1, 2
Stones, use of, in yard, IV. 4
Training a horse, VIII. 13
Trotting, VII. 11
Vice, III. 10
Walking, VII. 10
Washing, V. 6–9
Yard, stable, IV. 4

HUNTING

Achilles, I. 2, 4, 16; VI. 13
Aeneas, I. 2, 15
Agility of hare, V. 31
Alcathus, I. 9
Amphiaraus, I. 2, 8
Antilochus, I. 2, 14
Apollo, I. 1; VI. 13
Artemis, I. 1, 11; VI. 13; XIII. 18
Asclepius, I. 2, 6
Atalanta, I. 7; XIII. 18
Bag for carrying nets, etc., II. 9
Big game, hunting of, XI.
Boar hunting, X. 1 f.; hounds for, X. 1; description of nets for, X. 2 f.; risks of, X. 8, 12–16, 18, 20; strength of boars, X. 17
Breeding hounds, VII. 1 f.
Caltrops for deer hunting, description of, IX. 11 f.; setting, IX. 14 f.; for boar hunting, X. 22
Carthaginian flax, II. 4
Castor, I. 2, 13
Castorian hounds, III. 1
Cephalus, husband of Procris, I. 2, 5
Cheiron, I. 1, 3, 4, 8, 17; XII. 18
Cittus, Mt. (Khortiatzi), XI. 1
Colchian flax, II. 4
Cretan hounds, X. 1
Crops, hunting over, V. 34; XII. 6
Cudgel, VI. 11, 17
Deer, red, instructions for hunting, IX. 1 f.
Dew, effect of, on scent, V. 3
Diomed, I. 2, 13
Eagles, V. 16

Education, value of hunting in, II. 1; XII. 7, 14
Fawns, hunting the, IX. 1 f.
Flax, for nets, II. 4
Foxes, VI. 3
Frost, effect of, on scent, V. 1
Hare, hunting the, II. 2 f.; nets for, II. 4 f.; hounds for, III.; scent of, V. 1 f.; description of the hare, V. 30 f.; species of, V. 22 f.; eyesight of, V. 26 f.; agility of, V. 31 f.; hares in islands, V. 24; in mountains, marshes, plains, V. 17; habits and characteristics of the, V. 4 f.; fecundity, V. 13; tracking the, V. 15; VI. 8, 15 f.; VIII. 6 f.
Hayes for hare hunting, II. 4, 5, 7; setting up, VI. 9
Heracles, I. 9
Hesione, sister of Priam, I. 9
Hippolytus, I. 2, 11
Hounds, for hare hunting, III. 1; defective, III. 2 f.; the right sort, IV. 1 f.; trappings of, VI. 1; ailing, VI. 2; breeding, VII. 1 f.; colour, IV. 7; naming, VII. 5; training young, VII. 6 f.; skirters, VII. 10; for deer hunting, IX. 1; for boar hunting, X. 1
Hunters, praise of, I.; XIII. 11 f.
Hunting, advantages gained from, I. 1 f.; XII. 1 f.; and war, I. 18; XII; praise of, I.; XII.; in mountains, IV. 9 f.; over rough ground, IV. 10; time for, IV. 11; over crops, V. 34; at night, XII. 7; opponents of, XII. 10 f.; weather for, VIII. 1 f.
Keeper, net, II. 3; duties of, VI. 5 f.; X. 19; of hounds, IX. 2 f.
Islands, hares in, V. 24
Javelins for boar hunting, X. 3
Laconian hounds, X. 1
Leverets, V. 13
Locrian hounds, X. 1
Machaon, son of Asclepius, I. 2, 14
Meilanion, I. 2, 7
Meleager, I. 2, 10
Menestheus, son of Peleus, I. 2, 12
Mountains, hares in, V. 17; hunting in, VIII. 2 f.
Nais, Cheiron's mother, I. 4

513

INDEX

Nestor, I. 2, 7, 12
Nets, for hare hunting, II. 4 f.; setting up, VI. 5; for boar hunting, X. 2 f. *See* Keeper.
Nysa, Mt., XI. 1
Odysseus, I. 2, 13
Olympus, in Mysia, XI. 1
Outfit for hare hunting, II. 2
Palamedes, I. 2, 11
Pangaeus, Mt. (Pinari), XI. 1
Peleus, I. 2, 8
Periboea, daughter of Alcathus, I. 9
Phasian flax, II. 4
Pindus, Mt., XI. 1
Pleasures, mostly evil, XII. 7, 12
Podaleirius I. 2 14

Politicians, attack on, XIII. 10
Puppies, feeding, VII. 3, 4
Rain, effect of, on scent, V. 3 f.
Rhea, I. 4
Sophists, attack on, XIII. 1 f.
Spears, for boar-hunting, X. 3
Stakes, for nets, II. 6, 7
Telamon, I. 2, 9
Thebes, I. 8
Theseus, I. 2, 10
Thetis, I. 8
Toil, love of, I. 12; XII. 16, 17
Tracking the hare, VI. 8, 15 f.
Troy, I. 9, 13, 15
Virtue, personified, XII. 18–22
War, II. 1; XII.
Weather for hunting, VIII. 1 f.

INDEX

Constitution of the Athenians

Alliances, 495
Allies, in Athens' empire, 483–489, 501
Assembly, at Athens, 499, 501
Baths, 491, 493
Boeotia, 505
Comedy, at Athens, 497
Copper, 493
Council, at Athens, 479, 499, 501
Courts, see jurisdiction
Cyprus, 491
Dialects, 491
Dionysia, 501
Disfranchisement, 483, 505, 507
Dockyards, 501
Egypt, 491
Farmers, 495
Festivals, 499, 503; athletic, musical, dramatic competitions, 481, 483; see also under names of individual festivals
Flax, 493
Hephaestia, 501
Infantry, 487
Iron, 493
Italy, 491
Jurisdiction, 483–487, 501, 503
Legislation, at Athens, 501
Luxuries, 491

Lydia, 491
Magistracies, at Athens, 477, 501, 507
Messenians, 505
Metics, 479, 481
Milesians, 505
Navy, of Athens, 475, 481, 487–491
Non-Greeks, 491, 493
Orphans, 501
Panathenaea, 501
Peiraeus, one per-cent tax, 485
Peloponnese, 491
Pontus, 491
Prisoners, at Athens, 501
Promethia, 501
Shrines, 491, 501
Sicily, 491
Slaves, 479, 481
Sparta, 481; Spartans, 505
Thalassocracy, 489–495
Thargelia, 501
Timber, 493
Trade, 489–493
Tribute, in Athenian empire, 483, 501, 503
Trierarchs, 501
Wax, 493

515